WAQFS IN INDIA:
A STUDY OF ADMINISTRATIVE AND STATUTORY CONTROL

WAQFS IN INDIA:

A STUDY OF ADMINISTRATIVE AND STATUTORY CONTROL

M.A. QURESHI

GYAN

Published by

Gyan Publishing House
5, Ansari Road
Daryaganj, New Delhi-110002
Phone: 011-47034999, 9811692060
E-mail: books@gyanbooks.com

Distribution Network
gyanbooks.com
India, USA, Canada, UK, Australia

ISBN: 978-81-212-0282-4 (HB)

First Published, 1990

2nd Impression 2025

Printed at: Gyan Press, Delhi.

WAQFS IN INDIA:
A STUDY OF ADMINISTRATIVE AND STATUTORY CONTROL
Author: M.A. QURESHI

Preface

The religious, charitable and pious objects of a waqf are as old as the human society. The instincts of piety and benevolence can very well be traced even in those aboriginal tribes and races where the lights of learning and civilization have not yet reached. It is, therefore, maintained that the religious, charitable and pious objects of a waqf are not having origin in a particular system of jurisprudence, culture or civilization but it is to be found everywhere in one form or the other.

The law relating to waqfs is an important branch of Islamic jurisprudence. The knowledge of this subject to all of those who are interested in this branch of law. In India, there exists more than a lakh of public waqfs. These waqfs are having an annual income of more than rupees five crores. This is apart from family waqfs.

It is known to all that in our country this pious institution is not functioning properly. The income of these waqfs is not utilized according to the wishes of the settler. The resources of of these waqfs besides helping the preservation of cultural, charitable and philanthropic institutions can contribute to the educational and economic uplift of the community. In most of the cases mutawalli have either managed to transfer waqf properties or utilizing the waqf resources themselves.

The Central Government has a special waqf section in the secretariat to look after the waqf affairs. In states this function has been assigned to Waqf Commissioners and Waqf Boards. The present system at state level is far from satisfactory. The Waqf Boards and Waqf Commissioners are not paying adequate attention to the development of urban waqf properties under their management. One of the serious difficulties faced by them is to make their ways in the expenses of litigation. The author has made valuable suggestions to eradicate this evil. The author has also proposed for the establishment of a Waqf Tribunal in every State for deciding waqf cases.

The Central Waqf Council is also not an effective body. It takes long time in deciding cases. The Council can raise substantial amounts through donations and grants for financing educational schemes. The Council can increase its income by way of issue of bonds and debentures for procuring necessary finances.

The institution of family waqfs also needs immediate attention of the government as well as of the public particularly Muslims. These waqfs are looked upon by mutawallis in management as though they were waqfs for their own benefit only. They tend to ignore the rights and interests of other beneficiaries. This important subject has been discussed in detail in a separate chapter. The author has made valuable suggestions to improve the status of family waqfs.

The adverse effects of the laws of Estate Duty, Income Tax and Land reforms *etc* are also causing anxiety to Muslims. These laws are not clear. Too much discretionary power has been given to the officer concerned to exempt or not to exempt any waqf property from the purview of these legislations.

According to the Constitution, India is a secular state. Articles 25 to 30 of the Constitution guarantee religious freedom to all the people of India. Keeping in view the recent trends in the country the author has made a comprehensive study of this subject. It is submitted that the future of the country depends solely on the implementation of the policy of secularism. It has been seen that the state is not strictly following the policy of secularism. It is submitted that there is no other alternative but to follow the policy of secularism rigidly.

There is no provision under the Waqf Act, 1954, under which the Central Government can ask the State Waqf Boards/ Commissioners to supply required information. Consequently, the waqf section of the Central Government finds it impossible to function effectively. It is, therefore, necessary that a thorough survey of waqfs laws be made and suitable amendments be introduced.

At present there is no uniform waqf law in the country. The Central Waqf Act, 1953, is prevalent throughout the country except the states of West Bengal, Uttar Pradesh, Jammu & Kashmir and in some parts of the Maharashtra. Dargah Khwaja Saheb at Ajmer is governed by a separate Central Act. Under these circumstances different interpretation of the identical provisions is but an expected outcome. It is again submitted that only passing of legislation will not do. It is necessary to build up public opinion in favour of such legislation. In fact, Muslims should themselves become conscientious about the protection of their pious property. In the last I express my sincere thanks to the Indian Council of Social Science Research, New Delhi for providing me assistance in the conduct of research of this work.

M.A. Qureshi

Contents

1

History and Development of Waqfs

General Observations

The Muslim institution of waqf is an ancient and one of the most important branch of Islamic jurisprudence. The institution of waqf deals with the religious, social and economic life of Muslims. The waqf property is the national asset. There are waqfs which not only support mosques, imambaras *etc.*, but they also support schools, colleges, libraries, hospitals and *musafir khanas*. The help given by these institutions is not only confined to Muslims. The members of other communities are also deriving the benefit from these institutions. Since there is no proper administration and control of these waqfs they are mismanaged. It is, therefore, necessary that waqfs should be maintained properly and their resources be utilised for the objects and the purposes of the dedication.

As already noted the institution of waqf is not new to Islam. Probably Islam was the first religion of the world which recognised and developed a legal expedient under the name of the waqf. The law of waqf permits an owner of the dedicated property to settle his property for the use of beneficiaries in perpetuity. It is a distinguishing feature of the socio-economic structure of Islam.

The origin of waqf is not related to any one particular single source. It is the result of combination of several factors and various elements which were intimately fused during the formative period of Muslim law. The root cause of the origin of the institution of waqf is devotion to the way of God. Everybody wants to acquire merit in the eyes of God. There is a strong desire to win divine approbation. This is the root cause of the origin and development of the institution.

Holy *Quran* does not say anything specifically regarding waqfs. *Quran*, however, deals with the charity. *Quran* says a Muslim should spend his wealth for the cause of Allah, and be not cast by his own hands to ruin. The likeness of those who spend their wealth in Allah's way is as the likeness of a grain which growth seven ears, in every ear a hundred grains. Allah giveth increase manifold to whom He will. At another place *Quran* says those who spend their wealth for the cause of Allah and afterward make not reproach and injury to follow that which they have spent, their reward is with Lord, and there shall no fear come upon them ; neither shall they grieve.[1] The likeness of those who spend their wealth in search of Allah's pleasure, and for the strengthening of their souls, is as the likeness of a garden on a height. The rainstorm suiteth it and it bringeth forth its fruit two-fold. And if the rainstorm suiteth it not, then the shower. Allah is seer of what ye do. Whatever alms or vow, it is within the knowledge of Allah[2]. *Quran* again says that those who believe and do good works and establish worship and pay the poor due, their reward is with their Lord and there shall no fear come upon them neither shall they grieve[3]. A person will not attain unto piety until he spends of that which he loves. And whatever is spent, Allah is aware thereof.[4]

At another place the following verse was revealed to Prophet Muhammad.[5]

> They ask thee (O Muhammad) what they shall spend, say; that which ye spend for good (must go) to parents and near kindred and orphans and the needy and the wayfarer. And whatever good ye do, Allah is aware of it.

According to Heffening, the origin of waqf is to be sought in the strongly marked impulse to charitable deeds which is the lame duck of Islam. There is a maxim that charity begins at home. This maxim was for the first time applied by Islam. Holy *Quran* says :

> Ye shall never attain to goodness till ye give alms of that which ye love, and whatever ye give, of a truth. God knoweth.[6]
>
> It is not righteousness that ye turn your faces to the east and the west ; but righteous is he who believeth in Allah and the last day and the angels and the scripture and the Prophets, and giveth his wealth, for love of Him, to kinsfolk and to orphans and the needy and the wayfarer and to those who ask, and to set slaves free; and observeth proper worship and payeth the poor due (*Zakat*). And those who keep their treaty when they make one, and the patient in tribulation and adversity and time of stress. Such are they who are sincere. Such are the God fearing[7].

It is said that before the advent of Islam waqfs did not exist in Arabia though all religions had commanded their followers to give alms but not to their own kinsmen and dependents. It was Islam which considerably widened the concept of charity. It was maintained by the jurists on Islamic law that help to oneself, one's dependents and other relatives was also an act of piety.

Under the Islamic law, property can be given in charity in any of the one of the following ways : –

(i) the whole property may be given away; or
(ii) the corpus may be retained and the income from it or the usufruct may be given in charity.

The later type of charity is commonly known as waqf. Once the property is given in waqfs, it cannot be transferred, inherited or sold away. No person shall have any proprietory right in it.

Apart from the above Quranic provisions, this pious institution was developed by Prophet Muhammad himself. The Prophet's words and acts have great reverence in the eyes of a Muslim. Bokhari himself has said that the institution of waqfs rests on the foundation of Hadis and both movables and immovables are fit subject matter of waqf. He dates the institution from the Prophet himself. He relates that the Prophet created the waqf of his own property and advised his companion (afterwards Khalifa) to make of his garden. It has therefore, been, said that the waqf in Muslim law has its origin with and from the Prophet himself.

Probably the earliest waqf was that of the house of Arqam, where Prophet stayed when Hazrat Omar declared Islam. Hazrat Arqan made the waqf for his children. During this period waqfs for religious purposes were also created.

According to another tradition the first Muslim waqf came into existence in the first year of Hijra. It is said that the piece of land in which historical masjid known as 'Masjid Nabvi' (in Medina) was constructed belonged to two orphans. This piece of land was dedicated by the orphans in waqf and the masjid was constructed.[8]

The learned work of Syed Ameer Ali[9] *Mahomedan Law* is an authority on the subject under discussion. He says that according to Ghayat-ul-Bayan is founded on the rule laid down by the Prophet himself under the following circumstances, and handed down in succession by Ibn Auf, Nafe and Ibn Umar, as stated in Jamma-i-Tirmizi. Omar had acquired a piece of land in the canton of Khaibar, and proceeded to the Prophet and sought his counsel, to make the most pious use of it ; whereupon the Prophet declared 'tie up the property (Asl or corpus) and devote the usufruct to human beings, and it is not to be sold or made the subject of gift or inheritance; devote its produce to your children, your kindred, and the poor in the way of God'. Accordingly, Omar dedicated the property in question and the waqf continued in existence for several centuries until the land turned barren. Prophet directed it should not be gifted to anyone nor it should be made available for testamentary or intestamentary disposition.

Prophet declared that the best of all pious offerings is a provision for one's self, so that one may not fall into need and the giving of *sadaqah* should commence with those whose subsistence is obligatory.

The Prohpet of God has declared that a pious offering to

one's family (to provide against their getting into want) is more pious than giving alms to beggars.

Support of one's self, his children and family is the first duty and necessity.

In giving charity, commence with those whose maintenance is obligatory on you.

And the Prophet declared that a man giving subsistence to his family is giving *sadaqah.*

Giving alms to the poor has the reward of one alms, but that giving to kindred has two rewards.[10]

There is also another tradition. According to this tradition Prophet wished to purchase gardens from the Banu Nadjdjar in order to build a mosque. The owner of the gardens refused to take the purchase money and gave the land in the name of God.[11]

The book *Fathul-kadir*[12] is a work of great authority among Sunni Muslims. The book says that the law of waqf has its origin from the Prophet himself, who besides having prescribed the above rule to Omar, is reported to have declared that all human actions and with the life of the individual, except such benefactions as are perpetual in their character; and that, in accordance with these principles, trusts or dedications were frequent in the life time of the Prophet and in the early centuries of Islam.

There is also a tradition regarding family waqfs. Abu Talha gave to the prophet a garden which was situated in Medina. Prophet, however, returned the same to him. He directed that he should make it an endowment for his relatives. Accordingly Abu Talha gave the garden as a *sadaqah* for Ubaiy and Hassan.[13]

The institution of waqf acquired importance in the first century A.H. However, the legal rules were only developed during second century. During second century, there arose some basic differences in the juristic concept of waqf. These differences were reconciled by way of interpretation. There is a difference of opinion regarding the impact of Roman law on the institution of waqf. According to Heffening there was some foreign influence on the development of the institution of waqf. Henry Cattan says that the above statement of Haffening is not true. He says that the institution of waqf developed with Islam and there is no evidence that such a complex system of approrriating usufruct as a life interest to varying and successive classes of beneficiaries existed prior to Islam. He further says it is true that the separation of ownership from the usufruct was not a new legal concept, but the settlement of usufruct of prorerty on successive generations in perpetuity for an immediate or ultimate charitable purpose was not known to Islam in the first century. It only developed during the first three centuries of Islam.[14] Family waqfs also developed simultaneously.[15]

Previously, it was thought that only immovable property can be the subject of waqf. Later on, all types of property, movable and immovable, were made subject matter of waqfs. Apart from immovable and movable property, shops, warehouses, baths, mills, bakeries, soap and paper works, looms, gardens, farms and even villages were endowed by way of waqf. Vast pieces of land were very commonly dedicated to waqfs all over the Muslim world. In 1925, the Government of Turkey found that nearly three fourths of arable land of the country was under waqfs. In Algeira, one half of cultivable land was dedicated in waqf. In almost all the Muslim countries vast stretches of land are lying unused because of the reason that such land was dedicated in waqfs. Looking to this state of affairs, many countries have divested the land from the waqfs.

It is clear from the above discussion that Prophet himself laid down certain conditions for a valid waqf. However, in early days of Islam the law of waqfs suffered from great uncertainty. It was only during the second century after the flight that a body of rules based on Ijma were developed. These rules are the basis of the law of waqf. He directed that the asl (corpus) be so directed that it may never be sold. The dedicated property will not be the subject of gift or inheritance.

In the beginning there was no state protection to this important institution. The early Muslim rulers of Ummayad dynasty did not apply to the waqfs. It was only during the reign of Abbasia Khalifs of Bagdad[16] that state gave protection to this institution.

The property dedicated to waqf is not properly managed. Mutawallis are corrupt and they are not competent to deal with the property properly. This state of affairs is not new. In the year 1873, the Bombay High Court[17] observed that 'a waqf for a family settlement creates a perpetuity of the worst description, for it prevents the alienation of the house for ever, and necessitates its use in a manner which with the natural increase in the number of descendants would probably render impossible even if they would be willing (which could hardly be expected) to live amicably under one roof throughout all generations.'

TREATMENT OF WAQFS DURING MUSLIM RULE IN INDIA

The Hindus and Muslim religious institutions of public character in India have always been subject to secular checks and controls. The laws governing these institutions, scriptural or customary, impose a duty on the trustees to utilise the trust property to further the objects of the institution.

Even in ancient India Kautilya's *Arthshastra,* Asoka's edicts and other inscriptions and authoritative works 'definitely suggest that from very early times religious and charitable institutions in this country came under the special protection of the secular authority. In addition to supervision exercised by the Hindu kings over temples, they also use to interfere whenever there was mismanagement in them'.[18]

The conception of a state in the Muhammedan system is that of a commonwealth of all the Muslims living as one community under the guidance and direction of a supreme executive head called the Imam or the Caliph. The responsibility of administration rests with the Imam, but for the convenience of administration, he may delegate his powers to different persons. He may for instance, appoint ministers to whom he may delegate practically all his powers and faculties or only particular powers, or he may appoint them merely for the purposes of consultation and for executing orders. Similarly, he may appoint a person as Governor of a particular country with such powers as may be necessary. He may also delegate the exercise of his authority in the various departments of administration to different officers, such as the command of the army, administration of justice, revenue. But the Imam has no legislative powers at all though he may interpret the law. If he happens to be a jurist, but his interpretation will have no special authority by his position as Imam. He is bound by law, and by the decrees and orders of the court like any other citizen. The Imam is merely the representative or delegate of the people, from whom he derives his rights and privileges.[19]

The head of the state among the Muhammedans is the trustee of public property and in no sense its owner. Muslim rulers of that time made all possible efforts for the spread of Islam.

It was only during seventh century that Arabs invaded and conquered Syria, Egypt and Iraq. For a considerable long time Spain was also under the control of Muslims.[20] In Africa Muslims settled as tradesmen and gradually propagated the principles of Islam. In Asia Islam came by way of conquest of Persia. From Persia Islam advanced towards north. The people of Turkey adopted Islam The Ottoman Turks conquered Asia Minor and Asiatic Turkey. The Tatar carried Islam to Russia. Once upon a time Ottoman empire was ruling most of the states of the world. While writing the short history of the measurement of Muslim intelligence Huseyin Hilmi Islk[21] made following statement :

> The measurement of intelligence was done first by the Ottomans. I read in American literature that when the Ottoman Armies came upto Vienna the European states were frightened very much. They were terribly bewildered with the fear that Islam was spreading over Europe and Christianity was perishing. They endeavoured much in search of a solution for stopping the Ottoman attacks. One midnight the British ambassador in Istanbul cabled a message in Cipher. He could not wait till morning to give the good news. 'I found the reason why the Ottomans won victory after victory and the solution for stopping them.' And he explained as follows—
>
> The Ottomans never torture the prisoners of war but treat them like brothers. They test the intelligence of little

children no matter of which nationality or religion they are. Keen-witted children are selected and educated by qualified teachers in the school called 'Enderun' in the palace and being taught Islamic knowledge. Islamic morals, science and culture, they are brought up as strong enterprising Moslems. The distinguished commanders who caused the Ottoman armies to gain victory after victory and the outstanding men of politics and administration like (the two great Viziers) Sokullu and Koprulu were all these keen-witted children brought up in this manner. For stopping the Ottoman attacks, it is necessary to demolish these Enderun schools and their branches, the madarsas and to cause Moslems to decline in knowledge and science.

It has been said that the first entrance of Muslims in India came as a trading merchant. To encourage trade and in keeping with the then prevalent policy of religious toleration and eclecticism, the Muslims were given full religious freedom. Their religious property was fully protected. There is not even a single instance when any Muslim ruler had fought a religious war. There had been many wars between two Muslim rulers. These were only to show superiority. In spite of the fact that the Vijayanagar kingdom was continually at war with the neighbouring Muslim kingdom, there appears to have been great appreciation of each other's cultures. The Adil Shahi Sultans of Bijapur and Nizam Shahis of Ahmednagar freely patronised Maratha chiefs, and employed Hindu officers for their administration and Hindu troups in their armies.[22] Nizam Shahi of Ahmednagar gave great impetus to the Marathi language by making it the language of their official transactions The Hindu rulers of Vijayanagar reciprocated these feelings; they took Muslim troops in their employment, encouraged Muslim traders and built mosques for their worship. These endowments were looked after by rulers of that time.[23]

As regards northern India it is claimed that the settlement of Muslims was an act of force. In 1192, Shihab-ud-din Ghori won the second battle of Tarain and within fourteen years his general Bhakhtiyar Khalji had reached the bank of Brahmaputra. There is another side of the picture. In 1205, Sultan

Shihab-ud-din was signally defeated by the non-Muslim Qara Khital Turks at the battle of Ankhud, his officers and soldiers deserted him and he fled for refuge to the fort with about a hundred men.

In 1206 A.D., the Delhi Sultanate was established. After the establishment of Delhi Sultanate many waqfs came into existence. At that time state was providing fund for the maintenance of the waqfs. It has been said that Sultan Muhammad bin Tughlak appointed Ibn Battuta as the mutawalli of the waqfs in favour of the tomb of Sultan Qutb-ud-din. The income derived from the tomb was not sufficient for giving salary to the employees and, therefore, Sultan ordered for the financial help to the tomb.[24]

In 1218, Chengiz Khan started his march for the conquest of Muslim Asia and within forty years the Mongols had brought all lands up to the frontiers of Poland and Syria and had conquered India up to Lahore. There was a mass killing of Muslims by Mongols. There remained without exaggeration not a hundred souls alive.[25] The Muslim inhabitants of important cities like Samarqand, Bokhara, Tirmiz, Khwarazm, Naishapur, Merv were butchered in such a manner that only a few beggars were left. When Chengiz Khan marched from Samarqand to the bank of the Indus, no one along the route of his march was allowed to survive.[26] In 1300 A.D., however, almost all the Mongols in Muslim land accepted Islam. The Mongol conquest of Muslim Asia and South Western Europe were having deep impact on all Asian states and of the Empire of Delhi. A large number of refugees, who belonged to administration, got employment under Iltumish but were later on liquidated.

These endowments were looked after by the rulers of that time. It has been said that Sultan Muizuddin San Ghaur dedicated two villages in favour of Jama Masjid of Multan.[27]

When Muhammad-bin-Qasim conquered Sindh, he gave to Hindus absolute freedom of worship. Vaidya says 'even in religious matters they kept their promises'.[28] The question whether those who had accepted subjection and payment of tribute for freedom of religious worship should be allowed to build their idols was referred to Hajaj and even that stern and cruel man said, 'since we have accepted their tribute we must allow them freedom of their own worship'. Like the Prophet and the four Caliphs, Muslim rulers in India also allowed this freedom. There is no doubt that Muslim invaders who differed from the Hindus both in race and religion, like Mahmud of Ghazni and Muhammad Ghori violated the sacred places of the Hindus, but this violation was more for acquiring wealth than for religion. However, there were Muslim rulers who were actuated by pure bigotry. This policy of Muslim rulers was under attack. For example, when Sikander Lodi wanted to stop the pilgrimage at Thaneswar and massacre the pilgrims, courtiers asked him to consult the theologians before starting on a murderous venture. One Ulema named Mian Abdullah of Ajodhan, an eminent theologian, strongly protested against the mad scheme of the Sultan. He opined that any interference in the religion of the Hindus was against the law of Islam. Sikander was so much enraged at the reply that he clutched his dagger and told Mian Abdullah that he would first cut his (Abdullah's) throat at and then massacre the Hindus. The theologian was not at all perturbed. 'By the will of God', he said, 'one must die on the appointed day, but in the presence of a tyrant, one always despairs of one's life'. The Sultan quieted down and a great tragedy was averted.[29] The Muslim kings and the British government also pursued the policy of correctional intervention to save the institutions from mismanagement and neglect.

During the regime of Delhi Sultanate in every village generally a mosque was constructed. Some piece of land and rooms *etc.* were also attached to the mosque. The mosque was maintained out of the income of the village. This was the duty of the villagers to look after the mosque and the attached property. The Hindus were also granted waqfs by the government. It was the duty of the Moulvies to maintain proper accounts. The accounts maintained by the Moulvies were audited by the government auditors.

It was a custom among Muslim kings to appropriate villages and lands to religious men in order to provide means for the maintenance and repair of their tombs. But these endowments were destroyed, and the grantees were reduced to distress. Sultan Alauddin was another reformer of waqfs. He carefully repaired all the tombs and restored the lands and villages after bringing into c ltivation such as had been laid waste.[30]

Sher Shah Suri[31] also followed the policy of religious toleration and equal justice among his subjects. Ishwari Prasad says that Sher Shah enunciated a policy to encourage education among his Hindu subjects. He granted them waqfs and allowed them a free hand in their management. For his liberal and beneficent policy he was liked by his subjects of all castes and creeds.

The Mughal emperors of India provided themselves on their love of equity, and regarded the administration of justice as an important duty which the sovereign could not afford to neglect.[31] The holy *Quran* declared that the unjust shall not prosper. The splendour and delight of the garden of this world, and the verdure and fruitfulness of the fields of this each depend upon the flow of the stream of the equity and justice of kings.[32] The duty of a Muslim king to do justice in person was recognised as early as the time of the early Caliphs. The Caliph was the head of judiciary and it was his duty to grant audience to his subjects with a view to redressing their grievances. Every Tuesday at the Jharoka the Mughal emperor sat in judgment where even the poorest man's complaint was heard.[33]

Mughals allowed the Hindus to be the political equals of Muslims. The Mughals were national kings, and never regarded their non-Muslim subjects as rebels. According to Father Catrou, Akbar granted the fullest liberty for the preaching of Christianity throughout his empire. The Christians were permitted to practice their ceremonies freely in public. He allowed that the internment of a Portuguese should take place attended by all the pomp of the Roman catholic religion.[34] This policy was slightly changed during Shah Jehan and Aurangzeb. During his time grants were made from the public treasury for the repairs of the mosques. The pay to Imams, of criers to the daily prayers and of readers of the Khutha was disbursed from the same source. A large amount out of the public revenue was distributed by way of alms, pensions and allowances to the doctors of religion.[35]

Prince Dara Shikoh, the elder brother of Emperor Aurangzeb, was an accomplished scholar and a great admirer of Hindu philosophy and Sanskrit learning. The Persian translation of the Upanishad, was made under his supervision. It was only by this translation that scholars came to know about this great treasure of Indian philosophy and created a desire for greater exploration of Hindu culture. Under his patronage several famous Sanskrit works were translated into Persian including the *Bhagwad Gita* and the *Yog Vasistha.* Earlier the *Ramayana* and the *Mahabharata* had been translated into Persian under orders of Akbar as also quite a number of other Sanskrit works.[36]

During Mughal rule also waqfs were established and the old waqfs were given full state protection. The term waqf was used for the religious endowments of all communities and the waqfs were looked after by the Mughals without any discrimination of caste and creed. The Sadr-u-Sadur and Sadr-e-Aala were responsible for the proper administration of waqf property by the mutawalli. Sadr-us-Sadur was the Chief Ecclesiastical Officer. He was having power to appoint Sadrs and Muftis. They were required to keep strict and constant watch on the functioning of the mutawallis. In suitable cases, they were also removed. During Muslim rule kings were taking personal interest in the creation and upkeep of waqfs.[37]

Sadr-us-Sudur was also having the power to grant land for waqf purposes. They were in charge of lands, devoted to ecclesiastical and benevolent purposes and possessed an almost unlimited authority of conferring such lands independently of the king.

In each district Sadr-e-Sarkar were constituted. The main job of these court was to check the Sanads (certificates) of mutawallis of shrines and passing bills for payment to charitable endowments. Later on, Mughals placed waqfs under the control of Sadr-e-Sarkar.

There were officers known as Sadr-e-Subah. These officers were supervising the waqf property. They were known as the chief ecclesiastical officers. Diwan of the province was responsible for the collection of dues on charitable endowments.

Sadr Subah were responsible for the proper maintenance of waqfs. Provincial Sadr were not authorised to collect due from waqf properties.

During Mughal rule property was frequently dedicated to non-Muslims for religious purposes. Aurangzeb granted Inam land, free from all dues and taxes, to the Brahmans. A royal order was also issued for the protection of a religious preceptor of the Hindus. Aurangzeb was very liberal in protecting the religious places of Hindus. The following royal orders were made for guaranteeing religious freedom of Hindus.[38]

> At this auspicious time an august firman was issued that whereas Maharajadhiraj Raja Ram Singh has represented to the most holy, and exalted court that a mansion was built by his father in Mohalla Madho Rai, on the bank of the Ganges at Benares for the residence of Bhagwant Ghoshain who is also his religious preceptor, and as certain persons harass the Goshain, therefore, our Royal command is that after the arrival of our lustrous order, the present and future officers should direct that in future, no person shall in any way interfere or disturb the Goshain, so that he may continue with peace of mind to offer up prayers for the continuance of our God given Empire that is destined to last for all time. Consider this as an urgent matter.
>
> Dated 17th Rabi 11, 1091 A.H.

At this auspicious time an august firman was issued that as two plots of land measuring 588½ dira situated on the bank of the Ganges at the Beni Madho ghat in Benares (one plot is in front of the house of Goshain Ramjivan and on the back of the central mosque, and the other is higher up) are lying vacant without any building and belong to Bait-ul-Mal, we have, therefore, granted the same to Goshain Ramjivan and his sons as Inam, so that, after building dwelling houses for the pious Brahmans and holy faqirs on the above mentioned plots, he should remain engaged in the contemplation of God and continue to offer up prayers for the continuance of our

Empire that is destined to last for all time. It is, therefore, incumbent on our illustrious sons, exalted ministers, nobel Umaras, high officials, dargahs, and present and future kotwals, to exert themselves for the continual and permanent observance of this hallowed ordinance, and permit the above mentioned plots to remain in the possession of the above mentioned person and of his descendants from generation to generation, and to consider him exempt from all dues and taxes, and not to demand from him a new sanad every year.

During Mughal period Christians were also having full religious freedom. Alexander Hamilton writes that during Aurangzeb's period Christians were free to build churches and propagate their religion.[39] In 1626 A.D. Jahangir ordered that twelve bighas of land in Mozang at Lahore be given to Father Joseph la Castro for the construction of a Church. This land was free from all revenue and imperial taxes. In the fourteenth year of Aurangzeb's[40] reign a parwanah was issued with the seal of Fida Khan, exempting the fathers from all taxes.[41]

During Mughal period Jains and their religious places were also protected. In the second year of Shahjahan's reign a sanad of general protection to the Jains from obstruction in their religion was issued. In the 30th year of the reign of Shahjahan, Murad Bux, a subedar of Gujarat, granted a sanad reciting that the village of Palitana was granted as an Inam to Shantidas, a Jain Jeweller.[42]

Guru Gobind Singh, after the battle at Chankur, sent a petition in Persian verse to Aurangzeb who expressed his regrets and, it is alleged, issued a firman declaring that the Sikhs were a harmless people, having no enmity with any sect, and ordering that no one was, thereafter, to interfere with them.[43]

The early Turkish Sultans of Delhi gave full religious liberty to their non-Muslim subjects. This policy was also followed by Muslims. Hindus were allowed to follow their religion according to their wishes. They were allowed to bow before their idols, blow their conches, bathe in the river Jumna, and take out their religious processions without any let or hindrance by the state.[44] During this period Hindus were at liberty to construct new temples. Three images of the

Jaina sect, discovered in Etah, contain dated records of their installation in the year v.s. 1335/1278. A fragment of bilingual inscription in Persian and Sanskrit found in the purana qila of Delhi records the endowment of 12 bighahs of land to a temple dedicated to Sri Krishna.[45]

The Muslim kings refrained from enforcing Islamic law which favoured extermination of idolators. The Brahmanabad settlement between the Hindus and Muhammad Ibn Qasim the earliest Muslim invaders deviated from orthodox Islamic law and permitted the inhabitants of Brahmanabad . . . to repair the temple of the Budha and pursue their religion to worship their God.[46] The settlement commanded—nobody must be forbidden and prevented from following his own religion. They may live in the houses in whatever manner they like. Iltutmish accepted and acted on the advice of Junaidi that as the country had been conquered only recently and as the Muslims were very few in number, it would be inadvisable to pursue a policy that might create disturbances.[47] Balban too was guided by similar political considerations. Allauddin Khilji was of the opinion that 'policy and government are one thing, and rules and decrees of Islamic law are another'. Royal commands belonged to the Sultan. Islamic legal decrees rest upon the judgment of the Qazis and Muftis.[48]

The testamentary advice of Babur to Humayun urging him to shed religious prejudice, protect temples, preserve cows, and administer justice properly is in this tradition.[49] A Portuguese Manrique observed—here every man has liberty to profess his own religion freely.[50] He described an incident which portrays vividly the Mughal administration's respect for the religious susceptibilities of the Hindu. He says that one of his Muslim followers who had killed a peacock was caught and was punished with the amputation of his hand. A local official who commuted the sentence to whipping, explained that the emperor determined to let the Hindus living according to their laws and customs and to tolerate no breach of them.

The relations between the Hindus and the Muslims in medieval India were too complex to break any such generalisation. But it can be safely said that there was no communal animosity though the two lived as distinct cultural groups professing and practising different religions. Therefore, there were no Hindu Muslim riots, even when the Sikh, Maratha and Jat uprisings led to enormous conflicts between these communities and the Mughal state. Mukhia says there was non-occurrence of communal riots at the social level even in the worst days of Aurangzeb's tyranny.[51] During Muslim rule, Hindus were completely allowed to preserve their personal laws. There was complete protection to their religious property. Rajendra Prasad says that the attitude of the Muslim conqueror had on the whole been one of toleration and there had been continuous effort to deal with the Hindus fairly.[52]

In medieval India neither secular nor theocratic policies were prevalent. They employed the state machinery not for the propagation but for the exploitation of religion, and they refrained from enforcing the orthodox Shariat and from imposing Muslim law on the Hindus. The Hindus and the Muslims were not assimilated or integrated but they lived together in amity as two separate cultural groups professing and practising two different religions. United by common economic interests Hindu and Muslim subjects jointly rebelled against Muslim kings on more than one occasion. They did not resort to killing each other during the several revolts and rebellions against the Muslim kings—not even during the days of Aurangzeb.

Of course, Muslim and Hindu rulers adopted the policy of tolerance ; but there was no separation between state and religion. Construction of new mosques and Madrasas, maintenance of the existing ones, patronage of the theologians and scholars, appointment to religious officers were regarded as the proper functions of the ruler, which were carried out by one of the state department. Ziyauddin Barni, a noted writer, says that it is wonderful to note that Allauddin Khilji could be a success despite his policy. The policy of Allauddin Khilji was non-conformist.[53]

It is, therefore, clear that whatever might have been the circumstances it is certain that it was realised by all the rulers that they cannot rule the country unless and until the followers of all religions feel themselves that their lives, property, religious endowments are secured.

Under the British rule

The policy of the British government was not to interfere in the religious affairs of the local inhabitants. The Britishers were of the opinion that any control of religious institutions was, in fact, an exercise of sovereign power as it was traditionally understood in Indian terms. Ganapati Iyer[54] says :

> For, the policy of the company was, undoubtedly, not to create suspicion among the natives who were left in the enjoyment of their own laws and customs and were given their own courts to decide disputes among themselves. In fact, there was an implied, if not express, agreement when the natives came to live with the Europeans in the factories that they would be left in the undisputed enjoyment of their rights and that their laws & co. would be respected and given effect to.

However, Britishers could not follow this policy of non-interference for a long time. This was considered to be the duty of the government to look, manage and protect the religious endowments. These institutions were under the special protection of ruling authority. In Rameshwar Pagoda's case[55] their lordship of the Judicial Committee observed that there can be little doubt that the superintending authority was exercised by the old rulers. Mr. Nelson in his Madura Manual says—

> The principal pagodas with their enormous establishments, their officiating priests *etc.*, were managed by Dharma karta or trustee and manager for life who as stated above was usually a monk and a Guru . . . . . The Dharma kartas held but little communication with one another and recognised no earthly superior except the king himself. Each was independent of all control and acted altogether as he pleased. This freedom led naturally to gross abuses and the king was compelled occasionally to interfere in the management of some of the churches.[56]

A similar view was expressed by West J. in *Manohar Ganesh* v. *Lakhmiram*.[57] He said that the State in its secular executive and judicial capacity habitually intervened to prevent fraud and waste in dealing with religious endowments.

It is relevant here to discuss the case of *Rajah Mutt Ramalinga Setupati* v. *Perianayagam Pillai*.[58] In this case, the Privy Council, while explaining the provisions of the Madras Regulation VII of 1817, referred to Nelson's Madras Manual and made the following observations :

> It was abundantly clear from this letter that long before Regulation VII, the British government not only assumed the power to superintend the management of the property and affairs of pagodas throughout the peninsular but exercised its authority through the agency of its collectors.
>
> It was further observed—
>
> that before that Regulation the British government by virtue of its sovereign powers, assumed as former rulers of the country had done, the right to visit endowments of this kind and redress abuses in their management.

The main motive of the Britishers was to collect revenue.[59] The English concept of trust was not introduced by Britishers immediately. The Indian courts accepted gradually the English classification of trust.[60] However, the validity of an endowment was determined on the basis of Hindu law.[61] It was only on the basis of Hindu law that the Privy Council in *Ranchoordass* v. *Parvati*[62] disallowed bequests in favour of dharma. Once the validity of an endowment was established, trust notions were introduced to superintend its governance, even though the Succesion[63] and Transfer of Property[64] Acts were applicable in certain cases. However, the provisions of Trust Act, 1881 were not specifically made applicable to Hindu religious institutions.

The Anglo Hindu law seems to have superimposed English notions and recognised a whole range of proprietary interests. In Bengal and Madras Regulations were passed for having control over religious endowments.[65] Under the Madras Regulation a Board of Revenue was constituted to superintend all religious endowments.[66] It operated through agents in each district.[67] The agents informed the Board[68] about all unjust appropriations,[69] reported the names of present trustees and managers[70] and of various vacancies that had been created.[71] In certain cases, the Board was having power to fill in vacancies.[72] The board also had powers to ensure that the property was used for the purposes for which it was dedicated[73] In the last, the Regulation provided that they were designed only to ensure a fair administration and not to give the government an interfering leeway.[74]

In Bombay the Regulation (XVII) of 1827 was passed. The Bombay regulation was similar to the Regulation of Madras. The Bombay Regulation was withdrawn and a strict policy of non-intervention was followed from the year 1842. In *Advocate General* v. *Vishvanath Atmaram*[75] it was objected that if questions regarding Hindu temples were decided by civil courts, it would virtually amount to propagating the Hindu religion and that such questions were, therefore, not within the place of civil courts. The Bombay Sudder Court (consisting of Yardley, C J and Jackson J) refused to accept the above contention and said that the Supreme Court had jurisdiction to interfere in cases of Hindu and Mahomedan charities and religious institutions.

In *Narayan* v. *Chintamani*[76] it was said that in India there exists no state church and where the Hindu and Mahomedan religions are more amply recognised, civil courts cannot refuse to interfere in cases of Hindu and Mahomedan charities and religious institutions and there exists a stronger reason for British Indian courts exercising jurisdiction over matters connected with such charities and religious institutions than for English courts over dissenting charities. In *Manohar Ganesh Tembekar* v. *Lakhmiram Govindram*[77] a similar view was expressed by Birwood J. He said that civil courts have jurisdiction to enforce trusts for charitable and religious purposes, having connection with Hindu and Mahomedan foundations. From the very beginning it was considered the duty of the courts to protect all trusts and it was the duty of the sovereign to protect his subjects in the enjoyment of their religion.

Where a trustee of a temple failed to perform certain

festival which it was the usage of the temple to perform and it was either sought to remove the trustee for breach of trust or to compel the trustee to do the act, the court could interfere.[78] Similarly where a mutawalli of a mosque pronounced the word 'Amen' in a loud or low tone when engaged in prayer, and it was objected that this was contrary to the usage of the institution, courts must try the correct practice. The courts keeping into consideration the usage of the institution and the Muslim law had to decide whether the practice of saying 'Amen' loudly was correct or it should be said slowly.[79]

Similarly, where a person was expelled from caste either by the caste at a meeting[80] or by a religious superior[81] and such person had not the right to enter a temple, the courts from the very beginning had jurisdiction to try the cases.

It is, therefore, clear that even during British period courts were not hesitant in looking after the religious affairs of Indians. The Government of India, Act, 1919, authorised regional legislatures to ensure proper management of these institutions.

REFERENCES

1. *Quran* para 2, Sura 35 : 262.
2. *Quran* para 2, Sura 35 : 270.
3. *Quran* para 2, Sura 36 : 277.
4. *Quran* para 3, Al-Imran Sura 9 : 92.
5. *Quran* Surah 2 Ver 215.
6. *Surah* 3, Ver 92.
7. Surah 2. Ver 177.
8. See Shibli Naumani, Seerat-un-Nabi, Vol. II (Azamgarh, 1352 AH)
9. Vol. 1, p. 125 ; see also *Encyclopaedia of Islam*, p. 1097. Fyzee in his book *Outlines of Muhammadan Law* p. 265 has also cited this illustration.
10. Syed Ameer Ali, *Mahomedan Law*, Vol. I Pp. 214-16 ; K.P. Saxena, *Muslim Law*, p. 461.
11. S. Athar Hussain, *Waqf Laws and Administration in India*, p. 6.
12. Mamal-et-Din el Siwasi (died in 861 A.D.) who was the author of the above book also gave a list of waqfs created by the Prophet himself, and his companions. The waqf by the Prophet himself of a piece of land which he had acquired in the Canton of Khaibar for the support of travellers, the waqf of Omar of the land called Sammagh in the same canton for his children, kindred, and the poor, of Zabair ibn Awwam for his daughters ; of Akram in favour of his son ; of Abu

Bakr in favour of his children ; of S' aad ibn Abi Wakkas of his lands in Medina and Egypt for his children 'which still exists' ; and of Osman of his lands called Boruah, 'which still continues.'

13. Bukhari, Wasaya, Bab. 17.
14. Henry Catton, *Law of Waqf in the Middle East* ed. by Majid Khadduri and Liebesny, Vol 1 p. 205 (1955).
15. See *Encyclopaedia of Islam* p. 1100. The encyclopaedia contains an example of family waqf which can be made by Shafii of a house in Fustat for his descendants.
16. 750—1258 A.D.
17. *Abdul Ganne Kasem* v. *Hussein M. Rahimtulla*, 1873 10 Bom HCR 7.
18. The Report of the Hindu Religious Endowments Commission, May 10, 1962.
19. Abdur Rahim, *Muhammadan Jurisprudence*, Pp. 383-384 (1963).
20. From 711 to 1492.
21. *The Religion Reformers in Islam*, p. 1.
22. See Chakravarty A., *Hindus and Mussalmans of India*, p. 13.
23. Tara Chand, *Influence of Islam on Indian Culture* (1946).
24. R.P. Tripathi, *Some Aspects of Muslim Administration*, (Allahabad) (1936) and (1964) p. 59.
25. See *Tarikh-i-Jaha Gusha*, Vol. II, p. 177.
26. *Rauzat-us-Safa*, vol. V. p. 38-39 ; *Tarikh-i-Jahan Gusha*, vol. I, p. 15.
27. Who reached his zenith of power during 1185-95 A.D.
28. C.V. Vaidya, *History of Medieval Hindu India*, (Poona, 1926) Vol. 1, p. 180.
29. Zahiruddin Faruki, *Aurangzeb and His Times*, p. 111.
30. See Shams Siraj Afif, *Tarikh-e-Firoz Shahi*, (Elliot and Dowson), Vol. III, p. 353-55.
31. Abul Fazl's *Ain-e-Akbari*, translated by H. Blochmann, Vol. III, p. 399,
32. Elliot, *History of India* ; Rustom Ali, *Tarikh-i-Hindi*, (Reign of Muhammad Shah) Vol. III, p. 43.
33. Sir Thomas Roe in Purchas, *His Pilgrims*, B.S. Purchase.
34. Father F. Catrou, *History of the Mughal Dynasty*, p. 108.
35. Elliot *etc.*, *History of India* ; Bakhtawar Khan, *Mirat-i-Alam* Vol. VII, p. 159 ; Ram Prasad Khosla, *Mughal Kingship and Nobility* (Reprint) 1976.
36. A. Chakravarty, *Hindus and Mussalmans of India*, p. 15.
37. Tripathi *etc.*, *Twarikhe-Daulat-e-Sher* Medieval India Quarterly, Vol. 1 No. 1, July-September issue, p. 63.

38. See Zahiruddin Faruqi, *Aurangzeb and His Times*, p. 132.
39. 1098 Hijra ; See Zahiruddin Faruqi, *Aurangzeb and His Times*, p. 132.
40. 1672 A.D.
41. *Journal of the Punjab Historical Society* p. 200.
42. Zahiruddin Faruqi, *Aurangzeb and His Times*, p. 136.
43. *Id* note 42, p. 138
44. *Tarikh-i-Firoz Shahi*, Pp. 216-17 ; Nizami A.K., *Some Aspects of Religion and Politics during the Thirteenth Century*, p. 320.
45. Nizami, supra 45, p. 320, Professor Nizami has cited following material in support of his statement. V.S. Agarwal's article. A note on Medieval Temple Architecture, Jr. of the United Provinces Historial Society, July (1943) Pp. 112-117 ; Reports of the Archaeological Survey of India 1909-10, p. 131 and 1923 p. 92.
46. Elliot *etc.*, *The History of India* as told by its own Historians, Vol.1, Pp. 185-6 ; Rajendra Prasad, *India Divided*, 1946, p. 81.
47. S.M. Ikram, *Muslim Civilization in India*, (1964), Pp. 11-12.
48. *Supra* note 46, Vol. III, p. 183.
49. Rajendra Prasad, *supra* note 46, p. 37.
50. *Supra* note 47, Pp. 235-36 ; see also Terry in Fichs, *Early Travellers in India* (ed. by W. Foster), p. 315.
51. Harbans Mukhia, *Medieval Indian History and the Communal Approach*, p. 34.
52. *Supra* note 46, p. 81.
53. J.M. Shelat, Traditions of Indian Historiography and the problems arising from them. An inaugural address to the annual session of the Madhya Pradesh Itihasa Conference, 1970.
54. Ganapati Iyer, The law relating to Hindu and Mahomedan Religious Endowments, p. 1.
55. LR 1, IA 299.
56. Part III, Chapter 7, p. 162.
57. ILR 12 Bom 247.
58. (1874) 1 IA 209.
59. See the case of Collector of *Murshidabad* v. *Bishwanath Rai* (1807) 6 I D (Old series) 170 ; *Ramtonoo Mullick* v. *Ramgopal Mullick* cited by Macnaghten—Considerations on the Hindoo Law, 346 (1824).
60. See *Ganga Bai* v. *Thavur* (1863) 1 BHCR 71; *Bombay* v. *Commissioner* (1892) 16 Bom 217 ; *Saiyad Hussain Matira* v. *Collector*, (1897) 21 Bom. 48 at 52 ; *Monie* v. *Scott* (1914) 4 Bom. 281 at 292.
61. See Das Merces v. Hyde 6 Hyde 65 ; *Andrews* v. *Jeakim* (1859) 2 Bom LR 148 (CJ) ; *Judah* v. *Judah* (1890) 5 BLR 433 ; *Khushal chand* v.

Mahadevji (1875) 12 BHCR 244 ; *Rupa Jagshet* v. *Krishnaji* (1885) 9 Bom 169 ; *Jewan* v. *Shah Kuberuddin* (1841) 2 MIA 390 ; *Sonatu Bysack* v. *Juggal Kishore* (1859) 8 MIA 66 ; *Juggur Mohinder* v. *Sakheemoney* (1871) 14 MIA 289.

62. (1899) 26 I A 71.
63. See *Lala Hem Chand* v. *Pearey Lal* (1943) 1 MLJ 11 at 14 (PC).
64. *Narasimhan* v. *Venkatalingam* (1927) 50 Mad 687 (FB).
65. See Regulation XIX of 1810 (Bengal) and Regulation VII of 1817 (Madras).
66. See section 2 of the Regulation VII of 1817.
67. Section 7
68. Section 8.
69. Section 9.
70. Section 10.
71. Section 11.
72. Section 13.
73. Sections 3-5.
74. Section 10.
75. (1855) 1 BHCR p. 9.
76. (1881) ILR 5 Bom 393.
77. (1887) ILR 12 Bom 27.
78. *Subbaraya* v. *Chellappa* (1881) ILR 4 Mad 315.
79. *Fazul Karim* v. *Mawla Baksh* (1891) 18 Cal 448, 18 I A 59.
80. *Keshav Lal* v. *Bai Girja* (1899) ILR 24 BU.
81. Appaya v. Padappa (1898) ILR 23 Bom 122.

2

Waqf Law and Administration of Waqfs in India

General Observations

The chief sources for the early doctrines on the law of waqf are *Mudanwana of Sahnun.*[1] This book contains the opinions of Malik[2] of Ibn Qasim.[3] This book also contains information in respect of other early authorities of Medina. The book *Kitab Ahkam-al-waqf* by Hilal[4] contained information on the principles propounded by Abu Hanifa,[5] Abu Yusuf[6] and other authorities. The other important books which contain information in respect of waqf are *Kitab-al-siyar-el-kabir* of Shaibani and *Kitab-al-Umn* of Shafi.[7]

The legal meaning of 'waqf' according to Abu Hanifa is the appropriation of a particular article (corpus) in such a manner as subjects it to the rules of divine property. The immediate consequence of dedication is that the waqif will cease to have any right over the property which he has dedicated and the Almighty will become the owner of the property. Abu Hanifa was also of the opinion that a waqif is free to dedicate his property in waqf and the profit which may be derived from that property will be applied for the benefit of mankind. He said that waqf signifies the appropriation of any particular things (corpus) in such a way that (a) the appropriator's right in it shall continue, and (b) the advantage of it go to some charitable object or it is the detention of a specific thing (corpus) in the ownership of the waqf or appropriator, and the devoting or appropriating of its profits or usufruct in charity, on the poor, or other good objects in the manner of an ariyat or commodate loan. From the definition mentioned above, it is clear that under the Hanafi school waqif's right of ownership continues even after dedicating the property and he was free to dispose it off according to his will.

The principles propounded by Malik are very important. *Habs fi Sabil Allah* is given an important place and according to this doctrine both movable and immovable property can be given in waqf. According to Hanafi doctrine waqf can be made only of immovable property. Hilal in his book *Kitab ahkan-al-waqf* says that a Muslim cannot make a sadaqa of animals, merchandise and garments. A Muslim can validly make a gift of mules, weapons, horses and land *etc.*

Under Shafi school. a waqf is permanent dedication of property. The profits or use is only devoted to the purpose for which the waqf was created.

There was an impact of Medinese doctrine on Maliki school. Maliki school recognises a temporary habs in favour of few particular persons. After the death of such person or persons, the property will revert back to the original owner or his heirs.

Hilal states that 'the people and judges of Basra have always insisted that every waqf must finally go to the poor' and that some lawyers demand that the poor should be explicitly mentioned on the ultimate beneficiaries of each waqf.[8]

Under Hanafi school, a waqf must be made under a legacy. A waqif can make only one third of the estate and it can be revoked by the benefactor during his life time. Abu Hanifa further said that for a valid waqf, the ownership must be transferred to some one other than the owner and a transfer to the indeterminate body of the poor could not be envisaged. He further said that a waqf can be created in favour of one's own relatives or to one's poor neighbours.

There is an identity of views between Hanifee and Maliki schools on the question of the validity of a waqf. However, there is a slight difference between the two. Maliki school recognises the taking of possession on behalf of the poor by an appointed administrator. On the other hand, Hanifi school says that the presence of the poor even as ultimate beneficiaries will invalidate a waqf even though the subject matter of such waqf can be handed over to a determined first beneficiary.

The definition of waqfs is analogous to the definition given in section 2 of Mussalman Waqf Validating Act, 1913. The literal and primitive meaning of the word waqf is 'detention' or 'stoppage'. Up to the time of Abu Hanifa, it was not clear as to in whom did the ownership of the property vest. Juristically, a waqf means (i) the tying up of corpus (property) in perpetuity and (ii) devoting the usufruct (benefit), (iii) for pious or charitable purposes. We can call it a 'pious endowment.'

Abu Hanifa says that waqf means the appropriation of a specific thing (corpus) in such a way that (a) the appropriator's right in it shall continue and the advantage of it go to some charitable object. In other words, it is the detention of a specific thing (corpus) in the ownership of the waqf or appropriator, and the devoting or appropriating of its profits or usufruct in charity, or the poor, or other good objects in the manner of an ariyat or commodate loan. There are two important elements in his definition. Firstly, the right of the owner continues and secondly the usufruct is to be devoted to some charitable or pious purpose.

Khwaja Mohammed Noor J. held in a case,[9] 'The legal meaning of waqf according to the accepted doctrine of the Hanafi school is the extinction of the proprietor's ownership in the thing dedicated and its detention in the implied ownership of God in such a manner that the profits may revert to and be applied for the benefit of the mankind.

The following are the main ingredients of a waqf under the Hanafi school :

(i) The right of the owner continues even after dedication;

(ii) Immediately after the dedication of the property, it becomes irrevocable. Unless and until there was a decree of court or it was a testamentary waqf ;

(iii) The dedicated property must expressly purport to be in perpetuity; and

(iv) where the object c waqf fails, or is such that it may fail, waqf is void.

Abu Yusuf was the most favourable disciple of Abu Hanifa. The views expressed by Abu Yusuf were followed by later jurists. Abu Yusuf maintains that waqf signifies the extinction of the appropriator's ownership in the thing dedicated and the detention of the thing in the implied ownership of God, in such a manner that its profits may revert to or be applied for the benefit of mankind.[10] The dedicated property can neither be sold nor given nor inherited. The views of Abu Yusuf are generally prevalent in India. In *Jeewan Doss v. Shah Kubeer-Ooddin*[11] it was said that immediately after the creation of a waqf the owner shall have no right in the dedicated property. Such property can neither be sold nor given nor inherited. The case of Jeewan Doss was followed in *Vidya Varuthi* v *Balusami Ayyar*.[12] In this case, the Privy Council maintained that after the creation of waqf, right of the waqif is extinguished and the ownership is transferred to the Almighty. Fatawai Alamgiri declares that 'decrees in this country are given according to Abu Yusuf.'[13]

It can, therefore, be said that the following are the necessary ingredients for a valid waqf :

(a) *Religious or pious motive* : A merely secular motive would render the dedication a gift or trust, but not a waqf. The ownership will rest in the God.

(b) *Permanent nature* : Waqf is a permanent endowment. A pious dedication which is not permanent may be a sadaqa but can not come under the category of waqf. The dedicator will have no right in the property.

(c) *Utilisation of usufruct* : The ultimate benefit of the waqf should go to the mankind.

Imam Muhammad[14] says that the right of the waqif does not cease in property until he has appointed a mutawalli and delivered its possession into his hands. This was not the opinion of Imam Shafii and Abu Yusuf. Abu Yusuf and Imam Muhammad maintained that waqf is the tying up of the substance of a thing under the rule of the property of Almighty God, so that proprietary right of the waqif becomes extinguished and is transferred to Almighty God for any purpose by which its profits may be applied to the benefit of His creatures. Imam Muhammad was of the opinion that the right of the waqif was extinguished immediately he made the declaration. In modern India, the definition given by Abu Yusuf is considered to be the correct definition.

It is clear from the above that there is a vast difference between the views of Abu Hanifa and two of his disciples. According to Abu Hanifa the ownership of a waqf vests in the waqif, while his disciples Abu Yusuf and Imam Muhammad maintained that it abates in favour of God. Imam Shafi was also of the same opinion. In India, the views of Abu Yusuf are generally followed .

Shia Law

Sharia-ul-Islam deals with the Shia law. Shia school defines the term waqf in a different manner. Under the Shia law also a waqf is made for pious, religious or charitable purpose. The Shiites, hold that ownership of waqf vests in beneficiaries. The main aim of the waqf is to provide maximum benefit to mankind. Ameer[15] Ali says that according to the definition given by Sharai-ul-Islam waqf is a contract the fruit or effect of which is to tie up the original and to leave its usufruct free. He further said that the waqf or subject of appropriations is transferred, so as to become the property of mowakif aleh (or persons on whom the settlement is made) for he has a right to the advantage or benefits to be derived from it.

The above definition has two elements——(i) tying up or immobilisation of the corups, the subject matter of the waqf, and (ii) the use of the usufruct for certain purposes for the benefit of mankind. It is not clear from the above definition as to in whom does the property vests.

This definition is similar to that of given by Abu Hanifa. Abu Hanifa maintained that after the dedication of property in the waqf, the ownership is not transferred from waqif but remains in him as in ariyat[16]. Tyabji says that according to Shiite authorities, the corpus shall belong to the beneficiaries. Under Shia law, the ownership of waqfs property vests in God Almighty.[17] According to Sharai-ul-Islam a waqf can not be revoked.

The above definition was followed in *Kassimiah Charities* v. *Secretary, Madras State Waqf Board.*[18] In this case the term waqf was defined as the detention of the corups in the ownership of God in such a manner that its profits may be applied for the benefit of His servants. The objects of dedication must be pious or charitable. In a waqf there is extinction of the proprietor's ownership and detention in the implied ownership of God.[19] Immediately on dedication the property in the dedicator is divested and vests in the Almighty.[20]

One of the important ingredient of waqf is that it should be made with a religious motive—a desire to approach God. In *Abdul Wahab* v. *Sughra Begum*[21] it was said that approach to God may be made only by an act that is meritorious in Islam. In this case a family waqf was created for the salary and pension of servants. The waqf was held as valid.

Definition of waqf according to ancient jurists

Islamic law jurists have defined the term waqf in their own way. There is no idendity of opinion amongst different jurists on this point. According to Ameer[22] Ali waqf literally means detention, stopping or tying up. In Macnaghten's[23] *Principles and Precedents of Mohummadan Law* waqf is defined to be endowment, that is, appropriation of certain property to religious or useful, or what we should call, generally charitable purposes. If land is the subject matter of the waqf, the profits are dedicated to religious objects. Wilson[24] has given his definition in another way. According to him waqf is made of specified property and the property is permanently devoted to specific objects. Mulla[25] has followed the definition given in the Mussalman Waqf Validating Act, 1933. He says waqf means the permanent dedication by a person professing the Mussalman faith of any property for any purpose recognised by the Mussalman law as religious, pious or charitable.

It has been maintained that the above definition is for the purpose of the Act and is not necessarily exhaustive.[26] Though the definition is not exhaustive it brings out the dominant elements of waqfs.

Under such circumstances, a complete definition cannot be given unless and until the three important ingredients are included :

(i) the motive of dedication must be religious, a merely secular motive would render the dedication a gift or a trust ; but not a waqf ;

(ii) it is a permanent endowment, a pious gift, which is not a permanent foundation, may be a sadaqa, but cannot in law be termed as waqf ;

(iii) the usufruct is to be utilised for the good of mankind.

It is relevant here to mention the few definitions given by Pakistani courts. In *Abdul Hamid* v *Fateh Muhammad*[27] it was said that waqf means tying up the corpus and devoting the usufruct to some pious object and that the waqf property is not to be alienated in any way *i.e.*, gift or inheritance. The court further said that if the corpus of the dedicated property is intended to be consumed, the dedication will not be a waqf. In another case *i.e.* in *Gholam Hosain Sherazee* v *Province of East Pakistan*[28] it was said that it is well settled that once a waqf always a waqf and it cannot change in character merely because it is sometimes described by another name. Though there is a good deal of similarity between a waqf and a trust, there are also vital and substantial differences between them.

Law before the passing of the Mussalman Validating Act, 1913

It will not be out of the way to mention here the provisions of the Mussalman Waqf Validating Act, 1913, and the judicial opinion which was prevalent before the passing of the above mentioned Act, Before the passing of the Mussalman Waqf Validating Act, 1913 the Privy Council had diverged materially from Hanafi texts. In *Abul Fata Mahomed Ishak* v. *Rasamaya Dher Chowdhury*[29] the Privy Council characterised a family waqf as a gift (i) for which the donor exercises no self-denial ; (ii) taking back with one hand what he appears to put away with the other, (iii) forming the centre of attraction for accumulation of income and further accessions of family property ; (iv) carefully protecting so-called managers from being called to account ; (v) seeking to give to the donors and their family the enjoyment of property, free from all liability to creditors ; (vi) and not seeking the benefit of others beyond the use of empty words.

Their Lordship further said that they have endeavoured to the best of their ability to ascertain and apply the Muslim law as known and administered in India, but they cannot find that they have endeavoured to the best of their ability to ascertain and apply the Muslim law as known and administered in India, but they cannot find that it is in accordance with the absolute, and as it seems to them extravagant, application of abstract precepts taken from the mouth of Prophet. The Privy Council said that the creation of a family endowment was not a religious and meritorious act. It was said that the perpetual application of the surplus income in the acquisition of new properties to be added to the family estate was not a charitable purpose.

It may be noted here that it is only under Abu Yusuf's exposition of Hanafi law that waqif can benefit from a family waqf and therefore, the above criticism cannot apply to a waqf made in accordance with any other exposition of the law. It is again submitted that the donor exercises no self-denial. Even under Hanafi school the waqif reserves the life interest to himself. The waqif will not be able to deal with the corpus of the property. Under the family waqfs the whole profit goes to only few people and it may cause them great inconvenience in unforeseen times of need.

There are certain circumstances under which a Muslim woman and orphan will not have the right of inheritance in the deceased's property. Family waqfs can help them. Under family waqfs provision can be made for their maintenance. The women are often given shares with the other descendants and unless it is otherwise provided men and women share equally.

Position after the Passing of the Act

On account of the decision of the Privy Council in Abul Fata's case there arose a movement for the introduction of an act providing for the validity of such a waqf as valid. Consequently, the Government of India was constrained to pass the Mussalman Waqf Validating Act, 1913. This piece of legislation came into force on March 7, 1913.

Definition under the Mussalman Waqf Validating Act, 1913

As already discussed, under the Mussalman Waqf Validating Act, 1913, a waqf is defined as a permanent dedication by a person professing the Mussalman faith of any property for any purpose recognised by Muslim law as religious, pious or charitable. The preliminary benefit of the waqf property might be reserved—(a) for the maintenance and support wholly or partially of the waqif's family, children or descendants, and also (b) in case the waqif is a Hanafi, (i) wholly or partially for his own maintenance and support during his life time or (ii) for the payment of his debts out of the rents and profits of the property dedicated ; and the ultimate benefit above referred to may be postponed until after the extinction of his family children and descendants.

The Act further provides that nothing in the Waqf Act, 1913 affects any custom or usage whether local or prevalent among Muslims of any particular class or sect.

Nothing in the Waqf Validating[30] Act, affects any right, title or obligation or liability already acquired, accrued or incurred before 25 July, 1930.

Waqfs created before the passing of the Mussalman Waqf Validating Act, 1913, were validated by the Waqf Act of 1930, so that Waqf Act of 1913 was deemed to apply to waqfs created before its commencement[31] providing that nothing contained in Waqf Act, 1930 was deemed in any way to affect any right, title, obligation or liability already acquired, accrued or incurred before 25 July, 1930.[32] In *Khajah Solehman* v. *Salimullah*[33] it was said that Waqf Act, 1913, was not retrospectively effective. The Act was applicable only to those waqfs which came into existence after March 7, 1913.

The Waqf Act, 1913, did not effect any custom or usage

whether local or prevalent among Muslims of any particular class or sect. But Section 2 of the Shariat Act, 1937, says that 'notwithstanding any custom or usage to the contrary, in all questions (save questions relating to agricultural land) regarding (i) question relating to agricultural land and (ii) charities and charitable institution, and charitable and religious endowments, but (iii) not regarding other waqfs'.

In *Ma Mi and another* v *Kallander Ammal*[34] the Privy Council said that the definition given in the Mussalman Waqf Validating Act of 1913 is for the purpose of the Act, and is not necessarily exhaustive apart from the Act. It was, therefore, necessary for the validity of a waqf that the intention of the waqif must be religious, the dedication must be permanent and the profits derived from the waqf property shall be utilised for the uplift of mankind.

Definition as given under the Waqf Act, 1954

The definition given under this Act is more elaborate.[35] Under this Act, a waqf means a permanent dedication by a person professing Islam of any movable or immovable property for any purpose recognised by the Muslim law as pious, religious or charitable and includes—

(i) waqf by user ;

(ii) mashrut-ul-khidmat ; and

(iii) a waqf alal-aulad to the extent to which property is dedicated for any purpose recognised by Muslim law as pious, religious or charitable.

A waqf for the benefit of dedicator, his family and descendants, generation after generation violates the rules against perpetuity and, therefore, such a waqf will be void.[36]

A waqf can be created either by a Muslim or by non-Muslim.[37] The only condition is that the object of the waqf is one which is recognised by Muslim law as pious, religious or charitable and his own religion treats the object in the same manner. In clause (1) of Section 3 the words 'professing Islam' have been intentionally included. In case these words were excluded from Section 3 sub clause (1) all charitable and many pious endowments of other communities would have come within the purview of the Act. The reason for this assumption is that the purposes for which they stand are also regarded as charitable or pious under the Muslim law.

In 1964, the Waqf (Amendment) Act was passed. This Act removed the above defects of the Waqf Act, 1954. The Waqf (Amendment) Act, 1964 treats all grants made for religious, pious and charitable purposes including Mashrul-ul-khidmat as waqf and also permanent dedications made for mosques, *dargahs*, *imambaras*, *takias*, *musafirkhanas*, *etc*., by non-Muslims. Under Section 3 (1) of the Waqf Act, 1954, these dedications were not treated as valid object of waqf though it is maintained that under the Muslim law, these dedications were regarded as valid object of waqf.

Land used for the purpose of prayer and also for Muharram festival[38] from time immemorial was treated as waqf. In such cases, evidence of express dedication shall not be necessary.

The definition given in the Waqf Act, 1954 is an exhaustive definition, Section (1) of the Waqf Act, 1954 says that waqf means the permanent dedication by a person professing Islam. It means dedication of property for charitable and pious endowments of other communities will not come within the category of waqf. It may, however, be noted here that Section 66-C of the Act provides that non-Muslims can make a waqf, provided the object of waqf does not come into clash with the spirit of Islam.

The Waqf Act 29 of 1954 has been so amended in the state of Tamil Nadu (Madras) Waqf (Supplementary) Act 19 of 1961 as to include in the definition of the word 'waqf' all property given or endowed by any person professing any religion for the support of (1) mosques, *idgahs*, *imambaras*, *dargahs*, khanqas or maqbaras, (ii) graveyards and (ii) charities of persons professing Islam.

Madhya Pradesh Public Trusts Act, 1951

Section 2 (8) of the M.P. Public Trusts Act,[39] 1951 says that 'waqf means a permanent dedication by a person professing of any Islam movable or immovable property for any purpose recognised by the Islamic law as pious religious or charitable and includes a waqf by user, but does not include any waqf, such as described in Section 3 of the Mussalman Waqf Validating Act, 1913 under which any benefit is for the time being claimable for himself by the person by whom the waqf was created or by any member of his family or descendants. This definition includes the following—(i) permanent dedication ; (ii) by a person professing Islam; (iii) of any property whether movable or immovable; (iv) for the purpose which is recognised as pious, religious and charitable by Islamical law; (v) but it can not be a private or family waqf.

The definition given above is exhaustive and extensive. This definition consists of the word 'means' and 'includes'. The word 'means' is connotative of the exhaustiveness of the definition whereas the word 'includes' means the extension of the normal meaning of the word which is sought to be defined. It can, therefore, be said that the word, 'includes' enlarges the normal ambit and scope of a word. It embraces into it certain other things which are not normally included by it. The first part of the definition in both the Acts is identical. However, the later part of the definition given in Waqf Act, 1954 and the definition given in M.P. Public Trusts Act, 1951 are quite different. The definition given in the M.P. Public Trust Act, 1951, is inclusive in negative term, whereas the definition under the M.P. Public Trusts Act directs as what shall not be included in it. However, the Waqf Act, 1954 says what shall be deemed to be included in it.

As far as the general Muslim law of waqfs is concerned the definition given under the Waqf Act or under the M. P. Act is not exhaustive. The definition has been made limited for the purpose of this Act only.[40] The purpose of the Act was not to derogate the provisions of Muslim law.[41]

As noted above the provisions of Section 2 (8) of the M. P. Public Trusts Act, 1951 are identical to the provisions of Section 2 (13) of the Bombay Public Trusts Act. In *Alimiya* v *Syed Mohammed*[42] the Gujarat High Court held that waqf by immemorial user is not the same thing as 'waqf by user' mentioned in Section 2 (19) of the Trusts Act. The difference between the two expressions is two-fold. The first is that waqf before 1950 was required to be arising out of a permanent dedication of any property by a person for a pious, religious and charitable purpose recognised by Islamic law. The Indian courts have laid stress on the permanent dedication which can also be inferred from the evidence relating to immemorial user of the property for such purpose. The definition as is given in M.P. Public Trusts Act, 1951 does not say about waqf by immemorial user. It only deals with regard to permanent dedication of property, which also includes a waqf by user.

KINDS OF WAQFS

Waqfs can be of three kinds *i.e.* public, quasi-public and private.[43] Where the property is dedicated for the use of common man, it is known as public waqf. The most common examples of public waqfs are bridge, well, road *etc.* Where the object of the waqf is two-fold, the waqf is known as quasi-public. In the case of quasi-public waqfs the primary object of the waqf is partly to provide for the benefit of particular individuals or class of individuals which may be the settlor's family and partly to public. In the case of private waqfs, benefit is given to private individuals, including the settlor's family or relations.

The restrictions which are applied in the case of public waqfs are also applicable in the case of private waqfs. Muslim law makes no distinction between public and private waqfs.[44] Under both the systems, property is permanently dedicated in the name of God. The property becomes inalienable.

CHARACTERISTICS OF A VALID WAQF

Dedicated property vests in God

The creation of a waqf is essentially based on the legal fiction being that the property vests in God, in perpetuity, but income from the property is permitted to be utilised for certain specified purposes which under the Muslim law are recognised as pious or religious. It was said by Ameer Ali in *Vidya Varuthi Thirtha* v *Balusami* Ayyar[45] that the institution of waqf owes its origin to a rule laid down by the Prophet of Islam, and means 'the tying up of property in the ownership of God the Almighty and the devotion of the profits for the benefit of human beings. Once the dedication of property is made to the waqf, the ownership of the waqif is extinguished and it is transferred to God. Shia law is also identical on this point. Under the Shia law the property of waqf vests in God.[46] This question was recently decided by the Supreme Court in *Mohammad Ismail* v *Thakur Sabir Ali*.[47] In this case the question was when a waqf is governed by the Mussalman Waqf Validating Act, 1913 (*i.e.* when the waqf is a family waqf), then in whom does the property vest ? The Supreme Court held that even in the case of family waqf (alal-aulad) there is a transfer in favour of God in whom the waqf property vests. A similar view was taken by Justice Kirty in *Moather Raza* v *Joint Director Consolidation*.[48] It was said that there is nothing in the Mussalman Waqf Validating Act, 1913 from which it can be said that in the case of a family waqf, the property does not vest in God Almighty or the waqf itself, but vests in the mutawalli or mutawallis.

In *Mariamma* v *Andhuni*[49] there was a dedication of the family house by way of waqf for the performance of certain religious purposes and hence the property belonged jointly to the original heirs (including the father of the first plaintiff and the husband of the second defendant). It was provided that in accordance with our religious practices for the religious good of our family and also for the salvation of the soul of our deceased ancestors Moulood should be read in the family house on the 12th Rabi-ul-Awwal of each year and one chapter of the *Quran* should be recited in the family house everyday. It was also provided that the property should be free from alienation in favour of strangers and that it should not be burdened with debts, attachments and injunctions and that subject to the above provisions it had been allotted jointly to (the father of the first plaintiff, the first defendant and the husband of the second defendant).

It was argued by defendants that since the family home had been declared a waqf and thereby rendered incapable of partition, a valid waqf was created by the dedicator.

The Division Bench of the Kerala High Court rejected the above argument of the defendants. The High Court held that there was no valid dedication. The three brothers, owners of the house, never divested themselves of ownership in favour of God Almighty, in fact the property was retained by them, purportedly, jointly.

Customary Law

The general rule is that the properties of endowments and waqfs do not belong to the head of the institution. However, under special custom the head of the institution may become entitled to hold private property. In Amir Begum v Mehr Bibi[50] this special custom was recognised. It was held that the Mujawars of the shrine of Data Ganj Baksh are entitled to hold private property.

The dedication must be permanent

It is necessary for the validity of a waqf that the property should have been dedicated for ever. If the waqf has been created for a specified period say for 20 years, there shall not be a valid waqf. A waqf for limited period is void.[51] The purpose for which a waqf is created must be of a permanent character. Hanafi school of Muslim law says that if the dedication was not temporary, it shall be presumed that the dedication was final.[52] It appears that the opinion of Abu Yusuf was impliedly accepted in the Mussalman Waqf Validating Act, 1913. It can, therefore, be said that perpetuity is an essential condition for the validity of a waqf. Waqf for limited periods are unknown to Muslim law. In *Habib Ashraf* v *Syed Wajihuddin*[53] it was said that if the waqf name contains a condition that in case of mismanagement the property should be divided among the heirs of the settlor, the dedication shall be treated as invalid. Even in the case of a family waqf the ultimate benefit must be expressly or impliedly reserved for the poor or for any other purpose recognised by Muslim law as religious, pious or charitable purpose of a permanent nature. Thus a gift of usufructuary mortgage by the mortgagee is void, being of temporary nature. On the same principles a waqf of the house standing on land leased for a fixed term is also void. No valid waqf can be created of the property which does not belong to the settlor absolutely. In *Rahman* v *Baqridan*[54] it was said that if the waqif is only a usufructuary mortgagee and has no permanent control over the property, the dedication will not come under the category of waqf. In *Mst Peeran* v *Hafiz Mohammad*[55] the house was given on lease for a fixed period. It was held that the dedication was invalid as the dedication could not be said to be of property of a permanent character.

The Shia school of Muslim law maintains that when a waqf was restricted to particular time or made dependant on some quality of future occurrence, it was void.[56] There are some Shiite authorities who hold the view that the waqf property will revert to heirs of mauquf alaihi (beneficiaries), Some Shiite authorities hold the view that such a waqf will be void *ab initio*.[57]

In *Mohammad Abdulla* v *Abdul Rehman Jitakar*[58] it was said that all schools of Muslim law recognise the waqfs mentioned above. However, the object of such waqfs must be religious, pious or charitable. The waqif should clearly show his intention to establish a waqf for charitable, religious or pious purposes. A dedication for the benefit of wife, daughter and descendants of daughter and no provision for religious, pious or charitable object was held to be void.[59]

The recent case on the point is *Yora Karaddi Mallareddi* v *Syed Amanullah Hussain*.[60] In this case it was said that there must be substantial dedications of the usufruct of the property to religious, pious or charitable purposes. A mere intention to make a waqf is not sufficient. The declaration shall be made contemporaneously with the act of dedication. The founder of the waqf is not required to use the word waqf. There must, however, be intention of the donor to set apart any specific property or the proceeds thereof for the maintenance or support in perpetuity of a specific object or of a series of objects recognised as pious by Muslim law. In *Mariamma* v *Andhuni*[61] it was held that the provision regarding 'Moulood' did not amount to one recognised by Muslim law as religious, pious or charitable. It was also held that the provision for reading of the Quran in the private house of a person does not constitute a valid object for creation of a waqf.

The permanent dedication of property may be express or implied. It is, however, not clear as to under what circumstances a waqf can be treated as impliedly permanent. Abu Hanifa and Imam Muhammad are of the opinion that it should be specifically provided that the ultimate benefit must go to the poor. Abu Yusuf is of the opinion that it may be given impliedly, and this may be done by the mere use of the word waqf. Ameer Ali[62] says that once property is dedicated by way of a waqf, the right of the waqif or the founder automatically stands extinguished forever, and therefore, where appropriate and technical words are used, the dedication will be treated as impliedly permanent. Where the waqif has used the term waqf or mawkufa, the waqf will be implied, and the ultimate benefit will go to the poor, even though not specified. The views expressed by Ameer Ali were referred by Madras High Court in *Syed Ahmed* v *Julaiha Bibi.*[63] The Bombay High Court in *Nizamuddin* v *Abdul Gaffar*[64] followed the opinion of Abu Haneefa and Imam Mohammad. The matter was referred to the Privy Council and the Privy Council held that in the absence of ultimate gift to charity, the deed was not valid as a waqf.[65] The words 'permanent dedication' therefore, includes the following three things :

(i) dedication must be of permanent nature in the sense that the dedication should be irrevocable ;

(ii) secondly, the dedicated property must belong to the settlor absolutely ; and

(iii) dedication must be eternally and not limited.

Irrevocability

There was no unanimity of opinion on the question of revocation of a waqf. It has been said that once constituted validly a waqf cannot be revoked. Abu Hanifa says that a waqf is revocable unless confirmed by a court decree or is testamentary.[66] He is, therefore, of the opinion that in order to make a waqf irrevocable, the waqf should deliver the property to the mutawalli and then claim it back on the ground that the declaration was not binding. This fierce dispute may be submitted to a Qazi who would render a judgment establishing irrevocable character of the waqf. The principle propounded by Adu Hanifa is not absolute. He has made an exception in favour of a mosque and testamentary waqf coming into effect by reason of the death of the testator. Imam Muhammad maintains that once possession of waqf property has been given to the mutawalli, it is irrevocable. Abu Yusuf and Shaybani, both Abu Hanifa's disciples took a contrary view. According to Abu Yusuf, Malik Shafii and Hanbal, mere declaration is sufficient to make a waqf irrevocable. The opinion expressed by Abu Yusuf is generally followed in India.

Under Shia law, a waqf is revocable unless possession of the dedicated property is transferred either to the beneficiaries or mutawalli.

As already noted, delivery of possession is one of the important element of a valid waqf. A waqif has no right to revoke the waqf if all other conditions of waqf were fulfilled.[67]

In *Ma Mi* v *Kallendar Ammal*[68] it was said that if waqf was perfected by transfer of possession, the donor will have no power to revoke. In *Fatamabibi* v *Advocate General*[69] it was said that when a waqf was created by a living man, it could not be revoked. A waqif had a right to make changes till the waqf is complete in all respect ; but after the completion of the waqf the waqif had no right to make changes in the waqf.[70]

If in the waqfnama a condition is stipulated that the waqif reserves to himself the right of revoking the waqf or that the waqf will stand revoked on the happening of any event, then such a waqf is void. A waqf must not be subject to option. There was a difference of opinion as to whether waqif can reserve the right to revoke or alter the revocation later on. In *Fatamabibi* v *Advocate General of Bombay*[71] it was said that Abu Yusuf and Imam Muhammad had disagreed on whether right of revocation or alteration may be validly reserved in dedication.

In *Qassamally* v *Currimbhoy*[72] it was said that Imam Muhammad was of the opinion that dedication subject to option to revoke was void. Abu Yusuf was of the opinion that option limited for three days was permissible.[73] He said within three days the waqif could dispose of property by way of sale and other transfers of property.[74] It has been said that in the modern industrial age the three days period is immaterial and, therefore, a waqif may be allowed to revoke the dedication within three days. It may be noted that Abu Yusuf and Imam Muhammad were of the opinion that dedication for masjid with option for revocation (whether or not restricted to three days) operates as irrevocable dedication and, therefore, the option will be void. The Muslim law says that where Muslim jurists of authority have expressed dissenting opinions on the same questions, the court will adopt that view which is, in the particular circumstances most in accordance with justice. In *Sheikh Muhammad Mumtaz* v *Zubeida*[75] it was said that in choosing between conflicting opinions the principles of justice, equity and good conscience should be given full consideration.

It has been held that if the dedication in one way involves results which our law considers prejudicial to the public interests or immoral, it is our duty to decide the other way.[76]

It has also been said that when all three Imams differ, opinion of Yusuf used to be given preference by the Qazis owing to his experience as chief Qazi.[77] In *Abdul Sattar* v *Advocate General of Bombay*[78] the waqfnama contained a condition that at any time the waqf could be revoked by a deed or a will or a codicil by any one of the two waqifs, the waqf was held void.

Now the question arises as to whether the waqif can make a provision in the waqfnama that he will have the right to make addition or alteration in the beneficiaries and in their respective shares. It has been judicially held that the dedicator of the property in waqf possess the power to make a provision in the waqfnama that he will have a right to make addition and alteration in the beneficiaries and in their respective shares. Such a condition does not amount to the revocation of the waqf.[79] In Ma Ekhin Maung Sein[80] it was said that the waqif may reserve power to alter rules, *etc.*, relating to management. A power may be reserved to the waqif to alter the trusts, and to substitute new trusts of a charitable nature or to alter the rules relating to administration. A waqif may, at the time of dedication, reserve to himself the power to alter the beneficiaries either by adding to their number or excluding some and to increase or reduce their share.[81] A similar view was taken in *Sibte Rasul* v *Sibti Nabi.*[82] It was said that the waqif can make a provision in the waqf-deed to alter beneficiaries and their shares. Subsequently, it was said that there cannot be a power to alter the objects of a waqf.[83] It may be noted here that he will have no right to reduce the shares as to withdraw any part of the property from the waqf. The dedicator has also no power to substitute an invalid condition for a valid purpose.

A power may be reserved to the waqif to exchange the waqf land for other land, or sell it and purchase another land. So that the land so taken in exchange or purchased becomes subject to the waqf. In *Saleh Knan* v *Madar Saheb*[84] it was said that where there is no power to vary investments, leave of the court may be obtained. In proper cases, the court may grant leave for such purposes.

It has been a matter of dispute as to whether the subsequent mutawallis will have the power to alter the trusts, exchange the waqf property *etc.* According to Abu Yusuf if dedication empowers waqif to exchange land for another, waqif may not exchange land more than once.

A dedication purporting to reserve power to sale the waqf property and to use its proceeds on the waqf will be void.[85]

In *Mohammad Esuf* v *Maulvi Abdul Sathur*[86] the land was granted in inam in trust for the construction of a mosque. The land was resumed by government and regranted to the trustees in their individual capacity on full assessment. It was held that there was no extinction of trust and, therefore, the grantees were bound to hold the land in trust.

It has been said that before the advent of Islam appropriations were for ever, but our law has rendered them otherwise.[87] Abu Hanifa maintained that a waqf to be revocable unless there was a decree of the court confirming it. Abu Hanifa maintained that once Prophet Mohammad said 'Property cannot, after the decease of the proprietor be detained from division among his heirs'. According to Abu Hanifa the effect of providing the above provision is that a person who has declared a waqf may resile from his declared intention and acts, notwithstanding that he may have acted upon such declarations, so long as he has not obtained an order of the court confirming his declaration.

The opinion of Abu Hanifa is not shared by other classical jurists of Muslim law. The opinion of Abu Yusuf and Imam Muhammad is opposed to Abu Hanifa's opinion. Whether a waqf was recoverable or not previous to Islam it is under Muslim law irrevocable, because though a voluntary transaction, it brings an iwaz to the waqif in the form of approach to God (Qurbat) and, therefore, such transactions were irrevocable.

A testamentary waqf stands at a different footing. A testamentary waqf can be revoked by the waqif at any time before his death.[88] The reason is that a testamentary waqf is nothing more than a bequest and, therefore, it can be revoked. In *Syed Abdulla* v *Syed Zamin*[89] it was said that a waqf created during marzul-maut stands on the same footing. A testamentary waqf comes into existence after the death of the waqif. A testamentary waqf is, therefore, not invalid on the ground that the deed contains a clause under which it is stipulated that the waqf will not come into existence if the waqif is blessed with a child.

In *Janabli Sardar* v *Sobha Khatun*[90] it was said that where at the time of the creating a non-testamentary waqf the waqif reserves to himself the power to revoke the same, the waqf will be invalid.

The waqif may reserve the power to amend the waqf. The waqif can not, however, claim the absolute power to change the objects of the waqf.[91]

Perpetuity

It is deemed to be against public policy—both in Hindu and Muslim laws—that property should be tied up for an indefinite period of time and rendered incapable of being freely dealt with. Under the English law, the doctrine of perpetuity means that 'every future limitation (whether by way of executory devise or trust) of real or personal property the vesting of which is postponed beyond lives is being twenty-one years afterwards (including a further period of gestation where it exists) is void.[92] The object of the perpetuity rule is to prevent the mischief of making property inalienable, but when the disposition is in favour of purposes beneficial to the public, an exception is made to the application of the rule on grounds of public policy. In English law, therefore. it is well settled that valid and proper charitable trusts are exempted from the rule against perpetuities by making charity a trustee; and if the charity is not to get any benefit from the property but is merely to hold it as trustee for the performance of a condition in favour of non-charitable objects, such conditions will be void.

Under the original texts of Hindu law, there is no mention of the subject of perpetuities. The early decisions of the Indian High Courts and the Judicial Committee were against applying the English law of perpetuity to bequests made by Hindu testators. The leading case on the point is *Juggatsundary* v *Manickchand.*[93] In this case the Judicial Committee said that the extent of the testamentary powers of the Hindus must be regulated by the Hindu law. The same principle was affirmed by Sir Barness Peacock C.J. in *Gobardhan Bysack* v *Sham Chana.*[94]

Abu Hanifa is of the opinion that an express mention of perpetuity is necessary to complete a waqf. Imam Muhammad is also of the same view. Abu Yusuf is, however, of the view that a waqf shall be presumed to be perpetual.

Fatwai Alamgiri says that perpetuity is also among the conditions of waqf according to all opinions, though according to Abu Yusuf the mention of it is not a condition, and this is not correct.[95] Radd-ul-Mukhtar and Fath-ul-Kadir are of the same opinion. . . and when the waqf has become valid for the poor by implication, on further mention of perpetuity is needed for that purpose never fails, and sadr-ush-shahim says that all the jurists decide according to Abu Yusuf, and we also decide according to him.[96] Radd-ul-Mukhtar says that 'it is stated in the Durrar ul Ahkan that perpetuity is a condition by consensus, but according to Abu Yusuf its mention is not necessary . . . . and if a man says, 'I make this dedication on my children and adds nothing further, it is valid.

Dedication may be express or implied

The dedication may be express or implied. Abu Yusuf said that the waqif may provide in the waqfnama or a deed or he may make an oral dedication. The validity of a waqf may be presumed on account of immemorial user or by legal inference or presumption from the course of conduct and the attached circumstances when there is no evidence that a person even executed a waqfnama nor any direct evidence of oral dedication, yet the inference can be drawn of the dedication from the history of the matter the dealings with the property in dispute, the admissions and assertions made relating thereto.[97]

Abu Yusuf says that if the intention of creating a waqf is shown the dedication of property will be presumed to be perpetual and ultimately for the benefit of the poor.[98] In *Syed Ahmad* v *Julaikha Bivi*[99] it was said that wherever the term 'waqf' is used, permanence will be presumed as a matter of law, and the ultimate benefit will go to the poor though unnamed.

In *Abdul Fata Mohammad* v *Russomoy*[100] the Judicial Committee of the Privy Council said that family waqfs created in perpetuity were to be invalid as they infringed the rule against perpetuity. It was, therefore, held that private waqfs could not be made in perpetuity. However, after passing of the Mussalman Waqf Validating Act, 1913, the family waqfs created in perpetuity were held as valid. This Act enabled Indian Muslims to create waqfs for indefinite period, for the maintenance and support of his family, children or descendants, provided that the ultimate benefit was expressly or impliedly reserved for the poorer for any other purpose recognised by the Muslim law as religious, pious and charitable.[101] Section 4 of the said Act says that no such waqf shall be deemed invalid merely because the benefit reserved therein for the poor or other religious, pious or charitable purpose of a permanent nature was postponed until after the extinction of the family children or descendants of the founder of the waqf.

It is not necessary that the parpetuity of its objects should also be perpetual. The income of waqf must be applied for charitable purposes, In case, it is not possible to fulfil the object of waqf or object being such that it may fail, the waqf shall be void according to Abu Hanifa and Imam Muhammad. Abu Yusuf, however, says that in such cases the benefit shall be derived by the poor.

As already noted, it is the mandatory provision of the

law that the income of the waqf property must be applied for charitable purposes. There may be cases where the income of the waqf property may be applied for purposes other than charitable. In such cases the whole property has to be devoted to the charity free from the said charges. In *Muhammad Raza* v *Yadgar Hussain*[102] it was said that if the charges are on a specific portion of the property and the said portion never goes to charity at all, or the charity with reference to it is illusory and the said portion has not otherwise been dedicated by way of waqf at all ; then on failure of those charges the property is free of any trust and must result to the original owner or his heirs.

Dedicated property should yield permanent result

Under the Muslim law every kind of property can be dedicated as a waqf. However, it is necessary that it must admit yielding permanent benefit and therefore, the dedication of a building, standing on the lease hold land would not constitute valid dedication.[103]

Waqf property cannot be alienated

Waqf property vests in God and no human being can alienate it for his own purposes.[104] The dedication of property must be permanent. It is a concomitant to the doctrine of permanency of waqfs that once the properties are dedicated to God they cannot be alienated either by the waqif or by the mutawalli.[105]

The heirs of the waqif and mutawalli have no right to inherit the property of the waqf.[106]

The waqf property is also not liable for sale and execution of a decree based on private debts due by the mutawalli.[107]

The interest of the waqif or mutawalli in the property (if any) is not such as can be sold in execution of such a decree ; but a receiver of the rents and profits may be appointed when the mutawalli is entitled to remuneration or maintenance out of them.[108]

In *Rajindra Narain* v *Sundarar Bai*[109] it was said that the right to future maintenance cannot be attached and sold but receiver can be appointed to recover rents and profits of villages to pay the maintenance and to apply balance towards decree.

In *Mir Mahbuballi* v *Ahmada Bai* receiver was appointed for the benefit of the judgment creditor, of rents and profits of inalienable and unattachable jagir granted for maintenance. The court made suitable allowance for judgment debtor.

It may be observed here that only that part of the property will be inalienable which has been actually dedicated in waqf. Where part only of a property is dedicated, the portion that is not dedicated may be alienated and inherited. In *Dalrymple* v *Khoondkar Azeezul Islam*[111] an endowment may be wholly waqf where all profits arising there from devoted to religious purposes. But when the office of mutawalli is hereditary, the incumbent has a beneficial interest in the property, we look upon it as a heritable estate burdened with certain trusts, the proprietory right of which is vested in the mutawalli and his heirs, and in such a case there appears no sufficient reason why the incumbent should not exercise a right possessed by other proprietors to grant leases even in perpetuity.

In *Mohammad Ahmed Saeed* v *Kishorilal*[112] it was provided in the waqf-deed that waqfs right was reserved to transfer part of dedicated property for payment of his debts.

The above rule is not absolute, and in certain circumstances, it is permissible that a mutawalli may alienate the waqf properties a mutawalli may sell or grant a lease of the waqf properties, with the prior permission of the court. The waqf property may be given in exchange if the property of equivalent value is received by the mutawalli. The waqf property may be sold subject to compulsory reinvestment of the price in another property. if the right of exchange or sale was originally reserved by the waqif in the waqf instrument.[113] The waqf property can also be alienated if the original property falls into ruins or ceases to produce any benefit and, therefore, it is not possible to fulfil the objects of the waqf. In the above referred cases the courts will grant permission of the alienation of waqf property and the sale is considered to be incidental.

By a person professing Islam

Section 3 (1) of the Waqf Act. 1954 defines waqf as follows :

> Waqf means the permanent dedication by a person professing Islam of any movable or immovable

property for any purpose recognised by the Muslim law as pious, religious or charitable and includes :

(i) a waqf by user ;

(ii) granted (including mashru-ulkhidmat) for any purpose recognised by the Muslim law as pious, religious or charitable ; and

(iii) a waqf-alal-aulad to the extent to which the property is dedicated for any purpose recognised by Muslim law as pious, religious or charitable and 'waqf' means any person making such dedication.

It is clear from the definition that any person making dedication of any movable or immovable property must be a person professing Islam and that the dedication must be for any purpose recognised by the Muslim law as pious, religious or charitable.

Ameer Ali[114] says that according to the classical jurists of Islam even non-Muslims could make waqfs. A similar view has been expressed by Mulla.[115] Mulla says that under the Mohammedan law, a non-Muslim may also create a waqf for any purpose which is religious under the Mohammedan law provided it is also lawful according to his own religious creed.

The Indian courts have also approved the creation of waqfs by non-Muslims. However, the law is not free from doubt. Some courts have expressed the view that a waqf can be created by non-Muslims. But other courts have not agreed to this view. In *Fazlur Rahman* v *Anath Bundhee*[116] a contract for valuable consideration was in question and a Hindu agreed to set aside property for the benefit of Muslims. It was held that such a contract was illegal because the Muslim law of waqf does not contemplate a waqf for the mosque being made by non-Muslims. It was, however, maintained that non-Muslim can also make a waqf provided that the purpose of the waqf is neither repugnant to Islam nor opposed to the settlor's own creed.

The Nagpur High Court also followed the observations of Ameer Ali. In *Moti Shah* v *Abdul Ghaffar*[117] the court said that all persons who are competent to make a valid gift are also competent to constitute a valid waqf. The law only requires that the object for which dedication should be lawful according to the creed of the dedicator as well as the Islamic doctrines.

The matter was again discussed by the Patna High Court in *Mst. Mundaria* v *Shyam Sunder*.[118] The facts, in brief, of this case are discussed as under :

In 1901, one Rai Kashi Prasad, a Hindu by caste established a private imambara over a piece of land. The plot was under dispute. The waqif, Rai Kashi Prasad, himself became the Khalifa and used to keep a tazia at his own cost in the Imambara during Muharram festival. The subordinate judge held that under Muslim law only persons professing Islamic faith can make a valid waqf. While coming to this conclusion, the learned subordinate judge relied on Muslim's book entitled Mohammedan Law. According to Mulla a waqf can be created by only such a person who was professing the Mussalman faith. The waqf can be created for any purpose recognised by the Muslim law as pious, religious and charitable.

In *Saraswati Ammal* v *Raja Gopal Ammal*[119] the Supreme Court was required to consider whether samadhi was a religious purpose under the Hindu law. The Supreme Court held that the question what is a religious purpose under the Hindu law must be determined according to Hindu notions. Under Hindu law religious or charitable purposes are not confined to purposes which are productive of actual or assumed public benefit. A dedication, under the Hindu law, must be determined according to Shastras. The court said since then other religious practices and beliefs may have grown up and obtained recognition from certain classes, as constituting purposes conducive to religious merit. If such beliefs are to be accepted, it must at least be shown that they have obtained wide recognition and constitute the religious practice of a substantial and large class of persons. However, the belief of one or more individuals is not sufficient to enable them to make a valid settlement permanently typing up property. It was said that the heads of religious purposes determined by belief in acquisition of religious merit cannot be allowed to be widely enlarged consistently with public policy and needs of modern society.

It was, therefore, concluded that keeping in view these facts into consideration, the setting up of an Imambara cannot be considered a religious purpose under the Hindu law ; and, therefore, Rai Kashi Prasad being a Hindu, could not lawfully make any waqf in respect of an Imambara. In this case, the Patna High Court held that a non-Muslim can dedicate only a public waqf, and not a private waqf (*e.g.* an Imambara).

Under Section 66-C of the Waqf Act, 1954 a non-Muslim can dedicate his property in favour of existing Wqfs. However, he cannot create a new waqf. Under the Islamic law, it is necessary that a waqf must be lawful according to the creed of the dedicator as well as the Islamic doctrines. A Muslim is, therefore, not allowed to make a waqf the purpose of which is not under the Islamic law pious, charitable or religious. A Muslim cannot create a waqf in favour of an idol or temple *etc.* Similarly, a Hindu cannot make a waqf for mosque. Baillie[120] has taken the problem in a different way. He says that a valid waqf can be created for the education of non-Muslims or in favour of non-Muslim poor and destitutes or for the shrouds for the dead or digging of graves *etc.*

Section 66 (c) of the Waqf Act, 1954 was introduced by the Amendment Act 24 of 1964. Perhaps, this amendment was introduced by the legislature having noticed the lacuna in the definition of 'waqf' brought within the purview of Waqf Act, 1954, all properties including those donated by persons not professing Islam by the said Amendment Act. Section 66(c) of the Act read as follows ;

> Notwithstanding anything contained in this Act where any movable or immovable property has been given or donated by any person not professing Islam for the support of a waqf being—
>
> (a) a mosque, *idgah, imambara, dargah, khankah* or a *maqbara* ;
> (b) a Muslim graveyard ;
> (c) a choultry or a *musafirkhana*, then such property shall be deemed to be comprised in that waqf and be dealt with in the same manner as the waqf in which it is so comprised.

This Act is made applicable to properties given or donated by persons not professing Islam for the support of certain waqfs. It is, important to note that non-Muslims can give their property for the maintenance of certain waqfs, but they cannot create a new waqf.

As noted above, by this amendment the definition of the waqf in the Waqf Act, 29 of 1954, has been enlarged. Now the word waqf includes all property given or endowed by any person professing any religion, other than Islam for the support of (i) mosques, *idgahs*, *imambaras*, *dargahs*, *khanqah* or *maqbaras*, (ii) graveyards of persons professing Islam. It is clear from the above definition that a waqf by a non-Muslim for endowing a mosque *etc.*, would be valid. But as far as Madhya Pradesh Public Trust Act, 1951 is concerned the amendment has no effect and the position under the Public Trusts Act remains unchanged and the dedication of any property by non-Muslims would not constitute a valid waqf.

Paras Diwan[121] says that in view of the clear provisions in the statutes, and in view of the fact that waqfs essentially form part of the personal law of Muslims, the Nagpur view is not correct. The present writer submits that it is true that non-Muslims can make a waqf ; but they are precluded from dedicating their property for the purpose of the waqf. The reason for holding such opinion is that waqf implies a religious motive, an act meritorious in accordance with the faith of the waqif. In case the property is dedicated by a Hindu, no question of religious motive would arise. The present writer submits that every person who wants to dedicate his property in waqf wants to acquire merit in the eyes of God. Again, Hindu law does not prohibit Hindus from dedicating properties in a waqf. It is, therefore, submitted that there does not appear to be any irregularity if the dedication is made by non-Muslims for religious, pious or charitable purposes.[122]

The position of a waqf is not clear if the property was dedicated to a Muslim shrine by non-Muslim and there was no waqfnama nor the name of the waqif was shown in the registers. In such cases no presumption of lawful origin can be drawn in the absence of any evidence as to the person that created the waqf. In *Mohammad Mazaffarlmusavi* v *Bibi*

Jabeda Khatun[123] the Privy Council was concerned with the presumption of real existence of necessity to alienate the temple property in the absence of proof of such necessity after a lapse of nearly 100 years. In this case, the Privy Council said :

> The presumption of an origin in some lawful title, which the courts have so often readily made in order to support possessory rights, long and quietly enjoyed, where no actual proof of title is forthcoming, is one which is not a mere branch of the law of evidence. It is resorted to because of the failure of actual evidence. . . . . The presumption is not an 'open sesame' with which to unlock in favour of a particular kind of claimant a closed door to which neither the law nor the proved facts would in themselves have afforded any key. It is the completion of a right, to which circumstances clearly point, where time has obliterated any record of the original commencement.

In *Mazhar Hussain* v *Adiya Saran*[124] the Privy Council observed as follows :

There is no evidence that Haidar Baksh ever executed a waqfnama and no direct evidence of any oral dedication by him. But if the proper inference from the history of the matter, the dealings with the properties, the litigation that has affected it and the admissions and assertions made by the respondents predecessors-in-title is that Haidar Baksh purchased the villages in the names of Maiku Lal and Bahadur Lal on the express footing that they were to be an endowment of an existing waqf consisting of the mosque, grave and imambara, their lordships do not doubt that all the requirements of Shia law necessary to the valid creation of a waqf attaching to the villages were satisfied.

In *M.S. Waqf Board, Madras* v *Khazi Mohideen*[125] the Madras High Court made the following observations :

> Another question of fact raised is as to whether the grant has been made by a Muslim or a non-Muslim. Really there is no evidence on record either way. The plaintiff stated that the grant had been made by a Hindu ruler.

But that statement cannot be accepted as evidence and that is a statement of only his case and nothing more. The plaintiff himself had to concede in cross examination that he did not know who was the grantor, whether the grantor was a Muslim or a non-Muslim. No documentary evidence had been placed either by the plaintiff or by the defendant in order to find out who the grantor was. Due to complete lack of evidence regarding this aspect, the burden of proof becomes important. Alagiri Swami J has held that the defendant namely the Board has to prove that the grant was made by a Muslim, if it wants to support its case that the property is waqf on the ground that it has been granted by a Muslim. . . . . . Therefore, it is the defendant Board which wants to establish that the property is waqf should shoulder the burden of proof initially. As there is no evidence on either side, the conclusion of the learned Judge that it has not been proved that the grant had been made by a Muslim has to be accepted as correct.'

In *A.P. Waqf Board, Hyderabad* v *M. Somaiah*,[126] a waqf was created in favour of a Muslim shrine by a non-Muslim. There was no waqfnama and it was not certain who was the waqif of the waqf. On the other hand, it was shown that a non-Muslim donated the properties for the maintenance of the Darga. As already noted, under the Muslim law, a non-Muslim may also create a waqf for any purpose which is religious under the Muslim law provided it is also lawful according to his own religious creed. But the definition of 'waqf' in the waqf Act, 1954, limits the applicability to waqfs dedicated by persons professing Islam.

In the above case, it was contended by the respondent that dedication was for the worship at the tomb of a saint, Hazrat Niamatullah and, therefore, the dedication was not for a purpose not permitted by Hindu law.

It was said by Justice Chennakesav Reddy of the Andhra Pradesh High Court that it is clear from the definition of waqf in Section 3 (i) Waqf Act that any person making dedication of any movable or immovable property must be a person professing Islam and that the dedication must be for any purpose recognised by the Muslim law as pious, religious or charitable. Section 3 (1) itself indicates that properties donated or given by the non-Muslims for the maintenance of certain waqfs are brought within the purview of the Act, but the Section does not enable non-Muslims to create a waqf.[127]

Waqf by long user

A waqf can also be created by antiquity. Where a particular piece of land was used as a waqf property and there is no evidence to show how and when the alleged waqf was created the waqf may be established by evidence of user.[128] In *Abdul Rahim* v *Fahr Mohammad Shah*[129] it was held that where the ancient history in respect of the nature and character of a particular property is not available, a decision will have to be based on such evidence as may be gathered from its use and environment as also how the public regarded the property and the conduct of the parties in relation thereto. It was further held that where the mosque and other properties were within one compound with one gate and were so interconnected as to form part of one property and it was admitted that the mosque was waqf, the court was entitled to raise a presumption that the other properties also were waqf and that the mere fact that a person was described in the record of rights as owner or describes himself as mutawalli of a private mosque or Imambara would not make that property his own.[130] But where the plaintiff, a Hindu talukdar is in possession of the land and enjoying the fruits of the land and the land is shown as grove in village papers, the grove cannot be presumed to be a waqf by user, even though the grove contains same kachha graves of the members of the defendant's family.

Recently, the Madhya Pradesh High Court held that in view of certain admissions made by the defendants as well as their predecessors and other evidence on record, the suit property was waqf property.[131] A piece of land may be used as a mosque, or other religious place for a considerable time, the land becomes waqf though there is no evidence of express dedication. The Supreme Court of India[132] also expressed the view that a land adjacent to a mosque would become waqf by user if it had been used by the public for religious purposes along with the mosque. In the same case the Supreme Court further held that where the original mosque, which is proved to be a waqf property, an area is added by the mutawallis by way of construction of rooms and this area is used by the public for religious purposes along with the old mosque then if the area has been made into a separately demarcated compact unit for a single purpose, namely collective individual worship in the mosque, it must be regarded as one unit and be treated as such and the whole becomes accordingly waqf by user.

In Khati's[133] case the Orissa High Court held that 'a waqf normally requires express dedication, but where there is no evidence to show how and when the alleged waqf was created, the waqf may be established by evidence of user ; if land had been used from time immemorial for religious purpose, such as a Masjid, the land is constituted waqf, though there is no evidence of express dedication ; the title of the original owner is extinguished and the ownership of the property vests in God and accordingly the public character of the institution may be presumed. Land used from the time immemorial for the purpose of masjid and for its courtyard which formed part and parcel of Masjid and for celebration of Muharram festival constitutes a waqf by user.'

In another case public prayers were held on a piece of land with the permission of the owner of the land. It was held that a valid waqf was constituted by long user.[134] If the property was used as a mosque for a considerable long time and worship was also performed in it, the court will infer that it does not stand by leave and licence of the owner of the site but that the land is dedicated properly and no longer belongs to the original owner.[135]

A burial ground may be established as waqf by evidence of user. But where the evidence shows no more than certain persons, many years ago, used it as a burial place, it does not amount to an evidence of public user and hence does not constitute a waqf.[136] In *Bashir Ahmed* v *Abdul Jabbar*[137] the Patna High Court elaborately dealt with this matter. It concluded that for proving a land as graveyard by user, the claimant must prove the number of instances, the character of the burial and the extent of it from which the court can infer that the plot of land in question was necessarily used as a public burial ground. Therefore, the question of the period for which the land has been put to such use would not be such as to take it back to time immemorial. It is therefore, necessary that for the validity of a waqf, there should be the proof of dedication or of user otherwise the property shall not be a waqf property. In another case[138] a mosque was constructed in a private house. It was held that a waqf was not established because the common Muslims were not allowed to worship. It can, therefore, be said that 'user' must be by public and not by only individuals of a family. Where a platform was used as a praying place, not by the general public but by the Muslim inhabitants of an ahata, it was held that the property was a private and a mosque cannot be built on that piece of land.[139] Where an Imambara was constructed and 'majlises' were celebrated and Quran Khani was done and the building had never used as a residential house, it was held that by presumption a waqf came into existence.[140] It may, however, be noted here that mere burial of a saint on a particular spot will not be sufficient for the validity of a waqf. Similarly, in another case a saint was buried on a particular piece of land. Annual Urs (anniversary) was also held. There was no objection from the side of the owner of the land. Subsequently, a question arose whether under such circumstances, the land can be treated as waqf property. The Lahore High Court held that the burial of a saint on a particular spot would not be sufficient for the validity of a waqf even though Urs was held and there was no objection from the side of the owner of the land.[141] In Mohammad Sahib Qureshi's[142] case the servant of the mosque (Mouzzin) was living in a particular house. The house was situated at some distance from the mosque. In fact, the owner of the house granted licence for residential purposes. Subsequently, is was not claimed that the house was a waqf property. It was held that the property in personal occupation of the moulvi of the mosque under lease and licence would not become waqf property by user.

If documentary evidence is relied upon to establish waqf by user the entries in government records was held sufficient for the validity of a waqf. The Judicial Committee of the

Privy Council[143] held that when a certain piece of land was shown in the khasra as 'Kabiristan' and graveyard, this *prima facie*, at all events means that the land was a graveyard in the sense known under Muslim law. The Privy Council further said that where a khasra is the instrument which at all events embodies a right and there is no other document which creates title the khasra and the map are not merely historical materials but are instruments of title or otherwise the evidence of right. If waqf by user is to be established on the basis of the evidence of user, the land does not become waqf necessarily and immediately upon the burial of a single person.[144]

A description in a settlement register of a site as a kabristan is *prima facie* evidence that it is a public graveyard in the sense known to Muslim law. Where such a graveyard was used for a long time, it will be presumed that a waqf was established. Mere fact of a few burials many years ago will not come under the category of graveyards because there was no evidence of public user.[145] In Mohammad Kasim's case the Madhya Pradesh High Court said that in order to prove dedication by evidence of burials in a land and to justify the inference that the land is a cemetery, it is necessary to prove a number of instances adequate in character, number and extent. The evidence that the property was used for such purpose will not be sufficient. The claimant should prove that the entire property was used for such purpose. It will make no difference even if the land which is alleged to be graveyard is having only one survey number and the person who alleges it to be a graveyard must prove that every part of it is a graveyard.[146]

If a piece of land was used as a muslim graveyard and the entries to that effect were made in the revenue registers, it was held that a perfect waqf was established.[147] The court further said that it makes no difference that for the past few years the land was not used as graveyard.

A public graveyard is a waqf property and, therefore, it can not be transferred even if it was closed by Municipality.[148] Muslim community has a right to require the demolition of a house built on an abandoned graveyard in contravention of the original purposes of the waqf.[149] The building of a temporary hut by the custodian of the graveyard does not amount to an assertion of title hostile to the waqf.[150]

In one case the waqif claimed the right of graze even after dedicating the property in waqf. It was held that when the land was given in waqf for the purpose of graveyard, the rights of the former owner will immediately come to an end and he will have no right to graze his cattle on it.[151]

For a valid graveyard it is necessary that there must be good number of burials. In Baqar Khan's case a site described in the revenue register as a grave was shown.[152] It was owned by a Hindu Zamindar. It was held mere entry in the revenue register was not sufficient for a valid waqf. The existence of a few graves will not justify the presumption of a dedication.[153] It is true that a burial in a plot will not make the land waqf, the general presumption is that the part of the site where the dead body was buried was dedicated with the consent of the owner so that the grave is waqf and the Muslim community had access to it.[154] If there was no evidence of user such a claim for a private grave would seem to be of doubtful validity.

In Mohammad Kasim's case one portion of the land was used from time immemorial as graveyard. The other portion of the land was quite separate and distinct. It was in the possession of the mutawalli and there were no burials in the built portion. It was held that the whole piece of land in the graveyard could not be considered waqf property. The built portion was the private property of the mutawalli.[155] There is nothing wrong if a non-Muslim dedicates a plot of land for the purpose of a Muslim graveyard. A Hindu can validly establish a waqf.[156]

It may be noted here that under the Shariat law, waqf by user is only a mode of proof of dedication. If we turn our attention to the literature of Islamic jurisprudence we see there is no provision for waqf by user. It only presumes the existence of one if its origin is not known and no other proof of dedication is forthcoming.

Till 1969, a common trend regarding waqf of antiquity was prevalent. It was only in the case of *Panjab waqf Board* v *Ambala Panchayat Garhi Brahmin*[157] that the Panjab and Haryana High Court laid down certain criteria for a valid waqf. These rules are quite different from the old rules meant for determination of waqf by user. The High Court also made some very important observations. The result of these observations has been that the future of waqf by long user has become uncertain. In this case the village in which the land was situated was predominently a Hindu village. There were very few number of Muslims living and after partition of the country there were none. No dead body was buried in the graveyard since 1947. The persons along with the Panchayat Deh and Gram Sabha took possession of various plots and constructed houses thereon. The main question was to decide whether the property involved in the case was an old graveyard or not. While delivering judgment, the High Court observed :

> Most of the rulings which had been cited before learned single judge were of the years prior to the partition of the country or from far off states that have not been directly affected by the partition of the country in 1947, in the same manner in which this part of the country is affected. The conditions brought about by the partition of the country could not have been foreseen or visualised by the courts that decided the cases which has been cited. Any observations made in those rulings were intended to dispose of only those particular cases and these observations have to be taken in the context in which they were made. The courts could not have had under contemplation the unusual or unforeseen conditions or the deterioration in the law and order situation that followed the partition of the country in far off states or places. It is true that the burying of a few dead bodies could consecrate a piece of land but this observation apparently does not take into consideration the fact that the land has been built upon.
>
> The conversion of consecration of any secular property into waqf by user would of necessity be a long drawn-out and gradual process lasting over a period of years and it is not necessary that the process takes only one direction or keeps a uniform place. In some of the cases discussed in the judgment under appeal, the slow process had been continued from time immemorial before a waqf by user was found to have been established. There can be circumstances that arrest

the advance or progress of the process or which may give it a turn in the wrong or opposite direction. The process has reach a stage when it can be said to have become absolute ; a stage of non-return where after the process cannot take a turn for the worse . . .

. . . . .where a party is relying upon user as evidence of dedication of any property as waqf. we have also to keep in mind that this user had been discontinued at a particular point of time...

'On the basis of the entries in the records of rights it can be said that a few dead bodies had been buried in this piece of land during a period of 25 years to 40 years before the partition of the country but the circumstances are such that we can believe that the user of this land for this particlar purpose was discontinued for about two decades after the partition of the country, apparently because the minority community had evacuated from the villages. It can not be said that the user before the partition of the country had lasted upto a point of no-return and if the land could assume a certain character by user over a period of years, then the discontinuation of that user at a particular time could have cured the land of its consecrated character as waqf so as to justify the vesting of this land in the Gram Panchayat for the benefit of the present residents of the village. The minority community that could have occasion to use the land as a graveyard. The consecration of the land by the burying of a few dead bodies has come to an end with the desecration and the obliteration of all traces of these graves and the land has cured by continued disuser of the character that it may have acquired by indifferent user as a graveyard for a few decades before the partition of the country.

The Waqf Inquiry Committee in its report on waqfs said that from the above observation of the Panjab High Court it appears that law a laid down by some High Courts outside Punjab on waqfs by user should be applied subject to the changed conditions in Punjab as a result of the partititon and could be modified, if necessary. It is submitted here that in the Muslim jurisprudence there is no degree of consecration depending upon the locality where the dedicated property is situated. It is also very strange to note that because there had been a partition of the country and there were riots in Punjab the basis for the interpretation of Muslim law on waqfs or for its application in Punjab had become different from what was obtaining in the rest of the country. It means that according to this view a mosque or graveyard which happens to be situated in Punjab may not enjoy the same degree of inviolability as those which are situated in other parts of the country, without there being anything in law to warrant the discrimination.[158]

Waqf by user and immemorial user

There exists a difference between waqf by user and immemorial user. Mulla[159] says if land has been used from time immemorial for a religious purpose, *e.g.* for a mosque or a burial ground or for the maintenance of a mosque, then the land is by user waqf although there is no evidence of an express dedication. According to Mulla the waqf by immemorial user is confined to only three classes of waqfs, namely. mosque, burial ground and maintenance of mosque. This term will not include other kind of waqfs. On the other hand no such reservation is to be found in waqf by user. The above distinction was maintained by Gujarat High Court in *Alimiya* v *Sayed Mohammad.*[160] The court observed that—

> the fact remains that even if it were to include waqf by immemorial user, it cannot mean the same thing as we have in the definition of waqf given in Section 2 (19) of the Act as including 'waqf by user.' The difference, however, lies in two fold manner. The first is that waqf before 1950 was required to be arising out of permanent dedication of any property by a Muslim person and that was to be for a pious, religious or charitable purpose recognised by Islamic law. The judicial decisions also require that permanent dedication has to be there but that can be inferred from the evidence relating to immemorial user of that property for such purpose. That inference would obviously be rebuttable, But if we read the present definition it keeps intact

the first part *i.e.*, about permanent dedication of the property, it speaks of waqf by user only. Thus in view of the present definition of waqf under Section 2(19) of the Act, one can take proceedings under the Act on such material for being able to show any property as waqf by user.

It can, therefore, be said that under the M.P. Trust Act, 1951 the definition of the word waqf has been widened.

Waqf-alal-aulad

A Muslim can create a waqf for the maintenance and support wholly or partially of his family, children descendants or and a Hanafi Muslim can also create a waqf for his own maintenance and support during his life time or for the payment of his debtsout of the rents and profits of the property dedicated. In all cases, the ultimate benefit must expressly or impliedly be reserved for the poor or for any other purpose recognised by Muslim law as religious, pious or charitable of a permanent character.[161] The Madhya Pradesh Public Trusts Act, 1951 has excluded waqf-alal-aulad. Under Section 2(8) of the M.P. Public Trusts Act, 1951 a Muslim can create a waqf for the pious, religious or charitable purpose but the definition does not include any waqf, such as is described in Section 3 of the Mussalman Waqf Validating Act, 1913 under which any benefit is for the time being claimable for himself by the person by whom the waqf was created or by any member of his family or descendants. The other Acts have also recognised the validity of waqf-alal-aulad.[162]

CAPACITY OF THE WAQIF TO MAKE A WAQF

Age of majority and soundness of mind

For the validity of a waqf it is necessary that the waqif must be free, must be adult. and must be possessed of understanding.[163] The Indian courts have held that under Muslim law, a waqf can be created by any person who has attended the age of majority and is of sound mind and there is no fraud, undue influence, coercion,[164] *etc.* The waqif must possess good health. He shall not be suffering from death illness.[165]

In Muslim law the age of puberty is the age of majority.[166] There are special provisions for specified juristic acts, such as marriage and wills, and the law of the different schools is not uniform on these points. The shari-ul-Islam mentions 'a report which favours the legality of charity' by 'one who has attained ten years only,' but 'the preferable opinion is stated to be that waqf by him' is forbidden because the inhabitation under which he is placed by reason of his youth is not removed until he has attained to puberty and discretion, implying that puberty is the period of life after which waqf is permissible because then the person is competent to act. [167]

The age of majority of Indian Muslims is governed by two laws *i.e.* the personal law of Muslims and the Indian Majority Act. The capacity of Muslims to act in the following matters namely, marriage, dower, divorce and adoption is not affected by anything contained in the Indian Majority Act of 1875, but is governed by the Muslim law. In *Sadiq Ali* v *Jai Kishore*[168] it was said that the Muslim age of puberty is none. Apart from marriage, dower, divorce and adoption, there is no law stating in terms the effect of a person being a minor. Similarly, there is no law laying down that non-attainment of the age of majority incapacitates the minor from doing any act in the law whatever. It is not clear as to what will be the consequences of the acts which are neither expressly excepted from the effect of the Majority Act, nor expressly covered by some such enactments as the Indian Contract Act. In *Rajindra Narain* v *Suroda*[169] it was that said every act done by a minor is not necessarily null and void. Those acts which are prejudicial to his interests can be questioned and avoided by him after he reaches his age of majority.

As regards the age of majority the law is not uniform. Competence to enter into one transaction may be attained earlier than another. The Indian Majority Act itself is not uniform. At some places it says that a person will attain the age of majority if he or she has attained the age of 18 years. But the same law will not be applicable if a guardian was appointed for the minor. Under such circumstances a boy or girl will attain the age of majority at the age of 21 years. It may be observed here that the Indian Majority Act is silent that in the absence of any special law to the contrary, non attainment of majority will incapacitate the person in question in regard to all acts in the law. The Act specifically lays down that with regard to specific juristic acts, such acts should only be done when the person concerned has attained the age of majority.

The Indian Majority Act governs capacity in regard to waqf unless making a waqf be taken as a religious rite or usage. The question may depend on the aims and objects of a particular waqf. It is not clear the creation of waqf is a religious rite or usage or the disposition of property. Islam directs his followers to donate some share of their properties for the welfare of mankind. However, for attaining this pious work it is necessary to establish a waqf. This can be done by donations.

Formerly it was thought that a minor could not make a valid waqf. However, in *Fatma Bibi* v *Advocate General*[170] it was said that a minor can very well make a waqf. In Fatma Bibi's case a Muslim girl of 14 years made a waqf. Later on, after the demise of her husband she used for the declaration that the waqf made by her was void since she was minor at the time of the making of the waqf. It was held that though the dedication by a girl of 14 years was not to be upheld without enquiry yet the transaction never having been questioned by her husband. The court further said that for the last five years she never questioned the validity of the waqf. In fact, during these years she accepted the profits of the estate from the trustees. The court, therefore, refused to accept the contention of the lady. In *Delroos Banoo Nawab Asghar*[171] a deed executed by pardanashin lady was set aside on the ground that it was not proved that the consequences of waqf were explained to her. The guardian of a minor can not make a waqf on his or her behalf, such action will be a nullity at law.

Waqfs established by Pardanashin Ladies

The rules governing pardanashin ladies are quite different. Since they are presumed to be ignorant and infirm and they can be easily influenced the Indian courts have taken a rigid view in respect of waqfs made by pardanashin ladies. In ***Delroos Bano B gum*** v ***Nawab Asghar Ali***[172] the Calcutta High Court opined that under ordinary circumstances the waqif is presumed to know the consequences of his acts (i.e. the act of creating the waqf), but in this case the matter was somewhat different. The defendant was a pardanashin Muslim lady unable to read and write. Therefore, it was not possible for her to understand the result of the dedication which she intended to make. The court, therefore, held that no waqf was created by the pardanashin lady.

In case there arises any dispute as to whether the pardanashin lady established a waqf or not, the burden of proof will lie on the other side to prove that all consequences were explained to the lady, she gave her property in waqf freely and without any influence. In *Farid-un-Nissa* v *Mnkhtar Ahmad*[173] the court cancelled the waqfnama since the other party failed to prove that the contents of waqf were explained to her.

On the other hand, where a lady with a certain amount of education, who subscribes newspapers, manages her affairs and even appears in courts is not a pardanashin lady. A waqf made by such a lady will be valid. In *Fatima Bibi* v *The Advocate General*[174] a Sunni Muslim lady created a waqf for herself and alal-aulad. Subsequently, she wanted to revoke the same. It was held that she could not do so.

Ownership

It is also necessary that the waqif must have the power to give his property in waqf.[175] It is also necessary that at the time of making the waqf, the property must belong to the waqf. He must be the owner of the property. The basic principle of Muslim law has been construed by Indian courts in the following manner. The transfer must not be fraudulent or dishonest. A waqf created by a widow under a fraudulent waqf deed on her deceased husband's heirs, was held to be invalid even against her own share in the property.[176] In *Masihuddin* v *Ballabh Dass*[177] A usurped certain property belonging to B and purported to dedicate it. A thereafter purchased it from B, the rightful owner of the property. The waqf was held void. However, if B the rightful owner has given his ratification, the waqf shall be valid. In order to create a waqf, it is, however, not necessary that the waqif should have full proprietary interest in the property. The permanent dominion over the subject matter of the waqf will be sufficient.[178]

A waqf may be made of the property which has been given in possession to the waqf pursuant to an agreement to purchase it provided that the sale is completed eventually.[179] In *Rahiman* v *Baqridan*[180] the waqf dedicated the land which was already leased and the term of which was not expired. The waqf was held valid. It may, however, be noted that a mere leasehold cannot be dedicated as waqf.[181] Similarly the waqif cannot make a waqf of the right to money under a decree.[182]

Payment of Debt

Under the Hanafi law a waqif is competent to make a provision for the payment of his debt ; or for his own maintenance, out of the income of the property which he dedicates as waqf. Ithan Ashari and Ismaili laws are quite different on this point. Under Ithan Ashari[183] and Ismaili[184] schools a waqif cannot make a provision for the payment of the debts.

Section 3(b) of the Mussalman Waqf Validating Act, 1913, recognised the doctrine of Hanafi school that a Hanafi Muslim can make a provision for the payment of his debts. Section 3(b) of the above mentioned Act says that 'where the person creating a waqf is a Hanafi Musalman, also for his own maintenance and support during his lifetime or for the payment of his debts out of the rents and profits of the property dedicated. In number of cases the Indian courts have enforced this provision.[185]

In *Abdul Karim* v *Rahimbai*[186] the High Court of Bombay said that a Hanafi waqif is empowered to reserve only a portion of the income of the waqf as might be necessary for his maintenance. He is, however, not entitled to reserve the whole income for his maintenance. This decision of the Bombay High Court was not followed by other courts of India.[187]

A waqif is also competent to make the provision that in future this shall be his discretion to change any of the beneficiaries.[188]

After the completion of a waqf, dedicator has no right to withdraw any portion of the dedicated property. The dedicator has no right to withdraw even a very small portion of the waqf property.[189]

Advantages and Disadvantages of Waqf

Those who believe in Islam and wants to come more closer to God, they must given some part of their wealth to poors. They should donate their property perpetually for charitable and pious purposes. Prophet Muhammad declared that the best of all pious offerings is a provision for oneself so that one may not fall into need, and that giving sadaqah should commence with those whose subsistence is obligatory. The best way for helping poors is to constitute a waqf.

By establishing waqfs a man can come more near to his creature. The Holy Prophet again declared that the best of all the pious offering is a provision for one self, to the children, and finally to the needy relatives, and that the gift should commence with those whose subsistence is obligatory. He said that giving alms to the poor has one reward, but giving to poor kindred has two rewards. The idea is that the people did not want any one to be in want.[190] The waqf to some extent ameliorates poverty.

It is submitted that there are more disadvantages than advantages of this pious institution. This is natural that when a father makes a provision by way of waqf for the education of his children the children will have no enthusiasm to improve themselves. It has also been seen in many cases that if people are having sufficient funds by way of family waqf, they will have no interest to improve their conditions. The condition of waqf property is also miserable. Most of the waqfs were established more than 100 years back. Now their conditions have become pitiable. Mutawallis and other persons who are responsible have paid no attention for the proper repairs of such buildings. The condition is the worst in respect of agricultural lands. Agricultural land deteriorates in the course of time ; no one is concerned with keeping it in good trim ; the yield lessens, and even perpetual leases come to be recognised. Keeping all these facts into consideration Fzyee[191] has said that the institution of waqf as a whole has been an unmixed blessing to the community. Again the process of civil administration of justice in India is very slow. There are several cases pending for the last twenty years. This also includes waqf cases. It is, therefore, necessary that suitable reforms be introduced in the matter.

Suit for the Declaration that property is Waqf

A suit under section 92, Code of Civil Procedure is a suit of special nature which presupposes the existence of a public trust of a religious or equitable character. Section 92 of the Code provides that in the case of any alleged breach of express or constructive trust created for public purposes of a charitable or religious nature, or where the direction of the court is deemed necessary for the administration of any such trust, the Advocate General or two or more persons having an interest in the trust and having obtained the consent in writing of the Advocate General may institute a suit, within the local limits of whose jurisdiction the whole or any part of the subject matter of the trust is situated. In the aforesaid suit the plaintiff must pray for one or more of the reliefs that are mentioned in the section.

Recently, the Allahabad High Court held that in order to maintain a suit under section 92 it must be shown that there exists a trust for public purposes of a charitable or religious nature ; that there is a breach of such trust or that the direction of the court is necessary for the administration of the trust and the reliefs claimed in the suit must be one or more of the reliefs mentioned in the section. Where any of these conditions is absent section 92 would have no application to the suit. If the suit does not relate to a public trust but relates to private properties owned by an individual or to a private trust section 92 would not apply.[192]

Formerly, there was a conflict of opinion as to whether section 92 of the Code of Civil Procedure will be applied in the case of waqfs or not. The waqfs are substantially created for the common man. The suit under section 92 must be in a representative capacity and not to vindicate private rights. It has been said that the waqf may create intermediate private rights but if there is substantial benefit for charity, the suit, if it is to vindicate public rights will fall within section 92 and the the consent of the Advocate General is a condition precedent. Therefore, to attract the provisions of section 92 of the Code of Civil Procedure it must be established that the beneficial interest is vested in an uncertain and fluctuating body of individuals and the trust is of a permanent character.

A suit for the declaration that property belongs to a waqf

can be brought by Muslims interested in the waqf without the sanction of the Advocate General. The provisions of section 92 of the Code of Civil Procedure, 1908 will not be applicable in such a suit.[193]

In *Sughra Bibi* v *Haji Kummu Mian*[194] it was said that even a worshipper will have the right to file a suit for possession of a trust property where the trustee has alienated the trust property and would not proceed to recover possession of the same or has disabled himself otherwise from maintaining suit in respect thereof, or declines to institute a suit. A similar view was taken in *Amir Jain* v *Shaik Sulaiman Sahib.*[195]

In *Mahmud Ilahi* v *Dawn Trust*[196] it was said that where a declaration is sought that a property is not waqf, section 92 of the Code of Civil Procedure will not apply and a separate suit must be filed.

The provisions of section 92, Code of Civil Procedure are not applicable in the case of waqf-alal-aulad.[197]

DEFINITION OF SOME IMPORTANT TERMS

Waqif

The waqif is the owner of the property who dedicates his property in the name of God for religious, charitable or pious purposes. Section 3 of the Mussalman Waqf Validating Act, 1913, says that it is lawful for any person professing the Mussalman faith to create a waqf which in all other respects is in accordance with the provisions of the Mussalman law. In such waqfs the ultimate benefit should be expressly or impliedly reserved for the poor, or for any other purpose recognised by the Mussalman law as a religious, pious or charitable purpose of a permanent character. The Indian courts have held that it is not always necessary that the dedication must have been made for religious purposes.[198] When the owner of any specific property declares in good faith that he 'makes waqf' of it, or that he 'dedicates it in perpetuity by way of sadaqa or charity, he is called the waqif, or the founder of the waqf, or the settlor, or dedicator,' and is said to 'make a dedication or declaration of waqf or to dedicate the property,' or 'to create a waqf' or 'to make a settlement' by way of waqf.[199]

Ameer Ali says that according to the classical jurists of Islam even non-Muslims could make waqfs.[200] The waqif must be major at the time of making the waqf. A guardian on behalf of minor is not competent to make a waqf and such a waqf even if purported to be made is void.[201] A waqif can appoint mutawalli. He can also formulate the scheme for succession to the office of mutawalli.

Waqf Deed

A waqif can dedicate his property in waqf either orally or in writing. In case the waqif has dedicated his property by way of a deed, the deed is known as waqfnama. In *Mohammad Yasin Rahmat Ilahi*[202] it was said that the legal effect of oral waqf or waqf in writing will be the same. A waqif can create waqf in any of these to ways.

While interpreting a waqf deed (waqfnama) the intention of the waqif is the foundation stone. The waqfnama should be interpreted in accordance with the intention of the waqif and the words used in the waqfnama should not be given any special treatment. In *Asheerooddeen alias Kalla Miah* v *Drobo Moyee*[203] it was said that where the declaration was made in accordance with the English forms used in conveyancing and the operative words are clear, the preamble will not control them. In case there exists any custom to the contrary, that custom should be proved.[204]

In *Bikani Mia* v *Shuk Lal Poddar* [205] the word 'generation' was interpreted. The court laid down the following two rules for interpreting the word 'generation' :—

(i) In case the waqf deed says that only one or two generations of the descendants will be the beneficiaries, the benefit of such waqf will be enjoyed by such generations only ; and

(ii) In case the waqf deed contains three or more generations, the benefit will be enjoyed by all beneficiaries and the rule of perpetuity will be applied in such cases.

There is a difference of opinion on the question of interpretation of the term 'nearest relatives.' While interpreting this term, the following persons should be included in the order shown below.

Shia law does not maintain any difference between male and female as far as the law of inheritance and waqf is concerned. This school, therefore, does not give any priority to males over females. The following persons shall come within the definition of the term 'nearest relatives' :

(a) descendants howsoever low together with the father and mother ;

(b) grandparents, and brothers (and sisters)[206] together with the descendants of the brothers (and sisters) howsoever low ;

(c) paternal and maternal uncles (and aunts) in the order of inheritance.

Under Hanafi law, the following persons will come with the definition of 'nearest relatives'[207] :

(a) sons and daughters ;

(b) parents ;

(c) grand children ;

(d) grand parents ;

(e) great grand children ;

(f) great grand parents ; and

(g) brothers and sisters.

The term 'masculine gender' means males as well as females, unless a contrary was mentioned by the waqif in the waqf deed.[208]

Beneficiary

The beneficiaries of the waqf property must be persons who can be identified easily. In case the waqif has dedicated his property to persons who are having some perpetual ingredients, or the ingredients are such that the same can not be acquired once they are lost, the benefit should be given to only those people who are having such ingredients. For example if the waqif says that I dedicate my property to my blind or one eyed children ; or on my minor children ; or on my male children, the beneficiaries will be only these persons. No other person will be able to enjoy the fruit of that waqf[209]. On the other hand if the ingredients of beneficiary can be lost for sometime and they can again be seen, all identifiable presons should be treated as beneficiaries. For example, the waqif may say as follows—I dedicate by way of waqf for my children living in London ; or who are poor ; or who are married ; or professing Islam. In such cases the beneficiary will be all those persons who at the time of the accrual of income fulfils the above qualifications.[210]

Child

The ordinary meaning of the word 'child' is a young human being or offspring. The waqif of a waqf can dedicate his property, the fruits of which will be enjoyed by his children. Sometimes, it becomes difficult to say as to what is the exact meaning of this word. This word will include only those children who were in existence at the time of dedication or it will also include those children who were born later on. In *Abdul Latif* v *Abadi Begum*[211] it was said that the term 'child of the waqif' includes both the children in existence at the time of dedication, and after born children. However, this term will not include those children who were merely acknowledged by their parents and whose paternity is not known.[212] The grand-children and remoter descendants will also not come under the category of 'child of the waqif'. This rule is not absolute. There is one exception to this rule. The grandchildren of the waqif will come under the category of children if there was no child living at the time of the dedication, but if the child of a son (or other agnatic descendant) is living such a child or descendant will come within the definition of 'child of the waqif'. The child of daughter will not come under the category of 'child of the waqif'. Where there was no descendant in the first and second generation, the children of third or any lower category will be treated as child of the waqif.[213] The child of daughter will not come under the category of 'child of the waqif'. Where there was no descendant in the first and second generation, the children of third or any lower category will be treated as child of the waqif.[214]

The word heir means a person who is entitled to inherit property. The word heir means heirs generally, not such heirs alone as are also issues.[215] The words heirs and issues may be so used that each must be understood as heirs who were also issues.

The word 'nasabd' means only agnatic descendants.[216]

The term 'Nasl' and 'Zariat' means all descendants *i.e.* those persons who have descended from an ancestor. This term includes both males and females, near and remote.[217] It is not necessary these persons must be in existence at the time of the dedication. A person born later on will also come under this category.

In English language, the substitute of the term 'Aulad' is children. The children may be only males or only females ; or males and females both. However, the children of females will not come under the category of Aulad.[218]

The term 'Ahfed' includes the descendants of females as well as males.[219]

As regards the terms Aulad-dar-aulad there is a difference of opinion between Hanafi school and Shia school. The Hanafi school does not include the sons of a daughter. On the other hand, Shia school includes the sons of a daughter.[220]

The term 'Khandan' includes only legitimate offspring. However, the rule is not absolute. There is an exception to this general rule. There may be cases where the term aulad will include illegitimate children also.[221]

The word 'Qarabat' is a very wide term. It is not restricted to relations by blood. It includes relations by affinity also. The term includes all those persons who are related to dedicator through a common ancestor. A person from the father's side or the mother's side will come under this category. A person within the prohibited degree will also come under this category.

In English language the word 'Yatim' means orphan *i.e.* a person who is minor and whose father has died. A minor will be 'Yatim' even if his or her mother and or grandfather is alive but father is dead.[222]

WAQF PROPERTY

The Dedication must be of any grant of Property

The property dedicated is known as the subject of the **waqf** or the waqf property or dedicated property. Formerly, it was that though the subject matter of the waqf consisted of properties of a permanent nature, such as land, fields, gardens, *etc.* There are cases where it was held that movable property cannot be the subject matter of the property. The position was clarified by the Mussalman Waqf Validating Act, 1913. In India, except for cases where it was held that the land or immovable property alone could be subject matter of waqfs courts have held that a waqf can be made even of movable property. The Indian courts have followed the proposition of Abdur Rahim[223] who in his book *Muhammadan Jurisprudence* said that the dedicated property should possess two characteristics *i.e.*, (i) it must be mal, tangible property and (ii) it must be capable of being used without being consumed.

Waqf of Movable and Inmovable Property held Valid

It was said by the Calcutta High Court[224] that waqf of shares in a joint stock company was not valid. With the passage of time, the thinking of the people also changed. It was said that a valid waqf can be made not only of immovable but also of movable property.

In *Fatmabai* v *Ghulam Hussain*[225] the Bombay High Court said that a valid waqf could not be made of movables, unless the movable were accessory to the immovable property, such as cattle attached to agricultural land and implements of husbandary, or unless a waqf of movables was allowed by custom.

The above view of the Bombay High Court was followed by the Madras High Court in *Kadir Ibrahim* v *Mahomed.*[226]

Usufructuary Mortgage in property not Valid

The leading case on this point is *Rahiman* v *Mst Baqridan* In this case it was held that a usufructuary mortgage in immovable property cannot be subject of waqf.

In the above case it was further said that usufructuary

mortgagee is not the owner of mortgaged property and has no permanent control over that property.

Gradually, all sorts of properties were made subject matter of the waqf, and waqfs were validily made of animals. Even a camel was made the subject matter of the waqf. A stage was reached when all types of movable properties which were unconsummable by use were made subject matters of waqf. In *Abu Sayid* v *Baker Ali* it was said that a valid waqf may be made of movable and that a waqf even of coins or shares in a joint stock company was not invalid.

The position was made clear after the passing of the Mussalman Waqf Validating Act, 1913. Section 2(i) of this Act is very wide and includes every kind of property. The Act of 1913 lays down that a waqf may be made of 'any property' and the Waqf Act, 1954, also lays down that waqf may be made of any immovable or movable property. It has been judicially held that government promissory notes could be validly given in waqf.

In *Mirza Yakub* v *Mirza Rasul Baig* the waqf of cash money was held as valid.

Waqf of the Proprietary rights of a Groveholder held Valid

The propriety rights of a groveholder was held a valid subject matter of waqf. It was said that a groveholder has permanent dominion and full property right over the trees.

Offerings made in a shrine held Valid

The offerings made in a shrine are valid subject matter of waqf.

Waqf of cash money held Valid

Prior to the Waqf Validating Act, 1913, there were conflicting rulings of various High Courts in India as to whether a valid waqf could be made of money. The High Courts of Calcutta and Madras held that money cannot be the subject matter of waqf unless they are accessory to some immovable property of which waqf was being made. The Allahabad High Co rt held to the contrary. However, after the Waqf Validating Act, 1913, 'any property' would mean every movable as well as immovable.[228]

Waqf of money Decree

After the passing of the Mussalman waqf Validating Act, 1913, Indian courts have declared waqf of any property as valid. The courts have taken into consideration the necessity and wants of social life of Indian Muslims. It already noted in majority of the cases the courts have treated the waqf of movable property, government promissory notes, shares in joint stock companies and even money *etc.* as valid. In *Ghulam Mohiuddin* v *Hafiz Abdul Rashid*[229] the Allahabad High Court took a different view. It was said that the waqf of money decree is not valid. The court held that in the case of waqf of simple money decree, money may or may not be ultimately realised from the judgment-bebtors ; at any rate the recovery of any amount under the decree is problematic. Therefore, a waqf of money decree was declared as invalid. It was further said that if there was a custom to the contrary then such a waqf will be valid.

Waqf of the leased Property held Valid

The property which was already leased can be the subject matter of a valid waqf. It may, however, be noted that a mere leasehold cannot be dedicated as waqf.[230]

Waqf of the Mortgaged property held Valid

A waqf may validly be made of the property subject to mortgage.[231] But a usufructuary mortgagee cannot validly make a waqf of his rights.[232] The reason given by the court was that since he was not the owner of the property he was not competent to make a gift. A waqf which constitutes the part of a transaction to play fraud on the heirs is void and totally ineffective.[233]

Waqf of Dower debt held not Valid

The property which the dedicator intents to dedicate must be certain and specified with a reasonable clarity. An uncertain property can not be the subject matter of valid waqf.[234]

Waqf of right to Usufruct

Under Shaffi and Shia schools a waqf can be made of the land and everything from the use of which any benefit can be derived.[235] In *Hashim Haroon* v *Gounsalisha*[236] a waqf of a a debt due to donor under a simple mortgage was held as void.

Things which admits of use without destruction of subject held valid object of Waqf

Everything which admits of use without destruction of subject, everything lawfully saleable, because such articles as admit of usufruct resemble land, houses or arms, may be the subject of waqf.[237] The Shia law says that absconded slave cannot be the subject of waqf as he cannot be delivered.

Waqfs in respect of Animals held Valid

There exists a group of decisions in which the courts have accepted the validity of waqfs for animals of various kinds, usually domestic animals of the waqif, and also for some inanimate objects, usually memorials. Such waqfs present unusal difficulties from the standpoint of theory, in that objects benefited cannot enforce them. It will, therefore, not be wrong to call them as imperfect or unenforceable waqfs.

In *Puran Atal* v *Darshan Das*[238] the waqf of sheep along with their wool and milk was held as valid. Similarly, the dedication of trained dog or cat may validly be given in waqf[239]. It is, however, notable that on account of certain reasons Islam does not approve dogs as good animal to be kept in the house. The validity of the waqf of a dog is, therefore, very much doubted.

There are numerous English cases where the English courts have declared creation of trusts in favour of animals as valid.[240] The best judicial exposition of the principle is that of North, J., *in Re.* Dean. In that case a testator had devised his freehold estates, subject to an annuity of £ 750 and a term of fifty years in favour of his trustees, to the use of the plaintiff for life. He also gave his horses, ponies and hounds to his trustees, directing them to apply the annuity for the period of fifty years, if the horses and hounds, should so long live, for the maintenance of the horses and hounds, and the stables and kennels in which they lived. North J. held that the trust was good during the lives of the animals, and to the objection that there was no *cestui que* trust who could enforce the trust, he said —

> There is not the least doubt that a man may, if he pleases, give a legacy to trustees, upon trust to apply it in erecting a monument to himself, either in a church or in a churchyard, or even in unconsecrated ground, and I am not aware that such a trust is in any way invalid, although it is difficult to say who would be a *cestui que* trust of the monument. In the same way I know of nothing to prevent a gift of a sum of money to trustees upon trust to apply it for the repair of such a monument. In my opinion such a trust would be good, although the testator must be careful to limit the time for which it is to last, because as it is not a charitable trust, unless it is to come to an end within the limits fixed by the rule against perpetuities, it would be illegal. But a trust to lay out a certain sum in building a monument, and the gift of another sum in trust to apply the same to keeping that monument in repair, say for ten years, is, in my opinion, a perfectly good trust, although I do not see who could ask the court to enforce it. If persons beneficially interested in the estate could do so, then the present plaintiff can do so ; but, if such persons could not enforce the trust, still it cannot be said that the trust must fail because there is no one who can actually enforce it.

The waqfs for non-human beneficiaries are lawful and the persons incharge act properly if they carry them out, but the non-human object may not enjoy the benefit of the waqf for a period longer than the perpetuity period. Where a life is selected, it must be human life and not the life of an animal which may be the object of the waqf. Where the settlor selects no human life, he is confined to the absolute period of twenty one years.

Waqf of Property which is under Contract of Sale

A settlor can make a waqf of the property which he expects to receive under a contract of sale. The contract of sale may be completed subsequently.[241]

WAQF OF MUSHA

There is no agreement of opinion amongst different schools of Muslim Law on the question of waqf of Musha. According to Imam Muhammad the waqf of Musha in property which is capable of division is not valid. He was of the opinion that for the validity of a waqf, actual possession was necessary.[242] On the other hand, Abu Yusuf of Hanafi school was of the opinion that the Musha (undivided part of property) may be dedicated in waqf.[243] Therefore, the dominant Hanafi opinion (which does not insist on transfer of property in a waqf by the settlor to a mutawalli) does not prohibit waqf of a Musha, *i.c.* undivided portion of a longer property, which is capable of being separated from it. He maintained that a waqf of Musha, whether capable of division or not, could not be made for a mosque or a burial ground, as continuance of a participation in anything is repugnant to its becoming the exclusive right of God. The Indian courts have followed this principle.[244]

The above Hanafi opinion along with two exceptions were enforced in India in number of cases. In *Peeran* v *Hafiz*[245] however, the High Court of Allahabad took a different view. The court recognised the validity of the waqf of Musha for the maintenance of a mosque.

In *Mazhrool Haq* v *Puhraj Ditaree*[246] the dedication was made for the following purposes ;

(i) expenses of masjid ;
(ii) alms to mendicants ;
(iii) education of poor ;
(iv) surplus for marriages, burials and circumcision of mutawalli's family.

The above dedications were held valid. It was said that dedication in favour of a mosque, will not become void by there being a charge upon the profits of items which must lapse in the course of time, leaving the whole benefit to the moseque. In this case dedication for expenses of masjid, alms to mendicants, education of poor, surplus for marriages, burials and circumcision of mutawalli's family was held valid.

Tyabji[247] says that dedication in favour of a mosque, does not become void because there being a charge upon the profits of items which must lapse in the course of time, leaving the whole benefit to the mosque. In *Peeran* v *Hafiz*[248] it was said that a waqf of Musha for the maintenance of a mosque is valid.

It is clear that one of several heirs of a deceased Muslim are not at liberty to make a valid waqf of his undivided share of the inheritance for a mosque or burial ground though he is at liberty to do so for other purposes. The Judicial Committee of the Privy Council once said that if one of several heirs takes possession of the woole property and delivers possession of it to the trustees of a mosque for the benefit of the mosque, though it be without the consent of the other heirs, the waqf will be valid to the extent of his own share.[249] A waqf for the endowment or construction of mosques or burial grounds will be valid dedication.[250] Mulla[251] says that the cases referred above are of a waqf of a Musha for purposes other than a mosque or a burial ground. A waqf of a Musha or burial ground is invalid for the reasons stated by Abu Yusuf. It has been maintained in Pakistan that a waqf of Musha for the upkeep of a mosque is not invalid.[252]

THE BENEFICIARY

Beneficiary means the person or persons who will enjoy the benefit from the property dedicated in waqf. By establishing a waqf a man can come more near to God. Once Prophet said that the best of all the pious offering is a provision for one self, to the children and finally to the needy relatives and the gift should commence with those whose subsistence is obligatory. He declared that giving alms to the poor has one reward but giving to poor kindred has two rewards.[253] By creating waqf a Muslim can acquire merit in the eyes of God in this world and hereafter. A waqf may be created for the benefit of any person or class of persons or for any object of piety or charity.

A waqif can validly make a waqf for the benefit of the following persons :

(i) for the affluent and the indigent alike ; or
(ii) for the indigent only ; or

(iii) for the affluent to begin with but ultimately for the indigent.

Beneficiary need not be Poor

It may, therefore, be noted that it is not necessary that a man must necessarily be poor to get benefit of a waqf. The benefit may be derived by any person irrespective of the fact that he is not poor. It is, however, true that when all other purposes fail, the relief of the poor shall be the ultimate purpose of every waqf.[254]

Under Muslim Law, the following can be the expected beneficiaries—

(i) the waqif himself;
(ii) the family and descendants of waqif; and
(iii) general public.

Waqif as Beneficiary

According to Hanafi school, a waqif can make a provision that he will take some or the whole of the usufruct for his life or for a lesser period. Under Hanafi school a waqif can also provide for the payment of his debts. Hanafi school maintains that the interest in the dedicated property continues in some measures even after the creation of waqf. He can, therefore, be allowed to share the usufruct of the property with others. But Abu Yusufu and Imam Muhammad states that once validly dedicated will become the property of God. The Ithna Ashari school and Imam Mohammad, are not in favour of such a reservation in respect of the settler. They maintain that the waqif has no right to receive the benefit of the dedicated property and the possession of the dedicated property should also be given to the beneficiary. It has, therefore, been said that where the waqif has once relinquished his proprietary rights in favour of God, he will have no right to take any benefit from such property.

A waqf to pay profits to waqif during his life time without power of anticipation has been held to be valid.[255] Similarly, a waqf for mosque with a condition to pay Rs. 2.00 p.m. to daughter was held valid.[256]

The waqif can lawfully become the first mutawalli of the

waqf property. He can provide in the waqf deed that he will be the mutawalli. In Abadi Begum's[257] case, a case under Ithna Ashari school, the waqif, a Shia lady provided in the waqf deed that she will be the first mutawalli and that she will get Rs. 1500.00 as remuneration per annum. It was also provided that the succeeding mutawallis shall get Rs. 350.00 per month. The waqf was held as invalid. However, under Hanafi school and also under Mussalman Waqf Validating Act, 1913-30 such a waqf will be treated as valid.

Under Shia Law, a waqif can become the beneficiary if he has made an appropriation for the poor and has himself become poor. It is the requirement of a valid waqf that it ought to be made with intention of acquiring spiritual benefit after death.[258]

A beneficiary may or may not be related to the waqif. Reservation, therefore, of a benefit of any person cannot by itself invalidate a waqf. Formerly, it was maintained that a waqf in favour of strangers, though coupled with a substantial and immediate grant for charitable purposes was invalid.[259] This view was not followed by Mysore High Court in *G. Venkataswami* v *Mir Zahid*.[260] The High Court said that a waqf shall not be void only because some benefit was reserved in favour of the waqif or some other person. Under Hanafi Law, such a waqf will be treated as valid. The waqif can make his servants as beneficiaries.[261] Since a waqf can be made by a non-Muslim also, he can also be the beneficiary. This is subject to the rule that an alien enemy cannot take the benefit of waqf. This rule of Muslim Law has no relevance in India.[262]

Waqif's family as Beneficiary

A waqf[263] for the benefit of the waqif's family and his descendants, if created exclusively for their benefit, would be invalid. Before the passing of the Wakf Act, 1913, a waqf was treated valid if there was a substantial dedication of the property to charitable uses at some period of time or other. Where the primary object of the waqf was for the aggrandisement of the family and the gift to charity was only illusory, the entire waqf would be invalid.[264]

The above anomaly was removed after the passing of the

Waqf Validating Act, 1913. This Act provides that a waqif can make a waqf for the benefit of the family even if the gift to charity is illusory but the ultimate gift should necessarily go to charity.

Under section 3 clause (a) of the aforesaid Act beneficiary means a person or object for whose benefit a waqf is created and includes religious, pious and charitable objects and any other objects of public utility established for the benefit of the Muslim community. It is submitted that the definition of beneficiary as it is given in section 3 (a) has restricted its scope. The use of the words 'objects of public utility established for the benefit of the Muslim community' was not necessary at all. These words were already included in the preceding clause and includes religious, pious or charitable objects. Clause (1) of section 3 of the Waqf Act, 1954, contains no such restriction and, therefore, these words had made the definition of beneficiary inconsistent with the definition of waqf.[265]

Formerly, section 3 (a) of the Waqf Act, 1954, contained the words 'objects of publie utility established for the benefit of Muslim community.' These words were causing difficulty. It was generally felt that the benefit can be derived only by the Muslim community. It was, however, maintained as far as charity is concerned Islam makes no distinction between Muslim and non-Muslim among the recipients of charity. Whenever there is an injunction or inducement in the Quran and Hadith as charity, the recipients are stated as the poor, indigent, orphans, travellers, the downtrodden and poor neighbour without making any distinction on the basis of religion, caste or creed. To remove this confusion few words were substituted. The words 'objects of public utility established for the benefit of Muslim community' were deleted and the words 'objects of public utility sanctioned by Muslim Law were added.

Right of the Beneficiary to grant lease *etc.*

According to Shia Law the subject of waqf vests in the beneficiaries. The Sharai-ul-Islam says the beneficiaries themselves having only a life interest cannot in any event grant a lease for a longer period. Shia Law permits the beneficiaries under a waqf to make a lease of the waqf property or otherwise transfer or alienate it, for the period during which they are entitled to its benefit, but so that such lease or transfer or alienation does not prejudice the rights of any succeeding beneficiaries. Shia Law contemplates beneficiaries taking more active part in management of waqf property. It was said that Hanafi Law expects all administration to be done by the mutawalli.[266]

Right of the Beneficiaries to take Simultaneously and Equally

Where, under a dedication several objects or beneficiaries are entitled to take the benefit, they will take simultaneously and in equal shares. However, the above principle will not be applied if the waqfnama says otherwise.

Consequences of the failure of the first Beneficiary—Waqf Void

Under Shia Law if the beneficiary who in point of time, is to benefit in the first instance, fails the waqf will become void and will carry no force.[267] In case some of the objects of the waqf could not be fulfilled, the validity of the other objects is not thereby affected.[268]

It may be noted here that the failure of the prior object may accelerate a later. To clear the above observation, following observation which is given in Fatawai Alamgiri may be noted. It may be noted that endowment in favour of temple is void.[269] If a non-Muslim says, 'devote the produce to such a temple, and then if the temple is ruined, the produce should be given to faqirs and the indigent and not to the temple'. The object of a waqf may be non-existent in two ways—firstly, the beneficiary may be non-existent when the waqf is made, when it is called waqf munqata-ul-awwal (cut off initially) and secondly, the persons for whom the waqf is made, may cease to exist after the creation of the waqf, when it is called waqf munqata-ul-wasat (cut off in the middle). A man may make a waqf for the children born of his lions ; if he was not having any child at the time of making the waqf. This kind of waqf will come under the category of maqata-ul-awwals and the rents and profits will be applied to the poor. If the children are born to him afterwards then the rents and profits will be paid to them.

Shia and Shafii schools speifically says that for the validity of a waqf the beneficiaries must be in existence at the time of making of the waqf. This is not sufficient.[270] They must be competent to hold property and distinctly indicated.[271] It has been said that a waqf without mentioning the original beneficiary capable of enjoying it immediately will be void.

Creation of Waqf where benefit will be derived by Succession of Persons

The law on this subject is not free from doubt. The Shia and Shafii schools of Musliw Law recognises the dedication purporting to be for the benefit of succession of persons. The Shia and Shafii schools of Muslim Law recognises such dedication if the first beneficiary is, at the time of the dedication, in being, and competent to benefit under a waqf. If the waqf was created in favour of one not in existence in succession to a person actually in being, it would be quite good. It will make no difference if the succeeding beneficiary is not in being or otherwise not competent so to benefit.[272]

There is a difference of opinion on the question as to whether the dedication of property will be valid if at the time of dedication the beneficiary was not in existence or otherwise not competent so to benefit. The Sharai-ul-Islam says that the more approved Shiite opinion is that the waqf fails, notwithstanding that the next succeeding beneficiary is in existence, and competent so to benefit, though some authorities insist that the dedication ought to be sustained so far as it concerns the persons in being.

Hanafi school permits the shifting of benefit. This school says that a person can make a waqf in respect of persons who are not in existence or who cannot be ascertained at the time of the dedication. In such cases the benefit will go to the poor or to the other religious, pious or charitable object to which the benefit is ultimately dedicated. On the failure of the said person, to the object next entitled under the dedication to succeed to the benefit. As soon as he comes into being, the benefit will accrue to him.[273] For example, if one should make a settlement on the heirs of Zeyd, and Zeyd is living, there is nothing for his heirs, and the whole produce passes to the poor (because his heirs cannot be ascertained while he is living, but only after his death). 'But if Zeyd should die' (in which case his heirs could be ascertained) 'the whole of the produce must then be divided among his existing heirs, according to the number of them, males and females sharing alike, and if some of them should die, their shares would belong to those alive at the time of the coming of the produce (the produce or usufruct being something rhat accrues from time to time) while if one survived, half of the produce would be for him and the other half to the poor.[274]

In Abdul Wahab's case[275] it was said that when the object of the waqf is to benefit any specified persons or class of persons they are called the beneficiaries under the waqf and the waqf is said to be created or dedicated for their benefit. In this case the salary and pension paid to waqif's servants was held as valid thougn the name and amount was not specified.

Power of the Court to grant permission for the disposition of Waqf Property

The courts have given power to grant permission for the sale, mortgage *etc.* of the waqf property. The Bahr-ur-Raiq[279] says that even if there is a condition that waqf property should never be changed, Cadi can authorise changing and replacing it, if advisable.[277] The Bahrur-Raiq maintains that under the following circumstances the court may grant permission :

(1) the waqf[278] property being reduced to such a condition that the objects of the waqf cannot be given effect to, so that the beneficiaries are unable to derive any benefit from it, in which case it is provided that the Cadi may order the sale of the property, and direct that the sale proceeds be invested in the purchase of another property.

(2) to the sale of property dedicated to a mosque (not the mosque itself), provided that the property has become unless for the purpose of the mosque ;

(3) the Fatawai-Kazi Khan[279] suggests that in some cases waqf property may be sold, and another purchased out of the sale proceeds merely because the variation of the investment would be beneficial to the waqf.

The court possess the discretion in appropriate cases to grant permission for the sale of original waqf property.[280] The court can grant permission in spite of the fact that the dedication contained a provision that the property dedicated should not be changed or replaced. Before granting permission for the disposal of property, court must be satisfied as to mutawalli's right of indemnity against waqf property.[281] Where the waqif provided that the property will not become waqf during the life time of tenant, the dedication cannot be held valid.[282]

In *Commissioner of Waqfs, Bengal v Haji Rashid Ali Dina*,[283] it was said that the Mussalman Waqf Validating Act, 1913, undoubtedly authorised a postponement of the ultimate gift to charity, which would not have been valid under the original law. However, it should not abrogate the rule of contingency under the Muslim Law. It was said that where the deed of waqf provides that the ultimate gift to charity should take effect only if a certain person dies without leaving any issue, the rule of contingency under Muslim Law would affect such disposition, and the position in that respect is not altered by anything in the Mussalman Wakf Validating Act, 1913.

The provisions of Shafii school of Muslim Law are similar to that of Hanafi law. Under Shafii Law a waqf which depends on the happening of certain things is void. A waqf to come into operation on the death of the waqif is vaild, it is to be treated on the same footing as a testamentary waqf.[284]

The Shia Law on the point is also the same. In Syeda Bibi's case[285], (a Shia case) it was said that a contingent waqf will not be valid. A widow and her sons made a dedication for their inheritance. Some of the sons were minors. It was held that the waqf was wholly invalid. The court further observed that the dedication could not take effect at once for it depended upon the minors attaining majority and doing likewise.[286]

In Aga Ali's[287] case the waqf deed provided that it shall come into force from the date of its registration. The waqf was held as contingent and, therefore, void. It may be noted here that the waqfnama merely provided that it was not complete till the waqif had taken a further step. The further step was taken when the deed was in fact registered. Immediately after the completion of registration all elements of contigency disappeared. The principle laid down in Aga Ali's case was overruled in *Baker Ali* v *Aniuman Ara's* case.[288]

Waqfs for life interest Valid

The waqfnama may provide that income of the waqf property should be utilised for limited interests or for life interests or for the benefit of a succession of persons, during their lives, or during specified periods. It is also not necessary that at the time of the dedication the said persons were not in existence. A waqf will not be governed by the rule against perpetuity.[289] The successive future life interests in favour of unborn persons was held valid. It was further held that there seems to be no rule of Hanafi Law under which the first beneficiary should be in existence.

The Waqf Act of 1913 is silent as to whether a provision can be made in favour of others than members of the family, children and descendants of the waqif. Fatawai Alamgiri says that a provision in respect of strangers may be made.[290]

A dedicator can very well provide in the waqfnama that on the happening of a certain future event, a beneficiary therein named will have no right to take any benefit.[291] A person can make a hiba of his property in favour of his daughters with the condition that such of them as marry shall be excluded from the benefit of such hiba. However, on her becoming a widow, she will again be entitled for such right.[292]

Shia Law maintains that the waqif has the right to reserve to himself the right of adding to the beneficiaries any person who may born later on. However, he will not be able to exclude any person from the benefits.

A waqif can very well make a provision for his unborn child.[293] The following example will not be out of way to mention here ;

In a waqf for the waqif's child (aulad), and after his, upon the poor, or on any child and the children that may be born to me, and when they fail, upon the poor,' the child who may be in the existence at the time of the produce, enter into the benefit of the waqf notwithstanding that there may be no child in existence at the time of the dedication.[294]

Application of Income

It is the general rule that the income of the waqf property should be applied according to the directions of the waqf-nama. In the absence of any direction in the waqfnama the income has to be used under the following four heads in order of priority.[295]

1. The waqif[296] must try his best to maintain the waqf property. He should spend the money for its preservation. The income of waqf to be spent on necessary repairs. Fatawai Alamgiri says right to produce accrues to beneficiary when produce exceeds actual expenses, including land taxes and compulsory cesses——— which are a debt for which the crop is liable.[297] Tyabji says that where under the dedication, repairs are not the first charge of the income, the court may suspend the application of the income to the objects, specified and order the repairs to be made thereout ; but the mutawalli is not authorised to do so without any order of the court.[298]
2. The income of the waqf may be applied on the objects of the waqf.[299]
3. The income should be applied to the objects which are necessary for the general purpose of the specified objects.[300]
4. Under Hanafi[301] Law, Abu Yusuf always assumes that the ultimate destination of waqf is the benefit of the poor. The Waqf Act, 1913, implies that other objects may be mentioned as fit objects for the ultimate benefit. Tyabji says that the income should be applied for the benefit of the poor, or other object recognised by the Muslim Law as religious, pious or charitable object of a permanent character, for which the ultimate benefit

of the waqf property has been expressly or impliedly reserved.[302]

COMPARISON BETWEEN WAQF AND OTHER IDENTICAL INSTITUTIONS

There are certain common elements in a waqf as well as in a trust, but a Muslim waqf has its own distinctive features and is quite different from a debettur or a trust. The institution of waqf is religion oriented. In India, the concept of waqf was introduced only after the arrival of Muslims. Therefore, in many documents where Muslim influence was predominent, the expression waqf was introduced to express dedication.

Justice Ameer Ali[303] explained the difference a between waqf and English trust in the following words :

> the Mohammedan Law owes its origin to a rule laid down by the Prophet of Islam ; and means the tying up the property in the ownership of God, the Almighty and the devotion of the profits for the benefit of human beings. As a result of the creation of a waqf, the right of 'waqif' is extinguished and the ownership is transferred to the Almighty. The manager of the waqf is the Mutawalli, the Governor, the superintendent, or curator. But in that capacity, he has no right in the property belonging to the waqf ; the property is not vested in him and he is not a trustee in the legal sense.

It is, therefore, clear that the main purpose of a waqf is religious, pious, or charitable. Unfortunately, the Indian courts have overlooked this very aspect of waqfs.

This question was again considered by the Privy Council in Vidya Varuthi Thirtha's case.[304] Justice Ameer Ali, who delivered the Judgment of the Board made the following observations :—

> It is to be remembered that a trust in the sense in which the expression is used in English Law, is unknown to the Hindu system pure and simple. Hindu piety found expression in gifts to idols and images consecrated and

> installed in temples to religious institutions of every kind, and for all purposes considered meritorious in the Hindu social and religious system, to Brahmins, Goswamis, sanyasis *etc*...when the gift is directly to an idol or a temple, the seisin to complete the gift is necessarily effected by human agency. Called by whatever name, he is only the manager or custodian of the idol or institution
> In no case is the property conveyed to or vested in him, nor is he a trustee in the English sense of the term although in view of the obligations and duties resting on him, he is answerable as a trustee in the general sense for maladministration.

It is, therefore, clear that the religious endowment under Hindu Law differs from the concept of trust known to English law. The main object of a trust is to create a public religious charity in a non-religious secular sense.

After coming into force of the Central Act, the Supreme Court[305] clarified the status of waqfs in the following words ;—

> At this stage it is necessary to distinguish between waqf recognised by Muslim Law and religious endowments recognised by the Hindu Law on the one hand and public charitable trusts as contemplated by the English law on the other.

Similarly, there exist basic difference between the Muslim Law of trust and the English law of trust. A Muslim can lawfully create a trust. In Nizam of Hyderbad's case, the court was required to decide whether the trust executed by Nizam was a waqf according to the Central Waqf Act, 1954 (Act 29 of 1954) or it was a public charitable trust falling outside the said Act. The court, after examining the document by which the trust was created, held it was not a waqf. It was a secular comprehensive public charitable trust.

A mutawalli is not the absolute owner of the waqf property. Therefore, the waqf property claimed by him stood on a different footing than that when a person claimed secular property as plaintiff.

The case of *Hazeva Khatoon* v *Abdul Lataif*[306] and others is important not only for understanding the nature and character of a waqf and the position of the mutawalli but is also important for understanding the nature and character of a suit by a mutawalli. In the aforesaid case, Justice P.N. Mukherjee made the following observations :—

> It must be remembered that a Mutawalli as such, has no right or interest in the waqf properties and the same do not vest in him but vest in God Almighty. From this point of view, the claim to the office involving, as it does, in the present case, a claim to the possession of the same, would be sufficient for maintaining the suit without a prayer for possession or recovery of possession of the connected properties...The prayer for declaration of right to the office along with the prayer for injunction restraining the defendant from interfering with his occupation of the same or exercise of rights there under, amounts, in essence, to a claim for recovery of the office itself and as such the instant suit must be held to be maintainable.

In *Mohammad Ishak* v *Mohammad Amin*[307] it was held that the plaintiff was undoubtedly suing as mutawalli and he wanted to recover possession of properties, admitted by the defendant to be waqf properties, solely in that capacity. The mutawalli is not the owner and can be called upon to value his suit in accordance with his estimate of what the value of his rights as mutawalli of the properties would amount. In another case, the Calcutta High Court held that interest claimed by the plaintiff as a mutawalli cannot be valued at the same figures as his interest as full owner. There is no objective standard for determining the market value of the waqf properties.[308]

In the case of a trust it is not necessary at all that the property should be dedicated permanently. On the other hand, in the case of a waqf the dedication of the property must be permanent. Except in the case of Hanifees, a waqf is not entitled to take any benefit in the waqf property. On the other hand, in a trust, the settler himself can lawfully take an interest.

In the case of a waqf, the property vests in God, the mutawalli is merely the manager or superintendent. The property is not vested in him. It has been, therefore, said that a deed by which a mutawalli is appointed does not need to be registered. He is trustee only of the usufruct. The corpus is 'tied up' (made waqf of) but not transferred to him but to God. In the case of a trust, the property is absolutely vested in him. The mutawalli may ask for reasonable remuneration, which the trustee may not. In the case of Debattar, the property vests in the deity who has a juristic personality.

A waqf is created for religious, pious and charitable purposes. The dedication may also be made for the purpose of settler's family, children and descendants. This is the mandatory requirement for the validity of a waqf. In the absence of religious motive the dedication will not be lawful. The dedication without religious motive will be treated as trust. The ultimate benefit of the waqf property except in cases of general public utilities or charities must go to Muslims. Except the Hanafi Law, the waqif may not reserve to himself any benefit under a waqf. The author of a trust can lawfully become a beneficiary.

The objects of a waqf must be such as would be valid in the eye of Islam, that which is not, is prohibited by Islam. Therefore, a waqf cannot be created for the purpose of erection and maintenance of a Christian church or a Hindu temple. A waqf may be created only for charity though its preliminary object may be a family settlement. On the other hand a trust can be created for any lawful object. In the case of a waqf the position of a mutawalli is more analogus to that of a receiver or manager appointed by the courts. The mutawalli may be considered to be the holder or trustee of the usufruct only for the beneficiaries. He is given control over usufruct alone. Once a waqf comes into existence it becomes perpetual, irrecoverable and inalienable.

A trust can be established of any transferable property. Here the Waqf Act of 1913, has brought the law of waqf and trust on the same footing.

A mutawalli of waqf has not been given so much wide

powers as are given to a trustee. Under sections 16, 20, 36 and 40 of the Indian Trust Act, trustees have been given very wide powers. The position of mutawallis is more analogous to that of receivers and managers appointed over property in England.

A waqf is perpetual. It is also irrevocable. The property of the waqf cannot be transferred.

In the case of waqf, general charitable intention may be presumed and the cypres doctrine will be applied unless a particular charitable intention is disclosed which cannot be given effect to. A trust can be established for the benefit of its author when it is incapable of execution, or it does not exhaust the trust property.

There is also a difference between a gift (hiba) and waqf. The following is the main distinction between them.

In the case of hiba the ownership of the property passes from one human being to another. In the case of waqf immediately on the completion of a waqf, the waqif will cease to have any control over the property. The title of the property shall belong to the Almighty God.

Ordinarily, for the validity of gift delivery of possession is necessary. In a waqf *inter vivos* no delivery of possession is necessary. It is created by a mere declaration of endowment by the owner.

In the case of gift absolute right in the property is transferred to the donee. In the case of waqf there is no need to transfer property right absolutely.

The object of hiba is limited with regard to which it is created. A waqf can be created only for religious, charitable or pious purposes. Muslim Law also recognised family waqfs.

Distinction between Waqf and Sadaqa

The leading case on the point is *Ramanadham* v *Vada Levvai.*[312] In this case a distinction was made between a waqf and the trust. In a waqf, the legal estate or ownership is not vested in the trustee or mutawalli but it is transferred to God.

In the case of a sadaqa, the legal estate and not merely the beneficial interest passes to the charity to be held by the trust appointed by the donor.

The trustee of a waqf cannot alienate the corpus of the property, except in cases of necessity with the court's permission or when authorised by the settler to do so.

In sadaqa both the corpus and the usufruct are given away and the trustee can sell the property.

Distinction between Sunni and Shia law of Waqf

The following is the difference between a Sunni and Shia law of waqf :—

Sunni Law	*Shia Law*
1. The property dedicated in waqf vests in God.	The beneficiaries becomes the owner of the property.
2. Family waqfs are recognised. The waqif may reserve the entire income for himself and his family and descendants.	The waqifis at liberty to reserve the usufruct for his family and descendants but not for himself.
3. Mere declaration is sufficient for the validity of a waqf.	Delivery of possession is necessary for the validity of a waqf. Delivery of possession is not necessary in the case of a waqf by a father or grandfather. In the case of a waqf for mosque, mere formal dedication and permitting public prayers is enough for the validity of a waqf.
4. It may be provided in the waqf deed that the personal debts may be realised from the income of the waqf property.	It is not permissible for the waqf to make provision for payment of personal debts charged on the property.
5. A waqif may himself appoint as the first mutawalli of the waqf property. He can also appoint any other person as mutawalli.	A waqif can appoint himself as the first mutawalli of the waqf property if the property was not transferred. However, after that in the absence of any provision in the deed the

Sunni Law	*Shia Law*
	beneficiaries are entitled to administer the waqf.
6. Where there are more than one beneficiary and the first beneficiary is not available, the waqf shall be valid. The next beneficiary shall be entitled to enjoy the fruits of the property.	Under such circumstances, there shall not be any valid waqf. The existence of first mutawalli is necessary.

Distinction between a Waqf and Hindu Religious Endowment

The Muslim institution of waqf is based on basically different concept from those of the Hindu religious and charitable endowments. The aim of the waqf should be religious. A secular aim will render the waqf invalid. The other ingredient of a valid waqf is that the dedication of property must be permanent. In the case of waqf, the ownership of the waqf property belongs to the Almighty.

The Hindu piety found expression in gifts to idols and images consecrated and installed in temples, in gifts to maths and dedications to other religious institutions and for pious and charitable purposes. In short for all those purposes considered meritorious. In the words of Paras Diwan[310] when properties are dedicated to a temple, a math or any other religious or pious, or charitable institution, or purpose the property vests in the idol which is considered to be a juristic person, when dedication is made to a temple, in the math which is regarded as a juristic person, when dedication is made for a charitable purpose such as for a school or hospital. The Shebait of the temple, the mahant of the math, or the manager of the institution, is not the owner of the property. They are not even the trustees. It may, however, be noted that the above mentioned persons are answerable like a trustee in the general sense for maladministration and mismanagement.[311]

REFERENCES

1. d 240.
2. d 179.
3. d 191.
4. d 245.
5. d 150.
6. d 182.
7. d 204.
8. S. Athar Husain, *Waqf Laws and Administration in India*, p. 9.
9. *Syed Shaha Mohammad Kazim* v *Syed Ali Saghir AIR* 1932 Pat 33 : 11 Pat 228 : 2 PIT 817 : 13 IC 417.
10. See Hedaya pp. 231-34.
11. (1840) 2 MIA 390.
12. (1921) 48 IA 302.
13. S. Ameer Ali, *Mahomedan Law*, Vol. I, (2nd ed.) p. 156.
14. He was also the disciple of Abu Hanifa. He should not be confused with Prophet Muhammad, the founder of Islam.
15. *Supra* note 12, p. 497.
16. *Muslim Law*, (4th ed) p. 494.
17. See *Moatar Raza* v *Joint Director, Cansolidation, AIR* 1970 All 509 (FB).
18. *AIR* 1964 Mad 18 ; See also *Moti Shah* v *Abdul Gaffar Khan AIR* 1956 Nag 38.
19. *Mariam Bi* v *Jaffar, AIR* 1973 Mad 191.
20. *Ahmed Ariff* v *Commissioner of Wealth Tax, AIR* 1971 SC 1961.
21. (1931) 54 All 455.
22. *Supra* note 12.
23. p. 69.
24. See Wilson, *Anglo-Muhammadan Law* (6th ed) 1930.
25. *Punjab Waqf Board Commissioner, Patiala Division,* 1974 PLR 467 ; *Madras State Board Kazi Mohiuddin Shariff,* 1974 MCJ 253 ; see also *AIR* 1966 All 201 : *AIR* 1974 Pat 141 : 1907 ILR Bom 31.
27. (1958) PLD Lah 824.
28. (1967) PLD Dacca 1.
29. (1894) 22 IA 76 (PC).
30. XXXII of 1930.
31. *viz* before March 7, 1913.
32. The date of the comemncement of the Waqf Act, 1930

33. (1932) 49 I A 153 (Cal)
34. (1926-27) 54 I A 23
35. Sub-clause (10) of section 6 of the Bengal Waqf Act, 1934 says that a waqf means a permanent dedication by person professing Islam of any movable or immovable property for the purpose recognised by the Muslim Law as pious, religious or charitable and includes a waqf by user. The waqf-al-aulad is differently defined in the Bengal Act.
36. *Mohammad Ismail* v *Sabir Ali*, *AIR* 1962 SC 1722.
37. V.V.V.K.R *Yachandra Bahadur Varu* v *The Andhra Pradesh Waqf Board*, *AIR* 1978 AP 156. In this case it was said that section 3 (h) includes any person who has a right to worship or right to perform any religious rite in any religious institution or to participate in any religious institution.
38. *Khalil Ahmad Khan* v *Malka Mehar Nigar*, *AIR* 1954 All 362.
39. Analogous laws—section 2 (19) of the Bombay Public Trusts Act, 1950 is *Ad verbatim* same as given in section 2 (80) of the section 2 (8) of the M.P. Public Trusts Act, 1951.
40. *Supra* note 34.
41. *Mst. Penan* v *Hanif Mohd.*, *AIR* 1966 All 201.
42. *AIR* 1968 Guj. 257
43. *Supra* note 13, p 218 ; *Mohammad Shafiq* v *Mohammad Mujaba*, (1929) 51 All 32.
44. *Khalil Ahmad Khan* v *Mehar Nigar*, *AIR* 1954 All 362.
45. *Supra* note 12.
46. *Allaha Rakhi* v *Shah Mohammad*, *AIR* 1934 PC 77.
47. *Supra* note 36.
48. *Supra* note 17.
49. (1979) K.L.T. 231.
50. 38 P R 1883.
51. Hedaya, 234.
52. Id.
53. (1933) 144 IC 654 : *AIR* 1933 Oudh 222.
54. (1936) 11 Luck 735, 160 I C 495 ; see also *Abdul Quavi* v. *Asha*, *AIR* 1962 All 364.
55. *AIR* 1966 All 201.
56. Bail 11, 218.
57. Id.
58. (1907) 9 BLR 998.
59. *Amrutal Kalidas* v *Sheik Husain*, 11 Bom 492, 504.
60. (1972) 2 An WR 327; see also *AIR* 1922 PC 123.

61. *Supra* note 49,
62. *Supra* note 13, p. 232.
63. (1947) ILR Mad 480; see *Tengamali* v. *Fathima AIR* 1960. Mad 487.
64. (1888) 13 Bom 264.
65. See also *Ruqia Begum Surajmal*, *AIR* 1939 All 401 : *Mohammad Ali* v *Dinesh Chandra AIR* 1940 Cal 517 ; *Ghulam Mohamuad* v. *Ghulam Hussain*, *AIR* 1932 PC 81.
66. See Henry Catton, *Law of Waqf in the Middle East*.
67. Hedaya, *supra* note 51, p. 231-232 ; Bail 1. 550 (558) 212 : Abdul in *Abedally Hyderbhai* v. *Advocate General of Bombay*, (1956) 48 BLR 631.
68. *Supra* note 34.
69. (1881) 6 Bom 42.
70. *Syed Ali Zamin* v. *Syed Muhammad Akbar*, (1928) 7 Pat 468-426. 477 ; *Baqaullah* v *Ghulam Siddique*, (1935) 33 ALJ 647, *Masuda Khatun* v *Mohammad Ebrahim*, (1931) 59 Cal 402, 434 ; *Abdul Wahab* v *Sughra Begum*, (1931) 54 All 455.
71. *Supra* note 69.
72. (1911) 36 Bom 214.
73. Bail 1. 557.
74. *Supra* note 51, p 238.
75. (1889) 11 All 460 : 19 I A 205 ; see also *Musa Baba* v *Badesaheb* (1937) 39 BLR 1108 ; *Ebrahim* v *Bai Asi*, (1933) 58 Bom 236.
76. Re *Hoylee Row* v *Jagg*, (1911) 1 Ch 179, 187.
77. *Abdul Kadir* v *Salima*, (1886) 8 All 149.
78. *Supra* note 67 ; see also *Kulsom Bibi* v *Golam Husain*, (1905) 10 CWN 49 ; *Khajah Hossein* v *Shahzadee*, (1869) 12 WR 334, 346; *Hamira Bibi* v *Zubaida Bibi*, (1916) 43 I A 294, 301-302.
79. *North Sylhet Local Board* v *Gazanfar Ali*, (1949) 54 Cal WR 53. 80
80. (1924) 2 Rang 495, 506.
81. *Abdul Wahat* v *Mst Sughra*, *supra* note 70.
82. *AIR* 1934 All 74.
83. *Supra* note 44 ; see also *Rashindunnissa* v *Ata Rasool*, *AIR* 1958 All 67-72.
84. *AIR* 1954 Mad 143.
85. *Supra* note 69.
86. (1918) ILR 42 Mad I62 (FB).
87. *Supra* note 10, p. 232.
88. *Muhammad Ahsan* v *Umardaraz*, (1906) 28 All 633.

89. (1889) 13 Bom 555, 560.

90. (1938) 177 1 C 307 : (1838) AC 257.

91. *Rashidunnissa* v *Ata Rasool, supra* note 83.

92. See *Cadell* v *Palmer*, (1833) 1 Cl. & F 372.

93. (1857) 1 Boulnois 266.

94. Bourke, 282.

95. *Supra* note 13, p. 187.

96. Id.

97. *Mazhar Husain* v *Adiya Saran, AIR* 1948 PC 42.

98. *Supra* note 13, p 142 ; Bail 1. 558 ; *Ramandhan* v *Vada Leval*, (1911) 34 Mad 12, 18-20.

99. *AIR* 1947 Mad 480.

100. (1894) 22 Cal 619 : 22 I A 76, 86.

101. Section 3.

102. (1929) 51 I A 192 (Cal).

103. *Mst Peeran* v *Hafiz Mohd, AIR* 1966 All 201.

104. Fatwai Alamgiri, Vol 11, p 454 ; Radd-ul-Mukhtar, Vol III, 888 ; Hadaya, Vol II, p 888 ; Fath-ul-Kadir, Vol II, p 454 ; supra note 13, p 383.

105. Supra note 11 ; *Dayal Chand* v *Keramut*, (1871)) 16 WR 116 ; *Hidaitoonnissa* v *Afzal Hossein*, (1870) 2 N.W. 420 (Shia case) ; *Kuttayan* v *Mammanna Ravuthan*, (1912) 35 Mad 681 ; *Ismail* v *Mohammed*, (1893) 20 Cal 834 ; *Abdur Rahim* v *Narayan Das*, (1922) 50 I.A. 84 ; *supra* note 34.

106. *Jaafar Mohiuddin* v *Haji Mohiuddin*, (1863) 2 Mad HCR 19 ; *Fegredo* v *Mahomed*, (1871) 15 WR 75.

107. *Supra* note 5 ; *Mahabir Prasad Marwari* v *Syed Shah Mohammed Yehyea*, (1935) IIR 15 Pat 88 ; *Shah Mohammad Nain* v *Mohammad Naim* v *Mohammad Shamsuddin*, (1926) ILR 2 Luck 109 : *Sattappa* v *Mohammed Saheb*, (1935) ILR 60 Bom 516 ; *Shilandranath Patil* v *Hadi*. (1931) ILR 59 Cal 586 ; *Bikani Mia* v *Shuklal Poddar*, (1892) ILR 20 Cal 116.

108. See *Mir Mahbuballi* v *Ahmada, AIR* 1933 Nag 256 ; *Nawab Bahadur of Murshidabad* v *Karmani Bibi*, (1932) 58 I.A. 215.

109. (1928) 52 I A 262

110. *Supra* note 8.

111. (1858) SDA Cal 586.

112. (1932) 30 AIJ 44.

113. *Supra* note 18.

114. *Supra* note 13, p. 200.

115. *Supra* note 25, p. 198.

116. (1911) 16 CWN 114.
117. *Supra* note 18.
118. *AIR* 1963 Pat 98.
119. *AIR* 1953 SC 491.
120. Baillie, *Digest of Moohummudan Law*, Part I, (2nd Ed, 1875, p 561.
121. Paras Diwan, *Muslim Law in Modern* India, p 244.
122. See *Muhammad Raza* v *Yadgar Hussain*, (1924) 51 I.A.X. 192. In this case it was held that a grant of villages by Raja Raghoba Bhosle to a Muslim physician as mukhasa for the Imambara of Pir Hussain for ever was alleged to be a waqf.
123. *AIR* 1930 PC 103.
124. *Supra* note 97.
125. *Supra* note 26.
126. *AIR* 1980 AP 199.
127. See *Md. Mazaffarakmusavi* v *Bibi Jabeda Khatun*, *supra*, note 123 ; *Mazhar Hussain* v *Adiya Saran*, *supra* note 97 ; *Sarswathi Ammal* v *Rajagopal Ammal*, *supra* note 119 ; M.S. *Waqf Board* v *Khazi Mohideen*, *supra* note 26.
128. *Khati* v *Mirza Hussain*, *AIR* 1962 Ori 95 ; *Ramzan* v *Basarath*, *AIR* 1953 Pat 138 ; *Mehraj Din* v *Ghulam Mohammad*, *AIR* 1931 Lah 607 ; *Abdul Rahim Khan* v *F.M. Shah*, *AIR* 1964 Nag 401.
129. *Id.*
130. *Baonder Khan* v *Reghvindra Pratap*, *AIR* 1934 Oudh 263.
131. *Anjuman Islamia* v *Najim Ali*, *AIR* 1982 MP 17.
132. *Mohammad Shah* v *Fashihuddin Ansari*, *AIR* 1956 SC 713.
133. *Supra* note 38.
134. *Syed Mahar Hussain* v *Haji Ali Mohammad*, *AIR* 1934 Bom 257 : (1934) 36 Bom LR 526 : 152 IC 50.
135. *Supra* note 128.
136. *Ghulam Muheedin Khan* v *Abdul Majeed*, *AIR* 1957 AP 941 ; K. *Raushan Din* v *Mohammod Shariff*, *AIR* 1936 Lah 87.
137. *AIR* 1968 Pat 29.
38. *Khalil Ahmed* v *Sheikh Mohammad supra* note 44 ; see also *Musaheb Khan* v *Rajkumar Bakshi*, *AIR* 1938 Oudh 238 : (1938) CWN 937 : 177 IC 718.
139. *Mst. Mamik Devi* v *Habibullah*, *AIR* 1936 Lah 876.
140. *Sajjad Ali* v *Jagmohandas*, *AIR* 1927 Oudh 534.
141. *Ali Mohammad Khan* v *Ali Akbar Khan*, *AIR* 1924 Lah 58.
142. *State of Madras* v *Mohammad Sahib Quraishi*, *AIR* 1963 Mad 39.
143. *Ballabh Das* v *Noor Mohammad*, (1936) 40 CWN 499.

144. *Imam Baksh Munawar Din* v *Narasingh Puri*, (1938) 17⁵ IC 1005.
145. *Qadir Baksh* v *Saddullah*, (1938) 173 IC 260 ; see also *Ramshan Din* v *Muhommad Shariff*, (1936) 161 IC 650.
146. *Abdul Gaffoor* v *Mohammad Kasam*, (1968) JIJ 225 (SC).
147. *Anur Singh* v *Badar Din*, *AIR* 1940 Lah 119 : (1940) 188 IC 877.
148. *Abdul Gafoor* v *Rahmat Ali*, *AIR* 1930 Oudh 245 : (1930) 122 IC 326.
149. *Ehsan Baig Rahmat Ali*, *AIR* 1935 Oudh 47 : 152 IC 798 : (1934) 10 Luck 547.
150. *Ramzan* v *Mohammad*.
151. 149 IC 966.
152. *Mahabir Prasad* v *Mustafa*, *AIR* 1937 PC 174 : (1937) 41 CWN 933 ; 168 IC 418,
153. *Baqar Khan* v *Babu Raghindra Pratap Sahi*, *AIR* 1934 Oudh 263 : (1934) 9 Luck 568 : 148 IC 433.
154. *Siraj Ahmad Khan* v *Gaya Prasad*, *AIR* 1939 All 219 : (1939) ALJ 115 :
155. *Supra* note 146 ; see also *Abdul Gafoor* v *Hakim Ali*, *AIR* 1959 All 1978.
156. *Motish* v *Abdul Khan*, *AIR* 1955 Nag 1000; see also Arur (supra note 147).
157. *Punjab Waqf Board* v *Ambala Panchayat Garhi Brahmin*, *AIR* 1969 Pun 344.
158. *Interim Report*, 1973 p. 8.
159. *Supra* note 25, p. 184.
160. *Supra* note 42.
161. See section 3 (1) (iii) of the Waqf Act, 1954.
162. For detailed study please see Chapter 'Family Waqfs'.
163. *Supra* note 13, p. 156.
164. See *Mirza Fida Rasool* v *Yakub Beg*, *IR* 1925 PC 101: 87 IC 702: *Fazlur Rahman* v *Anath Bansi*, *supra* note 116.
165. *Ali Hussain* v *Fazal Hussain Khan*, 23 IC 477.
166. See Hunter, *Roman Law*, p. 608. Under the Roman law puberty was the age of majority but legislation altered its effects.
167. *Supra* note 16, p. 508.
168. (1928) 30 BLR 1346.
169, (1871) 15 WR 548.
170. *Supra* note 69.
171. (1875) 15 Beng L R167 .
172. Id. see also *Hussain Bai* v *Zohra Bai*, *AIR* 1960 MP 60. In this

case their lordship of the Madhya Pradesh High Court held that in the case of a deed executed by a pardanashin lady, it must be proved that it was explained to her and she understood clearly its implication, and mere reading of the document to her is not enough : *Inche Noriah* v *Shaik Allie*, (1929) AC 127 ; *Abdul Mannan* v *Mutawalli Janebali*, *AIR* 1956 Cal 584.

173. *AIR* 1925 PC 204 : (1925) 52 I.A. 342.

174. *Supra* note 69 ; see also *Davinder Singh* v *Mst Lachhmi Devi*, (1930) Lah 985 ; *Kali Bax Singh* v *Ramgopal Singh* 41 I A 23 ; *Faridunnissa* v *Mukhtar Ahmed*. *AIR* 1925 PC 204.

175. *Haider Hussain* v *Sudama Prasad*, *AIR* 1940 Oudh 18, 15 Luck 30.

176. *Nosh Ali* v *Shamsunnissa*, *AIR* 1939 All 319.

177. (1912) 35 All 68 see also *Commissioner of Waqf* v *Mohammad Mohsin AIR* 1954 Cal 463 : (1953) 58 CWN 22; *Ehsan Baig* v *Rahmat Ali* (1934) 10 Luck 547; *Mohd Ali* v *Dinesh Chander Roy*, *AIR* 1940 Cal 417.

178. *Mohammad Abu Zafar* v *Israr Ahmed*, *AIR* 1976 All 366.

179. In *Mst Bismilla Begum* v *Mohammad Ali*, *AIR* 1827 Oudh 162, it was said that if the sale was completed subsequent to dedication waqf was held as valid.

180. *Supra* note 54.

181. *Supra* note 55.

182. *Kadir Ibrahim Rowthar* v *Mohammad Rahimudolla*, (1909) 33 Mad 118 ; see also (1933) 60 IA 116.

183. See *Abadi Begum* v *Kauiz*, (1926) 54 I.A. 33.

184. See Fyzee, *Campendium of Fatimid Law*, section 335.

185. *M. Zain* v *Nurul Hasan*, *AIR* 1924 All 113 ; *Jinjira Khatoon* v *Mohammad Fakhrullah*, *AIR* 1922 Cal 429.

186. *AIR* 1946 Bom 342.

187. *Faqir Mohammad* v *Abida*, *AIR* 1952 All 127 (FB) ; *M. Sabir* v *Tahir*, *AIR* 1957 All 94; see also Mulla, *Mahomedan Law*, *supra* note 25, p 210.

188. *Supra* note 21.

189. *Supra* note 44.

190. J.M. Riazuddin, *Law of the Waqfs*, p 2.

191. A.A.A. Fyzee, *Outlines of Muhammadan Law*, (Fourth ed. 1981), p. 278.

192. See *Dhirendra Singh* v *Dhanai*, *AIR* 1983 All 216 ; Swami *Parmamanand Sarswati* v *Ranji Tripathi*, *AIR* 1979 SC 2141 ; Kailash *Chand* v *Bhupal Nath*, *AIR* 1973 All 238.

193. *Muslim Orphange* v *Khatoon* Bi, *AIR* 1958 Mys 28.

194. *AIR* 1969 SC 884.

195. (1968) 11 M.L.J. 559.

196. PLD 1950 Kar 15 : (1950) P. Sindh 25 (a Pakistani case).

197. See *Mohammad Jacco* v *District Collector*, *AIR* 1962 Ker 343. In this case it was held that the consent in section 92 is dispensed with by section 55 (1) of the Waqf Act only in the case of suits instituted by the Board. An application by any person or authority other than the Board for sanction to the District Collector is maintainable.

198. *Supra* note 54.

199. *Supra* note 16, pp. 488-89.

200. *Supra* note 13, p 200. The opinion of Ameer Ali was followed by the Nagpur High Court in *Motishah* v *Abdul Gaffoor*, *supra* note 18. In this case the Nagpur High Court held that non-Muslims can validly make waqfs but the objects for which the dedication is made should be lawful according to the creed of the dedicator as well as the Islamic doctrine ; see also *Madras Waqf Board* v *Kazi Mohiuddin Sharif supra*, note 26.

201. See *Commissioner of Waqf* v *Mohammad Mohsin*, *supra* note 176,

202. *AIR* 1947 All 520.

203. (1876) 25 WR 557 ; see also *Advocate General* v *Fatima*, (1872) 9 BHCR 19 ; *Bali Ram* v *Mohammad Afzal*, *AIR* 1948 PC 168.

204. See *Mohammad Ismail Afzal* v *Molla Dawood*, (1916) 43 I.A. 127. In this case it was held that the plea of usage can be taken into consideration while deciding the validity of the appointment of a mutawalli ; see also *Freedhari Doss* v *Mundikishore Doss*, (1867) 11 MTA 405 438.

205. *Supra* note 107.

206. See *Bibi Akhtari* v *Diljan Ali*, *AIR* 1993 PC 11 : 28 CWN 545 : 71 IC 621 : MIJ 359.

207. Bail I. 577 (589) ; see also *Bibi Akhtari* v *Diljan Ali*, Id.

208. *Supra* note 16.

209. Bail I. 569 (578).

210. Bail I. 569.

211. (1934) 61 I A 322 (Oudh).

212. Bail I 568 (para 2) (577).

213. Bail I 570, (para 2) (579) ; 571, (para 2) (580).

214. *Hya-on-nissa* v *Mafnkkir-ul-Islam*, (1805) 1 SDA (Cal) 106.

215. *Nawab Hyder-Hussain* v *Nawab Faghfur Mirza*, (1905) 32 I.A. 175 *Begum* v *Nawab Sahib Mirza*, (1889) 16 IA 175.

216. Bail II 221.

217. Bail I. 572.

218. Bail I, 568(para 2) 577.

219. *Supra* note 23, p 342; Macnaughten also cited the case of *Sheikh Karimuddin* v *Nawab Mir Syed*, Bom 119.

220. *Supra* note 206.

221. Bail , 568 (para 5) 577.

222. *Supra* note 13, p. 285.

223. Abdur Rahim, *Muhammadan Jurisprudence*, (1911) p 307.

224. *Kulsum Bibi* v *Ghulam Hussain, supra* note 77 ; *Abdul Shakur* v *Abu Bakr, supra* note 226.

225. (1907) 9 BLR 1337.

226. (1909) 33 Mad 118, 4 IC 136.

227. *Supra* note 54.

228. *Mirza Yakub* v *Mirza Rasul Bai, supra* note 226 ; *Abdul Shakur* v *Abu Bakr, supra* note 226 ; see also *Abdul Hamid* v *Fateh Mohammad* PLD 1958 Lah 824. In this Pakistani case, it was held that a waqf of cash will be valid provided the fund was not intended to be consumed.

229. *AIR* 1947 All 127, ILR (1947) All 334, (1947) ALJ 232,

230. See *Hashim Ali* v *Hamidt Bcgum, supra* note The waqi dedicated the land which was already leased and the term of which was not expired. The waqf was held valid ; see also *Peeran* v *Hafi* ,AIR 1966 All 201.

231. See *Jinjira* v *Mohammad, supra* note 185.

232. See *Abdul Qavi* v *Ashraf Al* , Ali, *AIR* 1922 Cal 429.

233. see *Har Prasad* v *Fayam Ahmed*. *AIR* 1933 PC 83 : (1933) 60 IA 116, 142 IC 217. In this case a waqfnama was executed by a widow as part of a transaction which was a fraud on the heirs of her husband. It was held that the waqf was void and cannot be enforced ever against the share which she inherits.

234. See *Nosh Ali* v *Shamsunnissa Bibi, AIR* 1939 All 319. It was held that the dower debt cannot be the subject of a valid waqf.

235. See *supra* note 16, p 537.

236. *AIR* 1942 Sindh 137.

237. *Supra* note 10.

238. (1911) 9 ALJ 709.

249. Bail 11, p 213.

240. See Re Dean (1889) 41 Ch. D. 552. In this case a trust by will for the maintenance of the testator's horses or dogs was held valid;

Mussett v *Bingle*, (1876) W.N. 170 ; *Re* Chardon, (1928) Ch. 464 ; *Re* Chamber's Will Trusts (1950) Ch 367 ; Re Wightneick's Will Trusts, (1950) Ch. 260 ; *Pettingall* v *Pettingalliel* (1842) 11 L.J. Ch. 176 ; Re Thompson, (1934) 1 Ch. 342.

241. See *Har Prasad* v *Fayaz*, *AIR* 1933 PC 83.

242. *Supra* note 10, p 233.

243. See Droit Musulman, Statute Personnel, et. Des Successions, (1895) Tome II, 176.

244. For waqf of Musha see *supra* note 34 ; *Ambalavana Pandari Sanntdhi* v *Meenakshi*, (1920) 47 IA 191 ; *Pande Har Naryan* v *Suraj Kanwari*, (1921) 48 I,A. 143 ; *Sheikh Mahmmed Ahsanulla* v *Amarchand Kandu*, (1889) 17 I.A. 28 ; *Mahomed Hasan* v *Mohammed Ibrahim*, (1903) 5 BIR 624 ; *Abdul Razak* v *B. Jimbabai*, (1911) 14 BLR 295 ; *Hussein Bahi* v *Advocate General*, Bombay, (1920) 22 BLR 846 ; *Mohammad Irfan* v *Mohammad Tahir*, (1933) 31 ALJ 97.

245. *Mohommad Ayub* v *Amir Khan*, *AIR* 1939 Cal 268 ; *Mohammad Badrul a Shah Hassan*, *AIR* 1935 All 278.

246. (1870) 13 WR 235.

247. *Supra* note 16, p 540-41.

248. *Supra* note 103 ; see also *Mohammad Ayub* v *Amir Khan supra* note 247.

249. *Muhammad Mumtaz* v *Zubaida Jan*, (1889) 11 All 460, 16 I.A. 205 ; seel also *Abdul Rahman* v *Maung Muto AIR* 1932 Rang 65 : 138 IC 851.

250. Note 247.

251. *Supra* note 25, p 173.

252. *Yunus Mia* v *Ftroz Ahmed*, (1951) Dacca 576 ; PLD (1952) Dacca 206.

253. *Supra* note 190, p 2.

254. *Supra* note 191, p 252.

255. Note 69.

256. *Tafazzal Begum* v *Majidullah*, (1923) 5 Lah 59.

257. *Abadi Begum* v *Kaniz*, (1926) 54 IA 33.

258. *Mohammad Qasim* v *Mohammad Mehdi*, *AIR* 1937 Oudh 465.

259. See *Ismail Haji* v *Umar*, *AIR* 1942 Bom 155.

260. *AIR* 1973 Mys 145.

261. *Ghulam Mohammad* v *Ghulam Hussain*, *AIR* 1932 PC 81 ; *Hashim* v *Iffat Ara*, *AIR* 1942 Cal 142 ; *Akhtar Bano* v *Kanhayalal*, *AIR* 1941 Oudh 492.

262. *Supra* note 13, pp 193-275.

263. *Bibi Kubra* v *Jainandan Prasad*, *AIR* 1955 Pat 270.

264. *Supra* note 29.

265. See *Zain Yar Jung* v *Director of Endowments*, *AIR* 1963 SC 985 ; *Kassimiah Charities* v *Secretary, M.S. Board*, *AIR* 1964 Mad 18.

266. *Mst Altmunnissa Bibi* v *Mohammad Abdur Rahman*, *AIR* 1938 All 485 : (1938) ALJ 727 : 177 IC 205.

267. Bail 11. 214.

268. Bail 1-553 (561) ; see also *Bikani Mia Shuklal Poddur*, *supra* note 107 ; *Zamandhan* v *Dada*, (1910) 34 Mad 22 ; *Kalub Hossein* v *Mehrum Bee* (1872) 4 N,W. 155, 159 ; *Nizamuddin* v *Abdul Gafur*, (1988) 13 Bom 264 ; *Syed Mohammad Kazim* v *Syed Abi Saghir*, (1931) 11 Pat 288

269. Waqf Chapter I, Bail 1, 553 : see also *Fatima Bibee* v *Ariff Ismailjee*. (1881) 9 CLR 66.

270. Bail II. pp 214-215.

271. Bail II, p.214 ; Minhaj 231.

272. *Mohammad Ahsanullah* v *Amarchand Kandu* (1889) 17 LA 28 : 17 Cal 408.

273. Bail I.574-5.

274. Fatwai Kazi Khan, III 316 ; *supra* note 13, p. 322 ; see also note 16, p 574.

275. *Supra* note 221.

276. V-241.

277. *Mahomed Ismail Ariff* v *Ahmed Mowala*, (1916) 43 IA 127.

278. Bahrur-Raiq, V 223, 237 ; Fatwai Kazi Khan, III 302, 883.

279. III 302, 383.

280. *Zubaida Sultan Begum* v *Dawood Ismail Makra*, (1936) 1 Cal 90.

281. *Sayed Arsad Hussain* v *Smt Naresh Nandini*, (1936) 40 CWN 584.

282. *Mst Ali Begum* v *Badrul Islam Ali*, (1938) 65 IA IA 298 (Lah)

283. *AIR* 1958 Cal 413.

284. *Hussain* v *Salah*, *AIR* 1953 Hyd 195.

285. *Syeda Bibi* v *Mughal Jan*, (1902) 24 All 23 ; see also *Baqar Ali Khan* v *Anjuman Ara Begum*, (1902) 35 All 236 : 30 I.A. 94.
286. *Mahabir Prasad* v *Mustafa*, *AIR* 1937 PC 173 : (1937) 35 CWN 933: 268 IC 418.
287. *Aga Ali* v *Alaf Hasan*, (1892) 24 Ali 420.
298. *Supra* note 288.
289. *Saadat Kamal* v *Attorney General*, (Palestine), *AIR* 1939 PC 185 : (1939) AC 508 (PC) ; see also *Musharraf Begum* v *Sikender Jahan Begum* (1928) 51 All 410 ; *Abdul Wahab* v *Sughra Begum*, *supra* note 70.
290. Bail 1. 580 (579).
291. Bail 1. 589.
292. *Latafatunnissa* v *Shaharbanu*, *AIR* 1932 Oudh 108.
293. Bail 1. 566-8.
294. *Supra* note 16, p. 536.
295. Id p 529.
296. *Supra* note 10, p. 236.
297. *Jaffar El Edroos* v *Mahomed E Fdros*, (1936) 39 Bom LR 277 ; Re *Casamally* v *Peerbhai*, (1906) 30 Bom 391 ; *Haehtm Ali Khan* v *Hamidi Begum*,AIR 1942 Cal 180, 46 CWN 561, 74 Cal LJ 261.
298. *Supra* note 10, p. 236.
299. *Supra* note 16, p. 559.
300. *Supra* note 16, p. 530 ; *Jugalmoni* v *Chowdhrani Ranjani Bibi* (1884) 10 Cal 533.
301. *Khajah Hossein Ali* v *Hazra Begum*, (1869) 12 W.R. 1344.
302. *Supra* note 16, p. 530.
303. *Vidya Varuthi Thirtha* v *Balusami Ayyar*, 48 I.A. 302 (1920-21) ; see also *Doyal Chand Mullick* v *Keramut Ali*, (1871) 16 W.R. 116, 1187 ; S.A.M. Habibullah, *The Law of Waqfs*, (1976), p. xiii.
304. *Supra* note 306.
305. *Zainyar Jung* v *Director of Endowment*, *supra* note 268.
306. 75 CWN 114.
307. AIR 1948 Cal 312.
308. *Hafiz Mohammad Fateh Nasib* v *Hazi Abder Rab*, AIR 1951 Cal 191 : 57 CWN 820.
309. *Supra* note 98
310. Paras Diwan, *Modern Hindu Law*, Chapter XVIII, see also *Pramath nath* v *Pradyumma Kumar*, (1925) I.A. 245 ; *D.A.V. College* v *S.N.S High School*, School, *AIR* 1972 P & H 245 (FB).
311. See *Vidya Varuthi Tirtha* v *Balusami Ayyar* supra note 306 ; ***Zain Yar Zuni*** v *Director of Endowment*, *supra* note 268.

3

The Object and Purpose of A Valid Waqf

The following are the essentials of the objects of a valid waqf :

Object must be lawful

The object of waqf means the purpose for which a waqf has been created by the waqif. A waqf may be for religious, pious and charitable purposes. It may be created for the benefit of any person or class of persons, or for any object of piety or charity. Property is dedicated to get reward in the next world. The words 'piety and charity' are not having restricted or narrow meaning. These terms can be interpreted in a very wide way. Every purpose which is recognised as 'good or pious' more under Islamic theology than law will come under this category. Every good purpose which God approves, or by which approach to Him is attained is a fitting purpose for a valid and lawful waqf. Ameer Ali says that a pious act may be a smile in a neighbour's face or help to the weary[1]. According to Fyzee a pious act can be recognised only by consulting Shariat. He says that a valid waqf may be created for a school or a hospital or a mosque ; but gambl-ing house, or a wine shop, or a shop for the sale of ham or bacon cannot be valid objects of a waqf[2].

The objects of a waqf can be divided into follow ing three parts :

(i) purpose of the waqf ;
(ii) beneficiaries ; and
(iii) waqf-al-aulad *i.e.* family waqfs.

Purpose of the Waqf

The purpose of a valid waqf must be religious, charitable or pious. The people generally dedicate property for obtaining the approval of the Almighty or a reward in the next world. Quduri maintains that though the poor be named in a waqf yet they will take on failure of the objects named.

Religion is not merely an opinion, doctrine or belief. It has its outward expression in acts as well, and religious practices or performances of acts in pursuance of religious belief are as much as a part of religion as faith or belief in particular doctrines[3]. In *Abdul Razak* v *Ali Baksh*[4] the Lahore High Court said that religious purposes are known to every Muslim having been defined in the *Quran* and explained by the Prophet Mohammad. It cannot at all be said that a waqf meant for religious purposes in any way vague or indefinite and hence invalid. Ameer Ali[5] says that religious purpose does not include such dedications as solely for the worship of God, 'which is an unmeaningful phrase in Islam. He further observes that the service of man and the good of humanity constitute pre-eminently the service and worship of God. Everything which is dedicated to God is in reality for the good of mankind; and everything which is dedicated for the good of human beings, individually or collectively, is for the service of God. Ameer Ali again observes that the requirement 'solely to the ownership of God cannot be defined precisely. It is difficult to understand the meaning of this comprehensive dictum. Keeping this fact into consideration, a waqf to an Imambara, to a Khankah, or to a dargah *etc* was declared as void. It is absolutely in contravention of the Muslim Law.

The Mussalman Waqf Validating Act, 1913, says that a waqf shall be valid if the purpose of such a waqf was religious, pious or charitable. It is submitted here that these are the English terms and it is not possible to give a precise and concise definition of these terms. The plain meaning of religion is the system of belief and the worship, behaviour *etc.* Pious means the showing and feeling deep respect for God and religion. Lastly, charity means kindness, generosity, help to the poors *etc.* It is clear from these definitions that the meaning of these terms is not plain and can be interpreted in different manner by different persons. On the other hand, the Islamic terms are definite and having more broader meaning. A purpose may not come within the category of these terms, yet dedication may be lawful under the Muslim Law. It is, therefore, submitted that a concise and precise definition of these terms should be given by the legislature and courts.

Under Muslim law, the ultimate object of a waqf is the benefit of the poor. Though poor may not be mentioned in a waqf yet they will take on the failure of the object named. The object of a valid waqf may be preliminary *viz.* such as must in course of time cease and come to an end (*i.e.* single person or member of collective groups), and if so, the preliminary objects must be followed by ultimate perpetual and never failing objects.

Under Mussalman Waqf Validating Act, 1913, the aim of the waqf must be recognised by Muslim Law as religious, pious or charitable. The language used in the Waqf Act, 1954 is also the same. The Act says that a waqf may be created for any purpose recognised by the Muslim Law as pious, religious or charitable and includes (i) a waqf by user, (ii) mashrut-ul-khidmat, and (iii) a waqf for alal-aulad to the extent to which the property is dedicated for any purpose recognised by Muslim Law as pious, religious or charitable.

There are several charitable purposes that are recognised by Muslim law as valid objects of waqfs. The term 'charity' is a very wide term. The preamble to the Statute 43 Eliz. C. 4 contains the following list as charitable objects :

(i) relief to aged persons ;
(ii) the maintenance of sick and manned soldiers and mariners ;
(iii) the maintenance of school of learning ;
(iv) free school and scholars in universities ;
(v) the marriage of poor maids ;
(vi) help of young tradesmen ;

(vii) handicrafts men and persons decayed;
(viii) the relief or redemption of prisoners of captures ;
(ix) the aid or ease of any poor inhabitants concerning and payment of taxes ;
(x) the repairs of bridges, ports, seas' banks and highways.

Prior to the passing of the Mussalman Waqf Validating Act of 1913, and at present in respect of territories in India to which the Mussalman Waqf Validating Act (6 of 1913) does not extend, (*i.e.* the former part B states which included the then state of Saurashtra, the then state of PEPSU, the state of Rajasthan the state of Madhya Pradesh and the state of Kerala) the following formalities should be fulfilled.

(a) the subject of the waqf had to be substantially dedicated to a charity. In *Abdur Rahim* v *Narayan Das*[6] it was said that if half of net income to be devoted to specified pious purposes, the waqf will be valid.
(b) a dedication could contain provisions for the family of the waqif, or for the benefit of specified individuals other than the waqif and the members of his family or for the benefit of objects that are not charitable provided that the property was substantially dedicated to charitable purposes and the charity was not illusory either by the small proportion that it bore to the whole waqf property, or from the uncertainty and remoteness of the time when the provisions relating to charity were to take effect.
Mere charge upon profits of estate of certain items which in course of time must necessarily cease, being confined to one family and which after they lapse, will leave whole property intact for original purposes for which endowment was made, does not render the endowment invalid under Muhammadan Law[7]. Again it was said that a waqf may be illusory, whether from its small amount, or from its uncertainty and remoteness[8]. These decisions were overruled after the passing of the Mussalman Waqf Validating Act, 1913.
(c) a perpetual dedication could not lawfully be made for the family of the waqif ; a provision for the benefit of

the poor or other charitable object on the extinction of the waqif's family, was deemed too remote to validate the dedication.

As regards the provision for the benefit of the poor or other charitable object, the courts have discussed the law elaborately in number of cases[9].

As regards remoteness, it was said in *Mahomed Ahsanulla* vs *Amarchand Kundu*[10] that settler used the word waqf merely as veil to cover arrangement for aggrandisement of family, and to make property inalienable. In *Mahomed Abdulla Jitakar* v *Abdul Rahiman*[11] Jitakar it was said that in respect of making provisions for the family of the waqif, there was no difference between Hanafi and Shafii Law.

Section 2 (1) of the Mussalman Wakf Validating Act, 1913, says that the purpose for which a waqf may be created must be one recognised by the Muslim Law as religious. pious or charitable. The term charity includes the following :

(i' maintenance and support wholly or partially of waqif' family, children or descendants ; and

(ii) if waqif is Hanafi, maintenance and support wholly or partially of waqif's children or descendants and (b) his own maintenance and support during his life time or payment of his debts out of rents and profits of property dedicated.

In *Ramanandhan* v *Vada Leevai*[12] it was said (a case before the passing of the Mussalman Validating Act, 1913 that charitable, pious or religious purposes must be understood in their ordinary and natural meaning, *i.e.* in sense analogous to that of English law.

The charitable intention of the waqif may be of two kinds *i.e.* general and particular. A general charitable intention means a desire to devote certain property in any event to charity. A particular charitable intention means the usufruct of the waqf should be used for some paramount desire or purpose.

The provision for the performance of Haj every year out of the income of the waqf property was held to be valid if the ultimate object of the waqf was perpetuity for the poor,[13]

A provision that a waqf be made to bestow every year in charity (in expiation) instead of the sins of omission of the dedicator was held valid if the ultimate object was a perpetuity for the poor[14]. A waqf can be made for *jihad*, or religious wars[15]. The question as to what objects of waqfs are valid and what are not has come before the High Courts in a number of cases[16]. Mulla has given the following long list of valid waqfs :

1. The dedication[17] of property for mosques and provision for *imams* to conduct worship therein;
2. The construction[18] of colleges and provision for professors to teach in colleges ;
3. The construction of bridges, aqueducts and caravanserais[19]. In Mariam Bai v M. J. Abdur Rahman Sait[20] a secular trust of a public or charitable nature, *e.g.* a maternity hospital was held as valid waqf.
4. The assistance[21] to the poor so that they may be able to go to Mecca for observing Haj;
5. It was held in *Bibi Jan* v *Kalb Hussain*[22] that a waqf for celebrating the birth of Ali Murtaza was valid. In *Ramanadhan* v *Vada* it was held that customary fateha for ancestors alms giving was a valid object of waqf.[23] It has been held that celebrating the death anniversary of the settler and members of his family and performance of annual fateha of the settler and of the members of his family are valid object of waqf. The provision for the performance of ceremonies at the grave of an individual or at the tomb of a saint is a valid object of waqf.[24]
6. In *Haji Abdul* v *Haji Hamid*[25] it was held that a provision for keeping tazias in the month of Moharram was a valid object of waqf. The due and proper observance of the annual festival of the Muharram has been held to be a valid object of waqf.[26]
7. In *Syed Ali* v *Syed Muhammad*[27] Ali it was held that a waqf for camels and duldul for religious processions during Muharram was a valid object of waqf.
8. It has been judicially held that a provision for the repairs of Imambaras was a valid object of waqf[28],

9. In *Mohammad Kazim* v *Syed Ali*[29] it was held that a provision for the maintenance of a Khankah was held to be a valid object of waqf.
10. A provision[30] for celebrating the death anniversaries of the settler and of the members of his family were held as valid waqf. This is also not in accordance with the principles of Muslim ecclesiastical law. Islam has nowhere permitted the establishment of these waqfs. It is, therefore, submitted that the courts should reconsider the previous judgments and a waqf for celebrating the death anniversary of waqif and his relatives be declared as invalid.
11. In another case[31] the reading of Quran in public places and also at private houses was held to be a valid object of waqf. But the recital of Quran at private tombs is not held to be valid object of waqf. It has been held that if there was no distribution of alms, the reading of the Quran and the performance of ceremonies for the benefit of the soul of the settler, there was no valid object of the waqf. The Madras High Court held that recitation of Quran and *fateha* etc. for the deceased waqif cannot unless coupled with alms giving to the poor be a valid object of waqf. The Bombay High Court in *Abdul Karim* v *Rahimabai* held that waqif's direction to spend a specified sum (out of the dedicated property) on feeding persons belonging to his community was not a valid object of waqf.[32]
12. The construction[33] of a robat or free boarding house for pilgrims at Mecca was held as valid object of waqf.
13. A provision[34] for the maintenance of poor relations and dependants was held as valid object of waqf. It has been said that a waqf for *fateha* and for *amar-i-khair* including the maintenance of poor relations was not void for uncertainty.
14. Performance[35] of qurbani with sacrifice of one goat in the month of *Bakra-idd* (*Id-duz zuha*) in the name of settler was held as valid object of waqf.

15. The payment[36] of money to faqirs *i.e.* to poor was held as valid object of waqf.
16. A grant to Idgah was also held as valid object of waqf[37].
17. A provision[38] for a dargah or shrine of a pir which has long been held in veneration by the public was held as valid waqf.
18. A provision[39] for the performance of ceremonies known as Kadam Sharif was held to be a valid object of waqf. This object of a waqf has also not been recognised by the Muslim Law. The Indian courts have recognised these kind of waqfs without verifying the basic tenets of Islam. We, therefore, submit that our courts should reconsider the old judgments and after making necessary examination, the same may be declared as invalid.

The provision regarding maintenance of dargah is also not in accordance with Islamic principles. Islam does not direct Muslims to establish and maintain dargah as a valid object of waqf. It is, therefore, respectfully submitted that Indian courts should examine these cases in the light of Quranic provisions.

The courts have also recognised the valid object of waqf of the performance of annual *fateha* of the settler and of the members of his family[40]. In *Badrul Islam* v *Mst Ali Begum*[41] it was held that provisions for residence in the waqf property of the waqif's brother and his descendants was valid object of a waqf. An assurance in perpetuity for the benefit of a community was held as valid object of waqf.[42] Similarly, a provision for burning of lamps in a mosque was held as valid object of waqf. A provision for endowing a teacher for a school was held as valid object of waqf[44].

It is submitted that some of the waqfs mentioned above are not within the spirit of Islam[45]. The Indian courts recognised them as valid object of waqf even without going into the depth of the religious aspect of these waqfs. It will be clear from the study of these cases that Indian courts have expressed doubts regarding the validity of some of the waqfs.

The object of a valid waqf must be to help the poors. If a waqf was made for the mankind the waqf will be held as void. The reason is that by this waqf the rich and the poor both will be benefited[46]. On the same lines a waqf for the people of Baghdad and when they fail for the poor was held as void.

In *Mukarram Ali* v *Anjuman-un-nissa*[47] a waqf was created in favour of waqif's son. The property was transferred in the name of son. It was provided by the waqif that out of the income of the property the son should support his descendants and kindred who may be in need of help and subject thereto for certain charitable objects. It is clear from the above that the object of the waqf was charitable and, therefore, the waqf was held as valid.

In *Phul Chand* v *Akbar Yar Khan*[48] the waqif dedicated property yielding Rs. 850.00 per year, for (a) the benefit of his family, (b) charities according to the custom of the family. This was the case when Waqf Act, 1913, was not into force. It was held that if the customary charities required expenditure of Rs. 500.00 per year, the dedication would be valid. The court further said that in the following cases the waqf would have been declared as void. However, such waqfs would be valid under the Waqf Act, 1913 :

(i) if they did not incur more expense than was becoming in a Muslim family of the same position as that of dedicator to give in charity; or

(ii) if the amount to be expended in charities is left entirely to the discretion of the mutawalli.[49]

The facts and question of law decided in *Kulsum Bibi* v *Golam Hossein*[50] are also relevant to note here. In this case, the waqif dedicated his four houses valued at Rs 1, 50,000/- in waqf. He appointed his son as mutawalli. The following provision was made in the waqf deed :

(i) the dedicator and his son and all succeeding mutawallis should have a right of residence in the largest house;

(ii) dedicator's wife and her children should have the same right;

(iii) the rates, taxes, *etc.*, be paid out of the income of the waqf property.

(iv) the net income should then be divided into three equal parts to be spent respectively, for

(a) the repairs and maintenance of the waqf property;
(b) expenses of a mosque;
(c) feeding of learned men from Mecca, Medina, Baghdad, Samarqand, Bukhara and other places noted for learning;

(v) that the said house should, subject to the rights under clause (i) be for the accommodation of the said men.

It was held that the dedication was a valid waqf.

Objects partly valid and partly invalid

A waqf may contain partly valid and partly invalid objects. Under the English law, expressions which are too wide (such as philanthropic or benevolent purposes) by their vagueness and uncertainty make the whole bequest invalid. Under Muslim Law, if the wider expression includes purposes which are valid objects of waqf, as well as purposes which cannot validly form objects of waqf, the valid object prevails, the rest shall be rejected. Under Muslim Law, only the valid objects are given due consideration and the other part of the deed will be deleted.[51] In other words, the Indian courts have formulated the following doctrine in resolving the valid and invalid objects of waqfs :

(a) where the waqf deed contains the full details about the dedicated property...the portion meant for invalid purposes shall revert to the waqif;
(b) where the portions of the dedicated property has not been mentioned and it is not possible to separate valid and invalid objects,...the property will be applied to those of the specified purposes as are valid.

Where there is a mere implied reservation for charity to come into effect after the family of the waqif becomes extinct the implication that benefit should be reserved for charity is enough. In *Abdul Sattar Ismail* v *Abdul Hamid*[52] the Madras High Court observed that the whole income of such a waqf can be applied to the valid objects. The fact that a certain portion of the deed cannot be given effect to, does not make the whole deed invalid.

In *Abdul Karim* v *Rahimabai*[53] the Bombay High Court said that where a waqf is created for mixed purposes, some of which are lawful and some are not, it is valid as to the lawful purposes, but invalid as to the rest. The property dedicated for invalid purposes will revert to the waqif. Where the property is not specifically dedicated to an object which fails, the whole amount will be devoted to the valid objects of charity[54].

It may not be out of the way to mention here that the law with reference to charitable settlement is different from that of other settlements *i.e.* from resulting trusts. The settlements to charitable purposes are an exception from the law of resulting trusts.[55] The court said that where a person makes a valid gift and expresses a general intention of charity, but either particularises no objccts, or such as do not exhaust the proceeds, the court will take upon itself to execute the general intention, by declaring the particular purposes to which the fund shall be applied. Where in consequence of an increase in the value of the estate, an excess of the income subsequently arises, the court will order the surplus, instead of resulting to be applied in the same or a similar manner, with the original amount. Under the Muslim Law an ambiguity or indefiniteness will not invalidate the waqf.

There also exists a group of decisions in which the English courts have declared valid the trusts which were having mixed objects. In *Gott* v *Nairne*[56] the testator gave £ 12,000 to his trustees to invest either wholly or partially in the purchaser of an *advowson,* and until the occurrence of a specified event, they were to present some fit person to the living, but subject thereto, the *advowson* was to be held in trust for A. Until purchase, the fund was to be accumulated with the income for twenty one years, following which, if the *advowson* had not then been purchased, the whole of it was to belong to A. Similarly, if the event contemplated occurred before the advowson was purchased, or if a balance remained after purchase, the whole, or the remainder of the fund was to be given to A. In view of these facts, A claimed the transfer of the fund with accumulations, as a beneficiary absolutely entitled, under the rule in *Sounders* v *Vautier*[57]. In Re Hooper[58] the testator directed that his trustees should hold a certain sum to devote the income 'so far as they can legally do so' for the care of certain graves and monuments in cemeteries, and a tablet and window in a church, with a gift over to certain other persons. Since some of this was manifestly not charitable, the question was whether the trust was good in whole or in part. Justice Maugham, held that as regards the tablet and window this was a valid charitable trust, and as regards the graves, this was not charitable, but good for a period of twenty one years.

These decisions were criticised. It was said that all trusts which are not charitable must have a *cestui que* trust. In support of this the following observations of Grant, M.R., in Morice v Bishop of Durham[59] have been advanced :

> There can be no trust over which this court will not assume control; for an uncontrollable power of disposition would be ownership and not trust. If there be a clear trust, but for uncertain objects, the property that is the subject of the trust is undisposed of and the benefit of such trust must result to those to whom the law gives the ownership in default of disposition by the former owner. But this doctrine does not hold good with regard to trusts for charity. Every other trust must have a definite object. There must be somebody in whose favour the court can decree performance.

In England, the Master of the Rolls has insisted on three certainties of a trust. It says if the objects are uncertain, the trust must fail. There has been a disposition in the modern cases to regard the observations of Grant, M.R. as meaning that a trust must have definite human or charitable objects and by construing them in this sense, they have been effectively employed, as will be shown, to prevent the development of purpose trusts.

Ameer Ali[60] says that the principle of law laid down in *Morice* v *Bishop of Durham*[61] cannot be applied to trusts or consecrtions under the Muslim Law. This proposition was criticised as based on misapprehension of the principle. It is submitted here that it is not correct to take every disposition by way of charity for charity. A disposition cannot be held to be waqf unless its object is charity. Again there does not seem to be any reason as to why the English doctrine of cypres cannot be applied to Muslim law cases also.

In *Advocate General* v *Hormusij*[62] it was said that if a trust 'for good purposes unspecified is construed as exempting the trustee from all judicial control, it is not trust at all, but a beneficial bequest to him personally.

Lord Hardwick's observation in Lewin Trusts[63] appears to cover the case under consideration, where the general intention to devote the property to waqf is expressed but the particular objects are not specified. Tyabji says that the Muslim law does not differ on this point from English law, nor does the difficulty that the state should estimate the goodness of different purposes by a Muslim standard seem formidable[64].

In the last it is submitted here that now under varied statutes relating to public trusts and waqfs, a public trust will not fail on account of uncertainty, or some of the objects being invalid or incapable of execution. Similarly, the doctrine of cypres has been very widely extended under those statutes.

In *Saklat* v *Bella*[65] it was said that the income of the waqf property should be applied according to the directions of the waqif. It will be malversation to apply funds set apart for public or charitable uses, for persons who are not objects of the trust. The objects of the trust must have all the benefit they require. In case some surplus remains there, it must be left to the court to make a cypres application of it. In *Syed Ahmad* v *Hafiz Zahid*[66] it was said that where the object of such a trust or charity is the rendering of some convenience or service of such a nature that it will not hurt the lawful recipients if others share with them, the trustees may, but they are not bound, to exclude persons who have no legal title to share. They can give the benefit of the convenience or service to other persons and the court will not interfere in such matters. However, such persons should neither be in large number nor so disorderly or unpleasant in their habits of those for whom the endowment was created.

Invalid objects of Waqfs—Purpose must not be Prohibited by Islam—Waqf for the Construction of church *etc* held Void

The waqif of a waqf can dedicate his property only for those purposes which are not prohibited by Islam.[67] Fatwai Alamgiri says that there be a nearness, that is, some relation between the appropriator (waqif) and the objects of the appropriation[68]...else how can the act be done with a religious motive ? Fatawai Alamgiri further says that appropriation by a Muslim or a *zimmi* for a temple, or a church or for the poor of the enemy will not be valid. Under Muslim Law only Muslim can make a waqf and, therefore, waqfs must have nearness to Islam.[69] But, under the law of Islam, non-Muslims may make a waqf for purposes 'which have nearness to themselves'—though they may not make waqfs for a temple or 'house of fire'[70].

A Muslim is not permitted to make a waqf for the erection, repair or support of a place of worship in accordance with the tenet of a religion other than Islam, but the benefit of no human being (though a non-Muslim or an apostate, provided that he is not an alien enemy) is prohibited by Islam.[71] An appropriation for Jewish synagogues or Christian churches will not be valid. Similarly an appropriation in favour of fornicators or highway robers, or drinker of wine or for the copying of what are now called the Towreet and Injeel is not valid.[72] But appropriation by an infidel be lawful.

Tyabji says that apart from the above exception, even though a non-Muslim should make the waqf to his son and his descendants, and then to the poor, on condition that if any of his children become Muslim they shall be excluded from the charity, the condition would be binding ; so also if he should say, whoever turns to any other religion than Christian is excluded would be paid.[73] It has been said that when a Christian makes a settlement (waqf) upon his children and his children for ever, so long as there are any descendants, or makes the ultimate destination to the poor as is customary and some of his

Children become Muslim, they are nevertheless to receive the waqf property.[74]

A Muslim is prohibited to make a settlement on an alien enemy, though a blood relation ; but he make it on a zimmi or infidel subject, even though a stranger in no way related to him.[75]

Islam rejects the proprietary rights in tombs

A dedicator can make a waqf for the tomb of a saint.[76] However, a waqf cannot be made for the repairs and upkeep of a private tomb.[77] It is not clear whether the tomb can be owned or not. In *Mahomed Oosman* v *Essack Saheb Mohammed*[78] itwas said that Muslim law does not permit the ownership of tombs. It is astonishing to note that at one point Islam enjoin special reverence for the remains of the dead, it strongly disapproves of any proprietary rights in them. Islam rejects the proprietary rights in tombs as superstitions. However, in many cases courts have allowed the proprietary rights over tomb. In *Mst Zinat* v *Mst Aimna and Karam Din*[79] it was said that tombs are property. It is submitted here that the courts in India should give a clear outline of approach. In India, there are tombs which are having handsome income and the misappropriation of that income is very common.

Certainty of Objects—Views of classical Muslim jurists on certainty of Objects

The doctrine of certainty is not familiar to Muslim law. This doctrine can be divided into two period. According to the classical jurists of Islamic law, a waqf with uncertain object was held as valid. Prophet and his associates never pleaded that a waqf will be void because of uncertainty. The only emphasized that the dedication must not be repugnant to the Shariat. However, it was not said that in the absence of specific description of purposes the waqf itself would fail. It was maintained that it is not at all necessary to mention in the waqf deed the object of the waqf clearly and precisely. In *Sheikh Ramzan* v *Ramzan*[80] it was said that it is not necessary that the objects should be mentioned in the waqf deed. Where the objects are specified, it will not be necessary to name the sum to be spent on each object.[81]

Certainty of Objects after the Establishment of British rule in India

After establishment of British rule in India English law was introduced. They were not conversant with the basic principles of Hindu and Muslim laws. These judges were not knowing Sanskrit or Arabic language, the knowledge of which was necessary for properly understanding Hindu and Muslim laws. A man may have a good knowledge of the one tongue, and considerable familiarity with the colloquial employment of the other, and yet the quite incapable of accurately rendering even a simple legal passage from the latter into the former, still less from the former into the latter. The English judges were, therefore, having no other alternative but to apply the principles of English law through the doctrine of justice, equity and good conscience.

Basic Principles of English Law on certainty of Objects

According to English law the object of a trust, whether private or public must be certain, otherwise the trust will be void for uncertainty. Under the English law certainty of objects implies two things (i) that the recipients should be identifiable with certainty (ii) that the interests they take should be discoverable. Therefore, gifts for charitable or philanthropic purposes fail. So, where personal property was given to 'A' with the hope that he would continue it in the family, it was held that the objects of the bounty were too uncertain for the trust to be enforced.[82]

Another example of a trust which failed for lack of certainty of objects is provided by *I.R.C.* v *Broadway Cottages* Trust[83] where the court of Appeal held that a trust for such members of unascertained class as the trustees should select was void.

In recent years, cases involving the problem of certainty of objects have been referred frequently before the courts, particularly when trusts have been made for the benefit of past and present employers.[84] The uncertainty of objects may frequently be a problem in determining whether a charitable trust has established. If the fund has been appropriated exclusively to charitable purposes, then it does not matter if the objects are uncertain. The trust will be applied to charitable purposes; but if the fund is to be applied, partly to charitable, and partly to non-charitable purposes (*e.g.* 'to charitable or benevolent purposes'), the entire gift will fail for uncertainty.[85]

Under English law of trust mere expressions of benevolence, such as 'deal justly with' are insufficient to raise any trust. Secondly, if the donor makes the gift in absolute terms (*e.g.* by using the words 'unfettered' or 'unlimited' in respect of the gift it will be difficult. If not impossible, to construe subsequent precatory words as creating a trust.[86] Thirdly, although in some cases, uncertainty of object can be considered apart from uncertainty of words which may create a trust, in numerous cases the two appear together and uncertainty of objects will raise a doubt whether the words used were intended to be construed imperatively, but were inserted solely to guide the donee in his use of the property.

Though the provisions of Indian Trust Act, 1882 were not applicable in the case of waqf but many Indian courts overlooked it and applied the provisions of Indian Trust Act, 1882, in waqf cases. The result of the treatment of the subject was the emergence of conflicting judicial opinion. It is notable that even in free India the position is more or less same.[87]

The case of *Morice* v *The Bishop*[88] of Durham made a very deep impact on the law of waqf and trust in India. It was said by Lord Eldon that a bequest for 'such objects of benevolence or liberality as the executor should most approve was too vague to be enforced. In *Knight* v *Knight*[89] it was said by Lord Langdal that for the validity of a waqf the three certainties must be there. A trust for charitable or benevolent purposes was void because it was not certain.[90] It has been also judicially held that a trust for charitable or philanthropic purposes would be void for want of certainty.[91] The insertion of the phrase 'for such charitable or public purposes as my trustees things proper' has been held to be void for want of certainty.[92]

The judicial Committee of the Privy Council[93] has said that a gift by a Hindu for *dharam*, an expression equivalent to 'charitable, religious or philanthropic purposes' would be void for uncertainty. The facts, in brief of this case are as under. A Hindu bequested his property in trust and directed the trees to act in such manner as they think proper for preserving his name, so that his money might be used for some religious and charitable purposes after his death. This trust was declared as uncertain.

Under these circumstances the Muslim law was influenced by these decisions. There are many cases where the Indian courts declared waqfs as void for want of certainty. Ameer Ali[94] says that the law declared in *Morice* v *Bishop of Durham* will not be applicable to Muslim law of waqf.

In *Ganga Bai* v *Thaver* the court was required to interpret a Will which was made by a Khoja. The gift was written in English. The words used in the Will were 'to be disposed of in charity as my executors right' were construed to create a valid trust ; but if the Will was written in Indian language and the word 'dharam' is used, the word is vague and uncertain, not comprehended in the word charity as understood in the English language, and the court will uphold the trust or legacy. It was, therefore, held that a bequest by a Khoja Muslim for 'dharma' was void for uncertainty.

A waqf for such charitable objects as the trustees should think proper and for such purpose as that the settler should obtain certain bliss therefrom would be void for uncertainty.[96]

The Allahabad High Court[97] has said that a waqf for *fateha* and for *amar-i-khair* including the maintenance of poor relations was not void for uncertainty. Similarly in another case[98] it was said that a waqf for '*khairat*' or for '*khairati kam*' was valid, and no specification of the object of charity was necessary. The court, however, maintained that whether a waqf for *umare khair* or *kare khair* was valid depended upon the construction of these words, as to in what sense there have been used and if these words were used to denote benevolent purposes, then the waqf would be void for uncertainty.

In *Mariambi* v *Fatmabai*[99] the Bombay High Court said that a bequest for *khairat* was void for uncertainty. The court said that a bequest by a Muslim for *dharam kherat etc.* can not be held as valid objects for want of certainty. The court further said that the word *khairat* is Arabic and from Arabic anguage this word has been derived by Gujrati language. In Arabic language the word *'khair'* means 'good' and *'khairat'* means good works, alms, charities. The court held the waqf as void for want of certainty.

In *Sheikh Ramzan* v *Mst. Rahmani*[100] it was said that a waqf would be void for uncertainty, unless it can be said that when a Muslim dedicates his property by way of waqf for 'good works', it must be taken that the dedication is for purposes recognised by the Muslim law as religious, pious, or charitable within the meaning of Section 2 (1) of the Waqf Act. However, the above observations of Oudh High Court was followed by Lahore High Court in *Punjab Sindh Bank* v *Anjuman Himayet Islam.*[101] In this case the court said that the use of the words of the proviso to Section 3 of the Waqf Act, 1913, 'religious and charitable objects' is not a sufficient specification of the object. Later on, same High Court changed its previous ruling in *Mohammad Afzal* v *Din Mohammad.*[102] In this case, the Lahore High Court said that the words *Mazhbi our khairati kam* meaning religious and charitable works, were sufficient to say that the object of the waqf was valid, and therefore, the waqf was not void for uncertainty.

The Privy Council upheld the above decision in Beliram *Choudhary and Brothers* v *Mohammad Afzal*[103]. In *Fazal Din* v *Karam Hussain*[104] the waqif made a dedication of his property for the benefit of the Muslim community on the occasions of rejoicings and mournings. The dedication was held as valid. In this case the congested conditions of the settlor's town was construed and it was said that these words mean the provision for buildings for accommodating marriage funeral parties. A waqf for *kare-kher* which means any good act is void for uncertainty unless a waqf for *kare-kher* in construed to mean 'purposes recognised by Muslim law is religious, pious or charitable.' But this decision was overruled by a Full Bench where it was held that the charitable purpose highly commendable according to the Hanafi schools of Muslim law were not sufficient to constitute a valid waqf. In *Ahmadi Begum* v *Badrnn*[105] Nissa the chief court of Oudh said that a dedication in general terms for 'charitable purpose' highly commendable according to Hanafi school of Muslim law was not a valid dedication. The Allahabad High Court held that the word *khairat* is crystal and a waqf can be created for the purpose of *khairat.*[106]

In *Hashim Ali* v *Iffat Ara Hamidi Begum*[107] the question was regarding the interpretation of words such as 'religious, pious or charitable' as used in the proviso to Section 3 of the Waqf Validating Act, 1913. The Calcutta High Court said that the use of the above words without specification of the object of charity will not invalidate a waqf as it contemplates an ultimate gift effective in law and that the ultimate benefit in a waqf alal-aulad can also be impliedly reserved for the poor or for any purpose of a permanent character. It is not necessary to express these words expressly in the waqf deed. The court further said that it is apparent from the waqfnama that the waqif wanted to dedicate his property in waqf and in case there was no descendants of the settler to take the benefit of the waqf property, the property would be used for charitable purpose. As regards the words 'ultimate gift to proper acts of charity' the courts declare them as valid since these words indirectly meant a gift to poor and if a gift to poor had been emphasized by all Muslim jurists.

In *Abdul Karim* v *Rahimatbāi*[108] a Muslim created a waqf. The waqif directed to pay money to *sayyads i.e.* descendants of the Prophet Mohammad. The waqf was held to be void for want of certainty. The court said it would not be possible to ascertain who were the descendants of the Prophet's family. In another case[109] the question was regarding the interpretation of the words 'maintenance and support'. It was said that the word maintenance means lodging, boarding, clothing and other necessaries of life. The term 'support' means not only maintenance, but also includes other expenses to the convenience of the beneficiary.

In *Garib Das* v *M.A. Hamid* [110] the Supreme Court of India was required to consider this question again. In this case under the waqfnama a Muslim settled his whole and entire property to the mosque and madarsa at mohalla Nathnagar and the surplus of usufruct thereof was to be spent on the same. It was provided that there were two mosques at Nathnagar. It was said by the Supreme Court that if the matter stood at that there was a scope for holding that the waqf was void for uncertainty, but there was another document in which the waqif had clarified by identifying the mosque that he meant out of the two. The Supreme Court held the waqf was not invalid for uncertainty.

DOCTRINE OF CYPRES

Time is not static. It is always changing. There can be waqfs whose income cannot be applied to the desired objects because of change of circumstances or lapse of time or for any other reason. In such cases the courts may apply the income of the waqf to the objects which are similar to the objects desired by the waqif. In other words the doctrine of cypres shall be applied by the courts only to those cases of waqfs where a valid waqf deed specified (with certainty) valid purposes but they happened to fail.[111] According to Abu Yusuf the validity of a waqf cannot be challenged merely because that the object of waqf could not be achieved. According to Wajizul-Muhit,[112] if a man were to say, 'this my land is mouqoofa (dedicated) or muharrama (consecrated) or mahboosa (tied up)' it would constitute a valid waqf according to Abu Yusuf.

It is not always possible for the waqif to mention in the waqf deed precisely and concisely the objects of the waqf. Formerly, it was thought that reasonable certainty is not necessary for the validity of a waqf. As already stated according to ancient jurists, once a man made a waqf, even without mentioning the purpose for which the income was to be applied, it was a lawful dedication. Before the passing of the Waqf Act, 1913, it was thought that if the income of the waqf property could not be utilised according to the wishes of the waqif, then it would be applied for other valid objects. Where the settlor's real intention was to make a family settlement the word 'waqf' was considered a mere verbal fiction on his part, which did not change the nature of the property, nor subject it to waqf ; the settler being held to have intended not to create a valid waqf but a family settlement, disclosing nothing like a general intention to devote the property to purposes that are valid objects of waqf, on which the court could proceed cypres. It has been said that even in the case of charity, if the settler does not give the land or the whole rents of the land, but noticing the property to be of a certain value appropriates part only to the charity, the residue will then, according to the circumstances of the case, either result to the heir at law, or will belong to the heir at law, or will belong to the donee of the property subject to the charge, if the donee itself is an object of charity.[113]

The other view which is said to be modern is that the purposes of a trust must be indicated with reasonable certainty; if they are not, the trust fails. There is very little difference between English and Muslim doctrine of cypres. The English doctrine of cypres is comparatively narrow than the Muslim doctrine of cypres.

It has been held that a bequest for uncertain and vague objects shall be invalid.[114] In an Indian case the Judicial Committee of the Privy Council[115] followed the above opinion and said that a waqf of 'good objects' in general was void.

Ameer Ali[116] was, however, of the opinion that the principle of law propounded in *Morice* v *Bishop of Durham* cannot be applied in Indian cases. He maintained that mere vagueness of uncertainty in waqf will not be sufficient for treating the waqf as void. In the absence of explicit directions on the part of the waqif, the Hakim (administrator) has the power of framing a scheme by himself or in consultation with the benficiaries for the administration of the waqf. He further said that where the dedication is to a religious or charitable institution, which in course of time, ceases to exist, the property so dedicated instead of reverting to the grantor or his heirs, would be applied...to some other religious or pious institution, similar in character to the one which has failed, or to any other object by which benefit may accrue to human beings. Tyabji has also supported the opinion of Ameer Ali.[117] On the other hand, Wilson and Mulla were not in favour of this opinion.

Under the circumstances discussed above, conflict of opinion is bound to prevail. It may, however, be noted that in majority of the cases, the opinion expressed by Ameer Ali and Tyabji was followed. It has been said that once it is plain that the waqif was having *bonafide* intention to create a waqf, and to divest himself completely of the property, it shall be said that a valid waqf may come into existence in the following circumstances :

(i) where the objects are not specified at all ;
(ii) where the objects fails as impracticable ; and
(iii) where the objects are partly valid and partly not valid.

In the first two cases, the doctrine of cypres will be applied. In the third case the valid objects may be accepted by the court and the others rejected.

The main aim of the doctrine of cypres is to determine judicially the purpose to which waqf money can be applied and which is very near to the wishes of the waqif. It is, however, notable that Muslim law does not prescribe any machinery for such determination. Waqfs are generally created for helping the poors and, therefore, where the aim of a waqf is not necessary at all to ascertain exactly the intention of the waqif. In such cases doctrine of cypres should be applied and the funds of the waqfs be applied for those purposes which are near to the intention of the waqif.

It may again be noted that doctrine of cypres does not give to the courts arbitrary power to apply the income of the waqf according to their sweet will. The courts are not expected to apply the waqf property or its income to other purposes, simply because they considered them to be more expedient or more beneficial than that the settler had directed.[119] The courts are not given the extra territorial power to apply this doctrine.

Cypres doctrine of Shia Law is much broader than Hanafi doctrine of cypres. It has been maintained where it is not possible to ascertain the intention of the waqif, the income of such a waqf may be applied for good purpose generally. In such cases preference shall be given to an object which is near to the object of the original waqf. It has also been said that when a specific charitable waqf fails, the waqf property may be applied for the benefit of the poor and for pious acts and objects which may be dear to God.

This principle is known as doctrine of cypres. The *Sharaiul Islam*[120] says :

> If one should make an appropriation for a maslahat, or object of general utility, which has ceased to be used, it is to be applied to any good and pious purpose. And if it is for such purposes generally, it is to be expended on the poor and indigent, and in any other way by which an approach is made to Almighty God.

Abdur Rahim[121] says that 'if however the specified objects be limited or happen to fail, but a general charitable intention is to be inferred from the words of the grant, the waqf will be good, and the income or profit will be devoted for the benefit of the poor, and in some cases to objects as near to the objects which failed, as possible'.

The literal meaning of the word cypres is as near as possible the doctrine lays down that if a charitable intention has been expressed by the dedicator, a waqf (or trust) will not be allowed to fail because the object specified by the settler has failed, in such a case the income will be applied for the benefit of the poor or to objects as near as possible to the object had failed. This principle is identified to the English doctrine of cypres, and the principle underlying the doctrine of cypres if deeply rooted in Muslim law. Tudor[122] says that 'the cypres principle is the outcome of the rule that ambiguity or indefiniteness, which in any other case would be fatal, is no objection to a charitable intention, that is to say, where he has manifested a desire in any event to devote a fund to charity, that intention is carried into effect, although no definite purposes are named, or although the objects which are named are incapable of being effected.

In England, the Charities Act was passed in 1960. This Act has introduced some important extensions of the cypres doctrine.

Whether or not a general charitable intent has been shown is a question of construction of the particular gift.[123] The decision upon the existence or non-existence of a general charitable intent, where (as is usually the case) it is not expressly stated, have established some fine distinctions, which often depend upon the terms of a particular gift.

Where there is an absolute gift by will to a charity which comes to an end after the testator's death, then the gift is also applicable cypres.[124] Under the English law the following are some instances of cypres application where a general charitable intent has been shown :—

(i) impossibility or impracticability of purpose ;
(ii) specific purpose has never existed ;
(iii) specific purpose ceases to exist before the testator's death ;
(iv) specific purpose ceases to exist after the testator's death.

Where the charitable intention of the waqif can be ascertained very well, the waqf will not fail on account of the reason the objects of the waqf could not be achieved. For the application of this doctrine it is necessary that original waqf should be a valid waqf.[125] A waqf which is already void for uncertainty cannot be validated by the application of this doctrine.[126] It has been also said that a waqf alal-aulad which was invalid may be turned into a public waqf[127] by applying the doctrine of cypres.

In one Pakistani case[128] fund was collected for establishing a missionary university. However, on account of unavoidable circumstances sufficient fund could not be collected for the same purpose. It was held that a waqf cannot fail because the object was not achieved.

A further example of the application of the above rule may be noticed in yet another decision involving a construction of 'general charitable intention.' It was said that where apart from the use of the word waqf, a general charitable intention is shown or rather the intention shown that in any case the property is to be dedicated by way of waqf, which implies both (i) that the waqif, ownership is divested, and (ii) that the ultimate benefit is expressly or impliedly reserved for purposes recognised by Muslim law as religious, pious or charitable. It was further said that if the object mentioned in the waqfnama was illegal, the income of the waqf shall be utilised for some other recognised objects of charity.[129]

If the waqfnama does not mention any object and the waqif takes no step to give effect to the dedication to utilise the property for objects which may lawfully be the objects of a waqf, it will be presumed that the waqif never intended to dedicate his property in waqf.

In another case the court was required to construe the words 'will' and 'gift'. A Khoja Muslim executed a Will. The Will was written in English. He said that the fund of the dedicated property should be disposed of in charity as his executor shall think right. The will was held as valid.[130] When the[131] court in the exercise of its charitable jurisdiction is called upon to adjudicate between the conflicting claims of dissident parties in communities held together or distinguished by some religious profession or denomination, the rights of the litigants will be regulated by reference to what upon inquiry, turn out to have been religious tenets and opinion held by the community in its origin, or at its foundation. A dedication for the benefit of a community of persons, holding particular religious tenets, will ensure for the benefit of the persons professing the religious tenets held by the said community in its origin, so long as they exist, and the secession even of a vast majority of those who originally formed the said community does not mean that the said object was failed, nor will it affect the operation of the dedication.

The doctrine of cypres was also applied in a case where the descendants of a person referred to as the second Sajjadanashin, were paid certain allowances, payments being based entirely on the practice which clearly came to be prevalent owing to the misconduct of a succession of men in charge of the trust properties.[132]

Where a person has dedicated his property in the way of God, it shall be applied to whatever is productive of reward in a future state. Under such circumstances the income of the dedicated property may be applied for religious warfare, the greater and lesser pilgrimages and the erection of masjids *etc.*[133]

Fatwai-Alamgiri maintains that if the waqif has given

directions to the administrator that he may give the produce as he pleases, the waqf will be treated as valid.[134]

The Sirajul Wahaj says that if the waqif has not mentioned the object of the waqf clearly ; but it is apparent that the waqif intended to make a waqf the dedication will be treated as waqf.[135]

As regards the application of doctrine of certainty it is submitted that the English law of certainty cannot be applied in Muslim cases. Where a waqf fulfils all the requirements of law it should be treated as valid. Since, the law in specifically laid down a waqf should not be declared void merely because it was void under the English law.

The doctrine of cypres should be applied in the following cases :

(i) where only the word is used and no specific purpose is mentioned ;

(ii) the purpose of the waqf is mentioned in a broader sense.

It is respectfully submitted that the whole law depends on the intention (*niyat*) of the parties. Where the intention is clear the Muslim law should be applied.

REFERENCES

1. S Ameer Ali, *Mahomedan Law*, Vol 1, (3rd ed). p 213.
2. Fyzee AAA, Qutlines of Muhammadan Law, (Fourth Ed.) p 294.
3. See *Ratilal Panachane* v *State of Bombay*, (1954) SCR 1055.
4. *AIR* 1646 Lah 200.
5. *Supra*, note 1, p 217-18.
6. (1922) 50 IA 84, 89.
7. *Muzhurool Huq* v *Puhraj Ditarcy*, (1869) 13 W.R. 235.
8. *Abdul Fata Mohammad* v *Kussomoy*, (1894) 22 I A 76 ; see also Muhammad Munawar v Rosulan Bi, (1899) 21 All 329 ; Mahomed Ibrahim v Abdul Latif, (1912) 37 Bom 447.
9. See *Abdul Fata Mahomed* v *Russomoy*, *Supra* note 8, *Murtuzai* v *Jamuna*, (1890) 13 All 261 ; *Maulvi Saipid Muhammad Munawwar* v *Razia*, (1905) 32 I.A. 86.
10. (1889) 17 I.A. 28 : see also *Abdul Ganne* v *Hussein Miya*, (1873) 10 BHCR 7.

11. (1907) 9 BLR 998
12. (1909) 34 Mad 12. For elaborate definition of charity, see *Ibrahim Khan* v *Ahmad Sayed Khan*, (1910) 7 ALJ 761.
13. See *Fatmabibi* v *Advocate General*, (1881) 6 Bom 42.
14. See *Assobai* v *Noorbai*, (1905) 8 BLR 245.
15. Bail 1, 565 (575).
16. Mulla, *Mohammedan Law*, (18th ed) p. 193-194.
17. Baillie Digest of Mohammadan Law p. 574.
18. Id.
19. Hamilton, Hedaye, p. 240.
20. AIR 1973 Mad 121.
21. *Supra* note 9.
22. (1909) 31 All 136, 1 IC 763 ; see also Syed Ismail v Hamidi Begum, AIR 1921 Pat 125.
23. *Supra*, note 12.
24. *Abdul Shakur* v *Abu Bakkar*, AIR 1930 Bom 191.
25. (1903) 5 BIR 1010.
26. (1915) 42 Cal 933.
27. AIR 1928 Pat 441 : (1928) 7 Pat 426 : 116 IC 525.
28. *Sayid ismail* v *Hamidi Begum* Supra note 22.
29. AIR 1932 Pat 33 ; 136 IC 417 : (1932) ILR 11 Pat 238 ; see also *Ghulam Rasul* v *Chief Acministrator of Waqfs*, PLD 1966 Lah 978. In this case the Pakistan court held that the upkeep and maintenance of Khanqah was valid object of waqf.
30. *Sattar Ismail* v *Hamid Sait*, AIR 1944 Mad 504 : (1944) 2 MLJ 92.
31. Id.
32. AIR 1948 Bom 342.
33. *Mohammad Yusuf* v *Mohammad Sadiq*, AIR 1933 Lah 501 : (1933) ILR 14 Lah 431 : 144 IC 271.
34 *Mukarram* v *Anjuman-un-Nissa*, AIR 1924 All 223 : (1923) 45 All 152.
35. *V.M. Mohin* v *Waqf Board* ; AIR 1968 Mad 243.
36. *Abdul Karim* v *Rahimabai*, *supra* note 32.
37. *Kulsombi* v *Mohammad Abdul Sattar*, AIR 1948 Nag 183.
38. *Sunni Central Board of Waqf* v *Sirajul*, AIR 1954 All 88 ; see also *Ghulam Ali* v *Sultan Khan*, AIR 1967 Ori 55.
39. *Phul Chand* v *Akbar Yar Khan*, (1896) 19 All 211.
40. *Mutukana Ana Ramanadhan Chettiar* v *Vada Levvai Marakayar*, (1909) 34 Mad I2 : 14 IA 21, see also supra note 34.
41. (1935) ILR 16 Lah 783.
42. *Advocate General* v *Yusufali*,, (1921) 24 BLR 1060.
43. *Gobinoda Chandra* v *Abdul Majid*, AIR 1944 Cal 163 ; see also *V.M. Mohin* v *Waqf Board*, Madras *Supra* note 35.
44. *Mazhar Husain* v *Abdul*, (1911) 33 All 400 : 9 IC 753.
45. For example, waqf for celebration of death anniversities of the waqif and of his relations ; performance of a customary religious ceremony *i.e.* Kadam Sharif, performance of Urs or fateha etc.

46. *Fatwai Alamgiri*, Bail 1, 575.
47. *Supra* note 34.
48. *Supra* note 39.
49. *Mujibunnissa* v *Abdul Rahim*, (1900) 28 I.A. 15
50. (1905) 10 CWN 449, 485
51. *Supra* note 44.
52. *Supra* note 30.
53. *Supra* note 32.
54. *Mst Ruqia Begum* v *Sarajmal*,, (1936) ALJ 231.
55. *Morice* v *Bishop of Durham*, (1804) 9 Ves. 399, 405.
56. (1876) 2 Ch. D. 278.
57. (1841) 4 Beav. 115 ; see also *D. Alton* v *Gibbons*, (1917) 1 Ir. R. 448., *Pirbright* v *Salwey*, (1896) W.N. 86.
58. (1932) 1 Ch. 38
59. *Supra*, note 55.
60. *Supra*, note 1, p 324.
61. *Supra*, note 55.
62. (1905) ILR 29 Bom 375.
63. (1911) (12th ed), p 183.
64. Tyabji, *Muslim Law*, (Fourth ed), p 568.
65. (1925) 53 IA 45, 55.
66. AIR 1934 All 732.
67. Rex v Lady Portiongton, (1712) 1 Salk 162. It was said that the king as head of the Commonwealth is obliged by the common law... to see that nothing be done to the propogation of a false religion.
68. Bail I, 552
69. *Putli Kunwar* v *Janki Das*, (1924) 46 All 813.
70. Bail I, 552 (560-561). supra note 64.
71. Bail II. 215 ; see also *Meer Mohammad Israel Khan* v *Shastri Charan Ghose*, (1892) 19 Cal 412 ; Ameer Ali citing from Fathul Qadir.
72. Bail II, 215 (para 3).
73. *Snpra* note 64, p 570.
74. Bail 1. 552.
75. Bail II. 215.
76. *Supra*, note 42.
77. See *Mahmed Gosman* v *Essack S.M.* AIR 1938 Bom 184 ; *Sarswathi Ammal* v *Rajgopal Ammal*, (1954) SCR 277.
78. Id.
79. (1917) 52 PR 421.
80. AIR 1932 Oudh 71 : (1932) 7 Luck 300 : 135 IC 372.
81. *Mutu Ramanadan* v *Vara Levai*, 39 IC 235 : (1917) 44 IA 21 : ILR 40 Mad 116, 122.
82. *Harland* v *Trigg*, (1782) 1 Bro C.C. 142.
83. (1955) 1 Ch. 20.
84. See Re Hain's Settlement (1961) 1 W.L.R. 440

85. Re Sutton, (1885) 28 Ch. D. 464 ; *Williams* v *Kershaw*, (1835), 5 Cl. & F III ; *Chichester Diochester Diocssan Board* v *Simpson*' (1944) AC 341.
86. *Meredith* v *Heneage* (1824) 1 Sin. 542.
87. See *Faqir Mohammad* v *Abda* , AIR 1952 All 127 ; *Mohammad Afzal* v *Din Mohammad* AIR 1946 Lah 300 ; *Mukarram* v *Anujman-un nissa, Supra* note 34 ; *Sheikh Ramzan* v *Rahman, Supra* note 82 ; *Abdul Shakur*, v *Shakur*, AIR 1930 Bom 191 ; *Syed Shah* v *Syed*, AIR 1932 Pat 33 ; *Mohammad Yusuf* v Azimuddin, AIR 1941 All 235 ; *Beli Ram* v *Afzal*, AIR 1948 PC 168 ; *Hashim Ali* v *Iffat Ara*, AIR 1942 Cal 180 ; *Syed Ahmed* v *Julaiha*, AIR 1947 Mad 176.
88. supra note 55.
89. (1840) 3 Beaven 148.
90. Re Riland, (1881) W.N. 173.
91. Re Macduff, (1896) 2 Ch. 463.
92. *Blair* v *Duncan*, (1902) AC 37 ; Grimond v Grimond, (1905) AC 124.
93. *Ranchodas* v *Parvatibai*, (1899) 23 Bom 725 : 26 IA 71 (a Hindu ca.
94. *Supra*, note 1, p 218.
95. (1863) 1 BHCR (OC) 71.
96. *Shanabuddin* v *Sohanlal*, (1907) PR 75 ; *Advocate General* v Hormusji, *Supra* note 62.
97. *Supra*, note 34.
98. *Muhammad Yusuf* v *Azimuddin*, *Supra* note 86.
99. *AIR* 1929 Bcm 127 : (1928) 31 BLR 135 : 116 IC 242.
100. *Supra*, note 80.
101. AIR 1935 Lah 596 : (1935) 158 IC 937.
102. AIR 1947 Lah 117.
103. AIR 1948 PC 168, Pak LR 1949 Lah 1, 50 BIR 674, 61 MLW 713, (1948) ALJ 422
104. AIR 1936 Lah 81 : (1936) 162 IC 404.
105. (1940) 15 Iuck 586 : (1940) OWN 689 ; 189 IC 391.
106. *Muhammad Yusuf* v *Azimuddin*, AIR 1941 All 443.
107. (1942) 46 CWN 561 : 74 CLJ 261.
108. (1946) 31 BLR 67.
109. AIR 1952 All 127,
110. AIR 1970 SC 1035.
111. *Hashm Ali* v *Iffat Ara*,, AIR 1942 Cal 180.
112. *Supra*, note 1, p 150.
113. *Supra*, note 80.
114. *Supra* note 55.
115. *Supaa*, note 92.
116. *Supra*, note 1, p 325.
117. *Supra*, note 64, Note 27.
118. See Wilson, *Anglo-Indian Muslim Law*, (6th ed)., p 322 and see also Mulla, *Mahomed Law*, *Supra* note 16, p 196-97.
119. *Supra* note 3.

120. Bail II. 216.
121. Abdur Rahim, *Muhammadan Jurisprudence*, p 305.
122. Tudor. *Charities* (4th ed) (1906), p 140.
123. Per Parker, J. In Re Wilson. (1913) 1 Ch. 314.
124. Re Selvin, (1891) Ch. 373.
125. *Supra*, note 37.
126. *Punjab Sindh Bank* v *Aujuman Himayat Islam*, (1935) 158 IC 987.
127. *Mohammad Sabir Ali* v *Tabir Ali*,, (1954) 2 All 556.
128. *Abdul Hamid* v *Fateh Muhammad*,, PLD 1958 Lah 824.
129. *Supra* note 12.
130. This case has been discussed in detail at *supra* note 95.
131. *Advocate General Mohammad* v *Hussain*, (1866) 12 BHCR 32.
132. *Sajjada Shah* v *Shah Habib*, (1919) 53 IC 677, 680.
133. *Supra* note 64, p 561.
134. Bail 1, 588.
135. *Supra* note 1, p 150.

4

Various forms of Waqfs and Waqf Properties

A. MOSQUES

Its object

In Islam mosques are having special significance. These are the places where five time *Namaz* be offered to *Allah tala*. These are also meant for enhancing Muslim brotherhood and cooperation. The word mosque has also been included in the definition of public trust under the M.P. Trust Act, 1951. The other objects of a mosque are as follows :

(i) for arranging religious and theological sermons ; (*milad-sharif etc*) ;
(ii) religious and theological instructions ;
(iii) performance of marriages *etc* ; (*Nikah*)
(iv) recitation of the Quran (*Quran-khwani*) ;
(v) birth day celebration of Prophet Muhammad (Id-*Miladun-Nabi*) ;
(vi) mourning for the martyrs of Kerbala (*Majlis*) ;
(vii) religious type poetic symposium, (*Natiya-khwani, etc*)

Mosques can be divided into following two kinds :

Public mosque

A public mosque is meant for common Muslim. It is a fundamental right of every Muslim to offer his *Namaz* in a public mosque. He cannot be denied this right on the ground of not belonging to a particular sect or denomination who have founded the mosque or were managing the said mosque[1].

In the case of a public mosque, every Muslim is entitled to perform his devotion. For a valid mosque, it is necessary that property should be dedicated to God and it should be separated from the ownership of the waqif. The proprietary[2] right of the waqif in a building or ground set apart for prayer becomes extinguished either on the declaration of the waqif that he has constituted it as a mosque or consecrated it for worship, or on the performance of prayers therein or thereon. According to Abu Hanifa and Imam Muhammad, a waqf of mosque shall be valid only if a dedication of property was made, possession was delivered to the mutawalli. It is also necessary that the waqif shall permit public Namaz to be offered once in it with Azan. Hedaya says separation is necessary because without that the mosque is not made special to God, and prayer is necessary, because delivery is requisite according to Abu Hanifa and Muhammad[3].

On the basis of above, it can be said that the following canditions must be fulfilled for the validity of a waqf :

(i) the building must be separated from the other properties of the waqif ;

(ii) a way must be provided to the mosque ; and

(iii) either public prayers must be said or possession must be delivered to the mutawalli[4].

It is, therefore, neeessary that the mosque must be provided with a separate way and either the possession of the mosque should be handed over to the mutawalli or public prayers must be said. Ameer Ali[5] says that where a mosque has been validly dedicated, the right of the waqif in the property will immediately be extinguished. In Ithna Ashari law, the dedication is complete were a formal declaration has been made and prayers have been said. Where in a room some people offered prayers for some months, but it is not proved that they offered in congregation, the user of the property by offering prayers is not for such a length that an inference of dedication by the owner may be made. The mere fact that a mosque was built on the suit property by some unknown person from funds without knowledge of the owner cannot prove dedication[6].

There are two necessary conditions for the validity of dedication of property for mosque *i.e.* the site for the mosque must be publicly appropriated and in that place Muslims shall commence observing *Namaz*[7]. For the validity of a mosque it is necessary that mutawalli should be given the delivery of possession of the dedicated property[8]. Appointment of *Muezzin*[9] or *Maulvi* is not necessary[10]. The existence of structure called *Mehrab* and *Minar* cannot be conclusive evidence that the building in question is mosque[11].

Under Shia law a waqf is complete if the waqif has dedicated the property in waqf and has allowed the prayers[12]. This is the duty of the waqif not to participate in the income of the waqf property. The waqif should not have any kind of interest in the waqf property. In case the waqif makes any such reservation, the dedication will become void[13]. A waqif can himself become the mutawalli[14].

The waqif cannot impose a condition that he will be at liberty to revoke the dedication. In such cases the dedication will be valid and the condition will be void[15].

Establishment of the Mosque in respect of Namaz by all sects is a Fundamental Right

It is a fundamental right of every Muslim to offer his *Namaz* in a public mosque. This is based on the principle that all Muslims believe in the unity of God and in the prophethood of Mohammad. Even then, in India, it has been repeatedly agitated that mosque can be established to a particular sect or to the followers of a particular school.

A mosque is the house of Almighty and every person should have the right to enter into the premises of the mosque. Of course, he must observe the rules and regulations of the mosque. He should not disturb the peaceful working of the mosque[16].

The above principle that mosque cannot be restricted to the

members of any particular sect was discussed in series of cases. In *Queen Emperor* v *Ramzan* a Wahabi Muslim was prosecuted under section 296, Indian Penal Code for uttering the word 'amin' aloud in a Hanafi mosque while the prayers were being offered. It was held that a mosque cannot be restricted to the follower of a particular school or madhhab. It was further said that if the dedication is complete the restriction is bad and it will be open to all Muslims, whatever their school or sub-school may be. In this case Justice Mohmood of Allahabad High Court delivered a strong dissenting judgment. He observed that it is indisputable matter of the Muhammadan Ecclesiastical law that the word 'amin' should be pronounced in prayers after the Sura Fateha or the first chapter of the Quran. There, however, exists difference of opinion among the four Imams as to whether it should be pronounced aloud or in a low voice. According to Hedaya, saying of 'amin' after reading the first part of the Quran is mandatory. There is, however, difference of opinion among Imams as to whether 'amin' should be said loudly or slowly. According to Imam Shafii 'amin' should be said loudly. The followers of the other two Imams, namely Malik and Hanbal, also maintained that the word 'amin' should be pronounced aloud. On the other hand, Hanafi school maintains that the word 'amin, should be pronounced very slowly. It is a fundamental principle of the Muslim law of waqf that when a mosque is built and consecrated by public worship it ceases to be the property of the building and vests in God. Every Muslim has the legal right to enter it and perform devotions according to his own tenets so long as the form of worship is in accord with the recognised rules of Muslim Ecclesiastical law. The defendants, therefore, were fully justified by law in entering the mosque in question and in joining the congregation and they were strictly within their legal rights in saying the word 'amin' aloud. Applying the same principle, Ameer Ali[18] says that a mosque does not belong to any particular sect. It is open to all Mussulmans to go in and offer their adoration to the Almighty. A mosque may be erected by members of a particular sect. But the other sects including Shias will have the right to go into the mosque and observe prayers. The Mutawalli has no right to stop the entry of any person so long as he is the worshipper of God, and does not interpret or distrub the worship of others from coming and offering his adoration to the Almighty.

There is no such thing as Shia mosque or a Sunni mosque or a mosque of any other sectarian denomination... even where a mosque is appropriated to a particular sect, the rights of the Muslim of the other sects to offer prayers therein cannot be shut out, although as a matter of public expedience and to avoid conflicts arising from sectarian bias, these rights may not be exercised.[19]

A further example of the application of the rule may be found in yet another decision of the Allahabad High Court in *Mohammad Wasi* v *Bachan Singh*.[20] In this case some Hanafi Muslims of the town of Mahmoodabad (UP) in their representative capacity filed a suit against their Shia (Ihna-Ashari) co-religionists to restrain them permanently from certain ceremonies which they were performing within the precincts of the mosque. A group of Sunni Muslims refused to associate themselves with the plaintiffs and were impleaded as party defendants. It was argued that masque was built by Hanafi Muslims. *Namaz* was also observed according to the Hanafi faith. After sometime Shias also started performing other ceremonies known as *gahwara* and *taziadari*. The Hanafees objected to the performance of this ceremony and tried to restrain them from observing this ceremony. The lower court dismissed the suit and since the case involved very important question of Muslim law it was referred to the Bench of three judges. The full bench upheld the decision delivered by the lower court and dismissed the suit. The full bench said that a mosque is dedicated for the purpose that any Muslim belonging to any sect can go and say prayer therein. It can not be reserved for Muslims of any particular denomination or sect. A Muslim of any sect can go into a mosque and say his prayers at the back of the congregation in the manner followed by him so long as he does not do anything malafide to disturb the others. It may be noted here that in this case the mosque was not appropriated to any particular sect. The court, therefore, said that when a mosque is not appropriated to a particular sect, there is no doubt that it may be used by any Muslim for the purpose of worship or customary religious ceremonies without distinction to sect. A Muslim will have a cause of action if he is deprived from entering and performing prayers in the mosque.

It is, therefore, clear that a public mosque is a place of worship for the Muslims and regardless of their sect or denomination or as to who had founded the mosque, they are entitled to offer their prayers in the mosque. It is a fundamental right of every Muslim to offer his *Namaz* in a public mosque. He cannot be denied this right on the ground of not belonging to a particular sect or denomination who have founded the mosque or were managing the said mosque.[21]

Head of Sect has no Power to Exclude others for Saying Prayers

The head of a particular sect has no power to exclude others for saying prayers. To the same effect are the observations of Justice Tyabji of Bombay High Court. He said that the only way of ensuring peace and religious freedom to all would be by laying down that the practices followed peacefully and without objection for years at a place of worship should not be disturbed on the ground that it is being objected to by some people because they claimed that it was repugnant to the true tenets of their faith. The court further said that the religious head of a mosque could not be given arbitrary power to exclude the entry of any particular sect.

No Division like Sunni Mosque or Shia Mosque

Under the Muslim law there is no division like Sunni mosque or Shia mosque.[22] As submitted earlier every Muslim has the fundamental right to enter into the mosque but he cannot disturb the peace of the mosque. The statement that all mosques are mosques is not easy to decide. If a mosque was dedicated to any particular sect, the difficulties may arise in allowing the members of other sects.

Ceremonies other than Prayers can be performed in a Mosque by members of other Sects

It has been judicially laid down that ceremonies other than prayers can be performed in a mosque by members of other sects. A mosque may be under the control and management of Hanafi sect. The Ahl-i-Hadith (one sect of Sunnis) may be allowed to pray separately in the same mosque. It was held by Division Bench that while every Muslim is entitled to offer prayers in a mosque as an individual because the mosque is the House of God. It can, however, be said that sect has an inherent right to form a separate congregation and offer prayers and as the relations between two groups were strained it was not possible to allow Ahl-i-Hadith to pray as a separate eongregation with the Hrnifees at the same time.[23] It was further held that there is no difference between Sunni mosque or Shia mosque. In Sifat Ali Khan v Ali Mian[24] the following observations were made :—

> Mohammedans of the Ahmadia sect are entitled to enter into a Sunni mosque if they please and to offer up prayers with the regular congregation behind the Imam chosen by the members of the congregation, but they are entitled to pray in a separate congregation behind an Imam of their own in a mosque which has always been used by orthodox Mohammedans.

In another case the members of one sect sought to perform certain ceremonies other than prayer in the mosque. The members of the other sect objected to the performance of the ceremonies. It was held that right to offer prayer is a legal right for the enforcement of which a Muslim can seek the help of the court. It was also said that a particular sect can hold the ceremonies in the mosque and nobody can prohibit them, but it can direct that these should be performed in a way as not to disturb the prayer.[25]

Members of one sect can join in Congregational Prayer, but they cannot arrange separate Congregational Prayer

The members of one sect have the right to join in congregational prayer. However, they have no right to arrange separate congregational prayer. No difficulty shall, however, arise if the mosque is not appropriated to any particular sect.

The question for interpretation was whether a Shafie Muslim will have a right to observe congregational prayers alongwith Hanafi Muslims.[26] It was held that a Shafie Muslim may join in a congregational worship, though the majority of worshippers in the congregation were Hanafis and he could not be prevented from taking part in the service because the Shafie practice is to pronounce 'amin' in a loud voice and the Hanafi prononce to utter the word softly. It was also said that Muslims of the Wahabis sect have the right to worship in a mosque built primarily for the use of Hanafis and generally used by them though their views in the matter of ritual differs from those of the Hanafis. However, the members of one sect cannot arrange separate *azan* and separate congregational prayers, against the wishes of the other sect, who was already having prayers in praticular manner as it would lead to insurmountable difficulties and continual friction.

Similarly, a Shia Muslim may worship in a mosque where the rest of the congregation are Sunnis but they are not entitled to have a separate call to prayers or to hold a congregation behind an Imam of their own, and there is no rule of Muslim law to entitle the members of a new sect to pray[27] as a separate congregation behind an Imam chosen by themselves. It may, however, be noted here that no particular sect has the right to observe worship before an Imam of their own choice in a mosque where the majority is of some other sect.[28]

Establishment of Mosque for the Residents of a Particular Locality

There is a difference of opinion as to whether dedication can be validly made for the use of a mosque by the residents of a particular locality. Fatawai Alamgiri holds the view that dedication with such a condition will be void.[29] It says persons belonging to other locality will also be allowed to observe prayers. A mosque cannot be dedicated with an effective reservation for a particular sct or class of people.[30] Under Shafie law a masjid may be dedicated with a reservation that it will especially be destined to a particular rite.[31]

The judicial opinion in India is not in favour of sectarian mosques, or reservations in dedications excluding other Muslims from the right to pray mosque. The Indian courts are of the opinion that every follower of Islam has the right in good faith to enter any mosque and offer up prayers according to his own religious tenets. So long as he has no intention to cause, and does not in fact cause, disturbance to others. No one sect or portions of the Muslim community can restrain any other from the exercise of this right.[32]

The Judicial Committee of the Privy Council has said that the followers of each of the four sunny schools have the right to worship with each other.[33] The Privy Council also said that since the parties failed to show that a fallower of Abu Hanifa could do wrong in following a practice recommended by any other of the four Imam, they cannot be allowed to observe prayer according to their sweet will. The Privy Council further said that merely pronouncing 'amin' and refaiddin (raising arms when saying Allah Akbar in prayers) does not disquality an Imam from Imamat.[34] This principle was against reiterated by Allahabad High Court. The Allahabad High Court said that a mosque cannot exclusively be used by any particular sect of Sunni Muslim. In fact, a mosque is a place where every Muslim possess the right to go and observe prayers.[35] Justice Mahmood[36] of Allahabad High Court also took a similar approach.

It was said by Justice Katju of Allahabad High Court that 'the general permission may be confirmed in the circumstances of the present case to every inmate of the Police Lines regardless of the fact whether he may be a member of the Police force and may be living within the premises of the police lines without any distinction or rank of office that he may be holding. There may be a mosque within the restricted area of a defence establishment which has security regulations and where admission may be restricted to all the members living within the premises of the area.' It was further held that merely observing Friday prayers does not convert a private mosque into public mosque. It was also said that a Muslim who does not reside in such area could not claim to enter the restricted area and claim the right of entrance in the mosque.

The above opinion of Justice Katju does not appear to be correct. Merely establishing a mosque in defence or police area cannot be construed that it is a private mosque. It is the right of the state to restrict the entry of persons for defence purposes. But this does not change the character of the mosque. It is again submitted that any person who is living in that particular area, though he may not be police/defence personnel cannot be restricted from entering into the mosquc. Muslims living in other locality, can, However, be restricted from entering into the mosque.

The dedication of waqf property to mosque is always final and it cannot be revoked later on. Imam Muhammad was of the opinion that if a mosque falls to decay and is no longer used for prayers, its old material will revert to waqif or his heirs.[38] On the other hand, Abu Yusuf was having a different opinion. He was of the opinion that under the circumstances mentioned above, the land and old material of masjid in ruins will not revert to waqif or his heirs.[39]

Private Mosque

Strictly speaking under Muslim law there can be no private mosque. After dedication, the property becomes public property. However, a Muslim may establish a mosque for the purpose of his family only.[40] In the case of a private mosque common man may not be allowed to enter into the mosque. For the purpose of Friday Namaz 'Azan' is necessary. However, where there is no Azan or Iqamat but unrestricted entry into the mosque to Muslims in a particular locality in which the mosque is situated the mosque will not cease to be a private mosque.[41]

In *Khalil Ahmed* v *Shaikh Mohammad*[42] it was said that among Muslims also private mosques can he established. There can be place of offering prayers by family as against Muslim congregational prayer. The best example of private mosque can be mosques in the Red Fort at Delhi and Agra where the members of the Moghul royal family used to offer prayers in the mosque situated within the four walls of their forts. Such private mosque do not become waqf property.

Juristic Status of Mosques

The concept of artifical or juristic personality (Shaksiyt-e-itebari) is well known to Muslim jurists of the past. In India, however, there has been a conflict of judicial opinion as to whether a mosque is a juristic person or not. In the opinion of Lahore High Court a mosque was a juristic person, and therefore, he could sue and be sued.[43] A contrary view was taken by the Privy Council.[44] The Privy Council said that a mosque is not a juristic person and, therefore, a suit cannot be brought against the mosque. Since the case is an important one, it is proposed to give brief facts of the case :—

In the year 1722, a structure was constructed for the purpose of a mosque. However, on account of certain circumstances, from 1762 the building and adjacent land was in occupation and possession of Sikhs. In the year 1849 Punjab became the territory of Britishers and at that time the mosque building and the property which had been dedicated therewith were in the possession of Sikhs. Mahants of Sikh shrine (gurdwara), and the mosque building was used by the custodians of the Sikh institution. In the year 1927 Sikh Gurdwaras Act (Punjab Act VIII of 1925) was passed. Consequently to the passing of this Act the old mosque building and land adjacent thereto were included as belonging to the Sikh Gurdwara. The case went before the Sikh Gurdwaras Tribunal in 1928. The Muslims claimed that the land and the property had been dedicated for a mosque and did not belong to the gurdwara. It was held by the tribunal that the claim failed by reason of adverse possession and previous, and in the result, the property and building were given into the custody of the defendants, and on 7th July, 1935, the building was suddenly demolished by or with the connivance of its Sikh custodians.

A suit was brought against the Shiromani Gurdwara Prabandhak Committee and the Committee of Management for the notified Sikh Gurdwaras at Lahore. It was claimed in the suit that a declaration should be made to the effect that the building was a mosque in which the plaintiffs and all followers of Islam had a right to worship.

The suit out of which the appeal arose was brought by 18 plaintiffs, the first being the mosque itself in the sense of the site and building, suing next friend, and the other plaintiffs, including minors and women. These persons claimed that they had a right to worship in the mosque. The Privy Council in its judgment said that it was not necessary to decide whether in any circumstances, or for any purpose, a Muslim institution could be regarded in law as a juristic person ; but it was sufficient to hold that suits can not competntly be brought by or against such instituions as artificial persons in the British Indian courts. The Privy Council did not decide as to whether a mosque could for any purpose be regarded as a juristic person. In *Mohammad Shafiuddin* v *Chaturn Bhuj*[45] the Rajasthan High Court held that a mosque is not a juristic person.

As already noted earlier, the juristic personality is not a new thing for Islam. It was very well known to classical Muslim jurists. It appears they deliberately excluded mosque from the purview of juristic personality merely on the ground that it should be controlled by human beings.

On the basis of discussion it can be said that Indian courts are not in favour of sectarian practice. The Indian courts have not favoured reservations in dedications excluding other Muslims from the right to pray in any mosque. This rule is, however, not absolute. There are cases, though very few, where courts have allowed the entry of any particular sect on the ground that among Muslims also there are religious communities which possess property and place of worship. In *Akbar Ali* v *Mohammed Ali*[46] the court allowed the use of masjid for the exclusive use of a particular community. It cannot be disputed that a mosque is the house of God and, therefore, every Muslim can visit the mosque and offer prayers according to his own religious tenets, so long as he has no intention to cause, and does not in fact cause disturbance for others.

As a matter of practice, no one who is not a member of a particular *jamaat* even enters the mosque belonging to it, without being invited to do so or obtaining leave, and without conforming, within the precints of the mosque, to the amenties observed by the members of the *Jamaat* in possession of the mosque.

Usually, the following questions will arise if a Muslim is debarred from entering into a mosque :—

(i) If the person in charge of a mosque, were proceeded against in a court of law for a breach of trust on the ground that the doors of the mosque were locked up, and not opened except to members of the *Jamaat.*

(ii) Whether they will be liable for breach of trust if the real object of the waqf were to benefit not their own *Jamaat* but all Muslims. Yes.

(iii) Whether[47] persons habitually attending a particular mosque can be prevented by the others from praying in their own way.

(iv) Whether a devout Muslim of another school in good faith wishing to enter the mosque and pray can be prevented from doing so.

(v) Whether a Muslim of another community wishing to enter a mosque in good faith, can be prevented from doing so.

As already noted, the Indian courts are not in favour of sectarian mosques. It will be apparent from the above discussion that all Muslims are brothers and they have the right to enter in to the mosques.

APPOINTMENT OF IMAM

Under Muslim law, the provision regarding appointing authority of an Imam is not clear. Ordinarily the Mutawalli possess the capacity to appoint an Imam of the mosque. The Calcutta High Court[48] has held that a *de facto* mutawalli shall have the right to appoint an Imam. Where the mutawalli is not available, the appointment can be made by the descendants and relatives of the waqif.

An incompetent Imam can be removed by the Qazi on the report of the congregation.[49]

Use of loudespeaker in a Mosque not a Legal Right

Muslims have no inherent right to use loudespeakers in their mosques, and the state has the discretion to stop the use of loudespeakers for worship in mosques in public interest.[50]

Idgah

Muslims have been directed to observe Id prayers (*i.e.* Namaz of Id-ul-Fitr and Id-uz-Zuha) slightly away from the locality of the residents. For this purpose only an Idgah may be established. It is a place comprising a compound or lawn, where Id pryers may be performed.

It has been said that for the purpose of management *etc.* there exists no difference between a mosque and an Idgah and, therefore, an Idgah shall be governed by the law relating to mosques.[51]

MUSLIM MONASTERY LIKE INSTITUTIONS

Khanqah

A Khanqah may be called a Muslim monastery. It is a place where faqirs, dervishes and saints *etc.* congregate for religious instruction and devotional exercises. A Khanqah must be housed in a dargah or be independent institution in themselves not associated with any saint's tomb, The institution of Khanqah exists throughout the country. A *dervish* or a *sufi* of particular sanctity may settle in some locality ; so long as he has not attained sufficient importance, his place of abode is called a *takia* or *astana* according to his position in public estimation. His pious life and teachings attract public notice, disciples gather round him, and a place is constructed for their lodgment, and the *takia* grows into a *Khanqah.*[52]

Khanqah is an institution which is similar in many respects to a math where religious instruction is given according to Hindu faith.[53] A *Khanqah* is founded by a man who has devoted most of his time in prayers and who has by virtue of prayers acquired certain name and fame.[54] On the place where he founded *Khanqah* teaching is given by the founder. After his death, if he is buried there, the place is generally known as resting place, *takia* or abode.

Many of the *Khanqahs* are waqfs and are governed by the law of waqfs. In south India an institution identical to *Khanqas* is *pallivall.* Though every *Khanqah* or *takia* is not a waqf, one may become waqf by endowment or user.[55]

It has been said that it is a private property in the sense an institution managed by the members of the founder's family. *Khanqah* is a private property and the property is controlled by the family members of the dedicator. The main aim of this institution is to manage the property, receive offerings, initiate and instruct disciples and hold *urs* (annual fair).[56] Khanqahs and shrines have been held to be waqf property.[57]

A *Khanqah* may also come into existence by long usage or by dedication. Later on, it becomes a waqf. Multan shrine of Mai Pall Daman is the best example of waqf by user.

Khanqahs are also looked after by the *Mujawar* and *Khadims*. The head of this institution is known as Sajjadanashin, meaning spiritual superior. Sajjadanashin is a spiritual head and teacher of religious doctrines and he has certain spiritual head and teacher of religious doctrines and he has certain spiritual duties to perform.[58]

It is regrettably noted that the institution of *Khanqah* is grossly mismanaged. The whole offerings of the *Khanqah* is generally taken by the persons who are looking after *Khanqah*. State has so far not been able to take concrete steps to control their authority by democratising the scheme of administration and whenever government has tried to check the evils, the management reacted to these efforts of government. In *Ikramul Haq Shah* v *Rajasthan Muslim Waqf Board* the Rajasthan government decided to appoint a receiver to look after the administration of Miskeen Shah's dargah at Jaipur. The appointment of receiver was vehemently protested by the Sajjadanashin and, therefore, government reviewed the appointment of the receiver. In place of receiver government decided to constitute a committee of management, the chairman of which was the Sajjadanashin. The Sajjadanashin of the dargah was not satisfied with the appointment of the committee and he resorted to a writ of *quo warranto* directed against the Rajasthan Waqf Board. The petition was dismissed by the single judge and, therefore, the Sajjadanashin filed a special appeal to the Rajasthan High Court. The appellant originally claimed the institution as dargah. However, in appeal he described it as Khanqah. The High Court reviewed the case law relating to the nature of a Khanqah and the authority of the head of a *Khanqah*. The High Court said that a *Khanqah* was a monastery where *dervishes* and other seekers after the truth congregate for religious instructions and devotional exercises.

As regards the authority of the chief of a Khanqah the

High Court confirmed that his position was just analogous to that of a mahant of a Hindu *math* who exercises both religious and secular powers of management over the institution. The High Court refused to accept the shrine as miskeen Shah's dargah with the status of a Khanqah nor its Sajjadanashin with the position of a Hindu mahant. The High Court also said that a decision on these issues required detailed factual investigations which were not within the jurisdiction of the writ petition.

Takia

Muslim law recognises *Takia* as a valid object of waqf. The plain meaning of *takia* is resting place. It may be a tomb or a burial ground. Takia may be a place of assembly in a village and is devoid of all religious connotation[60]. Sometimes it is a platform in a Muslim graveyard where prayers are offered[61].

It has been seen that a faqir builds his hut near a *takia* in a graveyard and takes up his residence there. In course of time he starts imparting religious instructions there, and starts calling it a *Khanqah*. Later on, the *faqir* may be able to collect disciples at his residence and ultimately it developes into a public institution of some importance.

Takia is a place where a *faqir* or dervish resides, before his pious life and teachings attract public notice, and before disciples gather round him, and a place is constructed for their lodgement[62]. Ameer Ali maintains that a *dervish* or a person who, by leading a pious life, has won the esteem and veneration of a neighbourhood, or a *Sufi* of particular sanctity has settled down is some locality. So long as he has not attained sufficient importance, his place of abode is called a *takia*. Afterwards when he attains sufficient importance it becomes '*astana*' which later on becomes *Khanqah* or *dargah*[63].

A *takia* has been recognised by law as a religious institution and a grant or endowment to it is a valid waqf or public trust for a religious purpose. Every takia is not necessarily a waqf, but some may become so by long user or by endowment[64]. Therefore, whether a particular property is *takia* or not would be a question of fact[65]. As already noted, a *takia* may be the object of a valid endowment or waqf. All properties belonging to a *takia* vest in God and become impartible and inalienable[66]. However, it is not necessary that a takia will always be a waqf property.[67]

A person may take the charge of graveyard and become the takiadar. But it does not mean that the property in the possession of the takiadar is waqf property. Some more proof is required to show that the property in the possession of the takiadar is a waqf property. A *faqir* or holy man builts a a hut and take up his residence near the takia or prayer platform in the graveyard and impart religious instruction and call the place a *Khanqah*. Inspite of all these things the khanqah was held not a waqf property[68].

A takia may also beeome waqf by long user or by an endowment[69]. In one case a faqir collected many disciples at his residence which was later on developed into an institution of public importance. It was held that the place of assembly of *faqirs* was a real *Khanqah* and such *Khanqahs* are takias and may be the object of a valid endowment[70].

Imambara

The establishment of an Imambara can be the object of a valid waqf. It is generally established by the members of the Shias (Ithna Ashari Shite faith) for the performanee of certain ceremonies at Muharram and other times. An Imambara can also be established by a Sunni for performing the holding of mourning sessions (majlis etc) raising of alms and *takias* and taking out the duldul as symbols of the flag, tomb and horse, respectively of the martyrs of Karbala. Generally an Imambara is established for private purposes. The establishment of a private Imambara is a domestic matter of the waqif. This may be established in a private house for the performance of certain Moharram ceremonies. It is not open to general public[71]. An Imambara may also be estalished for public purposes. The Indian courts have held that an Imambara is generally a private and not a public waqf and is also not a trust within the meaning of section 92 of the Civil Procedure Code. In *Mohammad Yusuf* v *Mohammad Shafi*[72] it was held that the provisions of section 92 of the Code of Civil Procedure are not applicable in the case of Imambaras. It was further held that the plaintiffs could not prove that members of the public were at liberty to place their own *tazias* in the Imambara in dispute or to convene a Majlis therein at their own pleasure and without the permission of the defendants. The plaintiff could only prove that members of the public were allowed inside the Imambara when the defendants chose to hold a Majlis or perform any other ceremony and throw the Imambara open to the public. It was, therefore, held that Imambara was not a public endowment.

Usually an Imambara is a private charitable object but evidence may be given that it was intended to be used by public and in that case it will form public waqf. The faith in Islam is necessary for creating an Imambara. A Hindu can not lawfully make a waqf in respect of the Imambara. The reason for this opinion is that Hindu may dedicate property for shastric purposes[73] It is submitted here that this opinion of Patna High Court is not correct. It needs reconsideration. This is also contrary to section 66-C of the Waqf Act, 1954. Under section 66-C of the Waqf Act, 1954, a non-Muslim can dedicate property in favour of certain Muslim institutions, including Imambara.

Cemetery (*Qabristan*)

Under Muslim law dedication of land for the purpose of using it as a burial ground by public is considered to be one of the pious and religious acts and, therefore, constitutes a valid object for waqf. There are two modes in which the property may be dedicated for the purpose of graveyard (i) express dedication as a burial ground, (ii) implied dedication to be inferred from actual user of land for the purpose of burying the dead bodies. In the case of express declaration, no difficulty arises but where there is no evidence of dedication, the question arises whether the fact of dedication can be presumed by user of the property as a graveyard by the public. Whether a particular piece of land is a graveyard or not is a question of fact.[74]

A cemetery is a consecrated ground and is not a private property, whether it is a burial ground or not depends upon number of person buried there or evidence of dedication derived from the testimony of witnesses or reputation. A cemetery once created continues to be so even though there remain no traces of the dead, not even the bones[75]. If the land was used as a burial ground for a long time it becomes waqf by long user, although there is no evidence of an express dedication. Therefore, cemeteries are waqfs either by dedication or by long user and are governed by the law of waqf.

Under Muslim law a graveyard or *qabristan* may come into existence by dedication of property. A graveyard may be either public or private. Where a graveyard is open for the burial of any Muslim it is a public graveyard. Where the use of the graveyard is confined to burial of corpses of the founder, his children, descendants and relatives, it is a private graveyard. With the passage of time a private graveyard may become public graveyard. Thus where members of public are permitted to be buried and the practice grows so that by instances adequate in character, number and extent, the presumption will be that the dedication is complete and the graveyard has become a public graveyard.[76]

There are cases when the courts are called upon to decide whether a particular site is or is not a graveyard. In such cases the courts have held as follows.

Graveyard by Long User

A graveyard can lawfully be established by long user. For establishing a graveyard by long user, it is not necessary that all the principles of Muslim law should have been applied. The establishment of graveyard by long user can be proved by applying the English doctrine of justice, equity and good conscience. It is not necessary to apply all the rules of Muslim law.[77] In *Abdul Rahim Khan* v *Fakir Mohammad Shah*[78] it was observed that where in a suit for a declaration that a property is waqf, the ancient history regarding the dedication of the property as waqf is not available, the decision can be based on such evidence as can be gathered from how the public regarded the property, its environment and the conduct of parties. If there are several instances of user of a land as a burial ground which are adequate in extent, number and character, such user would be an evidence of *qabristan*.[79]

In a Hindu populated village, where there are no Muslims nor any evidence of burial in recent times, nor presence of graves on the spot, the mere recording of a land in village papers as graveyard would not make it waqf property. In 1961, the Punjab Village Comman Lands (Regulations) Act and in 1974 the Haryana Municipal Common Lands (Regulations) Act were passed. The effect of these Acts was that a large number of waqf properties, particularly graveyards, were included in the *Shamelat Deh* (village common land). These were, therefore, taken over by the Panchayats in all the rural areas of the Punjab, Haryana and Himachal Pradesh and all the Shamlat lands in a Municipal area in Haryana vested in the Municipal Committees concerned. The Panchayats, therefore, started cutting trees and levelling graveyards so that the land may be made available for purposes of cultivation or construction.

On the other hand section 15 (1) of the Waqf Act, 1954, says that the general superintendence of all waqfs (including the evacuee waqfs) shall vest in the Waqf Board of the State. There was, therefore, direct conflict between the above mentioned state laws and the Waqf Act, 1954.

In the present case the land was recorded as *Shamelat deh* in the Jamabandis for the years 1909-10 and 1945-46. The land was used as graveyard. The village, where land was situated was having the population of Hindu community. The strength of Muslim was small. After partition of the country, all the Muslim left India and went to Pakistan. No dead body of Muslim was buried in the graveyard since 1947. Some of the members of the Hindu community took possession of various plots and constructed houses thereon[80]. The Panjab High Court held the fact that land recorded as *Shamelat deh* in the Jamabandis for the years 1901-10 and 1945-46 to the effect that the land has been used as graveyard does not necessarily make waqf by user. It was said that it cannot be said that the entry *ghar mumkin qabristan* is in accordance with the facts. The High Court held that—

> If no Muslim is living in the villages it cannot be understood how the entry in the Jamabandi that khasra number

247 is in possession of Ahle-Islam can be taken to be correct. There is no evidence of intention to create a waqf by anybody whatsoever in the present case, and only from an entry in the Jamabandi without proof of user, it can not be that land comprised in Khasra No 247 was waqf property and vested in the Punjab Waqf Board.

It is clear that the High Court itself found that the land in question was allowed to be used as graveyard between the year 1910-1946 and, therefore, a waqf-by-user came into existence. Once the intention of the owner of the land was to use the land as graveyard, and allowed it to be used as such, it can be said that a valid waqf came into existence. It was not necessary to dedicate the property expressly.

Since after 1947 there was no Muslim in the state it is not correct to argue that whether the property concerned was under the occupation of Ahle-Islam. The above decision is not in consonance with the provision of Muslim law of waqf. It is relevant here to discuss the law laid down by their Lordship of Privy Council in *Ballabh Das* v *Nur Mohammad*[81]. In this case Sir John Rankin said that 'when in the (khasra) document of 1868...one comes across a description of certain land by the word *qabristan* or graveyard, this *prima facie* at all events, means that the land is a graveyard in the sense known to the Muslim law.' There cannot be any exhaustively prescribed or described evidence to prove the existence of graveyard. It is, however, necessary that there should be number of instances of burials which may be adequate in character, number and extent so as to justify the inference that the plot of land is cemetery.

It is submitted here that if a particular piece of land is not used by Muslims as graveyard it does not mean that such a land has ceased to be a waqf land and any person can acquire and build the house on such land[81]. Muslims migrated to Pakistan leaving behind graveyards which are naturally now in disuse since 1947, could hardly mean that a waqf by user once created has come to an end simply because in later years no dead have been buried there.

A graveyard once created continues to be so even though

there remain no traces of the dead, not even the bones...(and although there is no evidence of an express dedication[83].

The matter was again examined by the Supreme Court of India in the case of *Mohammad S. Labbai* v *Mohammad Hanifs*.[84] The Supreme Court held that it is well settled that a conclusive proof of the graveyard is the description of the burial ground in the revenue record as public graveyard. Once a *qabristan* has been held to be a public graveyard then it vests in the puplic and constitutes a waqf and it cannot be divested by non user but will always continue to be so whether it is used or not.

The Supreme Court criticised the approach regarding Muslim law taken by the Indian courts. According to Muslim law it was the judicial misinterpretation of Islamic law. The Supreme Court observed—the most unfortunate part of the drama long in process is that the courts before whom the disputes came up for decision handed down judgments which were not strictly in accordance with the Shariat and the essential tenets of Mahomedan law.

In Utter Pradesh Land Management Committee (Gaon Samaj) was constituted. This Committee was required to take charge of all the land situated in the state of U.P. However, regarding recorded (in the revenue records) graveyards *etc.* was concerned, the Committee was directed not to object to the customary and traditional use of the land by the communities concerned. The committee was asked not to impose restriction on burial of dead bodies on such lands. The committee was not given right to cut away and sell the trees standing on such lands to the detriment of the recognised costomary user.

In case of violation of these directions by the Committees, necessary action against it or its members or chairman could be taken under sections 127 and 127-A of the U.P. Zamindari Abolition and Land Reforms Act, 1950.

Description of a site in a Settlement Register

Description of a site in a 'settlement register' as a *qabristan* is prima facie evidence of its being a public cemetery.[85]

Public Graveyard

A graveyard which is public cannot become the property of any private individual.[86]

Construction of House *etc.*

House or some pucca construction cannot be done on graveyard and the construction of a house shall not convert the graveyard into a private property. If a house is built on an obsolete graveyard the Muslim community has a right to get it demolished as it would be in contravention of the original purpose of dedication, It may, however, be noted that where only a temporary hut was built, the same may not be demolished.[87]

Public Cemetery

A public cemetery is a waqf and, therefore, even if closed by Municipal authorities it cannot be alienated.[88] It is the principle of Islamic jurisprudence that a dead once buried cannot be exhumed.[89] Ameer Ali maintains that when a body has been buried in the ground, whether for a long or short time, it cannot be exhumed without some excuse. But it may lawfully be exhumed when it appears that the land was usurped, or another is entitled to it under a right of pre-emption.

Process of Burial be Continuous

There must be the continous process of burials. Few cases of burial will not be sufficient for treating a place public graveyard. For constitution a place as graveyard there must be sufficient number of burials.[90]

Customary Law

In *Ram Rao Narayan Bellary* v *Rustom Khan*[91] certain land at Dharwar, which had formerly been used as a graveyard by the Muslim community, but which had been disused as such for twenty or thirty years, was sold by the owner to defendant 4, who thereupon commenced to prepare the foundations of a house which he proposed to built upon it. The Muslims brought a suit alleging that the Muslims of Dharwar were accustomed to religious rites and ceremonies at the graves in the social land. It was held by Mr Justice Fulton that by the custom of the country, founded on a sentiment which may almost be described as universal, the ground in which human relics are interred is regarded as for ever sacred. The members of the family of the dead are in the habit of performing certain religious services at their tombs. The ownership of the land may be vested in others, but the permission to bury in the land, granted must be subject to the custom of the community

Under the customary law, a Muslim tomb cannot be said to be waqf[92]. Mere burial of a saint does not create a waqf in the absence of a dedication, express or implied, to bublic religious uses[93].

Grant of Land Revenue

A grant of land revenue for the remuneration of a village *moulvi* does not constitute a waqf or endowment. The land is partible and heritable and if the holders does not perform the duties of the office, government enforces its objects by levying full assessmsnt[94].

INSTITUTIONS LIKE SHRINES AND THEIR SERVANTS

Dargah

Dargah is a burial place of saints.[95] Tyabji maintains that the a dargah is the shrine or tomb of a person honoured after his death as a saint. The *dargahs* are the tombs of great Muslim divines of the past, mostly having superstructures. It is a place where a Faqir or darvish or saint is buried and to hold anniversary *fateha* and *urs* at such tomb is well known object of Muslim charity[96].

The pilgrims *zaerin* belonging to various communities and from different parts of the country visit and pay respect. There are few very famous *dargahs* in India. Even pilgrims from abroad are attending these dargahs. Some of these dargahs are not having the grave of saints. The Dargah of Hazratbal in Kashmir is one of the famous *dargah* of India. It is claimed that this *dargah* is in possession of Prophet Mohammad's hair (*mu-e-mubarak*). There are also buildings where foot prints or finger prints of Prophet are preserved.

Dargah is a Persian word. It means the king's court, a

port, portal, gate, door. It also means lower threshold, a court before a place or great house, a large bench or place for reclining upon[97]. It is a shrine or the tomb of a Muslim saint. It is a place of resort and prayer[98]. The term *dargah* is a respectful term applied to the shrine of a Muslims saint[99].

It appears that an endowment to a dargah is not mentioned among the religious and charitable objects, nor is it mentioned in connection with waqfs. It may be made clear that dargahs are not the place of God. Muslim, believe that Prophet Muhammad was not in favour of erecting an elaborate mausoleum or excessive outlay for a tomb. It appears that this was only the reason that Mughal emperor Aurangzeb chose a simple grave of earth even without bricks and mortar.

In this sub-continent, even amongst Sunni Muslims there is a separate group of persons know as Ahle-Hadis and Wahabis. They are fundamentalists. They only believe in the teaching of *Quran* and Prophet Muhammad. They are not in favour of pilgrimage and paying regard to *dargahs*. However, other Sunnis pay great to these places. They believe that these saints can be very much helpful in performing their difficult work. It is astonishing to note that in spite of the Prophet's disapproval of building tombs, great reverence is paid all over the sub-continent to such tombs.

These dargahs are treated as waqf and are governed by the rule relating to waqfs. The relevant case on the point is Syed *Shah Abdul Latif Mohideen Kadiri Sajjatha Shiba Hadulla Sahib* v *Muhammad Labai.*[100] In this case a great saint named Mohideen Jelani once pass through Tirenelveli district and performed penance at a place which later on came to be known as 'Mohideen Andavar Pallivasal.' A building was also built there. This building was identical to Hindu temple. The place was famous not only amongst Muslims, Christians and Hindus but also regard the place as sacred and pay visit through out the year. Many rites performed at that place were of Hindn character. The income of the endowment is spent on dailty cleaning, lighting, maulaudh, fatiha, incense burning annual Qanthuri and Moharram festival and Santhana Kudam and Annadhanan for Paradesis and faqirs. The endowment was also having income from droppings in the Santhana Kudam during festivals, hund collections, rentral from shops *etc.*

The place was described in the register as mosque and not dargah. There is also a *mehrab* and a place where regular prayers are held.

It was held that the institution was not a dargah and, therefore, the first defendant was not a Sajjadanashin. He was, however, more than a mutawalli and something less than a Sajjadanashin. He can be said to be swami and the mutawalli of the Pallivsal. In this case a distinction was made between a dargah and mosque. It was said by the Madras High Court that *mehrab* is an essential part of a mosque. However, it is not an essential part of a dargah. In a dargah no call is made for prayers. On the other hand, in the case of mosque there is a call for prayer (*Asan*). The term dargah may include the whole group of buildings of which the tomb is the nucleus.

There exists difference between a dargah on the one hand and a mosque or khanqah on the other hand. A mosque or khanqah may be established just adjacent to the dargah. The property may also be dedicated for their maintenance and upkeep. In such cases both a mujawar and a matawalli may be appointed for the proper administration of dargah and mosque etc. respectively.

Dargah of Khwaja Muinuddin Chishti, Ajmer

A group of Hanafi Muslims consider the Dargah Khwaja Muinuddin Hasan Chisty, Ajmer as a very high spiritual place. Thousands of visitors daily come to dargah for paying regard to Khwaja Sahib. They also give Nazars to dargah. In this way daily collection is made in the Dargah. For a very long time this amount was misappropriated by the Khadims. Looking to the state of affairs, the Government of India was constrained to pass two legislations, one in the year 1936 and the other in the year 1955. It is relevant here to mention an interim Act. The name of the Act was Dargah Khwaja Saheb, (Emergency Provisions) Act, XVII of 1950. This Act as well as the Act of 1936 were repealed by Act XXXVI of 1955.

Historical Background

It has been maintained that Khwaja Muinuddin Hasan Chisti was born in or about 536 A.H.[101] in Sijistan. After finishing his religious education he came to India and settled at Ajmer[102]. On the first of Rajab in 1236 A.D. Chisti, (anything between 93 and 97), retired into his cell and was found dead on the sixth day when it was opened. He was burried in the kachcha tomb and remained there until the 15th century, when the Khilji Sultan of Malwa made it pucca and built a dome over it. Akbar defeated the Malwas in 1563, and built the tomb and granted 18 villages for the Dargah.

Khwaja Syed Fakhruddin and Sheikh Mohammad Yadgar, were devoted followers. These followers looking after the grave of Khwaja Saheb. The descendants of Syed Fakhruddin are known as Syedzadas while those of Sheikh Mohammad Yadgar as Sheikhzadas. Later on they were known as Khadims. From the very beginning these Khadim were entitled to receive Nazars (offerings). Formerly, the offices of the dargah's mutawalli and sajjadanashin was one and the same. Tubsequently, this was separated. The Mutawalli was looking after the secular administration and managements of endowed properties. On the otherhand Sajjadanashin was required to see the spiritual and religious functions[103]. The Dargah is having properties which was given by Mughals and other emperors of India. The total annual income of dargah from various sources is approximately Rs. 10 lacs. The estimated annual total expenditure may come to Rs. 4 to 5 lacs.

Succession to Khwaja Muinuddin Chishti

The disputes over money were and are, and predictably will continue to be, for as fat a share as possible of the spoil of cold, ironically enough rooted in asceticism and austerity. The case presently before the Supreme Court was sequel to litigation dating back to May 1948. The Sajjadanashin seat fallen vacant because new 'dewan' Syed Alley Rasul Ali Khan had migrated to Pakistan in September 1947. In the meanwhile, the orginal plaintiff died. Two of the heirs, Bashiruddin and Abdul Aziz whom the country had ruled were closest in propinquity to the risen of primogeniture, died but before than may had given up their claims, due to their believing that he was too illiterate to run the spiritual affairs of the sect.

Presently, the Sajjadanashin or the dewan sahib is in his haveli by virtue of a stay obtained from the Supreme Court, after having lost his case in the Rajasthan Hige Court[104]. Strangely enough the right to succession being agitated in the court was for the jagir, first class of dilwara, Hokran and Krishna pura, a temporal entity which had disappeared many years ago following the merger of the former princely in the new union of India and in the wake of the implementation of anti zamindari laws.

It is all so anachronic, but so bitter and so fierce. And it is all so self-contradiction and anti podal to the teachings of Chisti. But it is all used and is likely to continue in future also. After the defeat of Malwas Akbar rebuilt the tomb and granted eithteen villages to the *dargah*. This was the new beginning of the predominance after temporal over the spiritual. Later on, Akbar issued a direction stating that the Khwaja had left no heirs and he appointed dewan of his own choice. However, this direction of the Akbar carried no force. There was no dearth of heirs. They claimed their right of succession to the dewani and all of them centred around the right of primogeniture in propinquity—a case more of propinquity than primogeniture. After Akbar, Jahangir gifted more villages to the dargah and separated the temporal and spiritual affairs, bifurcating the functions of the Sajjadanashin and the mutawalli. Then Aurangzeb, gifted land in Hyderabad. By 1637 A.D., the income of the dargah was Rs 25,780 per annum a very large sum of money then to be spent according to the royal decree.

Money began pouring in, and cupidity grew in direct proportion to the prosperity of the shrine. The troubeld history of Ajmer, in a way, led to exoduses and influxes and they all had a cumulative effect on the fortunes of the dargah's estate and finances.

The Arab gulf money has also added to the prosperity of the dargah. The revenue from money orders sent from devotees in far away places, undisclosed for perfectly understandable reasons, has gone up many fold.

The Administrative and Statutory Control of Dargah

In the year 1863 Religious Endowments Act was passed. Under section 7 of this Act a Dargah Committee was constituted.[105] There were five members in this Committee. Their term of office was for whole life. Out of the five members, four were beneficiaries and, therefore, no concrete results could be achieved. This Committee continued to function till 1936 when it was dissolved after passing of the Dargah Khwaja Saheb Act of 1936. This Act provided for the establishment of a new committee of 25 members. The committee consisted of local and outsider members. The outsider members were not able to protect the interest of the dargah. Then again out of local members, four were beneficiaries. The result was that this committee also failed to protect the interest of the dargah. The Government of India, therereof are decided to go through into the affairs of the dargah. The Committee of Enquiry was constituted in the year 1949. The Committee recommended that the administration of the Dargah should be entrusted to a committee of five Sunni Muslims. This committee should appoint a manager (*nazim*) who will look after the day today administration. The committee also recommended that no person having any beneficial interest in the dargah shall be appointed as member of the committee.

These recommendations of the Committee were incorporated in the Dargah Khwaja Saheb Act, 1955. This Act does not lay down any qualification for committee members. These members were appointed by the Central Government for a period of five years.[106] The power to appoint Nazim was retained by the Central Government.[107] There is a provision for the appointment of large number of members from outside of Ajmer. Of course, it is a good provision from the point of view of administration. However, proportion between local and outside members must be maintained. Neither the committee should consist of all local members, nor it should consist all members from outside members can not take such interest which the local members may take.

The Problem of Nazar

In the past there had been controversy whether the

Khadims, the Dargah Committee and the Sajjadanashins have the right to receive *nazar*. It was argued by the Khadims and Sajjadanashine that they were entitled to receive *nazar* on religious and historical grounds. The claim of the Dargah Committee was based on section 14 of the Dargah Khwaja Saheb Act, 1955.

From the very beginning these *khadims* and *sajjadas* were receiving *nazar*. There were number of farmans and sanads that testify to the right of the khadims to receive *nazar*. There were also cases of controversy between khadims regarding the distribution of *nazars*.[108]

There are also instances when the income from *nazar* was even diverted from the general charitable purposes to the exclusive use of the khadims.[109]

During British rule, khadims were taking *nazar* and this right of the khadims was never questioned by the Britishers. The law suits relating to nazars were decided by English judges according to the mutual agreement reached between the parties. In one case the Sajjadanashin received some *nazar* to the exclusion of khadims. They claimed a share on the basis of an agreement that all offerings to the shrine were divisible in equal shares between the khadins and the sajjadanshin.[110] This claim of the khadims was approved. The courts never questioned the right of the khadims to appropriate the nazar and that the courts were of the opinion that the nazars presented at the dargah was for the use of the khadims and others and they never called upon the donors to give evidence of their intention.

One dispute relating to the share of the *nazar* was always between the khadims and the sajjadnashin. The Dargah Committee was never the party of the suit. The reason for exclusion was that nazar was not considered as a part of dargah endowments. The right of the khadims to receive *nazar* continued to be recognised till the middle of the twentieth century. In *Syed Altaf Husain* v *Diwan Syed Ali* the Dargah Committee claimed to a share in the *nazar*. The Privy Council said that there is a distinction between those articles such as *qabarposhes* (presented for the use of the dargah), and the other offerings which are made at the dargah. The Privy

Council said offerings made to dargah may be shared between the diwan (*sajjadanashin*) and the khadims. However, the articles present for the specific use of the dargah are the property of the dargah and these should go to the committee.

The practice of taking presents by the khadims and Sajjadanshin could not be checked effectively. They tried to take as much nazar as possible. In 1949, therefore, the government of India appointed the Ghulam Hasan Enquiry Committee. This Committee said immediately on the arrival of a pilgrim at the railway station, Ajmer, he is met by a horde of *khadims*. The pilgrim will be put to sale and whoever makes the highest bid becomes his *vakil* (guide). These sale proceeds are distributed among the khadims. The khadim who becomes the *vakil* was anxious to make as much profit as he could out of the transaction and tries to extort by all means fair or foul, the last paise out of his victim.[112] The committee called these khadims as 'Parasites.' The committee recommended that the offerings be shared mutually between the *khadims* and *sajjadanashin*.

The following recommendations were made by the committee :

Nazars, whether cash or kind, made at the *dargah* either inside the tomb or at any other place within the precincts of the *dargah* without any right of coshareship in the *khadims* or in any other person. Nazars and contributions for specific charities shall be collected in a box to be kept by the manager under the orders of the high powers committee at appropriate places appointed by it and no person, wheter khadims or any other, shall ask or receive, any *nazar*, in cash or kind, from any visitor within the precincts of the dargah. Contravention of this rule shall be an offence rendering the offender liable to ejetment from the *dargah* premises, and a fine not exceeding Rs 200/-.

Most of the recommendations made above were included in the Dargah Khwaja Saheb Act, 1955. Section 14 of the Act provides that it shall be lawful for the *nazim* or any person authorised by him in this behalf to solicit and receive on behalf of the *dargah* any nazars or offerings from any person. It was further provided that no other person shall receive or be entitled to receive *nazars* or offerings on behalf of the *dargah*. This has been clarified through his by-law 18. The by-law says that if a donor has failed to mention the purpose to which the offerings was to be put, it will be presumed to have been made for the maintenance of the Dargah.[113]

The legality of section 14 of the Dargah Khwaja Saheb Act, 1955 was challenged by the Khadims on the ground that it infringed a judicially recognised customary right of the *khadims* to receive nazar and was, therefore, repugnant to Article 19 (1) of the Constitution. The Supreme Court rejected this argument of the khadims.[114] The Supreme Court said offerings or *nazars* which are paid to the *dargah* and as such received on behalf of the dargah constituted Dargah Endowment and section 14 authorises the *nazim* or his agent to receive such offerings and prohibit any other person from receiving them. This section does not violate khadims judicially recognised right to receive offerings. The Supreme Court further said that even after coming into force of this Act pilgrims might and would make offerings to the *khadims* and there is no provision in the Act which prevents them from accepting such offerings when made.

The Supreme Court followed the classification of *nazar* into two categories made by the Privy Council in *Syed Altaf Hussain* v *Diwan Syed Ali*.[115] It observed that the offerings which were intended for the use of the *dargah* were treated (by the Privy Council) as constituting a class of offerings apart from other offerings which were divisible between the *khadims* and the *sajjadanashin*. In this way khadims' right to receive offerings was indirectly recognised. Of course, a distinction has been made between the *nazar* exclusively given for the use of the dargah or for the use of the khadims. It is, however, not easy to make distinction between these two offerings. The donors come to the Dargah from all parts of the country and they do not generally know this distinction.

Formerly. there was no penal provision for violating the provisions of section 14 of the Dargah Khwaja Saheb Act, 1955. The result was that exploitation of visitors and pilgrims continued unabated and offerings meant for its allied institutions were openly taken by khadims within the premises of the

Dargah.[116] Accordingly, section 14 of the Act was suitably amended. This amendment came in to force on 1st June, 1964. This amendment provides that making unauthorised soliciting or receiving of nazars punishable with fine upto Rs 1000.00. The Act, however, does not prescribe any prosecution. The result of this amendment was that even after passing of this Act, not a single prosecution could be launched.[117] By law-17 authorises the *nazim* to prohibit any khadim from entering the dargah for a period of seven days, if such *khadims* on enquiry held by the *nazim*, is found guilty of violating of any provision of the Act. It is, however, not easy to exclude any khadim from entering into dargah. The result of this slackness on the part of Dargah Committee is that three fourths of the total income of Dargah is taken by the *khadims* and *sajjanashins*. It has, therefore, become necessary that sincere efforts should be made for enhancing the income of the dargah. It is, therefore, submitted that an honest and sincere person should be appointed as *nazim*

Preparation of food in the Cauldrons (*degs*)

As soon as a person enters in to the dargah premises from the main gate he will find two big *degs* (cauldrons) on the right and left side of the main gate of the dargah. It is said that these degs were gifted by Mughals. The food is cooked in these degs whenever some visitor to the dargah volunteers to pay the cost. After the preparation of the food, the same is looted in a very peculiar manner. The following commnects were made by the Enquiry Committee regarding the preparation and looting of the food :

> All the men who take part in the looting of the deg, are swathed upto the eyes in clothes to avoid the effect of the scalding mess. When the cauldron is nearly empty, the inderkotis (a local sect) tumble in together and scrape it clean.... This custom or practice has been condemned by all right thinking Muslims. The treading upon cooked food intended for human consumption is not only an impious act but is obnoxious to human instincts—the sooner this practice is abolished the better.

It was further observed by the Committee that khadims were taking from Rs 5000.00 to Rs 2000/- for big and the small deg respectively, as *nazrana* or present from the pilgrims and will not allow the deg to be cooked unless the amount is previously deposited. The committee recommended for cooking the *deg* into the *dargah* treasury and no other sum by way of nazrana or gift to the *khadims*. This shall be the duty of the nazim to prepare the food under his supervision. After the preparation of the food the same may be distributed to the beggars and other persons. The food will not be allowed to be sold at any cost.

It is estimated that approximately Rs 10,000/- (this includes money, jewellery and other sundry articles) are annually dropped in the empty degs. This amount is also taken by *khadims*. Unfortunately the committee of enquiry also failed to make any comment on this important issue. The Dargah Khwaja Saheb Act, 1955 is also silent on this point. It does not contain any provision rcgarding this income.

MODES OF CREATING A VALID WAQF

Testamentary Waqfs

Waqfs made during death illness are governed by rules relating to testamentary waqfs. A waqf created during death illness (*marzul-maut*) is regarded as testamentary waqf. The position will be same even if the delivery of possession was made to the mutawalli.[119] There is no difference between Ithna Ashari and Hanafii law on this point. A waqf made in *marznl-maut* or death illness is subject to the legal incidents of a testamentary waqf.[120] Ameer Ali[121] says that if a waqf be constituted at a time when the waqif is suffering from the death illness and there is a clear indication of an intention on his part to transfer possession, it will take effect with reference to the entirety of the dedication, provided the heirs consent either before on after the waqif, otherwise the waqf will operate only in respect of one third of the testator.[122] If the waqf property is covered by one third of the estate, then it is valid as regards entirety of the dedication. If not, each provision will be given effect to with regard to its priority until one third of the estate is exhausted. The Shia and Sunni laws on this point are one and the same. Where a Muslim has disposed of his property by way of waqf and later on died, the transaction will take effect as a bequest and operates only with respect to one third of the property. However, if the waqif has recovered from his illness the waqf shall be valid as to the entire property.

Waqif to be Free from all Liabilities

It is a well settled principle of Muslim law that a Muslim can make a waqf only if he is free from all liabilities. The waqif must arrange for the payment of their debts before they make a gift or create waqf.[122] A Muslim who has to re-pay loan cannot make a valid waqf. Tyabji[123] says that Mufti Abu Saeed was asked, 'whether it was valid for a man to dedicate his property for the benefit of his descendants and thus avoid payment of his liabilities. He replied that it was not valid or or binding and that Cadis are forbidden from enforcing and register such trusts so far as the liabilities extend. It is, therefore, the first duty to arrange for the payments of their debts before they make gift or create waqf.[124]

A waqif can not evade his creditors. A dedication cannot be validly made so as to defeat or delay the rights of creditors; and dedication having such effect may be avoided by any creditor whose rights are defeated or delayed. Where a decree has been passed by the competent court, a waqif is not at liberty to create a waqf before the court's attachment order of some of his properties could be executed.[125]

It is a rule now firmly established, said Justice Sulaiman, that under Muslim law no person can make a waqf of his entire property without making arrangement for the payment of his debts. The provisions of section 53[126] of the Transfer of Property Act, do not in any way infringe any rule of the substantive Muslim law.

It is notable that it cannot however be said that a waqf will be void merely because waqif has failed to make arrangement for the creditors. The question whether a transfer was made with intent to defeat or delay the creditors is a mixed question of law and fact, and the dedication must depend upon a consideration of the entire circumstance surrounding the execution of the deed of transfer.[127]

In Bibi Kubra's case a Shia Muslim was having property worth more than rupees lakh. He also indebted to an extent of Rs. 795.00. He created a waqf of certain of his properties valued at Rs. 15,000/- and sold rest of his properties for Rs. 1,06,000.00 without paying the debt. This transaction of the Shia Nawab was challenged on the ground that the Nawab was not having bonafide intention.

The Patna High Court held that under Shia law, a waqf will not be valid unless the waqif divests himself of the ownership of the property as also its usufruct. The court refused to accept the plea that the Nawab was solvent enough to pay his debts at the time that the deeds of waqf executed so that he could have had no intention to defraud his creditors by the execution of those deeds.

No need of any particular Formality

The law does not prescribe any formality for the validity of a waqf. It is also not necessary that the waqf must use any express phrase or term requisite for the constitution of a waqf. Law looks to the intention of the donor alone.[128] Where the waqif intended to create a waqf, in whatever language it may be expressed or in whatever terms the wish may be formulated. It may, however, be noted that mere intention to create a waqf is not enough. Where the dedicator was having merely intention and no declaration of waqf nor delivery of possession was made, it was said mere intention to set apart property for the benefit of mankind is not sufficient to create a waqf, even if the income of the property is in fact applied to the intended purpose.[129] On the other hand, when a waqf is created by a document and is completed by delivery of possession, the settler cannot say that he never intended to create a waqf.

Waqfs from exception to ordinary rule of Muslim law which requires gifts to be perfected by possession and undoubtedly applies to waqf among Shias.[130]

In a Pakistani case, the Dacca High Court maintained that a mere declaration by a waqif is sufficient to complete a valid waqf. The court further said that if the waqf was made in good faith and with a real intention on the part of the waqif of divesting herself of the ownership of the waqf properties, then any subsequent malfeasance or misfeasance on the part of a mutawalli cannot invalidate such a waqf.

In an appeal before Lahore High Court, their lordship said that there is no set formula for creating a waqf. Clear intention for creating a waqf, declaration of waqif to that effect and appointment of mutawalli are the only requitsies for a valid waqf.[1:2] If there was only intention to constitute a waqf and neither the declearation was made nor delivery of possession was made, it was held that there came into existence no waof.[133] If the document purporting to create a waqf is invalid subsequent conduct providing the intention to treat the property as waqf cannot render the endowment valid.[134]

When a waqf has been validly created by a docum:nt or otherwise it is not open to the settler or his descendants to assert that it was not intended to be acted upon. If a waqf has been created by a document which establishes by its terms a religious or charitable trust, and it is completed by delivery of possession, later on the waqif will have no right to say that he was not having any intention to make a waqf. However, the waqif will always have a right to say that in fact no waqf came into existence and that the deed was not intended to be presumed to operate as waqf. The deed was fictitious and illusory.[136]

Ordinarily, on the basis of the waqf deed the court will presume the existence of the waqf. After the creation of waqf the waqif cannot say that it had not been acted upon. The onus of providing the contrary is on the person alleging that the waqf was not meant to be acted upon.[136] The Judicial Committee of the Privy Council said that if a person has executed a dead of waqf but without any intention of divesting himself of his ownership of the property the real intention being to utilise the document should it become necessary as a shield against any claims that any other person might have against him either then or at any future time, the deed cannot be given effect as a waqf.[137] The intention is always admissible if the waqf was not created by a document.[138]

Under Shafei law delivery of possession is not necessary

for the validity of a waqf.[139] Shia law is strict on the delivery of possession for the validity of a waqf. Under Ithna Ashari law actual delivery of possession of the dedicated property by or under the direction of the waqif at the time of dedication is absolutely necessary.[140]

Where the waqif dedicated the property by a document, the settler or his descendants cannot challenge the validity of the waqf. In such cases, the law will presume that a genuine waqf was created by the waqif. In such cases the burden of proof will lie on the person who alleges that there was no genuine waqf. However, in one case Supreme Court held that the settler and those claiming under him are at liberty to show that no waqf had been created and that the deed was not intended to operate as a waqf but was illusory and fictitious.[141]

For the validity of the waqf it is not only necessary that a waqfnama should have been executed. It is also necessary that after the writing of the waqfnama, other necessary steps should have been taken. In one case, one 'W' executed and registered a waqfnama. The waqfnama provided that the waqif made an endowment of the village of para to the rextent of Rs. 90.00 a month net profits for the use of the poor and the needy, designating his sons as mutawallis. The deed was registered. However, the waqif never tried to do other formalities so that a complete waqf would have come into existence. The property was not transferred to the mutawalli. It was held that Imam Muhammad's opinion on the question when the waqf is complete, must be preferred to that of Abu Yusuf. The waqif never employed the income for the religious and charitable purpose. The court, therefore, held no waqf came into existence.[142]

It is a rule now firmly established that the intention of the waqif must be found by reading the statute as a whole. The courts strongly lean against a construction which reduces the waqf deed to a futility. Waqfs which are written should be construed within the framework of the waqf deed.[143] In a case the waqif signed the waqf deed but he never handed over the possession of the property to the mutawali, it was held no waqf came into existence. In law the mere intention of the waqif carries no force.[144] In *Muhammed Ali Muhammed* v

Mst Bismillah Begum[145] a deed of waqf was executed, but the waqif was having no intention of divesting himself of his ownership of the property. In fact, his intention was to utilise the document against the creditors so that they may not be able to realise the outstanding debt from him. The Judicial Committee of the Privy Council held that under the circumstances mentioned above no real waqf came into existence.

It is also relevant here to discuss a Hindu parallel case. One Padmalochun executed on July 24, 1877, deeds purporting to divest himself of property and dedicated it to trustees for worship of family idols. Padmalochun died about three and half years after the execution of the deed. During this no change in accounts *etc.* was made. Similarly, no change in the business *etc.* was made. Everything appeared to have gone on in the same manner as if the deed was never executed except that family idol was removed to Padmalochun's house. It was held that no trust came into existence at all. The deeds were held to be merely fictitious or *benami*.[146]

A waqf made with intent to defeat creditors was only voidable at the instance of creditors not by a waqif or his heirs[147] In the modern industrial age, the argument as to whether the opinion of Abu Yusuf or of Imam Muhammed ought to be adopted carries much force. There are considerations which modify the views of both exponent and, therefore, expositions are brought very near to convergence.

For the validity of a waqf mere declaration is not sufficient. In case he is genuinely interested in making a waqf, he should do all such acts which will constitute a valid waqf. There is no need to keep a waqf secret. If a secret waqf has been established, the waqif can befool the common man. The common man will be under the impression that the waqif is the owner of the property and he will, therefore, advance the money to the waqif.

Tyabji[148] says that the waqif must either act himself as the mutawalli or must permit someone else to do so. He further says that when the waqif provides for the own maintenance and support during his life time these consideration gather additional weight. Tyabji further says that all these consideration *i.e.* the anomaly of allowing waqf without making the delivery, *etc.* help to make the exposition of the law by Abu Yusuf far more rigid in actual operation than a mere verbal statement and literal interpretation of it would indicate.

Today the saying of Imam Muhammad also carries no force. At one place he says that a waqf will be complete only if the mutawalli was appointed by the waqif. But on the other hand, he allows the waqif to become first mutawalli. The latitude of Abu Yusuf's exposition is greatly restricted and the stringency of Imam Muhammad is greatly relaxed. While trying to resolve this problem Tyabji[149] has made the following statement—

> Dedication by way of waqf is completed when the waqif makes a declaration in good faith with a real intention of divesting himself of the ownership of the property which he intends to dedicate as if he nominates another person as mutawalli such intention is ordinarily evidenced by delivery of the waqf property to him as mutawalli. Failure so to deliver needs at least some explanation. Want of such intention may be inferred if there is no explanation ; (b) the fact that no person is nominated as mutawalli, does not necessarily show a want of such intention ; it may (in proper cases) be presumed that the waqif himself intended to act as mutawalli, but this last presumption may be rebutted by evidence that the waqif did not act as such, and neither himself gave, nor requested (or permitted) another to give, any effect to his declaration, or by evidence of similar circumstances, and the circumstances may warrant the inference that the declaration was not made in good faith and that the owner had no intention of divesting himself of the ownership of the property in which case no valid dedication will take place.

Customary Law

The formalities for the creation of waqfs are regulated by Muslim law, though in some institutions custom may modify or prescribe some additional formalities. In customary law sometimes for Hindus religious and charitable endowments the word waqf is used. In *Khawaja Mahmud* v *Khawaja Md*[150] the Punjab Chief Court held that no pariticular ceremonies and rites are required for the creation of an endowment, the clear declaration of an intention is enough.[151] In Md. Hameed's case the Privy Council maintained that dedication may be inferred from the sorrounding circumstances. It has been held that mere declaration of an intention or agreement to create an endowment is not sufficient.[152]

Where the building was used as *thakardwara* for a considerable long time, the properties in dispute have always been treated as appurtenant to the *thakardwara* the property have all along devolved from guru to chela, the public fairs were held on the ground attached to the *thakardwara*, the properties were all along used for the purpose of *thakardwara* and for no other purpose and the land in revenue records was described as *Ghair mumkin mandir*, it was held that property was waqf.[153]

Waqf may be created either Orally or in Writing

Muslim law prescribes no specific form in which a waqf may be created. It is not necessary that a waqf should be made in writing.[154] It is only necessary that there must be some sort of declaration, either oral[155] or in writing.[156] Appropriate words showing any intention to dedicate property by way of waqf are necessary. Use of the word waqf is neither essential nor necessary. A waqf *inter voves* is completed by a mere declaration of endowment by the owner.[157]

Creation of Waqf Expressly or Impliedly

A waqf may be created either expressly or impliedly.[158] Fatawai Kazi Khan says "if a man says, 'this land is mauqoofa for God perpetuity.' it will create a valid waqf." A waqf may be treated as valid even though there was no mention of perpetuity.

"And if a man were to say, that this land is dedicated, consecrated, not to be sold, inherited or given by gift, all these words would create a waqf according to Abu Yusuf," says Radd-ul-Mukhtar.[159]

The word Waqf need not be mentioned in the Waqfnama

Again, it is not necessary for the validity of a waqf that the term 'waqf,' should have been used in the waqfnama.[159] The dedication as waqf may be implied in the terms of the settlement. This has been accepted by several courts.[160] It may, however, be noted here that for the validity of a waqf it is necessary that any specific words or specific formula should be used. Though oral waqf is permitted yet when the terms of a waqf are reduced to writing, no evidence can be given to prove the terms except the documents itself or secondary evidence of its contents, when it is admissible.[161]

The Conduct of Waqif is Material

The validity of a waqf can also be ascertained by circumstances—the statement and conduct of the waqif made in respect of waqf. Similarly, the statement and conduct of the successors of the waqif and the method in which the property has been treated are some of the circumstances which may be taken into consideration while determining the validity of a waqf.[162]

In case the waqf was created verbally but later on it was created by writing, no evidence other than the written document can be given.[163] A waqf can be proved by showing immemorial user of the property as waqf. It is not necessary on the part of the waqf to prove the writing by which a waqf was created. The existence of waqf will be presumed by indirect evidence also.[164]

Waqif may appoint Himself as the first Mutawalli

The founder of the waqf *i.e.* waqif is at full liberty to appoint himself as the mutawalli of the waqf property. In such cases no delivery of possession is necessary. It is also not necessary that the property should be transferred from the name of the donor as owner into his name as mutawalli. An apparent transaction must be presumed to be real and the onus of proving the contrary is on the person alleging that the waqf was not intended to be acted upon.[165]

As already noted a waqf may be oral or in writing.[166] A waqf *inter voves* is completed by a mere declaration of endowment by the owner. A dedicator is at liberty to make a waqf either verbally or in writing. A waqf created orally is equally valid.[167] Again it is also not necessary for the validity of a waqf that the term waqf should have been used in the waqfnama.[168]

It is necessary that any specific words or specific formula

should be used. However, the language of the waqf deed should be clear and unambiguous from which an intention to create a waqf is discernible. The dedication for the waqf may be inferred from long user by way of waqf.[169] It is not necessary in order to consitiute a waqf that the term waqf should be used in the grant, if from the general nature of the grant such a dedication can be inferred.[170] Where it is not clear whether a grant constitutes a waqf, the statements and conduct of the grantor and his successors, and the method in which the property has been treated are circumstances which though not conclusive, should be taken into consideration.[171]

TESTAMENTARY WAQF

There is unanimity of opinion amongst different schools of Muslim law on the question of creation of waqf by way of gift and will. Under all schools of Muslim law a waqf may be created *inter vivos* or it may be created by way of will. Generally a waqf is created during the death illness of the dedicator. Both the schools of Sunni and Shia law recognises this kind of waqf. Where a waqf is created by a will it is only up to the *bequeathable* one third [172] unless the heirs consent to it.[173] In one Shia case it was said that waqif will not be valid unless and until the heirs have given their consent. It makes no difference that the waqif had already given the possession of the property.[174]

Tyabji[175] says that in Hanafi law the benefit (if any) assigned to an heir of the waqif under a testamentary waqf is divisible and all his heirs in proportion to their rights of inheritance, notwithstanding any provision to the contrary contained in the waqf unless (after the death of the waqif) the heirs whose rights are affected by the said provisions consent to their being given effect to.[176] The position is quite different under the Ithna Ashari Shiite law. Under Shia law bequeathable one third is valid even without the consent of other heirs. The Sharai-ul-Islam is silent on this point.

Formerly, it was said that testamentary waqfs cannot be created by Shias.[177] The judicial Committee of the Privy Council, however, refused to accept this observation of Justice Mahmood in the above case. The Privy Council said that a Shia Muslim can also create a testamentary waqf.[178]

REFERENCES

1. See *Sarwar Husain* v *Additional Civil Judge, AIR* 1983 All 252 ; *Rangal Shah and others* v *Maula Jadal,* PLD 1960 Karachi (WP) 312 (A Pakistani case).
2. See S. Ameer Ali, *Mahomedan Law,* (2nd ed), p. 304 ; see also *Adam Sheikh* v *Isa Sheikh,* (1894) 1 CWN 76 ; *Nanhoobeg* v *Ghoolam Hussain* AIR 1951 Nag 394.
3. Hedaya, p. 239.
4. Tyabji, *Muslim Law.* Sections 514 and 521 ; see also *Musahibkhan* v *Raj Kumar Bakshi,* AIR 1938 Oudh 238.
5. *Supra* note 2, p. 393 ; see also *Mohammad Wasi* v *Bachchan Singh, AIR* 1955 All 68. In this case the character and nature of mosque was discussed in detail.
6. *Fais Mohammad* v *Kanhiyalal,* (1964) ILR 14 Raj 1944.
7. *Yakoob Ali* v *Lachman Dass,* (1874) 6 NW 80 ; *Khalil Ahmed* v *Shaikh Mohammad, AIR* 1965 All 320. In this case it was said that before a building could be called a public mosque, the requisite essentials are, that (i) the building must have been set apart as a mosque ; (ii) public prayers must have been said n it at least once a day ; and (iii) there must have been long user of the same as a place of worship by the public at large.
8. *Supra,* note 2.
9. A person appointed for calling *Azan* and maintaining mosque.
10. *Saiyad Maher Hussein* v *Haji Ali Mohammad,* (1933) 36 BLR 526, 534.
11. *Hasan Shah* v *Mohidin Shah,* AIR 1923 Bom 42.
12. Bail II 220 (Part I).
13. Bail I, 606.
14. *Tafazzal Beg* v *Majidullah,* (1923) 5 Lah 59.
15. Bail 1, 557.
16. The following are the relevant cases on this point. *Queen Empress* v *Ramzan,* (1885) 7 All 761 (FB) ; *Ataullah* v *Azimullah,* (1889) 12 All 494 (FB) ; *Jangu* v *Ahmedullah,* (1889) 13 All 419 ; *Fazul Karim* v *Haji Mowla,* (1891) 18 I.A. 59 ; *Mohammad Waqf* v *Bachhan Singh, supra* note 5 ; *Akbarally Adamji* v *Peerbhoy* v *Mahomedally Adamji Peerbhos,* AIR 1932 Bom 365 ; *Haji Mohammad Sayeed* v *Abdul Ghafoor,* (1955) AIR All 688 ; *Maula Bux* v *Hafizuddin,* AIR 1926 Lah 372; *Sarwar Husain and others* v *Additional Civil Judge, supra* note 1.
17. *Id.*
18. *Supra* note 2, p. 400 ; see also *Jangu* v *Ahmadullah,* (1891) ILR 13 All 419 (FB).

19. *Ragal Shah* v *Waula Jadal, supra* note 1.
20. *Supra* note 16.
21. *Supra*, note 1.
22. *Iqbal Begum* v *Syed Begum,, AIR* 1933 Lah 80 ; (1933) 140 IC 820 *Ataullah* v *Azimullah, supra* note 16 ; *Maula Baksh* v *Amir-ud-din, supra* note 16; *Sarwar Hussain* v *Additional Civil Judge, supra* note 1.
23. *Haji Mohammad Sayeed* v *Abdul Ghafoor, supra* note 16 ; *Sarwar Hussain* v *Additional Civil Judge, supra* note 1 ; *Sifat Ali Khan* v *Ali Mian, AIR* 1933 All 284.
24. Id., see also *Majlis-e-Islami* v *Sheikh Mohammad Nagoor, AIR* 1963 Ker, 49.
25. *Majlis-e-Islami* v *Sheikh Mohammad Nagoor, AIR* 1963 Ker, 49.
26. *Amir Hussain Shah* v *Hafiz Ghulam Rasul, AIR* 1936 Pesh 65 ; (1936) 161 IC 652; see also *Haji Mohammad* v *Abdul Ghafoor, supra* note, 16.
27. *Hakim Khalid* v *Malik Israfii*, (1917) 2 Pat I.J 108.
28. *Sifat Ali Khan* v *Ali Mian, supra* note 24 ; see also *Sarwar Hussain* v *Additional Civil Judge, supra* note 1.
29. See *Maula Baksh* v *Amir-ud-diun, supra* note 16.
30. *Kuttayan* v *Wamanna Rauthan*,, (1912) 35 Mad 681.
31. *Supra* note 4, p. 612.
32. *Attahullah* v *Azimullah, supra* note 16.
33. *Fazl Karim* v *Maula Baksh, supra* note 16.
34. *Muhammad Ibrahim* v *Ghulam Ahmed*, (1864) 1 BHCR 236.
35. *Jangu* v *Ahmudullah, supra* note 16.
36. *Attahullah* v *Azimullah, supra* note 16 ; see also *Haji Abdul Razak* v *Haji Adam Haji*, (1935) 37 BLR 603 ; *Fakir Mohomed Nanji* v *Agha Khan, AIR* 1930 Sindh 504 *Adam Haji Omar* v *Collector of Poona*, (1938) XVI Bom L.J. 54 ; *Ladha Sanani* v *Hasan Ismail, AIR* 1949 Kutch 17.
37. *Abdul Baqi* v *Chitanya*, AIR 1917 All 328.
38. *Supra* note 3, p. 240.
39. see *Kuttnyan* v *Mamonna Ratuthan*, (1912) 38 Mad 681.
40. *Musahibkhan* v *Raj Kumar Bakshi*, supra note 4; *Mohammad Yusuf* v *Mohammad Saffi,, AIR* 1934 Vll 1013 ; *Kaniz Mehdi Begum* v *Mriza Rasul Beg, AIR* 1918 Oudh 379.
41. *Supra* note 35.
42. *Supra* note 7.

43. Maula Baksh Hafiz-ud-din, *AIR* 1926 Lah 372.
Masjid Shahidgunj v *Gurdwara Prabandhak Committee*, *AIR* 1940 PC 116 : 116 ILR (1940) Lah 493 : 67 IA 251.
45. (1958) Raj L.W. 461.
46. (1931) 57 Bom 551; see also *Mohammad Esuf* v *Moulvi Abdul Sathar*, (1918) 42 Mad 161.
47. *Supra* note 16.
48. *Wajid Ali* v *Dadunnissa*, *AIR* 1947 Cal 282.
49. *Shakul Hamid* v *Mohammad Hussain*, AIR 141 Mad 42.
50. *Masud Alam* v *Commissioner of Police*, (1955) 59 CWN 293.
51. *Punjab Waqf Board* v *Mohar Singh*, *AIR* 1975 SC 1891.
52. See *Mohammad Kazim* v *Ali Saghir*, 4 Lah 15,
53. *Vidya Varuthi* v *Balusami Ayyar*, (1921) 48 I.A. 302, 312; *Mohiddin* v *Sayiuddin*, (1893) 20 Cal 810.
54. *Hussain Shah* v *Gul Mohammad*, (1925) 6 Lah 140.
55. *Maula Shah* v *Gul Mohammad*, (1924) 6 Lah 140 ; *Chhatkao* v *Gambhi* (1931) 6 Luck 452.
56. *Walayan Shah* v *Sardera*, PLD 1952 Lah 249 : (1952) Lah 624.
57. PLD 1949 Lah 249.
58. *Mole Shah* v *Ganesh Shah AIR* 1938 PC 22 : *Saycd Hussain* v *Durgah Cammittee*, *AIR* 1959 Raj 177.
59. *AIR* 1973 Raj 57.
60. *Supra* note 53.
61. *Jani* v *Bishan Singh*, AIR 1935 Lah 698.
62. *Sain Maula Shah* v *Ghane Shah*, AIR 1938 PC 202 : *Mohd* v *Shah Shamsuddin*, AIR 1948 Cal 159 ; *Mohiuddin* v *Sayiduddin*, *supra* note 51.
63. See S. Athar Hussain *et al.*, *Waqf Law and Administration in India* 2nd ed. p 151.
64. See *Maule Shah* v *Ghane Shah*, *supra* 62.
65. *Haji Ali* Mohammad v *Anjuman-e-Islamia*, AIR 1931 Lah 379 : (1931) 12 Lah 590.
66. *Shafiq-ud-din* v *Mahbnb*, AIR 1930 Lah 714, 125 IC 893.
67. See *Mohammad Ghouse* v *Madras State Waqf Board*, AIR 1966 Mad 439.
68. *Ali Shaht* v *Fateh Mohammad Mutawal*, AIR 1937 Lah 657, (1935) 159 IC 537.
69. *Sardar Ali* v *Gehna Sahan*, (1938) 40 BLR 1071 (PC) ; *Chutko* v *Gambhi supra* note 54.
70. *Sardar Ali* v *Gehno Shoh*, AIR 1933 Lah 444, (1933) 142 IC 847.
71. See *Delroos Banoo* v *Kazee Abdoor Rahman*, (1875) 23 WR 453.
72. *Supra* note 38.
73. *Mst Mundana* v *Shyam Sunder*, AIR 1963 Pat 98.

74. *Hasan Shah* v *Mohiuddin Shah, supra* note 11 ; *Radir Bux* v *Sadadul* AIR 1938 Oudh 77.
75. *Motishah* v *Abdul Gaffar*, AIR 1956 Nag 38.
76. *Mohammad S. Lobbia* v *Mohammad Hajifa*, AIR 1976 SC 1569.
77. *Ramzan Momin* v *Dasrath Raut*, AIR 1953 Pat 138 ; see also *Ghulam Mohldin* v *Abdul Majid*, AIR 1957 A.P. 941 ; *Abdur Rahim Khan* v *Fakir Mohammad*, AIR 1946 Nag 401 ; *Jhaolal* v *Ahmcd Ullah*, AIR 1934 All 335.
78. *Ibid.*
79. *Ramzan* v *Dashrath, supra* note 75 ; *Ghulam Mohidin* v *Abdul Maji ibid* ; *Mohammad Kasam* v *Abdul Gafoor*, AIR 1964 M.P. 227.
80. *Panchayat Deh* v *Panjab Waqf Board*, AIR 1969 Pun 344.
81. *AIR* 1936 PC 83.
82. See *Moti Shah* v *Audul Ghaffar, supra* note 73 ; *Arun Singh* v *Badar Din*, AIR 1940 Lah 119.
83. See Fyzee, *Outlines of Muhammadan Law*, (3rd ed), London, 1964, p. 318, citing *supra* note 73.
84. *AIR* 1976 SC 1569.
85. *Ballabh Das Nur Mohammad, supra* note 781; *Imam Baksh* v *Narsingh* AIR 1938 Lah 246.
86. *Pir Bux* v *Sher Mohammad*, (1969) ALJ 169 ; *Dost Mohammad* v *Chainraj* AIR 1940 Sindh 43.
87. *Ehsan* v *Rahmat Ali*, AIR 1935 Oudh 47 : ILR 1935 Oudh 47 : 152 IC 798 ; See also *Ramzan* v *M. Ahmed*, AIR 1936 Oudh 207 : 165 IC 104.
88. *Abdul Gafoor* v *Rahmatali*, AIR 1939 Oudh 245.
89. *Supra* note 83.
90. *Bashir* v *Abdul Jabbar*, AIR 1968 Pat 29 : *Mohammad Kassim* v *Abdul Ghafoor*, AIR 1964 MP 227 ; *Abdul Rahimt* v *Fakir Mohammad*, AIR 1946.
91. (1901) 26 BLR 198.
92. (1922) 4 Lah 15.
93. (1923) 4 Lah 133.
94. *Maktumsab* v *Dadabhai*, (1934) 36 BLR 1098.
95. *Supra* note 4, p. 491.
96 *A. Zimuddin* V *Sirdar Ali*,AIR 1927 Bom 387.
97. *Ghulam Muhammad* v *Abdul Rashid*, (1933) 14 Lah 558 ; *Zoolekha Bibi* v *Syed Zanul Abedin*, (1904) 6 BIR 1056, 1067.

98. Some of the well-known dargahs of India are—Dargah of Janab Khawaja Moinuddin Chisti, Ajmer; Dargah of Hazrat Nizamuddin Aulia, Delhi; Dargah of Haji Waris Ali Shah, Dewa, Barabenki, Dargah of Syed Salar Masood Ghazi, Bahraich; Dargah of Shaikh Salim Chisty, Fatehpur Sikri; Dargah of Tajuddin, Nagpur; Dargah of Haji Ali.
99. *Mohammad Oosman* v *Essak Mahomed*,, (1988) Bom 189 ; *Dargah* v *Syed Hussain*, (1962) 1 SCR 383.
100 (1958) 2 MLJ 199.
101. 1411 A.D.
102. For life history of Khwaja Saheb, see K.N. Nizami, *Tarikh Mashaikh e-Chist*, Delhi, 1952, p 146 ; *Encyclopaedia of Islam*, (New-Edition) Vol II, pp. 49-50.
103. See report of the Dargah Khwaja Saheb (Ajmer) Committee of Enquiry, Government of India, (1949) pp. 28-34 ; *Dargah Cammittee* v *Syed Hussain Ali*, (1962) 1 SSR 383.
104. *AIR* 1981 Raj 29.
105. See the Report of the Dargah Khwaja Saheb Committee of Enquiry, p. 73.
106. See sections 5 and 6 (1) of the Dargah Khwaja Saheb Act, 1955.
107. See section 9 of the Dargah Khwaja Saheb Act, 1955.
108. See Abdul Bari Mani, Ajmer, Asnad-ul-Sanadid, p. 14. This book contains another example regarding the distribution of nazar between khadims. In one case the matter was referred to the Adalat-ul-Aliya (High Court) at Fatehpur Sikri. The Adalat directed that they will distribute the income of nazar at the dargah—amongst themselves in accordance with the old usage without fail and no one will act contrary to what has been written here in the main text. This agreement was reaffirmed by Jahangir by way of farman.
109. See *Ibid.*
110. See the report of the Dargah Khwaja Saheb. p. 73.
111. AIR 1938 PC 71.
112. See report of the Dargah Khwaja Saheb, p. 57.
113. See by-law 18, Dargah Khwaja Saheb by-laws, 1958.
114. See *Dargah Committee* v *Syed Hussain Ali*, (1962) 1 SCR 416.
115. *Syed Altaf Hussain* v *Diwan Syed Ali*, AIR 1938 PC 71.
116. See Administration Report of the Dargah Hazrat Khwaja Saheb, Ajmer. (1961-62), and (1962-63).
117. See Administration Report of the Dargah Hazrat Khwaja Saheb, Ajmer, 1 (1963-64).
118. See Report of the Dargah Khwaja Saheb, p. 98.
119. *Ahmed* v *Rahim Bibi*, 30 All 238.
120. *Bibi Jinjira Khatun* v *Mohammad Fakhrulla*, AIR 1922 Cal 429 ; (1921) 49 Cal 477, 484.

121. See *Ali Hussain* v *Fazal Hussian Khatun*, (1914) 36 All 431 ; see also *supra* note 2, p. 531.
122. *Harprasad* v *Mohammad Usman*, AIR 1943 All 2.
123. *Supra* note 4, p. 509.
124. *Supra* note 120.
125. *Mohammad Ali* v *Bismillah Begam*, (1930) 35 CWN 324.
126. Section 53 of the Transfer of Property Act is as follows—

(1) Every transfer of immovable property made with intent to defeat or delay the creditors of the transferor shall be voidable at the option of any creditor so defeated or delayed. Nothing in this sub-section shall impair the rights of a transferee in good faith and for consideration.

Nothing in this sub-section shall affect any law for the time being in force relating to insolvency.

A suit instituted by a creditor (which term includes a decree holder whether he has or has not applied for execution of his decree) to avoid a transfer on the ground that it has been made with intent to defeat or delay the creditors of the transferor shall be instituted on behalf of, or for the benefit of, all the creditors.

(2) Every transfer of immovable property made with consideration with intent to defraud a subsequent transferee shall be voidable at the option of such transferee.

For the purposes of this sub-section, no transfer made without consideration shall be deemed to have been made with intent to defraud by reason only that a subsequent transfer for consideration was made.

127. *Bibi Kubra* v *Jainandan Prasad*, AIR 1955 Pat 270.
128. *Jewan Dass* v *Kubeer-oo-deen*, 2 MIA 390.
129. *Banubi* v *Narsingh Rao*, (1907) 31 Bom 250.
130. *Banubi* v *Kallandar Ammal*, (no 2) (1926) 54 IA 23.
131. *Yunus Mian* v *Firoz Ahmed*, PLD 1952 Dacca 206.
132. *Anjuman Islamic Punjab* v *Mubarak Ali Khan*, PLD 1967 Lah 1221.
133. *Banubi* v *Narsingrao*, (1907) 31 Bom 250 ; *Zafa Hussain* v *Mohammad Ghaisuddin*, (1937) 18 Lah 276 ; *Rahima Bibi* v *S. Mustafa*, (1938) 178 IC 83.
134. *Mahomad Shafi* v *Khadim Ali*, AIR 1944 Oudh 291.
135. *Masuda Khatun* v *Muhammad*, (1932) 50 Cal 402 ; 133 IC 657. AIR 1932 Cal 93 : *Ebratennessa Bibi* v *Sarat Candra* (1934) 37 CWN 892 ; *AIR* 1934 Cal 14.
136. *Gobind Chandra* v *Abdul Majid*, AIR 1944 Cal 163.
137. *Mohammad Ali* v *Mts Bismih Begum*, AIR 1930 PC 255 : (1930) 35 CWN 324 : 128 IC 647 : *Beli Ram Mohammad Afzal*, AIR 1948 PC 168.

138. *Muhammad Imdad* v *Mst Bismillah, AIR* 1946 All 468 : (1947) 227 IC 50.
139. *Pathu Kutti Umma* v *Nedungdi Bank Ltd.*, AIR 1937 Mad 731: 173 IC 699.
140. *P.G. Venkataswomy* v *Mir Zahid Hussain*, AIR 1973 Mys 148.
141. *Garib Das* v *Munshi Abdul Hamid*, AIR 1970 SC 1035.
142. *Muhammad Azizuddin Ahmad* v *Leg Ram*, (1893) 15 All 321.
143. *Sheikh Muhammad Ibrahim* v *Bibi Mariam*, (1928) 8 Pat 484.
144. *Zoolekha Bibi* v *Syed Zainul Abedin*, (1904) 6 BLR 1058, 1067.
145. *Mu* (1930) 35 *CWN* 325, 332 (PC).
146. *Watson and Co.* v *Ramchund Dutt*, 18 Cal 10.
147. *Zafrul Hasan* v *Farid-ud-din* AIR 1946 All 177, 47 Bom TR 239: see also *Syed Ali Zamin* v *Syed Akbar Ali Khan*, (1937) 64 IA 174.
148. *Supra* note 4, p. 517-18.
149. *Ibid.*,
150. 23 PR 1917.
151. See *Md. Hammeed* v *Mian Mahmud* (1922) 4 Lah 15.
152. *Ram Lal* v *Khushi Ram*, AIR 1949 EP 233.
153. *Lachhman Dass* v *Arya Pritinidi Sabha*, AIR 1932 Lah 603.
154. *Haji Nyee* v *V.U. Nagwe Zin*, AIR 1937 Rang 524 ; *Mohammad Abdul Aziz* v *Mahbub Singh*. AIR 1936 All 202.
155. *Rahim Baksh* v *Chamman Din*, AIR 1921 Lah 390 ; *Daw Ein* v *Daw Chan Tha*, AIR 1939 Rang 365.
156. *Mustafa* v *Amina Begum*, 2 ALJ 519 ; *Fakhruddin* v *Kifayat Ullah* (1910) 7 AAJ 1095 ; *Maryam Baj* v *Mohammad Jaffer Abdur Kahiman Sait*, AIR 1943 Mad 191 ; the other cases on the point are AIR 1945 Lah 554; AIR 1932 Pat 33 ; AIR 1943 Sindh 134 ; AIR 1937 Mad 73 ; AIR 1927 Oudh 113 ; AIR 1936 OWN 165.
157. *Haji Abdul Razak* v *Ali Baksh*, AIR 1945 Lah 554 ; *Mst Khorsheed Jehan* v *Kadim Ali*, AIR 1947 Oudh 17.
158. S. Athar Hussain *Waqf Laws and Administration in India* p. 115.
159. *Syed Ahmad* v *Jahaiha Bibi*, AIR 1947 Mad 480; see also *Mohammad Shafi* v *Khadim Ali supra* note 134 ; *Mohammad Hamid* v *Mian Mohammad*, (1922) 50 I.A. 92 ; *Wazir Khan* v *Hussain* 1929 Oudh 65 ; *Ramnandan* v *Vada Levvai*, 40 Mad 116 ; *Mir Mardan* v *Zari-Khan*, AIR 1926 Nag 337.
160. *Saliquntssa* v *Moti Ahmed*, (1903) 25 All 418 ; *Hamid* v *Mian Mahmood*, AIR 1922 PC 384; *Ram Rupe* v *Saran*, AIR 1936 Lal 283 ; *Khurshid* v *Qayyum*, AIR 1947 Oudh 17.
161. *Sheikh Mohammad* v *Bibi Mariam*, AIR 1929 Pat 410.
162. *Anjumon Islamia* v *Latafat Ali*, AIR 1950 All 109 ; *Mosten* v *Commissioner of Income Tax*, AIR 1955 NOC 3639 (Ass); *M. Raza* v *Yadgar*, AIR 1924 PC 109.

163. *Shaikh Mohammad* v *Bibi Mariam*, AIR 1929 Pat 410 ; (1929) ILR 8 Pat 484.
164. *Chief Administrator of Waqf* v *Rashi-ud-daula*, PLD 1961 (WP) Lah 993.
165. AIR 1970 SC 1035.
166. *Maryam Bai* v *Mohammad Jaffar*, AIR 1927 PC 985 ; AIR 1973 Mad 191; AIR 1945 Lah 554; AIR 1932 Pat 33; VIZ 1943 Sindh 134; AIR 1937 Mad 73; AIR 1927 Oudh 113; AIR 1936 OWN 165.
167. *Ali Mohammad* v *Mohammad Nasir*, (1929) 27 ALJ 517.
168. *Syed Ahmad* v *Julaiha Bibi*, (1947) Mad 480; see also Mohammad *Shafi* v *Khadim Ali*, *supra* note 134.
169. *Ballabh Das* v *Nur Mohammad*, AIR 1936 P C 837.
170. *Supra* note 128.
171. *Mohammad Raza* v *Yadgar*, (1924) 51 IA 192 : LIZ 51 Cal 446.
172. *Ghulam Mohammad* v *Ghulam Hussain*, (1931) 59 IA 74, 85 (All).
173. *Baboojan* v *Mohammad Noorul Haq*, (1868) 10 WR 375.
174. *Ali Hussain* v *Fazal Hussain Khan*, (1914) 36 All 43; see also *Nanhoo Beg* v *Ghulam Hussain*, AIR 1951 Nag 327.
175. *Supra* note, pp. 504-505.
176. Bail I. 601 (612), 602.
177. *Aga Ali Khan* v *Altaf Hussain Khan*, (1892) 14 All 429.
178. *Baqar Ali Khan* v *Anjuman Ara Begum*, (1902) 25 All 236 (PC).

5

A Socio-Legal Study of Family Waqfs in India

Historical background and development

A waqf can be of the following two kinds :—

(i) Public waqf—Where the waqf is one for the public purpose religious or charitable ; and
(ii) Private waqf—Waqf for the benefit (Waqf-al-al-aulad) of the settler's family and his descendants.

According to Ameer Ali, a Muslim can make a waqf for one's descendants. He says that so in the Wajiz-ul-Muhit. According to Abu Yusuf no such conditions (as are required by Abu Hanifa or Mohammad), are necessary ; so that if a person makes a waqf for himself, or for the mothers of his children (i.e. slaves who have borne him children), or for his own children, or makes a waqf of musha, it is lawful. This rule propunded by Abu Yusuf was followed in *Doe dem Juan Beebee* v *Abdollah Barber*[1].

The Shiahs and the Shafeis differ from the Hanafis on one point. According to the recognised and accepted Hanafi doctrine, the waqif may reserve the entire produce of the waqf property for his benefit during his life time—may in fact constitute himself the primary beneficiary of the trust. According to the Shias and Shafeis, the waqif can, if he is the mutawalli, receive the allowance reserved for the trustee. Imam Mohammad agrees with the Shias and Shafeis in holding that the waqif can not reserve for himself the entire produce of the waqf during his life time.

At the Muslim law this institution is given the same status as is given to public waqfs. The family waqfs are primarily based on Ijma, though traditions of the Prophet Muhammad are also cited in their favour. According to S. Murtaza Fazal Ali,[2] Judge of the Supreme Court of India, the Mahomedan law recognises the existence of a private trust which is also of a charitable nature and which is generally called waqf-al-aulad, where the ultimate benefit is reserved to God but the property vests in the beneficiaries and the income from the property is used for the maintenance and support of the family of the founder and his descendants. In case the family becomes extinct then the waqf becomes a public waqf, the property vested in God. A public waqf under the Mahomedan law is called waqf-*fi-sabi-lil-lah*.

Under the traditional Muslim law a waqf can be created exclusively for the benefit of the waqif's family. It is not necessary for the validity of the family waqf that it must have been pious, religious or charitable.

According to Islamic tradition, the Prophet of God declared that a pious offering to one's family (to provide against their falling into want) is more pious that giving alms to beggars. The most excellant of sadaqah is that which a man bestows upon his family.

The provision in the waqf for the maintenance of the family and relations of the waqif was itself considered to be a pious and charitable object under the Hanafi school of law, the waqif, the settler himself, can participate in the benefit accruing from the waqf. Therefore, as far as the Muslim law is concerned, there was absolutely nothing against a waqf being created exclusively for the benefit of the waqif, the members of his family and descendants because that itself was considered to be a pious and charitable act under Muslim law.[3]

According to another tradition of Prophet 'when a Muslim bestows on his family and kindred, hoping for reward in the next world, it become alms, although he has not given to the poor, but to his family and children'.

It is clear from the above traditions of Prophet Muhammad that a Muslim could lawfully create a waqf exclusively for the benefit of his family. In India this opinion of Muslim jurists continued till the introduction of English law. Unfortunately, the English notions of what constitutes charity had considerably influenced the decision of the Judicial Committee of the Privy Council in dealing with waqfs created by Muslims. The Judicial Committee of the Privy Council in its decision in *Abdul Fata Mahommed Ishak* v *Russnoy Rasamaya Dhur Chowdhri*[4] held that such a waqf can not be valid.

The English judges who were required to interpret and administer Muslim law and who were not having sound knowledge of this law held that there can be no waqf without charity. Before the passing of the Mussalman Waqf Validating Act, 1913, it was judicially held that family waqfs or waqfs-alal-aulad were not recognised by Muslim law. It was argued that family waqf is in fact not a waqf at all.

Since 1894 the Privy Council has regarded it as a concealed means for the aggrandisement of a family, which not only infringes upon the sacred rule against perpetuity, but in which the provision for charity is so illusory that the poor are not entitled to receive rupee till after the total extinction of a family ; possibly not for hundreds of years ; possibly not until the property had vanished away under the wasting agencies of litigation or malfeasance or misfortune.[5] This decision of the Privy Council was criticised mainly on the following grounds :—

(i) that it prevents the alienation, economic exploitation, and improvement of the waqf property ;

(ii) that the descendants of waqif are apt to multiply with the passage of time, with the result that after some generations, the income would have to be distributed in ever diminishing shares among scores of beneficiaries;[6]

(iii) that charitable aid often keeps people away from industry and lethargy breeds degeneration.[7]

It was, therefore, said by Fyzee that it is unfortunate that the opinion of Lord Hobhouse in Abdul Fata's case did not prevail in India.

Efforts of Sir Syed Ahmed Khan

Sir Syed Ahmad Khan was the member of the Legislative Council. In 1879 he prepared a bill which was known as Maswada Qanoon Waqf Khandane Ahle Islam. The main intention of Sir Syed was to establish the institution of family waqfs for the purpose of maintaining big estates among the Muslims and to avoid uneconomic fragmentation of property under the laws of inheritance. He proposed the following conditions for the applicability of the Act :—

(i) that the waqif must be a Muslim and resident of British India. He may belong to any particular sect ;

(ii) that the waqif should be the absolute owner of the property proposed to be given in waqf. There should be an entry in the revenue records to this effects ;

(iii) that the property should consist of one or more villages, fetching an annual income of at least Rs. 10,000.00 ;

(iv) that the property shall be free from any encumbrance ; and

(v) that there should be no dues of land revenue against the property.[8]

The Bill, however, could not get success. It was approved by Muslim intelligentsia of the country. The Advocates of family waqfs supported this institution on the following grounds :—

(a) that family waqf helps many families to survive the vicissitudes of fortune and its dissolution could have a serious impact upon real estate, resulting in grave financial difficulties and complication[9] ;

(b) that the concept of charity in Islam is very wide and includes the act of giving property to one's own descendant, also ; and

(c) that the family waqfs were expressly approved by the holy Prophet and was followed by his devotees,

In *Abdul Ganee Kassim* v *Hussian Miya*[10] it was said that to constitute a valid waqf there must be a dedication of property solely to the ownership of God or to religious or to charitable purposes. If a waqf does not fulfil this condition, the waqf was not held to be valid. It was said that a waqf for a family settlement creates a perpetuity of the worst description, for it prevents the alienation of the house forever, and necessitates its use in a manner which the natural increase in the number of descendants would probably render impossible, even if they should be willing (which could hardly be expected) to live amicably under one roof throughout all generations. The absurdity of the settlement is sufficiently shown by the circumstances that even during the life time of the executing parties, family quarrels arose which rendered it impossible for them to continue to live together. The rule discussed above was overruled in *Luehmiput* v *Amir Alam.*[11] It was help in this case that a private waqf may be made subject to certain limitations.

Kinds of Waqfs before the passing of Mussalman Waqf Validating Act, 1913

Before the decision of the Privy Council in Abdul Fata's case, the following two kinds of waqfs were prevalent in India :—

(i) Waqf created exclusively for the benefit of the settler, his children, descendants and kindred in perpetuity. Muslim law never recognised such waqfs as valid. For instance, where under the waqfnama a settler settles property for the benefit of his wife, daughter and descendants of the daughter. In *Abdul Gaffar* v *Nizamuddin*[12] it was said that since in such waqfs no benefit is given to charity, the waqf shall be void. Even after passing of the Mussalman Waqf Validating Act, 1913, such type of waqfs are not recognised.

(ii) A waqf for the benefit of the settler, his children and descendants as well as for charity. This type of waqfs can be divided into two categories—(a) a waqf where there is substantial dedication of property for charitable purposes at some period of time or other, however, remote it may be. Before the passing of the Mussalman

> Waqf Act, 1913, such waqfs were held as valid. If there was no substantial dedication of property for charitable purposes, such a waqf will not be treated as valid. In *Mahommed Ahsanullah* v *Amarchand Kundu*[13] a waqf was created with the condition that every small income of the waqf property should be used for religious and charitable purpose and that the most of the income should be used for the welfare of settler's family and his descendants. The court held that the main purpose of the settlement was the aggrandisement of the settler's family, and the gift to charity was illusory.

In *Fazlur Rahim* v *Mahommad Obedul*[14] the creation of waqf was held to be invalid. In this case the waqf was having annual income of Rs. 1,558.00. Out of this income Rs. 146.00 were to be applied for religious and charitable purposes, and the rest should be utilised by settler's descendants. The waqf was held invalid.

Till 1899, it was generally believed that a waqf was valid if it was established for the benefit of the settler's family children and descendants and for charity if there was a substantive dedication of the property to charitable uses at some period of time or other. In the year 1894, the Judicial Committee of the Privy Council gave a judgment on the law of family waqfs.[15] This decision of the Privy Council changed all the previous decisions. The facts of this case were as follows.

Two Muslim brothers executed a deed purporting to make a waqf of their immovable property for the benefit of their children and their descendants from generation to generation, and on total failure of this descendants, for the benefit of widows, orphans, beggars and the poor. They themselves appointed first mutawallis of waqf. The trial court held that the waqf was valid. On appeal, the High Court reversed the decision. In appeal, the Privy Council, upheld the decision of the High Courts. Their Lordships of the Privy Council held that the gift to charity was illusory, and that the sole object of the settler was to create a family settlement in perpetuity, and that the provision for the settler's family was therefore, invalid. Their Lordship said :—

> As regards precepts, which are held up as the fundamental principles of Mahomedan law, their lordships are not forgetting how far law and religion are mixed up together in the Mahomedan communities, but they asked during the argument how it comes about that by the general law of Islam, at least as known in India, simple gifts (hiba) by a private person to remote unborn generations of descendants successions that is of inalienable life interests, are for bidden ; and whether it is to be taken that the very same dispositions, which are illegal when made by ordinary words of gifts, become legal if only the settler says that they are made as waqf in the name of God, or for the sake of the poor. To those questions no answer was given or attempted nor can their Lordships see any.

In this way the dissenting opinion of Justice Ameer Ali in Bikani Mias's[16] case upholding the validity of such waqfs was brushed aside on the ground that it was based 'upon texts of an abstract, character and upon precedents very imperfectly, stated' was overruled.

In *Phul Chand* v *Akbar Yar Khan*[17] a Muslim dedicated certain properties in waqf. The average annual income of the dedicated property was Rs. 850.00 for the purpose of performing *fateha* and *kadam sharif* ceremonies. Rupees 500.00 were approximately used for religious purposes. The Allahabad High Court declared the waqf as valid.

In *Rukayya Banu* v *Nazira Banu*[18] the settler constituted a waqf and the same was having an income of Rs. 10,000.00 annually. Out of Rs. 10,000.00, Rs. 456.00 were applied to charity and the rest to go to settler's descendants. The waqf was held as invalid.

In *Mutu Ramnanandan* v *Vava Levvai* two Muslim brothers executed a deed under which they conveyed the land approximately of Rs. 20,000/- in trust. A provision for the *fateha* for ancestors and to alms giving was made. The rest of the amount was required to be utilised for the benefit of the settler's sons and their descendants without power of alienation. The court estimated Rs. 600.00 per annum for *fateha* and alms giving. The total income of the trust estate was estimated at Rs. 1500.00 leaving a balance of Rs. 900.00 for the benefit of the settler's descendants. The Privy Council held that though two fifths of the income was to be devoted to the charity, and three fifths was to go to the family, the effect of the deed was to give the property in substance to charitable uses, and that the deed was, therefore, valid.

In one case a waqf was created for the benefit of his wife, daughter, and descendants of the daughter. There was no provision in the waqfnama for the application of the income in the event of the family becoming extinct. It was held that the waqf was not a valid waqf. This case was also decided before the passing of the Mussalman Waqf Validating Act, 1913. Now under the Act, this kind of waqf can be validly created[19]. The moment waqf deed is executed the descendants of the settler become's entitled to share the waqf property. The heirs of the beneficiary cannot be deprived of the shares belonging to him[20].

The Shariat Act was passed in the year 1937. Section 2 of the Shariat Act specifically says that the principles of Muslim law will be applicable in the case of waqfs also. Before the passing of the Shariat Act, 1937, matters relating to waqfs were decided on the basis of justice, equity and good conscience. Now any question in respect of waqf *etc* should be decided on the basis of Muslim law. There is nothing in the Shariat Act to affect the Privy Council decisions previous to the Musslaman Waqf Validating Act, 1913, as they expressly interpret what was held to be the Muslim law on the subject of waqf[21].

The decision of the Privy Council in Abdul Fata's case caused great dissatisfaction in the Muslim community. There arose a movement for introducing appropriate legislation in the matter so that the provisions of Muslim law should be restored and Muslims should be allowed to make waqfs for their families. Muslims protested by way of writings[22] petitions,[23] resolutions,[24] momorials, quarrels in the Legislative Council[25] and learned opinion[26].

It may, however, be noted that persons who agaitated for state interference and legislative measure were so much enamoured of Muslim personal law. Who were the men behind this agitation ? Were they all really fighting for a Muslim cause as they pretended ? Really, among the men behind the move many were the men of money who never wanted self-denial but self-aggrandisement and that they wanted really was accumulation of capital, avoidance of Muslim law of inheritance and validity of a testamentary succession couched in the language of a waqf. It was argued that the decisions were encroachment on personal law of the Muslims.

The agitation launched by Muslims was so strong that the government allowed a private bill to be introduced into the Legislative Assembly. The private bill was introduced by Mohammad Ali Jinnah. He was supported by such men as The Hon'ble Mr. Faizulbhoy Currimbhoy (son of Sir Currimbhoy Ebrahim, the Baronet of Bombay), Hon'ble Malik Umar Hayat Khan, Sir Abdul Karim Ghaznavi and others. It was contended by those who took the plea that Privy Council decision was an interference in personal law of the Muslims, boldly asserted that there is no reason why the interference of the Government of India should not be sought.

In the Legislative Council, Sir Ali Imam gave full support to the waqf bill introduced by Mr. Jinnah. In the Legislative Council[27] he argued :—

> 'I am of the opinion that sanction should be given to introduce the Bill. Mohammadan feeling is very strong on the subject. The Privy Council ruling is known to have taken an erroneous view of the Mohammadan Law of Waqfs. To ask the Mohammadans to go again to the Judicial Committee of the Privy Council to enunciate the correct law this time is to hope against hope. That committee pride itself on never having reversed its decision. I venture to think Mohammadan non-official members of the Legislative Council will support Mr. Jinnah to a man. I have grave apprehension that withholding sanction to introduce the Bill will cause much dissatisfaction among the Mohammadans.

It may, however, be noted that the bill was not supported by all Muslims. There were Muslims who though differed with the Privy Council view opposed legislative interference. It was argued that interference of the government of India on a question of personal law was not desirable. They preferred review by Privy Council instead of government action. It was also argued that the bill had the inherent danger that waqf might be created under the Bill which may favour particular members of the family. Justice Ameer Ali was of the opinion that the Privy Council should again be moved for making certain reservations. He thought that Privy Council decision could be changed, but the men of money were not satisfied at all. They wanted accumulation of money. They made agitation as if Privy Council decision was responsible for the disruption and ruin of the many Mussalman families.

Mr. Vijay Raghavacharia also supported the Bill. He denied as 'absolute fiction' the claim that the proposed law was waqf according to Mohammadan law and said it is immaterial for me whether it is Mohammadan law or a new law altogether' and expressed his sympathy with the feeling of advanced party of our Mussalman friend that they should have a law of primogeniture and paid compliments to Messrs Jinnah and Co. for their shrewdness and ability in shaping their religion according to necessity.[28] The remarks of late Vijay Raghavacharya are not wholly correct. It is true that they tend to create primogeniture. However, it is wrong to say that a family waqf (waqf-al-aulad) is wholly absolutely fiction. It cannot be denied that waqf-al-aulad in some or other has been prevalent since the time of the Prophet Mohammad himself.[29] The waqfs were not made with an intention to deprive somebody entitled to inheritance. They were mainly created to tie up the property for beneficial use of oneself or dependants or a particular dependant or for putting particular property for the use of particular person.

A uslim is not legally allowed to dispose of more than one third of his property by way of will. There may also be circumstances where it may be necessary to provide for such close relation who are not heirs or successors in law for example, widow or children of a predeceased son or of a predeceased brother or a disabled relation not entitled to inheritance *etc.* In such cases the creation of family waqfs can be of very much use. It cannot, however, be denied that family waqfs are generally created for family aggrandisement and depriving some legal heirs or others.

The Waqf Validity Act, 1913 was passed more than eight decades back and the main aim of the passing of this Act was to save Muslim families from ruination. The experience of the working of this Act shows that it was mainly used to deprive the daughters or some other legal heirs of a deceased Muslim, who were entitled to receive shares under Mohammadan law.[30]

The main object of this piece of legislation was to remove the barriers which were imposed by the Privy Council in Abdul Fata's case so that Muslims should have the right to make a family waqf. However, this Act was not retrospective. The Act did not apply to waqfs created before the passing of the Act. The legislature, therefore, passed another enactment in the year 1930. This Act gave a retrospective effect to the Waqf Act of 1913. The result is that the Waqf Act of 1913, applies also to waqfs created before the Act. The Waqf Act of 1913, restored the law of the Shariat in India and to overrule the law as laid down by the Privy Council. The effect of this Act is that howsoever illusory the waqf for charity may be, ultimate benefit is given to charity, the waqf is valid. Before the passing of the Mussalman Waqf Validating Act, 1913, it was thought that the gift to the poor should not be too remote nor it should depend on the total extinction of all the descednats of the settler.

The Act of 1913, contains an usual interpretation clause which *inter alia* defines waqf. This definition of the word 'waqf' is only for the purpose of this Act. It is not a general definition. Section 2 of the Act says that waqf means the permanent dedication by a person professing the Mussalman faith of any property for any purpose recognised by the Muslim as religious, pious or charitable.

Power of dedicator to create a Waqf and make Reservation for Himself

The Hanafi school of Muslim law says that a person who has dedicated his property in waqf will have the right to make a provision in the waqfdeed that during his life time he will be having the right to take out the income of the waqf for his maintenance.

Section 3 of the Mussalman Waqf Validating Act, 1913, says that it shall be lawful for any person professing the Mussalman faith to create a waqf which in all other respects is in accordance with the provisions of Mussalman law, for the following among other purposes :

(a) for the maintenance and support wholly or partially of his family, children or descendants, and

(b) where the person creating waqf is a Hanafi Mussalman, also for his own maintenance and support during his life time, or for the payment of his debts out of the rents and profits of the property dedicated.

Before the passing of the Act of 1913, the power of the dedicator to make provision for himself was not settled. The Act of 1913, recognised this right. Even after passing of this Act the matter was not settled. This point will become more clear from the discussion of the following cases. In *Ma E Khin* v *Maung Sein*[31] it was said that a Hanafi Muslim may reserve even the whole income for himself for his life. Here the liberality of Hanafi school does not end. The school has given more powers to the waqf. A Hanfi waqif can even make a provision that his debts be satisfied out of the income of the waqf property. A similar view was taken by Allahabad High Court in *Khalil-ud-din* v *Shri Ram*[32]. In this case it was held that under the Hanafi law, the waqif may provide for the payment of his debts out of the income of the waqf property.

Shia law is quite different from Hanafi law. The Shia law does not permit a Muslim to make a waqf for his own benefit. A waqf created by a Shia Muslim will not be valid unless the settler divests himself of the ownership of the property and of everything in the nature of usufruct from the moment the waqf is created. A waqif has no right to reserve for himself a life interest in the income or any portion thereof[33].

In *Hamid Ali* v *Mujawar Hussain*[34] the Allahabad High Court said that if the settler reserves the whole income for himself, the waqf is wholly void. In case he had made reservations of a portion of the income *e.g.* one third, the waqf is void as to one third only of the corpus, but valid as to the remaining two thirds. However, in *Abadi Begum* v *Kaniz Zainab*[35] the Privy Council took a different view. The Privy Council said that such a waqf will be completely void. Their Lordship of the Privy Council approved the following four conditions for the validity of a waqf :

(a) it must be perpetual;
(b) it must be absolute and unconditional;
(c) the possession must be given to the mowkoof (beneficiary) and
(d) the property must be taken entirely out of the waqif or appropriator.

The rule of Shia school mentioned above is not absolute. There is one exception to this general rule. A waqif, under Shia school, can make a waqf for the maintenance of his family, children, and dependants.[36] A Shia Muslim may provide for the expenses of fast (roza), prayer (namaz), pilgrimage (Haj), Ziarat[37] *etc.*

A waqif may also reserve a life interest for a beneficiary in the usufruct of a property if the intention that the property should become waqf on the settler's death is clear.[38] In *Muhammad Ahsan* v *Umardaras* [39] the Allahabad High Court said that a provision that the endowment shall not take effect till the death of the settler's wife was valid. The opinion of Allahabad High Court could not stand for a longer time. In *Mst Ali Begum* v *Badrul Islam Ali Khan*[40] the Privy Council held giving of direction that certain property should become waqf after the death of a person surviving the testator was invalid. A Shia Muslim can validly make a provision for the payment of personal debts of the settler. However, he can make a valid waqf of property which is subject to a mortgage.

In one case the settler divested himself of all interest in the property. He himself appointed the mutawalli with uncontrolled powers of management.[41] The Privy Council said whether the waqif had divested himself is a question of construction of the waqfnama. This question should not be confused with the question whether there has been a transfer of possession or change in the character of his new possession.

In *Jinjira Khatoon* v *Mohammad*[42] a Hanafi Muslim lady constituted a trust and transferred her house to her husband. The lady directed her husband to pay the income of the house to her life and after her death to devote the whole of the income to certain charitable purposes. This waqf will be valid under the Hanafi school. However, this will not be valid under the Shia school.

In *Abdul Wahab* v *Mst Sughra*[43] a Hanafi Muslim executed a deed of waqf. As per the deed of waqf he directed that his debts should be paid out of the rents and profits of the waqf property. It was held that under the Hanafi school of Muslim law the waqf was valid. However, under the Shia school such a waqf will not be valid.

In another case a Hanafi Muslim executed a deed of waqf by which he reserved the whole legal and beneficial interest to himself during his life time. The waqf was held invalid. Chagla, J. (as he then was) said that a Hanafi Muslim is not to reserve for his absolute use during his life time the whole of the income of the waqf. The learned judge said that he is only entitled to reserve the income for his own maintenance and support.[44]

From the discussion made above it is clear that before the passing of the Act of 1913, a Hanafi Muslim was allowed to make a waqf and to eat out of the property endowed as waqf.

Ultimate Benefit must be for Charity

Under the traiditional Muslim law it is not necessary for the validity of a waqf that its object must be pious, religious or charitable. But the Indian court have held that piety and charity are part of Muslim faith. Pious and charitable institutions existed even before the advent of Islam. In the beginning there was no state protection to this important institution. Charity is one of the important ingredient of a family waqf. In the case of family waqf also, the ultimate benefit of the waqf property must be for charity. Section 3 of the Mussalman Waqf Validating Act, 1913, also provides that the ultimate benefit should be given expressly or impliedly for the poor or other religious, pious or charitable purpose of a permanent nature'[45] The Act recognised the support and maintenance of the waqif's family as one of the object of Muslim law. Before the passing of the Mussalman Waqf Act, 1913, charity was one of the essential ingredient of waqf. An exhaustive list of cases that might fairly be dealt with under the term charity, would be very long indeed. We can, therefore, do little more than call attention to some of the important cases. In *Mahommed Hamidullah Khan* v *Lolful Huq*[46] it was said that to constitute a valid waqf there must be a dedication of the property solely to the worship of God or to religious or charitable purposes. In *Fatima Bibi* v *Arif Ismailjee*[47] it was said that a waqf, the purpose of which is merely to create a family settlement without a charitable object shall be void.

The above principle was recently reiterated by the High Court of Allahabad in *Sabir Hussain* v *Smt. Hashmi Begum*.[48] It was said by Justice Deoki Nandan of High Court of Allahabad that a waqf can be lawfully created if ultimate benefit is reserved for religious, pious and charitable purposes of a permanent character recognised by Mussalman law.

In another case[49] a Muslim constituted a waqf and appointed Mutawalli. The property was also handed over to him. The following directions were given by the waqif to the Mutawalli :

(i) to defray out of the profits of the endowed land the expenses of a mosque ;
(ii) to give alms to medicants ;
(iii) to educate poor students ; and
(iv) to utilise the surplus for the marriages, burials, and circumcision of the members of A,B's family.

It was held that there was substantial charity in the waqf and, therefore, the waqf was held to be valid.

Before coming into force of Mussalman Waqf Validating Act, 1913, it was said that the gift to charity may be provided after the extinction of the line of descendants of the waqif. In *Bikani Mia* v *Shnklal*,[50] Ameer Ali dealt with the above subject very elaborately. He said that there had been an absolute consensus of opinion regarding the validity of waqfs on one's children, kindred and neighbours. There are minor differences. *viz.* whether a waqf can be created for one's self, whether the unfailing object should be designated, whether the property should be partitioned or not, whether consignment is necessary or not but so far as the validity of a waqf constituting one's family or children, the recipients of the benefaction, in whole or in part, is concerned, there is absolutely no difference. A waqf is a permanent benefaction for the good of God's creatures, the waqif may bestow the usufruct, but not the property, upon whomsoever he chooses and in whatever manner be likes, only it must endure for ever. If he bestows the usufruct in the first instance upon those whose maintenance is obligatory on him, or if he gives it to his descendants so long as they exists to prevent their falling into indigence, it is a pious act—more pious, according to the Prophet, than giving to the general body of the poor. He laid down that one's family and descendants are fitting objects of charity, and that to bestow on them and to provide for their future subsistencee is more pious and obtains greater reward than to bestow on the indigent stranger. In Bikani Mia's case the court said that when the waqif's descendants fail. it must go to the poor. It is an act by which nearness is obtained to the deity.

In *Fatma Bibi* v *Advocate General*,[51] Justice West observed that if the condition of an ultimate dedication to a pious and unfailing purpose be satisfied, a waqif is not made invalid by an intermediate settlement on the founder's children and their descendants. The benefits these successively take may constitute a perpetuity in the sense of the English law. But according to Muslim law, that does not vitiate the settlement, provided that ultimate charitable object be clearly designated.

The above opinion of Ameer Ali and West J. was not followed by the Judicial Committee of the Privy Council in Abdul Fata's case. In Abdul Fata's case the Privy Council refused to recognise theory of family waqfs. Consequently, the British Government was constrained to pass the Mussalman Waqf Validating Act, 1913. The Act of 1913 does not validate a waqf for alal-aulad which was void being violative of a statute which constitutes a code in itself. In another case[52] it was said by the Calcutta High Court that if the ultimate gift to charity would take effect on the extinction of the heirs howsoever the waqf would be invalid. However, if the gift to charity be postponed till after the extinction of the family, the waqf would be valid.

The controversy whether a family waqf should have pious, religious *etc.* character or not was not settled even after the passing of the various waqf legislations. In *Mahomed Mohin* v *Madras State Waqf Board*[53] a Muslim lady executed a deed of waqf. The deed provided for the enjoyment of income of certain property for herself and after her death to her near reliatives. It also simultaneously provided for religious objects and reserving ultimate benefit to charity. It was held that the deed was valid waqf-alal-aulad, transferring the ownership of property to God and not mere creating a charge in favour of charity. It was also said that a waqf-alal-aulad without there being some property in praesenti dedicated for any purpose such as pious, religious or charitable will not come within the scope of the waqf as contained in section 3 (1) of the Waqf Act, 1954. This view of Justice Venkataraman, was approved by a Bench of the Madras High Court in *Madras State Waqf Board* v *Mohammad Mahim.*[54]

A pure waqf-alal-aulad will not come within the scope of the Central Act, and only a waqf-alal-aulad in which some property has been dedicated in praesenti for the purpose recognised by Muslim law as pious, religious or charitable will come within the scope of the Act.[55]

The decision of Venkataraman, J. referred above was followed and approved by a Bench of the Patna High Court in *Asam Jafar Imam* v *State of Bihar.*[56] This was also a case of private waqf. The question was whether the Central Act had any application to such a waqf or not. It was observed that the provisions of the Act have been made applicable only for the properies which have been dedicated by Muslim la was pious, religious or charitable.[57] The Waqf Board will have jurisdiction only to the extent to which property has been dedicated for any purpose recognised by Muslim law as pious, religious or charitable and this must be in addition to the provision for the members of the family and descendants.

According to Justice Ismail of Madras High Court where under the terms of the waqf deed there is no provision for distributing any part of the income in praesenti to any person other than the members of the family, and the poor Muslims come in only in the event of the entire line in the family becoming extinct and so long as a single member of the family is alive, there is no chance of any poor person coming and taking the benefit under the waqf deed, and therefore, such a waqf shall be a waqf-alal-aulad simpliciter and consequently it shall be outside the scope of the Act and, therefore, section 36-A of the Waqf Act, 1954, has no application. Consequently, the Waqf Board can not come and complain under section 57 and seek to revoke the sanction already granted by the court.[58]

It is submitted here that atleast for some limited purpose the waqf was for purpose recognised by Muslim law as pious, religious or charitable and to that extent the provisions of Waqf Act, 1954, shall be applicable. The Waqf Board was, therefore, having a *locus standi* to ensure that the property was properly utilised. The court should have taken a broader view of the matter.

The ultimate Benefit must go to Beneficiary

Proviso to section 3 of the Mussalman Waqf Validating Act, 1913, further provides that the ultimate benefit in the case of family waqfs should expressly or impliedly, be reserved for the poor or for any other purpose recognised by the Mussalman law as religious, pious or charitable of a permanent character. Imam Abu Hanifa and his younger disciple, Imam Mohammad held the view that the ultimate objects of the waqf must be clearly specified else the waqf will not be valid. On the other hand, Cadi Abu Yusuf said that the ultimate benefit may be implied in favour of the poor.

This matter was also discussed by the Supreme Court in *Fazalul Rabbi* v *State of West Bengal.*[59] The Supreme Court made the following observations ;

> 'Now it is a matter of legal history that the waqfs in which the benefits to charity or religion were either illusory or postponed indefinitely, while the property so dedicated was being enjoyed from generation to generation by the family of the waqf, were regarded as opposed to the rule against perpetuities as contained in the Indian Succession Act and the Transfer of Property Act. This was so declared in a succession of cases by the Judicial Committee. Their lordships proceed at to observe the effect of these decisions in para 12, 'these cases led to agitation in India and the Mussalman Waqf Validating Act, 1913, was passed. It declared the rights of Mussalmans to make settlements of property by way of waqf in favour of their families, children and descendants. For the purpose of the validating Act the term "waqf" was defined to mean the permanent dedication by a person professing the Mussalman faith of any property for any purpose recognised by the Mussalman law as religious, pious or charitable. This gave a wider meaning to the word "waqf" but only for the purpose of taking them out of the invalidity which should have otherwise existed and which was already authoritatively stated to have so existed.'

In the last their Lordships concluded the effect of the Validating Act in the following words :

> ...but the intention of the Validating Act was not to give a new meaning to the word 'charity' which in common parlance is a word denoting a giving to some one in necessitous circumstances and in law a giving for public good. A private gift to one's own self or kith and kin may be meritorious and pious but is not a charity in the legal sense and the courts in India have never regarded such gifts as for religious or charitable purposes under the Mohammadan law.

On the basis of the above observations it can be said that even under general Muslim law waqf-alal-aulad cannot be considered to be public, charitable or religious objects.

The modern approach is that even if the document is absolutely silent as regards the ultimate object, the very use of the word waqf is a sufficient indication.[60]

Waqfs not to be Invalid by reason of Remoteness

Section 4 of the Mussalman Waqf Validating Act, 1913, says that no such waqf shall be deemed to be invalid merely because the benefit reserved therein for the poor or other religious, pious or charitable purposes of a permanent nature is postponed until after the extinction of the family, children descendants of the person creating the waqf.

On the basis of the above it can be said that the following are the main essentials of a family waqf :—

(i) it may be created wholly or partially for the family children and descendants of the settler ; and
(ii) ultimate benefit must go expriessly or impliedly, to poor or to a religious, pious or charitable purpose.

Section 4 of the Act had specifically repealed the law which was prevalent from the decision in *Abdul Fata Mohammad Ishak* v *Russomoy Dhur Chowdhary's case.*[61]

Under the Mussalman Waqf Validating Act, 1913, three terms have been used——family, children and descendants. The term 'family' is not easy to define. It had been given very wide interpretation. The term is not confined to those people who are dependant for their maintenance and support on the waqif. The Waqf Validating Act, 1913, is also silent on this point. Section 3 (a) of the Act allows a Muslim to make a waqf for the support of the family. Family in Mussalman Waqf Validating Act, 1913 means persons descended from one common progenitor and having a common lineage. The word 'family' has also been given a narrow meaning.

On the basis of above, it can be said that a person may belong to the family either because he is from a common progenitor, or if he is living under the same roof, and is being supported and maintained by the settler.

In *Ismail Haji Arat* v *Umar Abdulla*[62] it was said that the term family includes sister also. In this case the sister of the waqif was living and maintained by him. It was, therefore, held that she will come within the definitlon of the term 'family'.

In *Mohammad Azam Khan* v *Hamid Shah*[63] the nephews were living with the settler. The settler constituted a waqf for the maintenance of the settler's nephews and their descednants generation after generation. The waqf was held to be valid. It was held that nephews, their descedants and future generations shall be within the term 'family'. It was said that the word 'family' in section 3 (a) of the Mussalman Waqf Validating Act, 1913, is not restricted only to those person residing in the house of the settler for whose maintenance he was responsible, but was intended to be used in its broad popular sense, namely persons descended from one common progenitor and having common lineage, *e.g.* nephews of the settler and their descendants were included in the term, irrespective of whether they lived in the settler's house or whether the settler was responsible for their maintenance.

In another case it was held that the son of a half brother the son and grandson of a paternal uncle, and the son of a half sister, though not dependant on the waqif shall come within the category of family members.

The Allahabad High Court in *Abdul Qavi* v *Ashraf Ali*[64] said that the word 'family' in section 3 (a) has to be given a wide and not a restricted meaning and a person may belong to a family either if he is from a common progenitor or if he is living under the same roof and is being supported and maintained by the settler. In this case the daughter, of the waqif's sister, brought up and married by the settler was held to be a member of the waqif's family, but not her descendants.

In another case[65] the High Court of Allahabad treated daughter-in-law as the part and parcel of the family of the dedicator. In *Mubarak Ali* v *Ahmad Ali*[66] it was said that the term 'family' includes an adopted son who was residing with the settleras as a dependant relation. A Muslim is expected not only to maintain his children and descendants but also of the family of the waqif. A similar view was taken in *Beli Ram* v *Mohammad Afzal.*[67] In this case, the court said that the Mussalman Waqf Validating Act, 1913, authorises the maintenance of descendants but also of the family of the waqif.

It was said that waqif is fully competent to create a waqf especially for some heirs and he may deprive some of the heirs.

In *Aisha Bibi* v *Nabissa Sahib*[68] it was said by Ramaswami, J. that the word family means all the persons who live in a household and includes parents, children, servants, lodgers and boarders.

It is submitted here that in the light of the various decisions given above, our courts have failed to give a clear and precise definition of the word 'family'.

In *M. Eshaque* v *Maimuna Bibi*[69] the High Court of Calcutta examined the meaning of farzand, awalad, ba-farzandan, naslan ba'd naslin, batnanba 'd batnin.' The court said these words are having technical meaning and requires special knowledge of Muslim law.

It is lawful for the settler to make a waqf in respect of the members of the family and to exclude other members of the family. The various courts of India expressed this opinion in numbers of cases. Some of them are discussed as under :

In *Mst Mubarak Jan* v *Mst Taj Begum*[70] it was said that a valid waqf can be created in favour of only some members of the family or of some of the children or descendants whether males or famales and to the exclusion of others. In another case the court interpreted the above power of the settler narrowly. In *Rahiman Begum* v *Baqridan*[71] it was said that if there was no provision for the mainteance of the family a waqf for solely religious purpose, though valid as a waqf, is outside the Act even though the founder's daughter-in-law and after her, daughter are appointed mutawalli with the remuneration.

The legal history of the family waqf was again traced by the Indian Supreme Court in *Mohammad Ismail* v *Sabir*[72] Ali. Justice Wanchoo maintained that 'a waqf-alal-aulad must by it very nature be some kind of transfer of property by the persons making the waqf.' In this case a family waqf was constituted for the waqif and his descendants in respect of his talukdari property. The talukdari property is Governed by the Oudh Estates Act, 1899 which contains a rule against perpetuity. The Supreme Court held that the waqf was void. It was also held that the provisions of the Act of 1913 constitute the general law containing a rule against perpetuity (*e.g.* the Oudh Estates Act, 1869) may override it.

In *Thanga* v *Pappa*[73] the High Court of Madras was required to interpret the provisions of a waqf which provided for the descendants' maintenance and for charity. It was held by the High Court that where a waqf provides for the descendants' maintenance and for charity (concurrently), reservation for charity in the case of failure of descendants may be implied.

It has been the matter of debate whether the ultimate grant to the poor *etc.* must be express or may be implied. Under the Hanafi law, it must be express. This opinion of Hanafi law has been followed in India.[74] It may, however, be noted that section 3 of the Mussalman Waqf Validating Act, 1913, clearly says that the ultimate grant to the poor may be express or implied. In *Baqaullah* v *Ghulam*[75] the High Court of Allahabad said that where the ultimate grant to poor is not mentioned expressly, the same may be presumed from the terms of the dedication.

In *Abdul Rauf* v *Shamsul Haq*[76] the dedicator made a provision under which a person, along with other family members intervened. He was not entitled to be the beneficiary of a family waqf (between the primary beneficiaries and the ultimate object). It was held by the Allahabad High Court that the intervention of a person under the circumstances mentioned above, shall not invalidate the waqf ; it only accelerates the ultimate grant to charity.

A Muslim is competent to create family waqf by way of bequest. A bequest may contain certain defects. But on account of these defects the whole family waqf cannot be declared as void. A bequest shall remain binding to the extent it is valid under the law of wills. In *Mohammad Sabir Ali* v *Tahir Ali*[77] it was held that the creation of a interest in the whole of the property for the maintenance of the waqif was in consonance with the principles of Muslim law. A family settlement *inter vivos* also, which could not establish a family waqf, may remain binding as a family settlement.[78]

In *Rashidunnissa* v *Ata Rasool*[79] it was said that a Hanafi Muslim can make a waqf under which he can reserve his income for life in favour of the settler. However, the court said he create the successive life interest.

The rules in respect of the power of a waqif to determine the rights of the descendant beneficiaries are still governed by the Mussalman Waqf Validating Act, 1913. The courts have held that the provision that a widow will lose her share on remarriage is valid.[80] Similarly, the waqif can expressly provide the order of succession. In such cases the courts have held that it is not necessary on the part of the waqif to follow rules of Muslim law of inheritance.[81]

Where the waqif has failed to make a provision for the order of succession and the shares of the beneficiaries, the Indian courts have applied the following rules :[82]

(i) the descendants will take their shares per stirpes ;
(ii) the rule of double shares for male's will not apply.

The High Courts are having no unanimous opinion on the question of nearer excluding the remoter. In *Maqsood* v *Zahid*[83] the High Court of Allahabad held that this rule shall apply in each branch of the descendants. The Andhra Pradesh High Court, however, took a different opinion.

The Andhra Pradesh High Court in *Mazhar Ali* v *Bulan Murtaza*[84] however held that if a waqf was in favour of the descendants 'generation after generation,' the implication was that the nearer line or class took first, and after them the line next after. But the principle that the children of a predeceased son were excluded by their uncles and aunts did not apply to endowed property. But this is not a case of waqf, and much less of waqf made for the benefit of the settler's descendants. The sentiments of the Muslim law appear to be against the application of the rules of inheritance or principles of herediatry suceession to the administration of waqf property.

The courts are competent to enhance the amount of maintenance payable to a beneficiary of a family waqf under the waqf deed.[85]

Raja Mahmood Hasan of Asgharabad was a Shīa Muslim grantee of Uttar Pradesh, who died in the year 1939, at the age of 56. He was having two wives. At the time of his second marriage, he was a widower with ten children. At the age of 50 he married Siddique Fatima, a seventeen year old girl. At the time of his death he left his young widow, Rani Siddique Fatima (the appellant before the Supreme Court), one daughter by her and a number of children from an earlier marriage. The eldest son of the deceased was Mohammed Hasan. He was the respondent before the Supreme Court.

One Mst Sughra Begum was a Shia Muslim lady. On October 6,1921 she (waqifa) created a waqf of the entire properties dividing them in three parts. Raja Haji Saiyed Mohammad Mahmood Hasan was appointed by the waqifa as the mutawalli of the first part. His brother was appointed the mutawalli of the second part. The waqifa appointed herself the mutawalli of the third part. The dispute in this case related to a property concering part No 1. As already noted the plantiff was the second wife of the deceased Mahmood Hasan. In the year 1935, a permanent lease was executed on behalf of one Saiyed Anwarul Rahman in respcct of the disputed land in the name of the plaintiff. A nazrana of Rs. 786.00 was paid for the lease in her name, and thereafter the annual rent of Rs. 80.00 was also paid in the name of Rani Siddique Fatima. Between the two years 1937 and 1939 a Kothi (Bungalow) was constructed on the said land. The name of the bungalow was 'Mahmood Manzil'. The suit property in this litigation is the said Kothi together with the land appertaining to it.

There was also evidence that the raja made a will under which he declared that he has given the land and the bungalow to his wife Rani Siddique Fatima. He declared 'My wife Siddique Fatima has got a Kothi...by taking a perpetual lease. I and the estate have no concern with the same. It has been constructed by her with her own funds...'

It was claimed by the plaintiff that the disputed property belongs to her. The defendant was inducted as a tenant of the Kothi on and from 1st of March, 1947, on a rental value of Rs. 60.00 p.m. He paid rent upto May, 1950, but did not pay any rent thereafter. In the year 1952, the plaintiff served a notice on the defendant to pay the arrears of rent and delivered vacant possession of the Kothi. The defendant refuted the claim of the plantiff and asserted that the Kothi did not belong to her nor was he tenant of the same. Hence the appellant instituted the suit for realisation of arrears of rent, damages and recovery of possession of the suit property.

The contention of the respondent was that Raja Sahib, the first mutawalli of part No 1 had acquired the lease of the land and constructed the Kothi with the waqf fund as mutawalli of the waqf. It was a waqf property. After the death of the Raja, the respondent became the mutawalli of part No 1 including the Kothi in question. He occupied the Kothi as a mutawalli and not a tenant.

The trial court accepted the case of the defendant, rejected that of the plantiff and dismissed her suit. The Allahabad High Court dismissed her appeal. She preferred appeal before the Supreme Court on the grant of special leave.

It was claimed by the appellant Siddique Fatima that the Kothi was constructed out of the Savings which her husband used to pay to her. Subsequently, she demolished her case and claimed to be in possession of Rs. 50,000.00 at the time of the death of her husband which was paid by her husband from time to time. Thus she failed to explained as to out of which personal fund she claimed to have acquired the disputed property.

The only point on which the parties were at issue was with respect to the source of the money out of which the patta was obtained and the building constructed and the plantiff could succeed only if she proved that she had obtained the patta and built the kothi out of the money given to her by her late husband as pocket expense *etc.*

The Supreme Court through Justice Untwalia said it is undisputed that a valid waqf was created by Smt. Sughra Begum. It was also clear that except a portion of money which was to be spent for public, religious or charitable objects the waqf was primarily of a private nature for the benefit of the settler's family and the descendants, which is called waqf-alal-aulad. The ultimate aim of the waqf was to spend income, if any, in the service of the Almighty God.

It is important to note that all or most of the monies used for taking the lease, paying the annual rental and construction of the Kothi came from the income of the waqf estate.

The Supreme Court gave its judgment in favour of Mahmood Hasan, the eldest son of the deceased and rejected the claim of the widow Rani Siddique Fatima. The judgment of the Supreme Court is mainly based on the following two points :

That the raja's purported appropriation of various amounts from the income of the waqf estate, in the manner mentioned earlier for obtaining a permanent lease of the land and constructing a Kothi thereon for the benefit of Siddique Fatima, was in substance, a purchase of the property out of the funds of the waqf and was, in effect *ultra vires* the powers of the mutawalli by virtue of clause 24 of the waqfnama, and must be deemed to be a purchase of property, for the waqf estate corpus.

Clause 18 of the waqfnama reads :

> Syed Mahmood Hasan the mutawalli...is vested with the power to fix stipends for his children and their descendants and for his wives...whatsoever he pleases.

While interpreting the above clause, the Supreme Court emphasized on the obligation of a mutawalli to deal equally and justly with all beneficiaries of the waqf. The Supreme Court said that the Raja had exercised an impermissible preference in favour of his allegedly diverting a disproportionate part of the waqf income to the impugned transaction, to the prejudice of the other beneficiaries and thereby committed, malversation of the income or, in other words, an equitable fraud on the estate, which had to be undone. The Supreme Court further said it is difficult to conclude that the Raja was conferred an absolute power or discretion to fix any stipend for any beneficiary and no stipend for some beneficiary. Each beneficiary was entitled to share the usufruct of the waqf property per capita. The power given to the Raja under clause 18 had to be reasonably exercised within a reasonable limit of variation according to the exigencies and special needs of a particular beneficiary. He had no power to spend money quite disproportionately for the beneficiary—may she be his wife or young daughter or be he a young son. He had no power to spend money for acquisition of any immovable property for a beneficiary. No income from the waqf estate could be spent for acquisition of an immovable property. The money had to be equitably for the mainteance and support of each and every beneficiary.

It is clear from the above that the Supreme Court laid main stress on the breach of the equality rule and the imputation that the raja spent money disproportionately for the benefit of his wife as against the other beneficiaries namely his children. The emphasis made by the Supreme Court is in consonance with the principles of Muslim law. In the Muslim law, parents are directed to give equal treatment to his or her children or descendants in the matter of making gifts. The Muslim law treats each distribution of manafi or usufruct of a waqf to a beneficiary as *pro-tanto*, a hiba or simple gift.

As regards the equal treatment of settlers' descendants Tyabji[87] and Mulla have given different opinions. According to Tyabji the benefit of a waqf for a person's...descendants is taken per capita, males and famales taking equally and children of daughters being included. On the other hand, Mulla[88] says that where a waqf is made for the benefit of a settler's discendant but no rules of succession are laid down in the dead of waqif, the descendants take per stripes and not per capita and male- and females take equal shares.

It is humbly submitted here where the law is not clear the duty of the court is to see the intention of the waqif. Sometimes the rule of stripes and sometimes the rule of the capita may appear more just. Any of the rule may be applied on the basis of the circumstances of the case.

There is no Quranic authority on the basis of which it can be said that the wife and children be treated at par. The very idea seems repugnant to the Muslim law. Where the mother is given a very high status vis-a-vis the children (even the stepchildren). This high status extends to the period of widowhood. This principle is based on Quranic texts and the saying of the Prophet Muhammed. Rule of equality does not mean treating unequals as equals. Again the Supreme Court failed to take into consideration the point that the Raja intended to help his young wife. There does not appear to be any inquality. This judgment needs review in view of Article 15 of the Indian Constitution which prohibits discrimination on the basis of sex, *etc*.

Mutawalli as a Beneficiary

A mutawalli need not necessarily be also the beneficiary under the endowment. However, there may be cases where a person may be both the mutawalli and the beneficiary. But the claim to beneficial interest is separate from the office of mutawalliship. Under Muslim law, waqf is two-fold transfer simultaneously made; perpetual in both its aspects with religious motive pervading; the transaction as a whole consists of a transfer (i) of the usufruct[89] in favour of the beneficiary or objects of the waqf and (ii) of the substance in reality a renunciation of the substance metaphorically spoken of as a transfer of the substance to God. It was pointed out by the Privy Council in Vidya Varuthi's[90] case that waqf constitutes 'tying up of property in the ownership of God, the Almighty and the devotion of the profit for the benefit of human beings.' It can, therefore, be said that on such endowments under the Muslim law, the ownership in the property is wholly renunciated or vested in the God and the benefit which the beneficiaries derive come only out of the usufruct. Muslim law, it must be remembered makes a difference between Ayn (corpus) and manafi (usufruct) and the beneficial interest under the endowment is generally created out of such usufruct. As observed by Ameer Ali 'A waqf is a permanent benefaction for the good of God's creatures; the waqif may bestow the usufruct but not the property upon whomsoever he chooses and in whatever mannual he likes, only it must endure for ever.' Under these circumstances, it can be said that the beneficiary acquires no interest in the strict sense in the property itself though an interest in the usufruct arising out of such property is vested in the beneficiary. It was clearly said in Vidya Varuthi's case that even a sajjadanashin who has a larger interest in the usufruct acquires no right to the property belonging to the waqf. Again, in the case of *Abdur Rahim* v *Narayan*[91] the Privy Council said that on such an endowment the property itself is not chargeable according to the measure of interest which the beneficiary may have in the rents, and profits of the whole. Though, therefore, the beneficiary acquires no right in the immovable property yet his right to share the usufructs which are to accrue from such property in years to come creates an interest of a particular nature in the immovable property.

In the case of Mohammad Rustom Ali[92] the Privy Council held that the deed by which a mutawalli is appointed and vested with mutawalliship does not constitute a transfer to them the ownership of the property and as such it is outside the provisions of Indian Registration Act, 1977. The same view was re-affirmed by the Privy Council in still later decision in the case of *Alla Rakhi* v *Mohammad Abdur Rahim.*[93]

For a long time it was said that in case of a private waqf where the mutawalli is also the beneficiary, he is not a mere superintendent or manager but is the owner of the waqf property.[94] But the full bench of the said High Court overruled the said decision in *Motahar Raza* v *The Joint Commissioner of Consolidation*[95]. The full bench affirmed the opinion that the mutawalli acquires no right title or interest in the property itself but he is merely the holder of the office of a manager under the Muslim law.

The Supreme Court in the case of *Nawab Zainyar Jung* v *Director of Endowment*[96] accepted and approved the principle laid down in Vidya Varuthi's case in holding the mutawalli to be a manager, governor, superintendent or curator.

In *Zahra Khatun* v *Mohammad Jame Alam*[97] the plaintiff who claimed to be the mutawalli as also the benefieiary under a waqf-alal-aulad, brought the suit for a declaration that an order of the Commissioner of Waqfs recording the defendants as co-mutawalli was illegal and without jurisdiction and not binding on the plaintiff. It was alleged that the said defendants had transferred and or surrendered their beneficial interest in favour of the plaintiff and her predecessor and the plaintiff prayed for injunction restraining the said defendants from acting upon or giving effect to the said order or disturbing the plaintiff in her peaceful possession, enjoyment and management of the waqf properties.

It was held by Justice A.K. Sen of the High Court of

Calcutta that under Muslim law, the mutawalli does not acquire any right, title or interest in the waqf property but is merely the holder of the office of a manager, but where the mutawalli claims also the beneficial interest, his claim must be considered independently of the office of mutawalli.

Power of the Mutawalli of the family Waqf

At the Muslim law, the provision for the creation of waqf for the maintenance of waqif's family is not clear. Although in respect of the law applicable to waqfs there is some difference in regard to some matters between the Shia law and the various other schools of Muslim law applicable to Sunnis, in many fields the law is identical. After the passing of the Mussalman Waqf Validating Act, 1913, creation of a waqf for the purpose of the maintenance of the members of the waqf's family and their descendants was considered as a waqf created for charitable purpose.

Tyabji[98] has made the following observations :—

> According to Shia law the waqf is irrevocable after possession is given to the beneficiaries or the mutawalli. The settler divests himself of the ownership of the property and of everything in the nature of usufruct from the moment the waqf is created. In purely metaphorical sense the expression "ownership of God" is used but unlike Hindu law, since conception of a personal God is not recognised, there is no ownership of God or no property belongs to God in the jural sense, although "the ownership of the property" becomes reverted in God as he is originally the owner of all things.

In the opinion of Shia jurists such property was transferred to the beneficiaries or to the object of the waqf. The Supreme Court in Siddique Fatima's[99] case said that strictly the ownership of the waqf property has no jural conception with any exactitude. The corpus is tied down and is made inalienable only the usufruct and the income from the corpus of the waqf property is available for carrying out the objects of the waqf. In this connection it is relevant to quote Sharaiul Islam.[100] He says—

'Waqf is a contract the fruit or effect of which is (a) to tie up the original and (b) to leave its usufruct free.' 'The waqf or subject of appropriation (corpus) is transferred, so as to become the property of the mowkoof alehi, (or person on whom the settlement is made) for he has a right to the advantage or benefits (usufruct) to be derived from it.'

In the footnote at the same page occurs a passage which reads—

> But it should not be overlooked that question about ownership of property after dedication, refers merely to *scintilla juris* supposed to remain undisposed of, although entire usufruct, (all benefits, & Co.) are assigned away. Question in whom property rests, therefore, entirely academical.

A mutawalli is like a manager rather than a trustee.[101] The mutawalli, so far as the waqf property is concerned, has to see that the beneficiaries get the advantage of usufruct. We have already pointed out that under the Shia law the property does not remain with the waqif. It is transferred to God or to the beneficiaries. At page 554 of Tyabji's famous book *Muslim Law* it is stated :—

> The support and maintenance of the waqif's family, and Co. would seem under the Act to be deemed a purpose recognised by the Muslim law as religious, pious or charitable.

The above view was put forward by Justice S. Ameer Ali with great learning in his dissenting judgment in Bikani Mia's case. At page 593 he said as follows :

> The mutawalli has no ownership, right or estate in the waqf property; in that respect he is not a trustee in the technical sense; he holds the property as a manager for fulfilling the purpose of waqf.

According to Mulla in the case of a private waqf[102] the mutawalli is not a mere superintendent or manager, but is 'practically speaking the owner.' He is not bound to allow the use of the waqf property for objects which though laudable in themselves are not objects of the waqf[103].

Subsequently, the full bench of the Allahabad High Court in Moattar Raza v Joint Director of Consolidation,[104] U.P. camp at Bareilly overruled the earlier decision on the point. At pages 513-14 the court observed :

the legal status and position of a mutawalli under a waqf under the Musalman law is that of a manager or superintendent.

Tyabji[105] while discussing the powers of the mutawalli said that he may do all acts reasonable and proper for the protection of the waqf property, and for the administration of the waqf.

It is relevant here to discuss briefly the law regarding the distribution of income of the waqf properties amongst the beneficiaries. In Tyabji's book it is said that the benefit of a waqf for a person's sons and his children and the children of his children for ever so long as there are descendants, is taken per capita, males and females taking equally and the children of daughters being included[106]. In this connection Ameer Ali[107] has also made a very useful statement of law. He says that—

> It is lawful for a mutawalli with the income of the waqf to erect shops, houses, & co., which may yield profit to the waqf, as all this is for the benefit of the waqf. All properties purchased by the mutawalli out of the proceeds of the waqf become part of the original waqf estate.

In Siddique Fatima's[108] case it was contended that the right of the beneficiaries to get money out of the income of the waqf property for their maintenance and support was their property. In support of this case, the appellant cited the case of Ahmed G.H. Ariff v Commissioner of Wealth Tax.[109] In this case a waqf-al-aulad was constituted by the waqif. It was held that the aliquot share of the income provided for the beneficiaries was not meant for their maintenance and support. It was treated as asset and was, therefore, taxable. The court held that the citation of this case was irrelevant for the purpose of this case. In this case, however, the court discussed in detail the waqf property and the position of the mutawalli. It was said—

As mentioned before, the moment a waqf is created, all

rights of property pass out of the waqif and vest in the Almighty. Thereafter, the mutawalli has no right in the property belonging to the waqf. He is not a trustee in the technical ense, his position being merely that of superintendent or a manager.[110]

A beneficiary, under the Muslim law is not given discretionary power to discriminate between beneficiaries. Equality amongst all is a golden thread which runs throughout the Muslim law. The power given to a Mutawalli had to be reasonably exercised within a reasonable limit of variation according to the exigencies and special needs of a particular beneficiary. He had no power to spend money quite disproportionately for the benefit of one beneficiary. He had no power to spend money for acquisition of any immovable property for a beneficiary.[111]

In Siddique Fatima's case it was said that even acquisition of immovable property directly with the waqf fund is an accretion of the waqf property.

A mutawalli of a waqf although not a trustee in the true sense of the term is still bound by the various obligations of a trustee. He is like a trustee or a person standing in a fiduciary capacity, cannot advance his own interest of his close relations by virtue of the position held by him. The use of the funds of the waqf for acquisition of the property by a mutawalli in the name of his wife would amount to a breach of trust and the property so acquired would be treated as waqf property.

Under the English law the general rule is that a trustee must take heed of one beneficiary to the detriment of others. This rule implies that although a trustee may be the servant of all the beneficiaries, he is not the servant of any one of them, but an arbitrator, who must hold the scales evenly. In England, equity however, has always recognised the principle that if there is only a single beneficiary, who is *sui juris* and absolutely entitled, he may terminate and resettle the trust at his pleasure, and further more, if the trust at his pleasure, and further more, if the trustee incurs liabilities in carrying out his beneficiary's instructions, he can recover, not only out of the trust property, but against the beneficiary personally. The same position follows where all the beneficiaries, being *sui juris* and absolutely entitled, unite to instruct the trustee to deviate from the terms of his trust.[112]

The position of the mutawalli under the Muslim law is in any way different and all the beneficiaries are entitled to benefit equally, of course, subject to the special power conferred on the mutawalli.

Family Waqfs to Strangers—No settled Law

There is a conflict of opinion on the question whether family waqfs can be created in favour of strangers. Ameer Ali[113] says that a family waqf in respect of strangers shall be void. The matter was not settled even after the passing of the Mussalman Waqf Validating Act, 1913. This Act was not passed only to clarify the position in respect of family waqfs. The premable of the Act does not refer to a waqf under which individual strangers are preliminary beneficiaries. The Act does not say that the property will be dedicated permanently for charitable, religious and pious purposes.

In *Mohammad Afzal* v *Din Mohammad*[114] it was said by the Lahore High Court that if the waqif had created a family waqf and he proved that the life interest should be given to strangers, such a proviso shall be void, though the waqf shall be valid. The Judicial Committee of the Privy Council refused to accept the above decision as correct.

POSITION OF THE PRESENT DAY/STATUTORY AND ADMINISTRATIVE CONTROL OF FAMILY WAQFS IN INDIA

At present, in India the family waqfs are governed under the following Acts :—

(i) The Bengal Waqf Act, 1934 ;
(ii) The Bombay Public Trust Act, 1950 ;
(iii) The Jammu and Kashmir Muslim Waqf Act, 1959 ;
(iv) The Uttar Pradesh Muslim Waqf Act, 1960 ; and
(v) The Waqf Act, 1954.

The Bombay Act will not be applicable to a waqf if any benefit under it is reserved for the waqif or family. The U.P. Act will not be applicable if 75 per cent or more of whose income has been reserved for the waqif or his family. This rule is not absolute. There is one exception to this rule. Accordingly the exemption is subject to the conditions that if the mutawalli wrongfully sells or mortgages, or suffers to be sold in execution of a decree against himself, or otherwise destroys the whole or any part of the waqf property, the Waqf Board may apply all or any of the provisions of this Act to such waqf for such time as it may think necessary.[115]

According to Bengal Waqf Act, 1934 a waqf will be treated as waqf-al-aulad if 75 per cent or more of its income is reserved for the waqif himself or for the members of his family. Under section 32 of the Act a beneficiary can request the waqf commissioner to make an inquiry into the administration of such a waqf and to get its accounts audited. After necessary inquiry if the commissioner is of the opinion that the allegations of mismanagement are true, he may recommend to the state government to allow all the provisions of the Act to be applied to such a waqf.[116]

Under section 38 (2) the Commissioner can create a reserve fund from the income of such a waqf for the maintenance, expansion and repairs of the waqf property. Under the Act, it is the duty of the mutawalli of a waqf-al-aulad to furnish annually a statement of income and expenditure to the commissioner.[117] The Waqf Boards are getting 2 per cent as administrative charges.

The Waqf Act, 1954 and J&K Muslim Waqfs Act, 1959 are silent. They are not having provision like one in the Bengal and U.P. Acts. Under these Acts the Board or the Committee cannot intervene into the affairs of family waqfs beyond the extent such waqfs are dedicated to religious or charitable objects. This appears to be a self-defeating provision. If the intention behind the 1954 Act is to take 5 per cent contribution from the charitable portion of the income of such waqfs, then if the affairs of the whole waqf property are allowed to deteriorate beyond repair, the charitable portion of such family waqfs will also sink with the remaining waqf.[118]

Under the Bengal Act it is not obligatory on the part of the mutawalli to submit budgets of family waqfs. However, the Commissioner can pass order for the audit of the family waqfs. Under section 38 of the Bengal Act a beneficiary or any other person who is entitled under the waqf deed to receive pecuniary or other material benefits on his own account or on behalf of a religious or charitable institution, may request the commissioner to order the audit of accounts of a family waqf.

Section 34 of the Bengal Act says that if after inquiry under section 32 the commissioner is of the opinion that the affairs of any waqf-al-aulad have been mismanaged to such an extent as to make it desirable for the protection of the waqf property or in the interest of the beneficiaries that the waqf should be subjected to greater control and supervision, he may recommend to the state government that such waqf shall for a specified period be subject to the provisions of this Act which are applicable to waqfs other than waqf-al-aulad.

On the basis of above discussion, it can be said that there is no proper administrative or statutory control of family waqfs in India. There is no one common method of making survey of waqfs properties. Presumably the government is reluctant not to take any action only because the benefit of these waqfs is enjoyed only by few peoples. It is not a hidden fact that the property of these family waqfs has been misappropriated at a very large scale. There is an urgent need to introduce effective administrative policy throughout the country. There is no need for having more than one Act throughout the country.

The Waqf Boards and Commissioners of Waqfs (except in U.P. and Bengal) are not having complete reliable data regarding the family waqfs. While making survey Waqf Boards and Waqf Commissioners are not taking into account the family waqfs. It is, therefore, necessary that appropriate legislative steps be taken immediately.

REFERENCES

1. (1838) Foulton 345.
2. See *Radhakanta Deb* v *The Commission of Hindu Religious Endowments AIR* 1981 SC 798.
3. *T.N. Waqf Board* v *M. Ebrahim Musee, AIR* 1979 Mad 231.
4. (1894) 22 IA J6 (PC).
5. *Ibid.* see also a similar judgment of the Privy Council in *Razika Binti* v *Sharifa Binti Mohammad*, AC (1964) 15.

6. Majid Khaduri etc (ed), *Law of Waqf in the Middle East*, Vol I, (1955) Washington D,C., p. 217.
7. AAA Fyzee, Outlines of Muhammadan Law, (Fourth ed) p. 277.
8. Sir Tyed's proposed Bill on Waqf-al-aulad, 1 *Aligarh Law Society Review*, pp. 125-135.
9. These observations were made by the Committee of the Egyptian Parliament in 1946 for the revision of the Waqf Law in that country : see also S. Sulaiman Nadvi, Hayat-e-shibli, Azamgarh, 1943, p 536.
10. (1873) 10 BHC 7 ; see also *Mahomed Hamidulla* v *Lolful Huq*, (1881) 6 Cal 744.
11. (1882) 9 Cal 176 ; see also *Mahammad Ahsanullah* v *Amarchand Kundi* (1889) 17 Cal 498, 509, 17 I.A. 28.
12. (1892) 17 Bom 1 (PC).
13. *Supra* note 11.
14. (1903) 30 Cal 666.
15. *Supra* note 4.
16. 22 IA 86.
17. (1896) 19 all 211.
18. (1928) 55 Cal 448.
19. *Nizamuddin* v *Abdul Gafur* (1888) 13 Bom 264.
20. *Ghulam Rasool* v *Mst Noor Jahan*, AIR 1982 All 511. In this case the waqif created a waqf-ul-aulad in favour of his three sons and a daughter. The waqf deed provided that the income of the waqf property be distributed according to the share in the Shariat. The waqf deed also provided that every heir of the settler was entitled to be benefited by the waqf. They were also entitled to the benefit. One of the heir died during the lifetime of the settler.
21. Beli Ram v Muhammad Afzal, (1949) Lah 1, 50 BIR 674, *AIR* 1948 PC 168.
22. See Shibli Nu'mani, Waqf-e-aulad, Maqalat-e-Shibli, Vol 1, (Azamgarh) (1930), pp 82-104 ; S. Ameer Ali, *Mahomedan Law*, Vol II, (4th Ed), Calcutta (1912) pp 273-79 and 754-94 ; Moulvy Mohammad *Yusoof, Review of the Mahammadan Law of the Waqf*, Calcutta, (1906) published also as a supplement to the Cal Law Jr. Vol II.
23. E.g. petition submitted by Mohammad Yusoof (Judl) July 1907, Nos. 8-83, Part A.
24. Resolution No V, passed by the All India Shia Conference, III sitting held in December, 1909, and Resolution of the All India

Moslem League (1910). For this purpose please see Proceedings of the Home Department (Judl) March, 1910, Nos 163-167. Part A.

25. See proceedings of the Home Department (Judl) No 144 of 1910 and Nos 158-163, Part A ; Question asked by Mohammad Ali Jinnah in the Legislative Council on 18th February, 1910 and again on 25 February, 1910.
26. See the dissenting opinion of Justice Ameer Ali in Bikani Mias case, *Supra* note 16.
27. See proceedings of the Home Department (Judl) March, 1911, 182-183, Part A. It is relevant to note here that till now Abdul Fata's case has not been reversed by the Privy Council. See Fatma Binti Mohammad bin Salim' (1952) A.C. 1 PC ; *Razika Binti Abdulla* v *Sharifa Binti*, Mohammad, *Supra* note 5.
28. See S.A.M. Habibullah, *The Law of Waqif*, (1976) p. v.
29. S. Ameer Ali, *Mahomedan Law*, *supra* note 23.
30. See *Fatema Bintl Mohammad* v *Mohammad Btn Salim*, *Supra* note 28 ; see also A.A.A. Fyzee, *Outlines of Muhammadan Law*, p 302.
31. (1932) 2 Rang 495 : 88 IC 167.
32. (1934) 56 All 293 : 148 IC 294.
33. *Shabhan Mohd* v *Hemraj*, *AIR* 1942 Sindh1 4, ILR (1941) Kar 474 : 65 LA 198.
34. (1902) ILR 24 All 257.
35. (1927) S4 IA 33.
36. *Sibte Rasul* v *Sibte Nabi AIR* 1943 All 74 : (1942) AIJ 722.
37. *Mohammad Qasim* v *Mohammad Mehdi*, *AIR* 1937 Oudh 465 : 170 IC 629 : (1937) OWN 85.
38. *Mst Alt Begum* v *Badrul Islam Ali Khan*, *AIR* 1938 PC 184 : (1938) 65 LA 198.
39. (1906) ILR 28 All 633.
40. *Supra* note 39.
41. *Syed Ali Zamin* v Syed *Akbar Ali Khan*, (1937) 64 IA 158.
42. (1922) 49 Cal 477 ; see also Hamilton's Hedaya p. 237.
43. (1932) 54 All 455 : *AIR* 1932 All 248 : 136 IC 619.
44. *Abdul Karim* v *Rahimbai*, (1946) 48 BLR 67,
45. See *Fatima Bibi* v *Advocate General*, (1881) 6 *Bom* 402 *Amrit Lal* v *Shaikh Hussain*, (1887) 11 Bom 402.
46. (1881) 6 Cal 744.,
47. (1881) 9 OLR 66,
48. *AIR* 1980 NOC 134 (All).

49. *Mazhurool Haq* v *Puhraj*, (1980) 13 WR 235.
50. *Supra* note 16; see also *Amritlal* v *Shaikh Hussein*, (1887) 11 Bom 492.
51. *Supra* note 46.
52. *Mohiuddin Ahmed* v *Sofia Khatun*, (1940) 2 Cal 464 : 44 CWN 974.
53. *AIR*1968 Mad 243 : (1967) 1 Mad LJ 65.
54. (1971) 84 Mad WL 261.
55. G.M.A. *Bhaimia* v *Madras State Waqf Board*, (1968) 1 Mad LJ 410.
56. *AIR* 1975 Pat 48.
57. S 3 (1) (iii).
58. *Tamil Nadu Waqf Board* v *M. Ebrahim Musuee*, *AIR* 1979 Mad 231 : for superintendent or manager see *Hashim Hussain* v *Ahmed Raza*, 1974 All 305 (DB).
59. *AIR* 1965 SC 1722.
60. See *Syed Ahmed* v *Julaiha Bivi*, *AIR* 1947 Mad 480 ; *Mohammad H.* v *Iffal Pra*, (1947) ILR 2 Cal 16.
61. *Supra* note 4.
62. *AIR* 1942 Bom 441 : (1942) 44 BLR 256.
63. *AIR* 1947 All 137 : (1946) ILR All 585 ; see also *Badrul Islam Ali Khan* v *Mt Ali Begum*, *AIR* 1936 Lah 251.
64. *AIR* 1962 All 364.
65. *Musharraf Begum* v *Sikandar*, *AIR* 1928 All 40: 411C 583.
66. *AIR* 1935 *Lah* 414 : (1929) *LIR* 51 All 40 : 41 *IC* 583.
67. *AIR* 1948 *PC* 168 : (1649) *IIR Lah* 1 : 50 *BLR* 674.
68. *AIR* 1957 *Mad* 583.
69. (1949) ILR 1 Cal 333.
70. *AIR* 1938 Lah 453 : ILR (1938) 19 Sah 435.
71. (1936) 11 Luck 735 ; 160 IC 495,
72. *AIR* 1962 SC 1722.
73. *AIR* 1960 Mad 318.
74. *Mohammed Ali* v *Dinesh*, *AIR* 1940 Cal 417 ; *Sheikh Ramzan* v *Rahma AIR* 1932 Oudh 71 ; *Ruqaia* v *Sarajmal*, *AIR* 1936 All 404 ; *Ghulam Mohammed* v *Ghulam Hussain*, *AIR* 1932 PC 81.
75. *AIR* 1435 All 35.
76. 1969 All 616.
77. *AIR* 1957 All 94.
78. *Khajeh Soleman* v *Nawab*, *AIR* 1922 PC 107 : *Mohammad Irfan* v *Mohammad AIR* 1933 All 277 ; *Sekandar* v *Badruddin*. *AIR* 1935 Cal 792; Satifunnissa v Nazimuddin, AIR 1935 All 856.

79. *AIR* 1958 All 67.
80. *Latafunnissa* v *Shaher Bano*, CIC 1932 Oudh 108.
81. *Birjis Mahel* v *Humayun Raza*, *AIR* 1944 Pat 234.
82. *Syed Mohammed* v *Syed*,(1881) 6 Bom 88 ; *Sheikh Karimuddin* v *Nawab* (1885) 10 Bom 119.
83. *AIR* 1954 All 385.
84. *AIR* 1958 AP 8.
85. *Shahrukh* v *Enayet Hussain*, *AIR* 1975 All 452.
86. *Siddique Fatima* v *Mahmood Hasan*, *AIR* 1978 *SC* 1368 ; (1978) ALJ 635.
87. Cited by Supreme Court at p 1369 in the case under discussion.
88. Mulla, *Mahommadan Law*, ((18th ed) (1980) para 200, 223; see also Macnaghten's *Principles and Precedents of Mahommadan Law*, (1825) p 341 ; *Sayed Mahomod* v *Sayed Gobar*, (1881) 6 Bom 88, 90 *Abdul Ganne* v *Hussen Miyan*,(1873) 10 BHC 7 at 14 ; *Sheikh Karimudin* v *Nawab Mir Sayed*,(1885) Bom 19.
99. The word usufruct means the right of temporary possession, use or enjoyment of the advantages of property belonging to an other so far as may be had without causing damage and prejudice to this.
90. *Vidya Viruthi* v *Balusami*, *AIR* 1922 *PC* 123 : 48 *I.A.* 302 : 44 Mad 131 : 65 IC 101.
91. 50 *IA* 84.
92. *Muhammad Rustom Ali* v *Mushtaq Hussain*, 27 IA 224, 42 All 669, 612, 57 IC 329.
93. 61 *IA* 50.
94. *AIR* 1933 All 407.
95. *AIR* 1970 All 509.
96. *AIR* 1963 SC 985.
97. *AIR* 1978 Cal 133.
98. Tyabji, *Muslim Law*, (4th ed) Chapter X, p 523.
99. *Supra* note 86.
100. p. 494.
101. *Ibid*, p 498.
102. *i.e.* a waqf for the family of the founder where only the ultimate benefit is reserved to charity.
103. *Supra* note 90, p 224 ; see also *Hashim Hussain* v *Ahmad Raza AIR* 1974 All 305 (DB).
104. *AIR* 1970 All 509.
105. s.n. 100.
106. *Supra* note 100, section 545, p 606-608.
107. *Supra* note 23, p 472.

108. *Supra* note 88.
109. *AIR* 1971 SC 1691.
110. At page 1604-95.
111. *Supra* note 88.
112. George W. Keeton, *The Law of Trusts*, (Ninth ed) p. 329.
113. *Supra* note 30.
114. *Supra* note 22 ; see also *Ismail* v *Umar*, AIR 1942 Bom 155.
115. See section 2 (3) of the U.P. Muslim Waqfs Act, 1960.
116. See section 34 of the Bengal Waqf Act, 1934.
117. See section 52 of the Bengal Waqf Act, 1934.
118. See S. Khalid Rashid, *Waqf Administration in India* pp. 136-137

6

A Socio-Legal Study of the Role of Mutawallis in the Administration of Waqf Property

As soon as a waqf is created it becomes necessary to appoint a person who will look after the property of the waqf. This person is known as the mutawalli of the waqf property. The literal meaning of mutawalli is *nazir, qavyim.* He is responsible for carrying out the object of the waqf and to carry out the directions given at the time of its dedication. He is also responsible for the maintenance of the waqf property and for the realisation of outstanding waqf dues.

A mutawalli is a person or a body of persons entrusted with the management of a waqf. The mutawalli of a waqf is its superintendent. He is an agent who is bound to carry out the instructions laid down in the waqfnama, and who has to refer all discretionary matters to the Qazi. His position as a mutawalli is much better than a trustee, for his duties and obligations are far fewer and as a general rule he is under no liability to produce accounts.[1]

A mutawalli has the power of management and administration of waqf properties. He is entitled to the possession of all waqf properties. The servants and officers of the religious institution are subject to the control of its head. The deed of endowment usually provides for their salaries and remunerations[2]. The mujawar are servants of the khanqah and can be dismissed by the sajjadanashin.[3]

The office of mutawalli is different from trustee because he is not the owner of the waqf property. In India, in many judicial pronouncements the legal position of mutawalli was explained. In brief, the courts have asserted that :

(i) a mutawalli is not the owner of the waqf property;
(ii) he is only the manager and supervisor of the waqf property; and
(iii) his functions resemble those of a trustee but do not make him one.[4]

A mutawalli, during medieval period enjoyed very vast powers. Ibn Battuta was appointed mutawalli of waqfs of the tomb of Sultan Qutb-ud-din. Ibn Battuta was having the appointing power. He could appoint any number of persons. In fact he appointed nearly 450 persons to perform various duties. During this period a mutawalli was having power to enhance the amount already fixed by the head of the state. They were having discretionary power in the matter of appointment as well as in the matter of expenditure. The appointment of mutawalli was made on the basis of their honesty and sincerety. Only persons having good conduct and record were appointed. However, later on these persons became corrupt. It was the policy of the head of the state not to disturb honest mutawallis. During medieval period mutawallis were not considered totally state servants. They were guaranteed their independence in the working of the waqf property.

Under the mughal rule also mutawallis were given high status. So long as mutawallis were honest they were not disturbed. Their activities were checked either by Qazis or by the government auditors.

Shah Jahan was himself looking after the work of the mutawalli of Taj Mahal.[5] Mutawallis were required to maintain proper accounts of the receipt and expenditure of waqf property. These accounts were duly audited by the king's officials.[6]

After the passing of the Waqf Act, 1954, the position of mutawalli has been changed. A mutawalli is now under the double check of Board and the court. He is bound to file regular accounts to the Waqf Board. Any slackness on the part of the mutawalli to perform this duty will entitle the Board to take penal action against the mutawalli.

The appointment of a mutawalli of the waqf property is one of the important element of a valid waqf because in the absence of a mutawalli the wishes of the waqif cannot be fulfilled. In case a mutawalli is not appointed at the time of dedication, later on, it may become difficult to ascertain the intention of the waqif. It is, therefore, necessary that immediately on the dedication of property a mutawalli should be appointed.

Under Muslim law the office of mutawalli is mandatory. Abu Hanifa and and Imam Muhammad[7] are of the opinion that in the absence of a mutawalli, the dedication shall carry no force. On the other hand, Abu Yusuf is of the opinion that even in the absence of a mutawalli, the waqf shall be valid and the waqif himself shall become the mutawalli.

Under Shia law, where the object of the waqf is not to benefit specified individuals, but to promote works of general utility, and the waqif has not appointed any mutawalli, he himself becomes the mutawalli.[8]

On the creation of a waqf, all rights in the waqf property vest in God. The dedicator ceases to have any control over the property. The property is managed by mutawalli who is the manager, the governor, superintendent or curator but he is not the owner of the property, but merely the servant of God, managing the property for the good of His creatures.[9] Lord Summer said that mutawalli is not the owner of the waqf property.[10] The property belongs to the Almighty and is in very deed God's Acre. He is not the trustee for the waqf property and the property does not vest in him but vests in the Almighty.[11] He is not the owner of the property, but merely the servent of God, managing the property for the good of His creatures. He is the person who is appointed for the fulfilment of the object of the waqf, and the carrying out of the directions given at the time of its dedications.[12] This view was affirmed by the Supreme Court in Zain Yar Jung v Director of Endowments.[13]

A mutawalli is simply a manager of the waqf property. Sometimes he is also called as superintendent of waqf property, though he enjoys slightly better position than that of a mere manager or superintendent.

A mutawalli is also not the trustee of the waqf property,[14] in the English sense. The reason is he is not the owner of the property. He possess the power to manage the property as an individual. In a case pertaining to the private waqf, the Nagpur High Court said that the mutawalli is not a mere manager or superintendent but is practically speaking its owner.[15] This is his duty to see that the waqf property is used for the object mentioned in the waqf deed.

The mutawalliship of the waqf property is in the nature of a public office. A mutawalli is having the same rights of management as an individual owner is having in his property. He cannot be compelled for the use of property for the purpose not directed by the Waqf. In Syed Ahmad's case the Allahabad High Court said that the Muslim community of the locality where the mosque is situated cannot compel the mutawalli of the mosque to allow a school building to be constructed on the site attached to the mosque.[16]

As already submitted he is also not the trustee of the waqf property. The deed appointing mutawalli (trustee nama) does not purport to assign property to trustees. A mutawalli controls only usufruct and nothing else more.[17] They are trustees in the general sense that every man is a trustee to whom is entrusted the duty of managing and controlling property that belongs to another.

It will not be out of the way to mention here the difference between a mutawalli and trustee. On the one hand, a mutawalli is having legal, moral and religious duties and on the other, a trustee is having only secular duties. If a mutawalli disregards his above duties, he will be legally, morally and religiously responsible. It is true that he is not a trustee but he has duties similar to those of a trustee. He is answerable and responsible in case of mismanagement in the same manner as if he was the trustee thereof. If a mutawalli wrongfully deprived a beneficiary of the profits he is liable to pay interest on the amount in the same way as a trustee is bound to pay it.[18]

A mutawalli can sue and be sued in his personal capacity for the declaration that he is the mutawalli. It is not necessary for him to sue for the possession of property.[19] Since a mutawalli is a superintendent or manager of the waqf property he is entitled to sue for possession, though the property is vested in him.[20] The Muslim community can not compel the mutawalli of a mosque to allow a school building to be erected on a site attached to the mosque.[21]

A mutawalli has been given power to do all necessary repairs for the protection of waqf property. However, the mutawalli must use his power reasonably and he should not do any act which is not necessary. It is not easy to draw a clear cut line between the acts which are nacessary and the acts which are not necessary. This differs from case to case. It has been judicially said that a mutawalli has no power to make, or expend on, mere improvements, *e.g.*, the addition of a minaret to a mosque, unless it was necessary for the calls to prayers.[22]

The waqf property is not liable to attachment and sale in execution of a personal decree against the mutawalli. Similarly, the rents and profits thereof cannot be seized in execution.[23]

The office of mutawalli has also been saved from the attachment. His office cannot be attached in execution of a personal decree against the mutawalli.[24]

Creation of Waqf without Mutawalli

There was a difference of opinion on the question as to what will be the consequence if a waqf was created but no mutawalli was appointed. Imam Abu Hanifa and Imam Muhammad were of the opinion that no waqf could be established if the mutawalli was not appointed. The dedication would fail. Qazi Abu Yusuf was having some other opinion on the point. According to him dedication was lawful and the waqif became the mutawalli. A quite different view was taken by the Shia jurists. The Shia jurists were of the opinion that the dedication was effective and the beneficiaries were entitled to administer the waqf.

The Allahabad High Court[25] has said that it is not open to settler to change the character of the waqf while laying down new rules for the appointment of mutawalli.

Under Islamic law, courts have been assigned wide discretion. The courts like chancery courts of England keep a close watch on the action of the trustee. According to Justice Ameer Ali[26] in the case of a waqf of trust created for specific individuals or a determinate body of individuals, the Quazi whose place in the British Indian system is taken by the civil, court, has in carrying the trust into execution to give effect so far as possible to the expressed wishes of the founder. With respect to public waqfs, the Qazi's discretion is very wide. He may not depart from the intentions of the founder or from any rule fixed by him as to the objects of the benefactions ; but as regards management which must be governed by circumstances he has complete discretion. He may defer to the wishes of the founder so far as they are comfortable to changed conditions and circumstances, but his primary duty is to consider the interests of the general body of the public for whose benefit the trust is created. In this case, Mr. Justice Ameer Ali said that a certain section of the worshippers in a mosque had a greater right to manage and act as trustees, and the appointment of trustees was left to a committee which was to act under the general guidance of the court.

Mulla[27] says that the office of mutawalli is not hereditary and if a custom to that effect were set up, it would have to prove strictly. If the office of a mutawalli becomes vacant on account of death, removal of refusal to act as such, a new mulawalli may be appointed by the founder of his executor or by the court. The Madras High Court[28] has said that in appointing a mutawalli, other things being equal, the court would show a preference towards a member of the founder's family. It may, however, be noted here that this is not always the right of the member of the founder's family to be appointed as the mutawalli. The court can appoint any family member of the founder as mutawalli.

The mutawalli of a public waqf is the public officer. If there is a dispute between two persons regarding the appointment of mutawalli, the matter cannot be referred to arbitration.[29] Where 'A' claims that certain property and that he is the mutawalli thereof, and 'B' denies that the property is waqf property, an award made by an arbitrator that each shall be entitled to an equal share in the management and profits of the property until the matter is decided by the court is perfectly valid.[30]

Capabilities for the Appointment of Mutawalli

A person who has attended the age of majority and who is of sound mind can be appointed as mutawallii.[31] There is no bar of sex and religion in the appointment of the mutawalli. The person concerned must, however, be able to perform the duties perfectly. The following persons have been recognised to be appointed as the mutawalli—

(i) the founder himself (waqif),

(ii) his children ;

(iii) women ;

(iv) non-Muslims and

(v) Sunniites in a Shiite waqf and *vice versa.*

Appointment of Waqif as the Mutawalli

Ameer Ali[32] says that a waqif will not be the trustee unless he has reserved the trusteeship for himself at the time of consecration. Abu Yusuf is. however, of the opinion that consignment is not necessary in waqif so even when he does not (expressly) reserve the trusteeship for himself, he will still be the trustee. The opinion expressed by Abu Yusuf has been followed in many cases.

A waqif is competent to provide a scheme for succession to the office of mutawalli. He can nominate a successor by name, or he may indicate the class of persons who may succeed to mutawalliship. The founder may lay down the qualifications for the mutawalli. The settler may give power to the mutawalli to nominate the successor. The settler may provide in the waqf deed that the devolution to mutawalliship will be from generation to generation. The lineal descendants of the founder have no inherent right to be appointed as mutawalli. The Madras High Court has said that if the line of devolution is prescribed from generation to generation it does not follow that a female, or persons claiming through females are excluded though it may not be desirable to appoint a female owing to their habits and seclusion. In such cases, it cannot be said that women descendants are meant to be excluded, though it is different matter that the court may exclude female descendant from holding office on the ground that it would not be desirable in the interest of the waqf that a woman should hold the office.[33]

In *Shahr Banoo* v *Aga Mohammad*[34] the founder was a Shia Muslim and his lineal descendant who claimed to be appointed as mutawalli was a female of the Babi sect. The trial court accepted the claim of the female and appointed her as mutawalli. The aggrieved party appealed to the High Court. The High Court did not agree with the decision of the trial court. The High Court set aside the order of the trial court and appointed another person as mutawalli. The matter went in appeal. The Privy Council held that the decision of the High Court was correct. The female was removed from her office not because she belonged to Babi sect, but because as a member of the Babi sect she might not take zealous interest in carrying out the religious observances of the Shia school for which the trust was founded.

The Calcutta High Court was of the opinion that females heirs are competent to be appointed as mutawalli, and they will be appointed as mutawalli as and when the opportunity may arose. In this case a Muslim lady declared herself as the first mutawalli. She also directed that the succession to next mutawalli should be to the legal heirs of the second mutawalli.[35]

In *Mohammad Eshaque* v *Mohammad Amin* the judicial committee of the Privy Council held that the words 'bafarzandan' did not exclude the daughters of male descendants, but excluded the children of daughters. In this case the waqif appointed his son as mutawalli. It was also provided that the descendants (ba farzandan-parzandan) should succeed as mutawallis.[36]

A mutawalli can also be appointed by way of congregation. The dedicator mutawalli who has named a person to be his successor after his death can in his life time, appoint a third person as mutawalli. Such a person can act during the rest of the waqif's life but not thereafter. In *Ali Asghar* v *Fariuddin*[38] the waqif appointed himself as the first mutawalli. He also provided in the waqf deed that after his death, 'P' would be the mutawalli. Later on, the settler resigned from the office of mutawalli and appointed 'R' as mutawalli. 'P' questioned the validity of this appointment. It was held that 'P' questioned the validity of this appointment. It was held that 'P' was entitled to the office of mutawalliship only after the death of the settler, and if the settler resigned during his life time, he could fill the vacancy by nominating any person as mutawalli. The court further held that such an appointment would be valid only during his life time. On the death of the settler, 'P' would be entitled to mutawalliship.

The power of appointment does not include the power to remove from the office of mutawalliship. A waqif who has appointed a personas mutawalli will have no right to remove a mutawalli.

Under Shia law, a waqf will not be valid unless and until delivery of possession has been made to the mutawalli or to the beneficiaries. The waqif becomes *functus officio* immediately after he had transferred the property to the mutawalli. The waqif can appoint mutawalli after dedication of property and before transfer of possession. However, the waqif cannot appoint mutawalli after the transfer of possession. He can make an appointment, or settle a scheme at any time before the delivery of possession[39].

If the waqif has failed to appoint a mutawalli he cannot afterwards make an appointment or settle a scheme because immediately after the creation of the waqf the beneficiaries acquired the right to administer waqf property.[40]

Appointment of non-Muslims *etc* as the Mutawalli

Where the duties of a mutawalli are purely secular, a non-Muslim may be appointed as the mutawalli.[41] In case, the duties of a Mutawalli are in the nature of religious or spiritual, neither a female nor a non-Muslim can be appointed as a mutawalli.

Appointment of Sunni as a Mutawalli in a Shia Waqf

Muslim law does not prohibit a person belonging to a particular school of law to act as mutawalli for waqf belonging to the followers of another school of law. A Sunni may be appointed mutawalli of a Shia waqf. Similarly, a Shia Muslim can be appointed mutawalli of a Sunni waqf.[42] It may, however, be noted that the Indian courts have shown their restrain in some cases of this nature keeping in view the facts of those cases. In *Shahr Bano* v *Aga Mohammad Jaffar*, the court refused to appoint a female of Babi sects to be a mutawalli of a Shia waqf.[43]

Appointment of a Lady as Mutawalli

Quran has given to both males and females equal rights. But these rights have not been either interpreted or implemented correctly. There is no specific provision under which it can be said that ladies cannot be appointed as mutawalli. Muslim law does not exclude a woman from doing the temporal or non-religious duties of a mutawalli. A female or non-Muslim or a society may validly be appointed as mutawalli. But where the mutawalli has to perform religious duties or spiritual functions which cannot be performed by a female *e.g.* the duties a Sajjadanashin, or Kahatib or a Imam in a mosque or a Mauzzin a female or a non-Muslim is not competent to act as a mutawalli.

It was said by the Calcutta High Court that a womon was qualified for the appointment of mutawalli. However, she will not be eligible to be appointed as mutawalli if her duties involves religious functions. She will also not be eligible to be appionted as mutawalli if she cannot perform her functions in person.[44]

According to Allahabad High Court if the spiritual and secular duties can be separated and can be performed by a deputy, the female can remain in the office performing the secular duties alone.[45]

The Madras High Court has also said that secular duties can be performed by a woman or non-Muslims.[46] The Muslim law does not exclude a woman from doing the temporal or non-religious duties of a mutawalli.[47]

The only condition which Islam imposes for the appointment of mutawalliship is that he should be trustworthy, major and be able to understand the things properly. However, there is no mention in the religious books of Islam that the mutawalli must be professing Islam.[48]

Under Muslim law a *de facto* mutawalli can also be appointed. It has been said that a *de facto* mutawalli can file a suit for rent or for recovery of waqf property without establishing his *de jure* character.[49]

In Saadat Kamal Attorney General,[50] the Privy Council came to the conclusion that a sister was more prudent than her brother and therefore, the Council confirmed the appointment of sister as mutawalli in place of her brother.[50]

The Indian courts have held that where the mutawalli has to act also as Sajjadanashin, mujawar, imam or khatib, no woman can hold the office since the special duties of these functionaries cannot be performed by a woman.[51]

In *Kasim* v *Hajra Begum*,[52] the Calcutta High Court held that a woman can be appointed head mujawar of a astana or platform where Muharram ceremonies were performed.

The Nagpur High Court approved the validity of the appointment of a lady as mujawar.[53] This view was followed by Bombay High Court.[45] According to Bombay High Court a lady can be appointed as mujawar of a waqf. The Madhya Bharat High Court[55] also said that a lady appointed as mutawalli of a graveyard can be validly appointed. In this case the duties of a manager of graveyard were considered as secular. However, a lady will not be appointed as mutawalli if the administration of waqf requires a male, than a lady shall not be appointed as mutawalli.

In *Abdul Hamid* v *Abdul Aziz*[56] a Bengal Sunni Muslim was living in Bassein, a place which was quite distant from the waqf for which he was appointed mutawalli. He was, therefore, not able to perform his duties of mutawalliship. The court said that if it is required to chose from persons, then the court should chose a person on the basis of merit and a less qualified person should not be appointed as mutawalli.

According to Allahabad High Court males can be completely excluded from holding the office of mutawalli. In a case the Lahore High Court said that if a waqf was created exclusively for the benefit of females then males may be practically disqualified to be mutawalli of that institution. Under such circumstances only females may be appointed as mutawalli.[57] Where a succession is not made by inheritance and it is made by appointment, a minor cannot be appointed as mutawalli. However, a minor may be appointed as mutawalli provisionally for some time.[58] The Allahabad High Court again reiterated that a minor cannot be appointed as mutawalli. If a major cannot be appointed as mutawalli, the court should look after the waqf property.[59]

There was conflict of opinion on the question of appointing Shia mutawalli of the waqf made by a Sunni Muslim. It was thought that there was no wrong if a Shia Muslim is appointed mutawalli of a waqf made by a Sunni.[60] Later on, the opinion was changed. In Shahar Banoo's case[61] it was said that a lady can be appointed a mutawalli, but a Sunni Muslim cannot be appointed of a waqf established by Shia.

Appointment of Minor as Mutawalli

The waqif may appoint mutawalli, but it is essential that the person so nominated or appointed is a man of sound mind and not a minor. But where the succession to the office of mutawalli is by inheritance and not by appointment the position is quite different. The general rule is that a person appointed as mutawalli must be major (and that too according to Indian Statutory Law). In case of the appointment of a minor as mutawalli by way of succession, the whole waqf will not fail because of such minority. According to classical Muslim law, if waqif appoints minor as sole mutawalli, without adult, guardian, qazi shall appoint some other person to officiate minor as sole mutawalli. Where adult and minor are joint mutawalli qazi may either appoint some person to represent minor who should act with adult mutawalli, or may empower latter to represent minor.[62]

Ameer Ali while quoting *Fatwai Alamgiri* says that a minor can be appointed as mutawalli. However, he cannot act as mutawalli till he attains majority. He further says that a minor cannot be appointed as mutawalli but his office can devolve by virtue of a provision in the dedication to some such effect as that the tauliat should be confined to the male descendants of the waqif or the members of a particular family.[64] If the court feels that the person on whom office so devolves, he must appoint another person to discharge the duties during the minority of the person entitled.

The cases when a minor is allowed to be appointed as mutawalli needs reconciliation. It is submitted the intention of the waqif should be taken into consideration. It is presumed that the intention of the waqif must not be to appoint a minor as mutawalli. It is, therefore, submitted that a minor shall not be appointed to the office of mutawalli till he has attended the age of majority according to Indian Majority Act.

Mutawalliship is not Property

Under the Muslim law mutawalliship is an office. A mutawalli is not allowed to sell, mortgage or lease the waqf property unless he obtains the permission of the court which has the general powers of controlling the actions of mutawalli. The right to act as mutawalli is not heritable. In the case of *Mad Rustom Ali* v *Mashtaq Husain*[65] the Privy Council held that the deed by which a mutawalli is appointed and vested with mutawalliship does not constitute a transfer to them the ownership of the property as such it is outside the provisions of Indian Registration Act, 1877. The same view was reaffirmed by the Privy Council in still later decision in the case of *Alla Rakhi* v *Mad Abdur Rahim.*[66] The Supreme Court of India in the case of *Zainvarjung* v *Director of Endowment,*[67] accepted and approved the principle laid down in Vidya Varuthi's case in holding the mutawalli to be a manager, governor, superintendnet or curator. The law laid down in *Mohammad Qamar* v *SalamtiAli*[68] is also relevant to note here. It was said that in the case of family waqfs the mutawalli is not a mere superintendent or manager but is practically speaking the owner of the waqf property. But this opinion of Allahabad High Court was overruled by a full bench of the said High Court in *Moattar Raza* v *Joint Director of Consolidatian.*[69] The Full Bench said that the Mutawalli acquires no right, title or interest in the property itself but he is merely the holder of the office of a manager under the Muslim law. Therefore, cultivation of waqf land by a mutawalli must be treated as cultivation done in his capacity as manager or superintendent the waqf and the cultivation by him would be referable on behalf of God and it would be God's khudkost or that of waqf itself.[70]

The above issue was again agitated before full bench of Calcutta High Court in *Mt Zohra Khatoon* v *Janab Mohammad Jane Alam*.[71] In this case the Calcutta High Court said that it is not correct to say that holder of the post of a mutawalli is not the holder of mere office but is the holder of a property. Therefore, the claim of the plaintiff in so far as it is a claim to be declared the sole mutawalli is a claim limited to an office and is not a claim to the immovable property appertaining to the waqf estate of which the plaintiff claims to be the mutawalli.

Save and except as recognised by any custom, the law does not favour the right to act as mutawalli becoming heritable. When the mutawalli dies subject to an specific provision to the contrary in the deed of endowment, the waqf if still alive possesses the right to appoint another and in his absence his executor and in the absence of both it is the court that appoints the successor mutawalli. The mutawalli has no ownership right or estate in the waqf property, he holds the property as a manager for fulfilling the purpose of the waqf. Even a Sajjadanashin who has a larger interest of the usufruct has been held to have no right in the property endowed. These features, therefore, distinguish a mutawalli from a shebait and the elements which render shebaitship a property not being the mutawalliship cannot be considered as a property.

APPOINTMENT OF MUTAWALLI

Immediately on the creation of the waqf, the waqif cases to have any right over the dedicated property. The dedicated property vests in the almighty. The waqif can exercise the powers of a mutawalli. It has been said that the waqif of every Hanafi waqf can and that of every Ithna Ashari waqf must appoint the first mutawalli. A mutawalli may be appointed by the following persons.

(i) by the waqif himself;
(ii) by his executor;
(iii) nomination of successor by mutawalli;
(iv) appointment of successor's successors;
(v) by the mutawalli;
(vi) by the court;
(vii) by congregation.

By the Waqif himself

The founder of the waqf possesses power to appoint the first mutawalli and to lay down a scheme for the administration of the waqf and for succession to the office of mutawalli.[72] The appropriator has a right to reserve the superintendence to himself. If the waqif on the other hand, has reserved the right of management of waqf to himself, he can appoint mutawalli during his lifetime, whenever he thinks proper.[73]

As already noted a waqif can also nominate the names of his successors. In *Ghazenfar* v *Ahmadi*,[74] the Allahabad High Court said that the waqif has power to nominate the successor by or indicate the class together with power to nominate a successor after his death or relinquishment of office.

Where the office of the mutawalli is lying vacant, and the waqf deed is also silent on the mode of succession of mutawalli the waqif (if alive) or his executor (if any) can appoint a successor. Where the office of mutawalli is lying vacant and the mutawalli is suffering from marz-ul-maut, he can appoint a person his successor as mutawalli.[75]

In practice, the courts have allowed a mutawalli to appoint another mutawalli only in the case of private waqf. In the case of public waqfs, the courts are having more powers than the waqif. The Madras High Court[76] said that although the waqif has the first right to appoint an Imam of a dedicated mosque, but if the person he appoints is incompetent the court can, on the application of the congregation, appoint a more suitable person.

By his Executor

The power of appointing a mutawalli rests primarily with the waqif. In case, mutawalli has failed to exercise this right, his wasi or executor may appoint a person as mutawalli. Where there no executor, the mutawalli for the time being may appoint a successor on his death bed. The Orissa High Court said that where the waqif and his executor are dead, and the waqfnama is silent in respect of the appointment of mutawalli, the mutawalli for the time being may appoint a successor on his death bed. This power can be used only if the mutawalli is lying on the death bed. If he is having sound health, he will have no right to appoint a mutawalli.[77]

Nomination of Successor by Mutawalli

Under Muslim law the moment a waqf is created all rights of property pass out of the waqif and vest in the Almighty. The mutawalli has no right in the property belonging to the waqf : the property is not vested in him, and he is not a trustee in the technical sense.

The Supreme Court of India[78] also had the opportunity to deal with the rights of a mutawalli. Their lordship of the Supreme Court observed that—

> The mutawalli has no right in the property belonging to the waqf. He is not a trustee in the technical sense, his position being merely that of a superintendent or a manager. A mutawalli has no power, without the permission of the court, to mortgage, sell or exchange waqf property or any part thereof, unless he is expressly empowered by deed of waqf to do so.

It is thus clear that a mutawalli is not a trustee or manager but a superintendent of property. A mutawalli is further not the owner of the property, but merely a servant of God, managing the property for the good of his creatures. The founder of the waqf has the power to appoint the first mutawwalli and to lay down a scheme for the administration of the trust and for succession to the office of mutawalli. He may nominate successors by name or indicate any class, together with their qualifications, from whom the mutawalli may be appointed and may invest the mutawalli with power to nominate a successor after death or relinquishment of office.

Ameer Ali[79] has quoted the following passage—

> The mutawalli cannot, however, assign or transfer the office to any one, or appoint another during his life time, unless his own powers are general. Should he in his life time and in health appoint another in his place the appointment will not be lawfull and valid, unless the mutawalli has obtained the towliat with that condition, 'in a general manner.

Ameer Ali,[80] however, says that a waqif can empower the mutawalli to appoint his successor. This power is known as *towliat nama*, In such cases the mutawalli can appoint his successor even in good health.

It is also relevant here to note the observations of Baillie[81]—

> A superintendent may at death commit his office to another, in the same way as an executor may commit him to another...A superintendent while alive and in good health cannot lawfully appoint another to act for him, unless the appointment of himself were in the nature of a general trust.

Tyabji says[82] that 'the mutawalli may in acoordance with section 514 appoint a successor to succeed him at death, but he cannot validly transfer his office to another during his lifetime. An appointment or nomination made during the lifetime of the mutawalli is revocable like other testamentary dispositions.'

Mulla[83] has stated the aforesaid controversy in the following words —

> If the founder and his executor are both dead, and there is no provision in the wakfnama for succession to the office, the mutawalli for the time being may appoint a

successor on his death bed. He cannot, however, do so while he is in health, as distinguished from death illness, nor if the office goes by hereditary right.[84]

On the basis of law stated above, it is not clear whether Muslim law permits appointment of a successor by a mutawalli only on his death bed or he can appoint a mutawalli during his good health. It may be noted here that there is a difference between appointment and nomination. Appointment means to put in or choose for a position. It means the complete surrender of his office by the mutawalli, and the immediate transfer of the same in favour of the appointee. Nomination means to suggest or name (someone) officially for election to a position. In nomination the surrender of office does not take place immediately on the execution of document. The office goes to the appointee only after the death of the appointer.[85] The judgment of the Lahore High Court was challenged by means of an appeal before the Privy Council. Their lordships of the Privy Council allowed the appeal and reversed the judgment of the Lahore High Court on another point, but while dealing with the question of the right of a mutawalli to nominate his successor only on death bed, their lordships made the following observations :

> It certainly is not easy to see any rational basis for a rule which requires that an appointment to take effect on death shall be made only by one in mortal sickness when the appointer's judgment may well be impaired. Moreover, death may come without warning, or the expectation of death may not be realised. In the former case no appointment will be made and in the latter any appointment will be ineffective.

In another case before the Privy Council[86] same contention was raised. It was urged that the Muslim law prescribes that a nomination could be valid only if it was made while the incumbent was on his death bed, or was suffering from mortal sickness, but not when he was in good health. The Privy Council failed to give any final decision on the aforesaid controversy. The Privy Council observed that—

This contention, which appears to be supported by some authorities on the Muslim law would prevent a mutawalli from appointing his successor if he died suddenly without any expectation of death, and render ineffective any appointment made by him at a time when he was *not* on his death bed or suffering from such illness.

The rule on the basis of which it has been said that a mutawalli cannot appoint his successor excepting on death bed appears to be based on the principle against delegation of the powers of a trustee in favour of another. Although it is true that a mutawalli is not a trustee within the meaning of the Indian Trust Act, but the nature of the duties which he is required to perform are more or less the same. A mutawalli stands in fiduciary relationship and it is against the interest of society in general that such relationship should be allowed to be terminated unilaterally. It thus appears that it is on account of this reason that under the Muslim law a mutawalli is permitted to appoint his successor on his death bed—so that the mutawalli in office may not delegate his power to work as such during his lifetime. It is thus clear that Muslim law permits the appointment of a successor by a mutawalli to be effective after his death. Therefore, the appointment of a successor by a mutawalli in good health which would be effective after the death of the mutawalli does fall within the permissible limits of the Muslim law. According to Justice K.C. Agarwal of Allahabad High Court[87] the nomination of a successor by a mutawalli can be made even in good health to take effect on death. By nomination a mutawalli only proposes or selects his successor to exercise his duties as a mutawalli on his death bed. He does not part with or delegate his functions of a mutawalli during his lifetime. It is only this delegation or parting with duties by a mutawalli during his lifetime in good health that is prohibited.

In *Mohammad Khan Saheb* v *Kadir Beteha Sahib*.[88] one Amir Khan Saheb, the last man of the family of the original founder, made a settlement by which he endowed the mosque, with some other property, and appointed his foster son as the person entitled to enjoy the property endowed for charity, and to carry out the charity by means of its income. The validity of this appointment made by Amir Khan Saheb was subsequently challenged. It was contended that Amir Khan Saheb had no power to appoint him as successor. Justice Madhavan Nair of Madra High Court observed—

> ...it is well known principle of Mohammedan law, that in the absence of rules laid down by the founder of the mosque, the mutawalli for the time being may validly appoint a successor to himself. The present defendant was so appointed in 1879 and in my opinion he is a validly appointed trustee...

In *Ghazanfar Hussain* v *Mat Ahmadi Bibi*, a case before the High Court of Allahabad, a waqf deed dated 7th April, 1922, was executed by Mir Inayat Hussein, under which Mst Ahmadi Bibi was claiming to be in possession of the property as mutawalli of the trust. This claim was challenged by the plaintiff on number of grounds. The High Court found that Inayat Hussein was the founder of the trust and it was in this connection that the following observations were made—

> ...under the Mohemmedan law a mutawalli who is not the founder of the trust has no power whilest in health to appoint a successor or to formulate any scheme for succession to the office of the mutawalli, but this restriction does not apply to the founder of the waqf who in reason and equity ought to have a free hand in the matter of nominating a mutawalli for the administration of the trust in praesenti, and in laying down a detailed scheme as regards the succession to the office of the mutawalli...'

It is clear from the above case, that there is no doubt in respect of a founder of a trust to nominate at any stage he liked. The doubt may arise only in the cases where the mutawalli was not the founder of the trust.

In *Ali Asgar* v *Farid-uddin*[90] it was mainly contended that the settler had power to resign his own mutawalliship and to appoint another as his successor. It was in connection with this controversy the Allahabad High Court held that on the principles which had been deducted from the texts the waqif was himself the first mutawalli and he could appoint a successor.

In *Haji Sheikh Ali Mohammad* v *Mohammad Yusuf*[91] it was found that Mukarram Ali who had executed the document and appointed mutawallis was not in fact a mutawalli himself. In view of this finding that Mukarram Ali was not a mutawalli, the Orissa High Court observed that under Muslim law a mutawalli for the time being may appoint a successor on his death bed ; he cannot, however, do so while he is in health as distinguished from death illness.

The Lahore High Court[92] again said that a mutawalli has no right to nominate his successor, while in good health. The court held it is conceded that under Muslim law the nomination of a successor by the mutawalli for the time being is valid only if it is made while he was in death illness...' Again the Madras High Court[93] was faced with the problem of the rights of the founder to appoint a mutawalli. The Madras High Court said that—

> The Islamic law is clear on the question that when a founder has reserved to himself the power to assume the management of a waqf which he creates, on finding that the committee of supervision or other managers or office bearers have not discharged their duties, he has unfettered rights to assume the management of the trust himself or to appoint another trustee in the discretion for the property management of the trust...

The Andhra Pradesh High Court[94] also said that a mutawalli cannot appoint his successor when he is in good health or where the office goes by hereditary right.

The matter was again reviewed by Allahabad High Court.[95] A mutawalli in good health nominated his successor. The U.P. Waqf Board treated the nomination of a successor made by the erstwhile mutawalli as void since it was made during good health. The High Court reviewed the various relevant authorities and precedence on the subject and set aside the appointment when it held that the nomination was valid. The Court held that a mutawalli in good health can nominate his successor. The High Court held that the basis of which it has been stated that a mutawalli cannot appoint his successor excepting on death bed appears to be based on the principle against delegation of the powers of a trustee in favour of another...A mutawalli stands in fiduciary relationship and it is against the interest of society in general that such relationship should be allowed to be terminated unilaterally. It thus appears that it is on account of this reason that under the Muslim law a mutawalli is permitted to appoint his successor on his death bed so that the mutawalli in office may not delegate his power to work as such during his life time. Muslim law thus permits the appointment of a successor by a mutawalli to be effective after his death. So the appointment of a successor by a mutawalli in good health which would be effective after the death of the mutawalli does fall within the permissible limits of the Muslim law...

On the basis of various decisions discussed above, it can be said that a person can appoint mutawalli. Ameer Ali[96] has observed that 'in the law relating to waqf there are certain primary rules on which the principal doctors are in agreement. With regard to the subsidiary principles there is considerable divergence. The primary rules are (a) that the subject of the waqf should be dedicated in perpetuity ; (b) that all human right should be divested therefrom ; and (c) that it should be made non-heritable and inalienable. With regard to these there is consensus.' With regard to the subsidiary rules the same learned author[97] has observed that the Kazi is authorised to construe liberally the legal principles and to apply them in manner most consistent with justice and equity. These observations thus make it clear that there is scope for construing liberally the legal principles which may be applicable to the subsidiary rules relating to Muslim waqf.

The question of the right of a mutawalli to nominate his successor even when he his in good health is a matter to be governed by subsidary rules. Justice Mukherji of Allahabad High Court said[98]—

> It is a proposition of Mohammedan jurisprudence that where there are two opinions on a point of Mohammedan

law, the court should accept only that opinion which is in consonance with justice, equity and good conscience,[99]

Tyabji[100] says that it is not only in causes where there is a divergence of opinion that the principles of equity, justice and good conscience can be applied, but also, according to him, in other cases the aid of these principles can be taken.

By the Mutawalli

In the following cases a mutawalli on his death bed may appoint a person as mutawalli—

(a) where the waqif and executor are dead ;
(b) where the waqf deed is silent as to who shall be appointed as mutawalli ; and
(c) there is no positive custom regarding such devolution.[101]

As discussed earlier, the wishes of the waqif should be given paramounι consideration. In the absence of express provision in the waqfnama the office of mutawalli cannot go by hereditary right to the heirs of mutawalli.[102] A person who has appointed another person may not be able to remove the latter, unless the waqif whist confiding the trust, empowered him to assign the trust to another, and to remove the trustee.[103]

In the case of two or more mutawallis appointed jointly and the waqfnama is silent, the mutawalli shall be appointed on the basis of survivorship.[104] Where there are two mutawallis and one of them is dead, the survivor shall continue to be a mutawalli, unless there is a contrary direction in the waqfnama. The survivor also possess the power, on his death bed, to nominate his successor.[105] A mutawalli is empowered only to appoint his successor. A mutawalli has no powever to appoint his successor and so on and so forth.[106]

By the Court

A court of competent jurisdiction can appoint a person as mutawalli in the following circumstances—

(a) when a vacancy occurs and there is none to take the office of mutawalli ;

(b) when the mutawalliship devolves upon a minor.

A District Court is given the power of original jurisdiction. it can appoint a person as mutawalli only in a summary proceeding that is by means of a mere application.[107]

Though the courts are having power to appoint any person as mutawalli, but the courts are expected to honour the wishes of the waqif. The court can overlook the waqif's direction if it is neceessary in the interest of the waqif. The family member of the waqif cannot claim preference for the above appointment. The court can refuse to appoint the lineal descendants of the settler's family in case the court comes to the conclusion that his appointment as mutawalli will not be in the interest of the waqf.

The court's discretion in the matter of appointment of a mutawalli is very wide. It is analogous to the power of the chancery court superintending trustee's actions, Mr. Justice Ameer Ali[108] of the Privy Council distinguished between a private and public waqf. It is only in the case of a private waqf, the courts are required to give effect, so far as possible, to the wishes of the founder. However, in the case of public waqfs, the courts are having very wide discretion. Ordinarily, the courts are not expected to interfere with the intention of founder as regards the objects of waqf, but the courts are having full discretion in the matter of management. The courts are expected to give effeet to the wishes of the settler so far as they are conformable to the changed conditions and circumstnces but its primary concern and foremost duty is to take into consideration the interest of the general public for whose benefit the waqf is created. The courts are having discretion to vary or alter any rules fo management which it considers to be neither practicable nor in the best interest of the waqf. The courts can refuse to disregard any direction of the waqif if it feels that to do so will be in the interest of the waqf. Mr. Justice Ameer Ali maintained that even if the waqif makes a condition that the king or Qazi should not interfere in the management of waqf still the Qazi will have such powers for his supervision.

The interest of the waqf is the main consideration which a

court is rcquired to see while appointing a person as matuwalli. Keeping this fact into consideration the court can appoint a junior member in preference to a senior one or a non-descendant in preference to a descendant, if such an appointment is beneficial to the waqf.[109]

A waqif is fully competent to curtail the wide powers of the court. A waqif can make a provision in the waqf deed that a particular person cannot be appointed as mutawalli. In such cases the court should refrain from appointing him. Again, though the court possess the power to appoint a trustee directly without any recourse to section 92 of the Civil Procedure Code, a notice to the existing mutawalli should always be given.[110]

By Congregation

Appointment of mutawalli by congregation of the locality is made if the waqf is purely local.

The Waqf Board which is a body corporate is empowered of general superintendnece of all the waqfs existing in the state. Since, the Board is the only authority empowered, the approval of State Government is not required to make appointments to the Committee of management to be known Mutawallis. Section 63 of the Act does not empower the State Government to assume the power of the Waqf Board, nor does it enable the State Government to direct the Waqf Board to get the appointment of Mutawallis or Committee of Management of a waqf approved by the State Government. Such directions would be contrary to the provisions of the Act.

Where the State Government issues order either to appoint or accord approval to an appointment of Mutawalli, it does not have any legal force and is of no consequences.[111]

REMOVAL OF MUTAWALLI

Law before the Passing of Waqf Act, 1954

The following are the three ways for the removal of a Mutawalli—

(i) by the court;

(ii) by the Waqf Board; and

(iii) by the waqif himself.

By the Court

Ameer Ali says that the Qazi[112] has no power to remove a mutawalli merely on the complaint of the beneficiaries. He can remove the mutawalli upon proof of misfeasance or breach of trust.

It may, however, be noted that the court of competent jurisdiction can remove a mutawalli from his office. The power of the court to remove a mutawalli is unfettered and it can remove a mutawalli even against the wishes of the waqif. The Indian courts have the discretion to remove a mutawalli who is negligent towards his office. The courts can remove an insolvent mutawalli.[113] A mutawalli can be validly removed from his office if he has failed to make necessary repairs of the waqf property.[114] A mutawalli is removable from his office upon proof of misfeasance or breach of duty on his part even if the founder may have appointed him with the condition of non-removability.[115] The Calcutta High Court expressed the view that if a mutawalli neglects to repair the waqf premises, and allows them to fall iuto ruins, it amounts to breach of trust and he is liable to be removed from his office. Again, if a mutawalli has failed to produce accounts or pay taxes, without any just cause, he is guilty of misconduct and is liable to be removed from his office.[117]

Under Muslim law, taking of wine is strictly prohibited. Therefore, a mutawalli may be removed if he is proved to be addicted to drunkeness and such like vices[118]

While appointing new trustees and settling a scheme the court should keep into mind the wishes of the dedicators, the past history of the institutions, the way in which the management of the waqf was carried on *etc.* The court can give direction so that the affair of the waqf may be carried on property.[119]

Customary Law

Under the customary law, the manager of an institution may be expelled for misconduct or incompetency.[120] The worshippers of a mosque or the trustees of an endowment may possess the right to sue for the removal of a Mahant or to contest alienation of property belonging to the institution.[121] However, this right can be exercised only if there was a general or special custom to this effect.[122]

By the Waqif

It has been said that once a waqf comes into existence and a mutawalli is appointed, the founder ceases to have any power to remove the mutawalli unless such a power has been specifically reserved in the waqf deed.[123] It may, however, be noted here that this is not the settled law. There exists difference of opinion amongst classical jurists of Islamic law. Imam Mohammad says if the waqif has not reserved such right in the waqf deed, he cannot remove the mutawalli. According to Abu Yusuf waqif has such a right even without any such reservation.[124] In Fatwai Alamgiri also, the opinion expressed by Imam Mohammad has been followed. In India also, the opinion of Imam Muhammad has been followed in number of cases.[125]

The Madras High Court[126] expressed the view that a waqif cannot dismiss a mutawalli who has already taken charge of his office, unless he has reserved such a right under the waqf deed.

Where there is a dispute as to the right of a mutawalli to act as such and the Board has appointed some one in his place, his writ petition under Article 226 of the Indian Constitution will be premature during the pendency of inquiries conducted by the Board.[127]

Recently, the Madras High Court has held that the Waqf Board constituted under the Waqf Act, 1954 has no power to require the tenants by notice to pay rent not to the mutawalli but to itself merely because he has failed to submit accounts or his claim to the property is disputed.[128] It was further held that the Board is also not competent to interfere in the administration of a waqf during the pendency of proceedings for the removal of a mutawalli. This opinion of the Madras High Court is in consonance with the decision of the same High Court in *M. Mohammad Latif Sahib* v *Madras State Waqf Board*.[129]

It will also be relevant here to mention the provision of

the Madras Hindu Religious and Charitable Endowments Act, 1959. Sub-section (4) of section 53 of the Act says—

> Pending the disposal of the charges framed against the trustee, the appropriate authority may place the trustee under suspension and appoint a fit person to discharge the duties and perform the functions of the trustee.
>
> Again, sub-section (4) of section 64 provides that pending the settlement of a scheme for an institution, the Deputy Commissioner may appoint a fit person to perform all or any of the functions of the trustee thereof and define his powers and duties.

These are good provisions and can be very well provided in the waqf laws of India.[130]

REMUNERATION OF MUTAWALLI

Under Muslim law the office of mutawalli is honorary. A mutawalli cannot claim remuneration as of right. However, in practice a mutawalli is entitled for some remuneration. The remuneration of the mutawalli may be fixed either by the waqif or by the court. The following are the different modes of remuneration.

Remuneration as per Waqf Deed

The founder of the waqf can make a provision for the remuneration of the mutawalli in the form of a fixed alloance or otherwise.[131] The dedication may validly authorise the mutawalli, appointed by the waqif, and each succeeding mutawalli, to receive a specified remuneration for administering the waqf; provided that, in the absence of anything to indicate otherwise, the remuneration is receivable only by the first mutawalli, the succeeding mutawalli are not, without an order of the court entitled thereto.[132] The remuneration may be a fixed amount or may be the residue of the income of the waqf property after meeting all the expenses of the waqf. Where the waqf deed does not empower him, a mutawalli has no power to enhance the salary and allowances of the officers and servants of the waqf.

As regards the adequacy of remuneration it was said that one-third income of waqf villages was adequate remuneration.[133] On sixth net income has also been held to be adequate remuneration to the mutawalli.[134]

Remuneration as fixed by Court

In case the dedicator has failed to fix the remuneration of the mutawalli it can be fixed by the courts.[135] According to Ameer Ali[136] the general rule of Muslim law is that in fixing the salary of the mutawalli, regard should be given by the Quazi (now the courts) to the customary allowance at the time, but it should not exceed one tenth of the income.[137] A waqif is given the right to fix the amount of remuneration according to his fancy, but the courts can examine the adequacy of the amount fixed by the waqif.

The remuneration of a mutawalli is limited to the extent of waqf's income. In case, remuneration could not be paid to him, he will not be able to attach or sale the waqf property in execution of a decree. In *Ramanandan* v *Vada Levyai*[138] the Madras High Court said that if after utilising waqf income surplus fund, then the court can enhance the remuneration of a mutawalli.

The courts also possess power to enhance the remuneration if it comes to the conclusion that the amount fixed is meagre. If the amount[139] fixed by the founder is too small, the court may increase the allowance, but it must not exceed the limit of one tenth. A waqif has no right to fix the whole of the income of the waqf as remuneration of the mutawalli.[140]

The official trustee appointed by the dedicator is also entitled to receive remuneration. Section 9 of the Official Trustee Act says that if the dedicator was appointed an official trustee he will be entitled to receive in that behalf such remuneration as will be specified in the waqfnama. In case the official trustee was appointed as mutawalli by the court, his remuneration *etc* will be fixed according to the scales of commission given under section 11 of the Official Trustees Act.

Remuneration in Comparison to Other Debts

As regards the realisation of remuneration there is a difference in the process of realisation between a debt and the outstanding remuneration. The remuneration of the mutawalli does not create any right on the waqf property. In case the mutawalli was not paid his remuneration, he cannot proceed to attach the waqf property. He cannot dispose of the property by way of sale in execution of a personal decree against him for his private debts.[141]

Normally it is expected from the dedicator to fix the quantum of remuneration which shall be derived by the mutawalli. In case the dedicator has failed to fix the quantum of remuneration, the court may exercise its discretion and may fix the quantum of remuneration. According to Calcutta High Court[142] the court may fix a sum not exceeding one-tenth of the income of the waqf as remuneration. The above rule of one-tenth is not absolute. It may also vary. If after deducting religious and other allied expenses, there remains more funds than one-tenth he will be paid more than that.[243] One-third income of waqf villages has been treated as adequate remuneration.[144]

POWERS OF A MUTAWALLI

Under Muslim law a mutawalli has been given very wide powers. The discretion which has been assigned to a mutawalli is very wide. He can do all those acts which are reasonable and necessary for the protection and administration of the waqf properties under his supervision.[145] He can throw open the waqf property for purposes other than those, originally intended by the waqif. A mutawalli has been given power of management and administration of waqf properties. He has full power of applying the income of the waqf property for the purposes for which the waqf has been created. A mutawalli can appoint agents and servants to perform the ministerial acts necessary to carry out the duties of his office. A matuwalli is free to introduce any scheme which he considers shall be beneficial to the waqf. The beneficiaries cannot compel him to add any particular scheme.[146] It is lawful for a mutawalli to appoint his successor temporarily.[147]

A mutawalli has been given unlimited powers. He can himself appoint mutawalli of the waqf property. He may reserve the whole income for himself with a provision that it may be disposed of by him in any manner during his life time.

Construction of buildings on Waqf Property

It is lawful for a mutawalli to construct buildings on the waqf land. However, the construction must be beneficial to the objects of waqf. Fatawai Kazi Khan says—

> When the waqf land is adjacent to the houses in a town and people are inclined to rent the houses and the income would be greater by letting out the houses than by cultivation or planting trees, then the mutawalli may validly build houses and let them out, but the reverse is the case when the land is distant from the buildings of the town, in which case he is not entitled to build houses and let them out.

The grant of land for building purposes for the benefit of the waqf by Sajjadanashin has been held to be binding on his successor.[149] It is also lawful for a mutawalli to cultivate the waqf land if it is in the interest of waqf. Tyabji[194] says that—

(1) When the qayyin (or person in charge) of waqf lands desires to populate a village in it so that the inhabitants may increase therein, that they may protect it, and that the produce of corn may increase (their being required), then he is permitted to do so. An instance of this rule is when caravan serai is dedicated by way of for faqirs, as it is necessary to have a servant for sweeping and cleaning the serai, and for opening and closing the door, now the mutawalli gives a room to some person for his residence of by way of hire, is to do this work, and devote himself at to it. This is valid. This is in the Zahir.

(2) When the waqf land is adjacent to the houses in a town and people are inclined to rent the houses and the income would be greater by letting out the houses than by cultivation, or planting trees, then the qayyin may validly build houses and let them out, but the reverse is case when the land is distant from the buildings of the town, in which case he is not entitled

to build houses and 1st them out. This is in the Fatawai Kazi Khan.

Power to Mortgage, Charge Alienate, Lease out *etc*, of the Waqf Property

As already submitted a mutawalli is a manager or a superintendent of the waqf properties. He has, therefore, no beneficial interest in the waqf properties. He has no right to seal, or mortgage waqf property unless the waqfnama specifically provides for the same. A mutawalli can mortgage, charge or sell the waqf property after obtaiinng the permission from the court.[149] However, the waqif has the right to provide in the waqfnama that the mutawalli may be having power to dispose of the property. In *Abdur Rahim* v *Hachinur Raza* a mutawalli was removed on the ground that he made an unauthorised mortgage of waqf properties, and another person appointed as mutawalli. The new mutawalli tried to recover possession of the mortgaged properties from the mortgagee. It was argued that the mortgage was valid as to that portion of the properties which was settled for the benefit of waqif's family. The Judicial Committee refused to accept this contention. The Privy Council held that it was inconsistent with the basic concept of waqf.

In *Mohammad Usuf* v *Mohammad Afzal*[151] the waqf deed authorised the mutawalli to sale the property and utilise the proceeds for the construction and maintenance of a rest house at Mecca. It was held that the mutawalli could dispose of the property. The sale after the death of the waqif by the mutawalli according to the direction of the waqif has been held to be void against the heirs.[152]

In this connection, an amendment has been made in U.P. Section 49-A of the U.P. Muslim Waqf Act, 1960 lays down that even if the deed of waqf expressly authorises the mutawalli to transfer waqf property in given circumstances or otherwise, he cannot do so without the previous sanction of the Board. A retrospective permission is not contemplated by the Act. The waqif has power to empower mutawalli to mortgage, sale or lease out the property. If there is a necessity and there is no provision in the waqf deed the court may authorise the mutawalli to do so.

Alienation of Waqf Property with the Permission of the Court

It is a well established principle of law that a mutawalli can alienate or mortgage the waqf properties with the prior sanction of the court. However, a mortgage or alienation made without the sanction of the court is not void *ab initio*. The mutawalli may obtain the sanction of the court subsequently. The transaction is merely voidable.[153] Keeping this fact into consideration, the Calcutta, Madras and Allahabad High Courts and the Chief Court of Oudh have held that a mortgage made without the prior permission of the court may be retrospectively confirmed by the court. The Calcutta High Court[154] has held that the courts have the discretion to grant the approval of the mortgage retrospectively. Following this principle the Allahabad High Court confirmed a usufructuary mortgage by a mutawalli.[155] The Madras[156] and Orissa High Courts[157] have also confirmed the transaction of mutawallis retrospectively'. In all these cases the main basis for confirming the transaction of mutawalli was that the mortgage was necessary and it was in the interest of the waqf and that the pledge was not of the corpus put of the income. A beneficiary can challenge the unauthorised alienation. It is not necessary for him to bring a representative suit.[141] If a mutawalli was not having power to mortgage and he had mortgaged the waqf property the unauthorised mortgage cannot be partly valid.[159]

There is some difference of opinion among the various High Courts as to whether for obtaining permission of the court for alienating property, a suit was necessary or whether this can be done by putting in an application under the Trustees Act, 1866. Formerly, it was the judicial opinion of the courts that for the purpose of mortgage, lease *etc* of waqf property filing of separate suit was necessary. Merely filing of an application was not considered sufficient.[160]

In *Wazir Ali* v *Ladley Begum*,[161] a different view was taken. It was held that the sanction may be obtained on an application and that it is not necessary to bring a suit. In *Laung* v *Moolji*,[162] the Bombay High Court held that on a petition for appointment of new trustees, the Act is applicable to Hindus in Bombay. The Chief Court of Sindh,[163] was of the opinion that the procedure is by way of suit and not by way of application.

In *Thangu Chi* v *Ahmad Hussain* the Madras High Court held that any beneficiary, whose right was effected on account of the wrong action taken by the mutawalli, may bring a suit against the mutawalli for the possession of the waqf property. It is not necessary to file a representative suit.

Power of Mutawalli to grant Lease

Mulla says that a mutawalli has no power to grant lease of waqf property, if it be agricultural, for a term exceeding three years, and, if non-agricultural, for a term exceeding one year unless (a) he has been expressly authorised by the deed of waqf to do so ; or (b) where he has no such authority, unless he has obtained the leave of the court to do so : such leave may be granted even if the founder has expressly prohibited a lease for a longer term.

Ameer Ali[167] says that neither the *cestui que* trust nor the administrator can grant a lease of the waqf proerty for a longer period. According to Sidi Khalil, two years, according to others three years, is the longest term for which a lease may be given unless it is given to the next beneficiary, when it may be for ten years. The lease may, however, be extended if the property needs repair. It is a recognised principle that property held as waqf must be kept in good repair, and that future beneficiaries can in order to preserve their rights, oblige the usufructor to lease the house that is fälling into ruin and to apply the rent wholly to its reconstruction or repairs.

It will be relevant here to refer Tyabji's observation[168] on the subject under discussion. He says that subject to the provision of the various waqf acts, which empowers the statutory authorities created under the said Act, the mutawalli may obtain the sanction of the court for the sale or mortgage of waqf property by an application under the Indian Trustee's Act, XVII of 1866. But otherwise the sanction must be obtained by instituting a suit.

At another place[169] the learned author says that now statutory authorities created under various waqf statutes have drastically curtailed and regulated the powers with regard to alienation of waqf properties.

The recent trend in India is to grant long lease. Kamila Tyabji[170] says that the mutawalli's right to create long leases has been greatly increased in the modern law. This is in keeping with the general law of lease, where custom has long abrogated some of the more irksome rules including in a certain cases, the rule that the lease ended on the death of either party.[171]

In *Abdul Rahman* v *Abdul Hussain*[172] the Calcutta High Court said that under the Muslim law a mutawalli cannot grant lease of waqf property in the absence of express authority in the waqf deed or leave of the court obtained for the purpose... such lease being wholly invalid cannot be enforced even against the persons granting it. A similar view was taken by the Madras High Court.[173] The Madras High Court observed that a mutawalli has no power to grant a lease of waqf land for more than three years without the sanction of the Qazi. It was, however, made clear in that case that lease granted by the mutawalli in respect of waqf for more than three years, without the sanction of the court are not void *ab initio* under the Mohammadan law but only voidable, and are operative and binding on the mutawalli granting them unless they are declared to be otherwise. The court further observed that a mutwalli was justified in giviug the waqf property on long lease if it was necessary for the waqf property.

However, it may be noted here that there are numerous cases wherein a contrary view wat taken. It was held that under the Muslim law the leave of the court may be necessary for making a lease for a period exceeding one year, but such lease in the absence of sanction of the court would not be void if it is found to be for the benefit of the waqf. It means an alienation made by a mutawalli without the leave of the court can not be struck down as void if it is found to be for legal necessity or in the interest of the beneficiaries. The Calcutta High Court also took a simila view. In *N:mai Chand Adbya* v *Golam Hussain*'[174] a mortgage of the waqf property was made by the mutawalli on account of pressing necessity without the permission of the Qazi. Later on the validity of the transfer was challenged in a suit and the court found that the mortgage of the waqf properties was for urgent necessity and was proper. For that reason it was held to be a valid mortgage in law, in so much as it might be taken to have been retrospectively approved by the court.

In *Afzal Hussain* v *Chhedilal,*[175] the Allahabad High Court also followed the above opinion. The Court said that—

> On a review of all these rulings we are of the opinion that the distinction drawn in ILR 37 Calcutta 179 (i), is a distinction which we should follow and that in the present case the validity of the mortgage was one which should have been sanctioned by the District Judge if an application had been made to him previous to the execution of this superdnama.

It was further pointed out that—

> The transaction was, therefore, clearly one intended to preserve the waqf property. Under these circumstances we have no doubt that a District Judge would have acted correctly in giving sanction for the superdnama.

In these cases the criterion applied was as to whether on a review of all the circumstances it could be said that the transaction was actually for the benefit of the waqf and in case such circumstances were brought to the notice of the court and leave asked for on their basis a good case for grant of sanction would have been made out or not. The ratio of 37 Calcutta 176 and 1939 Allahabad 792 was adopted and approved by Bombay High Court.[176] It was held that—

> Under the Mohammadan Law it is competent to a mutawalli to lease for a long term the waqf property with the sanction of the court and even if such sanction is not obtained, the court has the power to grant retrospective sanction if it is satisfied that the transaction is for the benefit of the institution.

It was remarked by Justice King that—

I see no distinction in principle between antecedent and subsequent sanction in the case of a long term lease if a mortgage by a mutawalli can be validated by subsequent sanction as in 37 Cal 179 and 57 Allahabad 727. The test in both the cases is the same *viz.*, necessity or benefit to the institution.

Prior to the passing of the Waqf Act, 1954 the view of the Indian courts was quite different. The Madras High Court[177] painted out that the object of the sanction was evidently to provide safeguard against improper alienations and that purpose would be impliedly served by insisting upon sanction of the court, either previous or subsequently, so long of course as there is an assurance that the transaction could be examined on its merits and there is an enquiry as to whether it is supported by legal necessity or benefit to the trust. Thus if the parties were able to prove the necessity, the transaction will be held as valid.

The Orissa High Court[178] also expressed the view that in the absence of any express provision in the waqf deed a mutawalli was not entitled to make any alienation of the waqf property even for legal necessity, without the permission of the court, but in appropriate cases alienation might be permitted with retrospective effect and that such alienations were only voidable and not void *ab initio*.

However, after the passing of the Waqf Act, 1954 and also under section 14 of the M.P. Public Trust Act, 1951 a prior sanction would be necessary before a transfer can be validly effected by mutawalli. Similarly, a mutawalli can not sell the land dedicated to the samadhi of a Muslim saint without prior sanction of the court and such sale being nullity if in pursuance of such a sale, the transferee enters into possession and remains for the statutory period, he can acquire a title by prescription.[179]

It is submitted that if legal necessity or benefit to the institution or beneficiaries is proved, the transaction must be upheld notwithstanding the fact that the alienation was not initially made with the sanction of the court.

A lease for longer duration may be granted if the waqf deed specifically permits him to do so. Leases for longer period should be given with the prior permission of the court. The court/waqf Board has power to sanction leases in the interest of waqf, even if the lease deed specifically prohibits a mutawalli to do so.[180]

A mutawalli can also give waqf land on lease if it was required for legal necessity In *Kumari Shaida Begum* v *Delhi Iron Company, Lucknow*,[181] the Allahabad High Court held that sanction of lease can be given retrospectively if the transaction is one for legal necessity or for the benefit of the waqf or the beneficiaries the sanction if sought for subsequently may be given a retrospective oparation. In Shaida Begum's case one Mohammad Ishaq Khan, mutawalli executed a lease deed dated 8th December, 1947 in favour of Delhi Iron and Steel Company Ltd., Ghaziabad, for a period of 50 years. The property in suit forming the subject matter of the lease was a part of the waqf property. It was contended that the mutawalli was not competent to grant lease for more than a year since he did not obtain the prior sanction of the court. After referring to many learned works, Justice Shukla observed—

> The correct position of law is that an alienation by a mutawalli whose validity is challenged for want of sanction of the court must be judged on the touch stone—as to whether such transaction was for legal necessity or for the benefit of the waqf or the beneficiaries. If it is so found the other subsidiary questions are immaterial *viz* as to whether the sanction was actually asked for and accorded, if so, by the District Judge or any other civil court. If the finding about the transaction being for the benefit of the institution is recorded in a civil suit wherein its validity is impugned, it has substantially the same effect as if the transaction was made with the sanction of the appropriate court. In these circumstances, therefore, the alienation cannot be struck down as invalid and must be upheld.

In *Ram Dhari* v *Janki Ram Singh*[182] it was said that where a mutawalli executed a deed which was not permitted under the Muslim law or exceeded the right given to him under the law the deed cannot become void *ab initio*, but is voidable. The lease deed shall be a valid document unless it is avoided by the persons concerned.

In *Fathuddin Ahmed* v *State Waqf Board*[183]A the Madras High Court said that the Waqf Act gives specific powers to the Board for granting lease for a term exceeding three years such a provision bars the jurisdiction of civil court to take congnizance of an application asking for sanction of such lease.

If the waqf was of a considerable antiquity and was not known as to when the permanent lease was granted, the court can make a presumption of a lost and unrecorded permission of the Qazi.[184]

Power to contract Debt

Normally, it is not lawful for a mutawalli to contract a debt. However, he may contract a debt for the purchase of necessary articles for the waqf. The mutawalli may contract debt when he is lacking in waqf funds, otherwise he is not competent to incur a debt.

A creditor advancing money to a mutawalli for carrying out the purpose of the trust has no right to be indemnified out of the trust property. A creditor of a mutawalli is not in a better position than a creditor of the shebait of a Hindu endowment.[185]

A decree passed against the mutawalli will not be binding against waqf properties unless it specifically says so.[186] The waqif has the right to fix the amount of remuneration of the officers and servants of the waqf. The mutawalli has no power to enahance the remuneration of the officers and servants of the waqf. However, the court has power to increase the remuneration in suitable cases.

Power of the Mutawalli to appoint Imam

An Imam can be appointed by the following persons—

(i) by mutawalli himself;
(ii) by the waqif's descendants and members of his family:
(iii) by congregation.

As a matter of fact mutawalli has full power to appoint

an Imam. There is no difference between *de jure* mutawalli and *de facto* mutawalli. The Calcutta High Court[187] said that the *de facto* mutawalli has the power to appoint an Imam and also to dismiss him on proper grounds. In the absence of mutawalli, Imam should be appointed by the waqif's descendants and members of his family. In case the Imam is found to be not capable of performing his duties the congregation is entitled to appoint a competent person as an Imam. However, before selecting a person the congregation shall take the prior approval of the Qazi in respect of the removal and appointment of the Imam. An Imam may be removed by congregation.[188]

It has been said that the provisions of the Religious Endowments Act, 1863, does not apply to mutawalli appionted by a committee. Such a mutawalli is merely a servant of the committee.[189]

Power to nominate his Successor

A mutawalli may appoint his successor by way of will. The waqif may validly nominate the successor to the office of mutawalli by name, or indicate the class of persons from whom the mutawalli may be appointed, and may invest him with power to nominate the successor after his death or relinquishment of the office.[190] A mutawalli may appoint his successor by will even when he is in good health.[191]

A mutawalli possesses power to appoint a successor to himself.[192] It has been said that there is no such power of appointment in the congregation or devotees as such.[193]

There may be cases where on account of certain unavoidable circumstances, it was not possible for a mutawalli to appoint his successor. In much cases, the waqf property may, after the death of the last mutawalli, be administered by his executor as his legal representative.

The waqif possesses right to lay down rule as to the success of mutawalliship. Where the waqif has failed to lay down rules as the succession of mutawalliship, the same may be done by his executive. In the absence of the executor, court may lay down rule as to the succession. Tyabji[194] says that the waqif can expressly provide that no mutawalli shall have the power to appoint his successor.

In the absence of the waqif and his executor and the

silence of waqfnama on the question, the mutawalli may appoint his successor on his death bed, or when incapacitated from discharging the duties of his office, but he will not be able to do so when he is in good health or where the office goes by hereditary right.[195]

The authorities relating to the appointment of a mutawalli under the dedication to appoint a successor to himself, are not quite clear and require some attention. It is generally presumed that a mutawalli possesses the power to nominate his successor.[196] In this connection, the following rule may be noted—

(i) When the superintendent has died, and (a) the appropriator is still alive, the appointment of another mutawalli belongs to him, and not to the judge; and (b) if the appropriator be dead his executive is preferred to the judge. However, (c) if he had died without naming an executor, the appointment of an administrator is with the judge.

On the basis of above observations we can say that the power to appoint successor is given to three persons namely, the waqif, his executor and lastly the court.[197] It may be noted here that it is not clear whether the last mutawalli can nominate his successor or not. Notwithstanding this position, it has been said that—(ii) A mutawalli on his death bed may appoint any person his successor. This power of the mutawalli is similar to the power of an executor.

The statement made is overlapping. Serial number (ii) says that generally mutawalli has no right to appoint a successor to himself. However, during his life time he may appoint his deputy.[198] Where there is no power to the mutawalli to appoint a successor and the power has not been specifically reserved, the mutawalli may appoint a successor on his death bed but not otherwise.[199]

It may be noted here that the power of the mutawalli to appoint his successor does not in any way effect the power of the proper authorities to appoint his successor. There may be cases where there will be no proper authority and in such cases the appointment made by the last mutawalli on his death bed will be final.

A mutawalli while alive and in good health, cannot lawfully appoint another to act for him, unless the appointment of himself were in the nature of a general trust.[200] Where the superintendent desires on his death bed, to bequeath the superintendance to another it is allowable for him to do so; but he would not be authorised to appoint a successor in his life time and during health; unless the consignment of the superintendence to him have been general, that is, with permission (from the appropriator or his executor, as he may have received it from either) to confer it on another; in which case he may be authorised to appoint a successor during health.[201]

On the basis of the above construction, it may be said that the mutawalli has power to appoint, if he is authorised to appoint but not otherwise. The present author submits that the above statement is not correct. It is submitted that each case is having its own circumstances and, therefore, each case should be decided in the light of the circumstances of the case.

A mutawalli can not transfer his office to another person during his life time. In *Pir Ahsanullah* v *Pir Ziauddin*[202] it was contended that nomination of successor can only be valid if made while incumbent was in death illness but not in good health. A mutawalli has no power to transfer office unless expressly authorised by waqif. However, he may apooint his deputy.[203]

An appointment or nomination made during the life time of the mutawalli is revocable like other testamentary disposition.[204] The office of mutawalli is not legally saleable and any custom to the contrary is opposed to public policy and, therefore, void.[205]

A mutawalli has no power to appoint his successor's and so on and so forth.[206]

Succession among Descendants

Where a waqf is made for the benefit of the settler's descendants, but no rules of succession are laid down in the deed of waqf, the descendants take *per stipes*, and not per capita and males females take equal shares.[207] In *Maqsood Ali* v *Zahid Ali*[208] the Allahabad High Court held that as each branches off, the shares should be divided between the various branches, but in the same branch the nearer should exclude the more remote,

The Andhra Pradesh High Court[209] has taken a different view. The High Court held that the rule of exclusion of remoter by nearer heirs does not apply to endowed property. The court said that if the waqf was established in respect of the descendants 'generation after generation', the implication is that the nearer line or class takes first, and after them the line next after. Where there are no such words as 'generation after generation' the profits are to be divided equally among all the descendants.

The waqf deed is a gift and the waqif has the right to mention the order of succession. It has been held[210] that a waqf will not be invalid only because such provisions are contrary to the rules of inheritance.

Since the office and duties of mutawalli are akin to that of a trustee, a mutawalli can not claim adverse possession against the waqf property.[211]

In short, he is a manager and governor of the waqf property without having any interest in it but as regards his obligations and duties he is answerable like a trustee.

REGISTRATION OF WAQIF AS MUTAWALLI

Under Muslim law, a waqif can declare himself as the first mutawalli of the waqf. He is at liberty to resign from his office and to appoint another person as his successor. Where the waqif has reserved the power of appointing a mutawalli, he is entitled to appoint a mutawalli, but he is not entitled to dismiss him, unless he has reserved to himself the power to do so.[212] According to Justice Brand there is nothing in Muslim law which prevents the appropriator or waqif, who is himself the first mutawalli, from resigning his office, and out of his own residuary or general powers as waqif or appropriator, appointing has own successor provided that thereby he does not oust any express power already conferred by the deed of waqf.[211] The Pakistani courts have held th t after the creation of waqf appointment of mutawalli, the waqif has no power to alter the arrangement and remove the mutawalli who was appointed by him. This restriction is not absolute. There is one exception to this general rule. The waqif has right to make a provision in the waqf deed that he will be having power to dismiss the mutawalli. However, the power of appointment does not mean that the waqif possess power to remove him also.[214]

Power of the Court

As already submitted a waqf can be divided into public and private. As regards the private waqfs the courts are under duty to approve all such acts which were desired by the waqif. In the case of public waqfs the courts have been given very wide discretion. Broadly speaking the courts should act as per the direction of the settler. It has been maintained that the Mussalman law, like the English law, draws a wide distinction between public and private trusts. Generally speaking in the case of a waqf or trust created for specific individuals or a determinate body of individuals, Qazi, whose place in the British Indian system is taken by the Civil Court, has in carrying the trust into execution, to give effect, so far as possible to the expressed wishes of the founder. With respect, however, to public religious or charitable trusts, of which a public mosque is a common and well known example, Qazi's discretion is very wide. He may not depart from the intentions of the founder or from any rule fixed by him as to the objects of the benefaction; but as regards management, which must be governed by circumstances, he has complete discretion. He may defer to the wishes of the founder so far as they are conformable to changed conditions and circumstances, but his primary duty is to consider the interests of the general body of the public for whose benefit the trust is created.[215]

It is, therefore, clear that the courts are not bound to follow the directions given by the settler if the courts come to the conclusion that it is not possible to do so. In a case before Patna High Court, the waqfnama provided that a particular person should be appointed as mutawalli during the minority of a mutawalli. It was held that the court was not bound to appoint that particular person as mutawalli if he had repudiated the waqf.[216]

The District Court has no power to remove a *de facto* mutawalli and to appoint a receiver in a summary proceedings.[217]

As already submitted, mutawallis are required to act within four corners of the directions of the waqif. In case he has not followed the direction of the waqif on the ground of change in the circumstances, the courts have power to examine the genuineness of the statement made by the mutawalli. The Kerala High Court has also said that the mutawalli has to carry out the provisions of the waqf strictly. The court should decide on the evidence available whether the interest of the public to whom the mosque is dedicated require a change in the object of the foundation.

Again, the Orissa High Court reiterated that a member of the public by completing the construction of the mosque and by making improvements in it, whether with his own funds or funds raised by public subscriptions, cannot disentitle the person who has the right to its mutawalliship and himself become the mutawalli.[218]

In a Pakistani case[219] it was said that dependants can spend amount on the maintenance of mosque. But it does not mean that the management of the waqf property has been handed over to the defendants.

An application is sufficient for questioning the validity of appointment of mutawalli. It is not necessary to bring a suit under section 92 of the Civil Procedure Code.[220] It has however, been said that though it is not necessary to file a separate suit for the appointment of mutawalli, it is necessary that before making the appointment the court should issue notices to all persons interested.[221]

Office of Mutawalli not Hereditary

Under Muslim Law the office of mutawalli is not hereditary. However, this rule is not absolute. There is one exception to this general rule. Success to the office of mutawalliship or Sajjadanashin is also governed by custom.[222] Thus the Sajjadanshin of the shrine of Hazrat Khawaja Khawind Mahmud at Lahore is nominated by the existing Sajjadanashin and on his death, the Murids and worshippers of the shrine and mutaqids (believers) assemble and formally recognise the successor and duly instal him into the office.[223] The necessary requisites is a valid custom shall be application in the case of the claim of mutawalli on hereditary basis. The custom must be proved strictly.

Before the passing of the Shariat Act, 1937, courts were of the opinion that the office of mutawalli is hereditary. After the passing of this Act position has been changed.

A person may be appointed mutawalli by way of primogeniture. The word primogeniture means by descent to eldest son and his son. When eldest son pre-decease father or is incapable of succeeding because insane and grand son of last office holder (son of eldest son) preferred to junior son. For this purpose also, the person concerned must prove the custom. In a case before Madras High Court the plaintiff proved that he was lawful successor by hereditory right, and office not enjoyable by several heirs in common and, therefore, the succession must be by primogeniture and in the absence of evidence to contrary by lineal primogeniture.[224] The court accepted the contention of the plaintiff.[225]

Mahomed Oosman v *Essak Sale Mohammed* a Muslim claimed the office of Mujawar of a dargah on hereditory basis. The Bombay High Court refused to accept the contention of the plaintiff on the ground that the Muslim law does not know the office of mujawar a dargah.

Where a custom is set up that the said right devolves by primogeniture, it must be proved not only that each successive mutawalli has been uniformly his predecessor's eldest son, but also that he succeeded by right of primogeniture and not by appointment.[226]

Where the waqif has prescribed essential qualification for the appointment of mutawalli or Sajjadanashin it will be presumed that the above office was not hereditary. The reason for this opinion is that it will not be always possible for the family members of the waqif to possess such qualifications.[227]

In *Ghulam Hussain* v *Altaf Hussain*,[228] the Calcutta High Court held that where a committee was appointed under section 7 of the Religious Endowment Act, 1863, the powers exercised by the waqif and the committee respectively are not determined by the general Muslim law, they are derived from the sovereign powers of the government.

The endowed properties cannot be dissociated from the office and reference to one is sufficient to attract the other. The Judicial Committee of the Privy Council[229] has said that in the case of a hereditary office, the endowed properties cannot be dissociated from the office and reference to one is sufficient to attract the other. The matter has indeed been clarified further and put beyond doubt in the recent decision of the Supreme Court.[230] In this case the scope, effect and intent of Article 124 of the Limitation Act was examined and explained exhaustively.

In *Hazera Khatoon* v *Abdul Latif*[231] a suit was filed for declaration that the plaintiff respondent was the mutawalli of the waqf estate and for a permanent injunction, restraining the defendant from interfering, *inter alia*, with the management of the disputed property by the plaintiff as mutawalli. It was said by Justice P.N. Mukherjee of Calcutta High Court that a mutawalli has no right or interest in the waqf properties and the same do not vest in him but vest in God Almighty. From this point of view, the claim to the office, involving a claim to the possession of the same, would be sufficient for maintaining the suit without a pray for possession or recovery of possession of the connected properties.

de facto MUTAWALLI

Where the proper mutawalli is not available, any other person can act as a mutawalli. This person is known as the *de facto* mutawalli. Any person who for the time being manages the property of a waqf will be governed by the rules determining powers, duties and limitations of mutawallis.[232] In *Zahoor Ahmed* v *M.P. Waqf Board*[233] it was said that any person who for the time being manages or administers the waqf property would be a mutawalli. It has been contended that the status of a *de facto* mutawalli is unknown in Muslim law. The Madras High Court[234] held that the concept of a *de facto* trustee or trustee *de son tort* is not foreign to Muslim law, nor is there any prohibition against a person becoming a *de facto* mutawalli by taking the charge of the waqf and purporting to manage the waqf property. It was held in that case that such person can collect rents and profits and reimburse himself for the expenses incurred for such collection. This decision was again followed in another case.[235] Here it was held that no difference lies whether a *de facto* mutawalli collects rent through

through court by instituting a suit or otherwise them by legal process.

In *Abdul Rahim Khan* v *Ramzan*[236] the Allahabad High Court held the institution of *de facto* mutawalli is a recognised office under the Muslim law. The Court further held that a *de facto* mutawalli can sue without establishing his *de jure* character. This principle was followed by the Madhya Pradesh High Court.[237] In this case the owner of a house created a waqf and constituted himself a mutawalli of the waqf property. Thereafter he appointed certain persons as his agents and entrusted to them the power of management including the right of bringing suits against tenants. The plaintiff sued for eviction of a tenant of the waqf property. The defendant pleaded that the suit was not maintainable in the name of the plaintiffs, who only held a power of attorney.

Justice A.P. Sen (now Judge of the Supreme Court) held that ordinarily it is the lessor alone who has the right to bring a suit for ejectment and the agent cannot bring a suit for ejectment in his own name, but in this suit the plaintiffs were under the terms of the power of attorney constituted *de facto* mutawallis of the waqf property. They can not be called agents simpliciter. They were is reality the *de facto* mutawallis with certain powers.

It is also relevant here to discuss in detail the case decided by Calcutta High Court[238] on the point under discussion. In this case the question was whether the founder or waqif under the Muslim law, after he has dedicated his property to the Almighty and made provision for the appointment of a mutawalli, can subsequently alter the arrangement arrived at, or remove the mutawalli appointed by him, if he had reserved the power in himself when he created the waqf. After referring to the Fatawai Alamgiri, their lordship stated that reservation of such a power is necessary before the waqif can discharge a mutawalli appointed by him when he created the waqf.

In short, the courts in India have laid down following principles with regard to the power of a mutawalli in the administration of waqf property :

(a) a mutawalli[239] can in his personal capacity sue for a declaration that the applicant is the mutawalli of the waqf ;

(b) where[240] a decree has been passed against a mutawalli in his personal capacity the property of a waqf is not liable to sale or attachment ;

(c) a mutawalli[241] is empowered to file a suit in the court of law for the possession of waqf property ;

(d) the court[212] shall inform to all interested persons were any vacancy of a mutawalli has to be filled up ;

(e) the court[243] is competent to fill up the vacancy of mutawalli merely on the application. No separate suit is necessary for this purpose ;

(f) the possession[244] of a mutawalli cannot be adverse to the waqf.

(g) the mutawalli[245] can obtain the permission of court for alienating the property, merely filling the application for it. It is not necessary for him to file a separate suit for this purpose.

Mujawar

A mujawar is appointed for looking after the dargah. He is the servant of Muslim shrine. He is the caretaker of a shrine or mosque, or similar institution. He may also be responsible for properly maintaining the shrine.[246]

A mujawar acts as an intermediary or intercessor between God and man. This claim of the mujawar is not acceptable to fundamentalists. In *Mohammad Oosman* v *Essak Sale Mohammed*[247] the claim of a mujawar to act as an intermediary or intercessor between God and man was not recognised. It has been, therefore, said that the office of a mujawar is not hereditary. It can only be hereditary by way of long user or custom.

Duties

His main duty is to sit by the tomb, to read *fateha* to devotees, to invoke blessings for the *pir* for the devotees, to keep lights burning at the shrine, to put up incense, to place flowers on the tomb, to weigh children, to put *ghilaf* (covering) on the tomb and to act generally as intermediary between the devotees and the pir.

Sajjadanashin

A Sajjadanashin is the spiritual superior. This term consists of two words *sajjada* and *nashin*. The term *sajjada* means the carpet used by Muslims for prayers and *nashin* means sittings. He takes precedence on the carpet during prayers. A Sajjadanashin is a person who looks after the *khanqah*. The status of a sajjadanashin is higher than that of a mutawalli. He is the head of the institution. He can exercise jurisdiction over the mutawalli's management. But when he is also a mutawalli he, in that capacity, cannot exercise any power better than that of a mutawalli.

There exists difference between the office of a mutawalli and sajjadanashin. The office of mutawalli is secular but the office of sajjadanashin is spiritual. He is required to perform certain spiritual functions.[248]

The office of sajjadanashin is identical to that of a Hindu Shebait who exercises both religious and secular powers of management over the institution. A Hindu mahant is a spiritual superior in whom reside all powers of the institution as its head, the same cannot be said of the sajjadanashin of the Muslim religious institutions.

A Sajjadanashin is the teacher of religious doctrine and rules of life, and the manager of the institution and the administrator of its charities and has ordinarily speaking, right in the surplus income than a mutawalli.[249] He is the mutawalli of the *khanqah*. His office resembles that of Pallivasal in south India. All sajjadanashins are not necessarily the mutawallis of the properties of institutions as the office in such institutions is distinct and different.[250]

The greatest significance of the office of sajjadanshin is that the settler can himself declare as the first mutawalli of the *khanqah*. After his death the spiritual line is continued by a succession of Sajjadanashin.[251] Thus a chain of preceptors (called a *silsila*) comes into being, and the followers are known as *murids*. They pay homage not only to the founder but also to the whole line including the present incumbent called *peer oromurshi*.

In the absence of a scheme of succession in the waqfnama the succession to the office of Sajjadanashin is governed by custom. There is a custom that an electoral body consisting of faqirs and murid elect a competent person as Sajjadanashin.[252]

Sometimes by usage or custom a sajjadanashin has the power to nominate his successor. In the absence of any instructions in the waqfnama or custom, the court has power to appoint a Sajjadanashin. In appointing a Sajjadanashin, the court should take into consideration the spiritual traditions of the Khanqah.[253]

The original founder possesses the right to nominate his successor. The successor will have the same rights. In theory, the most illustrious disciple is to be installed as Sajjadanashin. However, in practice the office has become hereditary. The hereditary character of Sajjadanashin was also recognised by the courts of India also. In *Syed Shah M. Kazim* v *Syed Ali Saghir*,[254] their lordship said that on the death of a Sajjadanashin, his seniormost son shall be entitled to the office of Sajjadanashin. In this case a Sajjadanashin was found worthless and he was, therefore, removed from the office of mutawalliship, but was allowed to retain the spiritual office (Sajjadanashin) which was considered to be hereditary. The office of sajjadanashin of Dargah Khwaja Sahib Ajmer is hereditary and is governed by the rule of primogeniture.[255] A sajjadanashin is removable, if it is shown that he is a man of such a low morality that his continuance as superior of a sacred shrine is repugnant and undesirable.[256] The court can also separate the office of the sajjadanashin from that of the mutawalli.

It has been seen that in some *dargahs* and *khanqahs*, the sajjadanashin is entitled to a share in the offerings made at the tomb. The above right is attached to the office of sajjadanashin, and the successors of sajjadanashin are also entitled to receive that share as long as he holds the office. In *Altaf Hussain* v *Ali Rasul*[257] the Judicial Committee of the Privy Council held that both the Sajjadanashin and Khadims (servitors) were entitled to a share in the offerings made to the tomb. But the offering of qabar poshes belonged to the dargah and were its property, and as such must be kept by the sajjadanashin as trustee.

Where the waqf deed is silent on the point discussed above, the office of sajjadanashin will be filed up by observing the custom. The relevant case on the point is *Maule Shah* v

Ghane Shah.[258] In this case the validity of the 'bhek' custom was challenged. The word 'bhek' means an electoral body consisting of faqirs and murids instal a competent person generally a son or nominee of the late Sajjadanashin. The Privy Council held that the delegation of the power by 'bhek' to elect a Sajjadanashin was a valid delegation and, therefore, the appointment was held as valid.

While appointing Sajjadanashin this is the duty of the court to see the spiritual tradition of the family. Preference should be given to the descendant of the founder.[259] If the waqf deed is silent in respect of the appointment of Sajjadanashin can nominate his successor.[260]

Distinction between Sajjadanashin and Mutawalli

A Sajjadanashin is the head of the institution and his status of a sajjadanashin is higher than that of mutawalli. During medieval period there was a separation between the office of of mutawalli and sajjadanashin. During Mughal period persons having good conduct were appointed as mutawalli. Sajjadanashins were appointed from amongst the descendants of the saints.[261] A sajjadanashin has the right to exercise supervision over the mutawalli's management.[262] The nature of his office is sacred.

A mutawalli has no power to borrow money for the purpose of carrying out the objects of the trust. However, if there is any necessity, he may obtain the prior sanction of the court.[263] A sajjadanashin may be removed from his office on account of his misconduct. A sajjadanashin must have attained the age of majority for holding the office of sajjadanashin. A minor cannot be appointed as mutawalli.[264]

In *Mohammad Oosman* v *Essak*,[265] Justice Abdur Rahim decided the issues whether functions of sajjadanashin in any way are of a spiritual nature and distinct from those of ordinary mutawalli and found that the functions of the so-called sajjadanashin's office were not of spiritual or religious nature in any sense and that they had no disciples and no doctrines of sufism or anything to teach. All that they had to do was to conduct the annual *urs* and to offer *fatihas* at tombs and none of these could be said to be functions incapable of being performed by other Muslims. Justice Rahim further said that it is superfluous to retain the office of the so-called Sajjadanashin in addition to that of a trustee or mutawalli.

The term sajjadanashin is an absolute misnomer in connection with this institution.

A sajjadanashin has the right to share in the offerings made at the tomb. The right of the sajjadanashin to receive offerings is a right attached to his office and each successive incumbent of that office entitled to receive that share as long as he holds the office.[266] In the absence of any express provision in the grant or proved custom members of the family of the founder have no right to share in the surplus offerings ; though the sajjadanashin may in his discretion make an allowance to indigent members.[267]

THE ROLE OF QAZI IN ISLAM

The institution of qazi is of great importance in Islam. Since the religion and law are connected to each other qualifications for his appointment were that he should be a Muslim, having good character and sound knowledge of law. After the advent of Islam, Prophet Mohammad and the early Caliphs decided many matters in person. Later on, it was not possible for them to give judgement in each and every matter. The cases were, therefore, sent to qazis who were looking after the civil as well as criminal cases in accordance with the sacred law. Qazi, in fact, was a religious judge working under the guidance of the shariat.

Immediately after the death of the Prophet no qazi was appointed. Abu Bakr himself administered justice. This tradition was prevalent during Prophet's time. Afterwards, Abu Bakr delegated his judicial functions to Umar. Umar during his caliphate appointed first qazi. He maintained that the majesty of law was supreme, and that the administration of justice must be above the suspicion of subservience to executive authority.

During the reign of Umayyads also qazis were appointed. The appointment of qazis was made to meet out the new conditions which came on account of the advent of Islam. Qazis administered pre-Islamic as well as Islamic law. Qazis were considered to be the delegate of the governor. The governors were having full authority over his province, administrative and judicial without any conscious distinction of functions and he could and in fact regularly did, delegate his judicial authority to his legal secretary, the qazi.

The earliest qazis were very capable men. Their decisions laid the basic foundation of Islamic law. Whenever there was provision or confusion on any particular point they delivered judgments according to their own discretion. Their judgments was based on sound opinion. While delivering judgments they also took into consideration the custom which was prevalent at that time.

During the Mughal rule they were the bedrock of administration. In every town one qazi was posted. They were looking after the waqf property. They were assigned the duty to try waqf and trust cases. From the time of organisation of provincial administration under Akbar to the times of the Britishers paraganah qazis were appointed regularly. He was the official who exercised on the spot supervision over waqfs.[268] In villages waqfs were maintained by village Mullahs. Ultimately, mutawallis were responsible to look after the administration of waqfs under them. The kings were not generally interfering in their affairs. Above all king was looking after the waqf property. They were supervising the waqf property. Whenever they felt, they intervened in the administration of the waqfs. In appropriate cases they directly intervened to correct the irregularities in the matters of waqfs. It has been reported that Akbar removed several qazis on the ground of misappropriation of waqf fund and bribery.[269]. Akbar separates spiritual and temporal functions of the dargahs. For better administration of waqfs, he appointed mutawallis instead of sajjadanashins because he was knowing that sajjadanashins were having special place.

Since the powers of qazi under the Muslim system of law are vested in the courts under the British Indian system and that for that reason, the District Judge, as the principal civil court of original jurisdiction has a general power of nominating a mutawalli when there was vacancy in the office, in a summary procedure.[270]

Duties of a Qazi

Qazis were appointed to give justice to the common man. This was the duty of the qazis to treat every person, high or low, rich or poor, with the equality. Even after judgment the qazi felt that an error had crept in, he should not stand on his dignity, but should review his judgment.

It is debatable whether the duties of a qazi are purely secular one, unconnected with any religious duties or not. The matter was discussed by eminent writers as well as there are number of cases which are discussed here.

In Wilson's Glossary, qazi is mentioned as 'A Mohammadan Judge,' an officer formerly appointed by the government to administer both civil and criminal law, chiefly in towns, according to the princples of Quran. Under the British authorities the judicial functions of the qazis in that capacity ceased, and, with the exception of their employment as the legal advisors of the courts in cases of Muslim law, the duties of those stationed in the cities or districts were confined to the preparation and attestation of deeds of conveyance and other legal instruments and the general superintendence and legislation of the ceremonies of marriage, funerals, and other domestic occurrences among the Mohammadans.

In Hedaya[271] it is stated that it is the duty of the sovereign to appoint fit persons to the office of qazi, that he must decide the claims relating to property and that he must attend funeral and visit the sick.

Tyabji[272] says that much confusion is frequently caused by a failure to distinguish the person referred to in the texts as Cadi (*viz.*, the judge appointed by the state) from the person designated Cadi in our times. In India and Pakistan viz. an officiant at the performance of marriage and similar ceremonies.

In this connection it is relevant to discuss the observation of Mulla.[273] He says that the Mahomedan law does not regard the office of Qazi as hereditary. A claim to such a right, though supported by custom, is not one that can be recognised by a civil court. The learned author also observed that a Qazi may be appointed by the government or by some internal arrangement amongst the Mahomedans of each locality. In support of his statement, the learned authority has mentioned the following cases.[274]. A qazi has been assigned dual functions. He is required to perform secular as well as religious functions. Formely, there was a difference of opinion regarding his functions. In few cases, courts, held a qazi was required to perform only secular duties. But in subsequent cases it was held that he also performs religious duties.

In *Mahomed Ismail Ariff* v *Ahmed Moola Dawood*[275] their lordships of the Privy Council observed as follows :—

> Generally speaking, in case of a waqf or trust created for specific individuals or a determinate body of individual the qazi, whose place in the British Indian system is taken by the Civil Court, has in carrying the trust into execution to give effect so far as possible to the expressed wishes of the founder. With respect, however, to public religious or charitable trusts, of which a public mosque is a common and well known example, the Kazi's discretion is very wide. He may not depart from the intentions of the founder or from any rule fixed by him as to the objects of the benefaction ; but as regards management which must be governed by circumstances he has complete discretion. He may defer to the wishes of the founder so far as they are conformable to changed conditions and circumstances, but his primary duty is to consider the interests of the general body of the public for whose benefit the trust is created. He may in his judicial discretion vary any rule of management which he may find either not practicable or not in the best interests of the institution.

These observations do indicate that a Qazi not only was previously exercising the powers of a Civil Court but also managing public religious or charitable trusts. The matter was again discussed in *Kasam Khan* v *Kaji Abdulla*.[276] In this case Justice Fawcet made the following observations :—

> There is undoubtedly evidence to justify the finding that until the dispute about the Darga, the Kazi community at

Pawas invariably officiated at religious rites of the Mahommadan community at this village.

Exactly after ten years Justice Tyabji of Bombay High Court discussed the matter in *Sattappa Gurusattappa* v *Mohammad Appalal Kazi*.[277] He said :—

> The word qazi is etymologically derived from the root word for decreeing, ordaining or judging, and qazi signifies one who gives decisions. It is the technical designation for a judge (civil as well as criminal) in the texts. In addition, however, to his strictly judicial functions the qazi used (by amenity) to perform other functions such as officiating at marriages, superintending talaks, (occasionally keeping marriage records) and perhaps leading ceremonial prayers. These latter are the only functions now discharged by qazis in British India. Though Islam does not as a rule recognise an ordained priesthood or clergy, or require their administration for the office of any religious ceremony, and though the services of the qazi cannot of course be forced on anyone, yet by most persons the presence of some religious officiant is considered desirable (or in a vague sense obligatory) and there is hardly any normal marriage at which the qazi or a religious dignitary is not present. It is thus obvious that the qazi's office entails in India the rendering of services to the community. This fact must not induce a closing of eyes to the fact that when the ancient texts speak of a qazi they refer to a judicial office having entirely differnt functions from those of the religious officiant now spoken of as a qazi, and the applicability of the original texts to the question whether the office now known in India as that of a qazi should be hereditary may not be incontrovertible.

This judgment was carried in appeal. But the judgment in the appeal does not specifically dealt with the question as to whether the qazi performs religious duties or not. From the observations of Fawcett, J. in *Kasamkhan* v *Kazi Abdulla*[278] and Tyabji,[279] J. in *Sattappa Gurusattappa* v *Mohammad Appalal Kazi* and of the Privy Council in *Mohammad Ismail Ariff* v *Ahmed Moola Dawood*[280] it appear that a qazi does perform some duties of a religious nature like performing marriages and leading prayers in mosques. The Kazi Act, 1880 (Act XII of 1880) has also recognised the religious functions of the kazis. The statement and objects of this Act reads as follows :—

> Under the Muhammadan Law the Qazi was chiefly a Judicial Officer. His principal powers and duties are stated at some length in the Hedaya, Book XX. He was appointed by the State, and may be said to have corresponded to our Judge or Magistrate. In addition, however, to his functions under the Muhammadan Law, the Qazi in this country, before the advent of British rule, appears to have performed certain other duties, partly of a secular and partly of a religious nature. The principle of these seems to have been preparing, attesting and registering deeds of transfer of property, celebrating marriages, and performing other rites and ceremonies. It is not apparent that any of these duties were incumbent on the Qazi as such. It is probably that the customary performance of them by him arose rather from his being a public functionary and one known by his official position to be acquainted with the law, than from his having as Qazi, a greater claim to perform them than any one else.

Such was the position of the Qazi in this country under Native Government. On the 'introduction of the British rule Judges and Magistrates took the place of Qazis and the Qazi in his judicial capacity disappeared ; but the British Government, though no longer recognising the judicial functions of the Kazi, did not abolish the office. By certain regulations passed from time to time, the appointment of Qazi-ul-kuzaat and Qazis by the State was provided for, and the performance of their non-judicial duties was recognised by law. In the case of Bengal, indeed, certain additional duties were imposed on them. The duties of the Qazi under these regulations comprised some or all of the following, *viz.*—

(a) preparing and attesting deeds of transfer and other law papers ;

(b) celebrating marriages and presiding at divorces ;
(c) performing various rites and ceremonies ;
(d) superintending the sale of distrained property and paying charitable and other pensions and allowances.

In the course of subsequent legislation, the first and last of the above duties devolved on officers especially appointed for the purpose, and there remained nothing to be performed by the Qazi but the second and third, which were purely ceremonial. Under these circumstances it appeared no longer necessary that the Government should appoint these officers. Accordingly, in 1864, Act XI of that year, all the Regulations relating to the appointment of Qazis by Government and the duties to be discharged by them were repealed but in order that it might be clear that no interference with the ceremonial functions of these officers was intended, a section was added to that Act as follow—

> Nothing contained in this Act shall be construed so as to prevent a Qazi-ul-Quzaat or other Qazi from performing, who required to do so, and duties or ceremonies prescribed by the Muhammadan Law.[281]

Certain of his duties having thus survived the passing of Act XI of 1864, the Qazi is still a functionary of considerable importance in the Mohammadan community. What was originally in some sense an accidental adjunct of his judicial office has become his principal and only duty, and in some parts of the country at least, the presence of a qazi at certain rites and ceremonies appears now to be considered by Muhammadans essential from their point of view.

In the Preamble to the Qazi Act, it is stated as follows—

> Whereas by the Preamble to Act No XI of 1864 (an Act to repeal the law regulating to the offices of Hindu and Muhammadan Law officers and to the offices of Qazi-ul-Quzaat (among other things) declared that it was inexpedient that the appointment of the Qazi-ul-Quzzat, or of city, town or pargana Kazis should be made by the Government, and by the same Act the enactments relating to the appointment by Government of the said

officers were repealed ; and whereas by the usage of the Muhammadan community in some parts of (India) the presence of Qazis appointed by the Government is required at the celebration of marriages and the performance of certain other rites and ceremonies, and it is therefore expedient that the Government should again be empowered to appoint persons to the office of Kazi.

The aforesaid extracts from the Statement of objects and Reasons and the Preamble to the Qazis Act, clearly show that a Qazi holds a position of considerable importance in Mohammedan community and that his presence at the celebration of marriages and at the performance of certain other rites and ceremonies, considered essential by Mohammedans.[282]

Appointment of Qazi

Under section 2 of the Qazis Act, 1880, it is the State Government that has to appoint a Qazi after consulting the principal Muslim residents of such local areas. In Mohammad *Abbas Ali* v *Waqf Board*[283] it was contended that the Waqf Board has no power to appoint a Qazi. This contention was, however, rejected. In practice, there are two ways for appointing a Qazi. A Qazi may be appointed either by the State Government or by some internal arrangement among the Muslims of each locality.[284]

Office of Qazi not Hereditary

The office of a Qazi is not hereditary.[285] Any person who claims the office of Qazi as hereditary must prove the custom under which he is claiming the office.[286] In the absence of such custom the court will not recognise the office as hereditary.

REFERENCES

1. Kamila Tyabji, *Limited Interests in Muhammadan Law*, (1946) p. 124.
2. *Md Zahur* v *Najibulla*, 154 PR 1881.
3. *Fakira* v *Meher Singh*, 6 PR 1911.
4. *Hashim* v *Ahmed Raza*, *AIR* 1974 All 305 ; *Saadat* v *Advocate General*, Palestine, *AIR* 1939 PC 185 ; *Vidya Viruthi* v *Baluswami*, (1921) 48 IA 302.
5. See Abdul Hamid Lahori, *Badshah Namah*, Vol II, p. 330 (1868).
6. See S. Khalid Rashid, *Waqf Administration in India*, pp. 4-6.
7. *Nabinnissa* v *Liaqat Ali*, (1928) 50 All 830 ; see also *Ma Ekhin* v *Maung Sein*, (1924) 2 Rang 495.
8. See Tyabji, *Muslim Law* pp. 582-83.
9. *Vidya Viruthi* v *Balusami Ayyar*, *supra* note 4.
10. *Abdur Rahim* v *Narayandas*, (1922) 50 I.A. 84, 90.
11. *Sadar Kale Hanum* v *Attorney General for Palestine*, *AIR* 1939 PC. 185-189 : (1939) AC 508 ; see also *Syed Mustafa Peeran Sahib* v *State Waqf Board*, *AIR* 1969 Mad 66.
12. *Muhammad Zain* v *Nurul Hasan*, (1932) 45 All 682.
13. *AIR* 1963 SC 985.
14. *Ahmad G. Arif* v *Commissioner of Wealth Tax*, Calcutta, *AIR* 1971 SC 1691.
15. *Mohammad Qamar* v *Salamat AIR* 1933 All 407,
16. *Syed Ahmed* v *Hafiz*, *AIR* 1934 All 732.
17. *Muhammad Rustom* v *Mushtaq Hussain*, (1920) 47 I.A. 224.
18. *Kishwar* v *Zafar*, (1933) 55 All 164 : 146 IC 733.
19. *Muhammad Jafar* v *Muhammad Taqi Khan*, *AIR* 1933 Oudh 517, (1934) 9 Luck 170, 145 IC 1003.
20. *Daw Ein* v *Daw Chan Than*, *AIR* 1939 Rang 365, 186 IC 210.
21. *Re* Cassamally, (1906) 30 Bom 591.
22. *Ibid.*
23. *Muhammad Yakub* v *Ali Muhammad*, PLD 1957 Lah 544.
24. *Sarkum* v *Aahman Buksh*, (1896) 24 Cal 83, 91.
25. *Khalil Ahmed* v *Malka Meher Nigar Begum*, AIR 1954 All 362 (FB).
26. *Mohammad Ismail* v *Ahmed Moolla*, (1916) 43 I.A. 127, 134-35.
27. Mulla, *Mahomedan Law*, (18th Ed), section 206, p. 233.
28. *Asha Bibi* v *Nabinssa Sahib AIR* 1957 Mad 583.
29. *Muhammad Ibrahim* v *Ahmed*, (1910) 32 All 503 : 6 IC 219.
30. *Moazzan* v *Raza*, *AIR* 1924 All 818 : (1924) 46 All 856, 81 IC 851.
31. *Syed Hasan* v *Mir Hasan*, (1917) 40 Mad 543 ; *Abdul Salam* v *Abdul Aziz*, *AIR* 1944 Cal 299.
32. S. Ameer Ali, *Muhammadan Law*, p. 346 ; see also *Ruggan* v *Dhanno*, (1927) 49 All 257.
33. *Syed Mohammad Ghouse* v *Sayabiran Sahib*, (1935) 68 MLJ 684 ; 156 IC 757, *AIR* 1934 Mad 638.
34. (S1906) 34 I.A. 46, 34 Cal 118.
35. *Waris Ali* v *Sheikh Shamshuddin*, (1936) 63 CLJ 573.

36. *AIR* 1948 Cal 312 ; see also *Abdul Awal* v *Abdul Mannan*, PLD 1960 Dacca 90. In this case it was held that the District Judge as the Principal Court of original jurisdiction has by virtue of his powers as a Qazi, a general power of appointing a mutawalli when there is a vacancy in the office, in a summary proceedings.
37. *Khagum Khan* v *Mohammad Ali*, *AIR* 1955 AP 209.
38. *Supra* note 11.
39. *Syed Ali* v *Syed Mohammad*, *AIR* 1928 Pat 532 ; (1928) 7 Pat 468, 110 IC 12.
40. *Ghulam Ali* v *Mohammad Ali* (1933) 144 IC 467. A Shia case.
41. S. Ameer Ali, *Mahomedan Law*, *supra* note 32 ; *Sheikh Abdul Mannan* v *Muttawalli* of Sur Janebali, *AIR* 1956 Cal 584.
42. *Dyal Chand* v *Karamat Ali*. (1871) 16 WR 116.
43. (1906) 34 IA 46 : 34 Cal 118.
44. *Amiranessa Bibi Hatam Ali Khan*,(1933) 37 CWN 697.
45. *Supra* note 25.
46. *Shaikh Musthan Sahib* v *Balrami*, *supra* note 41.
47. *Moinuddin Bibi* v *Ratnavali*, 51 MIJ 598 ; *M.M. Husain Faroki* v *Syed Abdul Haq*, *AIR* 1932 Mad 485.
48. Bail 1. 591.
49. *Abdul Rahim Khan* v *Mohammad Shafi*, 1970 MLJ 968 ; *AIR* 192 Mad 69,
50. *AIR* 1939 PC 185.
51. *Mohammad Osman* v *Essak* (1937) 39 BLR 502.
52. *Kasim* v *Hajra Begum*, *AIR* 1920 Cal 800 ; see also *Munnavari Begum* v *Mir Mahapalli*, (1918) 41 Mad 1033.
53. *Mohammad Bhai* v *Wazirbi*, *AIR* 1947 Nag 31.
54. *Abdul Aziz* v *Mohammad Ibrahim*, *AIR* 1941 Bom 238.
55. *Abbas Ali* v *Mohammad Shah*, *AIR* 1951 MB 92.
56. (1934) 13 Rang 27.
57. *Tafazal Beg* v *Majidullah* *AIR* 1924 Lah 432, (1923) 5 Lah 59.
58. *Kaniz Zohra* v *Saiyed Muzataba*, (1923) 2 Pat 819.
59. *Supra* note 7.
60. *Supra* note 42.
61. *Shahar Banoo* v *Aga Mohammad*, (1906) 34 DA 46.
62. Ameer Ali, *supra* note 32 RS. *Ejaz Ahmed* v *Khatun Begum*, (1916) 39 All 228.
63. Ameer Ali, *supra* note 32.
64. *Piran* v *Abdul Karim*, (1891) 19 Cal 203.
65. *Supra* note 17.
66. *AIR* 1934 PC 77, 61 IA 50.
67. *Supra* note 13.
68. *Supra* note 15.
69. *AIR* 1970 All 509.
70. See also *Mst Allah Rakhi* v *Shah Mohd.* *AIR* 1934 PC 77 ; *All Zamin* v *Akbar Ali*, *AIR* 1937 PC 127.
71. *AIR* 1978 Cal 133.

72. *Ghazanfar Hussain* v *Ahmedi*, *AIR* 1930 All 169 ; (1930) ALJ 109, 123 IC 369.
73. Ameer Ali, *Mahomedan Law*, *supra* note 32, p. 352 ; see also *Advocate General* v *Fatima Begum*, 9 BHCR 19 ; *Sheikh Mastan* v *Balarani Reddi*, *supra* note 41.
74. *Supra* note 72.
75. See *Kamms* v *Allah Baksh*, *AIR* 1941 Lah 36 ; *Ali Mohammad* v *Yusufu*, *AIR* 1962 Ori 111.
76, *Shekuilul Hamid* v *Kazi Mohammad Hussain*, *AIR* 1941 Mad 42.
77, *Supra* note 75.
78. *AIR* 1971 SC 1691.
79. *Supra* note 39, p. 359.
80. *Ibid*
81. Baillie, *Mohammedan Law*, p. 604
82. *Supra* note 8, p. 516.
83. *Supra* note 27, para 206, p. 233.
84. See also Baillie, *Digest of Moohummudan Law*, (1865), Part I p. 604 ; *Piran* v *Abdool Karim*, *supra* note 64 ; *Zoolekha Bibi* v *Syed Zynul Abedin*, (1904) 6 BLR 1058 ; *Mt Kammon* v *Allah Baksh* (1941) 193 1C 323, *AIR* 1941, Lah 36 ; *Ali Mohammad* v *Mohammad Yusuf* *supra* note 75 ; *Hakim Khan* v *Sahebjan Skhib*, *AIR* 1935 Mad 1040 ; *Muhammad M. Hussain* v *Syed Abdul Huq*, *supra* note 4.
85. See the opinion of Justice Din Mohammad in *Haji Abdul Razak* v *Ali Baksh*, *AIR* 1946 Lah 200.
86. See *Ahsanullah Shah* v *Ziaddin*, 1937) ALJ 585.
87. *S.H. Hussain* v *S.A. Raza*, (1973) ALJ 843.
88. *AIR* 1926 Mad 466.
89. *Supra* note 72.
90. *AIR* 1947 All 261.
91. *AIR* 1962 Ori 111.
92. *Mst Kammon* v *Allah Baksh*, *AIR* 1931 Lah 36.
93. *Sheikh Masthan Saheb* v *Balram Reddi*, *supra* note 41.
94. *Mazhar Ali* v *Ghulam Murtaza*, *AIR* 1958 AP 8, 14.
95. *Hashim Hussain* v *Ahmad Raza*, *supra* note 4 ; see also *Khaliq Ahmed* v *Siddiqi Ahmad* *AIR* 1974 All 382.
96. S. Ameer Ali, *Mahommedan Law*, Vol 1, p. 259.
97. *Ibid*, p. 258.
98. *Aziz Bano Mohemmed Ibrahim* *AIR* 1925 All 720.
99. See Preface, Vol II, Ameer Ali's *Mohemmedan Law*, p. 7.
100. Tyabji, *Muslim Law*, (fourth ed), para (sic).
101. *Supra* note 91.
102. *M. Hussain* v *Syed Abdul Haq*, *AIR* 1942 Mad 485.
103. *Supra* note 96, p. 359.
104. *Commissioner of Waqf* v *Asraful Alam*, *AIR* 1975 Cal 162.
105. *Haji Abdul Razak* v *Shaikh Ali Baksh*, *AIR* 1948 PC 163.
106. *Amjaddulla Siddiqui* v *Mirza Nizamuddin Baig*, *AIR* 1982 AP 3.
107. *Abdul Alim* v *Abir* Jan, (1928) 55 Cal 1284 ; Bibi *Zohra* v *Bibi*

Habibunnissa, AIR 1940 Pat 9 ; *Allah Rakhee* v *Nasiruaddin AIR* 1943 Oudh 278 ; *Mohammad Ali Khan* v *Ahmad A. Khan, AIR* 1945 All 818 ; see also *Mohammad Bhai* v *Wazirbi,* sunni 53 ; The court held that where the court is required to remove a mutawalli and in his place another person has to be appointed. The appointment can only be made by means of a suit filed under section 92, Civil Procedure Code or under section 14, read with section 18 of the Religious Endowment Act, 1863.

108. *Supra* note 26.
109. *Shahr Bano* v *Agha Mohammad Jaffar,* (1906) 34 IA 46, 34 Cal *Kalandar Batcha* v *Jailani Sahib, AIR* 1930 Mad 554.
110. *Elahi Baksh* v *Mohammad Ghouse, AIR* 1933 Lah 27, 34 PLR 81.
111. *Jamia Masjid Magadi Town* v *Karnataka Board of Waqfs, AIR* 1981 Karn 37.
112. *Supra* note 32 ; see also *Ghulam Hussein* v *Ajit Azam Todallah Sahib* (1860) 4 MHCR 44 ; *Siddiq Ahmed* v *Syed Ahmed, AIR* 1945 *supra* note 41 ; *Mian Jan* v *Fakir Mohammad,* PLD 1960 (WP) Kar 420 ; *Bhurruck Chandra Sahu* v *Ghulam Shurruff* (1868) 10 WR S58 ; *Ghazanfar Hussain* v *Ahmadi Bibi, supra* note 72 ; *Mohammad Abdul Gant* v *Mst Kulsum Nissa, AIR* 1945 Cal 328, 49 CWN 271.
113. *Mohamedally* v *Akberally, AIR* 1934 PC 53, (1934) 36 Bom LR 386
114. *Supra* note 24.
115. *Sidiq Ahmed* v *Syed Ahmed, supra* note 112 ; *Khalil Ahmed* v *Malika Mehar, supra* note 25 ; see also *Mohd Ali* v *Akbar Ali, Ibid.*
116. *Saheb Baksh* v *Ghulam,* 22 CWN 605.
117. *Shah Najibuddin Ahmed* v *Amir Husan Khan, AIR* 1934 Pat 44.
118. Fath-ul-Kadir cited by Rud-dul-Mukhtar, Vol III, p. 640 referred in Ameer Ali *Mahommadan Law, supra* note 32.
119. *Muhammad Yusuf* v *Muhammad Sadik,* (1933) 14 Lah 431.
120. Wilson. *Digest of Anglo Muhammadan Law,* (2nd Ed.) paras 332, 333 ; 81 PR 1869, 105 PR 1892 : 3 PR 1899, 53 PR 1904 ; 15 PLR 1905, 13 PLR 1906, 6 PR 1911, compare 1 ILR 1 Mad 235, VI Cal Reports 265, ILR XIII Mad 214 and XXI Mad 179.
121. 81 PR 1869 ; 2063 of 1880 ; 75 PR 1884 ; 94 PR 1885 ; 66 PR 1892 87 PR 1892 27 PR 1897 ; 122 ; PR 1820 ; 7 PR 1908.
122 122 PR 1890 and 52 PLR 1905
123. See *Siddique Ahmed* v *Syed Ahmed, supra* note 112.
124. *Khalil Ahmed Khan* v *Malka Mehar Nigar Begum, supra* note 25.
125. *Ghulam Hussain Sahib* v *Ali Ajan Tudallah Saib, supra* note 112 ; *Advocate General* v *Fatima Sultan Begum,* 9 BHCR 19 (23-24) ; *Haidatoonissa* v *Syed Afzal,* 2 NW 422 ; *Khalil Ahmed Khan* v *Milka Mehr Nigar Begum, supra* note 25.
126. *Shaikh Mustan* v *Balram, supra* note 41.
127. See *Mohd Mohiuddin* v *State Waqf Board, AIR* 1963 Mad 132.
128. *Mohd Shareef* v *The Superintendent* (*Waqfs*), *AIR* 1971 Mad 343.
129. WP No 972 of 1961 (Madras) decided in 1968 ; see also S. Khalid *Rashid, Waqf Administration in India,* p. 81.
130. See *Mohd Shrif* v *The Superintendent* (*Waqfs*) *supra* note 12. In

this case Justice Ismail (as then he was) of Madras High Court strongly pleaded for the amendment in the Waqf Act, 1954 on the line of the provisions in Madras Hindu Religion and Charitable Endowments Act, 1959.

131. *Syed Ismail* v *Hamidi*, *AIR* 1921 Pat 125.
132. *Supra* note 11.
133. *Jugatmoni* v *Romjani*, (1884) 10 Cal 533.
134. *Jinjira Khatoon* v *Muhammad Fakhrulla*, (1921) 49 Cal 477 ; see also *Delrus Banoo* v *Kazee Abdoor Rahman*, (1875) 23 WR 453.
135. *Mohiuddin* v *Sayiduddin* (1893) 20 Cal 810.
136. *Supra* note 32.
137. *Mumtaz* v *Advocate General*, *AIR* 1946 Oudh 244.
138. (1916) 40 Mad 116 (PC).
139. *Supra* note 32.
140. *Mahabir Prasad* v *Syed Mustafa Hussain*, *AIR* 1937 PC 174.
141. *Nawab Bahadur Murshid* v *Karnani*, (1931) 59 Cal 1 (PC) : see also *Sattappa* v *Mahomed Sahib*, (1935) 60 Bom 516 ; *Narayan Singh* v *Niranjan Chakravarti*, (1923) 51 I.A. 37 ; *Rajah Nilomonji Singh* v *Bakrannath Singh*, (1882) 9 IA 104.
142. *Supra* note 135.
143. *Syed Shah Muhammad Kazim* v *Syed Abi Saghir*, (1931) 11 Pat 289.
144. *Supra* note 133.
145. *Phate Saheb Bibi* v *Damodar Premji*, (1879) 3 Bom 84.
146. *Supra* note 16.
147. *Supra* note 91.
148. *Narsingh Das* v *Safiullah*, *AIR* 1954 All 773.
149. *Tyabji supra* note 8, p. 597 ; *Fatawai Alamgiri*, Waqf, Chapter v Bail I. 595.

149A. *Mohammad Kasam* v *Abdul Gafoor*, *AIR* 1964 MP 227.

150. *Anwar Reza* v *Hachinwi Reza AIR* 1945 Cal 189, 48 CWN 215, ILR 1944 (1) Cal 680, 221 IC 262.
151. *AIR* 1949 Lah 514.
152. *Supra* note 150.
153. *Shailendra Nath* v *Hade Raza*, *AIR* 1932 Cal 356.
154. *Nimai Chaud* v *Ghulam Hossein*, (1909) 37 Cal 179, 3 IC 353.
155. *Afazal Hussain* v *Cheddi Lal*, (1935) 57 All 727, 155 IC 791.
156. *Abdul Kadir* v *Kediric Sabha*, *AIR* 1953 Mad 143.
157. *Saleb Khan* v *Mader Saheb*, *AIR* 1954 Ori 239.
158. *Thangachi* v *Ahmed Hussain*, *AIR* 1957 Mad 194.
159. *Supra* note 11.
160. Halima Khatun, In *re*, (1909) 37 Cal 870, 7 IC 33. In this case the Calcutta High Court said that a mutawalli who was interested in obtaining the permission of the court for mortgage, sale or lease *etc.* should file a separate suit. Merely filing an application under the Trustees Act of 1868 was not sufficient. A similar view was taken by Bombay High Court in *re Kahandas Narayandas*, (1881) 5 Bom

154. The court held that the sanction may be obtained on an application under the Trustees Act, 1866.
161. *AIR* 1938 Cal 437 (1938) 177 IC 477.
162. (1919) 21 Bom LR 1111, 54 IC 455. A similar view was taken the Bombay High Court in *re* Kahandas Narayandas, (1881)5 E 154. The High Court held that the sanction may be obtained on an application under the Trustees Act.
163. *Re* Muhammad Ismail, *AIR* 1944 Sindh 183.
164. *AIR* 1957 Mad 194.
165. *Supra* note 27, p. 235. see also *Mayadhar* v *Orissa Board of Waqfs*, *AIR* 1966 Ors 208.
166. *Mayadhar* v *Orissa Board of Waqfs ibid*; Woozatunnessa, in the matter of (1908) 36 Cal 21.
167. *Supra* note 32.
168. *Supra* note 8, para 561, p. 626.
169. p. 559.
170. *Supra* note 1.
171. In *Askari Hussain* v *Counnilal* 28 ALJ 205 Justice Mukherjee said that it is a piece of substantive Muslim law that a mutawalli whether the waqf be a public or a private one, cannot practically speaking, transfer is very much limited indeed, cases may occur in which a transfer of a portion of the waqf property if timely made, would save the rest from distribution or loss. It is stated in the petition that the present case was like that. If the sanction of the Qazi has to be obtained, under the Muslim law, and if without a previous sanction being obtained, no purchaser may be forthcoming to purchase the property except at the risk of losing it eventually, it is necessary that the mutawalli should be in a position to obtain that sanction.
172. 40 CWN 585.
173. *Sundaramurthy* v *Chotti Bibi*, *AIR* 1942 Mad 641.
174. *Supra* note 154.
175. *Supra* note 155.
176. *Zafarbhai* v *Chagan Bhai*, *AIR* 1942 Bom 21.
177. *Supra* note 156.
178. *Supra* note 157.
179. *Gulamali* v *Sultan Khan*. *AIR* 1967 Ori 55.
180. *Shah Mohammd* v *Manzoor Ali*, *AIR* 1966 Pat 45.
181. (1971) ALJ 510.
182. *AIR* 1972 All 553.
183. *AIR* 1966 Mad 307.
184. *Mohammad Mazaffar-al-Musavi* v *Jabeda Khatun*, *AIR* 1930 PC 103, (1930) 57 IA 125, 57 Cal 1293, 123, IC 722.
185. *Supra* note 140.
186. *Zubaida Sultana* v *Dawood Ismail*, *AIR* 1937 Cal 402.
187. *Wajid Ali* v *Dadannessa Bibi*, *AIR* 1947 Cal 282, (1947) 5 CWN 1.
188. *Chaniur Rahman* v *Abdur Salam* PLD 1965 (WP) Pesh 27-A Pakis case.

189. *Supra* note 126.
190. *Ghazanfar* v *Ahmadi Bibi, supra* note 72 ; *Syed Ali Zamin* v *Syed Akbar Ali Khan*, (1937) 64 IA 158, 16 Pat 344, 41 CWN 709, 167 IC 884.
191. *Abdul Razak* v *Ali Baksh, AIR* 1946 Lah 200.
192. *Amir Ali* v *Syed Wazir*, (1905) 9 CWN 876.
193. *Khajeh Salimullah* v *Abdul Khair*, (1909) 37 Cal 263.
194. *Supra* note 8, p. 613.
195. *Supra* note 94.
196. *Ghulam Muhammad* v *Abdul Rashid*, (1933) 14 Lah 588.
197 *Fatmabai* v *Haji Musa*, (1913) 38 Mad 491, 21 IC 964.
198. Bail 1. 591.
199. *Mst Kammon* v *Allah Baksh, supra* note 84 ; *Akbar Ali* v *Iftikhar Ali*, PLD 1951 Lah 368, (A Pakistani case).
200. Bail 1. 593.
201. *Moohummad Sadik* v *Moohummud Ali*, (1798) 1 SDA (Cal) 17. A reference may also be made to Bahr-ur-Raiq, Tatarkhania, the Zahiria, the Himadia and the Fasul-ul-Amadia.
202. (1937) 41 CWN 624 (PC) (Sindh).
203. *Sheikh Abdul Manna* v *Mutawalli of Mst Janabli supra* note 4.
204. *Abdulla Edrus* v *Zani S.H E.* (1888) 13 Bom 555.
205. *Haji Ali Mohammad* v *Anjuman Islamia*, (1931) 12 Lah 590.
206. *Amjadulla Siddiqui* v *Mirza Nizamuddin Baig, AIR* 1982 AP 34.
207. *Abdul Ganne* v *Hussen Miya*, (1873) 10 Bom HC 7.
208. *AIR* 1954 All 385.
209. *Supra* note 94.
210. *Birjis Mahal* v *Humayun Reza*, (1944) 23 Pat 203.
211 *Mohd Shah* v *Fasihuddin, AIR* 1956 SC 713.
212. *Sheikh Masthan Sahib* v *Malarani, supra* note 41.
213. *Ali Asghar* v *Fariduddin, AIR* 1947 All 261 : 1946 All 661.
214. *Abdul Sobhan Bhuya* v *Wasim Bhuya*, (1950) Dacca 178 ; a Pakistani case.
215. *Supra* note 26.
216. *Supra* note 107.
217. *Saliuddin Ahmad* v *Mohiuddin Ahmad, AIR* 1948 Pat 374, (1948) 26 Pat 531.
218. *Ali Mohammad* v *Mohammad Yusuf, AIR* 1962 Ori 111.
219. *Haq* v *Anjuman-i-Islamia* PLD 1962 (WP) Lah 462 – a Pakistani case.
220. *Mohammad Bhai* v *Wazirbi, supra* note 53.
221. *Elahi Baksh* v *Mohammad Ghouse*, (1933) 141 IC 169.
222. *Mohammad Soleman* v *Tasaddaq Hassan, AIR* 1935 Cal 623 ; *Fatamabi* v *Haji Musa, supra* note 95.
223. *Supra* note 194.
224. *Secretary of State* v *Syed Ahmad Badsha*, (1921) 41 MIJ 278.
225. (1937) 39 Bom LR 502.
226. *Abdul Edris* v *Zain*, (1888) 13 Bom 555.
227. *Syedun* v *Allah Ahmed*, (1964) WR 327.

228. (1933) 61 Cal 80.
229. *Ghanasambandhu Pandara Sannadhi* v *Velu Pandaram*, 27 IA 69.
230. *Balkrishna Saralram Pujari Waghmane* v *Shree Dhyaneshwar Maharaj Sansthan*, *AIR* 1959 SC 798.
231. 75 CWN 114 ; see also *Mohammad Jafar Hussain* v *M. Taqi Khan* 1433 Oudh 517.
232. *Saleh* v *Madar*, *Supra* note 157 ; *Abdul Kadir* v *Kadiria Sabha*, *supra* note 156 ; *Afzal Hussein* v *Chhedilal*, *supra* note 155 ; *Nimai Chand* v *Ghulam*, *supra* note 154 ; *Jawahar* v *Aziz*, *AIR* 1956 *Nag* 257 ; *Syed Mustafa* v *Waqf Board*, *AIR* 1969 Mad 66 : *Abdur Rahim* v *Mandu* (1970) MPIJ 968.
233. (1967) JLJ : SN 927.
234. *Mst. Moideen Bibi Ammal* v *Rathnavelu Mudali*, *AIR* 1927 Mad 69.
235. *Chidhoo* v *Hainer Khan* 1955 MIJ 161.
236. *AIR*1929 All 508.
237. *Abdul Raheem* v *Mamdu*, (1970) MPLJ 971.
238. *Siddique Ahmad Chouhdary* v *Syed Ahmed Choudhuri aud others*, *supra* note 112.
239. *Jaffer* v *Taqi*, *AIR* 1933 Oudh 517 ; *Hazera* v *Abdul Latif*, *supra* note 29.
240. *Mohammed Ismail* v *Mohammed*, *AIR* 1921 All 224 ; *Shah Mohammad* v *Mohammad*, *AIR* 1927 *Oudh* 113.
241. *Vidyavaruthi* v *Baluswami*, *supra* note.
242. *Supra* note 110.
243. *Mohammad Bhai* v *Wazirbi*, *supra* note 53.
244. *Supra* note 209.
245. *Wazir* v *Ladli*, *supra* note 161 ; *Jan Mohammad* v *Mahmood*, *AIR* 1974 All 124.
246. *Allaha Rakhi* v *Mohammad Abdul Rahim*, (1933) 61 IA 50 (All) ; see also *Munnavaru Begam* v *Mahapalli* (1918) 41 Mad 1033 ; *Mohmmad Oosman* v *Essak*, (1938) Bom 184.
247. *Supra* note 51.
248. *Moulvi Shah* v *Ghare Shah*, (1938) 40 BIV 1071.
249. *Vidya Varuthi* v *Baluswami*, *AIR* 1922 PC 12.
250. *Ikramul Haq Saheb* v *The Board of Rajasthan Muslim Waqf*, *AIR* 1973 Raj 57.
251. *Syed Shah* v *Syed Api*, *supra* note 143. *Ghulam Rasul* v *Ghulam* Qutab-ud-din, *AIR* 1922 Lah 142.
252. Paras Diwan, *Muslim Law in Modern Iudia*, p. 242.
253. *Najihuddin Ahmed* v *Amir Hassan*, *AIR* 1934 Pat 443.
254. *Supra* note 143.
255. *Syed Saulat Husain* v *Syed Ilmuddin*, *AIR* 1981 Raj 29.
256. *Supra* note 250.
257. *AIR* 1938 PC 7I.
258. *AIR* 1938 PC 202, (1938) 40 BIR 1071, 42 ICWN 1018, 175 IC 454.
259. *Najihuddin Ahmad* v *Amir Hassan*, (1934) 153 IC 557,

260. *Ahmad Yar* v *Ghulam Nabi*, *AIR* 1942 Lah 65 : (1948) Lah 116.
261. See Irfan Habib, *The Agrarian System of Mughal India*, p. 313; Report of the Dargah Khwaja Saheb (Ajmer) Committee of Enquiry New Delhi, (1949) pp. 27-28.
262. *Sardar Ali* v *Gahana Shah*, *AIR* 1933 Lah 444 ; (1933) 142 IC 847 ; *Mohiuddin* v *Saviduddin* ;(1893) 20 Cal 810, 821.
263. *Mahabir Prasad Marwari* v *Syed Shah Mahmmad Yuhmia*, *supra* note 141 Secretary of State v Mohiuddin, (1900) 27 Cal 674.
264. *Piran* v *Abdool Karim*, *supra* note 64 ; see also *Ishtiaq Ahmed* v *Saiyid Masood*. (1908) 6 ALJ 632 ; Sujjada *Shah* v *Shaw Habit*, (1919) MWN 662, (1919) 53 IC 677, 682.
265. *Supra* note 223.
266. *Supra* note 254.
267. *Jaffar El Adroos* v *Mahommed El Edroos*, (1937) 39 Bom LR 277.
268. See M.B. Ahmad, *Administration of Justice in Medieval India*, (Allahabad) 1926, pp. 223-24.
269. See Blochmann, *Ain-i-Akbari*, Vol I (2nd ed) p. 279 (1927) ; see also Report of the Dargah Khwaja (Aimer) Committee of Enquiry, New Delhi, p. 18.
270. For the history as to how the courts came to acquire jurisdiction over the waqfs, see *Mohammed Ali* v *Ahmad Ali*, *supra* note 107.
271. *Commentary on the Mussalmans Laws* by Charles Hamilton, No XX at p. 334.
272. *Muslim Law*. (Fourth Ed), p. 393.
273. *Supra* note 27, p. 251.
274. Regarding office as not hereditary—*Jamal Walad Ahmed* v *Jam : Walad Jallahr* (1877) 1 Bom 633 ; *Daud Shah* v *Ismailsha* (1878) 3 Bom 72 ; *Baba Kekaji* v *Nassaruddin*, (1893) 18 Bom 103 ; Mohd *Isak Sahah* v *Najaruddin*, *AIR* 1962 Mys 253 ; regarding claim not recognised by civil courts—*Kasam Khan* v *Kazi Abdullah*, *AIR* 1962 Bom 153, (1926) 50 Bom 133, 93 IC 135.
275. 43 IA 127, *AIR* 1916 PC 132 9 p. 135.
276. *AIR* 1926 Bom 135.
277. *Supra* note 141 ; see also *Raja Valad Shivapa* v *Krishnabhat*, (1878-89) ILR Bom 232.
278. *Supra* note 273.
279. *Supra* note 274.
280. *Supra* note 272.
281. See section 2 of the Act XI of 1864.
282. *Abbas Ali* v *Waqf Board*, *AIR* 1979 AP 117.
283. *Ibid*.
284. *Supra* note 273.
285. *Mohammad Isak* v *Najaruddin*, *supra* note 271.
286. *Supra* note 273.

7

Waqf Legislation During Pre-Independence Era

It is somewhat anomalous that notwithstanding the existence of richly endowed Muslim mosques and religious institutions all over India, the subject of endowment has received a most niggardly treatment. There is no statement of law directly on the subject in the *Quran*. In Islam, priests and Qazis have been assigned very high status. They enjoy the high reputation for purity and piety of character. They are responsible for the management of the waqf property. Probably this was considered a sufficient safeguard against breach of duty so as to render detailed rules to regulate their conduct unnecessary. It was considered to be the duty of the king to enquire into the particular laws and usages of classes, communities and societies, and adhere to them if they are not repugnant to the laws of God. After the establishment of British rule, the religious institutions in India became orphaned. The waqf property was grossly misappropriated.

Since the government was not willing to interfere into the waqf affairs, the endowments were like a mess. Corruption and maladministration prevailed and there was no way to check it. Mostly the funds of the religious and charitable endowments of the province were being squandered or misappropriated. The Act of 1861 was not a good piece of legislation for controlling the waqf affairs.[1] It was, therefore, said that the Act of 1863 be amended.[2]

The Beginning of Change in the Attitude of the Government

The passing of the Charitable Endowments Act VI of 1890 by the Government of India shows the beginning of change in the attitude of the Government. It was accepted that the Act of 1863 had failed to prevent the malversation of waqf property. It was, therefore, thought that appropriate legislation be introduced to check the maladministration of waqf property. Therefore, several bills were introduced in the Council as well as in the Council of the Governor-General of India. The Charitable Endowments Act VI of 1890 was the result of these various bills. The main aim of this Act was to to administer public endowments of non-religious character. There was a provision for the appointment of a Treasurer of Charitable Endowments for the whole of the country, with a provision that State Governments could also appoint such officers for their respective states. A person in charge of the administration of a public endowment was entitled to apply to the appropriate government for the vesting of the endowed property or income thereof in the Treasures of Charitable Endowments. The government was authorised to make scheme for the administration of such estates. The government could take necessary steps in this direction only if request was made by appropriate person.

The relevant sections of the Charitable Endowments Act VI of 1890 are as follows :—

Definition

In this Act 'charitable purpose' includes relief of the poor, education, medical relief and the advancement of any other object of general public utility, but does not include a purpose which relates exclusively to religious teaching or worship.

Appointment and Incorporation of Treasurer of Charitable Endowments

The Central Government may appoint an officer of the Government by the name of this office to be Treasurer of Charitable Endowments for India, and the Government of any State may appoint an officer of the Government by the name of his office to be Treasurer of Charitable Endowments for the State.

A Definition of appropriate Government *etc.*

In the subsequent provisions of this Act 'the appropriate government' means, as respects a charitable endowment, the objects of which do not extend beyond a single state and are not objects to which the executive authority of the Central Government extends, the Government of the State and as respects any other charitable endowment of the Central Government.

Orders vesting Property in Treasure

(1) Where any property is held or is to be applied in trust for a charitable purpose, the appropriate Government, if it thinks fit, may, on application made as hereinafter mentioned, and subject to the other provisions of this section. order, by notification in the official gazette, that the property be vested in the Treasure of Charitable Endowments on such terms as to the application of the property or tne income thereof as may be agreed on between the appropriate Government and the person or persons making the application, and the property shall thereupon so vest accordingly.

(2) When any property has vested under this section in a Treasure of Charitable Endowments, he is entitled to all documents of title relating thereto.

(3) Omitted by A.L.O. 1937.

(4) An order under this section vesting property in a Treasurer of Charitable Endowments shall not require or be deemed to require to administer the property, or impose or deemed to impose upon him the duty of a trustee with respect to the administration there.

Scheme for dministration of Property vested in the Treasurer

(1) On application made as hereinafter mentioned, and with the concurrence of the person or persons making the application, the appropriate Government if it thinks fit, may settle a scheme for the administration of any property which has been or is to be vested in the Treasurer of Charitable Endowments, and may in such scheme appoint, by name or office, a person or persons, not being or including such Treasure to administer the property.

(2) On application made as hereinafter mentioned, and

with the concurrence of the person or persons making the application, the appropriate Government may, if it thinks fit, modify any scheme settled under this section, or substitute other scheme in instead.

(3) A scheme settled, modified of substituted under this section small, subject to the other provisions of this section, come into operation on a day to be appointed by the appropriate Government in this behalf, and shall remain in force so long as the property to which it relates continues to be vested in the Treasurer of Charitable Endowments or until it has been modified or another such scheme has been substituted in instead.

(4) Such a scheme, when it comes into operation, shall supersede any decree or direction relating to the subject matter thereof in so far as such decree or direction is in any way repugnant thereto, and its validity shall not be questioned in any court, nor shall a Court given, in contravention of the provisions of the scheme or in any way contrary or in addition thereto, a decree or direction regarding the administration of the property to which the scheme relates.

Provided that nothing in this sub-section shall be construcd as precluding a Court from inquiring whether the Government by which a scheme was made was the appropriate Government.

(5) In the settlement of such a scheme effect shall be given to the wishes of the author of the trust so far as they can be ascertained, and in the opinion of the appropriate Government, effect can reasonably be given to them.

(6) Where a scheme has been settled under this section for the administration of property not already vested in the Treasurer of Charitable Endowments, it shall not come into operation until the property has become so vested.

Mode of applying for vesting Orders and Schemes

(1) The application referred to in the last two foregoing sections must be made—

(a) if the property is already held in trust for a charitable purpose, then by the person acting in the administration of the trust, or, where there are more persons than one so acting, then by those persons or a majority of them ; and

(b) if the property is to be applied in trust for such a purpose, then by the person or persons proposing so to apply it ;

(2) for the purposes of this section the executor or administrator of a decased trustee of property held in trust for a charitable purpose shall be deemed to be a person acting in the administrator of the trust.

Bare Trusteeship of Treasurer

(1) Subject to the provisions of this Act, Treasurer of Charitable Endowments shall as such Treasurer, act in the administration of any trust where any of the property is for the time being vested in him under this Act.

(2) Such Treasurer shall keep a separate account of each property for the time being so vested, in so far as the property consists of securities for money, and shall apply the property or the income thereof in accordance with the provision made in that behalf in the vesting order under section 4 or in the scheme, if any, under section 5, or in both those documents.

(3) In the case of any property so vested other than securities for money, such treasure shall, subject to any special order with which he may receive from the authority by whose order the property became vested in him permit the persons acting in the administration of the trust to have the possession, management and control of the property, and the application of the income, thereof, as if the property had been vested in them.

Sections 2 to 8 of this Act make the Treasurer of Charitable Trusts responsible for applying the income in accordance with the scheme for the administration of the settled property.

It is clear from the discussion that the Act failed to fulfil its purpose. It was having very limited scope. It was the sweet will of the trustee as to vest or not to vest the property or income in the Treasurer. It appears that the trustees were not interested in exercising this power. There were very few instances when trustees exercised this power.[3]

The Charitable Endowments Act 1890, therefore, failed to achieve the object for which it was enacted. The government realised the deficiencies of the Act. The government, therefore, made some better provisions in the Code of Civil Procedure.

in some specified cases, two or more persons interested can bring a suit against a trustee, provided they obtain prior permission for doing so from the Advocate General. These provisions in the Code of Civil Procedure could not solve the problem. The factors responsible for its failure were costly litigation, slow-process and the obtaining of permission from the Advocate General.

Since there was no supervision or intervention from the side of the government waqf properties worth lacs of rupees gradually started decaying. Most of the income of the waqf was taken by the mutawallis and the common man was having no right to check misappropriation.

Movement for Statutory and Administrative Control of Waqfs

During the last quarter of the 19th century, it was generally argued that government must take necessary steps for the protection and preservation of waqf property. In 1902, the Calcutta Muhammadan Union wrote a letter to the Viceroy for introducing necessary legislation so that the waqf property be protected. This demand of the Calcutta Muhammadan Union was not accepted by the government.[4] An identical representation was again made to the government by the Secretary of the society for the preservation of waqfs and the support of widows in India. This demand of the society was also turned down.[5]

In the year 1910 an identical resolution was passed by the All India Muslim League. It was resolved that necessary legislation be passed for the preparation and publication of a statement of the number, general purposes and manner of Muslim endowments designed mainly for the public benefit.[6] This demand of the Muslim League was also rejected.[7]

The attitude adopted by the government was also criticised by the Indian members of the Legislative Council. It was said that government should submit a report showing the number and value of all Mahomedan religious and charitable endowments indicating how many of them were looked after the Governments.[8] This demand of the Legislative Council was also rejected by the government. It was said by the government that it was not bound to furnish information regarding waqfs.[9]

The dissatisfaction regarding waqf affairs was not only prevalent in India. It was also prevalent in England. Occasional questions regarding mismanagement of waqfs were put up in British Parliament. However the policy of the then government was very plain. The government considered waqf affairs as purely religious matter and therefore, it was not willing to interfere into the religious affairs of Indian Muslims.[10]

Changed Attitude of the Government

Since there was effective and continuous demand for the administrative and statutory control of waqfs, the government was constrained to change its policy of non-interference. In July 1913, the Viceroy received a message from the India Office. The message suggested that the old policy of non-interference should be discontinued. It was further suggested that steps be taken for introducing appropriate legislation on the subject of waqfs.

The Home Member Hon'ble R.H. Craddock was not ready to accord the above suggestion. He rejected the idea of appropriate legislation on the following grounds :—

(i) the extent to which a Christian Government with subject of different creeds should exercise control over the religious trusts of those creeds ; and

(ii) the extent to which interference with religious trusts would cause excitement and agitation among classes of the people whose views were not very certainly represented on legislative councils. He further said that instead of dealing matters of high policy and Imperial concern, the Provincial Legislatures should summon a conference of the various authors of the Bills. He also suggested that few jurists on the subject be also requested to attend the conference. The resolution adopted in the conference be placed before the Government of India for its consideration and final approval.

These views of Hon'ble R.H. Craddock was approved[11] by the Legislative Department. Later on the same was sent to the India Office where it was accepted. In this way the policy of the government of non-interference was changed.[12]

The Central and State legislatures have passed the following Acts for the proper administration of charitable and religious institutions including waqfs : –

(i) The Bengal Charitable Endowments Public Buildings and Escheat Regulation, 1810 ;
(ii) The Religious Endowments Act, 1863 ;
(iii) The Charitable Endowments Act, 1890 :
(iv) The Charitable and Religious Trust Act, 1920 ;
(v) The Bihar Waqfs Act, 1947 ;
(vi) The Bombay Mussalman Waqfs Act, 1935. This Act modified the application of the Waqf Act, 1923, as regard its application to Gujarat and Maharashtra ;
(vii) The Uttar Pradesh Muslim Waqf Act, 1960 ;
(viii) The Bengal Waqfs Act, 1934 ;
(ix) The Bombay Public Trust Act, 1930.

The main aim of these legislations was to provide better administration and supervision of waqfs. These Acts are not prevalent throughout the country. The first four statutes mentioned above does not apply to those waqfs which are governed by the Waqf Act, 1954. It is clear from the above that the provisions of the Charitable and Religious Trust Act, 1920, shall not be applied with the provision of the Waqf Act, 1954 are applicable.

In Bengal and Madras the right of the company of superintendence was recognised by passing separate statutes. In Bengal the Regulation 19 of 1810 was passed. In Madras the Regulation 7 of 1817 was passed. These Regulations recognised the right of the company of superintendence of all endowments and benefactions Hindu and Muslim, vested in the respective boards of revenue Regulation 19 of 1810 declared[13] that—

> It is the duty of every government to provide, that the endowments for pious and beneficial purposes be applied according to their real intention, the local agents are appointed to ascertain and report the names of trustees, managers, and superintendents, whether under the designation of Mutawalli or any other, and all vacancies, and to recommend fit persons where the nomination devolves on the government. That the Board of Commissioners

may appoint such persons or make such other provision for the superintendence, management or trust as may be thought fit.

The preamble of this regulation laid down that—

> Whereas considerable endowments have been granted in land by the preceding governments of this country, and by individuals, for the support of mosques. Hindu temples, colleges and other pious and beneficial purposes, and whereas there are grounds to suppose that the produce of such land is used in many instances contrary to the intentions of the donors—and whereas it is an important duty of every Government to provide that all such endowments be applied to the real interest and will of the grantor—the following rules have been framed.

The main effect of the passing of the Regulation of the Bengal Code, 1810 and Regulation VI, 1817 of the Madras Code, was that the general superintendence vested in the Board of Revenue and Board of Commissioner in the several districts subject to the overall control of the Board of Revenue It was the policy of the British Government not to interfere in the purely religious endowments. The Board of Revenue was having possession over the landed and other properties of mosques, Hindu temples, colleges. The policy of the British government not to interfere into waqf administration could not continue for a long time. The British government was constrained to interfere into waqf administration. There were cases of misappropriation of waqf money and, therefore, the government decided to control the waqf administration. There were cases where endowed properties, irrespective of their being religious or secular was encouraged.[14]

In 1859, the British government decided to assume the responsibility of managing the native endowments. It was said that it is the duty of the state to see that these institutions enjoy the equal and impartial protection. It was, therefore, said that the management or religious endowments should no longer be delayed.[15]

The Religious Endowments Act XX of 1863

In the year 1863, the Government of India decided to divest itself 'of all direct concerns with management of religious endowments.' For this purpose an Act entitled 'Religious Endowment Act (Act 20 of 1863)' was passed. This Act placed the religious endowments 'under the management of their respective community.'[16] After the passing of this Act, the British Government acquired the sovereign functions of superintendent over religious institutions Mahants and Mutawallis were immuned from submitting the accounts. They were given full freedom to manage these institutions according to their sweetwill.

This Act provided—Except in this Act, it shall not be lawful for any Government in India, or for any officer of any Government in his official character, to undertake or resume the superintendence of any land or other property granted for the support of, or otherwise belonging to, any mosque, temple, or other religious establishment, or to take any part in the managment or appropriation and endowment made for the maintenance of any such mosque, temple or other establishment, or to nominate or appoint any trustee, manager or superintendent thereof, or to be in any way concerned therewith.

As a result of this Act, the landed and other properties relating to mosques, temples or other religious establishments were transferred to trustees, managers, or superintedents, *i.e.* respective creed of the community. The Act made special provisions in respect of management of mosques, temples and other religious institutions and also in regard to right of successors of the managers mutawallis and the tenure of their office. Form these properties were under the control of Board of Revenue or local agents. Local committees were also appointed to exercise the powers of the Board of Revenue. This Committee was given the powers of the appointment of managers, trustees and superintendents. The Act of 1863 was applicable only to public religious endowment. It was not applicable to private institutions. Detailed provisions were made in respect of mosques, temples and other religious establishments. Rules were made to ensure proper management and to empower the superior court in the district to take congnizance of allegations of misfeasance against the managing authority. After the passing of this Act, judiciary was entitled to entertain waqf suits. A suit could be filed under section 92 of the Code of Civil Procedure against the mutawalli of mahant. But this provision was not very much useful. This was the beginning of communal politics and Parties that later dominated the political scene. In the beginning Qazis and Pandits were assisting Englis judges in the administration of justice. However, later on this practice was abandoned. Therefore, English judges were required to administer Muslim law. English judges were having very little knowledge of Muslim law. The taking of help of qazis was also no more in practice. The result was that in many cases justice was denied to the aggrieved party. Khan Bahadur Moulvi Mohammad Yusoof says that there was not a single case on Muslim law which was consistent wi'h the institution of the Muslim[17] law.

The Act of 1863 was most unsatisfactory. It produced disastrous results which could not be neutralised by subsequent legislation. There was no active supervising agency over the working of mismanagement. There was also misappropriation of temple funds.[18] Consequently other ameliorative measures including section 92 of the Code of Civil Procedure, 1908 were enacted.

Section 14—Persons interested may singly sue in case of Breach of Trust *etc.*

Any person or persons interested in any mosque, temple, or religious establishment, or in the performance of the worship of the service thereof, or the trusts relating thereto, may, without joining as plaintiff any of the other persons interested therein, sue before the Civil Court the trustee, manager, or superintendent of such mosque, temple of religious establishment or the member of any committee appointed under this Act, for any misfeasance, breach of trust or neglect of duty, committed by such trustee, manager, superintendent or member of such committees in respect of the trusts vested in or confided to them respectively ; and the Civil Court may direct the specific performance of any act by such trustee, manager, superintendent member of a committee, and may decree damages and costs against such trustee, manager, superintendent or member of a committee, and may also direct the removal of such trustee, manager, superintendent or member of a committee.

Section 15—Nature of interest entitling a Person to Sue

The interest required in order to entitle a person to sue under the last preceding section need not be a pecuniary, or a direct immediate interest or such an interest as would entitle the person suing to take any part in the management or superintendence of the trustee.

Any person having a right of attendance, or having been in habit of attending, at the performance of the worship or service of any mosque, temple or religious establishment, or of partaking in the benefit of any distribution of alms, shall be deemed to be a person interested within the meaning of the last preceding section.

This Act applies only to public religious endowments, but do not apply to private ones. It specifically makes provisions relating to management of mosque, temple or religious establishment as regards right of succession to trusteeship, tenure of office *etc.* When the object of the suit is to protect an endowment against misfeasance, breach of trust or neglect of duty, section 14 of the Act, which is quite general and applies to endowments created both before and after 1863[19] would apply. It lays down that the proceedings can be initiated by any interested person for the protection of mosque *etc.* Section 15 has further defined that the interest need not be pecuniary or direct.

Its Jurisdiction

The Act applies to all parts of India, except the Presidency of Bombay, and except some of the Scheduled Districts and also to the District of Canara in the Presidency of Bombay does not apply to the Presidency towns.

Object of the Act

The main object of the Act is to relieve the executive officers from the duty of governing non-Christian institutions. Previously the trustee, manager or superintendent of every religious establishment, not purely of private nature was either (i) nominated or confirmed by the State Government or some public officer, or (ii) appointed in the manner prescribed by the founder or usage, and he was under the supervision of the Board of Revenue. In the former case, the management was left with a committee of persons professing the religion, and the manager or the superintendent was responsible to the body, while in the latter case, the trustee, manager or superintendent was subject to no executive control ; but in both cases he came within the jurisdiction of the Civil Courts. Section 14 of the Act provide appropriate remedies for misfeasance or neglect of duty.

In *Jan Ali* v *Ram Nath Mundul*[20] it was held that the mosques, *etc.* to which this Act is applicable are those with which Regulation XIX of 1810 was concerned, and that the description of those establishments is to be found in the preamble to that Regulation, which speaks of 'endowments granted in land for the support of mosques, Hindu temples, colleges, and other pious and beneficial purposes,' and describes the mischief to be remedied as consisting in the misappropriation of the produce of those lands contrary to the intention of the donors, to the personal use of individuals in immediate charge and possession of such endowments. Hence it was laid down in that case that section 14 would be applicable, if the mosque in question was one for the support of which endowments in land had been granted by the Government or by individuals. On the other hand, the necessity for the sort of supervision contemplated would not arise in the case of a building destined exclusively for the domestic worship of the founder's family, even assuming a perpetual endowment of that kind to be valid.

For the enforcement of this section, it is not essential to show that the establishment existed in 1963, nor that the right of nominating or confirming the manager was vested in the Government.

Scope of the Act

Under Section 14 of the Act[21] or Section 92 of the Code of Civil Procedure, 1908, leave is not required for a suit by two local worshippers on behalf of the entire body of worshippers, for the avoidance of a permanent lease.[22]

A beneficiary of trust interested in the maintenance of a

mosque or other charitable institution, may without having recourse to the provisions of Order 1, rule 8 of the Code of Civil Procedure and without suing in a representative capacity on behalf of the other beneficiaries, sue for recovery of possession of property wrongfully alienated by the trustee and for the incidental declaration that the properties are subject of the trust and that they cannot be alienated, and can establish his right thereto or against a trespasser, to recover any portion of the property which has been misappropriated, without joining any other person who may participate with him in the benefit. When the consequential relief is made available to the plaintiff, he is not entitled to a mere declaration[23]. Therefore, any person or persons interested in the waqf may bring a suit under Act XX of 1863, or Section 92 of the Civil Procedure Code without joining other persons as co-plaintiffs for the removal of a mutawalli on the ground of misfeasance, breach of trust or neglect of duty.

Act XX of 1863 & Section 92 of Code of Civil Procedure

Section 92 of the Civil Procedure Code and Section 14 of Act XX of 1863 have got the same forms of relief and offer a choice to persons interested in the trust. They might proceed under either and are not bound to proceed under both.[24] But section 92 of the Code of Civil Procedure is wider and provides *inter alia* far settling a scheme which is a jurisdiction of a very wide and beneficial nature,[25] and contemplates more grounds of removal besides those mentioned in this section, *e.g.* unfitness, *etc*. Suits in which relief is asked for against strangers to the trust, whether alieness from the trustees or trespassers, are outside the purview of Section 92 of the Code.[26] This section empowers the Civil Courts to remove trustees for misfeasance, *etc.*, and it does not recognise any difference in respect of trustees, whether hereditary or selected.[27] The provisions of Section 92 are mandatory, and no suit could be brought for any of the reliefs in the section, except under the conditions laid down in it, saving at the same time the jurisdiction of the District Courts under the Religious Endowments Act. But a suit under this section can be brought only by the Advocate General or the State Government, or with his sanction by two or more interested persons. Section 92 of the Code of Civil Procedure and Section 14 are not mutually exclusive.

Other Provisions of Act XX of 1863

When a suit is instituted by a committee appointed by the Government under Section 7 of the Religious Endowments Act, the death of a member during the pendency of the suit has not the effect of making the suit infructuous. The surviving members can continue the suit for proceeding, as the Committee is not *ipso faeto* dissolved, when one of the members dies.[28] With regard to endowments falling under section 3, the powers of such Committee are very wide, and they act within their powers in making appointment of a mutawalli for a term, with conditions which are as much binding upon the person appointed as upon the members of the Committee. But the position of the said mutawalli is that of a servant of the Committee, and he is not a mutawalli under the Muslim law. The properties of the trust vest in the committee under Section 12, and the Committee can take over the management, and can appoint or dismiss the mutawalli (section 3). The mutawalli appointed under the Act cannot appoint his successor. The powers of the Committee appointed under Act XX of 1863 are not the powers exercisable under the general Muslim law by the waqif, but by the powers vested in the ruling power, the power exercised by the Board of Revenue under Regulation XX of 1810, and the power conferred upon the Committee under the Religious Endowments Act XX of 1863. The words 'manager,' 'trustee' and 'superintendent' used indifferently and indiscriminately in the Act are used to denote one and the same idea of management. The bonafides of the Committee can not be questioned when act are not shown to be detrimental to endowment, and no relief can be had against the Committee under Section 14. The remedies[29] provided by Section 18 are alternative.

Qazi Act, 1864 and Charitable Act, 1890

In the year 1864 the Qazi Act (11 of 1864) was passed. This Act abolished Hindu and Muslim law officers, who were appointed under Regulation XII of 1793.

In the year 1890, the Charitable Endowments Act was

passed. This piece of legislation was applicable to charitable endowments relating to relief of the poor, education, medical relief and advancement of any other object of general public utility. The Act provided that the finance of the religious institutions should be placed under a treasurer who shall be appointed by the Central Government for the whole of India. This Act excluded a purpose which related exclusively to religious teaching or worship. The Act was made applicable to waqfs also. The Act was applicable to those charitable endowments only which had been established for the relief of the poor, medical relief or any other object of general public utility. This Act was having a limited scope. The trustees were having the discretion to apply the property for vesting and settling of a scheme. Section 5 of the Act provided that if the objects of the trust do not extend beyond a single state and are not objects to which the executive authority of the Central Government in other cases, could frame a scheme for the administration of any property vested in the Treasurer of Charitable Endowments on the application of and with the concurrence of the persons making the application.

The Official Trustees Act (Act No 2 of 1913)

The main aim of the passing of this Act was to appoint Official Trustees. The Official Trustees could be appointed amongst the persons specified in Section 4 thereof.

The Mussalman Waqf Validating Act, 1913

For a sufficiently long time Indian courts refused to recognise a waqf for private purposes. In *Abdul Fata* v *Rasomoyya*[30] the Judicial Committee of the Privy Council invalidated secular waqfs. The Privy Council said that a waqf was valid if there was a substantial dedication of the property to charitable uses at some period or other but if the primary object of the waqf was the aggrandisement of the family and the gift to charity was illusory, whether from its small amount or from its uncertainty and remoteness, the waqf for the benefit of the family was invalid. In Abdul Mohammed's case, the Privy Council failed to understand the fundamental differences between a hiba and waqf. The Privy Council refused to be guided by the known precepts of Muslim jurists. The Privy Council said :—

> As regards precepts whlch are held as the fundamental principles of Mohammadan law, their lordships are not forgetting how far law and religion are mixed up together in the Mohammadan communities, but they asked during the argument how it comes about that by general law of Islam. At least as known in India, simple gifts (hiba) by a private person to remote unborn gen ration of descendants, succession, that is. of inalienable life interest are forbidden and whether it is to be taken that the very same dispositions, which are illegal when made by ordinary words of gift, become legal if only the settlers say that they are made as waqf in the name of God or for the sake of the poor. To those questions no answer was given or attempted to, no case their lordship see any.

The simple point which was missed by their Lordship of the Privy Council was that waqf was a disposition of property for consideration *i.e. sawab* alike hiba was the transfer of the property without any consideration. This judgment was criticised in all parts of the country. A large number of representations and memorials were submitted by leading Muslim personalities of India to the Viceroy and to Her Majesty's Government. The decision caused a great furore in the Muslim society and led to widespread resentment. Maulana Shibli wrote number of articles against this judgment. The judgment was even criticised in the Parliament. The judgment was in accordance with the law by which the Hindus and Muslims regulated their lives. Consequently, the Government passed Mussalman Waqf Validating Act of 1913.

The main aim of the passing of the above Act was to remove doubts regarding the validity of waqfs created by persons professing Islam in favour of themselves, their families, children and descendants and ultimately for the benefit of the poor or for other religious, pious or charitable purposes. The Act of 1913 defined the waqf as the permanent dedication by a person professing the Musalman faith, of any property, for any purpose recognised by Muslim law as religious, pious or charitable. It is necessary for the validity of waqf that it must be created both for the benefit of the settler's family, children and descendants and for charity. The Act made it lawful for a Muslim to create a waqf which in all respects is in accordance with law for the following among other purposes :

(a) for the maintenance and support, wholly or partially; of his family, children or descendants, and

(b) where the person creating a waqf is a Hanafi Muslim also for his own maintenance or for the payments of his debts out of the rents and profits of the property dedicated.

The ultimate benefit in the above mentioned cases must be expressly or impliedly reserved for the poor or for any other purpose recognised by the Muslim law as a religious, pious or charitable purpose of a permament character.

Under the Waqf Act, 1913, a waqf shall not be deemed to be invalid merely because the benefit reserved therein for the poor or other religious, pious or charitable purpose of a permanent nature is postponed until after the extinction of the family, children or descendants of the person creating the waqf.

It was said that the benefit of the family is in itself a religious and charitable object. The Act of 1913 still recognised waqfs created before the passing of this Act as invalid. In 1930, another Act was passed by which retrospective effect was given to the provisions of Act VI of 1913.

The Act of 1913 was not a complete enactment. There were many defects in that Act. The mutawallis were having arbitrary powers. They were treating waqf property as if it were their own. The most important defect was that there was no control over mismanagement of waqf property. They started a movement for introducing another piece of leglisation which may remove all these defects. It was maintained that trusts created for public purpose should be protected by the state and the state should make suitable legislation for supervising and managing these institutions.

Under the Act of 1913, a mutawalli of the waqf other than the 'waqf-alal-aulad', was required to submit to the court of

District Judge or other Civil Courts, a statement containing the following particulars :—

(i) description of waqf property ;
(ii) gross annual income ;
(iii) gross income accounted during the previous year ;
(iv) amount payable as revenue, taxes, cesses and rents ;
(v) estimate of annual expenditure ;
(vi) amount set apart as mutawalli remuneration and allowance to other persons (i) religious purposes ; (ii) charitable purposes and (iii) any other purpose.

Section 3 of Act VI of 1913 validates those waqfs which are primarily and wholly for the purpose of supporting and maintaining the family, children or descendants of the creator of the waqfs. Under the Act it is necessary that in case the family should one day become extinct there should be a provision in the waqf for the benefit of some religious, pious or charitable purpose. Section 3 (a) of the 1913 is applicable only in the case of private waqfs. This section is not applicable to those waqfs which are partly charitable and partly private. Therefore, an application under Sections 3, 5 and 10 of Act XVII of 1923 can be filed with respect to such a waqf by reason of the definition of waqf in Section 2 of Act 42 of 1923.[31]

Suits relating to Public Matters—Scs 92 & 93 of the Code of Civil Procedure

Sections 92 and 93 of the Code of Civil Procedure, 1908 lays down detailed procedure for taking action in case of breach of a trust set up for religious or charitable purpose and for issue of directions by the court for proper administration of the trusts. Section 92 of the Code says that in case of any alleged breach of any express or constructive trust created for public purposes of a charitable or religious nature, or where the direction of the court is deemed necessary for the administration of any such trust, or two or more persons having an interest in the trust and having obtained the consent in writing of the Advocate General, may institute a suit, whether contentious or not, in the principal civil court of original jurisdiction or in any other court empowered in that behalf by the (State Government) within the local limit of whose jurisdiction the whole or any part of the subject matter of the trust is situated, to obtain a decree—

(a) removing any trustee ;
(b) appointing a new trustee ;
(c) vesting any property in a trustee ;
(cc) directing a trustee who has been removed or a person who has ceased to be a trustee, to deliver possession of any trust property in his possession to the person entitled to the possession of such property[32] ;
(d) directing accounts and enquiries ;
(e) allocating the trust property or any part thereof or its income to any particular object of the trust ;
(f) authorizing the whole or any part of the trust property to be let, sold, mortgaged or exchanged ;
(g) settling a scheme ; or
(h) granting such further or other relief as the nature of the case may require.

Save as provided by the Religious Endowments Act,[33] 1961 no suit claiming any of the reliefs specified in sub-section (1) shall be instituted in respect of any such trust as is therein referred to except in conformity with the provisions of that sub-section.[33a]

Suit may be filed by Persons having interest in the Trust Property

The provisions of section 92 of Code of Civil Procedure, 1908 are also applied in the case of public waqfs. A public waqf is a trust for purpose of a charitable religious nature within the meaning of section 92 and if the reliefs specified in the section are claimed with reference to a waqf, the section applies.[34] A mutawalli was liable to be removed under section 92 of the Code of Civil Procedure.

In the year 1920, the Charitable and Religious Trusts Act was passed. Before the passing of this Act the Official Trustees Act of 1913, was in force. This Act was having very limited scope. The Act of 1920 was passed with a view to providing more effectual control over the administration of Charitable and Religious Trusts. There was no administrative machinery for supervising the administration of trusts. However, any interested person could apply to the court of the District Judge to direct the trustee to furnish required information in respect of the trust. The Act was also applicable in the case of waqfs if the entire benefit was utilised for public purposes.

The scheme of section 92 is comprehensive. It ensures proper administration of religious and charitable trusts including waqfs. Any interested person in trust has been given right to bring a suit against a trustee ıor his removal and breach of trust. However, section 92 allowed even some of them to file a suit with the consent of the Advocate General or of the Collector of the District. In *Syed Mazhar Hussain* v *Haji Ali Mohammad Jalaluddin*[35] it was said that the obligation to obtain consent was imposed to prevent an indefinite number of harassing suits being brought against trustees by different persons interested in the trust. Section 92 is also applicable to mutawallis. They are liable as trustees in the general sense for the administration of the trust fund or trust property. A mutawalli has no right to transfer except in certain exceptional circumstances recognised by Muslim Law and the fact that the purchaser is a bonafide perchaser for value without notice would afford no protection to him. He is a pure and simple trespasser.[36]

The Waqf Act, 1954 has not adversely affected the provision of section 92, Code of Civil Procedure. There is no provision in the Act which expressly says that the scheme framed under section 92 of the Code of Civil Procedure in respect of waqfs prior to the coming into force of the Act, shall cease to be operative on the coming into force of the Act, nor is there any provision which says that wherever such schemes confer certain powers or cast certain duties upon the court, such powers and duties shall be exercised and performed by the Waqf Board.[37]

Under section 92 a court can decide whether the property is waqf or not.[38] A court, under section 92 can decide the validity of mosques or khanqah's established for public purposes.[39] A suit may be filed either (a) by the Advocate General, (b) and outside the Presidency towns by the Collector or such officer as the State Government may appoint in this behalf, *e.g.* legal remembrancer,[40] or two or more persons having an interest in the trust and having abtained the consent of the Advocate General. Where the suit has been filed by any two persons interested in the waqf must have existing interest. The contingent interest will not solve the problem. The interest must be present and substantial. The residents of the locality in which a religious institution, such as a mosque is situated and for which it was originally founded the persons authorised by law to use it and the worshippers of the mosque are the persons interested as required by section 92 of the Code of Civil Procedure.[41] Any of the worshipper can file a suit against a trespasser for possession of trust property.[42] All persons deriving benefit under the waqf can file a declaratory suit against the mutawalli under section 42 of the Specific Relief Act, 1877.[43]

The founder of an endowment or his heirs cannot remove trustees and appoint new trustees without invoking the aid of section 92.[44] The standard of rectitude and accuracy expected from every trustee of charitable funds is of the highest, and that the standard must in all circumstances be maintained by courts, if the safety of the property held upon such trusts is not to be imperilled throughout the whole of India.[45]

Private trusts are not immune from the jurisdiction of the court. A court is competent to interfere to ascertain that no breach of trust is done. A suit can be filed for removing the trustee of a private trust and for the framing of a scheme. It may, however, be noted that the public or the ultimate beneficiaries have no such right to file a suit.[46]

The courts are having discretion to differ from the wishes of the waqif in view of the changed conditions and circumstances and for the interest of the general body of the public for whose benefit the trust was created. The courts are at liberty to follow or not to follow any rule of management which the courts may consider that the same may not be in the interest of the institution.[47]

Where the trustee in breach of the trust has improperly alienated the trust property to a stranger and the essence ofthe plaintiff's claim against such alienation is that he is a trespasser and the property of which he is in possession should be restored. The new trustee that is to be appointed by the court such relief is outside the scope of a suit under section 92 because a relief against a third party is not one of the reliefs specifed in toat section and cannot be brought within the words 'such further or other relief', which should be construed *ejusdem generis* with the previous clauses.[48]

Under the Muslim Law, the full legal and beneficial ownership of the property rests in the waqf. The mutawalli is a mere manager who has not the legal estate in him as in the case of an English trustee. The transferee from the mutawalli, therefore, does not get the legal estate and the question whether he purchase with notice of the waqf or not is really immaterial.

A mutawalli of the waqf has no right to transfer the property except in certain exceptional circumstances recognised by the Muslim Law. In the case of the transfer of waqf property, the transferee becomes a trespasser. Section 92 of the Code of Civil Procedure has been made applicable to mutawallis because of the obligations and duties imposed upon them.[49]

Where the purchaser had taken upon himself the duties of a trustee de son tort, relief under section 92 can be claimed. However, if the mutawalli purchased the property in his personal capacity and not on behalf of the waqf, he will be treated as trespasser. He will not be a trustee either actual or constructive. For the recovery of trust property, section 92 of the Code of Civil Procedure will not be applicable. The principles of English Law of a constructive trust are not at all applicable to such cases, but even if they are deemed to be applicable, the transferees from mutawalli cannot be held to be constructive trustees on these principles, which could make them proper parties to a suit for execution and administration of a trust which section 92 contemplates.[50] It is not necessary for all the plaintiffs to contest the suit actively.[51] A suit regarding the validity of a trust cannot be entertained under section 92 of the Code of Civil Procedure.

Under section 92, Code of the Civil Procedure Code a suit is not absolutely necessary in all cases of appointing a mutawalli. The court can appoint a mutawalli in certain circumstances, and if some mutawallis are living a notice to them is necessary before any appointment can be made. Where a person claims to be the trustee of a fund the proper remedy can be a suit under section 92 of the Code of Civil Procedure and not an application under the Trusts Act, 1822, sections 34[52] or 74.

The relief will be sought strictly on the basis of various forms mentioned in the section otherwise the permission of the Advocate General shall not be necessary.[53]

Where the plaintiff is trying to enforce any individual right then no sanction under section 92 of the Code of Civil Procedure would be necessary. However, if the plaintiff wanted to enforce public right then sanction under Section 92 of the Code of Civil Procedure would be necessary for the institution of such a suit.[54]

In *Imdad Ali Khan* v *Sardar Khan*[55] there was a kutcha mosque. The executant was not in a position to convert it into a pucca mosque. He executed an ikrarnama in favour of Muslim public at large. On some ceremonial occasions Muslim public of adjoining villages used to gather for prayers. The Muslim public made the mosque pucca at their expense by raising subscriptions from the public. It was held that the mosque was a public institution and endowment of land was a real waqf in favour of this public institution.

Under section 92 of the Code of Civil Proceudre action can be brought in respect of those charities only in which the public are interested. A Muslim waqf is a trust meant for public purposes of a charitable and religious nature.[56]

For filing a suit under section 92, there must either be a breach of trust or the direction of the court for the administration of the trust to bring the case within the scope of this section.

Suits be instituted in the Principal Civil Court of Original Jurisdiction

Section 92 says that suit may be instituted in the principal Civil Court of original jurisdiction or in any other court empowered in that behalf by the (State government) within the local limits of whose jurisdiction the whole or any part of the subject matter of the trust is situated. In *Prithipal Singh* v *Magh Singh*[57] it was said that suits under section 92 can be instituted both in the Principal Civil Court of Original jurisdiction as also in any other court empowered in that behalf by the State Government within the local limits of whose jurisdiction the whole or any part of the subject matter of the trust is situated. Provisions of section 92 do not envisage that such other courts are to be empowred by a gazette notification, Empowering by a gradation and distribution list of officers in the judicial department which is prepared and published by the State Government is sufficient compliance.

Grant of leave to file suit is not a mere irregularity which can be cured but is a condition precedent. The provisions of section 92 are mandatory in nature in that respect and the defendant cannot waive that right and confer jurisdiction on a court. In regard to the granting of leave to file a suit under section 92 the eourt does not have to write a reasoned order. It does not even have to give a notice to the defendant of an application for leave to file as the order granting leave is of an administrative nature.

Removing any Trustee

This is a mandatory provision and the reliefs specified in the section can only be enforced now by resort to the procedure of the section. The persons who have established endowment or their heirs cannot sue trustees for the due performance of the trust and to remove them and to appoint new trustees without invoking the aid of section 92 of Code of Civil Procedure.[58] A suit for the above relief cannot be filed without obtaining sanction under section 92 or 93 of the Code of Civil Procedure. Under sections 92 and 93 a trustee may sought to be removed for purchasing the waqf property or for a breach of trust, or wrongfully alienated trust property, or has been guilty of wanton waste and neglect, or he is incapable of managing waqf affairs.[59] In *Newaz Ahmad Khan* v *Hasanuddin Ahmed*[60] it was said by Calcutta High Court that setting on the title to a waqf property as his personal estate might not by itself be sufficient ground for the removal of a mutawalli from the office, if it is established that there was honest administration and management of the waqf, and in conformity with, and not in defiance of the trust for which a religious institution is established. According to Lahore High Court the mohunt of a waqf is an unfit person to continue in office if he denies the waqf character of the property and sets up an adverse claim to it.[61]

A mosque is a public property and, therefore, a person in charge of a mosque claiming it as his private estate be removed under section 92 of the Code of Civil Procedure. The Patna High Court removed a Sajjadanashin from the management of a waqf for gross mismanagement, but allowed him to retain the spiritual office of Sajjadanashin[62]

Suits for removing Trustees in Private Trusts

In the case of private charities the court can interfere to see that no breaches of trust are created. In such cases the members of the family can file a suit for the infringement of their right under section 9 of the Code of Civil Procedure. The public or the intended beneficiaries have no manner of right at all.[63]

Trust Property be Let, Sold, Mortgaged or Exchanged

Courts are having complete discretion in letting, selling, mortgaging or exchanging waqf property.[64] In such cases the primary duty of the court is to see the interest of the general body of the public for whose benefit the trust was created.

Settling a Scheme

Under this clause also courts are given very wide discretion. The courts can issue direction for the better administration of public trusts. It can direct the institution to act in a particular manner for the purpose of proper administration. The courts can take into consideration not merely the wishes of the waqif, but also the past history of the institution and the way in which it has been managed since inception in conjunction with others existing conditions that may have grown up since its creation.[65] In *Nizam-ul-Haq* v *Mohammad Ishfaq*[66] it was said that the District Judge can settle a scheme without sanction of the waqif. The court can refuse to frame a scheme if it comes to the conclusion that there was no case of mismanagement.[67]

Granting such further or other Reliefs as the nature of the Case may require

The scope of this section 92 sub-class (h) is very wide. It provides relief of the same nature as it provided for sub-clauses (a) to (g) of this section. Where the only relief claimed in a suit for a declaration that certain property is waqf property, the suit will not come within the purview of section 92 of the Code of Civil Procedure.[68] In *Abdur Rahim* v *Abu Mahommed Barkat Ali*[69] the Privy Council held that a suit can be filed for a declaration that property belongs to a waqf. For filing of such a suit the prior consent of Advocate General is not necessary. The Council further held that on general principles further or other reliefs should be taken to mean relief of the same nature as mentioned in clauses (a) to(g). Therefore, such a suit will not come within the scope of section 92, sub-clause (h).

Where a suit has been filed for one or more of the reliefs as mentioned in section 92 (1) as to a waqf for a public purpose, the prior approval of the Advocate General must be obtained. However, the above sanction shall not be necessary in a waqf which is not a public purpose. For instance, a suit in respect of a private imambara[70] or where the effect of a deed of waqf is to give the property in substance to the settlor's family.[71]

In *Shiv Dinshah Monekji* v *Shiv Jonetji Tijibhai*[72] it was said that section 92 (h) can be applied to remedy the infringment of an individual right or private right. The same shall not be applicable to establish the right of the public in respect of trust.

Suits to enforce Private Rights

A suit filed not to enforce the right of the public in respect of a public trust but to remedy the infringement of on individual right or a private right will not come within the definition of section 92.[73] Suits for the enforcement of private rights can be enforced in the ordinary manner. For example, a suit between two individuals each claiming certain rights as mutawalli over waqf property can be filed in ordinary manner.[74] According to the Allahabad High Court the right of a Muslim to use a mosque is a private not a public right and, therefore, a suit in the ordinary manner may be filed for claiming the right to use the mosque.[75] Suits against strangers or trespassers and transferees from trustees for a declaration that property in their hands is trust property and for possession have been held to be beyond the scope of section 92.[76]

Power and Competency of the Court under Section 92, Code of Civil Procedure

A suit under section 92 can be filed only in the principal civil court of original jurisdiction. Unless otherwise provided it does not include the Court of Additional District Judge appointed under Section 8 of the Civil Courts Act XII of 1887.[77] The State Government has no right to direct the transfer of a particular suit pending in a District Court to the court of a particular judge. The authority to decide the case must be general one.[78]

Sub-section (2) of Section 92

The requirements of this sub-section is mandatory. According to this sub-clause no suit claiming any of the reliefs specified in sub-section (1) shall be instituted without the consent of the Advocate General.[79] Where a suit under this section has been dismissed, the aggrieved person is not competent to file an appeal on his own account, the reason being that he was not a party to the suit.

Vacancy of Mutawalli may be filled up on an Application to Court

When there is a vacancy of mutawalli and there is no question of removing any trustee, the vacancy may be filled by an application to the court. A separate suit need not be filed under section 92 of the Code of Civil Procedure.[80] A District Judge may appoint a mutawalli by way of nomination but he has no power to appoint a mutawalli in a summary proceeding in place of another mutawalli. This is possible only by filing a suit either under the Religious Endowments Act, 1863 or under Section 92, Code of Civil Procedure. Where the dispute is between two or more persons regarding the office of mutawalliship, then it is a dispute of a civil suit. The appointment of a mutawalli by a District Judge in a summary proceeding is not appealable, and such appointment should be made in cases of emergency, and by the very nature of it must be subject to the result of any suit which may be instituted by any of the parties who claim adversely to one another to the mutawalli, or subject to the result of any suit which may be instituted either under section 92 or under the provisions of the Religious Endowment Act.[81]

Declaratory Suits

The parties can file a suit for the declaration that he is entitled for the office of mutawalli. He can also pray the court for an injunction restraining the defendants from preventing him to carry out his duties.[82] A declaratory decree is incapable of execution. Therefore, a mutawalli who has been declared under the declaratory decree to be entitled for certain property cannot get property under section 144 of the Code of Civil Procedure.[83] Under sections 92, a suit will not lie for removal of *de facto* or constructive trustees.[84]

Exercise of powers of Advocate General outside Presidency Towns

The powers conferred by sections 91 and 92 on the Advocate General may, outside the Presidency towns be with the previous sanction of the (State Government),[85] exercised also by the Collector or by such officer as the (State Government) may appoint in this behalf.

Section 93 of the Code of Civil Procedure deals with the powers of Advocate General outside Presidency towns. According to this section the powers conferred by sections 91 and 92 on the Advocate Genral may, outside the Presidency towns, be with the previous sanction of the State Government, exercised also by the Collector or by such officer as the State Government may appoint in this behalf.

The Charitable and Religious Trusts Act, 1920—The Religious Endowments Conference, 1914

On March 16, 1914, the Religious Endowments Conference was held in Delhi. The Conference was attended by 26 members. Home Member Sir Reginald Craddock was the President of this conference. The following points were submitted before the conference for its consideration :—

(a) Has the time arrived to reconsider the policy underlying the Act of 1863 ?

(b) In case the stage for a change has been reached,

should this be done for India as a whole, or by each province individually according to the state of local feelings in it.

(c) Is it possible to differentiate between religious and secular endowments in respect of the control to be exercised over them ?

(d) Assuming that intervention is considered proper, should this include the liability to publish regular audited accounts of all the trusts in order to afford to the public information as to the extent and method of management of these endowments ?

As regards the question number one it was said that the present law needed immediate change. It was said that the waqf property should be properly maintained and for this purpose legislation be passed. As regards question number two the conference was not having unanimity of opinion. According to one view instead of having one uniform law, the provincial legislature should be allowed to make their own law. This should be keeping in view of the circumstances of that province. The other opinion was that the Imperial Parliament should make a uniform Act which may be prevalent throughout the country. The conference also proposed that keeping in view the local requirements separate rules may be made.

As regards question number three the majority opinion was that such differention was not practicable.

As regards question number four there was general support among the members. The members differed on the questions such as audit should be compulsory for trusts or only of those which are having specified value. There was no unanimity of opinion as to whether the authority to appoint the auditors be judicial or executive ; the qualification of auditors, and the duties to be imposed upon them, that is, whether these should extend to administrative audit or be confined to the verification of such accounts as might be produced, *etc.*

It was also said that the term of office of members should be for five years and special concession in respect of court fee and costs be given for instituting suits against erring mutawallis.

Even this conference failed to change the attitude of the government. The government was of the opinion that Civil Courts were competent to deal with such matters and there was no need of separate legislation on the subject.[86] The members strongly criticised this attitude of the government. According to members if Civil Courts and Civil Courts alone were to be the agencies through which the aggrieved public was to seek redress, 'the evil will flourish very much the same as now'. It was said that unless and until trustees are made legally bound to keep and publish accurate accounts,[87] proceeding before the District Judge against them will carry no force. However, the government was not willing to make any law on the subject. The government was of the opinion that if any legislation is made it will amount to interference[88] into Muslim religion and will lead to agitation in the country. The government of India drafted a bill (Religious and Charitable Trusts Bill). In this Bill the Civil Courts were given power of supervision over endowments. This draft, however, could not be given the shape of an Act. In the year 1920 Charitable and Religious Trusts Act XIV was passed. This Act was not much used. This Act contained no provision under which trustees were legally required to publish accounts and to get these accounts audited. It was generally felt by the Muslims that government should make survey of the number of waqf properties in the country.[89] Mr. Justice Abdur Rahim was also of the opinion that an exhaustive survey was necessary[90] for devising an effective machinery for administering the endowments.

The Passing of the Charitable and Religious Trusts Act, 1920

In 1920, the Charitable and Religious Trust Act,was passed. The main aim of the passing of this Act was to provide effective control over the admnistration of Charitable and Religious Trusts. The Act also passed with an idea to provide safeguards irrespective of such trusts and to enable the trustees thereof to obtain the directions of a court on certain matters. The Act was also passed to make special provision for the payment of expenditure incurred in certain suits against the trustees of such trusts. The Act under discussion, applies only to cases where the entire benefit is allotted to public purposes. The provisions of this Act shall not be applicable in the cases where the purpose of the trust is partly private.

The Act does not provide any administrative machinery to exercise supervision on the administration of trustees. It was, however, opened to any person interested in the trust to apply to the court of the District Judge to direct the trustee to furnish the petitioner through the court, with particulars as to subject matter of the trust and the income belonging thereto and to get the accounts of the trust and of the income thereto. The interested party can examine the accounts of the trust.

Mussalman Waqf Act, 1923

The legislative steps taken by the government were not sufficient to remove the defects. Excepting the Mussalman Waqf Act, 1913, and 1920, all above statutes were of general nature. These Acts were not exclusively meant for waqf. Both trusts and waqfs of certain categories were governed by these Acts. In 1923, Government passed the Mussalman Waqf Act, XLII of 1923. The main aim of the Act was to make provision for the better management of waqf property and for ensuring the keeping and publication of proper accounts. Under section 3 of the Act a mutawalli was required to submit to the court of District Judge or other Civil Courts, a statement containing the following particulars :—

(i) description of waqf property,
(ii) gross annual income;
(iii) gross income accounted during the previous year;
(iv) amount payable as revenue, taxes, cesses and rents;
(v) estimate of annual expenditure;
(vi) amount set apart as mutawalli remuneration and allowances to other persons, (i) religious purpose, (ii) charitable purposes; and (iii) any other purpose.

According to section 4 of the Act the above statement was required to be furnished to the court. Any person who is interested in the waqf can ask for the supply of more particulars.

Under section 5 of the above Act a mutawalli was under the duty to submit before the court annually duly audited statements of account. Section 10 of the Act provided that a penalty up to rupees five hundred could be levied for furnishing false or untrue and misleading account or particulars.

Under the Mussalman Waqf Act, 1923, there is no provision for the investigation or determination of the nature and extent of waqf property. There is no uniform case law on this point. Before the Bombay Amendment Act, 1935, it was held that in proceedings under section 10 (the penal section) a magistrate can examine whether the property in question is waqf or not.[91] In Mahomed Husain's case, however, it was said that an inquiry under section 6 (i) is confined to cases where the existence of the waqf is admitted but where the existence of the waqf itself is disputed, the District Court has no power to inquire into its existence.[92]

Under the Mussalman Waqf Act of 1923 the District Judge is the proper authority to impose the penalty provided by section 10 regarding certain duties enjoined by the Act.[93]

It is clear from the above discussion that the aforesaid Act mainly provided relief to civil courts in all matters from the inspection of accounts, auditing and the imposition of penalty. The courts were already overburdened with the work and, therefore, it was not possible for them to effectively implement the provisions of the Act. These Acts failed to introduce any administrative machinery for the proper and effective control of waqfs. There was no administrative machinery to exercise proper supervision over the administration of waqfs. These Acts could not improve the functioning of the waqfs in India.

The courts were not having the jurisdiction to direct a mutawalli to file a statement of his accounts.[91] This defect of the Act was removed in Bombay by the Bombay Act XVIII of 1935. This Act added a new part III after section 6 which provided—Powers of the courts to call for particulars and statement of accounts from the mutawallis. There was, however, no legislation in the remaining part of the country. There was a provision for imposing penalty on defaulter mutawalli. But it was not effective.

The Act failed to prescribe any procedure in case the holder of the property denied its waqf character.[95] It was also not clear that in such cases the courts may be able to initiate enquiry under the Act as to the nature of the property. The various High Courts of India gave different opinions on this point.[96] Before 1945, the Bombay High Court expressed the view that a magistrate can go into the question of the nature of a property.[97] This difference of opinion was finally settled in Bombay by inserting section 6—C of the Amending Act XVIII of 1935. By this amendment courts were given power to make such enquiry. The Allahabad High Court held that in such cases courts can initiate enquiry.

The Mussalman Waqf Act, 1923, could not solve the existing problem. Even after the passing of this Act mutawallis continued to treat the waqf property as their own. There was no change in the misappropriation of waqf funds. There was, therefore, persistent demand for amending the existing waqf Act. Looking to the persistent demand, many state governments passed separate Acts so that the defects in the previous Act should be removed. The Bengal Government was the first to respond to this demand. The U.P. Government also passed U.P. Muslim Waqf Act of 1936. It may, however, be noted that even after the passing of these Acts, the defects could not be removed. The Mutawalli is still having dominant position in the waqf property. There is no control over his power.

The provisions of the Mussalman Waqf Act, 1923, and those of the Charitable and Religious Trusts Act, 1920 are overlapping. The provisions of the Charitable and Religious Trusts Act, 1920 are not applicable in the case of a waqf coming within the purview of the Bengal Waqf Act, 1934 and the U.P. Muslim Waqf Act, 1960. Before the passing of these Acts it was said that if the waqf is substantially for public purposes of a religious or charitable nature it will be covered by the Charitable and Religious Trusts Act, 1920. There were two ways opened to the aggrieved party. He was required to apply under that Act[98]. Where a waqf is partly for public purposes, than an application must be made under the Mussalman Waqf Act, 1923.[99]

The various Acts passed by the Central Government were not sufficient to control the maladministration of the waqf property. There was no control over the misappropriation of waqf money. There was persistent demand for bringing forward a more effective piece of legislation and setting up statutory Boards of public spirited persons who could exercise effective control over the activities of the mutawallis and the way they were managing the waqf institutions. Under these circumstances, various State Governments passed their own Acts[100]. The main feature of these various Acts was that statutory non-official Boards or Majlises were constituted for the purpose of effective administration of waqf in the states or territory. These Acts were not a complete code and there were many defects in these Acts. Ultimately the U.P. Muslim Waqf Act, 1936, was repealed and the U.P. Muslim Waqfs Act, 1960 was passed. The Bengal U.P. and Delhi Waqf Acts expressly repealed either the whole of the Mussalman Waqf Act, 1923 or certain provisions of it from their application to these Acts.

The Bengal Waqf Act, 1934

This piece of legislation was the first attempt to safeguard the interest of waqf property. This Act for the first time introduced the idea of formation of waqf boards and appointment of Muslim Waqf Commissioners. The Commissioners were made the President of the Board.[101] Sections 7 to 15 provide for the establishment and constitution of the Board, terms of office of members, their removal and filling up of vacancies. Sections 16 to 22 provide for the appointment of Commissioner of Waqf. There is, however, no provision for the separate waqf Boards for Shias and Sunnis. The representation of Shias was ensured by nomination[102].

Chapter III of the Act deals with powers and functions of the Waqf Board and the Waqf Commissioner.

Chapter IV provides for the enrolment and registration of waqfs. Sections 53 and 54 of the Act lay down that unless expressly empowered by the terms of the waqf deed a mutawalli cannot transfer waqf property without the prior sanction of the Commissioner.

Chapter IX of the Act deals with the finance. Section 59

of the Act provides that every waqf shall pay annually to the Board contribution not exceeding five per cent of its net income. This amount shall be known as 'Waqf fund.' This fund shall be utilised for meeting the cost of survey of waqf properties, or payment of any loan incurred under section 60, payment of salary etc. of the employees of the waqf.

Under chapter XII the State Government is authorised to make rules for carrying out the purposes of the Act regarding certain specified matters. The Board is also competent to make by-laws, with the prior approval of the State Government.

The Delhi Muslim Waqf Act, 1943

This piece of legislation came into force in the year 1943. Under the Act, two separate Majlises *i.e.* for Shia and Sunni waqf properties were constituted. Since in Delhi the Shia waqf property was very small, the Shia Majlis could neither build up any finances nor could it engage any staff. There were many defects in the Act, and therefore, with the approval of Delhi Administration, the Central Waqf Act, 1954, was introduced on Ist October, 1962 in Delhi territory. The Delhi Muslim Waqf Act, 1943 was, therefore, repealed.

The Bihar Waqf Act, 1947

The above Acts passed during pre-independence period exhibited good results. The Bihar government, therefore, decided to have its own local Act on waqf. A bill to this object was introduced in the Bihar Legislature in 1946. The Bill was then sent to a Select Committee. However, the Governor-General gave his assent in the early months of 1948. Under the Act, two Majlises for Shia and Sunni Waqfs were established. The Act suffered from many defects. The income derived by both the Majlises was not sufficient to have adequate machinery for exercising supervision over administration of waqf properties. The powers of the Majlises were not adequate. It had no power to decide whether a property was waqf or not. The Act did not give power for conducting a survey of waqf properties in the state. There was number of unknown waqf properties in the state which could not be ascertained. This had led to loss of revenue to the Majlises,

Majlises suffered from lack of fund. The Majlises were not able to make proper survey of the waqf property. There was no provision in the Act for the survey of waqf properties. In 1954. therefore, the Waqf Act, 1954, was made applicable to this state also[103].

The Bombay Public Trust Act, 1950

In Bombay no separate Act on waqf was passed. Only amendments to the Mussalman Waqf Act, 1923 were made. According to these amendments District Waqf Committees were established. The main job of these Committees was to advise and assist the court in all matters relating to the registration, superintendence, administration and control of waqfs.[104] These Committees were not independent bodies. These were directly under the control of the District Court.[105]

The Bombay Public Trust Act came into force in the year 1950. It applies to all the religious and charitable endowments in the state of Maharashtra and Gujarat with the exception of waqfs situated in the Maharashtra area of Maharashtra and Kutch area of Gujarat which are governed by the Waqf Act, 1954 and the Nanded Gurudwara which is governed by the Nanded Sikh Gurudwara Sachkhan Shri Hazur Apchalnagar Sahib Act, 1956. The provisions of the above mentioned Act are identical to the provisions of Waqf Act, 1954. However, there are certain basic differences between the two statutes. Under the Bombay Public Trusts Act, 1950, control over waqf is exercised directly by the State Government through a Charity Commissioner. The State Government also appoints Joint, Deputy and Assistant Charity Commissioners. On the other hand, under the Waqf Act, 1954, supervision over waqf property is exercised by a statutory non-official Board which functions under the control and guidance of state and central governments. The powers exercised by the Charity Commissioner under the Bombay Public Trusts Act, 1950, were challenged in *Rati Lal, Pannalal Gandhi* v *Bombay State*[106] on the ground that the powers of the Charity Commissioner were in violation of fundamental rights conferred by Article 26 of the Indian Constitution. The Bombay High Court rejected the above argument. It held that the provisions of the Act did not contravene the fundamental rights embodied in these articles and the whole Act was *intra vires* of the constitution. The matter went in appeal before the Supreme Court.[107] The Supreme Court held that certain sections and clauses of the Act were void but other provisions of it were *intra vires* of the constitution.

The court held that the provisions of section 44 of the Bombay Public Trusts Act, 1950, relating to the appointment of the Charity Commissioner as a trustee of any public trust by the court without any reservation in regard to religious institutions like temples and *maths* are unconstitutional and must be held to be void.

It was further held that the provisions of clauses (3) to (6) of section 47 of the Act to the extent that they relate to the appointment of the Charity Commissioner as a trustee of a religious trust like temple and math are unconstitutional and must be held to be void.

The Supreme Court said that the Charity Commissioner has no right to divert the trust property or funds for purposes which he considers expedient or proper, although the original objects of the founder can still be carried out. The diversion of fund may amount to unwarrantable encroachment on the freedom of religious institutions in regard to the management of their religious affairs. Therefore, clause (3) of section 55 was held as void.

Chapter III of the Bombay Act provides for some substantive laws in regard to trusts.

Chapter IV of the Act provides for the appointment of assessors to help the Charity Commissioner and his deputies in conducting enquiries. Chapter VII-A of the Bombay Act deals with regard to special provisions entrusting the management of temples, mosques and endowments created for a public, religious or charitable purpose which vests in the State Government and to District Committee of five to seven members.

The United Provinces Muslim Waqf Act, XIII, 1936

Section 85 (2) of the U.P. Muslim Waqf Act, 1960, provides that the U.P. Muslim Waqfs Act, 1936, as amended from time to time and the Husainaba Endowment Act, 1878, are hereby repealed.

Provided that this repeal shall not affect the operation of those Acts in regard to any suit or proceeding pending in any court or to an appeal or an application in revision against any order that may be passed in such suit or proceeding and subject thereto, anything done or any action taken in exercise of powers conferred by or under those Acts shall, unless otherwise expressly required by any provision of this Act, be deemed to have been done or taken in exercise of the powers conferred by or under this Act as if this Act were in force on the day on which such thing was done or action was taken.

The Dargah Khwaja Sahib Act XXIII of 1936

Khwaja Moinuddin Chisti was born in the town of Sanjar in Sistan (Iran) in twelfth century. On his father's side he was in direct line from Hazrat Ali, son-in-law of Prophet Mohammad. As he grew up, he decided to renounce the world and entered the service of a great mystic saint, Khwaja Usmani Harooni, who later invested him with the office of the Caliph and conferred upon him the sacred relic of the prophet—a staff, a rose, wooden sandals and a small carpet used for prayers. The Khwaja was further ordained to carry on the peaceful message of Islam on his mission in the year 1186.

From a very long time demand was made for the better management of this Dargah. This is one of the most famous dargah situated at Ajmer (Rajasthan). This Dargah is having very good source of income. However, there was no law controlling the affairs of dargah. In 1842 while the triangular feud between the Diwan or Sajjadanashin, the Mutawalli and the Khadims was in process, the Government of India decided to sever all connections with the dargah management. The result of this act of the government was that there occurred corruption at the mass scale. In 1867, therefore, the Government decided to appoint a Committee of five persons under the Act of 1863 to run the dargah administration. This Committee consisted of members from the three groups—members of the families of the Sajjadanashin and the Mutawalli. Two members were also from the family of the Khadims. There was one independent member also. He was the President of the Committee. The Committee failed to solve the problem. The Government was not happy with the state of affairs prevalent at that time. In 1882 looking to this state of affairs government consulted the law officers over the possibility of altering the constitution of the Committee. The legal position was that the constitution could not be changed unless the law itself was amended or the matter was brought before a Civil Court. The Government of India was not willing to interfere into the religious affairs of any community.[108]

It was however only in the year 1936 that the Dargah Khwaja Saheb Act was passed. This Act provided for a new Committee consisting of 25 members. Nine local and 16 outsiders were also made the members of this Committee. The main purpose of this constitution of the Committee was to stop the monopoly of the local members and to lessen the friction between the members.

The Dargah Khwaja Saheb Act, 1955

This Act was passed in the year 1955. Prior to the passing of this Act, there were two Acts—Dargah Khwaja Saheb Act, 1936 and the Dargah Khwaja Saheb (Emergency Provisions) Act 1950. There is a history behind the passing of the Dargah Khwaja Saheb Act, 1955. The same is discussed as follows :

Dargah Khwaja Saheb shrine is stituated in Ajmer. It is only the Muslim shrine for the administration and management of which a separate central legislation exists. Before the passing of the above Act, the khadims (attendants) and Sajjadanashin of the Dargah were managing the affairs of the Dargah. From the time of Mughals, Khadims were having the right to appropriate *nazar* presented to them. The Dargah was not properly administered by Khadims. They were misappropriating the funds. In 1949, the Government of India appointed a committee headed by Justice Ghulam Hasan. The other members of the Committee were Mohammad Yamin Khan of Meerut and Nawab Mahmud Yar Jung of Hyderabad. The Committee was required to enquire into and report into the administration of Dargah endowments. The Committee was also directed to examine and report regarding the provisions of the Dargah Khwaja Saheb Act of 1936. The Committee said as soon as a pilgrim gets down at the railway station, Ajmer, he is met by a horde of khadims. To avoid a conflict among the khadims the man is put to sale and whoever makes the highest bid becomes his *vakil*. The sale proceeds are distributed among the khadims. The khadim who becomes his vakil is anxious to make as much profit as he can out of the transaction and tries to extort, by all means fair or foul, the last pie out of the victim. On the recommendations of this committee Dargah Khwaja Saheb (Emergency Provisions Act XVIII of 1950 was passed. Subsequently the Dargah Khwaja Saheb Act, 1955 was passed by the Indian Parliament. The Act repealed all the previous related Acts *i.e.* Dargah Khwaja Saheb Act, 1936, and the Dargah Khwaja Saheb (Emergency Provisions) Act, 1950. It was provided in the Act that a Committee should be appointed to administer the Dargah endowments and to manage the shrine.[111] The Nazim or Secretary of the Committee was alone authorised to receive offerings on behalf of the Committee.[112] A provision was made for regulating the presence of Khadims in the Dargah.[113]

The khadims of the Dargah were not satisfied with the passing of this Act. In *Syed Hussain Ali* v *Dargah Committee*[114] Khadims alleged that the Act was unconstitutional. The Rajasthan High Court accepted this contention of the khadims. It struck down certain sections of the Act as *ultra vires* the constitution. The matter went in appeal.[115] The Supreme Court set aside the judgment of the Rajasthan High Court, and gave its verdict in favour of the Dargah Committee regarding the responsibility of the Dargah, management and appropriation of *nazar*. The Supreme Court held that when offerings are made and earmarked generally for the Dargah they belong to the Dargah and such offerings can be received only by the Nazim or his agent and by nobody else.

The Dargah Khwaja Saheb Act 1955, was not having any penal provision for the khadims who were violating the above Act. The Dargah Khwaja Saheb Amendment Act, 1964, added a clause to section 14 making soliciting or receiving of any *nazars* in contravention of the provisions of sub-section (1) punishable with fine extending to one thousand rupees.

In spite of the above legislations, khadims are continuing to collect money and at times extort all the offerings. Again, Dargah Committee could not provide alternative accommodation to the pilgrims, so that the khadims may not be able to extort money. It is here suggested that the Dargah Committee should start collecting funds for the construction of *sarai* for pilgrims.

The shrine has acquired national importance. Pilgrims all over the country are visiting the shrine. In addition to India, pilgrims from other countries are also visiting the shrine. It is, therefore, proposed that the shrine should be made a centre of religious and ethical learning. The Dargah Committee can also start some business out of the shrine. This will definitely increase the income of the shrine. The Committee should also try to provide educational facilities to the children of khadims. This process will slowly wean them away from the practice of soliciting offerings and to establish them properly in life. In this connection, it may be noted here that the Central and State Governments can also provide loan to the shrine for the above purpose.

The Hyderabad Endowment Regulation, 1939

Till the passing of the Central Act in 1954 the position was quite different in the states ruled by the native rulers. These rulers continued to exercise satisfactory superintendence impartially over Hindu as well as Muslim religious and charitable endowments. The state of Hyderabad was one of them. The Hyderabad Endowment Regulation was passed in the year 1939. The preamble of this Regulation laid down that.

> Whereas the management and security of endowed property is included in the duties of government, therefore it is necessary that some principle should be adopted, so that these duties may be discharged conveniently and efficiently and the intention of the person endowing the property that humanity should be benefited through the endowed property should be realised.

After the passing of the Waqf Act, 1954, the above Act has ceased to carry any force.

Under this regulation, all religious and charitable endowments, without denominational distinction came under state superintendence. The regulation declared that 'the management and security of all endowed property is included in the duties of government.' It required that all religious and charitable endowments be registered in the official book of endowments. Under section 2 of the regulation a superintendent

(Muntazim) was to be appointed by the government for the management of the endowments. The State Director of Endowments was appointed in that behalf by the State Department of Endowments. The Collectors and tahsildars, within their respective charges were local directors of endowments. The State Director of Endowments was responsible to the state government for the efficient management of the department. It was the duty of all the directors of endowments to safeguard, through the courts and otherwise all endowed property and to ensure that the same were being applied to proposes uses according to the original trusts.

REFERENCES

1. See proceedings of the Home Department (Public), January 1871, February 1913, Nos 132-151, p. 139.
2. See Resolution dated 28th October, 1871 ; see also Bill drafted the Orissa Native Commission and Madras Hiudu Religious Institutions Bill, 1878 ; Despatch No 630-T, dated 20/30 September, 1889 from the Government of India, July 1914, Nos 265-85, Part A, p. 48 (Simla Report).
3. See proceedings of the Home Department (Judicial) Apart 1909. No. 36-51, Part B.
4. See proceedings of the Home Department (Public), March 1903, No. 121, Part A.
5. *Ibid*, p. No 116 ; see also the representation of Anjuman-i-Himayat-i-Islam, No 116.
6. *Ibid*, (Judicial), March 1910, No 230, Part A.
7. See also newspaper *Watan*, Lahore, 22 August, 1902, p. 3. Cal 1 ; The Curzon Gazette, Delhi, September 1902, p. 2, Col 1 ; Ahsan-ul-Akbar, Calcutta, 24 October 1902, p. 7.
8. Proceedings of thhe Legislative Department, April 1902, Nos. 58 Part B.
9. Proceedings of the Home Department (Public), Nos 193-96 pp. 819-20.
10. Proceedings of the Home Department (Judicial) August, 1908, No 189, Part B, see also *ibid*, (Judicial) January 1913, No 62 Part B ; (Judicial) April 1913, Nos 128-29, Part B.
11. *Ibid*, October 1913, Nos 171-172, Part A.
12. See Ameer Ali, *Mohammadan Law*, Vol I, (4th ed), Calcutta (1912), p 441.

13. See *Jeewan Doss* v *Khuab Shleer-ood-Deen*, (1840) 128 MA 390 at p. 422.
14. Proceedings of the Home Department (Public), 23 September 1859, Nos 45-46, proceedings of the Home Department (Legislative) 20 September, 1845, No. 884; S. Khalid Rashid, *Waqf Administration* in India, p. 13.
15. Proceedings of the Home Department (Judicial), February 1913, No 151, p. 139.
16 See *Ramalinge* v *Perianayagum*, 1874 IA 209 ; *Vidya Varuthi* v *Baluswami*, (1921) 48 IA 302.
17. Khan Bahadur Moulvi Mohammad Yusoof, *Review of the Mohammadan Law af the Waqf*, Calcutta, (1906) p 113.
18. See Report of the Hindu Religious Endowments Commissioner (1961) Government of India, Ministry of Law.
19. See *Syed Diljan Ali* v *Bibi Akhtari* 4 Pat 741, *AIR* 1925 Pat 88 IC 1035, 1925 PISC 194, 7 PIT 4.
20. S Cal 32.
21. *Ganesh Singh* v *Ram Gopal*, 5 Beng LR App 55 ; *Dhurrum Singh* v *Kissan Singh* 7 Cal 767 ; *Fakhruddin* v *Ackeni 2* Mad 197 ; *Sheor Kunwari* v *Ram Parkash* 18 All 227 ; *Sivayya* v *Reddi* 22 Mad 223.
22. *Ashraf Ali* v *Muhammad Nuruiiama* 49 IC 355.
23. *Moulvi Muhammad Fahim-ul-Huq* v *Jagat Ballaw Ghosh*, 74 IC 403.
24. *Venkataranga Churlu* v *Krishnama Charlu*, 37 Mad 184, 20 IC 5 24 MIJ 1697.
25. *Hanoraj Laddashet* v *Anant Padmanabh Bhat*, 4 IC 514, 42 Bom.
26. *Kalyana Venkatamana Ayyangar* v *Kasturiranga Ayyangar*, 40 212, 31 MIJ 777.
27. *Fakurdin Sahib* v *Ackeni Sahib*, 2 Mad 197.
28. (*Prince*) *Gholam Hossain Shah* v *Altaf Hossain*, 1934 Cal 328, 58 CIJ 356, 150 IC 124 ; *Gholam Hussain Shah* v *Syed Muslim Hossain*, *AIR* 1934 Cal 348, 150 IC 124.
29. *Shah Najibuddin Ahmed* v *Amir Hossain Khan*, *AIR* 1934 Pat 448.
30. (1894) 22 Cal 619.
31. *Kadir Murthza Hussain* v *Mohammad Murthuza Hussain*, *AIR* 1943 Mad 234, (1942) 2 MIJ 672.
32. Inserted by C.P. Code (Amendment) Act 66 of 1956, section 9.
33. or by any corresponding law in force in the territories which, immediately before the 1st November, 1956, were comprised in Part B States.
34. A. U.P. amendment : In sub-section (1) after clause (b) the following clause was inserted by UP Act 24 of 1954— "(bb) for delivery of possession of any trust property against a person who has ceased to be a trustee or has been removed."

    See clause (cc) inserted by the later amendment of S. 92 (1) by Central Act, 66 of 1956.

Bangladesh and Pakistan—For 'State Government' read 'Provincial Government' and omit the words inside brackets marked 3, and 5.

Changes : The words 'public purposes of a charitable or religious nature' have been substituted for the words 'public, charitable or religious purposes' ; the words 'whether contentions or not' have been inserted and clauses (a) (b) and sub-section (2) have been added by the Code of 1908.

34. *Gobind Channra* v *Abdul Majid*, *AIR* 1944 Cal 163, 48 CWN 225, 78 CIJ 48, (1944) ILR Cal 339, 216 IC 143.
35. 36 Bom LR 526
36. *Supra* note 36.
37. *Amjadulla Siddiqui* v *Nizamuddin Baig*, *AIR* 1982 AP 342.
38. *Syed Mazher Hussain* v *Haji Ali Mohammad Jalaluddin*, *AIR* 1934 Bom. 257, 152 IC 50, 36 Bom AR 526 ; see also 24 Cal 418, 425 ; 33 Cal 789, 804 ; 32 Mad 141—Hindu cases.
39. See *Mohammad Kazim* v *Abi Sagir*, *AIR* 1932 Pat 33 : 11 Pat 288 ; 136 IC, 417.
40. *Muhammad Aziz-uddin* v *The Legal Remembrancer*, 15 All 321.
41. *Mahommad Ahmad Shah Mubarak Shah* v *Pir Atta Khan*, *AIR* 1934 Pesh 57, 152 IC 523.
42. *Pir Baksh* v *Mohammad Ibrahim AIR* 1932 Lah 493 (2), 138 IC 69 33 PLR 468.
43. *Mt. Niamatul Nissa* v *Hafizul Rahman*, *AIR* 1933 Oudh 261, 8 Luck 422, 10 OWN 393, 144 IC 473.
44. *Supra* note 21.
45. *Gulzarilal* v *Collector of Estate*, 58 IA 460, 53 All 910.
46. *Asha Bibi* v *Nabbisa Sahib*, *AIR* 1957 Mad 583.
47. *Fakhrunnessa* v *District Judge of 24 Parganas*, 47 Cal 592, 56 IC 479.
48. *Supra* note 38.
49. *Ibid.*
50. *Ibid.*
51. *Hashim Haroon* v *Gounsalishan*, *AIR* 1942 Sindh 137. *ILR* 1942 Kan 179.
52. *Elahi Baksh* v *Mahommed Ghaus*, *AIR* 1933 Lāh 27, 141 IC 169.
53. *Mohammad Sadiq Ali Khan* v *Kazim Ali Khan*, *AIR* 1934 Oudh 118]11 OWN 323, 150 IC 193.
54. *Muslim Orphanage* v *Khatood Bai*, *AIR* 1958 Mys 28 ; See also *Jawahar* v *Akbar Hussain*, 7 *All* 178 (FB) ; *Kazi Hasan* v *Sagum.*
55. *AIR* 1954 Ori 15.

56. *Muhammad Kazim* v *Abi Saghir*, *AIR* 1932 Pat 33, 11 Patna 288, 136 NV 417.
57. *AIR* 1982 P & H 137.
58. *Syed Dilijan* v *Bibi Akhtari Begum*, *AIR* 1925 Pat 543, ILR 4 Pat 741, 88 IC 1035.
59. *Jaygunnessa Bibi* v *Mujib Ullah Mahomed Pramanik*, 81 IC 850.
60. *AIR* 1936 Cal 262.
61. *Fazala* v *Zainul Abdin*, *AIR* 1932 Lah 359, ILR 13 Lah 162, 131 IC 632, 32 PIR 400.
62. *Syed Shah Mahomed Kazim* v *Syed Abi Saghir*, *AIR* 1932 Pat 33. 11 288 136 IC 417.
63. *Supra* note 48.
64. *Supra* note 49.
65. *Mahomed Ismail Ariff* v *Ahmad Moola Dawood*, ILR 43 Cal 1085, 48 IF 127, 55 IC 00.
66. *AIR* 1936 Lah 361.
67. *Advocate General* v *Yusuf Ali*, *AIR* 1921 Bom 336, 24 Bom LR 1060, 84 IC 759.
68. *Jamal-uddin* v *Mujtaba Husain*, 25 All 631, 635.
69. *AIR* 1928 PC 16, 55 IA 96, ILR 55 Cal 519, 101 IC 361, 32 CWN 482, 48 CLJ 55, 56 ALJ 464. 30 Bom LR 744, 54 MIJ 609 ; *Ghafoor Ali* v *Mohiuddin* 33 Bom LR 1575, 135 IC 806, AIR 1932 Bom 65.
70. *Asghar Ali* v *Delroos Banoo* (1877) 3 Cal 324.
71. *Muhammad Shafiq* v *Muhammad* (1929) 51 All 20, 111 IC 93, AIR 1928 All 660.
72. 33 Bom 509.
73. *Sir Dinsha Manekji* v *Sir Jamsetji Jiji Bhai*, 33 Bom 509, 529-30, 2 IC 701.
74. *Manijan* v *Khadem Husain*, 32 Cal 273.
75. *Jawahar* v *Akbar Husain*, 7 All 178.
76. *Abdur Rahim* v *Mahomed Barkat Ali*, *AIR* 1928 PC 16. 55 IA 96. 55 Cal 519, 108 IC 361.
77. *Mohabur Rahman* v *Haji Abdur Rahman*, *AIR* 1921 Cal 210, 48 Cal 53.
78. *Abdul Karim* v *Abdus Subhan*, 39 Cal 146, 13 IC 243.
79. *Supra* note 21.
80. *Abdul Hulim Abed* v *Abir Jan*, *AIR* 1928 Cal 368, ILR 55 Cal 1284, 110 IC 416, 32 CWN 835, 22 CIJ 577.
81. *Bibi Zohra* v *Bibi Habibunnissa*, *AIR* 1940 Pat 9.
82. *Sardar Ali Shah* v *Fateh Mahammad*, *AIR* 1935 Lah 657.
83. *Fateh Mohammad* v *Sardar Ali Shah*, *AIR* 1936 Lah 48.
84. *Abdul Rahim Khan* v *Fakir Mohammad Shah*, IR 1946 Nag 401 ; *Mahomed Hussain* v *Collector of Broach*. *AIR* 1945 Bom 157, 46 BLR 925, 219 IC 449, ILR (1945) Bom 257.
85. Substituted for 'Provincial Government, (by IAO 1950).
86. *Supra* note 2, (Legislative), July 1914, Nos 265-285 Part A, p 18.

87. *Ibid*, p. 23.
88. *Supra* note 2, (Judicial), July 1914, Nos 265-85, Part A, p. 2.
89. See proceedings of the Home Department, (Judicial), September 1913, No 13, Deposit.
90. See his foreword to Ganapathi Iyer's *Hindu and Mohammedan Endowments*, Madras, (1918) pp. 23.
91. In *re Sayenda Taher Saifuddin*, *AIR* 1934 Bom 169, (1934) 38 Bom 302, 36 Bom LR 311, 154 IC 940.
92. *Mahommed Husain* v *The Collector af Broach*, *AIR* 1945 Bom 157, (1945) Bom 257, 46 Bom LR 925, 219 IC 449.
93. *Kale Khan* v *Karim Rahman*. *AIR* 1935 Bom 207, 37 Bom LR 207, 156 IC 203.
94. See *Nasrullah Khan* v *Majid Ali*, (1930) 54 All 167 ; see also in *re* Waqf Paramathi Nemakkal Taluk, *AIR* 1946 Mad 146.
95. *Syed Ali Mohammed* v *Collector of Bhagalpur*, *AIR* 1927 Pat 189.
96. *Supra* note 96 ; see also *Mohammad Baqar* v *Mohammad Qasim*, *AIR* 1923 Oudh 210, 9 OWN 538 ; *Mohammad Hussain* v *The Collector of Broach AIR* 1945 Bom 157, 219 IC 449 ; *Syed Kamail Saheb* v *Eihikasna Sarguru*, *AIR* 1941 Mad 897 ; *supra* note 97.
97. *Supra* note 93.
98. *Syed Ali* v *Bibi Akhtari*, *AIR* 1931 Pat 354, (1931) P0 Pat 506, 134 IC 417. He could also file a suit under section 92, Code of Civil Procedure, see *Naihuddin Ahmad* v *Amir Hassan*, *AIR* 1434 Pat 443, (1934) 153 IC 556.
99. See *Shabbir Husain* v *Ashiq Husain*, *AIR* 1929 Oudh 225, (1929) 4 Luck 429, 117 IC 7391 *Ali Bakhtiyar* v *Khandkar Altaf Hussain*, *AIR* 1939 Cal 581, (1933) 60 Cal 790, 145 IC 638 ; *Emda Ali Chaudhari* v *Tabulla* AIR 1937 Cal 313, *Yusufally* v *Yusufally* *AIR* 1953 Bom 92, (1952) 54 Bom LR 702.
100. The State of Bengal was the first in passing the Bengal Waqf Act of 1934. This was followed by tne United Provinces Muslim Waqf Act XIII of 1936, the U.P. Muslim Waqf Act, 1936, the Delhi Muslim Waqf Act, 1943, the Mussalman Waqf (Bombay) Amendments to the Mussalman Waqf Act, 1923 Act, 1935.
101. See Section 8 (2).
102. Section 8 (d).
103. See notification dated 12th April, 1973.
104. Section 6L of the Amending Act, 1935.
105. Section 6M and 6-0.
106, *AIR* 1953 Bom 241.
107. *AIR* 1954 *SC* 388.
108. See the proceedings of the Home Department (Judicial) July 1914, Nos. 265-285, Part A, pp. 265-266.

8

A Socio-Legal Study of Waqf Legislation in India During Post-Independence Era (Waqf Act, 1954)

At the time of the independence of India, the administration of these important institutions was far from satisfactory. Except in few states the Mussalman Waqf Act, 1923, was prevalent throughout the country. Again after partition many important officials of the waqf left India. The worst affected state was Punjab. Most of the waqf property was unlawfully acquired by non-Muslims as there was no one to look after the property. However, there were few Indian Muslims who continued their efforts for a better waqf legislation. The persons who played active role in the making of the Act were Mr S.M. Ahmed Kazmi, President of the Anjuman Himayat-e-Islam, Punjab (a non-political organisation); Maulana Hafizur Rahman (President of the Jamait-ul-Ulema-i-Hind); Maulana Abul Kalam Azad (Union Minister of Education), two non-political organisations *i.e.* Idar-e-Islami and the Jamait-ul-Ulema-i-Hind played important role for the codification of Waqf Act, 1954. Mr Kazmi moved the private bill in 1952 which ultimately became the Waqf Act in 1954.[1]

The Waqf Act, 1954 was the first serious attempt made by the government for the administrative and statutory control of waqfs in India. The Act lays down a comprehensive administrative structure to ensure proper administration of waqfs in the country. The Act made a provision for the constitution of a Waqf Board. This Board has been given considerable power to control the administration of waqfs. Under the Act mutawallis have been made responsible for their acts. In case of default they can be penalised. Under the Act, the State Governments are required to Act as supervisor. The Central Government has been authorised to lay down the policies to be adopted by the Board.

On 13th March, 1953 the Bill presented by Mr Kazmi was referred to a Select Committee.[2] The Committee was of the opinion that there should be nominated Board instead of an elected Board. The Committee felt this will help the state government to give proper representation to various interests. In this way the State Government will be able to nominate suitable persons to the Board.[3]

The Bill contained a clause for the constitution of a Central Board. This idea of having a Central Board to look after the functioning of the State Waqf Board was not approved by the Committee. After making necessary changes the bill was passed. This Act is prevalent throughout the country except the states of Bengal, Uttar Pradesh and certain parts of Maharashtra and Gujarat. These states are having their own Acts.

The Public Waqfs (Extension of Limitation) Act, 1959

After the partition of the country much of the waqf property was unlawfully acquired either by the custodian or by displaced persons. Subsequently, some of the places of worship were given back to the Waqf Boards. However, there were still waqf properties occupied by unauthorised persons. Under these circumstances it was felt necessary that legal action should be taken for the restoration of such property. With a view to overcoming this difficulty Public Waqfs (Extension of Limitation) Act, 1959 was passed. This Act extended the period of limitation. Section 3 of the Extension Act says "where a person entitled to institute a suit of the description referred to in Article 142 or Article 144 of the First Schedule to the Indian Limitation Act, 1980, for possession of any immovable property forming part of a public waqf, or any interest therein has been dispossessed, or has discontinued the possession, at any time after the 14th day of August, 1947 and before the 7th day of May 1954, or as the case may be, possession of the defendant in such a suit has become adverse to such person at any time during the said period, then notwithstanding anything contained in the said Act, the period of limitation in respect of such a suit shall extend upto the 15th day of August, 1967".

The intention of the government was to give sufficient time for the filing of the suit so that the waqf property may be restored. Keeping this fact into consideration the above period was extended several times.

On reading Section 3 of the Extension Act, it becomes clear that the extension of time for filing suits is available only where dispossession is after 14th August, 1947 and before 7th May, 1954. If dispossession or commencing of the defendant's adverse possession is anterior to or subsequent to the said period, the benefit of the Extension Act is not available. In *A.P. Waqf Board, Hyderabad* v *Bowlat Bibi*[4] the defendant came into possession of the land on 1st June, 1954, and that was the date on which her adverse possession commenced. This was also the date on which the mosque was dispossessed. It was said that since the said date was beyond the period contemplated by Section 3 of the Extension Act, the benefit of the extended period of limitation was not available to the plaintiff.

It is thus clear that after the fall of Mughals no proper attention was paid to the waqf property. In fact during British period no attention was paid for the better administration of waqf mutawallis, therefore, got good opportunity to misappropriate waqf fund. Mutawallis were the main architect of this decay.

During British rule, Regulation XIX of 1810 and Regulation VI of 1817 were passed in Bengal and Madras respectively, The administration of the property was taken by the Englishmen directly. Later on, they realised that this could give adverse effect and, therefore, adopted the policy of non-interference. In fact both these attitude of the government were not desired. The government should have followed a middle policy. Even after the passing of the Act of 1923 Britishers were hesitant in interfering into the religious affair of Muslims.

The Waqf Act, 1954

Till 1913, there was no statutory control of waqfs in India. In the year 1913, Mussalman Waqf Validating Act was passed for the proper administration of waqfs. From 1913 to 1954 few legislative steps were taken for the administration of waqfs. However, these steps were not sufficient for the proper administration of waqfs. In the year 1954, Waqf Act was passed. This is the main central law on the subject which now applies in various states (excluding Jammu and Kashmir, Uttar Pradesh, Bihar and West Bengal). These states are having their own Acts and also in several union territories. The rules relating to management of waqfs, alongwith their judicial interpretation are to be applied subject to the statutory waqf administration that may in a particular place be applicable for the time being. The passing of the Waqf Act, 1954, was a landmark in the history of waqf administration. However, there were defects in this Act. To remove these defects the Waqf Act, 1954 was further amended by the Waqf Act, 1964. This Act was further amended by wqfs (Amendment) Act, 1984. The main provisions of Waqf Act, 1954 are as under :—

> Section 2 says that this Act shall apply to all waqfs whether created before or after the commencement of this Act. Except the J & K Act, all other Waqf Acts of various states lays down identical provisions. The J & K Act excludes from its purview Shia waqfs. (4A)

Waqf-al-aulad

Where the waqf was created for family purposes (waqf-al-auled) Waqf Act, 1954 and J & K Act will be applicable to the extent the property is dedicated to religious or charitable purposes.[5] According to Bengal Act at least 75 per cent or more of the total income must be reserved for private purposes or the waqf was created solely for the benefit or waqf and/or his family.[6] However, the Waqf Commissioner has been authorised to make enquiries into the affairs of such a waqf. If the Waqf Commissioner comes to the conclusion that the waqf was grossly mismanaged, he may recommend the state government to make the provisions of the Act applicable to such waqfs also for a specified period. This is applicable to waqfs other than waqf-al-aulad. Under the Bombay Act, such waqfs are completely exempt. The percentage of the income reserved for private and public waqfs carries no force.[7]

Section 3 of the Waqf Act, 1954, deals with regard to the definition of waqf. In comparison to the other local Acts the definition given under the Central Act is most exhaustive. Section 3 of the Waqf Act, 1954 says that a waqf means the permanent dedication by a person professing Islam or any other person. The words "or any other person" have been substituted by Waqf Amendment Act, 1984 of any movable or immovable property for any purpose recognised by Muslim law as pious, religious, or charitable and includes—

(i) a waqf by user ;
(ii) grants (including mashrut-ul-khidmat) for any purpose recognised by the Muslim law as pious, religious or charitable ; and
(iii) a waqf-al-aulad to the extent to which the property is dedicated for any purpose recognised by Muslim law as pious, religious or charitable.

It is not necessary for the waqf to dedicate property for each and every object of waqf. The waqf will be valid if the waqif has only prepared waqfnama providing dedication of property for pious, religious and charitable purposes and for purposes of the maintenance of the members of the family.[8] The use of the words 'person professing Islam' is deliberate. It appears this term has been used to exclude all charitable and pious endowments of other communities from the purview of the Act.

Section 3 and 66-C of the aforesaid Act are related to each

other. It is, therefore, necessary that Section 66-C of the Act be also discussed here. Section 3 of the Waqf Act, 1954, defines the word 'waqf' in such a way as to create an impression that a dedication by a non-Muslim could in no circumstance be a waqf.[9] Therefore, in 1964, the Waqf Act, 1954 was amended and a new Section entitled 66-C was introduced in the Act. The aim of this Section is to recognise the validity of waqfs made by non-Muslims. The permissible purposes of waqf as mentioned in the new Section 66-C were, however, not identical with those as laid down in Section 3, and that made all the difference.

This section says that person not professing Islam can dedicate his movable or immovable property and can create a waqf for the following purposes—

(a) a mosque, idgah, imambara, dargah, khanqah or a maqbara ;

(b) a Muslim graveyard ;

(c) a choultry or a musafirkhana.

The plain reading of the two sections show that there is similarity between them. But in fact Indian courts have failed to accord wide interpretation to these sections. In *Madras Waqf Board* v *Kazi Mohideen Sheriff*[10] dedication was made by non-Muslim in respect of 'kazi service.'

The Madras High Court refused to accept the waqf as valid. The court held that the purpose of the waqf was not covered by Section 66-C, though covered by Section 3. The court further held that even if the 'kazi service' intended by the non-Muslim settler was attached to a particular mosque it could not be a waqf under Section 66-C; though it would have bean a waqf under Section 3 if the settler were a Muslim. The court also said that the present dedication could be a waqf under Section 66-C if it were for the mosques generally (without stating 'kazi service' as its specific purpose).[11]

It is submitted that in the above case the Madras High Court took a very narrow view. The term 'mosque' be interpreted in a very wide way and it should include all those services to the community for which a mosque, can be lawfully used. It will be wrong to confine the scope of this term within the building and fixtures of the mosques.

The opinion of the Madras High Court in the above case was not followed by Andhra Pradesh High Court in *A.P. Waqf Board* v *Bowla Bibi*[11]. In this case the court said that it is a well settled principle of interpretation of statutes that no words in a statute should be construed as superfluous and unnecessary. The repeating of the second requirement while omitting the first requirement thus clearly indicates that the first requirement in the main limb of the definition does not apply in the case of such grants. It must also to be remembered that the definition clause having defined waqf proceeds to include certain other grants as well within the definition of waqf by widening the definition for the purpose of the Act.

In *A.P. Waqf Board* v *Somaiah*[11b] Justice Chennakesav Reddi observed that Section 66-C only centemplates a non-Muslim donating certain properties to an existing waqf, but he cannot create a waqf as such.

The above observation of Mr. Justice Reddi was not followed by the same High Court in *A.P. Waqf Board, Hyderabad* v *Bowla Bibi*[11c]. In this case the High Court said that the provisions of Section 3 and 66-C are not identical. The court said that the main limb of definition lays down to ingredients viz that the dedication should be by a person professing Islam and secondly that the dedication must be for any purpose recognised by Muslim law as pious, religious and charitable. Clause (ii) of Section 3 in the second half of the definition include grants (including mashrut-ul-khidmat) for and purpose recognised by Muslim law as pious, religious or charitable. The land would be a grant of the nature contemplated by Clause (i) even if it is assumed that the grant was in favour of the predecessor in interest of the vendor of the defendant. Now, in the case of such grants, it is not necessary that it should have been made by person professing Islam. The grant should only be made for religious, charitable or pious purpose.

The intention of the legislature for inserting Section 66-C was different. Section 66-C says that where any movable or immovable property has been given or donated by a person not professing Islam for the support of a waqf being (i) a mosque, idgah, imambara, dargah, khanqah or a moqbara; (ii) a Muslim graveyard; and (iii) a choultry or musafirkhana, then such property should be deemed to be comprised in the waqf and be dealt within same manner as the waqf in which it is so comprised. Another aspect of Section 66-C is that this Section deals with regard to properties being donated or given for the support of specified institutions, the definition of waqf is general and includes all purposes recognised by Muslim law as pious, religious or charitable.

The court said that on a proper construction of the definition it is not necessary in the case of grants contemplated by Clause (ii) of Section 3 in the definition that they should be proved to have been dedicated by a person professing Islam.

Where the dedication by a Hindu ruler has been made to the fakirs visiting the mosque and not to the mosque, the dedication neither constitutes a waqf within meaning of Section 33 (i) nor a deemed waqf within meaning of Section 66-C. Consequently, the provisions of the Waqf Act including Section 36-A would not apply to the dedicated property[11d].

The other local Acts are not having such a provision. The Bombay and Bengal Acts have retained the words 'person professing Islam' while defining waqf. Under the U.P. and Kashmir the dedicator need not be a Muslim. The law is also not clear on the point if rival claims arise about the waqf and non-waqf character in case of a dedication made in favour of a public charitable institution where the dedicator has died and is, therefore, unable to clarify his intent.

Under the U.P. Act the definition of the word 'waqf' has been considerably curtailed by the definition of the term 'beneficiary'. This word is confined only for the benefit of the Muslim community.

Section 3 deals with various definitions. Section 3 (i) of the Waqf Act, 1954 deals with the waqf by user. The Karnatak High Court has interpreted the term 'waqf by user' in the following manner[12] —

In order to hold that the property had become waqf by

user by applying the principle of lost grant, there must be satisfactory evidence to show that the grant itself was lost in antiquity and the evidence about it was not available and further that the property is being used as waqf property for a long time without interference. It is, therefore, clear that the mere existence of two or three graves on or near the suit land or the circumstances that urs was being carried on there for some time, even if true, is not sufficient to hold that it is waqf property without proof of dedication of the same for religious purpose.

SURVEY OF WAQFS

For a long time, it has been argued that complete survey of waqf property should be made. It is an essential pre-requisite for ensuring proper administration of waqfs and for building up the finances of the Waqf Board. The British government was not in favour of such survey. The British government felt that the survey would in many cases be keenly resented, and the object of which would almost certainly be misunderstood[13]. The Mussalman Waqf Act, 1923 as well as the local Acts of Delhi and Bihar also contained no provision regarding survey of waqfs. However, there was a demand for the making of the survey of waqf properties[14]. In his foreword Sir Abdur Rahim made a strong plea for an all India survey of religious and charitable endowments.

It was only in the year 1934 that a provision to this effect was made in the Bengal Waqf Act, 1934. Subsequently, a similar provision was made in the United Provinces Muslim Waqfs Act, 1936[15].

In India, there are about one lakh public waqfs, valued at more than a hundred crore of rupees. The vast resources of waqfs can be a strong instrument not for the preservation of religious charitable and philanthropic institutions but also for the educational and economic uplift of the Indian Muslims. It is a sad state of affairs that a large number of waqfs have succumbed to the processs of decadence resulting from neglect, misuse and malversation. It is again astonishing to note that the exact number of waqfs are still not known. There is a statutory provision that survey of waqfs shall be made. But till now no concrete attempt could be taken to know the exact number of waqfs.

Section 4 of the Waqf Act, 1954, says that a survey of the waqfs in a state will be carried out, if not already done, by the Commissioner of Waqfs appointed by the state government for the purpose. The commissioner may prepare a separate report of Sunni and Shia waqfs. The State Government shall forward the same report to the Waqf Board for its examination and publication. The Waqf Board after examining the report may publish the same in the state gazette. The Waqf Board may also give other particulars of the waqf property. Section 6 (1) of the Waqf Act, 1954, says that if a question arises whether a particular property is waqf or not or whether the waqf is Shia or not, any interested person may file a suit in a civil court of competent jurisdiction for the decision in the matter. The decision of the court shall be final.

The Waqf Act, 1954, U.P. Waqf Act and J & K Waqf Acts provides exhaustive provisions regarding the survey of waqf properties[16]. However, the Bengal Act is not so exhaustive. This Act provide only for the registration of the waqfs. This Act provides for the enrolment of waqfs on the application made by the Mutawalli or any person interested therein. According to the Bengal Act this is the duty of the Waqf Commissioner to make necessary inquiries before enrolling the waqf[17].

The Bombay Act does not contain any provision regarding the survey of waqfs.

Under Section 4 of the Waqf Act, 1954, Commissioner of Waqfs power is nothing more than to list out waqfs. Under Section 4, he cannot decide title dispute relating to any waqf property since that will amount to an unauthorised assumption of judicial power.[18]

It has been hold that the power of Waqf Commissioner to make survey is quasi-judicial. According to Justice A.P. Sen of the Supreme Court the power of the Commissioner to make a survey of existing waqf properties, carries with it, by necessary implication, the power to enquire as to the existence of a waqf.

It would be illogical to hold that while making a survey of waqf properties existing in the State Commissioner of Waqfs appointed by the State Government under sub-section (i) of Section 4, should have no power to enquire whether a particular property is waqf property or not. It will be clear that the words for the purpose of making a survey of waqf properties occurring in sub-section (i) of Section 4 is a key to the construction of the section. The ordinary meaning of the word 'survey' as given in the Random House Dictionary of English language, is 'to take general or comprehensive view of or appraise, as a situation'. If the Commissioner of Waqfs has the power to make a survey, it is but implicit that in the exercise of such power he should enquire whether a waqf exists. The making of such an enquiry is a necessary concomitant of the power to survey. It can, therefore, be said that the power of Commissioner to make survey is not only administrative but also quasi-judicial[19].

The Waqf Board has no right to alter or modify any decision of the Commissioner of Waqf in respect of the waqf property. The decision of the Commissioner is said to be judicial. The Waqf Board can merely check any clerical error, and can rectify such a mistake.

Due to some unavoidable circumstances, survey of waqf property could not be undertaken completely and these provisions remained unimplemented. The Inter-State Waqf conference held in New Delhi, 1960 advocated very strongly for a thorough survey of waqf properties. One of the delegates pointed out that in Andhra Pradesh alone, the number of registered waqfs was 3,300 while the number of unregistered waqfs stood at about 12,000[20]. The survey so far made reveals that till 1965 there were more than 34,189 waqfs in Andhra Pradesh. Similarly, in the Alwar district of Rajasthan, the survey revealed the existence of as many as 1965 waqf properties.[21] Pursuant to the recommendations of the conference, the state governments were requested to appoint Commissioner of Waqfs for making a complete survey of waqfs in their respective states.[22]

In case question arises, whether a particular property is waqf or not or whether it is a Shia or a Sunni Board or the mutawalli or any person interested therein may file a suit in a civil court for declaring that the property is waqf property. The decision of the court in such matter is final.

Functions of the Waqf Commissioners

The Waqf Commissioner has no power to declare whether a particular property is waqf or not. Only civil courts are competent to decide the matter.[23] It is relevant here to discuss briefly the facts of this case. In this case there was a building whose owner first mortgaged it and later on sold it to the petitioners. The defendants maintained that the building was waqf and the person claiming to be its owner was only its mutawalli. Therefore, he was not competent to sell the waqf property. The defendants, therefore, requested Waqf Commissioner, Rajasthan to declare the property as waqf, nullifying its sale and including it in the waqf list.

It was contended by the petitioner that the Waqf Commissioner has no right to decide whether a property was waqf or not. It was argued by the petitioner that this issue can be decided only by civil court.

The above argument was rejected by the Waqf Commissioner. Under these circumstances the petitioners filed a writ petition before the Rajasthan High Court requesting that the Waqf Commissioner be barred from holding any enquiry regarding the nature of property in dispute. The High Court said that under the Waqf Act, 1954, a Waqf Commissioner has obviously no jurisdiction either to decide any question relating to the title of the petitioners or to eject them without going to competent civil court. It seems what he contemplates to do so to hold an enquiry and to come to a finding if there is a case for going to a civil court under Section 6 of the Act. Therefore, he cannot bere strained from holding enquiry for that purpose.

The High Court said that the object of investing the power of a civil court in the Commissioner is to enable him to make proper survey of existing waqf properties...and not of these which have already become extinct.

It is submitted that the above opinion of Rajasthan High Court is not sound. It is within the competence of the Waqf

Commissioner to treat certain property as waqf property. After examining documents a Waqf Commissioner can declare any property as waqf. He can also include such property in the 'waqf list'. Unlawful alienation of waqf property can never make it extinct. A validly created waqf remains so in perpetuity and can extinguish only under certain circumstances which certainly do not include unlawful alienation.

The following observations of the Rajasthan High Court needs reconsideration—'If a person who is a non-Muslim...is in possession of a certain property, his rights, title and interest cannot be put in jeopardy simply because that property is included in the list published under section 2 of section 5.' The distinction made by the High Court between the properties held by a Muslim and non-Muslim is not based on any rational principles. The property can be unlawfully acquired by any person. It is not necessary for him that he must be a non-Muslim. It is not correct to assume that the intention of the legislature was not to apply this Act to non-Muslims. It is doubtful that the list published under Section 6 (4) of the Act does not become final.

It was on account of this judgment that Waqf Act was amended in the year 1969. According to Waqf (Amendment) Act, 1969, it is only on the basis of the waqf list prepared by the Commissioner that a suit in the Civil Court regarding the disputed nature of waqf may be filed.[24] It can, therefore, be said that the Commissioner of waqf is after making necessary enquiries, competent to include any property in the 'waqf list' provided such property was in existence at the date of the commencement of the Act. It will be better if the doubt is removed by way of amendment. It is proposed that the word 'existing' be deleted from Section 4 (i) of the Act.

In Radha Krishna's case the Rajasthan High Court further held that Section 6 of the Waqf Act, 1954, did not apply to a person who was not a party to the survey proceedings before the Waqf Commissioner. Publication of the Waqf list and the lapse of one year within which an appeal could be made did not extinguish his rights to property. The High Court also maintained that proper notice be given to such persons.

According to Madras High Court the publication of waqf lists in the gazette was hardly a substitute for notice because nobody is expected to look into the gazette everyday at the risk of losing his property rights.[25]

In Abdul Karim's case it was said by the Supreme Court that persons holding trust property and not being party to proceedings before the Enquiry Officer (under the Madhya Pradesh Public Trust Act) were not affected by the period of limitation laid down in the Act.[26]

It is, therefore, submitted that the judgment of the Rajasthan High Court in Radha Krishna's case needs reconsideration.[27]

Section 6 (i) of the Waqf Act, 1954, be broadly interpreted. The words 'persons interested in a waqf' be so construed that this cover such persons also who may not be party to survey proceedings before the Waqf Commissioner.

This submission has been followed by Waqf (Amendment) Act 1984.

The explanation inserted in section 6 says that for the purposes of this Section and Section 6—A, the expression "any person interested therein", Shall, in relation to any property specified as waqf property in a list of waqfs published, under Sub-Section (2) of Section 5, after the commencement of Waqf (Amendent) Act, 1984, shall include also every person who, though not interested in the waqf concerned, is interested in such property and to whom a reasonable opportunity had been afforded to express this case by notice served on him in that behalf during the course of the relevant inquiry under the Act.

A fresh section entitled Section 6—A. Power of Tribunal to determine disputes regarding waqfs was introduced by the waqf (Amendment) Act, 1984. This new Section says that any question arises whether a particular property is waqf property or not or whether it is a Shia waqf or a Sunni waqf, the Board or the mutawalli of the waqf or any person interested therein, may appty to the Tribunal having jurisdiction in relation to such property, for the decision of the question and the decision of the Tribunal shall be final.

Law of Limitation and Waqf Properties

Public waqf has been defined in Section 2 of the Act. The preamble described the Act to be an Act to extend the period of limitation in certain cases for suits to recover possession of immovable property forming part of public waqfs. Under the Limitation Act, the title of the true owners would be extinguished if the properties are in adverse possession for twelve years or more. After partition of the country, a number of waqf properties passed into unauthorised hands. Many of the mutawallis who were in charge of these properties had migrated to Pakistan and the few who stayed behind could not for various reasons institute civil proceedings for the recovery of possession of these properties. The result was that ever since the partition, a large number of these waqf properties had been in the possession of unauthorised occupants. Therefore, it was provided that the above provisions of Limitation Act shall not be applicable in the case of suits filed for the possession of waqf property. This provision was made with a view to enabling the Waqf Boards and other interested persons to institute suits for the recovery of the possession.

The period of limitation for recovery of possession of an immovable property forming part of public waqfs was in the first instance extended upto August 15, 1967. This date was extended upto 31st December 1970 by Section 2 of Parliament Act IX of 1969. In 1978 the government again passed the Public Waqfs (Extension of Limitation– Delhi Amendment) Bill, 1977, which seeks to extend the limitation period up to December 31, 1980, in respect of suit for recovering possession of immovable property forming part of public waqfs in Delhi.

The enactment of 1969 was challenged in the court of law on the ground of discrimination under Article 14 of the Indian Constitution.

It was held by a single judge of Allahabad High Court that Parliament extended the limitation in respect of suit for the recovery of possession of any immovable property forming part of public waqfs in every case where the dispossession had taken place at any time between August 15, 1947 and May 7, 1953. The provisions of the Act can not be said to be hit by

Article 14 of the Constitution because the Act applied equally to all the public waqfs as defined in the Act. The classification made by the Parliament was a valid one having regard to the peculiar conditions prevailing in the country between August 15, 1947 and May, 1953.[28]

SURVEY REPORT

The following is the brief survey report of the various states of India :

Madhya Pradesh

The erstwhile part 'C' state of Bhopal had appointed a Commissioner of Waqfs who conducted the survey of waqfs situated in Sehore and Raisen districts. After examining the report, the M.P. Waqf Board published a list of waqfs situated in the Districts of Sehore and Raisen in the government gazette as required under the Waqf Act. Although in terms of the provision to Section 6 (4) of the Waqf Act, the said list had assumed finality but the State government did not accept this position despite the fact that they were advised to do so by the government of India.[29]

In 1961, the Government of Madhya Pradesh appointed a Commissioner of Waqfs to undertake survey not only of waqfs situated in the integrating units of Mahakoshal, Madhya Bharat and Rewa region but also of Bhopal region where the survey had already been undertaken. A long period of 23 years has passed but the M.P. Waqf Board is not aware of the extent to which the survey has been completed so far and the request of the Board to be apprised of the same by the government was not approved.[30]

The inordinate delay in the completion of the survey of waqf properties is not only causing financial hardship to the Waqf Board but also adversely effecting the unserveyed waqf properties. It may be added that while on the one hand, the State Government is insisting on the Waqf Board to bear the initial expenditure incurred by government on the survey of waqf properties in the Bhopal region undertaken in 1961 and to pay the printing charges of survey list in the gazette, it has on the other hand refused to issue certificate under Section 7 (3) of the Waqf Act to enable the Board to recover the same from the mutawallis concerned. In view of this amount of Rs. 31,000 which was inadvertently paid by the Board to the State Government towards expenses on survey could not be recovered from the mutawallis.

United Provinces

Before 1937 the survey of waqfs in the United Provinces was made by the following personnel :

(i) The Waqfs Enquiry Committee. This Committee was presided by Hon'ble Justice Iqbal Ahmad (1929-30) ;
(ii) The District Judges (1934); and
(iii) The District Officers (1936).

The survey reports made by these offi cers was not of much help. The Enquiry Committee which submitted its report in 1930 stated that in United Provinces waqfs were having gross income of Rs. 39,95,218. However, when in 1936 District Officers submitted their report, they stated completely different figures from the one they had themselves furnished to the waqf committees.

The report submitted by the District Judges in 1934 was also not true. This was based on accounts filed in the courts by mutawalli under Section 5 of the Mussalman Waqf Act, 1923. The accounts submitted by the mutawalli were not completely true.

Keeping this fact into consideration a provision for making survey was made in the United Provinces Muslim Waqfs Act, 1936. A Chief Commissioner of waqf, two Assistant Commissioners and a seven member Advisory Committee to advise the Chief Commissioner were appointed. These persons were responsible for making the survey of the property.[31] Waqf Commissioners were also appointed to assist the Chief Commissioner of waqfs.[32]

The following procedure was adopted for making survey—

(i) The nature of waqf was determined on the basis of the waqf deed and where no such deed existed, by the help of the user or evidence of declaration.

(ii) The mutawallis of these waqfs were requested to submit the deed and/or to supply other information.

(iii) Mutawallis were given the opportunity to file objections against the 'factum of waqf, its nature and exemption.'

(iv) Where the income reported was so low with reference to the property and its situation that it appeared wholly improbable, local verification was made through the local member of the Advisory Committee or revenue staff by means of commission issued under Section 4 (4).

(v) The District Waqf Commissioners were deciding the waqf cases only during their spare time. They were busy in their own work and they were not able to pay full attention to the waqf cases.

(vi) The entire province was divided into three circles. One looked after by the Chief Waqf Commissioner, and the other two by the two provincial Assistant Commissioners. These persons were deciding dispute on the basis of spot inspections. They were also supervising the subordinate staff in collecting information.

The survey was completed on 31 October 1938. There were 8174 Sunni waqfs in the province. Out of these waqfs 5306 were subject to the Act and their total assessable income was Rs. 4,19,869.[33] The cost of making survey was Rs. 46,379.00. Due to shortage of staff, it was not possible for the Chief Commissioner or his assistant to do either the necessary field work or to look into individual cases.

Under Section 4 of the U.P. Waqf Act, 1960, survey of waqfs in the state has to be made. The survey work has been started and may be completed shortly.

For making complete survey it is necessary that Waqf Commissioners should have adequate staff to conduct surveys on his own to verify the authenticity of figures furnished by Revenue Officers. It is also necessary that care should be taken to verify the income of a waqf.

It is also necessary that thorough survey should be made of waqf by user. There are several small graveyards, mosques *etc.* with appertaining lands. With the rise in the cost of the land, these waqf properties have acquired significant importance. In the recent years, the property of waqf by user has been acquired frequently. It has, therefore, become necessary that proper records be maintained of this property. The present survey must pay full attention to unearth such properties so that suitable steps be taken for the restoration of such property.

It will be in the interest of the cause of waqfs if a survey of waqfs under illegal encroachment by private individuals or by government departments is also conducted.

Maharashtra and Gujarat

As far as survey of waqf property is concerned the States of Maharashtra and Gujarat are the worst sufferers. As already submitted the Bombay Public Trusts Act, 1950, is in force in these states. This Act does not contain any provision regarding survey of waqfs or trusts. It is absolutely necessary in the interest of the waqfs that proper and thorough survey of waqf properties in these two states be made. There can be two alternatives for attaining this object *viz*. either the Central Act, 1954, be made applicable to these states also or necessary amendment be made in the Waqf Act, 1954.

Andhra Pradesh

In Andhra Pradesh also no proper survey was made. Large number of waqfs were left out. In matters of valuation and income also the figures were unreliable. It was, therefore, decided by the State Government to make inspection of all waqfs. It was reported that there were 34,189 waqfs worth Rs. 27,50,80,007 and having an annual income of Rs. 50,72,223.[34]

Rajasthan

In Rajasthan also the Madras scheme was followed. The survey report submitted by the tahsildars neither disclosed the valuation nor correct annual income of waqf properties. This was only on account of the indifference showed by the Tahsil office.

Madras

In Madras the entire survey work was left to tahsildars

who were under the direct control of District Collectors. In each collectorate a clerk was paid an allowance of Rs 1500 per month for waqf duties. But nowhere were the survey reports properly checked. The tahsildars were not responsible to Waqf Commissioners and the result of this defect was that no proper survey of waqf property could take place.[35]

Survey of Waqfs under the Waqf Act, 1954

The agency employed by the State Government for conducting survey was not statisfactory. Therefore, the Central Government recommended to the State Governments for the appointment of the following persons as Waqf Commissioners :

(i) Waqf Commissioner ;
(ii) Additional Waqf Commissioners (two) ;
(iii) Assistant Commissioners in each Tehsil ;
(iv) Patwaris ; and
(v) Kanungos.

It was said that a satisfactory survey of waqf properties could only be made by the patwaris, kanungos and tahsildars. It was also said that for making proper survey of the waqf properties two Additional Waqf Commissioners of the rank of sub-divisional officers be appointed. It was further proposed that tahsildars should be appointed as Assistant Waqf Commisioners, and they will work under the direct control of Waqf Commissioner. Under the present scheme the Commissioner and Assistant Commissioner of waqfs obtained first hand information by making tours of tehsil headquarters and to his staff, especially the patwaris.

The tehsildars were instructed that income and expenditure of a waqfs should be confirmed by making spot enquiries and the income and expenditure accounts furnished by mutawallis should not be relied upon. It was also provided that full details be given regarding the property under illegal occupation.

Jammu and Kashmir

Under the J&K Muslim Waqf Act, 1959, the J&K

Government has appointed a special officer, Auqaf to conduct not only survey of Waqfs, but also to supervise waqf affairs in the state, to help constitute waqf committees, to settle waqf disputes, to undertake inspection of waqfs and so one. There are more than 10,000 waqfs in the state. These waqfs are having vast resources at their disposal. For conducting survey it is absolutely necessary that there should be full-fledged staff. Waqf properties to be surveyed are so spread out in the State that many of these were quite out of reach. It is, therefore, absolutely necessary that proper transport facilities be provided for making survey of the waqf property. Absolute reliance on revenue records may lead to some anomalies which vitiated the reliability of initial survey of waqfs made in the states of Madras and Rajasthan.

Muzrai Institution in Karnataka State

The erstwhile princely state of Mysore dedicated property for religious and pious purposes. The state government is having a separate department for looking after the property of this institution. Muzrai grants in favour of Muslim institutions numbering more than 400 have been surveyed as Muslim waqfs under the provisions of the Waqf Act, 1954. A list of waqf property of this institution has been published under Section 5 of the Act. Now the property of Muzrai institution is under the control of Karnataka Waqf Board.

Initial Payment of Cost of Survey of Waqfs

Under the Waqf Act, 1954, the conduct of survey is squarely the responsibility of the State Government. Under the scheme of the Act the expenditure on survey including charges on account of publication of waqfs list has initially to be borne by the State Government to be recovered subsequently from the mutawallis concerned. Chapter II of Waqf Act, 1954 abundantly makes the position clear which makes it obligatory for the State Government to appoint Commissioner, Assistant Commissioner and Additional Commissioner to prescrible particulars under which a list of waqfs is to be published, to issue certificate for recovery of survey charges from a mutawalli as arrears of land revenue *etc.* The Waqf Board comes in only for examining and publishing the list of waqfs based on the report of the Waqf Commissioner. The Act, vide Section 7 (i) makes mutawallis of waqf in the state and not the Waqf Board responsible for defraying the total cost of survey and that too after the survey has been completed and required proportion assessed by the Waqf Commissioner. Obviously, therefore, initial expenditure on conduct of survey has to be borne by no agency other than the State Government. This has been actually the practice throughout the country and each State Government/Government of Union Territory has borne/or in continuing to be or the initial expenditure on this account.

This section has also been amended by Waqf (Amendment) Act, 1984. Sub-Section (1) of Section 7 says that the total cost of making a survey including the cost of publication of the list or lists of waqfs shall be borne by all the mutawallis of the waqfs whose net annual income whereof exceeds one hundred rupees, in proportion to the net annual income accruing in the State to such waqfs such proportion being assessed by the Survey Commissioner.

Recently, the Government of M.P. asked the M.P. Waqf Board to bear even the initial expenditure on the Commissioner of waqfs and his organisation.[36] This is totally against the provisions of the Waqf Act, 1954. It is, therefore, submitted that the Government of Madhya Pradesh may take immediate action as per the law on the subject and in line with the practice and procedure being adopted by all the other states and union territories to which Waqf Act, 1954 is applicable.

It is submitted here that once the survey work of any particular area has been completed and whose lists have been published by the Waqf Board in the government gazette under Section 5 (2) of the Waqf Act, 1954, then it should not be allowed to be altered except on the order of the civil court of competent jurisdiction. By virtue of provisions of Waqf Amendment Act, 1969, the lists of waqfs published together or separately are to be treated as final and conclusive under Section 6 (4) of the Waqf Act, 1954, unless modified in pursuance of a decision of the civil court under sub-section 1 of Section 6 of the Act.

Evacuee Waqf Property—Waqf Commissioner's Power to ascertain whether Evacuee Property is Waqf or Not

Under the Administration of Evacuee Property Act, 1950, custodian of Evacuee Proporty can declare whether a particular property is the evacuee property or not. Under Sections 24 and 27 of the above Act respectively appeal and revision can be filed by the aggrieved person who is interested in the property. Section 28 gives finality to the order passed under Sections 24 and 27. Under Section 46 of the Act the civil or revenue courts shall have no jurisdiction to entertain or adjudicate upon question whether any property or any right to or interest in any property, is or is not evacuee property. In *Custodian* v *Jafran Begum*[37] it was said by the Supreme Court that before the authorities under the Act assume the duties of administration of evacuee properties, someone has to determine what properties are evacuee and that there is nothing in Section 7 to suggest that the custodian is incompetent to declare a property as evacuee property.

Under the Administration of Evacuee Property Act, 1950, custodian has exclusive jurisdiction to determine whether a property declared evacuee property was waqf property. The Administration of Evacuee Property Act, 1950, seems to debar the waqf commissioner from inquiring into the nature of any property declared to be evacuee property.

It is, however, not obligatory on the part of the custodian to furnish all necessary information material to the waqf commissioner regarding any disputed property. The custodian can refuse to furnish such information. It is, therefore, submitted that in case of any dispute whether the property is waqf or evacuee, it will be obligatory on the part of the custodian to furnish all necessary information regarding such disputed property.

Power of the Waqf Board to make Changes in the List

According to Section 4 (3) of the Waqf Act, 1954, the Commissioner shall after making such inquiry as he may consider necessary, submit his report[38] to the state government regarding : (a) the number of waqfs (in the state, or as the case may be, any part thereof) showing the Shia waqfs and Sunni waqfs separately ; (b) the nature and object of each waqf ; (c) the gross income of the property comprised in each waqf ; (d) the amount of land revenue, cesses, rates and taxes payable in respect of such property ; (e) the expenses incurred in the realisation of the income and the pay or other remuneration of the mutawalli of each waqf ; and (f) such other particulars relating to each waqf as may be prescribed.

On the other hand sub-section (1) and (2) of the Waqf Act, 1954, requires that on receipt of a report under Section (3) of Section 4, the State Government shall forward a copy of the same to the Board. Sub-clause (2) says that the Board shall examine the report forwarded to it and publish it in the official gazette, a list of waqfs (existing in the state) containing such particulars as may be prescribed. On the reading of these two sections it is clear that both the commissioner and Board are having equal functions.

It is not clear whether the Board is competent to effect changes in the waqf list prepared by the Waqf Commissioner and submitted to the Board. Recently, the Waqf section, Government of India sent a circular to the Secretaries, Waqf Board, empowering the Boards to make 'any changes' in the list of waqfs. It may not be out of the way to submit here that nowhere in the Act, Boards have been given this power. They have no right to make any change in the list supplied by the Waqf Commissioners. If there is any omission in the list, the Waqf Commissioner can be consulted. In case of disagreement the matter can be referred to some higher authority. The Board may, however, be empowered to effect changes in the waqf list where the commissioner has ceased to function after completing the survey.

Power of the State Government to effect Changes in Waqf List

Under the Act state government has no power to make any change in the list submitted by tne Waqf Commissioner. Section 5 (1) of the Act clearly says that on receipt of a report submitted by Waqf Commissioner the State government should forward a copy of the same to the Board.

Section 5 of the Waqf Act, 1954 says that the state government shall forward the same to the Waqf Board for its examination and publication. The Waqf Board after examining the report—may publish the same in the state gazette. The Waqf Board may also give other particulars of the waqf property.

Section 6(1) of the Act says that if a question arises whether a particular property is waqf property or not or whether the waqf is Shia or not, any interesed person may file a suit in a civil court of competent jurisdiction for a decision in the matter. The decision of the court shall be final.[39]

The suit must be filed within one year from the date of publication of the list of waqfs.

Waqf Property in possession of a Stranger—Stranger not bound to file suit within One Year

The words 'any person interested therein' appearing in sub-Section (1) of Section 6 have been a matter of controversy. The controversy has been, however, finally settled by the Supreme Court in *Muslim Waqfs Board, Rajasthan* v *Radha Kishan.*[40] The provisions of Section (1) of the Waqf Act, 1954 are identical to the provisions of section 5 (2) of the United Provinces Muslims Waqf Act. 1936. **In** *Sirajul Haq* v *The Sunni Central Board of* Waqf,[41] U.P., the Supreme Court was required to construe Section 5(2) of the above Act. The court interpreted the expression 'any person interested in a waqf' as meaning 'any person interested in what is held to be waqf', that is, in the dedication of a property for a pious, religious or charitable purpose.

Where a stranger who is a non-Muslim and is in possession of a certain property his right, title and interest therein cannot be put in jeopardy merely because the property is included in that pulished under sub-section (2) of Section 5 of the Waqf Act, 1954. The failure of such a person to institute a suit in a civil court of competent jurisdiction for decision of such question within a period of one year, as provided for under sub-Section (2) of Section 5 of the Act final and conclusive under sub-section (4) of Section 6.

The purpose of Section 6 is to confine the dispute between the Waqf Board, the mutawalli and a person, interested in the waqf. The word 'therein' in the expression 'any person interested therein' appearing in sub-section (1) of Section 6 must necessarily refer to the 'waqf' which immediately precedes it. It cannot refer to the 'waqf property'. Thus the list published under sub-section (2) of Section 5 will not bind a stranger who is in possession of the property merely because he happens to be a person affected by the publication of the list of waqfs.[42]

In *C. Kotaiah* v *Waqf Board of A.P.*,[43] it was said that Section 6 of the Waqf Act, 1954, contemplates suits to be filed only by Board or the Mutawalli or the persons interested in the waqf and that persons who do not fall within the above categories need not file the suit contemplated by Section 6. It was also said that the Commissioner, who makes survey under Section 4 cannot enquire and does not decide the question whether a particular property is a waqf or not. The publication of the list under Section 5(2) cannot be treated as conclusive on the question whether a particular property is a waqf or not.[44]

Central Waqf Council

Section 8A of the Waqf Act, 1954, provides that the purpose of advising on matters concerning the working of Boards and the due administration of waqfs, the Centrol Government may, by notification in the official gazette, establish a council to be called the Central Waqf Council. This is an advisory body. It consists of members not exceeding twenty appointed by the Central Government. There is no such provision in the U.P. Kashmir, Bengal or Bombay Acts.

The Council was given statutory status by the Waqf Amendment Act, 1964.

Section 8B says that the Central Waqf Council shall receive one per cent of the aggregate of the net annual income of the waqfs which every Waqf Board is required to pay out of its waqf fund. [See waqf (Amendment) Act, 1984]

Section 8D of the Act authorises the Central Government to make rules. Such rules may provide for all or any of the following matters, namely—

(a) the term of office of the procedure to be followed in the discharge of their functions by, and the manner of filling casual vacancies among the members of the council ;

(b) control over and application of the Central Waqf Fund, and

(c) the from and manner in which accounts of the Council may be maintained.

Section 9 provides that there shall be a Waqf Board in each state for the general superintendence of all waqfs in that state. State Government is empowered to establish Sunni and Shia (or common) Waqf Boards and prescribes details for their constitution, functions and finances.[45]

According to Sub-Section (2) of Section 9 the Board shall be a body corporate having perpetual suceession and a eommon seal with power to acquire and hold property and to transfer any such property. [Ins. by Act 34 of 1964, Sec 5]

Sub-Section (3) says that it shall be lawful for the Board to so re-organise its administrative set up in the state as to ensure better administration of the waqfs in the state.
[Subs, by Act 69 of 1984, Sec. 10]

The U.P. Act also contains the same provisions.[46] These Waqf Boards are established with a view to supervising the administration of waqfs in the state.

The Bengal Act provides for the establishment of an advisory Board headed by the Commissioner of waqfs.[47] This is the duty of the Board to help the Commissioner in the discharge of his administrative and supervisory duties.[48]

Under the Bombay Act the endowments are not administered by a Board. These are administered by Charity Commissioners. He is assisted by Joint, Deputy and Assistant Charity Commissioners.[49]

In Kashmir the status of the Board is quite different. It is having only an advisory character. The Government shall establish a Committee of waqfs for any area or for one or more waqfs in any area as may be specified in the notification. The Committee shall be a body corporate having perpetual succession and a common seal with power to acquire and hold property, subject to such conditions and restrictions as may be prescribed by or under this Act, and shall by the same name sue and be sued.[50]

Sunni and Shia Waqf Boards

Under the Waqf Act, 1954, separate Waqf Boards for Sunni and Shia can be established only if the proportion of either the income or the number of Shia waqfs in any state exceeds 15 per cent of the number or income of all other waqfs in the state.[51] Under the Bengal Act there can be eleven members in the Board. Out of these eleven members, State Government is empowered to appoint four Shia members to the Board.[52]

Establishment of Boards and their Functions

Sub-section (2) of Section 9 of Waqf Act, 1954 provides that rhe Board shall be a body corporate having perpetual succession and common seal with power to acquire and hold property and to transfer any such property subject to such conditions and restrictions as may be prescribed and shall by the said name sue and be sued.

Composition of the Waqf Boards

Section 10 of the Waqf Act, 1954, lays down that the Board shall consist of eleven members in the case of a state and the union territory of Delhi, and (b) five members in the case of any other union territory. The Chairman of the Waqf Board shall be elected by the members from amongst themselves.

Appointment of Members

Section 11 of the Waqf Act, 1954, provides that the members of the Board shall be appointed by the State Government from anyone or more of the following categories of persons.

(a) members of the State legislature and members of Parliament representing the State ;

(b) persons having knowledge of Muslim law and representing associations such as State Jamiat-ul-Ulamai-Hind or State Shia conference. The persons of Jamat-ul-Ulamai-i Hind may be Hanafees, Ahle Hadis or Shafai ;

(c) persons having knowledge of administration, finance or law ;

(d) mutawallis of Waqf situated within the state in the

of the appointment of mutawallis only one mutawalli shall be appointed to the Board.

Under the Bengal and U.P. Waqf Acts the position is different. In these two states members are appointed partly through nomination by the State Government and partly through election.[53]

Terms of Office

Section 12 of the Waqf Act, 1954, provides that the members of the Board shall hold office for five years. However, a member may continue to hold office until the appointment of his successor is notified in the official gazette.

Section 12 (1)(2) of the above Act provides for the appointment of a full time secretary. He is the chief executive officer. He is not the member of the Board. Identical provisions are also given in Kashmir and U.P. Waqf Acts.[54]

The Andhra Pradesh High Court[55] considered the scope of the proviso to Sections 12 and 50 of the Waqf Act, 1954. The petitioner questioned the validity of certain proceedings of the Waqf Board on the ground that the term of the office of the members had on the relevant date expired.

It was said by Justice Lakshmaiah that the proviso to Section 12 read with Section 20 of the Waqf Act saved the said proceedings. Proviso to Section 12 provides that 'a member shall, notwithstanding the expiration of his term of office continue to hold office until the appointment of his successor is notified in the official gazatte.' Section 50 says that 'no act or proceeding of the Board shall be invalid by reason only of the existence of any vacancy amongst its members or defect in the constitution thereof.' The provisions of the two sections are specific and needs no interpretation.

The main object of the Section 12 is to define the duration of the members of the Board and the object of the proviso is to see that there should not be any hiatus in the continuation of the membership. Therefore, what is sought to be provided for by the proviso cannot be said to have been dealt with by the main section itself. The proviso cannot be said to be invalid for the reason that it seeks to whittle down the effect of the main section.[56]

Disqualifications for being Appointed, or for continuing as a Member of the Board

Section 13 of the Waqf Act, 1954, deals with regard to the qualifications for membership of Waqf Board. The following are the five disqualifications for appointment and for continuing as a member of the Board :—

(a) if he is not a Muslim and is less than twenty-one years of age ;

(b) if he is found to be a person of unsound mind ;

(c) if he is an undischarged insolvent ;

(d) if he has been convicted of an offence involving moral turpitude and such conviction has not been reversed or he has not been granted full pardon in respect of office. [Amended by Waqf (Amendment) Act, 1984].

(e) if he has on any previous occasion, been removed from the office of a member, or has been removed by order of a competent court from any position of trust either for mismanagement or corruption. [Subs. by Waqf (Amendment) Act, 1984].

Meeting of the Board

Section 14 of the Waqf Act, 1954 consists of three sub-clauses. Sub-clause (1) says that the Board shall meet for the transaction of business at such times and places as may be prescribed. Sub-clause (2) of the aforesaid Act says that the Chairman, or in his absence, any member chosen by the members from amongst themselves shall preside at a meeting of the Board.

Sub-clause (3) of the Act says that all questions which come before any meeting of the Board shall be decided by a majority of votes of the members present, and in the case of equality of votes, the chairman or, in his absence, any other person presiding shall have a second or casting vote.

Functions of the Board

Section 15 of the Waqf Act, 1954, says that the general superintendence of all waqfs in a state, in relation to all matters, except those which are expressly required by this Act to be dealt with by the waqf fund shall vest (Subs. by Act 69 of 1984, S. 14) in the Board established for the state. This is the duty of the Board to exercise its powers so as to ensure that the waqfs under its superintendence are properly maintained, controlled and administered and the income thereof is duly applied to the objects and for the purposes for which such waqfs were created or intended. This is the duty of the Board to act in conformity with the direction of the waqf, the purposes of the waqf and any usage or custom of the waqf sanctioned by the Muslim law. The explanation says that in this Sub-section waqf includes a waqf in relation to which any scheme has been made by any court whether before or after the commencement of the waqf (Amendment) Act, 1984.

The dedication of property may be for religious, pious or charitable purpose. It is not necessary for the waqif to mention each and every object of waqf separately. In such cases the Waqf Board has to frame a scheme for the management of waqf. Under this scheme the dedicated property shall be allocated according to the wishes of the waqif. Unauthorised alienation is, therefore, invalid and the Waqf Board can recover the property from the alienee.[57]

Section 15-A deals with regard to this power to develop urban land which is waqf property. Under this Act the waqf Board has been given power to make special efforts for the development of waqf land situated in the urban area. For this purpuse the Board has to make application to the State Government specifying therein the nature of the work.

Section 15—B confers powers of inspection by waqf Commissioner or persons authorised by him. This section says that if any loss or damage has been caused to any waqf property, then the Waqf Commissioner or any other authorised person shall have power to inspect all movable and immovable waqf properties and their accounts *etc*. Such inspections can be made at least once in two years and the concerning waqf shall have a gross annual income of at least twelve thousand rupees. [For details See. Section 15—B of the Waqf Act, 1954].

Section 15—C deals with regard to the recovery of the amount determined under Section 15—B. Under Sub-Section (3) or Sub-Section (5) of Section 15—B this is the duty of the mutawalli or other person to make any payment or to restore the pessession of any property. If he has failed to do so then waqf Commissioner shall take appropriate stefrs for the recovery of possession of the property and shall also send a certificate to the collector to this effect.

Section 15 -B deals with regard to the conditional attachment of property by Tribunal. Where the waqf Commissioner comes to the conclusion that the mutawalli or any other person is about to dispose of the whole or any part of this property, or is about to remove the whole or any part of this property he may apply to the Tribunal for the conditional attachment of the said property. [For details See Section 15—D of the Act.]

Establishment of Committees *etc.*

Section 16 of the Waqf Act, 1954 also considers it necessary to establish either generally or for a particular purpose or for any specified area or areas committees for the supervision of waqfs.[58] Under the Bombay Act Committees can be established to manage every temple, mosque or endowment created for a public, religious or charitable purpose, which vests in, or the management of which vests in the State Government.[59]

The Waqf Board shall determine the functions of such committees from time to time. It is not necessary for the members of such committees to be members of the Waqf Board. The Waqf Board can choose few districts for the setting up of the committees. District Waqf Committees are generally required to perform following functions :

(*i*) supervising and safeguarding waqf property and the interest of the Board in the district;

(*ii*) compiling or maintaining a list of waqfs registered and unregistered in the district;

(*iii*) implementing the religious, educational, economic and other programme of the Board in the District;

(*iv*) supervising religious education, mosque, schools, grave, khanqas and other religious institutions in the district;

(*v*) maintaining lists of poor widows, orphans, destitutes and poor students *etc.*;

(*vi*) assessing requirements of books by the religious schools and wardwise libraries;

(*vii*) assessing the wardwise committees in discharge of their functions;

(*viii*) sending progress report and any other matter.

The power of the Waqf Board to constitute a committee has given rise to the following two questions :—

(*i*) whether Board can exercise this power to substitute such a committee in the place of a mutawalli who is effectively working ; or

(*ii*) the Board can constitute the committee only where a mutawalli has been removed and managements of the waqf taken over by the Board under section 43 and 43-A of the Waqf Act, 1954.

In *Andhra Pradesh Waqf Board* v *Hidayatullah*[60] the Andhra Pradesh High Court was required to answer, definite answer on this problem. In this case the Board had without taking any action for the removal of a mutawalli directed him to hand over the entire property of the waqf to a managing committee which had constituted under Section 16 of the Act.

The High Court refused to accept the action taken by the Andhra Pradesh Waqf Board as correct. The court held that unless recourse was taken to Sections 43 or 43-A of the Act, the mutawalli could not be divested of all his control over the property and asked to hand it over to any committee constituted by the Board.

In *Sheikh Abdul Latif* v *Commissioner of Waqfs*[61] the main question before the court was whether Section 27(1)(a) and (b) of the Bengal Waqf Act has given power which is to be exercised quasi-judicially or not. It was contended on behalf of the appellant that at least the power given in Section 27(1)(b)(c) (d) and (e) is not quasi-judicial in function but administrative function of the Commissioner of waqfs only. The appellant submitted that power given in Section 27(b)(c), (d) and (e) is administrative function in view of judgment reported in A.I.R. 1978 Cal 92-98. It is, however, clear that even the administrative function which affects other persons will be vulnerable to attack any application under Article 226 of the Constitution. It was, therefore, submitted that power under Section 27(b)(c) of the Act is administrative function and cannot be exercised by the Commissioner in a quasi-judicial way as it has done.

On the other hand, the respondent contended that all the powers under Section 27(1)(a), (b), (c), (d) and (e) are functions to be exercised in a quasi-judicial manner and not administratively. The High Court held that Section 27(1)(a) of the Bengal Waqf Act on the fact of it cannot but be quasi judicial. According to Calcutta High Court[62] the power, so far as the decision is concerned, under Section 27(1)(a) is a quasi-judicial power. His lordship held that so far as this decision is concerned the Commissioner discharged the quasi-judicial function. On reading Section 27(1)(a) of the Act it is quite clear that the Commissioner may investigate and determine the nature and extent of waqfs and waqf property, and call from time to time for accounts, returns and information from mutawallis and it cannot but be quasi-judicial, because it requires investigation as well determination of the nature and extent of the waqf and waqf property. The nature and extent of the waqf property *prima facie* means how income from the property has to be applied for the objects and purposes of the waqf and for such benefit of such class of persons for which such waqf is created or intended. This is exactly what has been stated in Section 27(1)(b) of the Act. According to the opinion of the Court Section 27(1)(b) of the Bengal Waqf Act is corollary to Section 27(1)(a) of the Act or in other words, in order to determine the nature and extent of the waqf the waqfnama must be considered and it must be shown how does it benefit and to whom the benefit is intended and what is the object of the waqfnama and how the income is to be spent on the said objects. All these require determination by the Commissoner of waqfs. Therefore, naturally this is a quasi-judicial power. The power under Section 27(1)(a) and (b) given to the Commissioner of Waqfs is the power which is to be exercised in a quasi judicial manner and not otherwise.[63]

A member of the committee constituted by the Waqf Board has been treated a landlord and he can file a suit for the eviction of waqf property. He can collect the rent from the tenants.[64]

In *Mohammed Dilawar Ali* v *A.P. Muslim Waqf Board*[65] an administrative committee was constituted under Section 16 of the Waqf Act, 1954. The Waqf Board delegated its power such as to appoint, remove or dismiss employees of Board to Committees. In consequence of this delegation of power the Committee terminated the service of an employee and sent the same for the ratification of the Board. This termination order was challenged on the ground of excess of delegation of power. The Andhra Pradesh High Court held that the constitution of administrative committee was not in conformity with the provisions of Section 22 of the Act and, therefore, it was illegal and void *ab initio*. The delegation of power to the committee was also not lawful. The Board was having no power to ratify the same.

Resignation of Chairman and Members

According to Section 17 of the Waqf Act, 1954 the Chairman or any other member may resign his office by writing under his hand addressed to the State Government. It is further provided that the Chairman or the members shall continue in office until the appointment of his successor is notified in the official gazette.

Removal of the Chairman or Members

Sub-clause (1) of Section 18 of the Waqf Act, 1954 deals with the removal of the Chairman and members of the Waqf Board. The State Government may by notification in the official gazette remove the Chairman of the Board or any member thereof if he becomes subject to any disqualifications specified in Section 13, or is incapable of acting or acts in a manner which the State Government, after hearing any explanation that he may offer, considers to be prejudicial to the interests of the waqfs ; or fails, without excuse sufficient in the opinion of the Board to attend three consecutive meetings of the Board.

A member of the Waqf Board can be removed. In *Akhtar Ahmad* v *State of Andhra Pradesh*,[66] the Andhra Pradesh High

Court held that where a member of the Waqf Board behaved in a discourteous manner towards the Chairman of the Board he was liable to be removed. But before removing him the Government must be satisfied that the conduct of the member was prejudicial to the interests of the waqf and, therefore, he was removed from the membership of the Waqf Board. A member of the Waqf Board is free to oppose the action of the Chairman. The opposition by members will not, however, always amount to prejudice the interests of waqfs. It was, therefore, held that if the discourteous conduct could not at all reasonably lead to the determination that it was prejudicial to the interest of the waqfs, it cannot be said that the consideration alleged to have been made by the Government was a reasonable and valid consideration. Hence, the Government's action removing any member for alleged discourteous action was not bonafide and was invalid.

Sub-clause (2) of Section 18 of the Waqf Act, 1654, says that where chairman of the Board is removed under sub-section (1) he shall also cease to be a member of the Board.

Filling of a Vacancy

Section 19 of the Waqf Act, 1954, lays down that when the seat of a member becomes vacant by his removal, resignation, death or otherwise, a new member shall be appointed in his place and such member shall hold office so long as the member whose place he fills would have been entitled to hold office, if such vacancy had not occurred.

Vacancies among members or defect in the Constitution not to invalidate acts or Proceedings of the Board

According to Section 20 of the Waqf Act, 1954 no act or proceeding of the Board shall be invalid by reason only of the existence of any vacancy amongst its members or any defect in the constitution thereof.

Secretary and other Officers of the Board

According to sub-cause (1) of Section 21 of the Waqf Act, 1954, there shall be a Secretary to the Board. He shall be a Muslim and shall be appointed by the State Government, in consultation with the Board. He shall be the Chief Executive officer of the Board and shall be under administrative control of the Board.[67]

The Board may appoint such other officers and servants as it may consider necessary for the efficient performance of its functions under the Act.[68]

Delegation of Power

Section 22 of the Waqf Act, 1954, says that the Board may delegate such of its powers and duties as it may deem necessary. This has become necessary because of the fact that meetings are held after a long interval. There are urgent and complicated matters which needs immediate attention. However the mode of delegation of authority is different.

The Board may delegate to the Chairman or any other member or to the Secretary or any other officer or servant of the Board or any Committee thereof, subject to such conditions and limitations as may be specified in the order, such of its powers and duties as it may deem necessary. The provisions in U.P. Muslim Waqf Act, and J & K Muslim Waqf Act are identical.[69] Under the Bombay Act, the State Government may delegate authority to the Charity Commissioner or any other officer.[70] Under the Bengal Act delegation can be made only to Chairman of the Board. The power cannot be delegated to any other person.[71]

In view of this provision, in every state, Waqf Boards have established small committees of their members for dealing with matters like administration, finance, property, religious affairs *etc.* These Committees work on the guidelines given by the Waqf Board.

It is the important principle of delegation of power that essential powers cannot be delegated. Therefore, the Board cannot delegate its essential powers.

Inspection of Records and Issue of Copies

According to sub-section (1) of Section 23 of the Waqf Act, 1954, any person can inspect the proceedings or other records in the custody of the Waqf Board. The Board may also issue copies of the same on payment of such fees and subject to such conditions as may be prescribed. According to sub-clause (2) of Section 23, all such copies be certified by the Secretary of the Board in the manner provided in Section 76 of the Indian Evidence Act, 1872. The powers conferred on the Secretary by sub-section (2) may also be exercised by such other officer or officers of the Board as may be authorised by the Board.[72]

Prevention of Disqualification for Membership of Parliament

Section 24 of the Waqf Act, 1954, lays down that merely becoming the Chairman or member of the Board will not disqualify a person to become members of parliament. The Section says that the offices of Chairman and members of a Board shall not disqualify and shall be deemed never to have disqualified, the holders thereof for being chosen as, or for being, members of Parliament.

REGISTRATION OF WAQFS

The registration of all waqfs properties is necessary, because this is the only way through which the Board may come to know about the creation of a waqf within his jurisdiction. There are two central legislations which lay down that a waqf must be got registered. These legislations are (i) The Waqf Act, 1954 and (ii) the Indian Registration Act.

Chapter IV of the Waqf Act, 1954, deals with regard to the registration of waqfs. Sub-section (1) of Section 25 of the Act says that every waqf whether created before or after the commencement of the Act shall be registered at the office of the Waqf Commissioner [Substituted by Waqf (Amendment) Act, 1984]. Application for registration shall be made by the mutawalli. The application for registration can also be made by the waqif or his descendants or a beneficiary of the waqf or any Muslim belonging to the sect.[73]

The application for registration has to be filed in the prescribed form and manner. The Waqf Commissioner [Waqf (Amendment) Act, 1984] may also specify the place where registration application can be filed.[74]

The application shall be accompanied by a copy of the waqf deed. Where the copy of the waqf deed is not available, the applicant shall give all necessary details as far as they are known to him.[75] The application of registration shall be signed and verified.[76] The Waqf Commissioner [Substituted by waqf (Amendment) Act, 1984] can request the applicant for the supply of more details[77]. The Board may make necessary inquiries regarding the genuineness and validity of the application and the correctness of any particulars.[78]

In the case of waqfs created before the commencement of this Act every application for registration shall be made within three months from such commencement in the case of waqfs created after such commencement, within three months from the date of the creation of the waqf. Every waqf registered under Section 25 before the Commencement of the waqf (Amendment) Act, 1984 shall be deemed to have been registered on such commencement at the office of the Waqf Commissioner. [Substituted by Waqf (Amendment) Act, 1984].

Every application for registration pending immediately before the commencement of the waqf (Amendment) Act, 1984 before the Board shall stand transferred to the waqf Commissioner. [Substituted by waqf (Amendment) Act, 1984].

Where a waqf was already in existence at the time of the commencement, the same shall be deemed to be registered. The Central Waqf Board may supply the application for registration purposes. Registration fees *etc.* has to be paid at the prescribed rates for registration. The application form should be accompanied alongwith a copy of the waqf deed. Where it is not possible to submit waqf deed, supply of full particulars of waqf will be sufficient. The application for registration should be signed by all applicants. They should also verify the contents given in the application form in the same manner as is required to be done in the Code of Civil Procedure, 1908, for the signing and verification of pleadings.

Section 26 of the Waqf Act, 1954, deals with the procedural matter. According to this Section, after the registration of the waqf, various entries are required to be made in the register of waqfs maintained by the Waqf Commissioner [Substituted by Waqf (Amendment) Act, 1984]. The Register of waqfs shall contain the following entries :—

(a) The class of the waqf;
(b) The name of the mutawalli;
(c) The rule of succession to the office of mutawalli under the waqf deed or by custom or by usage;

(d) Particulars of all waqf properties and all title deeds and documents relating thereto;

(e) Particulars of the scheme of administration and the scheme of expenditure at the time of registration;

(f) Such other particulars as may be prescribed.

Section 17 (1) (b) of the Indian Registration Act says that every waqfnama by which immovable property of the value of Rs. 10,000 or more is dedicated by way of waqf should be registered. If the dedicator (waqif) is himself appointed mutawalli, the registration of waqf is necessary. However, a trusteenama by which he appoints additional mutawalli does require registration if the document does not purport to transfer any interest in the property to them. In M. Rustom Ali's[79] case on 25th August, 1908, one Nawab Azmat Ali Khan executed a waqf deed under which he created a waqf. He appointed himself as the mutawalli of the waqf property. This document was registered under the Indian Registration Act.

On 9th November, 1908, Nawab Azmat Ali Khan again executed another document, called the trusteenama and this document was not registered. Under this trusteenama additional mutawallis of the waqf property were appointed. By the deed of trusteenama further directions were given to the mutawalli. It was provided that some mutawallis will act jointly with the dedicator, and others to act after his death. He died after about a month. After his death the mutawallis brought a suit to recover possession of the property from his heirs. Of course, the waqfnama was registered under the Indian Registration Act, but the heirs argued that it was not registered in a due manner as certain rules made under Section 69 of the Act were not followed.

It was held by the Privy Council that the document was duly registered. The trusteenama, however, was not registered and it was argued that, not being registered, it did not confer upon the mutawallis any right of suit. The Privy Council rejected this argument of the heirs. The Privy Council ruled that the document, even if read with the waqfnama did not purport to assign the property to the mutawallis, and did not therefore, require registration.

The main aim of registration is to ensure that all the relevant or important records relating to waqfs are maintained properly. It may, however, be noted that mere non-registration with the Waqf Board will not mean that the property is not the waqf property. Again, where a waqf property is in dispute, the registration without enquiry is ineffective. The Board is not competent to decide whether a particular property is waqf property or not. If a dispute is raised by a non-Muslim the Board cannot by simply entering the property in the register of the waqfs drive him to take recourse to a civil court.[80]

Sub-Section (2) to Section 26 was Substituted by Waqf (Amendment) Act, 1984. This new Sub-Section provides that the register of waqfs maintained immediately before the commencement of the waqf (Amendment) Act, 1984. Shall be deemed, on such commencement to be the register maintained by the Waqf Commissioner.

Section 26 -A was substituted by the waqf Commissioner can appoint executive officer. The Executive Officer shall exercise full control over the waqf property. He shall exercise his duties under the dircetion, control and supervision of the waqf Commissioner. While exercising his powers and discharing his functions the Executive officer shall not interfere with any religious duties or any usage of the waqf. [For details See Section 26—A of the Waqf (Amendment) Act, 1984].

Section 26—B was also substituted by waqf (Amendment) Act, 1984. Under this new section deals with regard to the powers of the Waqf Commissioner in respect of those waqfs which have ceased to exist the Waqfs Commissioner shall, if he is satisfied that the objects or any part thereof of a waqf have ceased to exist hold an inquiry to ascertain the properties and funds of such waqf. [For details See Waqf (Amendment) Act, 1984].

Section 27 of the control Act says that the Board may collect information regarding any property and if and question arises whether a particulars property is waqf property is waqf property or not or whether a waqf is a Sunni waqf or a Shia waqf, it may decide such question. [This section has been also amended by Waqf (Amendment) Act, 1984].

Registration is, however, not necessary in the case of a document appointing mutawalli, if it is executed subsequent to the completion of a waqf created through a written and duly registered deed.[81]

The Provisions of Section 25 (8) are Mandatory

An examination of these provisions reveal that every possible contingency to register a waqf and any of its properties has been visualised by the legislature and extensive and *suo moto* powers have been conferred on the Board to remedy every situation. The provisions of Section 25 are mandatory. The aim of the legislature was that no injustice, hardship or Inconvenience should be caused to the Board and the object of the statute will be furthered and will be achieved.[82]

Decision if a Property is Waqf Property

Under the various Waqf Acts wide powers are assigned to the Waqf Board and Committees to collect information regarding any property which they believe to be waqf property. Section 27 of the Waqf Act, 1954, gives powers to the Board to collect information about a property and to decide whether it is a waqf property or not and its decision unless revoked or modified by a civil court, is final. Similar power is given in Kashmir and U.P. Acts also.[83] In Bombay the power to decide whether property is waqf or not rests with the Deputy or Assistant Charity Commissioner.[84] Under the Bengal Act, Waqf Commissioner has to decide whether a property is waqf or not.[85] The aggrieved party can file a suit in the court of law.

If any of the properties are not included in a waqf that is already registered, the proper course for the Board is to collect such information under Section 27 of the Act and after making such enquiry as it may deem fit, decide that question in accordance with sections, the rules and the principles of natural justice. In deciding that question, it is open to the Board to rely on any information furnished by any person or any authority. The power conferred on the Board by Section 27 of the Act is a *suo moto* power to be exercised by the Board and cannot be exercised on any application made by Section 25 (8) of the Act.[86]

Power to Cause Registration of Waqf and to Amend Register

Under Section 28 of the Waqf Act, 1954, the Board may direct a mutawalli to apply for the registration of a waqf, or to supply any information regarding a waqf or may itself cause the waqf to be registered or may at any time amend the register of waqfs.

Notification of Change in Registered Waqfs

In the case of change in the mutawalli on account of his death *etc.* the incoming mutawalli is under the duty to notify the change to the Board[87]. In the case of any other change in any of the particulars mentioned in Section 25, the mutawalli shall, within three months, notify such change to the Board.[88]

A person who failed to apply for registration of waqf without any reasonable cause shall be punished under Section 41 of the Waqf Act, 1954.

Savings

Section 30 of the Waqf Act, 1954 is a savings section. According to this section if a waqf was registered before the commencement of this Act under any law for the time being in force it shall not be necessary to register the waqf under the provisions of this Act. The registration made before such commencement shall be deemed to be a registration made under this Act.

MUTAWALLIS AND WAQF ACCOUNT

Budget

This is the duty of the mutawalli to prepare and submit to the Board for approval a budget for the next financial year. The budget should contain the information regarding receipts and expenditure in respect of the waqf during the financial year. The budget should be prepared in the prescribed form[89].

Submission of Accounts of Waqfs

This is also the duty of the mutawalli to keep regular account of the receipts and expenditure of the waqf property. This is also his duty to submit to the Waqf Board the audited accounts of the waqf property. The information should be submitted in the prescribed form. It should contain particulars of money received and spent during the period of twelve months ending on the 31st day of March.[90] Under Section 41 of the Waqf Act, 1954, a defaulter mutawalli is liable to be punished.

Duty to Deposit Receipts in the Bank

A mutawalli is not expected to keep the waqf money with him. He should immediately deposit the money in his possession in the State Bank or in any scheduled bank or in the postal savings bank.

Audit of Accounts of Waqfs

As already submitted this is the duty of the mutawalli to submit accounts of waqfs to the Board. The account of waqfs submitted to the Board shall be audited and examined annually or at such other intervals as the Board may determine by an auditor appointed by the Board[91]. The auditor shall submit its report to the Board. This shall be the duty of the auditor to specify among other things, all cases of irregular, illegal or improper expenditure or of failure to recover money or other property caused by neglect or misconduct and any other matter which the auditors considers it necessary to report. The report shall also specify the name of responsible person for such expenditure or failure[92].

The cost of the audit of the accounts of a waqf shall be paid from the waqf fund[93].

Section 33 was also amended by the waqf (Amendment) Act, 1984. The amended Act provides the manner of audit of accounts of waqfs. It says that ;

(a) in the case of a waqf having no income on a net annual income not exceeding one thousand rupees, the submission of a statement of accounts shall be a sufficient compliance with the provisions of Section 32 ;

(b) the accounts of a waqf having a net annual income exceeding one thousand rupees, but not exceeding three thousand rupees, shall be prepared in the form of a statement of income and expenditure. This statement shall be audited triennially or at such other intervals by an auditor appointed by the Waqf Commissioner. [For further details see Section 33 of the Waqf (Amendment) Act, 1984].

Board to Pass Orders on Auditor's Report

The auditor's report will be examined by the Waqf Board. The Board may call for the explanation of any person in regard to any matter mentioned in the report and shall pass such orders on the report as it thinks fit[94]. Section 34 of the central Act has been amended suitably by Waqf (Amendment) Act, 1984.

Sums Certified due Recoverable as Arrears of Land Revenue

The outstanding amount mentioned in Sections 33 and 34 shall be certified by the Board. This amount shall be paid by the concerning person within sixty days after the service of a demand for the same issued by the Board. The Board is empowered either to modify or cancel such outstanding amount[95]. Where the person concerned has failed to pay the above outstanding amount within the stipulated time the same may be recovered as arrears of land revenue. However, before taking any legal action in the matter, a reasonable opportunity of being heard in person be given to the defaulter[96].

Duties of Mutawallis

Section 36 of the Waqf Act, 1954 says that a mutawalli shall have the following duties—

(a) to carry out the directions of the Board ;

(b) to furnish such returns and supply such information or particulars as may from time to time be required by the Board ;

(c) to allow inspection of waqf properties, accounts or records or deeds and documents relating thereto ;

(d) to discharge all public dues ; and

(e) to do any other act which he is lawfully required to do.

Section 36-A of the Waqf Act, 1954, says that notwithstanding anything contained in the waqf deed no transfer of any immovable property of a wakf by way of—

(i) sale, gift, mortgage or exchange ; or

(ii) lease for a period exceeding three years in the case of agricultural land or for a period exceeding one year in the case of non-agricultural land or building shall be valid without the previous sanction of the Board.

Identical provisions have also been inserted in the U.P. and Bengal Acts[97]. Under the Bengal Act the period of limitation for recovery by the Board, of the waqf property transferred in contravention of Section 53 of the Act shall be 12 years from the date of the Board's knowledge of such transfer[98]. This is a good piece of legislation and can be adopted in other Acts.

According to Section 72 (2) of the Bengal Act, a suit for the recovery of any waqf property wrongfully possessed, alienated or leased, shall not be deemed to have become barred by limitation if such suit was not so barred before the 15th day of August, 1947. There is no such provision in any of the statutes mentioned above.

A mutawalli has no right to grant permanent lease. He must obtain the prior approval of the Waqf Board. In *Ram Dhan* v *Janki Rai Singh*[99] the mutawalli of the waqf executed a permanent lease in respect of the property. The lessee built a kachcha construction on the leased land. The defendant was also said to have purchased the same land. The dispute was over the possession of the land resulting in proceedings under Section 145, Criminal Procedure Code.

It was said by the defendant that the mutawalli had no right to lease out the waqf property and as such the lessee has no power to execute the sale deed in favour of the plaintiffs.

The lower court decided the case against the plaintiff. The plaintiff preferred an appeal before the lower appellate court. The lower appellate court held that the grant of lease was a voidable contract. The lease deed was a good document unless it is avoided by mutawallis or beneficiaries.

The defendant was not satisfied with the judgement of appellate court and he filed an appeal before the High Court.

It was said by the High Court that under the Muslim law, the powers of a mutawalli are restricted. He has no right to execute a permanent lease without the permission of the Waqf Board. But if a mutawalli executes any deed which is not permitted under the Muslim law or exceeds the right given to him under the law, the deed would not become void *ab initio.* It would be a valid document unless it is avoided by the persons concerned. In the present case the lease deed in question was avoided by the mutawallis or beneficiaries.

The defendant also contended that deed of lease was not valid. It was said that the property which was given on lease was an agricultural land and, therefore, the lease cannot be created for more than three years, and in case it is for other purposes, the lease may not be created for more than one year unless the permission of the Waqf Board is obtained. The court pointed out that such lease deed, if executed, can be validated retrospectively by obtaining permission of the Waqf Board and by no stretch of imagination it can be said that the lease is void *ab initio.*

The High Court also examined the provisions of Section 24 of the Indian Contract Act. It was said that such a lease deed cannot be said to be void when its consideration or the object is not unlawful under Section 24 of the Indian Contract Act. The Supreme Court held that the lease deed in question was a voidable document and unless this lease deed was avoided, the lessee had a right to transfer his right to the plaintiffs.

For attracting the provisions of Section 36-A of the Waqf Act, 1954 it is necessary that there should be a lawful waqf in existence. In *T.N. Waqf Board* v *S. Syed Inam Saheb*[100] the dedication was made by a non-Muslim to the Fakirs visiting the mosque and not to the mosque. The Madras High Court held that since the land was not dedicated to the mosque, no valid waqf came into existence. Their lordship held that it was not necessary that prior permission under Section 36-A of the Waqf Act, 1954 should have been obtained before granting lease for 25 years.

Unlawful Transfer of Waqf Property and its Recovery

Section 36-8 (1) of the Waqf Act, 1954, says that in case the the mutawalli has not followed these provisions and has transferred any immovable property registered as waqf property, under Section 26, the Board can recover possession by issuing a certificate to the Collector of the District. This is a new provision which has come into force after the amendment of 1964. Formerly, the Board was allowed to sanction leases of waqf property for more than three years or mortgage or exchange of periods. It did not include sale and, therefore, where sale became necessary in the interest of waqfs, courts had to be approached.

Identical provisions are also given under the U.P. and Bengal Acts. These Acts debar a Mutawalli from transferring in any way immovable waqf property over a specified period. The transfer can be made only with the prior permission of the Board.[101]

This is the duty of the Collector to make an order asking the person concerned to deliver the property to the Board within a period of 30 days from the date of the service of the order.

The aggrieved party has been given the right of appeal. He can prefer an appeal to the District Court within whose jurisdiction the property was situated[102].

This is the mandatory requirement of natural justice that the aggrieved party must be given an opportunity of being heard. In the case of *Haji Nizamuddin* v *State of Uttar Pradesh*[103] the mutawalli granted a lease of the waqf property in favour of the petitioners. The Central Board of Waqfs received information that the property of the waqf had been let out in an unauthorised manner to the petitioners. The Controller of Waqf Board issued a show cause notice calling upon the petitioners to restore back the possession of the property to the waqf under Section 57-A of the Muslim Waqf Act, 1960.

According to Rule 9 (2) of the U.P. Muslim Waqfs [Recovery of Waqf Property] rules (1972) in such cases the aggrieved party must be given personal hearing before deciding his case. This opportunity of personal hearing is in addition to the opportunity of showing cause guaranteed under the Rules. In the present case the Board issued a 'show cause' notice to the petitioner. The petitioner expressly made a request for the opportunity of personal hearing. The Controller of the Board rejected the petitioner's prayer for personal hearing on the ground that the request for the personal hearing was made as a measure of delaying tactics.

It was said by K.N. Singh and P.N. Bakshi JJ of Allahabad High Court that it is well settled principle that when the statutory rules require an authority to give personal hearing to a person against whom action is to be taken the authority concerned must comply with the statutory requirement of the law and it is not open to it to by-pass the statutory procedure merely on the ground of delay. In our opinion, the Controller acted in contravention of statutory provisions in issuing requisition order to the Collector for the petitioner's eviction. The procedure followed by the Controller was in contravention of the provisions of the Act and the Rules framed thereunder as such the requisition order is rendered illegal and liable to be quashed.

Under the Bombay Act, lease of agricultural lands can be made for a period up to 10 years. For this purpose it is not necessary to obtain prior sanction of the Charity Commissioner[104].

The Kashmir Act is very liberal in this regard. Section 41 of the J & K Muslim Waqf Act, 1959 says that any waqf property such as agriculture lands, orchards, ahatas, houses, shops, vacant plots. Hujars, apartments attached to Khanquahs, Takias, and Sarias, may be leased out for a term not exceeding twenty years without the previous sanction of the Government.

It is notable that the grant of lease of the agricultural land for a term of twenty years is not desirable. As already noted under the Central, U.P. and Bengal Acts, lease of agricultural land can be made only for a period of three years without the previous sanction of the Board. It is, therefore, submitted that necessary amendment be made in the Act.

In *Subrat Shanker Bahadur* v *The Bihar Sunni Waqf Board*[105] the High Court of Patna was required to interpret the following wordings of Section 36-B (1) of the Waqf Act, 1954 —— 'any immovable property of a waqf entered as such in the register of waqfs maintained under Section 26'.

The question for construction was whether the expression

'entered as such' in the above provision qualify the preceding word 'waqf' or the preceding expression 'immovable property' of a waqf in its entirety.

Justice Madan Mohan Prasad Singh of Patna High Court said that the reference must be here to the immovable property of a waqf entered as such in the register of waqfs maintained under Section 26 of the Act. To hold otherwise would lead to anomalous results. It is true that any proceedings held by the Waqf Board, affecting the rights of the party, should conform to the strictest rights of any party and the strictest rules of natural justice.

The jurisdiction of the Board is limited to administration of waqfs. A Board can exercise jurisdiction only to persons claiming under waqfs. It has no jurisdiction over a stranger, enabling it to dispossess him of a property in his possession though it may be listed in its records as a waqf by claiming to exercise its powers under Section 36-B of the Waqf Act, 1954. In such cases, the remedy open to the Waqf Board is to file a civil suit for the possession of the property[106].

Mutawalli entitled to pay certain Costs from income of Waqf Property

Under Section 37 of the Waqf Act, 1954, a mutawalli is authorised to spend waqf money on certain contingencies. He is free to spend money on all lawful purposes. He may spend money under the following heads :—

(i) on account of furnishing any particulars of documents or copies, (under Section 25) ; or
(ii) on account of furnishing full and true statement of accounts, (under Section 32) ; or
(iii) on account of furnishing information of documents required by the Board ; or
(iv) on account of carrying out the directions of the Board.

Section 38 of the central Act says that where a Mutawalli refuses to pay or fails to pay any revenue, cess *etc.* the Board or where such refusal or failure occurs after the commencement of the Waqf (Amendment) Act, 1984, the Waqf Commissioner may dischange in dues from the waqfs Fund. Sub-clause (2) says that if the Mutawalli has failed to pay the dues then the Waqf Commissioner [Substituted by the Act of 1984] may recover the same as an arrear of land revenue.

Creation of Reserve Fund

The Waqf Commissioner [Subs. by the Act of 1984] may create and maintain a reserve fund from the income of a waqf. This reserve fund may be created for the following purposes :—

(i) for the payment of rent and of revenue, cess, rates and taxes due to the Government or any local authority ;

(ii) for the discharge of the expenses of the repair of waqf property ; and

(iii) for the preservation of the waqf property[107].

It is clear that under Section 38 of the Central Act in case of default by a mutawalli to pay revenue, cess rates or taxes the Commissioner can pay the dues from the waqf fund and recover from the mutawalli alongwith damages.

Extension of Time

The Waqf Act, 1954, empowers the Waqf Board to extend the time within which any act is required to be done by the mutawalli.[108]

This is also the duty of the mutawalli to discharge all public dues.[109]

Penalties

Section 41 of the Waqf Act, 1954, also contemplates control of the power of mutawallis. This section provides for severe panalties for a mutawalli who has violated the provision of the Waqf Act. Section 41 says that the following penalties may be imposed on a mutawalli who fails :—

(a) to apply for the registration of a waqf ;

(b) to furnish statements of particulars or accounts or returns as required by this Act ;

(c) to supply information or particulars as required by the Board;

(d) to allow inspection of waqf properties, accounts or deals and documents relating thereto;
(e) to deliver possession of any waqf property, if ordered by the Board or the court;
(f) to carry out the directions of the Board;
(g) to discharge any public dues ; or
(h) to do any other act which he is lawfully required to do by or under this Act.

He shall unless he satisfies the court that there was reasonable cause for his failure, be punishable with fine which may extend to one thousand rupees. By the Amendment Act of 1984 this amount has been raised to two thousand.

The Waqf (Amendment) Act, 1984 provides that if a Mutawalli has failed to apply for the registration of the waqf and this has been done which a view to concealing the existence of such a waqf or waqfs then he shall be punishable with imprisonment for a term which may extend to six months and also with fine which may extend to five thousand rupees. Sub-clausc (2) provides that no court shall take cognizance of an offence punishable save upon complaint made by the Board or the Waqf Commissioner or by duly authorised officer. It is further provided by sub clause (3) that only the court of Metropolitan Magistrate or a Judicial Magistrate of the First class shall entertain the cases mentioned above (Substituted by Amendment Act, 1984). Sub-clause (4) says that notwithstanding any thing contained in the Cr. P.C. the above referred fine shall be credited to the Waqf Fund. The court has also been given power to impose term of imprisonment in default of payment of fine. (Subs. by Amendment Act, 198-).

Besides the above duties, the Waqf Act imposes on every mutawalli a duty to apply to the State Waqf Board for registration of the waqf of which he is the mutawalli. It is immaterial whether the waqf was created before or after the commencement of the Waqf Act, 1954. The mutawalli is required to file the application in prescribed form. Section 29 of the Waqf Act, 1954 says that in case of any subsequent changes in the particulars or any change in the office of the mutawalli they have to be notified to the Board.[110] Section 41 of the Waqf Act. 1954, provides that if the mutawalli has failed to apply for registration or he failed to supply the particulars of changes, penal action will be taken against him.

The Waqf Board is fully competent to direct the mutawalli for the creation of reserve fund from the income of the waqf. The amount of this fund may be utilised for the payment of public dues *etc.* Similarly, a Waqf Board is competent to settle schemes for management of a waqf having no scheme.

Power to Appoint Mutawalli in Certain Cases

Under the Waqf Act, 1954, Waqf Board has been empowered to appoint *ad hoc* mutawalli for certain cases. The Waqf Board can appoint a mutawalli if there is a vacancy of mutawalli and there is no one to be appointed under the terms of the deed of the waqf.[111] It may, however, be noted that the Waqf Board has no power to appoint permanent mutawalli in respect of Afityat properties.[112] Similarly, the Waqf Board has no inherent power to dispossess a mutawalli or take over the administration of a mosque from the mutawalli, pending an enquiry into the application for removal of the mutawalli.[113] The Board can appoint a person only if there was no suitable person available to act as mutawalli.[114]

Before taking action under Section 42, a reasonable opportunity should be provided to the Board.

Under the Waqf Act, 1954, the power to appoint a temporary mutawalli has been given only to the Waqf Board. The State Government has no power either to appoint or accord approval to such appointment.[115]

The orders passed by the Waqf Board under Section 42 can be challenged in the court of law. A civil court can pass interlocutory orders. This power to pass interlocutory orders pending suit, necessarily extends to varying, modifying or suspending the orders of the Waqf Board passed under Section 42. But the Civil Court shall not do this except after hearing the Waqf Board, since it is the Waqf Board in which the statute has vested the power of supervision over the waqfs in the State.[116]

Removal of Mutawalli

All the Waqf Acts of India contain a provision for the removal of mutawalli. However, the provisions given in

Waqf Act, 1954, are comparatively elaborate and effective. This Act also lays down certain procedural safeguards, which may be taken into consideration.[117]

According to Section 43 of the Waqf Act, 1954, a Mutawalli may be removed if—

(a) he has been convicted more than once of an offence punishable under Section 41 ; or
(b) he has been convicted of an offence of criminal breach of trust or any other offence involving moral turpitude ;
(c) misappropriates or deals improperly with the properties of the waqf ; or
(d) he is of unsound mind or is suffering from other mental or physical defect or infirmity ;
(e) he has failed to pay, without reasonable excuse the contribution payable by him under Section 46.[118]

Where the Board has appointed a Committee to act as a mutawalli and that Committee has failed to perform its functions the Board may supersede the Committee and appoint any other person to act as the mutawalli.[119]

Formerly, there was no such provision and the Waqf Board was not having any right to take over direct management of waqfs in cases where the office of mutawalli is lying vacant and no suitable person is available.

The removal of a person from the office of the mutawalli shall not affect his personal rights, if any, in respect of the waqf property either as a beneficiary or in any other capacity or his rights, if any, as a Sajjadanashin[120]. It was held by Andhra Pradesh High Court that entries in Register of waqfs is conclusive proof of a person's right to office of Mutawalli or Sajjadanashin.[121]

It is the duty of the Waqf Board to observe all the principles of natural justice before removing a mutawalli from his office. The Waqf Board must conduct a proper enquiry into the matter in the prescribed manner. It is also necessary that the decision of his removal must have been taken by a majority of not less than three fourths of the members [122] of the Board. These are the mandatory requirements of the Act and the infringement of the procedure prescribed by Section 43

(4) and 45 read with Rule 23 of the Andhra Pradesh will be illegal.[123]

An aggrieved mutawalli can appeal before the State Government against the order to the Waqf Board. The decision of the State Government on such appeal shall be final and shall not be questioned in any court of law.[124]

After the removal of mutawalli under sub-sections (1) and (2) of Section 43 of the Waqf Act, 1954 the Board may by order direct the mutawalli to deliver possession of the waqf property to the Board or to any other authorised person or committee. For this purpose the Board has been given the status of the civil court. Therefore, the order passed by the Waqf Board shall be executed by the civil court as if it had passed the decree.[125]

The Waqf Act, 1954, further lays down that a mutawalli removed under Section 43 of the Act shall not be eligible to be appointed as a mutawalli of that waqf for a period of five years from the date of such removal.[126]

The U.P. and Bengal Acts are also equally elaborate in laying down various grounds for the removal of mutawallis, these Acts neither prescribe any specific majority by which the Board may take such decisions, nor do they lay down any period for which the mutawalli removed from his office may not be eligible for reappointment to the same office. The Central and Bengal Acts contain procedure for obtaining possession of waqf property from a person who was removed from the office of mutawalliship. There is no such provision in the U.P. Act.

Under the J&K Muslim Waqf Act, 1959, the Committee of waqf is empowered to effect his removal. Section 26 of the aforesaid Act lays down the following disqualifications for the appointment of mutawalli. According to Section 26 notwithstanding anything contained in any law, decree, order or deed, no person shall be qualified to be appointed or to continue as mutawalli if.

(i) he is not a Muslim ; or
(ii) he is a Government servant ; or
(iii) he habitually indulges in activities which are against Shariat ; or

(iv) he is otherwise ill-reputed or of bad character.

The first two disqualifications are not in consonance with the Muslim law. A government servant or non-Muslim can be appointed as mutawalli. Under the Muslim law if a mutawalli is required to perform religious duties then a non-Muslim cannot be appointed.[127]

Under the various Waqf Acts there is a provision for the removal of the mutawalli.[128] However, the Waqf Act, 1954 is more elaborate, effective and lays down certain procedural safeguards.

The U.P. and Bengal Acts do not lay down specific majority by which the Board may take such decisions. These Acts also do not prescribe any period for which the removed mutawalli may not be eligible for reappointment to the same office. The U.P. Act does not lay down any rules for obtaining possession of waqf property from a person who has been removed from the office of mutawalli.

The provisions in the Kashmir Act are also relevant to note here. Section 26 of the Act says that notwithstanding anything contained in any law, decree, order, or deed, no person shall be qualified to be appointed or to continue as Mutawalli if (l) he is not a Muslim.

The disqualifications regarding habitual indulgence in activities in contravention of Shariat ; or is otherwise ill reputed or bad character needs clarification. These sentences are vague. The term activities which are against Shariat are not easy to define. It is very difficult to establish which trade is prejudicial to or inconsistent with Sunna or Shariat.[129] It is not easy to make objective assessment of a person. Personal and subjective considerations are sure to crop in the determination of such cases resulting in biased and malicious decision by the Committee.

Under the Bombay Act, the Charity Commissioner is required to file a suit in the Civil Court for the removal of a mutawalli. Any two or more persons having an interest in the trust and having obtained the consent in writing of the Charity Commissioner can also file a suit for the removal of the mutawalli. These persons can bring a suit only in case of an alleged breach of public trust or where recovery of trust property is involved, or where the direction of the court is deemed necessary for the administration of any public trust.[130] This is a very expensive and time consuming remedy. It will also cause inconvenience. It is easily understandable that if a suit is filed for the removal of a mutawalli and the dishonest mutawalli is allowed to hold the post till the decision of the case, he will definitely misappropriate the waqf property. It is, therefore, necessary that this provision needs amendment.

It is also relevant here to note the provisions of the Bengal Act which also needs the immediate attention of the legislature. According to Section 75A of the Bengal Act a Mutawalli shall not be entitled to spend funds of the waqf estate of which he is a mutawalli for meeting any costs, charge or expenses, incurred by him in any suit, appeal or application or other proceedings for, or incidental to, his removal from office or the taking of any disciplinary action against him. The above provisions appear to be too much harsh. It is here submitted that the mutawalli be allowed to spent money on his defence out of waqf income. This amount may be realised from him if the court passes an order for his removal. In this way an indigent mutawalli will be able to defend himself. Where a mutawalli has lost his case in the lower court and has gone in appeal, he may be suspended and in his place a receiver may be appointed immediately. In such cases also certain amount (generally paid to the employees who are under suspension) may be paid to him so that he may be able to maintain his dependants.[131]

Assumption of Direct Management of Certain Waqfs by the Board

The Waqf Board can also assume direct management of the Waqf if no suitable person is available for appointment as mutawalli.[132] The Board may assume direct management of the waqf property in the following circumstances :

(i) where a vacancy in the office of the mutawalli exists but no suitable person is available who can be appointed as mutawalli ;

(ii) where the right of any person to act as mutawalli is in dispute ;

(iii) where the committee, appointed to look after the waqf property is not functioning properly. It has abused its powers or has failed in performing its duties.[133]

The Waqf Board is required to take following necessary steps before assuming direct management of a waqf :

(i) necessary enquiry regarding the affairs of the waqf be made ;
(ii) notice to this effect may be issued to the mutawalli ;
(iii) notification that action was taken under Section 42 be issued.[134]

The Kashmir, Bengal and Bombay Waqf Acts do not contain any such parallel provision. The Bombay Act bars the court from appointing a Charity Commissioner as trustee of religious trusts and prohibits the Charity Commissioner from accepting such trust if management of religious affairs is involved. Under the Act special committees may be appointed. These Committees may consist of persons belonging to the same community to which the endowment, purported to be directly administered by the Government belongs. These provisions were incorporated in the Act after the decision of the Supreme Court in *Ratti Lal* v *State of Bombay*.[135]

Under the U.P. Muslim Waqf Act, 1960 a waqf board has been given very limited power to assume direct control of the waqf property. The Board can assume direct management only if in the opinion of the Board, the Committee appointed by the waqif or any competent court or authority, is not functioning properly and satisfactorily. The Board after superseding the Committee may constitute a fresh Committee.

The Waqf Board may either supersede it and appoint a fresh committee, or may assume direct management of the waqf.

This is the duty of the Board to forward a copy of the order to the court or Munsif. Where there is no Munsif, the court of Civil Judge within whose jurisdiction the said property is situated or the said mutawalli resides and the court shall thereupon adopt and issue the order as if it were a decree made by itself in a suit[136].

Till 1971, the Board was required to refer such matters to the waqf tribunals. This was a very peculiar situation. Under the Act, Board was itself competent to decide as to who should be the mutawalli or even to assume direct management. It was surprising that the Board was under the duty to refer the matter to the tribunal for its award. However, the government realised the defect and the same was removed by an amendment[137].

Application for Inquiry

Under the Waqf Act, 1954, the Waqf Board can initiate inquiry against any waqf if it has received information in writing to this effect and it is satisfied that there are reasonable grounds for believing that the affairs of the waqf are being mismanaged[138]. While explaining the scope of Section 44 and 45 of the Act, the Andhra Pradesh High Court held that under these Sections the Board cannot appoint receiver. It also held that the Rule 10-A of the A.P. Waqf Act, 1974 was *ultra vires* of the Act.[139]

Inquiry by the Commissioner [Subs. by Amendment Act, 1984]

Under Section 45 of the Waqf Act, 1954, a Waqf Commissioner can make enquiry either on an application received under Section 44 or on its own motion. Sub-section (2) of Section 45 says that for the purposes of any inquiry under this Act the Commissioner or any person authorised by it in this behalf shall have the same powers as are vested in a Civil Court under the Code of Civil Procedure for enforcing the attendance of witnesses and production of documents.

Section 45 of the Act makes a special provision with regard to the procedure to be followed in an inquiry before the Waqf Commissioner or any other delegated authority. There are various inquiries contemplated by the different sections of the Act which are to be held for the purpose of effective control and supervision over the waqfs. Section 45 of the Act makes the Waqf Commissioner a Civil Court for the purpose of exercising certain powers under Code of Civil Procedure. The following are the few cases where inquiry may be envisaged under the different provisions of the Waqf Act, 1954.

Section 15 (n)	—to investigate and determine the nature and extent of waqfs *etc.*
Sections 44 and 45	—Enquiry relating to the administration of the waqf under Section 45, the Commissioner *suo moto* or on an application under Section 44 has no power to decide anything apart from matters realting to the administration of waqfs and has no jurisdiction to decide disputed question of title. [140]

The Waqf Commissioner as well as the provision of enquiry under the Act are the creation of the statute. The Waqf Act, 1954, has prescribed the procedure to be followed while exercising powers under the Act. The procedure prescribed by the Act includes partial application of the provision of Code of Civil Procedure and for the exercise of these powers the Board has been made a civil court. It may, however, be relevant here to discuss the provisions of Section 4 of the Code of Civil Procedure. Section 4 C.P.C. says that the provisions of the Code of Civil procedure shall not apply nor otherwise limit or affect any special or local law or any special jurisdiction or power conferred or any special form of procedure prescribed by or under any other law for the time being in force. It is, therefore, clear that where there is anything in conflict with special or local laws or any special procedure, the Code of Civil Procedure would not apply.

At present, legislation has created special forum and remedy. It also prescribes special procedure. While prescribing special procedure it is usual to extend certain provisions of Code of Civil Procedure.

In the modern industrial age, the job of the State is not only to maintain law and order. It is required to introduce extensive legislation on various aspects of lives of its subject. The legislature has, therefore, passed a number of enactments. The authorities under these Acts have been given the power of Civil Court. Under these Acts the legislature has laid down special forum, remedy and special procedure. Thus special procedure has been prescribed for the smooth functioning of the authorities established under the various Acts.[141] While prescribing special procedure the legislature has extended certain provisions of the Code of Civil Procedure. For certain purposes these various authorities have been given the status of Civil Court. It may, however, be noted that the various statutes have conferred limited powers upon the special tribunal.

In *Rama Swami* v *Madras Hindu Religious Endowment Board*[142] it was held that the provisions of the Code of Civil Procedure are not applicable to it. The Code of Civil Procedure deals with the procedural matter which is aimed at to provide machinery for advancing the substantial rights and in matters relating to procedure when all procedures should be accepted to be permissible unless it is prohibited by the Code of Civil Procedure either expressly or by necessary implication.[143] It is, therefore, clear that the provisions of Code of Civil Procedure are applicable only with respect to the specified matters. It is relevant here to discuss the various sections and orders contained in the First Schedule of the Code of Civil Procedure 1908.

Sec. 30 C.P.C.—Power to Order Discovery and the Like

Subject to such conditions and limitations as may be prescribed, the Court may at any time, either of its own motion or on the application of any party :—

(a) make such orders as may be necessary or reasonable in all matters relating to the delivery and answering of interrogatories, the admission of documents and facts and the discovery, inspection, production, impounding and return of documents or other material objects producible as evidence;

(b) issue of summons to persons whose attendance is required either to give evidence or to produce documents or such other objects as aforesaid;

(c) order any fact to be proved by affidavit.

Section 31—Summons to Witness

The provisions in Sections 27, 28 and 29 shall apply to

summons to give evidence or to produce documents or other material objects.

Section 32—Penalty for Default

The Court may compel the attendance of any person to whom a summons has been issued under Sction 30 and for that purpose may :—

(a) issue a warrant for his arrest;
(b) attach and sell property;
(c) impose a fine upon him not exceeding five hundred rupees;
(d) order him to furnish security for his appearance and in default commit him to the civil prison.

Section 75—Power of Court to Issue Commissions

Subject to such conditions and limitations as may be prescribed, the Court may issue a commission :—

(a) to examine any person;
(b) to make a local investigation;
(c) to examine or adjust accounts; or
(d) to make a partition.

Section 76—Commission to Another Court

(1) A commission for the examination of any person may be issued to any Court (not being a High Court) situated in a State other than the State in which the Court of issue is situated and having jurisdiction in the place in which the person to be examined resides.

(2) Every Court receiving a commission for the examination of any person under sub-section (1) shall examine him or cause him to be examined pursuant thereto, and the commission, when it has been duly executed, shall be returned together with the evidence taken under it to the court from which it was issued unless the order for issuing the commission has otherwise directed, in which case the commission shall be returned in lieu of such order.

Section 77—Letter of Request

In lieu of issuing a commission the Court may issue a

letter of request to examine a witness residing at any place not within India.

Section 78—Commission Issued by Foreign Courts

Subject to such conditions and limitations as may be prescribed; the provisions as to execution and return of commissions for the examination of witnesses shall apply to commission issued by or at the instance of :—

(a) Courts situated in any part of India to which the provisions of this Code do not extend ; or
(b) Courts established or continued by the authority of the Central Government outside India ; or
(c) Courts of any State or country outside India.

Section 132—Exemption of certain Women from personal Appearance

(1) Women who, according to the customs and manners of the country, ought not to be compelled to appear in public shall be exempted from personal appearance in Court.

(2) Nothing herein contained shall be deemed to exempt such women from arrest in execution of civil process in case in which the arrest of women is not prohibited by this Code.

Section 133—Exemption of other Persons

(1) The following persons shall be entitled to exemption from personal appearance in Court, namely :—

(i) the President of India ;
(ii) the Vice-President of India ;
(iii) the Speaker of the House of the People ;
(iv) the Ministers of the Union ;
(v) the Judges of the Supreme Court ;
(vi) the Governors of States and Administrators of Union territories ;
(vii) the Speakers of the State Legislative Assemblies ;
(viii) the Chairman of the State Legislative Councils ;
(ix) the Ministers of States ;
(x) the Judges of the High Courts ; and
(xi) the persons to whom Section 87B applies.

(2) Omitted

(3) Where any person claims the privilege of such exemption, and it is consequently necessary to examine by commission, he shall pay the costs of that commission, unless the party requiring his evidence pays such costs.

ORDER XI, CODE OF CIVIL PROCEDURE DISCOVERY AND INSPECTION

Rule 1 : Discovery by interrogatories

In any suit the plaintiff or defendant by leave of the Court may deliver interrogatories in writing for the examination of the opposite parties or any one or more of such parties, and such interrogatories when delivered shall have a note at the foot thereof stating which of such interrogatories each of such persons is required to answer. Provided that no party shall deliver more than one set of interrogatories to the same party without an order for that purpose. Provided also that interrogatories which do not relate to any matters in question in the suit shall be deemed irrelevant, notwithstanding that they might be admissible on the oral cross examination of witness.

Rule 2 : Particular Interrogatories to be Submitted

On an application for leave to deliver interrogatories, the particular interrogatories proposed to be delivered shall be submitted to the Court. In deciding upon such application the Court shall take into account any offer, which may be made by the party sought to be interrogated to deliver particulars, or to make admissions, or to produce documents relating to the matters in question or any of them ; any leave shall be given as to either for disposing fairly of the suit or for saving costs.

Rule 3 : Cost of Interrogatories

In adjusting the costs of the suit inquiry shall at the instance of any party be made into the property of exhibiting such interrogatories, and if it is the opinion of the taxing officer or of the Court, either with or without an application for inquiry, that such interrogatories have been exhibited unreasonably, vexatiously, or at improper length, the costs occasioned by the said interrogatories and the answers thereto shall be paid in any event by the party in fault.

Rule 4 : Form of Interrogatories

Interrogatories shall be in Form No 2 in Appendix C with such variation as circumstances may require.

Rule 5 : Corporations

Where any party to a suit is a corporation or a body of persons whether incorporated or not, empowered by law to sue or be sued, whether in its own name or in the name of any officer or other person any opposite party may apply for an order allowing him to deliver interrogatories to any member or officer to such corporation or body, and an order may be made accordingly.

Rule 6 : Objections to Interrogatories by Answer

Any objection to answering any interrogatory on the ground that it is scandalous or irrelevant or not exhibited bonafide for the purpose of this suit or that the matters inquired into are not sufficiently material at that stage, or on any other ground, may be taken in the affidavit in answer.

Rule 7 : Setting aside and striking out Interrogatories

Any interrogatories may be set aside on the ground that they have been exhibited unreasonably or vexatiously or struck out on the ground that they are prolix, oppressive, unnecessary or scandalous, and any application for this purpose may be made within seven days after service of the interrogatories.

Rule 8 : Affidavit in answer, filing

Interrogatories shall be answered by affidavit to be filed within ten days, or within such other times as the Court may allow.

Rule 9 : Form of Affidavit in Answer

An affidavit in answer to interrogatories shall be in Form No 3 in Appendix C, with such variations as circumstances may require.

Rule 10 : No Exception to be taken

No exceptions shall be taken to any affidavit in answers,

but the sufficiency or otherwise of any such affidavit objected to as insufficient shall be determined by the Court.

Rule 11 : Order to Answer or Answer further

Where any person interrogated omits to answer or answers insufficiently, the party interrogating may apply to the Court for an order requiring him to answer, or to answer further, as the case may be, and an order may be made requiring him to answer further, either by affidavit or by *viva voce* examination, as the Court may direct.

Rule 12 : Application for discovery of documents

Any party may, without filing an affidavit, apply to the court for an order directing any other party to any suit to make discovery on oath of the documents which are or have been in his possession or power, relating to any matter in question therein. On the hearing of such application the Court may either refuse or adjourn the same, if satisfied that such discovery is not necessary, or not necessary at that stage of the suit or make such order either generally or limited to certain classes of documents as may, in its discretion, be thought fit :

Provided that discovery shall not be ordered when and so far as the Court shall be of opinion that it is not necessary either for disposing fairly of the suit or for saving costs.

Rule 13 : Affidavit of documents

The affidavit to be made by a party against whom such order as is mentioned in the last preceding rule has been made, shall specify which (if any) of the documents therein mentioned he objects to produce and it shall be in Form No 5 Appendix C, with such variations as circumstances may require.

Rule 14 : Production of Documents

It shall be lawful for the Court, at any time during the pendency of any suit, to order the production by any party thereto, upon oath, of such of the documents in his possession or power relating to any matter in question in such suit, as the Court shall think right ; and the Court may deal with such documents, when produced, in such manner as shall appear just.

Rule 15 : Inspection of documents referred to in pleadings or affidavits

Every party to a suit shall be entitled at any time to give notice to any other party, in whose pleadings or affidavits reference is made to any document, to produce such document for the inspection of the party giving such notice or of his pleader; and to permit him or them to take copies thereof ; and any party not complying with such notice shall not afterwards be at liberty to put any such document in evidence on his behalf in such suit unless he shall satisfy the Court that such document relates only to his own title, he being a defendant to the suit or that he had some other cause or excuse which the court shall deem sufficient for not complying with such notice in which case the Court may allow the same to be put in evidence on such terms as to costs and otherwise as the Court shall think fit.

Rule 16 : Notice to produce

Notice to any party to produce any documents referred to in his pleading or affidavits shall be in Form No 7 in Appendix C, with such variations as circumstances may require.

Rule 17 : Time for Inspection when notice given

The party to whom such notice is given shall, within ten days from the receipt of such notice, deliver to the party giving the same as a notice stating a time within three days from the delivery thereof at which the documents or such of them as he does not object to produce may be inspected at the office of his pleader or in the case of bankers books or other books of account or books in constant use for the purposes of any trade or business at their usual place of custody, and stating which (if any) of the documents he objects to produce and on what ground. Such notice shall be in Form 8 in Appendix C, with such variations as circumstances may require.

Rule 18 : Order for Inspection

(1) Where the party served with notice under Rule 15 omits to give such notice of a time for inspection or objects to give inspection, or offers inspection elsewhere than at the time office of his pleader, the Court may, on the application of

the party desiring it, make an order for inspection in such place and in such manner as it may think fit :

Provided that the order shall not be made when and so far as the court shall be of opinion that it is not necessary either for disposing fairly of the suit or for saving costs.

(2) Any application to inspect documents except such as are referred to in the pleadings, particulars or affidavits of the party against whom the application is made or disclosed in his affidavit of documents shall be founded upon an affidavit showing of what documents inspection is sought, that the party applying is entitled to inspect them, and that they are in the possession or power of the other party. The Court shall not make such order for inspection of such documents when and so far as the Court shall be of opinion that it is not necessary either for disposing fairly of the suit or for saving costs.

Rule 19 : Verified Copies

(1) Where inspection of any business books is applied for, the Court may, if it thinks fit, instead of ordering inspection of the original books, order a copy of any entries therein to be furnished and verified by the affidavit of some person who has examined the copy with the original entries, and such affidavit shall state whether or not there are in the original book any and what erasures, interlineations or alterations :

Provided that, notwithstanding that such copy have been supplied, the Court may order inspection of the book from which the copy was made.

(2) Where on an application for an order inspection privileges is claimed for any document, it shall be lawful for the Court to inspect the document for the purpose of deciding as to validity of the claim of privilege.

(3) The Court may, on the application of any party to a suit at any time, and whether an affidavit of documents shall or shall not have already been ordered or made, make an order requiring any other party to state by affidavit whether any one or more specific documents, to be specified in the application is or are, or has or have at any time been, in his possession or power ; and, if not then in his possession when he parted with the same and what has become thereof. Such application shall be made on an affidavit stating that in the belief of the

deponent the party against whom the application is made has, or has at some time had, in his possession or power the document or documents specified in the application, and that they relate to the matters in question in the suit, or to some of them.

Rule 20 : Premature discovery

Where the party from whom discovery of any kind or inspection is sought objects to the same or any part thereof, the Court may, if satisfied that the right to the discovery or inspection sought depend on the determination of any issue or question in dispute in the suit, or that for any other reason it is desirable that at issue or question in dispute in the suit should be determined before deciding upon the right to the discovery or inspection, order that such issue or question be determined first, and reserve the question as to the discovery or inspection.

Rule 21 : Non-compliance with order for discovery

Where any party fails to comply with any order to answer interrogatorics, or for discovery or inspection of documents, he shall, if a plaintiff, be liable to have his suit dismissed for want of prosecution, and, if a defendant, to have defence, if any, struck out, and to be placed in the same position as if he had not defended and the party interrogating or seeking discovery or inspection may apply to the Court for an order to that effect, and an order may be made accordingly.

Rule 22 : Using answers to interrogatories at trial

Any party may, at the trial of the suit use in evidence any one or more of the answers or any part of an answer of the opposite party to interrogatories without putting in the others or the whole of such answer.

Provided always that in such case the Court may look at the whole of the answers, and if it shall be of opinion that any others of them are so connected with those put in that the last mentioned answers ought not to be used without them, it may direct them to be put in.

Rule 23 : Order to apply to Minors

This order shall apply to minors, plaintiffs and defendants

and to the next friends and guardians for the suit of persons under disablity.

Order 13 Rule 10 : Court may send for papers from its own records or from other Courts

(1) The Court may of its own motion, and may in its discretion upon the application of any of the parties to a suit, send for, either from its own records or from any other Court, the records of any other suit or proceeding, and inspect the same.

(2) Every application made under this rule shall (unless the Court otherwise directs) be supported by an affidavit showing how the record is material to the suit in which the application is made and that the applicant cannot without unreasonable delay or expense obtain a duly authenticated copy of the record or of such portion thereof as the applicant requires, or that the production of the original is necessary for the purpose of justice.

(3) Nothing contained in this rule shall be deemed to enable the Court to use in evidence any document which under the law of evidence would be inadmissible in the suit.

ORDER XVI C.P.C.—SUMMONING AND ATTENDANCE OF WITNESSES

Rule 1 : Snmmons to attend to give evidence or produce documents

At any time after the suit is instituted, the parties may obtain an application to the Court or to such officer as it appoints in this behalf, summons to persons whose attendance is required either to give evidence or to produce documents.

Rule 1-A : Production of witnesses without summons through Court

Where any party to the suit has, at any time on or before the day fixed for the hearing of evidence, filed in the Court a list of persons either for giving evidence or for producing documents, the party may, without applying for summons under R. 1 bring any such person, whose name appears in the list, to give evidence or to produce documents.

Rule 2 : Expenses of witness to be paid into Court on applying for Summons

(1) The party applying for a summons shall, before the summons is granted and within a period to be fixed, pay into Court such a sum of money as appears to the Court to be sufficient to defray the travelling and other expenses of the person summoned in passing to and from the Court in which he is required to attend, and for one day's attendance.

(2) *Experts.* In determining the amount payable under this Rule the Court may, in case of any person summoned to give evidence as an expert, allow reasonable remuneration for the time occupied both in giving evidence and in performing any work of an expert character necessary for the case.

(3) *Scale of expenses.* Where the Court is subordinate to a High Court, regard shall be had in fixing the scale of such expenses, to any rules made in that behalf.

M.P. Amendment—'*Exception*—When applying for a summons far any of its own officers, Government and State Railway administrations will be exempt from the operation of sub-rule (1).'

Rule 3 : Tender of expenses to witness

The sum so paid into Court shall be tendered to the person summoned, at the time of serving the summons, if it can be served personally.

M.P. Amendment :—

Substitute Rule 3 as under :—

3(1) The sum so paid into court shall, except in case of a Government servant or a State Railway employee, be tendered to the person summoned, at the time of serving the summons, if it can be served personally.

(2) Where a party other than Government in a suit requests the Court to summon a Government servant or a Railway employee as a witness or to produce official documents, the party shall deposit with the court a sum which in the opinion of the Court will be sufficient to defray the travelling and other allowances of the Government servant or the Railway employee,

as the case may be, as for a journey on tour and out of the sum so deposited the Court shall pay to the Government servant or the Railway employee concerned the amount of travelling and other allowances admissible to him as for a journey on tour.

Rule 4 : Procedure where insufficient sum paid in

(1) Where it appears to the Court or to such officer as it appoints in this behalf that the sum paid into Court is not sufficient to cover such expenses or reasonable remuneration, the Court may direct such further sum to be paid to the person summoned as appears to be necessary on that account and in the case of default in payment, may order such sum to be levied by attachment and sale of the movable property of the party obtaining the summons; or the Court may discharge the person summoned, without requiring him to give evidence; or may both order such levy and discharge such person as aforesaid.

(2) *Expense of witnesses detained more than oue day* :— Where it is necessary to detain the person summoned for a longer period than one day, the Court may, from time to time, order the party at whose instance he was, summoned to pay into Court such sum as is sufficient to defray the expenses of his detention for such further period, and in default of such deposit being made, may order such sum to be levied by attachment and sale of the movable property of such party ; or the Court may discharge the person summoned without requiring him to give evidence ; or may both order such levy and discharge such person as aforesaid.

M.P. Amendment—Insert the following between the words 'summoned' and 'as appears' in sub-rule (1) :

'or, when such person is a Government servant or a State Railway employee, to be paid into Court.'

Rule 5 : Time, Place and Purpose of attendance to be specified in Summons

Every summons for the attendance of a person to give evidence or to produce a document shall specify the time and place at which he is required to attend, and also whether his attendance is required for the purpose of giving evidence or to produce a document or for both purposes; and any particular document, which the person summoned is called on to produce, shall be described in the summons with reasonable accuracy.

Rule 6 : Summons to produce documents

Any person may be summoned to produce a document, without being summoned to give evidence ; and any person summoned merely to produce a document shall be deemed to have complied with the summons if he causes such document to be produced instead of attending personally to produce the same.

Rule 7 : Power to require persons present in Court to give evidence or produce document

Any person present in Court may be required by the Court to give evidence or to Produce any document then and there in his possession or power.

Rule 8 : Summons how Served

Every summons under this Order shall be served as early as may be in the same manner as a summons to a defendant and the rules in Order v as to proof of service shall apply in the case of all summons served under this rule.

Rule 9 : Time for serving Summons

Service shall in all cases be made a sufficient time before the time specified in the summon for the attendance of the person summoned, to allow him a reasonable time for preparation and for travelling to the place at which his attendance is required.

Rule 10 : Procedure where witness fails to comply with Summons

(1) Where a person to whom a summon has been issued either to attend to give evidence or to produce a document fails to attend or to produce the document in compliance with such summons, the Court shall, if the certificate of the serving officer has not been verified by affidavit, and may, if it has been so varified, examine the serving officer on oath, or cause him to

be so examined by another Court, touching the service or non-service or the summons.

(2) Where the Court sees reason to believe that such evidence or production is material, and that such person has, without lawful excuse, failed to attend or to produce the document in compliance with such summons or has intentionally avoided service, it may issue a proclamation requiring him to attend to give evidence or to produce the document at a time and place to be named therein; and a copy of such proclamation shall be affixed on the other door or other conspicuous part of house in which he ordinarily resides.

(3) In lieu of or at the time of issuing such proclamation or at any time afterwards, the Court may, in its discretion, issue a warrant, either with or without bail, for the arrest of such person, and may make an order for the attachment of his property to such amount as it thinks fit, not exceeding the amount of the costs of attachment and of any fine which may be imposed under Rule 12.

Provided that no Court of Small Causes shall make an order for the attachment of immovable property.

Rule 11 : Witness appears Attachment may be Withdrawn

Where at any time after the attachment of his property, such person appears and satisfies the Court—

(a) that he did not, without lawful excuse, fail to comply with the summons or intentionally avoid service, and

(b) where he has failed to attend at the time and place named in a proclamation issued under the last preceding rule, that he had no notice of such proclamation in time to attend, the Court shall direct that the property be released from attachment, and shall make such order as to the costs of the attachment as it thinks fit.

Rule 12 : Procedure if witness fails to appear

The Court may, where such person does not appear or appears but fails so to satisfy the Court, impose upon him such fine not exceeding five hundred rupees as it thinks fit, having regard to his condition in life and all the circumstance of the case, and may order his property, or any part thereof, to be attached and sold or, if already attached under Rule 10, to be sold for the purpose of satisfying all costs of such attachment, together with the amount of the said fine, if any.

Provided that, if the person whose attendance is required pays into Court the costs and fine aforesaid, the Court shall order the property to be released from attachment.

Rule 13 : Mode of Attachment

The provision with regard to the attachment and sale of property in the execution of a decree shall so far as they are applicable, be deemed to apply to any attachment and sale under this Order as if the person whose property is so attached were a judgement-debtor.

Rule 14 : Court may of its own accord summon as witnesses strangers to suit

Subject to the provisions of this Code as to attendance and appearance and to any law for the time being in force, where the Court at any time thinks if necessary to examine any person other than a party to the suit and not called as a witness by a party to the suit, the Court may, of its own motion, cause such person to be summoned as a witness to give evidence, or to produce any document in his possession, on a day to be appointed, and may examine him as a witness or require him to produce such document.

Rule 15 : Duty of person summoned to give evidence or produce document

Subject as last aforesaid, whoever is summoned to appear and give evidence in a suit shall attend at the time and place named in the summons for that purpose, and whoever is summoned to produce a document shall either attend to produce it, to be produced at such time and place.

Rule 16 : When they may depart

(1) A person so summoned and attending shall, unless the Court otherwise directs attend at each hearing until the suit has been disposed of.

(2) On the application of either party and the payment through the Court of all necessary expenses (if any), the Court may require any person so summoned and attending to furnish security to attend at the next or any other hearing or until the suit is disposed of land, in default of his furnishing such security, may order him to be detained in the civil prison.

Rule 17 : Application of Rules 10 to 13

The provisions of Rule 10 to 13 shall, so far as they are applicable, be deemed to apply to any person who have attended in compliance with a summons departs, without lawful excuse, in contravention of Rule 16.

Rule 18 : Procedure where witness apprehended cannot give evidence or produce document

Where any person arrested under a warrant is brought before the Court in custody and cannot, owing to the absence of the parties as any of them, give the evidence or produce document which he has been summoned to give or produce, the Court may require him to give reasonable bail or other security for his appearance at such time and place as it thinks fit, and, on such bail or security being given, may release him, and in default of his giving such bail or security, may order him to be detained in the civil prison.

Rule 19 : No witness to be ordered to attend in person unless resident within certain limits

No one shall be ordered to attend in person to give evidence unless he resides—

(a) within the local limits of the Court's ordinary original jurisdiction, or

(b) without such limits but at a place less than fifty or (where there is railway or steamer communication or other established public convenience for five sixths of the distance between the place where he resides and the place where the Court is situated) less than two hundred miles distance from the Court house.

Rule 20 : Consequence of Refusal of party to give evidence when called on by Court

Where any party to a suit present in Court refuses, without

lawful excuse, when required by the Court, to give evidence or to produce any document then and there in his possession or power, the Court may pronounce judgment against him or make such order in relation to the suit as it thinks fit.

Rule 21 : Rules as to witnesses to apply to parties Summoned

Where any party to a suit is required to give evidence or to produce a document to the provisions as to witnesses shall apply to him so far as they are applicable.

ORDER XVIII C.P.C.

Hearing of the Suit and Examination of Witnesses

Rule 1 : Right to begin

The plaintiff has the right to begin unless the defendant admits the facts alleged by the plaintiff and contends that either in point of law or on some additional facts alleged by the defendant the plaintiff is not entitled to any part of the relief which he seeks, in which case the defendant has the right to begin.

Rule 2 : Statement and production of Evidence

(1) On the day fixed for the hearing of the suit or on any other day to which the hearing is adjourned, the party having the right to begin shall state his case and produce his evidence in support of the issues which he is bound to prove.

(2) The other party shall then state his case and produce his evidence (if any) and may then address the Court generally on the whole case.

(3) The party beginning may then reply generally on the whole case.

M.P. Amendment—Add sub-rule (4)

'(4) Notwithstanding anything contained in this rule the Court may order that the production of evidence or the address to the Court may be in any order which it may deem fit.'

Rule 3 : Evidence where several issues are involved

Where there are several issues, the burden of proving some

of which lies on the other party beginning may at his opinion, either produce his evidence on those issues or reserve it by way of answer to the evidence produced by the other party ; and in the later case, the party beginning may produce evidence on those issues after the other party beginning may produced all his evidence, and the other party may then reply especially on the evidence so produced by the party beginning, but the party beginning will then be entitled to reply generally on the whole case.

Rule 4 : Witnesses to be examined in open court

The evidence of the witness in attendance shall be orally in open Court in the presence and under the personal direction and superintendence of the Judge.

Rule 5 : How evidence shall be taken in applicable cases

In case in which an appeal is allowed the evidence of each witness shall be taken down in writing in the language of the Court, by or in the presence and under the personal direction and superintendence of the Judge, not ordinarily in the form of question and answer, but that of a narrative, and when completed, shall be read over in the presence of the Judge and of the witness, and the Judge shall if necessary, correct the same, and shall sign it.

Rule 6 : When deposition to be interpreted

Where the evidence is taken down in a language different from that in which it is given and witness does not understand the language in which it is taken down, the evidence as taken down, in writing shall be interpreted to him in the language in which it is given.

Rule 7 : Evidence under Section 138

Evidence taken down under Section 138 shall be in the form prescribed by Rule 5 and shall be read over and signed and, as occasion may require, interpreted and corrected as if it were evidence taken down under that rule.

Rule 8 : Memorandum when evidence not taken down by Judge

Where the evidence is not taken down in writing by the Judge, he shall be bound as the examination of each witness proceeds to make a memorandum of the substance of what each witness deposes and such memorandum shall be written and signed by the Judge and shall form part of the record.

Rule 9 : When evidence may be taken in English

Where English is not the language of the Court, but all the parties to the suit who appear in person and the pleaders of such as appear by pleaders, do not object to have such evidence as is given in English taken down in English, the Judge may so take it down.

Rule 10 : Any particular question and answer may be taken down

The Court may, of its own motion or on the application of any party or his pleader, take down any particular question and answer or any objection to any question, if there appears to be any special reason for so doing.

Rule 11 : Remarks on demeanour of Witnesses

The Court may record such remarks as it thinks material respecting the demeanour of any witness while under examination.

Rule 12 : Questions objected to and allowed by Court

Where any question put to a witness is objected to by a party or his pleader and the Court allows the same to be put, the Judge shall take down the question, the answer, the objection and the name of the person making it, together with the decision of the Court thereon.

Rule 13 : Memorandum of evidence in unappealable Cases

In case in which an appeal is not allowed, it shall not be necessary to take down the evidence of the witnesses in writing at length : but the Judge as the examination of each witness proceeds, shall make a memorandum shall be written and signed by the Judge and shall form part of the record.

Rule 14 : Judge unable to make such memorandum to record reasons of his inability

(1) Where the Judge is unable to make a memorandum as required by this Order, he shall cause the reason of such

inability to be recorded, and shall cause the memorandum to be made in writing from his dictation in open court.

(2) Every memorandum so made shall form part of record.

Rule 15 : Power to deal with evidence taken before another Judge

(1) Where a Judge is prevented by death, transfer or other cause from concluding the trial of a suit, his successor may deal with any evidence or memorandum taken down or made under the foregoing rules as if such evidence or memorandum had been taken down or made by him or under his direction under the said rules and may proceed with the suit from the stage at which is predecessor left it.

(2) The provisions of sub-rule (1) shall, so far as they are applicable, be deemed to apply to evidence taken in suit transferred under Section 24.

Rule 16 : Power to examine witness Immediately

(1) Where a witness is about to leave jurisdiction of the Court, or other sufficient cause is shown to the satisfaction of the Court why his evidence should be taken immediately, the Court may, upon the application of any party or of the witness, at any time after the institution of the success take the evidence of such witness in manner hereinbefore provided.

(2) Where such evidence is not taken forthwith and in the presence of the parties, such notice as the Court thinks sufficient of the day fixed for the examination, shall be given to the parties.

(3) The evidence so taken shall be read over to the witness, and if, he admits it to be correct, shall be signed by him, and the Judge shall, if necessary, correct the same, and shall sign it, and it may then be read at any hearing of the suit.

Rule 17 : Court may recall and examine Witness

The Court may at any stage of a suit recall any witness who had been examined and may (subject to the law of evidence for the time being in force) put such questions to him as the Court thinks fit.

Rule 18 : Power of court to inspect

The Court may at any stage of a suit inspect any property or thing concerning which any question may arise.

ORDER XIX C.P.C.

Affidavits

Rule 1 : Power to order any point to be provided by affidavit

Any Court may at any time for sufficient reason order that any particular fact or facts may be proved by affidavit, or that the affidavit of any witness may be read at the hearing, on such conditions as the Court thinks reasonable.

Provided that where it appears to the Court that either party bonafide desires the production of a witness for cross-examination, and that such witness can be produced, an order shall not be made authorizing the evidence of such witness to be given by affidavit.

Rule 2 : Power to order attendance of deponent for cross-examination

(1) Upon any application evidence may be given by affidavit, but the Court may, at the instance of either party order the attendance for cross-examination of the deponent.

(2) Such attendance shall be in Court, unless the deponent is exempted from personal appearance in Court, or the Court otherwise directs.

Rule 3 : Matters to which affidavits shall be confirmed

(1) Affidavits shall be confirmed to such facts as the deponent is able of his own knowledge to prove except on interlocutor's applications, on which statements of his belief may be admitted.

Provided that the grounds thereof are stated.

(2) The costs of every affidavit which shall unnecessarily set forth of hearsay or argumentative matter, or copies of or extracts from documents, shall (unless the Court otherwise directs) be paid by the party filling the same.

ORDER XXVI C.P.C.

Commissions to Examine Witnesses

Rule 1 : Cases in which Court may issue Commission to examine witness

Any Court may in any suit issue a commission for the examination on interrogatories or otherwise of any person resident within the local limits of its jurisdiction who is exempted under this Code from attending the Court or who is from sickness or infirmity unable to attend it.

Rule 2 : Order for Commission

An order for the issue of a commission for the examination of a witness may be made by the Court either of its own motion or on the application, supported by affidavit or otherwise, of any party to the suit or of the witness to be examined.

Rule 3 : Where witness resides within Court's jurisdiction

A Commission for the examination of a person who resides within the local limits of the jurisdiction of the Court issuing the same may be issued to any person whom the Court thinks fit to execute it.

Rule 4 : Person for whose examination commission may issue

(1) Any Court may in any suit issue a Commission for the examination of :—

(a) any person resident beyond the local limit of its jurisdiction ;
(b) any person who is about to leave such limits before the date on which he is required to be examined in Court ; and
(c) any person in the service of the Government who cannot in the opinion of the Court, attend without detriment to the public service.

(2) Such Commission may be issued to any Court, not being a High Court, within the local limits of whose jurisdiction such person resides, or to any pleader or other person whom the Court issuing the commission may appoint.

(3) The Court on issuing any commission under this rule shall direct whether the commission shall be returned to itself or to any subordinate Court.

Rule 5 : Commission or request to examine witness not within India

Where any Court to which application is made for the issue of a commission for the examination of a person residing at any place not within India is satisfied that the evidence of such person is necessary, the Court may issue such commission or a letter of request.

Rule 6 : Court to examine witness pursuant to Commission

Every Court receiving a commission for the examination of any person shall examine him or cause him to be examined pursuant thereto.

Rule 7 : Return of Commission with depositions of witness

Where a commission has been duly executed, it shall be returned, together with the evidence taken under it, to the Court from which it was issued, unless the order for issuing the commission has otherwise directed, in which case the commission shall be returned in terms of such order ; and the commission and the return thereto and the evidence taken under it shall (subject to the provisions of the next following rule) form the part of the record of the suit.

Rule 8 : When depositions may be read in evidence

Evidence taken under a commission shall not be read as evidence in the suit without the consent of the party against whom the same is offered unless :—

(1) The person who gave the evidence is beyond the jurisdiction of the Court, or dead or unable from sickness or infirmity to attend to be personally examined or exempted from personal appearance in Court or is a person in the service of the Government who cannot in the opinion of the Court attend without detriment to the public service; or

(2) The Court in its discretion dispenses with the proof of any of the circumstances mentioned in clause (a) and authorises the evidence of any person being read as evidence in the suit, notwithstanding proof that the cause for taking such evidence by commission has ceased at the time of reading the same.

Rule 9 : Commissions to make local Investigations

In any suit in which the Court deems a local investigation to be requisite or proper for the purpose of elucidating any matter in dispute or of ascertaining the market value of any property, or the amount of any means profits or damages or annual net profits, the Court may issue a commission to such person as it thinks fit directing him to make such investigation and to report thereon to the Court.

Provided that where the State Government has made rules as to the persons to whom such commission shall be issued, the Court shall be bound by such rules.

Rule 10 : Procedure of Commissioner

(1) The Commissioner, after such local inspection as he deems necessary and after reducing to writing the evidence taken by him, shall return such evidence together with his report in writing signed by him to the Court.

Report and depositions to be evidence in suit. Commission may be examined in person.

(2) The report of the Commissioner and the evidence taken by him (but not the evidence without the report) shall be evidence in the suit and shall form part of the record ; but the Court or with the permission of the Court, any of the parties to the suit may examine the Commissioner personally in open Court touching any of the matters referred to him or mentioned in his report, or as to his report, or as to the manner in which he has made the investigation.

(3) Where the Court is for any reason dissatisfied with the proceedings of the Commissioner, it may direct such further inquiry to be made as it shall think fit.

Rule 11 : Commission to examine or adjust Accounts

In any suit in which an examination or adjustment of accounts is necessary, the Court may issue a commission to such person as it thinks fit directing him to make such examination or adjustment.

Rule 12 : Court to give Commissioner necessary Instructions

(1) The Court shall furnish the Commissioner with such part of the proceedings and such instructions as appear necessary and the instructions shall distinctly specify whether the Commissioner is merely to transmit the proceedings which he may hold on the inquiry, or also to report his own opinion on the point referred for his examination.

Proceedings and report to be evidence-Court may direct further enquiry.

(2) The proceedings and report (if any) of the Commission shall be evidence in the suit, but where the Court has reason to be dissatisfied with them, it may direct such further enquiry as it shall think fit.

Rule 15 Expenses of Commission to be paid into Court

Before issuing any commission under this Order, the court may order such (if any) as it thinks reasonab'e for the expenses of the commission to be, within a time to be fixed, paid into Court by the party at whose instance or for whose benefit the commission is issued.

Rule 16 : Powers of Commissioners

Any Commissioner appointed under this Order may, unless otherwise directed by the order of appointment—

(a) examine the parties themselves and any witness whom they or any of them may produce, and any other person whom the Commissioner thinks proper to call upon to give evidence in matter referred to him ;

(b) call for and examine documents and other things relevant to the subject of inquiry ;

(e) at any reasonable time enter upon or into any land or building mentioned in the order.

Rule 17 : Attendance and examination of witness before Commissioner

(1) The provisions of this Code relating to the summoning, attendance and examination of witnesses, and to the remuneration of, and penalties to be imposed upon, witnesses, shall apply to persons required to give evidence or to produce documents under this order whether the commission in execution of which they are so required has been issued by a Court situated within or by a Court situated beyond the limits of India, and for the purposes of this rule Commissioner shall be deemed to be a Civil Court.

(2) A Commissioner may apply to any Court (not being a High Court) within the local limits of whose jurisdiction a

witness resides for the issue of any process which he may find it necessary to issue to or against such witness, and such Court may, in its discretion, issue such process as it considers reasonable and proper.

Rule 18 : Parties to appear before Commissioner

(1) Where a commission is issued under this Order, the Court shall direct that the parties to the suit shall appear before the Commissioner in person or by their agents or pleaders.

(2) Where all or any of the parties do not so appear, the Commissioner may proceed in their absence.

As stated earlier Section 30 (b) of the Code of Civil Procedure, 1908, deals with regard to the issue of summons to persons whose attendance is required either to give evidence or to produce documents or other objects.

Section 32 of the Code empowers the court to secure the attendance of any person by coercive method by issuing warrant for arrest on attaching or selling his property or by imposing a fine or to order him to furnish security and in default thereof to commit him in civil prison.

Order XVI of the Code of Civil Procedure deals at length with the subject of summoning and attendance of witnesses. TheWaqf Board while holding enquiry can use and exercise all the powers but it cannot travel beyond the rules itself. Therefore, all the limitations which are applicable to the exercise of powers by Civil Court would equally apply to the Waqf Board also. The Board can impose a fine upon a witness who failed to appear before the court in response to a summon issued against him. Apart from this, the Board cannot impose fine.[144]

The Board cannot direct a witness to appear in person who is either exempted from personal appearance owing to privilege or position or being a pardanashin lady.

Order 18 of the Code of Civil Procepure deals with the manner of recording evidence and also its mode and order of production of evidence. Although in an inquiry the Board is not bound to follow the mode and order literally yet it would be necessary to follow the mode substantially.

Production of Documents

Section 45 of the Waqf Act, 1954, empowers the Board to ask any person for the production of documents relating to waqfs. This Section invests the Board with the powers exercisable by the Civil Court under the provisions of the Code of Civil Procedure. The provisions relating to production of documents are scattered in Code of Civil Procedure and besides Sections 30, 31, 32 the powers are further fully defined in Order 11 Rule 14, Order 13 Rule 10, Order 16, Rules 1, 6, 7, 10, 11, 12, 13, 15 and 18. According to Rule 14 of Order 11, the said Rule is an enabling provision and the court can exercise the power either *suo motto* or on application of the party.[145] It is necessary that the document must be in existence and in possession otherwise the party cannot be asked to produce the same.[146] The power can be exercised at any state of the case,[147] for non-production of document.[148] The Board cannot compel for the production of confidential documents like Income Tax returns *etc.*[149]

Under Order 13 Rule 10, Code of Civil Procedure court may send papers from its own records or from other courts. Every application made under this rule shall be supported by an affidavit showing how the record is material to the suit in which the application is made and that the applicant cannot without unreasonable delay or expense obtain a duly authentic copy of the record or of such portion thereof as the applicant requires, or that the production of the original is necessary for the purpose of justice. The documents so-called under this Rule, do not become part of the evidence in any proceedings unless they are admitted in evidence expressly.[150]

According to Order 16 Rule 1, the Court may issue summons to any person whose attendance is required to produce any document and such document may be produced by the person himself who is summoned to produce or he may cause the production thereof through any other person.[151] Under Rule 17 of Order 16 any person in a court may be ordered to produce any document then and there in his possession or power but the essential condition of the Rule being that the document must be in possession of the witness then and there.[152]

Rule 10 of Order 16 Code of Civil Procedure deals with coercive procedure to be adopted upon non-compliance with the directions contained in the summons. Rules 12, 13 and 15 are ancillary to Rule 10. These rules deal with the coercive process and its mode of enforcement. It was said in *Hirdey Narain* v *Emperor* that this rule is of penal nature and, therefore, it should be exercised cautiously.

Annual contributions payable to the Board

The main source of income of Waqf Board is contribution made by various waqfs in particular state. Section 46 of the Waqf Act, 1954, says that this shall be the duty of the mutawalli of every waqf to pay annually to the Board contribution not exceeding six per cent of the net annual income accruing in the state of the waqf as the Board may from time to time determine. The above contribution shall not be payable by the mutawalli of a waqf of which the net annual income does not exceed one hundred rupees.

The Waqf Board is given the power to reduce or remit such contribution for such time as it thinks fit.[153]

The mutawalli of a waqf may realise the contributions payable by him under sub-section (1) from the various persons entitled to receive any pecuniary or other material benefits from the waqf. However, the sum realisable from any one of such persons shall not exceed such amount as shall bear to the total contribution payable the same proportion as the value of the benefits receivable by such person bears to the entire net annual income of the waqf.[154]

Where the income of the waqf is available in excess of this amount payable as dues, the contribution shall be paid out of such income.

Sub-clause (4) of the Waqf Act, 1954, provides that the contribution payable under sub-section (1) shall be subject to the all outstanding dues of government and local authority *etc.* The arrears of these authorities be given first priority. The amount shall be recovered on a certificate issued by the Board after giving the mutawalli concerned an opportunity of being heard. The amount will be recovered as an arrear of land revenue.

The other Acts except Kashmir Act also contain more or less same provision. Under the Bengal and U.P. Acts also a contribution of six per cent of the income of every waqf has been prescribed.[165] Under the Bombay Act, a waqf is required to pay five per cent of the income of the waqf.[156]

Under the Bengal Act a waqf-al-aulad is required to pay only 25 per cent of the income of the waqf.[157]

Under the Kashmir Act, a waqf is not required to pay contribution from the income of the waqfs. In Kashmir a committee of waqf is in-charge of all income of the waqf properties within its jurisdiction and may freely spend it.[158] Therefore, in Kashmir the Committee of waqfs in an area does not require any assistance. Under the Kashmir Act a mutawalli is treated merely an agent. He is under the duty to carry out directions issued to him by the Committee.[159] These provisions of the Act are not in consonance with the principles of Muslim law and needs immediate attention of the legislature.

Under the Bengal Act, a waqf is required to pay 2 per cent contribution towards an Education Fund. There is no such provision in any other Act.

While computing the net income of a waqf the Central Act was allowing deduction on revenue, cess, rates and taxes payable to the Government or any local authority. In *G.M. Bhaimia* v *Madras State Waqf Board*[160] the Madras High Court also allowed deduction of expenses actually incurred in earning the income. However, the mutawallis took undue advantage of this decision. They claimed inflated costs. Therefore, Section 3 (g) of the Waqf Act was amended.[161] Now under the Act net income means gross income. Under the Act the old deductions have been retained.

The definition of the term 'gross income' under the Waqf Act, 1954, U.P. and Bengal Acts is same.[162] It is only under the Bombay Act that no deduction is allowed.[163] It is, therefore, submitted that necessary amendment be made in the statutes.

Under the Waqf Act, 1954, waqfs having an income of not more than Rs 100 are exempt from the payment of contribution. The other Acts are silent on this point. It is submitted that this is a good piece of legislation and can be inserted in other Acts also.

Under the land reform laws the States have fixed annuities in cases of religious and charitable endowment including waqfs. This amount is directly paid to the mutawalli from whom the Board demands the amount of contribution. It has been seen that considerable amount of contribution could not been realised.

Under the U.P. Act, the State Government is allowed to deduct on production of a certification to this effect by the Secretary of the Board, contributions payable by a waqf from the amount of annuity payable to it.[164] It is submitted here that this is a good piece of legislation and can be introduced in other Acts also.

Under sub-section (5) of Section 46 of the Waqf Act, 1954 if a mutawalli has received income of the waqf and has refused or failed to pay the contribution the same may be personally realised from him from selling any movable or immovable property belonging to him.[165]

The Bombay Act is also identical on this point.[166] However, it has gone one step further. It provides that if a trustee of a public trust has failed to pay the contribution the Charity Commissioner may direct the bank in which he or any person with whom any money belonging to the public trust are deposited, to pay the contribution from such money as may be standing to the credit of the public trust or may be in the hands of such person or may from time to time be recovered from or on behalf of the public trust by way of deposit by such bank or person and such bank or person shall be bound to obey such order. Every payment made pursuant to such order shall be sufficient discharge to such bank or person from all liability to the public trust in respect of any sum or sums so paid by it or him out of the moneys belonging to the public trust so deposited with the bank or person.

All lands belong to the state government. When a person acquires land from the state, he acquires it subject to the paramount right of the state to assess it for the purpose of revenue from time to time, according to the exigencies of administration, unleses by the grant the state has exempted the land from the liability.[167]

The State Government has, however, granted exemption to institutions of public religious or charitable nature from the payment of land revenue. According to sub-section (2) of Section 160 of the M.P. Land Revenue Code, 1959, the State government may grant such annuity not exceeding the amount of exemption from land revenue enjoyed by the holder as the State Government may consider reasonable for the proper maintenance or upkeep of such institution or for the continuance of service rendered by it. The Government will pay such annuity and the holder will pay the land revenue.[168]

There is also a provision of appeal. Any bank or person who has been directed to make the payment may appeal to the State Government. The State Government may after making necessary enquiry confirm, modify or cancel such order.[169]

Apparently this is a good provision and can be adopted in other statutes also.

Power of the Board to borrow

The Board can borrow money for giving effect to the provisions of the Act. The Board may 'however' obtain prior approval of the State Government for this purpose[170]

Waqf Fund[171]

There shall be a waqf fund. This fund shall consist of monies received as donations, benefactions, or grant received by the Board[172]. The Waqf fund shall normally be under the control of the Waqf Board. The Waqf Fund shall be applied for following purposes :—

(a) repayment of any loan ;
(b) payment of the cost of the audit ;
(c) payment of the salary and allowances of the Secretary and staff of the Board ;
(d) payment of travelling allowances to the chairman, members, secretary and staff of the Board ;
(e) payment of all expenses incurred by the Board in the performance of the duties *etc.*

After meeting out the above expenses the Board may use any portion of such balance for the preservation and protection of waqf properties or for such other purposes as the Board may deem it fit.

Budget of the Board

This is the duty of the Board to prepare a budget for the next financial year showing the estimated receipts and expenditure during that financial year.[173]

Accounts of the Board

This is the duty of the Board to maintain books of accounts *etc*[174].

Audit of the accounts of the Board

The accounts of the Board shall be audited and examined annually[175]. The auditors may be appointed by the State Government[176].

According to sub-section (2) of Section 51 this shall be the duty of the auditor to submit his report to the State Government. The auditor shall specify in his report all cases of irregular illegal or improper expenditure or of failure to recover money or other property caused by neglect or misconduct and any other matter which the auditor considers it necessary to report and the report shall also contain the name of any person who, in the opinion of the auditor, is responsible for such expenditure or failure and the auditor shall in every such case certify the amount of such expenditure or loss as due from such person. In short, the auditor has to report on the following matters—

(i) Whether and what are cases of irregularities ?
(ii) Whether and what are illegal or improper expenditure?
(iii) Whether there is any failure or omission to recover monies of the waqf?
(iv) Whether there is any failure or omission to recover property belonging to waqf ?
(v) Whether there is any wastage of money or other property and if so to what extent ?
(vi) Whether any illegal expenditure or failure to recover

money or property or any other loss or waste of the waqf property is due to non-feasance, misfeasance or malfeasance of the trustees ?

(vii) Whether there is any breach of waqf or any other person in the administration of affairs of the waqfs ?

(viii) Whether there is any misconduct of mutawalli or any other person in the administration of affairs of the waqf ?

(ix) Whether the accounts are maintained regularly and in accordance with the provisions of law ?

(x) Whether receipts and expenditure are properly and correctly shown in the accounts ?

(xi) Whether the cash balance and vouchers are in agreement with the accounts ?

(xii) Whether and what books were required by the auditor to be produced and whether they have been produced or not ?

(xiii) Whether an inventory of the movables of the waqf is maintained or not ?

(xiv) Who appeared before the auditor and furnished the requisite information sought for by the auditor ?

(xv) Whether any property or funds of waqf were applied for any object or purpose other than the objects of the waqf ?

(xvi) The amounts outstanding for more than one year and the amounts written off, if any.

(xvii) Whether tenders were invited for repairs or construction involving expenditure exceeding Rs. 5000/-.

(xviii) Whether any money of the waqf is invested contrary to the provisions of the Act ?

(xix) Whether there is any alienation of immovable property in contravention of the provisions of the Act. ?

(xx) Any other matter which the auditor may consider to mention looking to the expediency of a particular case.

State Government to pass orders on auditor's Report

The State Government shall examine the auditor's report and may call for the explanation of any person in regard to any matter mentioned therein, and shall pass such orders on the report as it thinks fit[177].

Sums certified due recoverable as arrears of Land Revenue

According to sub-section (1) of Section 53 of the Waqf Act, 1954, every sum certified to be due from any person by an auditor in his report under Section 51 unless such certificate is modified or cancelled by an order of the State Government made under Section 52, and every sum due on a modified certificate shall be paid by such person within sixty days after the service of demand for the same issued by the State Government.

Sub-section (2) of the above Section says that if such payment is not made in accordance with the provisions of sub-section (1), the sum payable may be recovered in the same manner as an arrear of land revenue. However, before taking any action the person concerned may be given an opportunity of being heard.

Section 53 is very widely worded. It includes every sum of money becoming due and payable under the Act. The Section covers all sums payable either on account of surcharge or fine imposed under the provisions of the Act. The present section makes the sum payable under the Waqf Act, 1954 as an arrear of land revenue for the purpose of recovery. It is, therefore, relevant to discuss in detail the provisions of recovery proceedings contained in the M.P. Land Revenue Code, 1959. Section 147 of the M.P. Land Revenue Code deals with 'process for recovery of arrear'. It reads as under—

An arrear of land revenue payable to Government may be recovered by a Tahsildar by any one or more of the following processes—

(a) by attachment and sale of movable property ;

(b) by attachment and sale of the holding on which arrear is due and where such holding consists of more than one survey number, or plot number by sale of one or more of such survey numbers, or plot numbers as may be considered necessary to recover the arrears ;

(bb) by attachment of holding on which arrear is due and letting the same under Section 154-A;

(bbb) by attachment of any other holding belonging to the defaulter which is used for the purpose of agriculture and letting the same under Section 154-A;

(e) by attachment and sale of any other immovable property belonging to the defaulter.

Provided that the processes specified in clauses (a) and (c) shall not permit the attachment and sale of the following namely—

(i) the necessary wearing apparel, cooking vessels, beds and bedding of the defaulter, his wife and children, and such personal ornaments cannot be parted with by any woman ;

(ii) tools of artisans and, if the defaulter is an agriculturist his implements of husbandary, except an implement driven by mechanical power and such cattle and seed as .may, in the opinion of the Tahsildar, be necessary to enable him to earn his livelihood as such ;

(iii) articles set aside exclusively for the use of religious endowments ;

(iv) houses and other buildings (with the materials) and the sites thereof and the land immediately appurtenant thereto and necessary for the enjoyment) belonging to an agriculturist and occupied by him.

Section 148 of the Code provides that the cost of recovery shall be the part of arrear. Section 149 provides for the enforcement of processes in other districts under clauses (a) and (c) of Section 147 of the M.P. Land Revenue Code, 1959. Chapter XI of the Code contains various other Sections which all deal with the mode of recovery and the various aspects and questions relating thereto. Section 147 (iii) is important to note here. Sub-section (iii) of Section 147 exempts articles set aside exclusively for use of religious endowments. Accordingly, even if a sum of money is to be recovered from the waqf, it cannot be recovered by sale of articles exclusively set apart for the use of religious endowments.

[No financial liability of Government].[178] This was repealed by the Waqf (Amendment) Act, 1964 (34 of 1964).

JUDICIAL PROCEEDINGS

Institution of suits under Section 92 of the Code of Civil Procedure, 1908[179]

The Waqf Board can institute a suit to obtain any of the reliefs mentioned in Section 92 of the Code of Civil Procedure, 1908, relating to any waqf. For filing a suit under Section 92, Code of Civil Procedure, the prior consent referred in Section 92 is necessary. The Board shall be necessary party in the suit relating to waqf property[180].

Section 55 of the Waqf Act, 1954, does not bar a suit by the managing committees of a mosque seeking an injunction against trespassers on the mosque land[181].

Sub-section (2) of Section 55 of the Waqf Act, 1954, says that no suit to obtain any of the reliefs referred to in Section 92 relating to any waqf shall be instituted by person or authority other than the Board without the consent in writing of the Board and for the institution of any such suit, it shall not be necessary to obtain the consent referred to in that Section, notwithstanding anything contained therein.

Provided that nothing in this sub-section shall apply in relation to any such suit against the Board.

Section 55 contemplates institution of scheme suits under Section 92 even after coming into force of the Waqf Act, 1954. The Act does not nullify, obliterate or affect in any manner the schemes framed by the court and in force on the date of the coming into force of the Act. According to Justice Ismail (as he then was) of the Madras High Court the scheme to be operative and that with respect to matters provided for by the scheme, it is the scheme that has to be implemented and acted upon[182]. The Waqf Board can apply for modification of an existing scheme under Section 55 of the Act, but the modification has to be and can be effected only by the court. It is always open to the Board to apply for modifications in accordance with law[183].

In *C.C. Peeran* v *State Waqf Board*[184] the scheme was framed by a civil court and which was in operation on the date of the coming into force of the Waqf Act, 1954.

It was said by Justice Venkatadri that on coming into force of the Act and in particular having regard to the language of Section 15 of the Act all the powers hitherto exercised by the Court under the scheme become exercisable and have to be exercised by the Waqf Board. It was, therefore, held that the plaintiff was bound to submit his accounts to the Waqf Board and also have it recognised according to law[185].

Institution of Suits

Section 73 of the Bengal Act, 1934 empowers the Commissioner to file a suit for the reliefs enumerated in Section 92. It Is not necessary for him to obtain the consent of the Advocate General, or for the reliefs referred to in Section 14 of the Religious Endowments Act, 1863, without the leave of the court. However, the consent of the Commissioner will be necessary if the suit is filed by other persons[186].

In *Mohammad Ghouse* v *Mohammad Yusuf*[187] the Division Bench of the Madras High Court was required to deal with the following issues :

Whether the mutawalli had failed to maintain proper accounts and whether he as manager had failed in his obligation by not keeping a reserve amount for the purpose of ultimate distribution of the net income to beneficiaries as directed (immediate distribution being impossible due to pending litigation) *inter se*. The beneficiaries alleged that for a considerable length of time they had been consistently appropriating a major part of the income towards monies allegedly advanced by him for the preservation and upkeep of the waqf properties.

For the validity of a waqf it is necessary that the corpus must be preserved in perpetuity. The usufruct, or net income after deduction for expenses of upkeep, remuneration of the manager, *etc.* must be distribution to the beneficiaries. This is the duty of the mutawalli to keep and render proper accounts.

The trial court was of the opinion that the manager has failed to perform his duties properly. The trial court found that although the manager could not pay anything to the beneficiaries (due to litigation pending regarding the respective shares due to them) 'he should have set apart and segregated a certain amount for (ultimate) payment to the beneficiaries' and that although 'the defendant may not be liable for non-payment of the income to the beneficiaries in the present suit' and even though misappropriation had not been proved 'there are circumstances which throw suspicion on the conduct of the defendant manager and the accounts maintained by him.'

The High Court rejected the above findings of the lower court on the ground that it reached in an impossible manner.

The High Court treated the plaintiff's failure to demand scrutiny of the accounts as conclusive in favour of the manager *inter alia*, that his accounts were in order. This attitude of the court, at least in the present case, is not appropriate in the case of waqfs which are the property of Almighty God and where the duty of the courts is to see that the waqfs are duly discharged. The elaborate discussion of the scope of a suit filed with the consent of the Waqf Board under Section 55 (2) of the Waqf Act, was not necessary at all.

The High Court of Madras held that the account books had not been scrutinised and adjudicated upon by the court below. The account books filed in the court from 1948 to 1970 have not been looked into and examined in a manner known to law. The High Court said that 'though the Books are in court the plaintiff did not request for a scrutiny of these accounts'. On this basis the High Court appears to have felt that the burden of proof on the plaintiff had not been discharged and the accounts submitted by the manager must be accepted as true and correct.

On the basis of this judgment it can be said that the High Court failed to make a satisfactory judicial probe into the affairs of the waqf before it. It appears that the waqf property was not properly managed by the manager. The court failed to scrutinise the account properly.

There was difference of opinion on the question of interpretation of Section 55 of the Waqf Act, 1954, and Section 92 of the Code of Civil Procedure. Prior consent in writing of the Board is necessary for instituting a suit for obtaining any of the remedies mentioned in Section 92 of the Code of Civil Procedure. Section 14 of the Religious Endowment Act, 1863, having been omitted by the Waqf Amendment Act, 1964.

Save as provided by the Religious Endowment Act, 1863, no suit in respect of waqf can be filed except in conformity with provisions of Section 92 of the Code of Civil Procedure. Section 92 says that if the relief sought by the plaintiff is in respect of a waqf for a 'public purpose' it shall be necessary for the plaintiff to obtain the prior sanction of the Advocate General for filing a suit. Two or more persons having an interest in the waqf may obtain the consent in writing of the Advocate General and may file a suit in the court of law. The parties can file the suit either in the principal civil court of original jurisdiction or any other court empowered in that behalf by the local government, within the local limits of whose jurisdiction on the whole or, any part of the subject of waqf is situated.

Under Section 92 of the Code of Civil Procedure the plaintiff can file a suit only for a 'public purpose'. A suit for breach of trust against the mutawalli's[188] removal or appointment of mutawalli[189] is a suit for public purpose and therefore the court's prior approval is necessary. It was said[190] that a suit in respect of private Imambara is not a suit in respect of a waqf for the 'public purpose'. If the suit was filed for the giving of delivery of property to the settler's family, no prior sanction of the Advocate General is necessary for filing the suit[191].

A mosque or a khanqah[192] is a waqf for public purpose and the suit in respect of it must be brought in accordance with the provisions of Section 92 of the Code of Civil Procedure.

In another case[193] the waqif dedicated his property in a waqf. He himself became the first mutawalli of the property. He also made a provision in the waqf deed that after his death the income was to be applied for the benefit of the mosque. The validity of this waqf was challenged. The court held that the waqf was valid. The court took into consideration the opinion of Abu Yusuf regarding the life interest. The court held that there was no difference between a waqf for a mosque and one for other charitable purposes. The court further said that it is also not necessary for a trustee to obtain sanction of the Advocate General under Section 92 of the Code of Civil Procedure for filing a suit against the stranger.

An important question as to whether Section 55 of the Waqf Act, 1954, has indirectly repealed Sections 92 and 93 of Code of Civil Procedure or Section 14 of the Religious Endowment Act, 1863, so far as waqfs are concerned. The Kerala High Court[194] has said that Section 15 and other Sections of the Act gives to the Board very wide powers and almost all the reliefs enumerated in sub-section (6) of Section 92, Code of Civil Procedure are within the powers of the Board. The Waqf Board is competent to grant the relief. In cases where the Board is not having the jurisdiction to grant permission, the Board is having two alternatives. The Board can either remove the civil court itself or grant permission to an interested person to file a suit. It was further said that so far as suits by private parties are concerned, Section 55 was meant to supplement and not to replace Section 92 of the Code of Civil Procedure and, therefore, apart from the consent of the Board, the consent of the Advocate General or the Collector as the case may be, shall be necessary for filing a suit.

The above ambiguity was realised by the legislature and, therefore, the Amendment Act, 1964 was passed. This amendment removed the above ambiguity. The Amendment Act, 1964 clearly states that the consent of the Board alone would be sufficient for filing a suit.

The Board's discretion to grant sanction is not a judicial or quasi-judicial decision. It is purely an administrative action and is, therefore, outside the purview of correction by the issue of a writ of certiorari[195].

Notice of Suits by the Parties against the Board

Section 56 of the Waqf Act, 1954 lays down that no suit shall be instituted against the Board in respect of any act purporting to be done by it in pursuance of this Act or of any rules made thereunder, until the expiration of two months next after notice in writing has been delivered to, or left at, the office of Board, stating the cause of action, the name, description and place of residence of the plaintiff and the relief which he claims, and the plaint shall contain a statement that such notice has been so delivered or left. Identical provisions are also made in Kashmir and U.P. Acts. Under these Acts also no suit shall be instituted against the Board in respect of any act purported to be done by it in pursuance of the Act or of any rules made thereunder, until the expiration of two months next after notice in writing has been conveyed to the Board[196]. This provision appears to have been made so that litigation may be minimised. The Board gets an opportunity to reconsider its decision. In this way a mutawalli is also prevented from initiating frivolous litigation.

The Bengal and Bombay Acts are silent on this important point. It is submitted that such a provision may be incorporated in these two Acts.

The court cannot make exceptions or qualifications to the explicit terms of Section 56 on account of consideration of hardship and absence of prejudice or detriment. A defect cannot be equated to a formal defect contemplated by Order 23 Rule 1 (3), Code of Civil Procedure. It is a radical defect going to the root of the claim of the petitioners. Section 56 is express, explicit, mandatory and admits of no exceptions. Therefore, the issue of a notice under Section 56 is a condition precedent to the institution of the suit itself. Cases where suits have been instituted without the issue of a notice in accordance with Section 59 are cases which clearly fall under Order 7, Rule 11 (d), Code of Civil Procedure.[197]

Notice of Suits, *etc.* by Courts

Section 57 of Waqf Act, 1954, deals with regard to the notice of suits, *etc.* by courts. Sub-section (1) of Section 57 says that in every suit or proceeding relating to a title to waqf property or the right of a mutawalli, the court shall issue notice to the Board at the cost of the party instituting such suit or proceeding.

Sub-section (2) of the same Section says whenever any waqf property is notified for sale in execution of a decree of a civil court or for the recovery of any revenue cess, rates or taxes, due to the Government or any local authority, notice shall be given to the Board by the

Court, collector or other person under whose order the sale is notified.

Sub-section (3) of Section 57 of the Act says that in the absence of a notice under sub-section (1), any decree or order passed in the suit or proceeding shall be declared void, if the Board, within one month of its coming to know of such a suit or proceedings applies to the court in this behalf. The question may arise whether the application under Section 57 (3) of the Act is required to be filed before the lower appellate court or before the High Court. According to Patna High Court such petition under Section 55 (3) of the Act is required to be filed in the High Court.[189]

Sub-section (4) of Section 57 says that in the absence of a notice under Section (2), the sale shall be declared void, if the Board, within one month of its coming to know of the sale, applies in this behalf to the court or other authority under whose order the sale was held. It has been judicially held that the absence of notice would not invalidate the proceedings under Section 4 (1) of the Waqf Act, 1954.[199]

The order passed by the High Court under Order 41, Rule 11 (1) of the Code is a decree. In *Secretary, Bihar State Sunni Waqf Board* v *Leela Devi*[200] the Waqf Board intended to get the decree set aside by filing a petition under Section 57 (3) of the Act. The order passed under Order 41 Rule 11 (1) of the Code is a decree.[201] In Leela Devi's case[202] the petitioner filed an application under Section 57 (3) of the Act to set aside the decree of the lower appellate court. Even if the decree of the lower appellate court is set aside, the decree of the High Court remains intact and, therefore, no purpose will be served to the petitioner in filing a petition under Section 57 (3) of the Act before the lower appellate court. It is also an admitted case that the petitioner filed such a petition after the High Court dismissed the appeal under Order 41, Rule 11 (1) of the Code. If it is so, the petitioner is required to file such a petition in the High Court and not before the lower appellate court. If there would have been no order under Order 41, Rule 11 (1) of the Code, then certainly the petitioner was entitled to file such a petition before the lower appellate court but so far as present case is concerned, the order passed, under Order 41, Rule 11 (1) of the Code is also a decree and, therefore, he is required to file such a petition before the High Court under Section 57 (3) of the Act and not before the lower court.[203]

The provisions of the Waqf Act, 1954, were made applicable to the State of Bihar since 12th April, 1973, and not before that. In the above referred case the appeal and the second appeal were dismissed after coming into effect of this Act. Hence, the petitioner is entitled to file such a petition before the High Court and not before the lower appellate court. The scheme of the Act is that no suit shall be instituted against the Board until the expiration of two months next after a notice in writing has been delivered at the office of the Waqf Board. Section 57 (1) of the Act provides that in every suit or proceeding relating to a mutawalli, the court shall issue notice to the Board. If no notice was issued to the Board under Section 57 (1) of the Act, any decree or order passed in the suit or proceeding shall be declared void, provided the Board files such a petition for setting aside the decree within one month from the date of knowing of such suit or proceeding. Therefore, the order passed by the High Court under Order 41, Rule 11 (1) of the Code on 27th January, 1978 in second appeal is the main decree which can be set aside by the High Court. The High Court can set aside the decree of the lower appellate courts as well. The lower appellate court cannot set aside the decree passed by the High Court under Order 41, Rule 11 (1) of the Code. The petition should, therefore, be filed in the High Court and not before the lower appellate court.

Whether under Section 57 (1) of the Act, the Court is required to issue notice to the Waqf Board as the suit or proceeding related to title to the waqf property. This question came for consideration before Rajasthan High Court in the *Board of Muslim Waqfs for Rajasthan, Jaipur* v *Bhanwar Chand*.[204] In this case the trustees of Khatargach sect instituted a suit on 20.3.1958, for declaration of title to and possession of 'nohra' against Managers of Masjid Khari, situated in Mohalla Teliwada alleging that the nohra belonged to Khattarga sect of Nagaur on which the defendants have taken unlawful possession. The defendants contested the suit on the ground that the nohra in dispute belonged to the Masjid and was under its possession for more than 60 years. The court decreed the suit on 31.7.1963. The defendants preferred the appeal on 28.8.1962 which was dismissed on 30.11.1963. The second appeal was also dismissed on 9.7.1969. Thereafter the Board of Muslim Waqfs for Rajasthan filed an application on 8.9.1969 under Section 57 (3) read with Section 151, Civil Procedure Code and prayed that the decree passed in second appeal be declared void as it was passed without notice to the Board, as the proceedings related to title to waqf property. The applicant contended that mutawallis informed the Board about decree on 2.9.1969. The Board was constituted on 6.8.1962. The application was silent about knowledge of first appeal or its decision.

It was said by Justice S.K. Mal Lodha of Rajasthan High Court that the Board was constituted on 6.8.1962, prior to the filing of first appeal (i.e. on 28.8.1962) and it was difficult to believe that the Board came to know of the suit only on 2.9.1969, (7 years after). Application thus was not within one month of knowledge of Waqfs Board.

It was further said that merely on the basis of list of waqf properties published under Section 5 (2), it would not be said that the suit was limited to title to waqf property, which was disposed of without notice under Section 57(1) of the Act

Proceedings under the Land Acquisition Act, 1894

Section 58 (1) of the Waqf Act, 1954, says that if in the course of proceedings under the Land Acquisition Act, 1894, or under any other law for the time being in force [Subs. by Amendment Act, 1984]. By waqf Amendment Act 1984, an explanation has also been inserted to Section 58 of the Act. it appears to the Collector before an award is made that any property under acquisition is waqf property, a notice of such acquisition shall be served by the Collector on the Board and further proceeding shall be stayed to enable the Board to appear and plead as a party to the proceeding at any time within three months from the date of the receipt of such notice.

Where the Board has reason to believe that any property

under acquisition is waqf property, it may at any time before the award is made appear and plead as a party to the proceeding.[205]

When the Board has appeared under the provisions of sub-Section (1) or sub-section (2), no order shall be passed under Section 31 or Section 32 of the Land Acquisition Act, 1894 without giving an opportunity to the Board to be heard.[206]

Any order passed under Section 31 or Section 32 of the Land Acquisition Act, 1894 without giving an opportunity to the Board to be heard shall be declared void, if the Board, within one month of its coming to know of the order, applies in this behalf to the authority which made the order.[207]

The Kashmir, Bengal and U.P. Acts also contain the same provision.[208]

The Bombay Act is silent on this point. Since this a good piece of legislation, it may be made applicable throughout the country.

Under the M.P. Land Revenue Code, 1959, where the area reserved for *abadi* is in the opinion of the Collector insufficient, he may reserve such further area from the unoccupied land in the village as he may think fit.[209] The provisions of the Land Acquisition Act, 1894[210] shall apply to such acquisition and compensation shall be payable for the acquisition of such land in accordance with the provisions of that Act.[211] Before a notification for acquisition of land for extension of *abadi* land may be issued, the conditions mentioned under sub-section (1) should exist. The Collector should form the opinion that the area reserved for abadi is insufficient. The other condition is that there should be no unoccupied land available for this purpose.

It is clear that the provisions of Section 243 of the M.P. Land Revenue Code are also applicable in the case of waqf property situated in rural areas. It is submitted that these provisions should not be made applicable in the case of waqf land situated in rural areas.

Commissioner to be made a Party to a suit or proceedings regarding a Waqf on its Application

Section 59 of the Waqf Act, 1954, says that in any suit or proceeding in respect of a waqf or any waqf property by or against a stranger to the waqf or any other person, the Commissioner [Subs. by Amendment Act, 1984] may appear and plead as a party to the suit or proceeding. The Kerala High Court said that the Mysore Waqf Board, as a party vitally interested in the upkeep, management and functioning of the waqf, has a right under Section 59, to appear and in case it desires to be impleaded as a party. The Waqf Board can approach the court during the pendency of those proceedings to be made a party thereto.[212]

Bar to Compromise of suits by or against Mutawalli

Section 60 of the Waqf Act, 1954, deals with regard to bar to compromise of suits by court against a mutawalli. Section 60 of the Act says that no suit of a waqf relating to title to waqf property or the rights of the mutawalli shall be compromised without the sanction of the Board. According to Madras High Court where the administration of a waqf is carried out in accordance with a scheme framed by the court in the course of a suit and the same is managed properly, no petition under Article 226, could be filed for any relief provided by the said scheme.[213]

A similar provision is also given under the U.P. Act.[214] In Bengal such a suit cannot be compromised without the sanction of each court and the Board,[215] Under the Bombay and Kashmir Acts, there is no such bar.

Power to make Application to the Court in case of failure of Mutawalli to discharge his Duties

Section 61 of the Waqf Act, 1954 deals with regard to the power to make application to the court in case of failure of mutawalli to discharge his duties. Sub-section (1) of Section 61 of the Waqf Act, 1954 says where a mutawalli is under an obligation to perform any act which is recognised by Muslim law as pious, religious or charitable and the mutawalli fails to perform such act, the Board may apply to the court for an order directing the mutawalli to pay to the Board or to any person authorised by the Board in this behalf the amount necessary for the performance of the Act.

Where the mutawalli has wilfully failed to discharge the duties assigned to him, the Board or any person interested in the waqf may make an application to the court and the court may pass such order thereon as it thinks fit.

In *Hamid Khan* v *Gowhar Bibi*[216] an application was filed under Section 61(2) of the Waqf Act for removing a mutawalli. The waqfnama provided that the District Court shall have jurisdiction to remove a mutawalli and appoint a new person. It was held that the application was not maintainable.

A new section entitled 61–A, Power of appellate authority to entertain appeal after the expiry of the specified period was inserted by the Waqf (Amendment) Act, 1984. According to this section where any period has been specified for filing of appeal, the appellate authority may entertain the appeal after the expiry of the said period.

Section 62 of the Act gives power to the Central Government to issue directions to the Waqf Board as it may think fit on questions of policy and for issuing such directions it may call for any periodic or other report or information from any Board through the Government of the State concerned.[217] While performing its duties the Board is guided by the directions issued under sub-section (1).

Directions by the State Government

Section 63 of the Act gives power to the State Government to issue directions on questions of policy to the Waqf Board. This power of the State Government is subject to any directions on questions of policy issued under Section 62. The State Government may give directions which it may deem fit and in the performance of its functions, the Board shall comply with any such directions.

Section 63 of the Act empowers the State Government to issue general or special directions to a Board constituted by it in the performance and functions of the Board. The general or special directions to be issued by the State Government, which, however, is subject to the policy directions of the Central Government, if any, issued under Section 62 of the Act, must relate to the performance and functions of a Board which are required to be complied with by the Board. But this power to issue general or special directions to Board in its working or in the performance of its functions cannot be construed as empowered the Minister for waqfs or the Government to interfere with the day today functioning of every waqf in the state. The Government cannot act as a manager, director, controller or supervisor of every waqf in the state.[218]

The State Government under Section 63, cannot stay the action taken by the Waqf Board for remission and non-payment of annual contribution and non-submission of settlement of account *etc.* For example, the M.P. State Government stayed the proceedings regarding remission and non-payment of annual contribution and non-submission of settlement of accounts of Jama Masjid, Katra Bazar, Sagar,[219] (M.P.). It is submitted here that the question of assessment and recovery of contribution is not policy matter and is not covered by Section 63 of Waqf Act, 1954. The Waqf Board has been given certain powers under the Waqf Act and can exercise these statutory powers without any restrictions. Issue of stay order is a judicial or semi-judicial power which can be exercised only when there is a specific provision to that effect in the Act.

In the case of *Haji Syed Md Hussain* v *State of Bihar*[220] the Division Bench of the Patna High Court comprising Chief Justice Singh and Justice Lalit Mohan Sharma said that the State Government has not been vested under the Waqf Act, 1954, with any arbitrary power to remove a mutawalli. The only purpose of Section 63 of the Act is to enable the Government to give lawful. special or general directions to the Waqf Board and the Board would in that case be bound to comply with them in the performance of its functions.

According to Patna High Court the language of Section 63 clearly suggests that what the State Government has been authorised to do is to give general or special directions to the Board and the Board would in that case, be bound to comply with them in the performance of its functions. It is not within the authority of the state to pass an order directly removing the mutawalli. The distinction between these two kinds of power is not formal in nature, it is vital in consequence.

Section 43 empowers the Board to remove a mutawalli from his office but only on specified grounds as detailed in sub-section (1) and that too only according to the procedure prescribed by Section 44 and 46 where they are applicable.

Section 45 require the Board to hold an enquiry in the prescribed manner and the procedure has been detailed in the rules framed under Section 67. Section 43 (1) indicates that there may be some cases in which the Board can pass an order of removal without holding a full-fledged enquiry as mentioned in Section 45. As for example, there may be a case where that mutawalli has been convicted of an offence of criminal breach of trust satisfying the conditions of clause (d). On the other hand, if there is any allegation against the mutawalli of misappropriating the property of the waqf, which the mutawalli does not admit, an enquiry will have to be held before coming to a finding on the disputed question. If that is not done, there will be a seriously violation of the principles of natural justice.

In the case of removal of mutawalli, the Board would not be justified in removing a mutawalli on the assumed ground of improper dealing with the property of the waqf, without holding an enquiry and without giving the mutawalli reasonable opportunity to meet the allegations. There does not appear to be any reason to depart from the plain grammatical meaning or Section 53 of the Act which indicates that the authority of the State Government is limited to give directions to the Board and not to pass order straight removing a mutawalli of a waqf.

The High Court, therefore, quashed the orders of the State Government, removing the mutawalli. It was left on the discretion of the authorities concerned to take action against the petitoner mutawalli according to law. He can be removed from his office if his case comes within the provisions discussed above.

Power to supersede the Board

Section 64 of the Waqf Act, 1954, is also very important. It gives to the State Government power to supersede the Board if the State Government is satisfied that the Board is unable to perform its duties or has persistently made default in the performance of the duty imposed on it or has wilfully and without sufficient cause failed to company with any direction issued by the central government or if the state government. is satisfied with the Board's continuance is likely to be injurions to the interests of the waqf. |Subs. by Amended Act, 1984] may also supersede the Board if it has exceeded or abused its powers. The supersession may be made for such period as the State Government may deem it fit. It is necessary for the State Government to give a reasonable time to the Board to show cause why it should not be superseded. This is also the duty of the State Government to consider the explanation and objections, if any.

The following shall be the main consequences of the publication of a notification of supersession—

(a) all the members of the Board shall as from the date of supersession, vacate their offices as such members ;

(b) all the powers and duties of the Board shall, during the period of supersession be exercised and performed by such person or persons as the State Government may direct and ;

(c) all property vested in the Board shall, during the period of supersession, vest in the State Government.

The State Government can also extend the period of supersession for such further period as it may consider necessary. It can also reconstitute the Board in the manner provided in Sections 10 and 11 of the aforesaid Act.

Section 64 gives to the State Government very wide powers which may be misused by it. The Act does not contain any guideline which the State Government may take into consideration while making an order of supersession.

The requirement that the State Government should give reasonable opportunity is not sufficient. In most of the cases State Government misused this power.

Protection of Action taken in Good Faith

Section 65 of the Central Act deals with regard to the bar of legal proceedings for Act done in good faith under the Act. This section says no suit or other legal proceeding shall lie against the Board or the Waqf Commissioner, Survey Commissioner [Subs. by Waqf (Amendment) Act, 1984] or any other person duly appointed under this Act in respect of anything which is in good faith done or intended to be done under this Act.[221]

The Commissioner, Auditor, *etc.* to be deemed to be Public Servants

Section 66 of the Central Act says that the Commissioner, every auditor, every officer and servant of the Board and every other person duly appointed to discharge any duties imposed on him by this Act or rules or orders made thereunder shall be deemed to be public servants within the meaning of Section 21 of the Indian Penal Code[222].

Special Provision for organisation of certain Boards

Section 66A[223] gives special power to the Government for reorganisation of certain Boards. Where on account of the reorganisation of State under any law providing for reorganisation of states [Subs. by Waqf (Amendment) Act, 1984] the functioning of the Board has been transferred to another State and, therefore, government come to the conclusion that the Board should be dissolved or be reconstituted and reorganised as an intra-State Board, Government may frame a scheme for such dissolution or reconstitution and reorganisation. The State Government may also prepare proposals regarding the transfer of the assets, rights and liabilities of the Board to any other Board. The government may also prepare a scheme of the transfer or re-employment of employees of the Board and the same may be forwarded to the Central Government. The Central Government may after consulting the State Government, approve the scheme with or without modifications[224]. The order may provide for all or any of the following matters, namely—

(1) the dissolution of the Board ;
(2) the reconstitution and reorganisation in any manner whatsoever of the Board including, the establishment *etc.* ;
(3) the area in respect of which the reconstituted Board or new Board shall function and operate ;
(4) the transfer, in whole or part, of the assets, rights and liabilities of the Board (including the rights and liabilities) under any contract made by it to any other Board or State Government and the terms and conditions of such transfer ;

(5) the substitution of any such transferee for the Board, or the addition of any such transferee, as a party to any legal procceding to which the Board is a party ; and the transfer of any proceeding pending before the Board to any such transferee ;

(6) the transfer or re-employment of any employee of the Board to or by, any such transferee. The terms and conditions of service applicable to such employee after such transfer or re-employment ;

(7) such incidental, consequential and supplemental matters as may be necessary to give effect to the approved scheme.

Where an order is made under this section transferring the assets, rights and liabilities of any Board, then, by virtue of that order such assets, rights and liabilities of the Board shall vest in and be the assets, rights and liabilities of the transferee.

Special Provisions for Establishment of Board for part of a State

Under Section 66-B, the State Government has been given special provision for establishment of Board for part of a State. It shall be lawful for the Government of the State to establish one or more Boards for such part or parts in which this Act is in force. The words any law providing for the reorganisation of any state as from the date on which that law comes into force were substituted by Amendment Act. 1984. Sub-section (2) of the same Section says where any such Board has been established and it appears to the government of the state that a Board should be established for the whole of the state. The State Government may dissolve the Board established for the part of the State or reconstitute and reorganise such Board or establish a new Board for the whole of the State and thereupon, the assets, rights and liabilities of the Board for the part of the State shall vest in, and be the assets, rights, and liabilities of, the reconstituted Board or the new Board, as the case may be[225].

Power to make Rules

Section 67 of the Waqf Act, 1954 empowers the State

Government to make rules to carry out the purpose of the Act. Under the aforesaid Act, the State Government can also make rules and procedures for the removal of the Chairman of the Waqf Board[226].

Accordingly the State of Punjab made Punjab Waqf Rules (1964). Under Rule 6 of the aforesaid rules, members of Board can remove the Chairman of the Board by passing vote of no-confidnece. In *Haji Anwar Ahmed Khan* v *The Punjab Waqf Board*[227] the petitioner Haji Anwar Ahmed Khan was the member of the Board. He was duly elected Chairman of the Board. Later on, the petitioner was removed by the members of the Board after passing of the no-confidence motion against him. The petitioner challenged his removal from the office of Chairmanship.

It was contended by the petitioner that there was no provision in the Act for passing a motion of no-confidence against the Chairman once he has been elected.

Justice Bhupinder Singh Dhillon said that it is accepted principle of common law relating to the removal of the holder of an office that the body which has authority to elect its Chairman, has the inherent and implied power to remove the Chairman[223].

Under Section 3 (e) of the Waqf Act, 1954, the word 'member' means a member of the Board and includes the Chairman. As is clear from the scheme of the Act and Rule 6 that after the members are appointed under Section 11 of the Act, the first meeting of the Board has to be convened by the Government as soon as possible by giving the members not less than 10 days' clear notice and in that meeting the Chairman has to be elected. It would thus be seen that there will be some time gap between the date of nomination of the members and the election of the Chairman. The Chairman continues in office on the strength of his being a member of the Board. It is, therefore, obvious that the period of five years shall start from the date when the members are nominated by the Government under Section 11 whereas the Chairman, in no case, can be there for complete period of five years. It will, therefore, be obvious that in view of the scheme of the Act, the word 'member' used in Section 12 cannot be held to include Chairman. Therefore, the tenure of the office of the Chairman is not fixed for five years and the same is at the pleasure of the members of the Board.

A meeting which has toconsider the motion of no-confidence against the Chairman should be convened by the Government and if the motion of no-confidence is carried, the members in the same meeting may be able to elect a new Chairman in accordance with Rule 6. In this view mere presence of the Chairman in the meeting convened otherwise than in accordance with Rule 6 for considering motion of no-confidence against the Chairman, would not disentitle him from claiming the relief against no-confidence motion especially when he protested that the members had no jurisdiction to pass No-Confidence Motion against him. Where there is no provision prescribing the procedure for convening a meeting for considering the 'No-Confidence Motion' against the Chairman, in view of the principles as contained in Section 21 of the General Clauses Act it would be legitimate to hold that the same procedure which is followed for electing the Chairman of the newly constituted Board, shall be followed for considering the No-Confidence Motion against the Chairman and if the No-Confidence Motion is carried, for electing the new Chairman. So also Rule 6 provides on quorum for the election of the Chairman. Since there is no provision of quorum as regards the meeting in which the Chairman has to be elected, the principles of common law would be applicable in this regard also, thus the Chairman has to be elected by majority of the members of the Board. It is, therefore, obvious that majority of the members or more would be able to elect the Chairman. Similarly, the motion regarding want of confidence in the Chairman, can also be carried if majority of the members vote for the motion[229].

Even after the removal of Chairman he continues in office till appointment of his successor is notified in official gazette.

Power to make Regulations

The Waqf Board can also make regulations not inconsistent with this Act or the rules for carrying out its functions under this Act[230].

The regulation may provide for all or any of the following matters, namely—

(a) the time and place of the meetings of the Board and the number of members required to form a quorum at its meetings;
(b) the procedure and conduct of business at the meetings of the Board;
(c) the constitution and functions of committees of the Board and the procedure for transaction of business at the meeting of such committees ;
(d) the allowances or fees to be paid to the Chairman or members of the Board or members of Committee ;
(e) terms and conditions of service of the officers and servants of the Board ;
(f) the form of application for registration of waqfs, further particulars to be contained therein and the manner and place of registration of waqfs ;
(g) further particulars to be contained in the register of waqf ;
(h) the books to be kept at the office of the Board ;
(i) the form in which, and the time within which, the budget of waqfs may be prepared and submitted by the mutawallis and approved by the Board ;
(j) the manner in which the accounts of waqfs may be kept and audited and the contents of the auditor's report ;
(k) the methods of calculating the income of waqf for the purpose of levying contributions under the Act ;
(l) fees payable for inspection of proceedings and records of the Board or for issue of copies of the same ;
(m) persons by whom any order of decision of the Board may be authenticated ;
(n) any other matter which has to be or may be prescribed.

Repeal and Savings

The main object of repealing and amending Acts is not to bring in any change in law but to remove enactments which have become unnecessary. Mostly, they expurgate amending Acts because having imparted the amendment to the main Acts, those Acts have served their purpose and have no further reason for their existence[231]. The repeal of amendment Act, therefore, has no repercussion on the parent Act which together with the amendments remains unaffected. The words "shall not apply to waqfs to which this Act applies" were substituted by Waqf (Amendment) Act, 1984.

A statute may be of two kinds *i.e.* it should be either perpetual or temporary. A statute is perpetual when no time is fixed for its duration[232]. A perpetual statute remains in force until its repeal. It may, however, be noted that a perpetual statute does not mean that it will never be repealed. It is prepetual in the sense that it will not be abrogated by efflux of time or by non-user[238]. A statute is temporary when its duration is only for a specified time. A temporary statute expires on the expiry of the specified time unless it is repealed earlier.

When a temporary Act expires, Section 6 of the General Clauses Act (Act X of 1897)[234] which in terms is limited only to repeal has no application.

The effect of expiry, therefore, depends upon the construction of the Act itself[235]. A temporary statute, even in the absence of a saving provision like Section 6 of the General Clauses Act is not dead for all purposes. The right or obligation resulting from the provisions of the temporary Act and their character may have to be regarded in determining whether the said right or obligation is enduring or not[236].

A power to make a law with respect to the topics committed to Parliament or State Legislatures carries with it a power to repeal a law on these topics. The power of a legislative body to repeal a law is co-extensive with its power to enact such a law and a legislature which has no power to enact a law on a particular subject matter has also not power to repeal the same.[237]

No repeal can be brought about unless there is an express repeal of an earlier Act by the later Act or unless the two Acts cannot stand together[238]. A repeal may, therefore, be by express words of a later statute or may be implied on considerations of inconsistency or irreconcilability of the provisions of an earlier statute with those of a later statute.

A statute after its repeal is as completely obliterated as if it had never been enacted[239]. It destroys all inchoate right and all causes of action that may have arisen under the repealed statute. Therefore, no proceeding under the repealed statute can be commenced or continued after its repeal.

Section 6 of the General Clauses Act applies to all types of repeals, the Section applies whether the repeal be express or implied[240] or whether it be repeal simplicitor or repeal accompanies by fresh legislation[241]. The Section also applies when a temporary statute is repealed before its expiry[242] but it has no application when such a statute is not repealed but comes to an end by expiry[243].

The effect of clauses (c) to (e) of Section 6, General Clauses Act is to prevent the obliteration of a statute in spite of its repeal to keep intact rights acquired or accrued and liabilities incurred during its operation and to permit continuance or institution of any legal proceeding or recourse to any remedy which may have been available before the repeal or enforcement of such rights and liabilities. The result is that the offences committed during the continuance of a statute can be prosecuted and punished even after its repeal. It may, however, be noted that any investigation, legal proceeding or remedy saved by clause (e) is only in respect of any right and privilege acquired or accrued and any obligation, liability penalty, forfeiture or punishment incurred within the ambit of clause (c) and (d) of Section 6[244]. Regarding other matters though acts done under the statute will not be invalidated after its repeal by virtue of clause (b) of Section 6, but they will be rendered abortive if no right was acquired or had accrued and no liability had been incurred prior to repeal[245].

The Waqf Board can also make regulations for carrying out its functions[246].

Section 69 of the Waqf Act, 1954, says that the following enactments, namely—

(1) The Bengal Charitable Endowments, Public Buildings and Escheats Regulations, 1810; (Bengal Regulation XIX of 1810);

(2) The Religious Endowments Act, 1863; (2 of 1863);

(3) The Charitable Endowments Act, 1890; (6 of 1890);

(4) The Charitable and Religious Trusts Act, 1920; (14 of 1920);

(5) The Mussalman Waqf Act, 1923; (42 of 1923) shall not apply to any Waqf to which this Act applies.

Sub-clause (2) of Section 69 further says that if immediately before the commencement of this Act in any state there is in force in that state any law which corresponds to this Act that corresponding law shall stand repealed.

It is clear from the above that the waqfs which are governed by the Act of 1954 are excluded from the application of the Waqf Act, 1923, and some other pre-1954 enactments relating to endowments and trusts.

It is, however, provided that such repeal shall not affect the previous operation of that corresponding law. Anything done or any action taken in the exercise of any power conferred by or under the corresponding law shall be deemed to have been done or taken in the exercise of the powers conferred by this Act.

The purpose of Section 70 of the Waqf Act, 1954, appears to be to remove any difficulty which may arise in giving effect to the provisions of the Act. The Central Government may, by order make such provisions, not inconsistent with the purposes of the Act, for removing the difficulty.

As already noted there are states where the Waqf Act, 1954 is not applicable. These States and their local Acts are as under—

(1)	Uttar Pradesh	—The U.P. Muslim Waqf Act, 1960.
(2)	Bihar	—Bihar Waqfs Act, 1947. This Act, was repealed in the year 1973. Now the Waqf Act, 1954 is also applicable in the State of Bihar.
(3)	West Bengal	—The Bengal Waqf Act, 1934.
(4)	Jammu & Kashmir	—The J & K Muslim Waqf Act, 1959.
(5)	Maharashtra	—The Bombay Public Trusts Act 1959. This Act is applicable in some parts of Maharashtra, which has already been discussed earlier.

In Tamil Nadu, in addition to the Waqf Act, 1954, state government has passed local legislation *e.g.* Madras Waqf (Supplementary) Act, 1961.

Dargah of Khwaja Moinuddin Chisti, Ajmer is not governed by the Waqf Act, 1954. There is a special Act which governs this shrine *i.e.* Dargah Khwaja Sahab Act, 1955.

Under the Jammu & Kashmir Muslim Waqf Act, 1959 the plaintiff[247] Suraj Ram filed a suit against the Waqf Committee for an injunction restraining them from evicting him from premises occupied by him allegedly as a tenant pursuant to proceedings earlier taken by the Waqf Committee against him. The Waqf Committee had passed a final order directing the plaintiff to vacate the said premises on grounds available under the said Act. This order was confirmed by the District Judge. It was admitted by the plaintiff tenant that he was the tenant of Waqf Committee and undertook to vacate the premises before the end of July, 1960

The main question before the court was whether the availability of two alternative procedures to the Waqf Committee—(one by way of regular suit and the other by summary proceedings under the Act) for evicting the plaintiff, who was a tenant of the Waqf Committee—rendered the summary procedure adopted by the Committee as discriminatory, unconstitutional and illegal by reason of Article 14 of the Indian Constitution.

Chief Justice Murtaza Fazal Ali of J & K High Court (now Judge of the Supreme Court) decided the case in favour of the Waqf Committee. He said that under Sections 43 and 44 of the Waqf Act, 1959, a procedure has been laid down which is almost as effective and exhaustive as that of a civil court. A tenant of Waqf property is given full and complete opportunity to defend himself and appeal against the order of the committee is also provided to the district Judge and the appellate order has been read final and cannot be questioned in any civil suit.

The judgment delivered by Murtaza Fazl Ali was in conformity to the equities of the case. It is, however, submitted that the above provision of the Waqf Act violates the constitutional guarantee of equal protection.

Under Section 11 of the J & K Muslim Waqf Act, 1959, a person is disqualified from being a member of the Waqf Committee if he is *inter alia* not a Muslim. For most of the functions of the Waqf Committee, this disqualification may be necessary and, therefore, justified. But the same disqualification may not be justified in view of Sections 43 and 44. Under these Sections, the Waqf Committee is vested with judicial or quasi-judicial powers, including powers to pass an order of eviction against any person including a non-Muslim in unauthorised occupation of any waqf property. Therefore, the above disqualification is undesirable. It is true that an appeal can be filed against the decision of the Waqf Committee, but the provision is no substitute for satisfactory judicial determination at the trial stage.

Removal of Difficulties[248]

If any difficulty arises in giving effect to the provisions of this Act, the Central Government may, by order published in the official gazette, make such provisions not inconsistent with the purposes of this Act, as appear to it to be necessary or expedient for removing the difficulty.

REFERENCES

1. See proceedings of the meeting of Muslim Members of Parliament held on September 6, 1953, New Delhi. (Ministry of S.R. and Company Affairs),
2. See Muslim Waqfs Bill, 1952, Part II; Section 2 of The Gazette of India, dated 26-7-1952.
3. See the Muslim Waqfs Bill, 1952 ; Report of the Select Committee p. 111.
4. *AIR* 1983 AP 63.

4A. Section 2 of the J & K Muslim Waqfs Act, 1959 says 'save as otherwise expressly provided, this Act shall apply to all waqfs whether created before or after the commencement of this Act. Provided that this Act shall not apply to any waqf created under or governed by the law applicable to Shia Muslims.

5. Section 3(i), (iii) and Section 3 (ii) of the Waqf Act, 1954 and J & K Muslim Waqf Act, 1959 respectively.
6. Section 6(ii) of the Bengal Act.
7. Section 2(19) of the Bombay Act.

8. *Tamil Nadu Waqf Board* v *Sannasi Munayathiriyan*, *AIR* 1982 Mad 293 ; *V. Mohammad Mohin* v *Madras State Waqf Board* *AIR* 1968 Mad 242.
9. It may, however, be noted that even before the passing of the Waqf Act, 1954, the judicial opinion was that a non-Muslim could lawfully create a waqf. See *Venkatasubbaray* v *Silar*, *AIR* 1930 Mad 582. In this case there was an endowment by a non-Muslim zamindar publicly made and recognised by the government. Wahace J. of the Madras High Court held that there could be no exception of any kind to the rule of Muslim law that no waqf can be endowed by a non-Mahommedan.
10. *AIR* 1974 Mad 255 ; see also *AIR* 1966 Mad 307.
11. See also *Tnmil Nadu Waqf Board* v *S. Syed Inam Saheb*, Mad 297.

11A. *AIR* 1983 AP 57.

11B. *AIR* 1980 VP 199, (1980) 1 Andh LT 467.

11C. *Supra* note 11A.

11D. *Tamil Nadu Waqfs Board* v *S. Syed Inam Saheb etc.*, *AIR* 1983 Mad 297.

12. *Mysore Board of Waqfs* v *K.S.L. Setty* *AIR* 1974 Kart 28.
13. See the proceedings of the Legislative Department, April 1908, Nos. 58-60, Part B.
14. See the Foreword of Sir Abdur Rahim in the book, *Hindu and Muhammadan Endowment* by P.R. Ganpathi, (Madras) (1918).
15. See Sections 4, 4A and 5 of the United Provinces Muslim Waqf Act, 1936.
16. See Section 4 of the Waqf Act, 1954, Chapter I—II of the U.P. and Chapter 2 of The J & K Muslim Waqf Act, 1959.
17. See Chapter IV of The Bengal Waqf Act, 1934.
18. See *Bangalore Corporation* v *Mysore Board of Waqfs*, *AIR* 1973 Mys 181.
19. *The Muslim Waqf Board, Rajasthan* v *Radha Kishan*, *AIR* 1979 SC 289.
20. See proceedings of the Inter-State Waqf Conference, 1960, p. 20.
21. An account of the survey of waqf properties and allied matters in Rajasthan, 1957-1964, p. 17.
22. See proceedings of the Inter-State Waqf Conference, 1960, p. 20.
23. See *Radha Krishna* v *State of Rajasthan AIR 1967* Raj 1.
24. See Section 6 (i) of The Waqf Act, 1954.
25. See W.P. 1142/66 decided by the Madras High Court on 7th April, 1969, (unreported judgement).

26. *Abdul Karim* v *Municipal Committee*, Raipur (1967) 2 SCJ 299 at 303.
27. See *City Corporation, Bangalore* v *Mysore Waqf Board W.P.* 4259/1968 decided by the Mysore High Court ; *Parwati Bai* v *Andhra Pradesh Waqf Board*, (1969) 11 A.W.R. 265. In these cases the judgment of Rajasthan High Court was followed.
28. *Ram Prasad* v *Magan Singh*, *AIR 1981* All 52.
29. *Vide* Ministry of Law and Justice letter No 6/1/72–Waqf dated 5.4.1972.
30. *Vide* GAD's memo No 1235/672/1/4 dated 4.3.1977.
31. See notification No 1309–(1)/IX168-37 dated 29 June 1937, issued by the Government of United Provinces.
32. See notification No 1309/IX-169-37, dated 17 June, 1937, issued by the Government of United Provinces.
33. See *supra* note 31.
34. *See* S Khalid Rashid, *Waqf Administration in India*, p. 65.
35. See an account of the survey of waqf properties.
36. Based on the letter No 1/12/71-Waqf, issued by the Officer on Special Duty (Waqf) Government of India, Ministry of Law and addressed to the Secretary, Government of M.P., General Administration Department, Bhopal.
37. Appeal No 772 of 1964 decided by the Supreme Court on 20-4-1967.
38. In respect of waqfs existing at the date of the commencement of this Act in the state or any part thereof.
39. See also sections 55 to 61 of the Act.
40. *AIR* 1979 SC 289.
41. *AIR* 1959 SC 198, (1959) SCR 1287.
42. *AIR* 1978 AP 34, (1977) APHN 182.
43. *AIR* 1978 AP 34 ; 1977 APHN 182.
44. *A.P. Waqf Board, Hyderabad* v *Bowlat Bibi* *AIR* 1983 A.P. 57, 62.
45. See also Sections 24, 46-54 ; 62-66.
46. See Chapter III of the U.P. Act.
47. See Section 8 (2) of the Bengal Act.
48. See Chapter II and III of the Bengal Act.
49. See Chapter II of the Bombay Act.
50. See Section 7, 8 and 13 of the J & K Muslim Waqf Act, 1959.
51. See Section 9 (1A).
52. See Section 8(2) of the Bengal Act, 1934.
53. See Section 11 of the U.P. Muslim Waqfs Act, 1960 and Section 8 (2) of the Bengal Waqf Act, 1934.

54. See Section 17 of the U.P. Muslim Waqfs Act, 1960 and Section 20 of the J & K Muslim Waqf Act, 1959.
55. See *V.J. Mahmood Naina* v *State of A.P.*, *AIR* 1976 AP 169.
56. *Ibid.*
57. *Tamil Nadu Waqf Board* v *Sannasi Munayathiriyar*, *AIR* 1982 N. 293 ; *V. Mohammad Mohim* v *Madras State Waqf Board, AIR* 1968 Mad 243, (1967) 1 Mad LJ 65.
58. Similar provision is also given in the U.P. Waqf Act, 1960. Section 17 in this Act has been incorporated with a view to taking care of the waqfs scattered throughout the length and breadth of a State.
59. Section 56-C of the Bombay Act. See also Chapter VII of this act.
60. *AIR* 1974 AP 287.
61. *AIR* 1982 Cal 288.
62. *AIR* 1944 Cal 206, (1944) 48 CWN 15.
63. *Sd. Abdul Latif* v *Commissioner of Waqfs*, *AIR* 1982 Cal 288.
64. *Mohinder Singh* v *Mohd Ibrahim*, *AIR* 1982 H.P. 95.
65. *AIR* 1967 AP 291, (1968) (1) (ALT 165, (1967) (1) An WR 221,
66. *AIR* 1964 A.P. 244.
67. Sub-clause (2).
68. Sub-clause (3).
69. Section 20 of the U.P. Act and S 21 of The J & K Muslim Waqf Act, 1959.
70. See Section 8 read with Chapter VII-A of The Bombay Act.
71. See Seetion 29 of The Bengal Act.
72. Sub-clause (3) of Section 23 of the Waqf Act, 1954.
73. Sub-section (2) of Section 25.
74. Sub-section (3) of Section 25.
75. Sub-section (4) of Section 25.
76. Sub-section (5) of Section 25.
77. Sub-section (6) of Section 25.
78. Sub-sections (7) and (8) of section 25.
79. *Muhammad Rustom Ali* v *Mushtaq Hussain*, (1920) 47 IA 224.
80. *AIR* 1967 Raj 1.
81. *Supra* note 79.
82. *Shah Mansur Peer Dargah and Others* v *State of Karnataka and Others*, *AIR* 1980 Karn 118.
83. See Section 23 (3) and 33 of The Kashmir and U.P. Acts respectively.
84. Section 19(i) and (ii) of The Bombay Act.
85. Section 46-A of The Bengal Act.

86. *Supra* note 82.
87. Sub-clause (1) of Section 29 of the Waqf Act, 1954.
88. Sub-clause 2
89. Section 31 of The Waqf Act, 1954.
90. Section 32 of The Waqf Act, 1954.
91. Sub-clause (1) of Section 33 of the Waqf Act, 1954.
92. Sub-section (2) of The Waqf Act, 1954.
93. Sub-clause (3) of Section 33, the Waqf Act, 1954.
94. Section 34 of The Waqf Act, 1954.
95. Sub-clause (1) of Section 35, Waqf Act, 1954.
96. Sub-clause (2) of Section 35 of the Waqf Act, 1954.
97. See Sections 49-A and 53(1) of the U.P. and Bengal Acts respectively.
98. Section 54-A of The Bengal Act.
99. *AIR* 1972 All 553.
100. *AIR* 1983 Mad 297.
101. See Section 49B and 54A of the U.P. and Bengal Acts respectively.
102. The Bombay Act is silent on this point. The U.P. Muslim Waqfs (Recovery of Waqf Property) Rules, 1972 contains exhaustive rules on the point.
103. *AIR* 1978 All 271.
104. Section 36.
105. *AIR* 1976 Pat 271.
106. Under the Kashmir Waqf Act, 1959, waqf committees are empowered to issue notice of eviction. In case the notice was not complied within 45 days, the committee or any officer duly authorised by the Committee may evict that person from, and take possession of the waqf property. In this connection the committee can also take the help of police. Under the Bombay (S. 41 (1) and Kashmir Acts (S. 36) no gift or sale of waqf property can be made.
107. Section 39.
108. Section 40.
109. *Commissioner of Wealth Tax* v *P.P. Waqf Board AIR* 1966 Ker 108.
110. Section 32 of the U.P. Waqfs Act, 1960 is identical to Section 29 of The Waqf Act, 1954.
111. Section 42.
112. *Syed Amjadullah Khodir* v *Muslim Waqf Board*, 1962 (2) An. W.R. 28 (NOC).
113. See *Dr. U.C. Mohammed Hashim* v *Tamilnadu State Waqf Board* (1980) 93 L.W. 546, (1980) (1) M.L.J. 235.

114. *Gulam Mohummed Mir Yaseen Ali* v *A.P. Waqf Board*, 1982 (1) ALT 70 (NRC), *AIR* 1983 NOC 43 (A.P.).
115. *Jamia Masjid Magadi* v *Karnataka Board of Waqfs*, *AIR* 1981 Kar 37.
116. *Supra* note 114.
117. For details see Sections 43 (4), (5) and (6) of the Waqf Act, 1954.
118. This clause became necessary because there were number of mutawallis who were not paying contribution to the Board and in some states heavy arrears have accumulated creating a difficult position for the Waqf Board. This provision, though may take time yet will definitely improve the financial position of Waqf Boards.
119. Section 43(2)
120. Sub-section (3) of Section 43 of the Waqf Act, 1954.
121. *Syed Niamutulla Quadri* v *A P. Waqf Board*, 1975 APHN 34.
122. Sub-section (4) of Section 43.
123. *Chhoteh Abdul Kader Saheb* v *A.P. Waqf Board*, 1981 (1) ALT 207.
124. Sub-section 4-A of Section 43 of the Waqf Act, 1954.
125. Sub-section (5) of Section 43 of the Waqf Act, 1954.
126. Sub-section (6) of Section 43 of the Waqf Act, 1954.
127. See *Sheikh Mastan Balvani Reddi AIR* 1953 959 ; *Sheikh Abdul Mannan* v *Mutawalli of Janebali*, *AIR* 1956 Cal 584 ; *Asad Raza* v *Waheecunnissa*, 57 IC 70.
128. See Sections 43 (4), (5) and (6) of the Waqf Act, 1954.
129. Section 26 (viii) of The J & K Muslim Waqf Act, 1959.
130. Section 50 of The Bombay Act.
131. Inserted by Section 14 of 1964 Act.
132. Section 43 read with Section 43. 43 (2) of the Act.
133. *Ibid.*
134. *Supra* note 114.
135. *AIR* 1954 SC 388.
136. Section 63 of the U.P. Muslim Waqf Act, 1960.
137. Section 66 of the U.P. Muslim Waqf Act, 1960, see also Amendment Act XXVIII, 1971.
138. Section 44 of The Waqf Act, 1954.
139. *Ghulam Sankadani* v *A.P. Waqf Board and others*, 1974 (2) An WR 372, 1974 APHN 283, 1974 (2) APIJ 118.
140. *Waqf Board, Hyderabad* v *Parvathi Bai*, *AIR* 1972 A.P. 333.
141. For example, Section 59 of the M.P. Public Trusts Act, 1951; Section 45 of the Waqf Act, 1954 ; *Spindles School Sati Tahilra-*

man *AIR* 1969 Delhi 7 ; *Munnalal Tiwari* v *Premehond Jain*, 1970 JIJ 718, *Umedi Bhhi* v *Collector*, 1969 MPIJ 680.

142. *AIR* 1935 mad 745.

143. *Thakarlal* v *Nathulal*, *AIR* 1964 Raj 140.

144. *Munnalal* v *Tara*, *AIR* 1929 All 850.

145. *Ibid.*

146. *Velayudham* v *Subramania*, *AIR* 1941 Mad 709.

147. *Puny Kalu* v *Shanker Kalu AIR* 1961 MP 348.

148. *See Shiv Sambhu* v *Raj Mohan*. *AIR* 1966 Tripura 16.

149. *Nagammi Achi* v *Alamelu Achi AIR* 1957 Mad 401 ; *supra* note 146.

150. *Gokul Prasad* v *Mahadevi Kaur*, *AIR* 1941 Oudh 341 ; *Jagannath* v *Kajoria AIR* 1951 Raj. 167 ; *Balwant Singh* v *Firm Raj Singh AIR* 1969 Punj 197.

151. *Netram* v *Bhagwan*, *AIR* 1941 Nag 159.

152. *Chinnaswami* v *Pichai Maricar*, *AIR* 1947 Mad 58.

153. Sub-section 2 of the Waqf Act, 1954.

154. Sub-section 3 of Section 46 of the Waqf Act, 1954.

155. See Sections 59 (1) and 34 of The Bengal and U.P. Acts.

156. Section 58 of The Bombay Act.

157. Section 59 1) of the Bengal Act.

158. Section 58 of the Kashmir Act.

159. Section 24 of the Kashmir Act.

160. (1968) MIJ 40 ; see also *Mohd. Ibrahim Sait* v *Kerala Waqf Board AIR* 1964 Ker 310.

161. The amendment was made by the Waqf (Amendment) Act, XXXVIII of 1969.

162. See Section 3(6) of the U.P. Act and Seetion 3(7) of the Bengal Acts.

163. See explanation (a) to section 58 of the Bombay Act.

164. Sec Section 35 of the U.P. Act, 1960.

165. See Section 34(5) of the U.P. Act and Section 59(1) of Bengal Act.

166. See Section 58 of the Bombay Act.

167. *Chintaman Rao* v *State of M.P.* 1971 ; R.N. 95 ; *Vinarjak* v *Collector*, Bombay, (1901) 26 Bom 339.

168. S. 160 of the M.P. Land Revenue Code, 1959 says—

(1) Every Muafi or Inam land wherever situated, which was heretofore exempted from payment of the whole or part of the land

revenue by a special grant from the Government or under the provisions of any law for the time being in force or in pursuance of any other instrument shall, notwithstanding anything contained in any such grant, law or instrument be liable from the commencement of the revenue year next following the coming into force of this Code, to the payment of full land revenue assessable thereon.

(2) Where any such Muafi or Inam land is held for the maintenance or upkeep of any public, religious or charitable institution, the State Government may, on the application of such institution in the prescribed form and made within such time as may be prescribed, grant to it such annuity not exceeding the amount of the exemption from land revenue enjoyed by it, as may be considered reasonable for the proper maintenance or upkeep of such institution or for the continuance of service rendered by it.

(3) The annuity granted under sub-section (2) shall be subject to such conditions as may be prescribed and may from time to time be reduced or withdrawn by the State Government.

(4) Where an application is made under sub-section (2) the recovery of land revenue from the institution concerned shall be stayed until the decision of the application.

169. See Section 59 (2) and (3) of the Bombay Act.

170. Section 47 of the Waqf Act, 1954.

171. Substituted by Act 34 of 1964, Section 17, for sub-section (1).

172. Section 48 (1) of the Waqf Act, 1954.

173. Section 49 of the Waqf Act, 1954.

174. Section 50 of the Waqf Act, 1954.

175. Analogous laws on this point are—S. 53 of the Andhra Pradesh Act ; S. 63 (4) of the Bihar Act ; S. 34 of the Bombay Public Trusts Act, 1950 ; S. 89 of the Madras Act ; S. 60 of the Orissa Act ; S. 34 of the Rajasthan Public Trusts Act, 1959 ; S. 53 of the A.P. Charitable and Hindu Religious Institutions & Endowments Act No XVII of 1966 ; S. 17 of the M.P. Trusts Act, 1951.

176. Sub-section (1) of Section 51 of the Waqf Act, 1954.

177. Section 52 of the Waqf Act, 1954.

178. Section 54 of the Waqf Act, 1954.

179. Substituted by Act 34 of 1964, Section 19 for Section 55.

180. Section 55(1) of the Waqf Act, 1954.

181. *Shahi Jama Masjid Merta* v *K.L. Bhagat*, *AIR* 1973 Raj 322.

182. *Palani Muslim Dharmaparipalana Sangam* v *Waqf Board*, (1957) 1 MLJ 201.

183. *Amjadullah Siddiqui* v *Mirza Nizamuddin Baig*, *AIR* 1982-A.P. 342, at p. 347.

184. *AIR* 1969 Mad 530.

185. See also *State of Madras* v *Mahalingaswamy Devastan*, ILR (1957) Mad 752 This was a case under the Madras Hindu Religious and Charitable Endowment Act, 1951. In this case a scheme was prepared before the coming into force of the above mentioned Act. The issue for determination was whether after the coming into force of the Act the Court continues to exercise the powers and performs the duties assigned to it under the scheme. The court held that all the powers conferred upon and all the duties placed upon the court in a scheme shall have to be performed from the date of the commencement of the Act, by the Area Committee, if there is one and in the absence of Area Committee by the Commissioner ; *Mayadhar* v *Orissa Board of Waqfs*, *AIR* 1966 Ori 208 ; *Narayana Murthy Acharya*, *AIR* 1925 Mad 411.

186. *Shahi Jama Masjid Merta* v *K.L. Bhagat*, *AIR* 1973 Raj 322

187. *AIR* 1976 Mad 371.

188. *F.A. Shihan* v *Abdul*, (1930) 58 Cal 474.

189. *Abdul Alim Abed* v *Abi Jan*, (1928) 55 Cal 1284.

190. *Asghar Ali* v *Delroos Banoo*, (1877) 3 Cal 324.

191. *Muhammad Shafiq* v *Muhammad*, *AIR* 1928 All 660 (1929) 51 All 30.

192. *Syed Shah* v *Syed Ali*, (1932) 11 Pat 288, 344-345.

193. *Amir Bi* v *Nilasandra Mosque*, *AIR* 1969 Mys 103.

194. *Mohammad Jacoe Sait* v *District Collector*, Trichur, *AIR* 1963 Ker 343.

195. *Abdul Kasim* v *Mohammad Dawood*, AIR 1964 Mab 247.

196. See Section 36 of the J & K Muslim Waqf Act, 1959, and Section 75 of the U.P. Muslim Waqf Act, 1960.

197. *Rahmat Bi* v *State Waqf Board*, *AIR 1982* Mad 202.

198. Secretary, *Bihar State Sunni Waqf Board* v *Leela Devi*, *AIR 1980* Pat 141.

199. *Mohammad Abdul Aziz* v *C. Bhumavva*, *AIR 1982* AP 357.

200. *Supra* note 200.

201. See *Batuk Prasad Singh* v *Ambica Prasad Singh*, *AIR 1932* Pat 238 ; *Annapu Ramanna* v *Ponduri Sreeramula* *AIR 1958* AP 768.

202. *Supra* note 200.

203. *Ibid.*

204. *AIR 1981* Raj 98.

205. Sub-section (2) of Section 58.

206. Sub-section (3) of Section 58.

207. Sub-section (4) of Section 58.

208. See Section 38 of the J & K Muslim Waqf Act, 1959; Section 74 of the Bengal Act, Section 67 of the U.P. Muslim Waqf Act, 1960.
209. Section 243 (1).
210. 1 of 1894.
211. Sub-section (3) of Section 243.
212. *Mysore Board of Waqfs* v *Mahboob Ali AIR 1962* Mys. 128.
213. *Fatheuddin Ahmed* v *State Waqf Board Madras, AIR 1966* Mad 307.
214. Section 69 of the U.P. Act, 1960.
215. Section 69 of the Bengal Waqf Act, 1934. This Section has been substituted by the Bengal Waqf (Amendment) Act.
216. (1977) APLJ 39 (NRC) ; (1977) APHN 317. In an unreported judgment of Andhra Pradesh High Court, a suit was filed for a declaration that the plaintiff is mutawalli of a dargah. Subsequently, Waqf Board and the government also became parties to the suit. Later on, the plaintiff and the Waqf Board entered into a compromise decree. There was no legal contract before the court so as to justify the passing of decree on foot of consent of parties. It was held there was no lawful agreement before the court so as to justify the passing of decree on foot of consent of parties. The Waqf Board is not the final arbiter in matters concerning waqfs because it functions subject to the control and direction of the State Government. When the latter vetoed the decision of the Waqf Board to enter into a compromise, there is an annulment of the subordinate body's decision. The compromise was entered non-est by reason of the action of the State Government and its opposition expressed in court to the latter's acceptance of the compromise. The compromise in question must be held to have been stripped to its base the amount the State Government acted under Section 63 notifying its direction that the compromise was not to be implemented—*Syed Akram Ali* v *Muslim Waqf Board, A.P. etc.* AAO 56/70 dated 30.8.1971 (unreported).
217. Substituted by Act 34 of 1964, Section 20 for Sub-section (1).
218. See *Masjid-e-Islammabad* v *The Karnataka Board of Waqf AIR 1981* Karn 154,
219. This is based on the letter No 131/1331/1 (4) dated 27th April, 1969, written by Secretary, Government of Madhya Pradesh, General Administration Department, Bhopal.
220. *AIR 1979* Act 103.
221. *S.J. Jafil* v *Aziz and other* 1969 (2) APLJ 206, ILR 1971 A.P. 558.
222. 45 of 1860.
223. Section 66-A was inserted by Act 34 of 1964.
224. Sub-section (2). This section has been amended by Waqf Amendment Act, 1984.

225. Inserted by Act 34 of 1864 Sec. 21

226. The State Government may particularly make rules in respect of the following subjects. (sub-section (2) of S. 67)

(a) the particulars which a list of Waqfs published under sub-section (2) of S. 5 may contain;
(b) the conditions and restrictions subject to which the Board may transfer any property;
(c) the regulation of the functions of the Boards;
(d) the terms and conditions of service of the Secretary of the Board;
(e) terms and conditions of service of the officers and servants of the Board;
(f) the form of application for registration of waqf, further particulars to be contained therein and the manner and place of registration of waqfs;
(g) further particulars to be contained in the register of waqfs;
(h) the books to be kept at the office of the Board;
(i) the form in which, and the time within which, the budgets of waqfs may be prepared and submitted by the mutawallis and approved by the Board;
(j) the manner in which the accounts of waqfs may be kept and audited and the contents of the auditor's report;
(k) the methods of calculating the income of waqf for the purpose of levying contributions under this Act;
(l) the circumstances in which, and the conditions subject to which, the Board may reduce or remit the contribution payable in respect of a waqf;
(m) the procedure to be followed in the recovery of any sum due under this Act as an arrear of land revenue;
(n) any other matter which has to be, or may be, prescribed;

227. *AIR 1980* P & H 306.

228. See also *Venkata Narayana* v *Deputy Registrar of Societies Eluru, ILR (1975)* AP 242.

229. See also *Dharam Singh* v *State of Haryana AIR 1974* Pun 99 1973 Pun LJ 554 ; *See Ram* v *Director of Panchayats*, (1974) Pun LJ. 52; *Hardatt Singh* v *Block Development and Panchayat Officer, AIR* 1976 P & H 122.

230. Section 68 (1) of the Waqf Act, 1954.

231. *Khuda Bux* v *Manager Caledonian Press, AIR 1954* Cal 484, p. 486. approved in *Jethanand* v *State of Delhi, AIR 1960* SC 89, p. 91.

232. See *Jotindranath* v *Province of Bihar, AIR 1949* PC 175 at 178.

233. *Hebbart* v *Purchase,* (1871) L.R. 3 P.C. 605 at p 650.

Metropolitan Police Commissioner v *Hammond*, (1964) 2 All E.R. 772 (H.L) at p 780.

234. Section 6 of the General Clauses Act, 1897—*Effect af Repeal*— Where this Act, or any Central Act or Regulation made after the commencement of this Act repeals any enactment hitherto made or hereafter to be made then, unless a different intention appears, the repeal shall not—

(a) revive anything not in force or existing at the time at which the repeal takes effect ; or

(b) affect the previous operation of any enactment so repealed or anything duly done or suffered thereunder; or

(c) affect any right, privilege, obligation or liability acquired, accrued or incurred under any enactment so repealed ; or

(d) affect any penalty, forfeiture or punishment incurred in respect of any offence committed against any enactment so repealed; or

(e) affect any investigation, legal proceeding or remedy in respect of any such right, privilege, obligation liability, penalty, forfeiture or punishment as aforesaid;

and any such investigation, legal proceeding or remedy may be instituted, or continued or enforced, and any such penalty, forfeiture or punishment may be imposed as if the repealing Act or Regulation had not been passed.

S. 6 A—*Repeal of Act making textual amendment in Act Regulation* Where any Central Act or Regulation made after the commencement of this Act repeals any enactment by which the text of any Central Act or Regulation was amended by the express omission, insertion or substitution of any matter then, unless a different intention appears the repeal shall not affect the continuance of any such amendment made by the enactment so repealed and in operation at the time of such repeal.

S. 7 *Revival of repealed enactments*—(1) In any Central Act, or Regulation made after the commencement of the Act, it shall be necessary for the purpose of reviving, either wholly or partially, an enactment wholly or partially repealed, expressly to state the purpose.

(2) This section applies also to all Central Acts made after the third day of January, 1868, and to a Regulation made on or after the fourteenth day of January, 1887.

S. 8 *Construction af references to repealed enactment*—Where this Act, or any Central Act or Regulation made after the commencement of this Act repeals and re-enacts with or without modification, any provision of a former enactment, then references in any other enactment or in any instrument to the provision so repealed shall, unless a different intention appears, be construed as references to the provision so re-enacted,

(2) where before the fifteenth day of August, 1947, any Act of Parliament of the United Kingdom repealed and re-enacted, with or without modification, any provision of a former enactment then references in any Central Act or in any Regulation or instrument to the provision so repealed shall, unless a different intention appears, be construed as references to the provision so re-enacted.

235. Steavenson v Olier, (1841) 151 E.R. 1024, pp 1026, 1027; see further *Spencer* v *Hooton* (1920) 37 T.L.R. 280; RV Ellis, (1921) (125 L.T. 397; *R.* v *Wicks*, (1946) 2 All E.R. 529, p. 531 ; *State of Orissa Bhupendra Kumar*, *AIR 1962* SC 945, p. 953.

236. *State of Orissa* v *Bhupendra Kurnar*, *AIR* 1962 SC 945.

237. *Ramkishna* v *Janpad Sabha*, *AIR* 1962 SC 1073, 1080, citing *A.G. for Ontario* v *A.G. for Dominion*, (1896) AC 348 (PC).

238. *M/s Mathra Prasad and Sons State of Punjab*, *AIR 1962* SC 745, p. 748.

239. *Keshavan* v *State of Bombay*, *AIR 1951* SC 128, pp. 131, 132; *State of Punjab* v *Mohar Singh*, *AIR 1955* SC 84 at p. 87.

240. *State of Orissa M.A. Tullocn & Co AIR 1964* SC 1284; p. 1294.

241. *Indira Sohanlal* v *Custodian of E.P.,.*, *AIR 1956* SC 77, p. 83.

242. *State of Punjab* v *Mohar Singh supre* note 241.

243. See effect of Expiry of temporary statutes, text and note 7.

244. *Director of Public Works* v *HO PO Sang*, (1961) 2 All E.R. 721 (PC) p 781.

245. *Ibid*, at p. 732; see also *Sonilal* v *Kanhaiyalal*, (1913) 19 IC 291 (PC) at p. 295.

246. Section 68 of the Waqf Act, 1954.

247. *Chairman Waqf Committee* v *Suraj Ram AIR 1976* J & K 14.

248. Inserted by Act 34 of 1964, Section 24.

9

Waqfs and the Constitutional Law of India in its Socio-Legal Perspective

Introduction

India is inhabited by various linguistic, religious, and cultural groups, so the judicial role becomes increasingly significant, in ensuring to the minorities a feeling of security and confidence, of consciousness of equality and of awareness that their rights are beyond the reach of the changing majorities. This judicial role in dispelling any fear from the minds of the minorities, a feeling of insecurity and aloofness, is intrinsically a part of social justice embedded in our constitutional policy behind safeguarding the interests of the minorities.[1]

The Constitution of India is based on secular principles. It is true that constitutionally India is a Secular Democratic Republic, yet we cannot lose sight of the fact that it is multi-religious state. It is a commonwealth of various religions. Therefore, difference of opinion and conflict is bound to prevail between different sections of the society. Indians are ignorant of the fact that religion is a matter for the individual conscience, practice and belief. It has no relation between state and individual. It cannot be a source of conflict between individuals and the State. Probably this fact was realised by Lord Buddha and he taught us the lesson of tolerance. After the advent of constitution the principle of tolerance was accepted as the basic feature of the Indian Constitution. The Indian Constitution guarantees to every person, equality, freedom of speech and expression, right to profess, practise, propagate and pursue religion according to his faith and belief. The Constitution provides equality before law[2], prohibition of discrimination on grounds of religion, race, caste, sex or place of birth[3], equality of opportunity in matter of public employment[4], freedom of speech[5], freedom of conscience and freedom of profession, practice and propagation of religion[6]; freedom to manage religious affairs[7]; freedom as to payment of taxes for promotion of any particular religion[8]; freedom as to attendance at religious instruction or religious worship[9]; protection of interests of minorities[10]; right of minorities to establish and administer educational institutions[11], *etc.*

The main aim of these provisions is to maintain a separation between the state and the religion. The Constitution makers felt this separation necessary since in India the followers of one or two religions are not living. India is the land of people having different language, culture and religion. The makers of the Indian Constitution were very far-sighted and they for maintaining the integrity of the country incorporated these provisions. Recently, in Sri Lanka many Tamil speaking people, who constitutes about 13% of the total population of that country were killed by the majority community *i.e.* by Sinhalese. This happened only because under the Sri Lanka Constitution the minority community *i.e.* Tamils have not been given equal rights. They are treated as second class citizens. In India, looking to the recent events in Punjab and Assam and in other parts of the country it has become necessary that the State should follow these provisions of the Indian Constitution rigidly. A distinction has, however, been always made between pure matters of religion and other religious matters, partaking of economic or social activities. In the case of former, state has no right to interfere. In the latter case, interference is permissible in the interest of public order, health, morality, *etc.*

The Nature and Scope of the Fundamental Rights

Since the advent of Indian Constitution there has been a large body of case law dealing with the fundamental rights set out in Part III of the Constitution. If some of these decisions have been criticised as less liberal than was contemplated, taken as a whole they indicate that the Indian fundamental rights are dynamic realities. The super-structure is rising on the foundations laid by the enunciation of the rights in the constitution, so that in the case of many of the rights, an estimate of their scope becomes impossible without reference to the case law, because the interpretation of the rights has often demanded an approach of a kind not contemplated by the ordinary rules of interpretation of statutes. The fundamental rights are not drafted in the same idiom. The Universal Declaration of Human Rights adopted by the General Assembly of the United Nations in 1948 did not profess to define these rights in terms, appropriate to their application by courts. They were stated in general terms, with qualification, except that they might be restricted to protect the rights of others they were a 'common standard of achievement' which all notions were 'to promote...by progressive measures'. They were, in fact, comparable to the Directive Principles in Part IV of the Indian Constitution rather than to the Indian Fundamental Rights.[12]

Equality before Law and equal Protection of Law within the Territory of India

Article 14 of the Constitution of India is based on the Fourteenth Amendment of the Constitution of the United States of America.[13] This article gives the guarantee of the Rule of Law. All the citizens are equal in the eyes of law and they should be given equal treatment. The state can, however, make a classification. A classification may not be merely arbitrary, but necessarily there must be a great freedom of discretion, even though it results in ill-advised, unequal and oppressive legislation[14]. The guarantee of the equal protection of the law means the protection of equal law. It forbids class legislation, but does not forbid classification which have upheld the validity of many different classification of persons.

The courts have said that a law applying to one person or one class of persons is constitutional if there is sufficient basis or reason for it. Therefore, the Madras High Court in *Lakshmlndra Thirtha Swamiar* v *Commissioner H.R.E.*[15] said that the classification of institution and endowments based on religion Hindu, Mohammadan and Christian cannot be said to be either arbitrary or unreasonable having regard to the object sought to be attained *viz.* the better administration and management of such institution.

The state is free to take up one set of institutions for legislative consideration at one time and enacting laws in respect of them, reserving the other types of institutions for consideration to a future date[16]. The confusion was made clear by the Supreme Court in *Moti Das* v *S.P. Sahi*[17]. It was said that while Article 14 forbids class legislation, it does not forbid reasonable classification for the purpose of legislation. In this case the constitutional validity of the Bihar Hindu Religious Trusts Act was questioned on the ground that the exclusion of the religious institutions of the Sikhs and the constitution of a separate religious Board for the Jains were discriminatory and violative of Article 14 of the Constitution. The Supreme Court rejected the above contention and held that there are some differences, between Hindus, Sikhs and Jains in some of the essential details of the faith which they profess and the religious practices they observe. The Supreme Court further said that there are also organisational differences in the matter of religious trusts between Sikhs, Hindus and Jains.

Freedom to hold Property

After coming into force of the Indian Constitution, stress was made for controlling and protecting the religious endowments. It was said that the Anglo-Indian laws were not sufficient. Looking to the fact that many waqfs were mismanaged, some amount of control or supervision over their administration was considered necessary in the interest of public as a whole. However, the state felt inability to make any law on the subject as it was considered to amount interference into the internal affairs of these institutions. It was said that under the Indian Constitution, state is not given the right to interfere in the establishment or maintenance of religious affairs. The various religious denominations are given liberty to manage them in accordance with the tenets of their religions. The state can interfere into the secular affairs of a waqf only on the grounds of public order, health and morality. It was not possible for the state to prevent the creation of religious trust. It cannot control the exercise of the manager's powers. Similarly, it cannot check that the capital and income of the endowed properties are used in the public interest.[18] It was argued that essential religious rights had to be protected. But at the same time it was said that there was a need for control. It was admitted that religious rights were to be protected and the exact scope of protection and control was left undefined.[19] Again, the move for control was revived. In the meantime, the Report of the Hindu Religious Endowments Commission, 1962 was released. This report was welcomed as a guideline for the control of both Hindu and Muslim endowments.[20]

The Indian Constitution does not define the term property. The courts held that those in charge of religious endowments were not really having property rights and, therefore, not amenable.[21]

The Commission on Hindu Religious Endowments in its report of May 10, 1962 made the following observations :—

> These laws have ensured a minimum degree of efficiency and a legitimate disposition and utilisation of the funds of the institution concerned. Where, however, there has been no legislation at all and the only possible recourse is to the ill-defined executive authority of the Government with a residual and ultimate resort to courts ...Under Section 92 of the Code of Civil Procedure, 1908, the position is not unsatisfactory.

The Commission said that in West Bengal which has no law relating to religious endowments, important temples were regarded as private property and 'no check or scrutiny of the resources is exercised or contemplated.'

All is not well with religious institutions even now. The Commission on Hindu Religious Endowments said :[22]

> A large number of witnesses have testified before us that many *mahants* and trustees have either alienated the property of the endowments to third parties or favoured dependents of nominees or treated such property as their own private property so that it may pass on to their own children or dependents of nominees or treated such property as their own private property so that it may pass on to their own children or dependents. In addition it is also complained that these *mahants* and trustees have neglected the temples in their charge—(and) there have been literally hundreds of cases in which the head of a mutt or the *dharmakarta*, shebait or trustee of a temple or othei religious foundations has burdened or alienated the properties of the mutt or endowment to the serious detriment of the trust. In most, if not all cases, some valuable consideration is alleged in the deed of alienation. The evidence before us is to the effect that generally such recitals are either false...colourable or *benami* transaction.

The above practice was not prevalent only among Hindu community. The same was also prevalent among Muslims. There were reports to the government of the misappropriation of property of the dargah at Ajmer. The government, therefore, appointed the Ghulam Hasan Committee. The report of the Dargah Khwaja Saheb (Ajmer) Committee of Enquiry[23] indicted the Khadims as 'parasites' and 'unscrupulous persons' trading in the name of the holy saint. The Committee exposed the glaring malpractices of the Khadims and others in respect of several matters connected with the Dargah.[24]

During the course cf debates in the Uttar Pradesh Vidhan Sabha, it was 'dens of vice' that every year donations from pilgrims valued at rupees ten crores were misappropriated[25].

Under these circumstances, if the reliligious institutions are left untouched by the legislatures then in other words government will be encouraging corruption and maladministration. Such freedom will certainly bring about the extinction through bankruptcy. In this state of affairs secular checks and controls are absolutely essential for the very survival of men of these institutions. The state has, therefore, undertaken the supervision of administration of the endowed property of religious institutions.

Looking to the above sorry state of affairs, state decided to control only public, religious and charitable trusts. The Regulations of 1810, 1817 and 1827, the Acts of 1863, 1890 and 1920, Section 529 of the Code of Civil Procedure, 1877, and section 92 of the same Code of 1908, the Orissa Hindu Religious Endowments Act, 1939, the Bombay Public Trusts, Act, 1950, and the Madras Hindu Religious and Charitable Act, 1951 were all applicable only to public religious institutions and endowments.[26] However, the state has not undertaken to take the control of private trusts and if state interference in the private trusts, the action of the state will be unconstitutional.

Articles 25 and 26 of the Indian Constitution guarantees right to freedom of religion. This guarantee has been again affirmed and supplemented by Articles 27 to 30 of the Indian Constitution. Articles 25 and 26 protect matters of religious doctrine of belief as well as acts done in pursuance of religion-——rituals, observances, ceremonies and modes of worship. The importance of these articles and particularly Articles 25 and 26 was discussed by Justice N. Rajagopala of the Supreme Court of India in *Sardar Syedna Taher Saheb* v *State of Bombay*[27] in the following words :

> ...these articles embody the principles of religious toleration that has been the characteristic feature of Indian civilisation from the state of history, the instances and periods when this feature was absent being merely temporary aberrations, besides, they serve to emphasize the secular nature of Indian democracy which the founding fathers considered should be the very basis of the constitution.

The word 'Religion' not defined

Articles 25 and 26 of the Indian Constitution guarantee right to freedom of religion. Article 25[28] guarantees to every person and not merely the citizens of India, the freedom of conscience and the right freely to profess, practice and propagate religion. This freedom is subject to power of the state to regulate the freedom on account of public order, health and morality. Further sub-clause (a) of clause (2) saves the power of the state to make laws regulating or restricting any economic, financial, political or secular activity which may be associated with religious practice. Under sub-clause (b) of this Artiele, state can make laws providing for social welfare and social reform even though they might interfere with religious practice.

The Constitution makers have deliberately not defined the term 'religion'. It is also not possible to lay down an exhaustive definition of this term which would be applicable to all classes of persons. In India religion is not necessarily theistic and in fact there are well-known religions in India like Buddhism and Jainism which do not believe in the existence of God or of any Intelligent First Cause.

In *Narayanan Nambudripad* v *State of Madras*[29] Justice V. Aiyar referred the following observations of Chief Justice Lathem which he made in *Adelaide Company of Jehovah's Witnesses Inc* v *The Commonwealth*[30]. These observations were made while dealing with section[31] 116 of the Australian Constitution.

> It would be difficult, if not impossible, to devise a definition of religion which would satisfy the adherents of all the many and various religions which exist, or have existed, in the world. There are the those who regard religion as consisting principally in a system of belief or statement of doctrine. So viewed religion may be either true or false. Others are more inclined to regard religion as prescribing a code of conduct. So viewed a religion may be good or bad. There are others who pay greater attention to religion as involving some prescribed form or ritual or religious observance. Many religious conflicts have been concerned with matters of ritual and observance. Section 116 must be regarded as operating in relation to all these aspects of religion, irrespective of varying opinions in the community as to the truth of particular religious doctrines, as to the goodness of conduct prescribed by a particular religion, or as to the propriety of any particular religious observance'.

After carefully examining the definition of religion given in *Davis* v *Benson*[32] the Supreme Court adopted the observations of Chief Justice Lathem in *Adelaide Co. of Jehovah's Witnesses Inc.* v *The Commonwealth*[33].

It is sometimes suggested in discussion of the subject of freedom of religion that, though the civil government should not interfere with religious opinions, it nevertheless may deal as it pleases with any acts which are done in pursuance of religious belief without infringing the principle of freedom of religion. It appears to me to be difficult to maintain this distinction as relevant to the interpretation of section 116. The section refers in express terms to the exercise of religion, and, therefore, it is intended to protect from the operation of any Commonwealth laws acts which are done in the exercise of religion. Thus the section goes far beyond protecting liberty of opinion. It protects also acts done in pursuance of relgious beliefs as part of religion.

The followers of a particular religion have faith in a system of beliefs and doctrines, which are regarded by those, who profess that religion, to be conducive to their spiritual well-being. A religion is not merely opinion, doctrine or belief, it has its outward expression in acts as well. It has been, therefore, said that religious practices or performance of acts in pursuance of religious beliefs are as much a part of religion as faith or belief in particular doctrine. Therefore, their lordship of the Supreme Court in *Ratilal* v *State of Bombay*[34] said that if the tenets of the Jain or Parsi religion lay down their certain rites and ceremonies are to be performed at certain times and in a particular manner, no outside authority has any right to say that these are not essential parts of religion and it is not open to the secular authority of the state to restrict or prohibit them in any manner they like under the guise of administering the trust estate. In Ratilal's case the provisions of Bombay Public Trusts Act, 1950 were challenged as violating Articles 24 and 26 of the Constitution. In this case two connected appeals were filed. In the first, the appellant was a *vahivtdar* or manager of a Jain public temple or *derasar*. In the second, the appellants were the trustees of the Parsi Panchayat. As regards the tenets of the Zoroastrian religion, the Supreme Court cited with approval the following observations of Justice Davar in *Jamshedji* v *Soonabai*[35]. In this case Justice Davar upheld the bequest of property by a Parsi for the perpetual performance of ceremonies like *Muktad, baj, yejushni, etc.*

> If this is the belief of the community—and it is proved undoubtedly to be the belief of the Zoroastrian community —a secular Judge is bound to accept that belief—it is not for him to sit in judgment on that belief—he has no right to interfere with the conscience of a donor who makes a gift in favour of what he believes to be the advancement of his religion and for the welfare of his community or of mankind.

A religion may not lay down a code of ethical rules for its followers to accept, it might prescribe rituals and observances, ceremonies and modes of worship, which are regarded as internal parts of religions and these forms and observances might extend even to matters of food and dress. It was, therefore, said that the guarantee under the constitution not only protects the freedom of religious opinion but it protects also acts done in pursuance of a religious belief which is very clear by the expression 'practice of religion' in Article 25[36]. There is, however, difference between the practices which are essential and integral part of religion and those which are purely secular practices[37].

Denominations, its Meaning and Significance

Under Article 26[38] of the Indian Constitution every religious denomination or a section of its has guaranteed right to establish and maintain institutions for religious and charitable purposes and to manage in its own way all affairs in matters of religion. These denominations or a section of it can also acquire and own movable and immovable properties and to administer such properties in accordance with law. In short, these institutions are entitled to administer themselves. The state can, however, make rules and regulations for the proper administration of these institutions. However, the state cannot make a law which may take away the whole right of administration.

The word denomination means a particular religious body with special beliefs different from those of others with the same religious faith.[39] It is a collection of individuals, classed together under the same name, (now almost always), especially a religious sect or body having a common faith and organisation and designated by a distinctive name.[40]

The Supreme Court referred the definition of 'denomination' given in the Oxford dictionary, namely, 'a collection of individuals classed together under the same name a religious sect or body having a common faith and organisation and designated by a distinctive name'. It further said that each one of the sects and sub-sects of Hindus could certainly be called a religious denomination.[41] This also includes among Muslim Sunnis and Shias. They constitute separate religious denominations. Hanafees, Shafees *etc.* are the sub-sects of Sunnis. Similarly, Daoodi Bohras community is a sub-sect of the Shias.[42] Article 26 contemplates not only a religious denomination. It also deals a section thereof.[43] Therefore, a Mutt or spiritual fraternity represented by it was a religious denomination under Article 26. Among Christians there are many denominations similarly among Muslims there are many denominations. The members belonging to each of these religions would be a denomination.

State can impose Restrictions in the Exercise of Right under Arts. 25 and 26

Under Articles 25 and 26 of the Indian Constitution state can impose restrictions on the grounds of public order, morality and health. Under Article 25 sub-clause (2) (a) state can regulate or restrict any economic, financial, political and other secular activities which may be associated with religious practice. Under Article 25 (2) (b) the state can make law for social welfare and reform even though such enactment might interfere with religious practices.

Religious Denominations' right to manage its own affairs but matters of religion and non-religion not clear

It is very difficult to differentiate between essential and

non-essential matters of a particular religion. The Supreme Court, therefore, said that the essential part of a religion should be primarily ascertained by referring to the doctrine of that religion. If the tenets of any religious sect of the Hindus prescribe that offerings of food should be given to the idol at particular hours of the day, that periodical ceremonies should be performed in a certain way at certain periods of the year or that there should be daily recital of sacred texts or oblations to the sacred fire, all these would be regarded as parts of religion and the mere fact that they involve expenditure of money or employment of priests and servants or the use of marketable commodities would not make them secular activities partaking of a commercial or economic character, all of them are religious practices and should be regarded as matters of religion within the meaning of article 26 (b). What article 25 (2) (a) contemplates is not regulation by the state of religious practices as such, the freedom of which is guaranteed by the constitution except when they run counter to public order, health and morality, but regulation of activities which are economic, commercial or political in their character though they are associated with religious practices.[44]

If, therefore, a comparison is made between the provision of Articles 26 (b) with 26 (c) and (d) it can be said that legislature cannot, under any circumstance, deprive a denomination to manage its own affairs in matters of religion. In such cases a denomination cannot be regulated by law. The legislature can, however, regulate a denomination's right to acquire, own and administer property as these are not matters of religion.

The expression 'matters of religion' is used here in a very wide sense. It is not limited to matters of doctrines or beliefs. It also includes acts done in pursuance of religion and, therefore, contains a guarantee for rituals and observance of ceremonies and modes of worship which are regarded as integral parts of religion.[45]

In *Dargah Committee, Ajmer* v *Hussain Ali*[46] the Supreme Court said that there exists essential difference between the practice which are secular practices, otherwise secular practices are apt to be clothed with religious form and may make a claim for being treated as religious practices.

The courts are competent to decide as to what constitutes an essential part of religion or religious practice with refers to doctrines of the particular religion and included as an integral part of the religion.[47]

Right of prayer in Mosque is a Fundamental Right

In view of the provisions in Article 25 and 26 of the Indian Constitution, it is open to any sect or school of thought among the Muslims to establish and maintain an institution for religious purpose. It is a fundamental right of every Muslim to offer his prayer in a public mosque. He cannot be denied this right on the ground of not belonging to a particular sect or denomination. To offer prayer only under the Imam of their choice cannot be said to be a fundamental right. The only fundamental right of a Muslim in a public mosque is to offer his prayers unrestricted by any right or by any particular rule of restraint. He shall have, however, no right to disturb any one else offering his prayer in the mosque. What particular rite will be followed and how it shall be done are matters of practice. This cannot be a fundamental right in the exercise of religious rites.[48]

The right of a denomination to wholly exclude members of the public from worshipping in the temple, though comprised in Article 26 (b), must yield to the overriding right declared by Article 25 (2) (b) in favour of the public to enter into a temple for worship. However, whether the right claimed on behalf of the temple is not one of general and total exclusion of the public from worship in the temple at all times but of exclusion from certain religious services, they being limited by the rules of the foundation to the members of the denomination, then the question is not whether Article 25 (2) (b) overrides that right so as to extinguish it, but whether it is possible so to regulate the rights of the persons protected by Article 25 (2) (b) as to give effect to both the rights. Where the denominational are such that to give effect to them would substantially reduce the right conferred under Article 25 (2) (b), then on the conclusion that Article 25 (2) (b) prevails as against Article 26 (b), the denominational rights must vanish. But where that is not the position, and after giving effect to the rights of the denomination, what is left to the public of the rights of worship is something substantial and not merely the husk of it, there is no reason why the courts should not so construe Article 25 (2) (b) as to give effect to Article 26 (b) and recognise the rights of the denominations in respect of matters which are strictly denominational, leaving the rights of the public in other respects unaffected. Therefore, the exclusive right of the members to worship at all times will be hit by Article 25 (2) (b) and cannot be recognised. The distinct right, namely, that during certain ceremonies and on special occasions it is only members of a certain community that have the right to take part therein and that on those occasions all other persons would be excluded, would clearly be a denominational right and protected by Article 26 (b).[49]

Protection of Articles 25 & 26 extends to acts done in pursuance of Religion

The protection of Articles 25 and 26 is not limited to matters of doctrine or belief. The protection also extends to acts done in pursuance of religion and, therefore, contain a guarantee for rituals, and observances, ceremonies and modes of worship, which are integral parts of religion.

The courts are only competent to decide as to what constitutes an essential part of a religion or religious practices. The courts will decide with reference to the doctrines of a particular religion and include practices which are regarded by the community as a part of its religion.[50]

Sardar Syedna Taher Saifuddin Saheb's case—The Bombay Prevention of Excommunication Act, 1949 was held void

After the Privy Council's decision in *Hasanal* v *Mansoorali*,[51] the Bombay legislature passed the Bombay Prevention Excommunication Act, 1949. The main aim of the passing of this Act was to prevent the practice of excommunication 'which results in the deprivation of legitimate rights and privileges of members of certain religious communication.' Under the Act a person was liable to be excommunicated on purely religious grounds.

The petitioner challenged the constitutional validity of this Act.[52] The majority opinion[53] held that the impugned Act violated Articles 25 and 26 and was void. However, Chief Justice Sinha declared the Act as valid. The Supreme Court held that the protection of Articles 25 and 26 was not limited to matter of doctrine or belief. It also extended to acts done in pursuance of religion. The court was competent to decide whether a practice was essential part of religion or religious practice. While deciding a particular practice, the courts took into consideration the doctrine of the particular religion and included practices which were regarded by the community as a part of its religion. As far as these practices were concerned the power of the management was recognised. The Supreme Court declared the above excommunication under the Act as invalid and, therefore, the head of the community was denied the power to excommunicate a member even on religious grounds. In this way the Act interfered with the right of the Dawoodi Bohra community under Article 26 (b) not depended on the preservation of civil rights. Similarly, excommunication was not prejudicial to public order, morality and health. The Act was passed with a view to restricting the right of the excommunication and, therefore, the community lost certain civil rights. Even then it cannot be said that the Act was passed with a view to providing social reform within the meaning of Article 25 (2) of the Constitution. The passing of the Act was a violation of Article 26 (b).[54] The following conclusion may be drawn from the judgment :

(a) the petitioner was having no right to excommunicate any member of the community ;

(b) after this decision of the Supreme Court, the main underlying principles of Article 25 and 26 become uncontroversial;

(c) where excommunication was itself based on religious grounds, such as lapse from the orthodox religious creed or doctrine or breach of some practice considered as an essential part of the religion, excommunication may held to be for the purpose of maintaining the strength of that religion;

(d) one of the most important effect of excommunication was that it will adversely affect on the social status of such member. He also lost his right to the enjoyment of property.

(e) Article 26 (b) was subject to clause (2) of Article 25. The Act did not come within the purview of Article 25 (2). The Act did not restrict the economic, political or social status of the member and it did not come within the purview of Article 25 (2).

The Act by depriving the head of the community of the power and the right to excommunicate and by penalising the exercise of that power, struck at the very life of the community by rendering it impotent to protect itself against dissidents and his malices. The Act violated the right to practice religion guaranteed by Article 25 (1). It also violated Article 26 because it interfered with the rights of the Dai as the trustee of the property of the denomination to administer that property so as to exclude dissidents from the beneficial use of it[55].

To own and administer Movable and Immovable Property

Article 26, clauses (c) and (d) provides to a religious denomination, the right to acquire and own property and to administer such property in accordance with law. The administration of its property by a religious denomination has been placed on a different footing from the right to manage its own affairs in matters of religion. The right to manage its own affairs in matters of religion is a fundamental right and therefore, cannot be abrogated by any legislative act. On the other hand, the right to administer its property by a religious denomination is not a fundamental right and, therefore, the legislature can regulate it by law. Therefore, if the question merely relates to administration of properties belonging to a religious group or institution, it is not a matter of religion to which clause (b) of the article would apply.[56]

State can check the unnecessary Expenditure

The state can check the expenses to be incurred in connection with the religious observations. This is a matter of administration of property belonging to the religious denomination and, therefore, the state is fully competent to control the expenses. The reason is that it could not be the injunction of any religion to destroy the institution and its endowments by incurring wasteful expenditure on rites and ceremonies. In this connection, the following observations of the Supreme Court[57] may, however, be noted :

> ...it is the fundamental right of a religious denomination to administer its properties in accordance with law and the law, therefore, must leave the right of administration to the religious denomination itself subject to such restrictions and regulations as it might choose to impose. A law which takes away the right of administration from the hands of a religious denomination altogether and vests it in any other authority would amount to a violation of the right guaranteed under clause (b) of Article 26.

Cow Slaughter Case

The majority of the world population is beef eaters. But on the other hand, in Hindu religion cows have been given special religious importance. Article 48 of the Indian Constitution directs the state to organise agriculture and animal husbandry on modern and scientific lines and shall, in particular, take steps for preserving and improving the breeds, and prohibiting the slaughter of cows and calves and other milch and drought cattle. Consequently, the various state governments prohibited the slaughter of cows by passing enactments. In *Mohammad Hanif* v *State of Bihar*[58] the question was whether the prohibition of cow slaughter affected the religious rights of Muslims. The appellant contended that the sacrifice of a cow on Id-ul-Zuha festival was necessary. In support of his argument he cited the provisions of *Quran*. He also contended that the sacrifice of the cow was a part of his religion.

Their lordship of the Supreme Court rejected the evidence adduced by the appellant as it was most unsatisfactory. It is not necessary that a particular religious practice must be universally prevalent. The courts may recognise the validity of those religious practices which are not universally prevalent and very few religious denominations are observing it.

As already noted, under Article 26 (d) it is the fundamental right of a religious denomination to administer properties in accordance with law and, therefore, the legislature cannot take away this right. The legislature can only impose restrictions and regulations[59].

Article 26 (c) and (d) does not provide any new right in any denomination or any section thereof. These clauses merely protect and guarantee the continuance of already existing right. Therefore, if the right to administer properties never vested in the denomination or had been validly surrendered by it or had otherwise been lost of it, Article 26 will not be applicable[60].

Acquisition of Waqf Property for public purpose has nothing to do with Freedom of Conscience

Some Hindus, and many Muslims draw no distinction between law and religion. Immediately after the advent of Indian Constitution an unsuccessful attempt was made impugn a provision of the U.P. Abolition of Zamindari Act as repugnant to Article 25 (1) in so far as it did not exempt waqf property from expropriation. The court said that Article 25 is expressly made subject to Article 31 and all other provisions in Part III of the Constitution. Acquisition of waqf property had noting to do with freedom of conscience or the right to profess religion ; the Mutawalli's right to profess his religion remained unaffected by the acquisition[61].

The state is free to acquire private property in accordance with the other provisions of the Constitution. The Constitution guarantees to religious denominations to own and acquire properties and administer them in accordance with law. However, such properties can be acquired by the state for public purposes. After such acquisition, the religious denominations cease to own property. Article 26 does not interfere with the right of the state to acquire property[62].

Shirur Mutt case—A case on Arts 25 & 26

After independence the leading case which considered the scope and extent of the rights conferred under Articles 25 and 26 was *Commissioner Hindu Religious Endowments Madras* v

Lakshmindra[63]. The case is also known as Shirur Mutt Case. The facts in brief of this case were as follows :—

The dispute arose out of a scheme in connection with a Mutt known as the Shirur Mutt. The petitioner was the head of this institution. The Endowment Board intended to introduce a scheme for the better administration of the Mutt. Consequently the Board called upon the petitioner to show cause why a scheme should not be framed for the proper administration of the trust. The petitioner filed a petition challenging the validity of the Madras Religious Endowments Act, 1927. In 1951, the Madras Religious and Charitable Endowments Act, 1951, was passed. At that time the petition was still pending. Therefore, the petitioner challenged the constitutional validity of the subsequent Act. It was contended that the various Sections of the Act offended the fundamental rights guaranteed by Articles 19 (1) (f), 25 and 26 of the Constitution. After carefully examining the various sections, the Supreme Court struck down Sections 21, 30 (2), 31, 55, 56 and 63 to 69 of the Act as infringing Articles 19, 25 and 26 of the Constitution. The Supreme Court also declared as *ultra vires* Section 76 (1) of the aforesaid Act. The legislature through the Act imposed a tax in the garb of a fee as such tax being beyond the competence of the Madras legislature. The Supreme Court said there is no reason why the word 'property' as used in Article 19 (1) (f) of the constitution should not be given a liberal and wide connotation and should not be extended to those well recognised types of interests which have the insignia or characteristic of proprietary right.

The court further held that the office of a Mahant is a property within the meaning of Article 19 (1) (f) of the Constitution and Mahant has got right to enjoy the property or beneficial interest therein and consequently if any provision interfering with this beneficial enjoyment of their property or with his performance of duties as a Mahant would be unreasonable restriction under Article 19 (1) (f) of the Constitution.

After the decision of the Supreme Court in the above case the Madras Act was amended in 1954. This amended Act was again challenged in *Sudhindra* v *H.R. & Cammissioner*[64]. It was held that Sections 30 and 31 of the Act suffer from the same defects which existed prior to its amendment. In *T.K. Lakshmana* v *State of Madras*[65] Section 44 (b) of the Madras Hindu Religious Act was challenged. However, this attempt was not successful. The Court held that the aforesaid Act was unconstitutionally valid.

Court may grant injunction for the Preservation of Peace

Where there is considerable heat, tension and possibility of breach of peace the proper course would be to see that the decree or interim order does not accentuate the problem. The Court may grant or not grant injunction. It may be granted where it would help in the preservation of peace and public order[66].

Provisions for proper working of the Endowments held Lawful

The state will not interfere only in religious matters. In secular matters state shall have full right to control the affairs of the institution.Provisions in Religious or Charitable Endowments Acts for carrying out the objects of any trust and for the better administration, protection and preservation of properties or for the better and more convenient discharge of the trustee's duty or for keeping accounts of gifts made to the head of a math and for utilisation of the same according to the customs and usages of an institution were held as lawful as they imposed reasonable restrictions in the public interest on trustees whose duty it is to carry out their trust. However, in considering the reasonableness of restrictions imposed on religious trusts the impact of Articles 25 and 26 must not be overlooked.

Act for proper working of the Trusts held Valid

In *Moti Das* v *S.P. Sahi*[67] the Bihar Hindu Religious Trusts Act, 1951 was challenged before the Supreme Court. The validity of this Act was challenged on the ground that it contravened Article 14 of the Constitution inasmuch as it makes discrimination between other sects of Hindu religion and Sikh religion, secondly on the ground that the enactment violates Articles 25 and 26 of the Constitution. The Supreme Court held that the state can treat Hindu, Sikh and Jain religious trusts differently because these trusts were not similarly situated. The legislature was free to recognise degrees of harm and to confine where the need is said to be the clearest. The concept of property that it could effectively be transferred from a personal to a personal public law context was confirmed. Justice S.K. Das held that a Shebaiti right was a right to property within the meaning of Article 19 (1) (f) of the Constitution. The Court held that Section 60 (2) which empowered the Endowments Board to alter the budget of any religious trust was *intra vires* the constitution but the wishes of the founder would be respected in all other cases.

Tilkayat Sri Govindlalji's case

In *Tilkayat Sri Govindlalji* v *State of Rajasthan*[68] Gajendragadkar, Chief Justice (for B.P. Sinha, Chief Justice K.N. Wanchoo, K.C. Das and J.C. Shah JJ) went one step further and held that a Tilkayat of a temple is a mere manager and no more. He relied on Ameer Ali's judgment in Vidya Varuthi's case and the Srirur Math's case to show that the Tilkayat has never claimed any proprietary interest in any part of the usufruct of the properties of the temple for his private personal needs and as such the proprietary interest was lacking. The office of Tilkayat is not a property within the meaning of Article 19 (1) (f) of the Constitution and, therefore, he was not entitled to the benefits of Article 31 (2) or 19 (1) of the Constitution. The Supreme Court further held that even if the office of Tilkayat be assumed to be that of a Mahant or Shebait, reasonable restrictions could be imposed by Article 19 (5) of the Constitution. Regarding Article 25 (1) of the Constitution with reference to the temple the court held that what is protected by Article 25 (1) and 26 (b) respectively are the religious practices and managing religious affairs and not secular affairs and if a practice in question is purely secular or the affairs, which is controlled, by statute, is essentially and absolutely secular in character, it cannot be urged that such provision contravenes Article 25 or 26 of the Constitution. Seervai says in such cases the real question is whether the religious denomination looks upon it as an essential part of its religion, and however irrational it may appear to persons who do not share that religious belief, the view of the denomination must prevail, for it is not open to a court to describe as irrational that which is a part of a denomination's religion[69].

In *P.B.N.C. Committee* v *Government of A.P.*[70] it was held that the appointment of a treasurer and the vesting of the properties in him for the purposes specified in the Charitable Endowments Act would not offend the fundamental rights of the members of the society.

Jagannath Ramanuja's Case

In *Jagannath Ramanuja* v *B.K. Patra*[71] it was said that any scheme for the administration of a Mutt must conform to the following requirements :

(i) A mahant of the Mutt had property rights in the endowment of the mutt. Accordingly, he should not be deprived of from the right of enjoyment of the property;

(ii) Where on account of levy of restrictions a mahant was not able to discharge his functions and consequently he was reduced to the level of a servant, such a restriction would be treated as unreasonable;

(iii) The main function of the mahant is to encourage and foster spiritual training and to strengthen the denominations of the particular school to which the Mutt belonged, any scheme in the administration of a Mutt should not hinder but should assist the mahant to achieve that purpose;

(iv) This is the right of the mahant to decide the essential rites and ceremonies of any particular sect. Outside authority has no jurisdiction to interfere in such matters;

(v) The state can control the scale of expenditure on such rites. But the administration of religious denominations must be enjoyed by the Mutt;

(vi) The mahant has been given very wide power to dispose of surplus income of a Mutt except in respect of the expenses for personal use connected with the dignity of his office. This power is absolute and cannot be taken away.

(vii) Provision for prior sanction of the Endowment Commissioner for fixing the standard scale of expenditure for the various rites and ceremonies has been held as valid. It will not amount to an unreasonable restriction on the mahant's right.

Article 25 and the right to carry *kirpan*

Explanation (1) to Article 25 lays down that the wearing and carrying of kirpans shall be deemed to be included in the profession of the Sikh religion. Therefore, Sikhs are allowed to carry or wear a kirpan. A law cannot prohibit the carrying of kirpan unless and until it is in public order. In this Article the word kirpan has been used in the plural in relation to Sikhs and emblems. It was not the policy of the legislature that in the name of religion a Sikh could carry any number of kirpans or swords as a religious emblem when one of the Sikh Gurus had orbained that the kirpan should be worn only as one of five named emblems. It was also not the policy of the legislature that a Sikh should possess without a licence any number of arms, for the possession of which others had to obtain a licence. It can, therefore, be said that a Sikh was entitled to possess only one sword or kirpan.[72]

Section 295 of the Indian Penal Code and Religious Freedom

Section 295 A of the Indian Penal Code prohibits the insult or attempt to insult the religion or religious belief of a class of citizens. The courts have given a broad and liberal interpretation to the right to practise and propagate religion. In *Ramji Lal Modi* v *State of U.P.*[73] their lordship of the Supreme Court held that Section 295 A, Indian Penal Code was protected by Article 19 (2). It would be absurd to suggest that an insult to the religion of an individual could have no bearing on public order so as to attract Article 19 (2), having regard to the provisions of Article 25 and 26, which while guaranteeing the freedom of religion, expressly made it subjeet to public order[74]. Under Section 295 A only deliberate and malicious acts or insult or attempt to insult the other religion are punishable. The intention of such insult should be to disturb public order.

The expression 'any object' held sacred by any class of persons in Section 295 of the Indian Penal Code were of general import and could not be limited to idols in temples or idols carried on the occasion of festivals, but included sacred books and any other objects which were regarded as sacred by any class of persons, whether such objects were actually worshipped or not[75].

A section of the public has no right to instal their own deities in a denominational temple

The right guaranteed under Article 25 (1) was not merely a matter of faith and belief but also of practice of rituals and ceremonies. In *Tejraj* v *State of M.P.*[76] the respondent installed a Shivling in a Jain temple and prohibited Jains from worshipping there. It was held that where the fact of a very old temple being a public Jain temple was admitted, and supported by documents, and there was no record of the temple having been dedicated to the Hindu public, the mere presence of a Shivling in the temple and the use of the temple by the Hindu community did not support the claim that the temple was also a Hindu temple. In this case it was proved that the temple was dedicated for the benefit of the Jain community and it was a public temple. The court, therefore, held that the members of the Jain community were having fundamental right under Article 25(1) to enter and worship there according to the principles and forms of their religion. The court further held that the state had no right to introduce a Shivling into the temple, and to prohibit the members of the Jain community from entering the temple and from worshipping except on the condition of Hindus being allowed to worship the Shivling. In this way the state violated the fundamental rights of Jain under Articles 25 (1) and 26 (b). The action taken by the state was not for maintaing public order, morality and health. In *Sanjib Kumar* v *Principal, St. Paul's*[77] College it was held that an educational institution under the control of a Christian Missionary Society could provide that all religious practices which were carried out inside its premises should be in conformity with Christian principles. The Principal of the college was, therefore, right in refusing to allow Saraswati pooja within the college premises.

In *Sri Venkataramana Devaru* v *State of Mysore*[78] the constitutional validity of the Madras Temple Entry Authorisation Act, 1947 was challenged. The object of the Act was to remove the disability of Harijans from entering into Hindu public temples. The appellant contended that the temple was a private temple. The Supreme Court was required to decide whether right of a religious denomination to manage its own affairs in matters of religion under Article 26 (h) could be subjected to, and controlled by, a law protected by Article 25 (2) (b). It was held that the expression 'religious institutions of a public character' occurring in Article 25 (2) (b) contemplated not merely a temple dedicated to the public as a whole, but also temples endowed for the benefit of sections of the public and included denominational temples also.

Seervai[79] says that the decision of the Supreme Court in Devaru's case and of the Madhya Pradesh High Court in Tejraj's case are conflicting but the conflict is merely apparent. According to Devaru's case a Hindu religious institution of a public character included not only Hindu temples open to all Hindus generally, but also included denominational Hindu temples, that is to say, a law providing for the throwing open of all Hindu temples to all classes and sections of Hindus would apply also denominational temples. It was, however, not possible for any section of the Hindu community to instal into a denominational temple different idols of their faith.[80]

In *P.S. Charya* v *State of Madras*[81] it was held that Shri Krishna Devaru Temple at Shivalli in Udipi was a public temple and a must. It was held that the Madras Temple Entry Authorisation Act, 1947 did not violate any provision of Part III of the Constitution.

Social Reform Laws among Hindus

With a view to making social change among Hindus the legislature passed few Acts. In 1944, the Legislature passed the Bombay Prevention of Hindu Bigamous Marriage Act.

The validity of this Act was challenged[82] on the ground that it violated Article 25 of the Constitution. This contention was not accepted. It was held that the Act was a good piece of legislation. The court said there is a sharp distinction between religious faith and belief, and religious practices. The court also said the Act was a measure of social reform covered by Article 25 (2) (b).

Acquisition or requisition of the Property of a Religious Denomination for Public Purposes

The leading case on this point in *State of Bihar* v *Kameshwar Singh.*[83] It was contended in this case that the dedication of property to certain religious institutitons is already public purpose and, therefore, such a property cannot be acquired for another public purpose. The Supreme Court rejected this argument of the appellant. The Supreme Court was of the opinion that property belonging to a religious institution would only change its form, namely from immovable property into money.

In *Prankrishna* v *Junior Assessor*[84] it was said that the provisions of the West Bengal Food Grains (Intensive procurement) Order, 1952 did not violate Articles 25 and 26, for, if the state could acquire property dedicated for religious purposes, it could equally acquire the usufruct thereof.

State can make law for better discharge of trustees

The state can also make law for the better and more convenient discharge of the trustee's duty.[85]

State can make law for properly keeping accounts

The legislature can also lawfully make law for keeping accounts of gifts made to head of a *math* and for the utilisation of the same according to the customs and usages of an institution.

Entry of Government officials into Religious Institutions

The state is fully competent to exercise full control over the secular administration of waqf as opposed to its religious administration. In the garb of exercising powers government officers are empowered to interfere in day today working of the endowment. There is a difference of opinion between High Courts of India as to whether the state officials are allowed to enter into the religious institutions. The subject has become more important because of the recent murder of Mr. Avtar Singh Atwal, DIG (Punjab) and an 11 years old boy. The police officer was not even in uniform at the time of his assassination. He had gone to the Golden Temple with his wife and children to offer prayers. In Ratilal's case the Court said that unlike the Madras provision invalidated in Lakshmindra, the Bombay provision required those entering a religious institution to give the trustees reasonable notice of their intended entry and to respect the religious practices and usages of institution.[86] But the Madras High Court declined to follow Ratilal in Swamiar as 'the Supreme Court had no occasion in the Bombay case to test the validity of the Bombay Act with reference to the fundamental rights of a Matadhipati. The Madras High Court invalidated the amended Section 21 of the Madras Act. The amended section empowered among others, a servant of a *math* authorised by the Commissioner in certain cases, and a police officer, not below the rank of sub-inspector, to enter a religious institution after if practicable, giving the trustees notice of the intended entry. The court held that even the members of denomination could not enter their *math* as of right and that the position of a Matadhipati 'is not that for instance of a trustee of a public temple'.

In *Tilkayat Shir Govindlalji* v *State of Rajasthan*[87] and *Narayan Doss* v *Neeladri Rao*[88] the Supreme Court and the Andhra Pradesh High Court respectively upheld the challenged provision permitting the entry of any person into the Nathdwara temple or the Hathiramjee *math* for the inspection of property and seizure of hidden documents related to an enquiry into the affairs of the *math*. The Supreme Court compared the challenged section with the provision of the Madras Act authorising inspection of trust property upheld in Lakshmindra and not with the invalidated Section 21 authorising entry into religious institutions. It observed that the challenged Section 27 empowered the state government to depute any person to inspect the property of the temple and its records, correspondence, plan and other documents. In Tilkayat Govindalji's[89] case, the court dismissed as 'far fetched and imaginary' the fear of the counsel for the temple that the state might depute a non-Hindu under this section and observed that the power of inspection the state might confer on a person 'is intended to a safeguard the properties of the temple and nothing more.[90] The Andhra Pradesh High Court[91] upheld the validity of Section 5 (b) of the Commissioner of Enquiry Act, which empowered a gazetted officer authorised by the Commission of Enquiry to enter any place or building to search and seize hidden documents relating to the enquiry. The court held that, unlike the Madras provision, the impugned section 'does not violate the sanctity of the institution nor is it likely to wound religious sentiment'.

In Gurdwara[92] case the concerned officer was authorised to enter any building or place. He was also authorised to make search and seize books of accounts according to the provisions of Sections 102 and 103 of the Code of Criminal Procedure. The main question before the Supreme Court was whether the principle of election was a matter of religion or not. The facts in brief of the case were as under.

The Sikh Gurdwara Act, 1925, was amended in the year 1959 and section 148-B was added. The amendment provided that till the constitution of a permanent board, that among others all members of the Interim Gurdwara Board, Patiala, and thirty-five Sikhs from the extended area, PEPSU, elected by members specified therein shall be members of the Gurdwara Prabhandak Committee. The petitioner attacked this Section as it violated Article 26 of the Indian Constitution because it introduced into the Gurdwara Prabhandak Committee more designated members and members elected by a limited Sikh electorate, which in turn was elected by Sikhs as well as by non-Sikhs. It was contended that a direct election of the members of the Committee by the entire Sikh community was itself a matter of the Sikh religion and, therefore, part of the content of the right guaranteed by Article 26 (b).

The court held that no authoritative text was placed before it to show that a direct election by the entire Sikh community was a part of the Sikh religion. It further held that the principle of direct election though democratic and desirable, could not be raised to the pedestal of religion and that to treat it as 'religion is tantamount to confusing with current politics.'[93]

The Bihar Act was challenged on the ground that the state legislature was not competent to enact a law which will have extra territorial operation. The Supreme Court, however, rejected this argument. The court held that it is a valid piece of legislation.[94]

Durgah Committee's case—Denominational right not created by Art 26 (c) & (d)

In the Durgah Committee's case the Supreme Court considered the validity of many of the important provisions of Durgah Khwaja Saheb Act, 1955. The court found that the 'denomination never had the right to administer the property'[95] of the Durgah and that 'the management of the properties endowed was always in the hands of officers appointed by the state and who were removable by the state at the state's pleasure.[96] The court, therefore, said :—

> It is obvious that Article 26 (c) and (d) does not create rights in any denomi ation or its section which it never had; they merely safeguard and guarantee the continuance of rights which such a denomination never had the right to manage the properties endowed in favour of a denomination institution, as for instance by a reason of the terms on which the endowment was created, it cannot be heard to say that it has acquired the said rights as a result of Article 26 (c) and (d), and that the practice and custom prevailing in that behalf, which obviously, is consistent with the terms of the endowment, should be ignored and management should now be given to the denomination.'

Therefore, the court upheld the constitution of the Durgah Committee under Sections 4 and 5 of the Act to manage and supervise administration of the endowed property.

The court held valid that offerings received on behalf of the Durgah formed part of the endowment and that only the

Nazim or any other authorised by him was entitled to solicit and receive offerings on behalf of the Durgah.

The court upheld[97] the power conferred on the committee to regulate the powers and functions of the khadims. It said that Section 15 provided that all the rites and ceremonies of the Durgah must necessarily be performed according to the tenets of the Chistia sect. Therefore, the Committee was not free to interfere with the religious affairs of the Durgah.

In Durgah Committee's case Justice Gajendragadkar overlooked material infirmities in the case of the respondents. He abided by the High Court's verdict that the Chistia sect whom the respondents purported to represent was a religious denomination even though he found that on theoretical consideration it was not a denomination. He also found that the respondents, who claimed that they alone were entitled to administer the property of the Durgah, challenged the inclusion of non-Chistia Muslims into the Durgah Committee and not the constitution of the Committee itself, and claimed proprietary interest over offerings from pilgrims only though the Durgah had other property also.

The case of Govindlalji[98] is identical to Durgah Committee's case. The facts of this case are as follows :

The Rajasthan Nathdwara Temples Act provided for constitution of the Nathdwara Temple Board, vested the ownership of the temple and its endowments, including offerings to the deity and their possession in the Board, spelled out the powers and functions of the Board, specified the grounds removal of the Goswami and President and ordinary members of Board and dealt with matters like budget and similar other affairs. The Board is empowered to manage the affairs and properties of the temple and to arrange for the conduct of daily worship and ceremonies and festivals in the temple according to the custom and usages of the Pushti Margiya Vallabhi Sampradaya.

The court found that 'the legislature was anxious to provide for the better administration of the temple properties and not to infringe upon the traditional religious ceremonies worship'. The court further held that administration of property was not a matter of religion and it was regulable according to the law enacted by the state.

It is also interesting to note that the Mahants can be removed from their offices under the statutory provisions. This was held in *S.T. Swamiar* v *Commissioner, H.R. & C.E.,*[99] *Mysore* and *Digyadarsan* v *State of Andhra Pradesh*[100]. The S.T. Swamiar case dealt with the validity of the provisions of the Madras Hindu Religious and Charitable Endowments Act. Section 52 (1) of this Act empowered the Commissioner and persons interested in the *math* to sue for the removal of a mahant for, among other things, wasting or employing for purposes unconnected with the *math*, its property and income. The court said that the mahant was not entitled to use the trust property for personal luxury or objects incongruous with his position as a mahant. Similarly, in Digyadarsan case the challenged provision of the newly enacted Andhra Act authorized the Commissioner to remove a mahant on any of the specified grounds after giving him a reasonable opportunity to defend himself.

In *Pandit Saligram Acharya* v *Pandit Raghva Charya*[101] the Patna High Court sustained the validity of the removal of shebait and the appointment of a receiver for the temple properties pending the appointment of a new shebait. In this case the shebait was removed from his office on account of mismanagement of properties and misappropriation of funds.

In *K.A. Samajan* v *Commissioner H.R. and C.E.,* Hyderabad[102] Justice Grover relied on the report of the Commission on Hindu religious Endowments to sustain the verdict of the High Court below :—

> In the report of the Hindu Religious Endowments Commissioner presided over by Dr. C.P. Ramaswamy Iyer... it has been pointed out that legislation relating to endowments became necessary in the state as a result of the almost invariable mismanagement of the endowment properties of temples by the trustees, misappropriation of the funds of the endowment for purposes unconnected with the original aims and objects of such endowments, utilization of the funds of the endowments by the trustees

or managers for their personal purposes *etc.* All this fully supports the decision of the High Court.'

In *Bashiruddin Ashraf* v *State of Bihar*[103] the provisions of Section 58 (1) and the penal provisions of Section 65, Bihar Waqfs Act, 1948 were held not to violate Article 19 (1) (g). Section 58 (1) required a Mutawalli of every waqf to prepare a budget and send it to the Majlis and Section 58 (2) and (6) conferred certain powers on the Majlis, which the court held did not in any way interfere with the waqf, and in any event were severable. Section 65 provided punishment for failure to prepare and furnish the budget to the Majlis. The petitioner who was convicted under Section 65 impugned the validity of Section 58 but the court held that the provisions as regards the preparation of a budget were necessary to ensure that a waqf was properly administered and that the income of the waqf was duly appropriated for the purposes for which the waqf was established. Section 58 was held as reasonable restrictions on the duties of the mutawalli as a person administering the waqf.

In *Hafiz Mohammad* v *U.P. Board of Waqfs*[104] it was held that the right of a mutawalli is not equivalent to that of a Mahant. It is a right to the management of the property and not a proprietary right. A mutawalli is having secular duties. He is not the head of a spiritual fraternity differing in all these respects from a Mahant.

Right to Acquire, Hold and Dispose of property—Art 19 (1) (f) of the Constitution

The Indian citizens have been guaranteed the right to acquire, hold and dispose of property[105]. No person shall be deprived of his property save by authority of law[106]. The right to acquire, hold and dispose of property is not absolute. It is subject to Article 19 (5)[107] of the Indian Constitution.

For claiming the right to acquire, hold and dispose of property, he must establish that the right which he claims is a right to property. Property is not defined in Indian law. Section 3 (26), General Clauses Act defines 'immovable property as including land benefits to arise out of land and things attached to the earth or permanently fastened to anything attached to the earth and Section 3 (36) defines movable property. Section 3, Transfer of Property Act defines 'attach to the earth' occurring in Section 3 (26) of the General Clause Act. Property consists of a bundle of rights some of which the law treats as themselves capable of separate acquisition and possession or enjoyment[108]. In *State of West Bengal* v *Subodh Bose*[109], Jagannadhadas J. said that in the context of Article 19 (1) (f) and Article 31 (2) only that can be called 'property' which can be the subject matter of acquisition or taking possession. Therefore, a bare individual right, out of the bundle of rights which go to make up property as being itself property within Article 31 (2), unless such individual right was itself recognised as property, *e.g.* an easement, a profits, *a-prendre*, and the like. However, a right to annual undertenures cannot itself be treated as property for it is not capable of independent acquisition or possession. The deprivation of such right is a restriction on the exercise of the main rights as regards the main property itself and must fall under Article 19 (1)(f) and(5)[110]. It may, however, be noted that the above proposition must be qualified when dealing with the rights of hereditary trustees of temples; or other religious institutions.[111]

The Indian Constitution has not defined the term property. The courts, therefore, gave liberal and wide meaning to the word property[112]. Property in its legal connotation means the sum of a bundle of rights and in the case of tangible property would include the right of possession, the right to enjoy, the right to destroy, the right to retain, the right to alienate and so on[113]. The courts recognised all types of interest which have the insignia or characteristics as property[114]. The term property does not only include the subject matter of ownership, but includes also the *dominium* or the right of ownership or of partial ownership[115]. It includes every possible interest which the party can have[116].

It may, however, be noted that all valuable rights are not property. The right of a mutawalli is not property[117]. Similarly, the right of a Tilkayat of Nathdwara to the possession and the management of the Temple property is not property[118].

In *Raj Kali Kuer* v *Ram Rattan*[119] Justice Jagannadhadas held that the right of a hereditary priest or pujari in a temple must also amount to property where emoluments are attached to such an office.

In *State of West Bengal* v *Subodh Gopal*[120], Chief Justice Patanjali Sastri of the Supreme Court held that Article 19 (1) (f) declares the citizens, right to own property and has no relation to the right to the property owned by him. It can, therefore, be said that protection of the concrete rights of property did not fall within the scope of the rights secured by Article 19 (1) (f). This opinion of their Lordship was not accepted by the Supreme Court in other cases[121], though the case was decided in the same year. In this case it was held that the clause applies equally to concrete as well as to abstract rights of property.

Money is the property and, therefore, no tax can be imposed save under authority of law. A tax not imposed in accordance with law would violate the fundamental right guaranteed under Article 19 (1) (f) of the Constitution[122]. A tax should not be confiscatory in character. It should not destroy the business of the person taxed[123]. The legislature is free to impose heavy tax. It will not infringe fundamental rights under Article 19 (1) (f)[124]. Similarly, the legislature can impose a tax retrospectively[125].

Reasonable Restrictions

Under Article 19 (5) state can impose reasonable restrictions on the acquisition, holding and disposition of property. The state may impose restrictions in the interests of the general public or for the protection of the interests of any Scheduled tribe. The state under Article 19 (1) (f) cannot impose restrictions arbitrarily. It was said in *K.K. Kochuni* v *State of Madras*[126] that there must be harmonious balancing between the Fundamental Right declared by Article 19 (1) (f) and the social control permitted by Article 19 (5). The phrase 'in the interests of the general public' are not justifiable. State can lawfully impose restrictions in the interest of the general public. For example, the Rent Control and Eviction Acts passed by the various state legislatures though imposing restrictions on the landlords to hold and dispose of property were held as lawful on the ground of their being necessary in the public interest in times of shortage of accommodation[127]. The Supreme Court has held as valid the consolidation of holdings as it was in the interest of the general public[128]. The State can also lawfully limit the size of holdings in the hands of a single individual to a specified limit[129]. A ban on possession, sale, consumption or use of liquor has been held as lawful restrictions[130].

In *Vivian Joseph Ferreria* v *Bombay Municipality*[131] a cess was levied on residential buildings including those which were in good and sound condition. The validity of this provision was challenged. Their Lordship of the Supreme Court upheld the validity of this provision as it was a reasonable restriction in the interest of the general public.

In *Jyoti Pershad* v *Union Territory*[132] their Lordship of the Supreme Court held that 'it was not suggested that slum dwellers would not constitute the general public and that if a legislation was designed to grant them protection, it could not be justified as one in the interests of the general public, because obviously the interests of such a vast number of the population in the country, their health, well-being and morals would, part even from themselves, necessarily impinge upon and influence, for good or evil, the health, safety, well-being and morality of the rest of the community as well'.

The Orissa Hindu Religious Endowments Act faced constitional challenge before the Supreme Court in *Sadesib Prakash* v *State of Orissa*[133] and Section 42 (1) (b), sub-section (7), Section 44 (2) and Section 74 (3) were particularly assailed. The Supreme Court held that enquiry under the present Act relating to framing of a scheme is itself in the nature of a judicial inquiry by judicial officer followed by a right of regular appeal to the High Court and, therefore, the provisions relating to the framing of schemes are not open to any of the constitutional objections and, therefore, perfectly valid.

Unreasonable Restrictions

There are several instances where the court has held that the restrictions imposed by the legislature on the use of property was unreasonable. In *Mahant Sri Jagannath Ramanuj* v *the State of Orissa*[134] Sections 38, 39, 46 and 47 of the Orissa Hindu Religious Endowments Act (Act No 4 of 1939) were challenged before the Supreme Court as offending the fundamental rights enshrined in Articles 19 (1) (f), 25, 26, 27 and 32 of the Constitution. Their lordship of the Supreme Court held that setting of a religious institution by an executive officer, without the intervention of any judicial tribunal, amounts to an unreasonable restriction upon the rights of property of the head of the religious institution and, therefore, Sections 38 and 39 of the Act were declared *ultra vires*. The court struck down the restrictions on the mahant's power to utilise the surplus income.

The Andhra Pradesh Charitable and Hindu Religious Institutions and Endowments Act, 1966 was challenged before the Supreme Court[135]. The main question for consideration before the Supreme Court was whether hereditary trusteeship is a property within the meaning of Article 19 (1) (f) of the Constitution. It was held by the Supreme Court that the office of the hereditary trustee was not in the nature of property as contemplated by Article 19 (1) (f). It was also held that the provisions of the Act do not infringe Articles 14, 19 and 26 of the Constitution. Such provisions are protected by Article 19 (5).

Rights held as not Property

The courts have held following rights as not Property :

(1) the right of a quasi-permanent allottee under the provisions of the Administration of Evacuee Property Act read along with the notification issued thereunder[136];
(2) the right of a Mutawalli[137];
(3) the right of the Tilkayat of the Nathdwara Temple to the possession and management of the temple property[138],
(4) The right of a landlord to eject his[139] tenants;
(5) The right of recognition[140] as a Ruler under Article 366 (22) and the rights that accrue by virtue of that recognition;

(6) the village offices abolished by the Mysore Village Offices Abolit.on Act, 1961[141];

(7) where the petitioner[142] acquired a colliery in transgression of the rules validly made under the Mineral Concession Rules, it was held that he did not have sufficient interest in the property to raise questions about the constitutional validity of r. 39, Coal Mines (Conservation and Safety) Rules, 1954. A person alleging a violation of his right to hold property must be able to establish his title to that property[143];

(8) where the alleged fundamental right of a petitioner was dependent on the question whether the property transferred to her was evacuee property, and where the decision of the authority having jurisdiction to determine that question had become final, she not having questioned it, and where such decision was not a nullity or could not be otherwise got rid of, she could not complain of the violation of her rights under Article 11 (1) (f)[144];

(9) If the right to property was lost before the coming into effect of the Constitution, Article 9 (1) (f) could not be invoked[145].

No levy of tax for the Promotion of any Particular Religion

Article 27 guarantees freedom as to payment of taxes for promotion of any particular religion.[146] Before the advent of Indian Constitution, the British Indian Government was maintaining an Ecclesiastical Department. The expenditure on this department was met from public fund. The framers of the Indian Constitution were very well knowing the role of the religion which it played before 1947 *i.e.* when India was divided into two sovereign States – India and Pakistan. In fact religion was responsible for the division of the country. Keeping in view the experience of the past the Indian Constitution makers deliberately provided that it shall be unconstitutional to pay out of the public funds any money for the promotion or maintenance of any particular religion or religious denomination. This is based on the principle of secularism. It is claimed that India is a secular but not an anti-religious state. The reason is that it guarantees the freedom of conscience and religion. Article 27 and 28 of the Indian constitution emphasize the secular nature of the state, for they secure to every person freedom from the payment of taxes for the promotion of any religion and freedom from attendance at religious instruction or religious worship in certain educational institutions.

Now under Article 27 of the constitution imposition of tax for the promotion or maintenance of any particular religion or religious denomination has been totally prohibited. This provision has immensely benefited the Hindu Religious institutions. The majority religious institutions in the country are of Hindus and they are not required to pay any tax *etc.*

Under the above article the main emphais has been placed on the word 'particular religion'. It appears that the State cannot levy tax for the promotion of any particular religion. It can, however, equally levy tax in the interest of all religions.

The state is competent to impose tax to ensure proper administration of religious trusts and institutions. Article 27 only forbade the appropriation of public money to the promotion or maintenance of any particular religion[147]. It can, however, levy a fee. There is a difference between tax and fee[148]. It was argued that the word tax in Article 27 was not confined to taxes proper but included fees also. This point was, however, not decided by the Supreme Court. Since India is a secular state the word 'tax' should be given liberal interpretation so that Article 27 may become more useful to the common man. No tax can be levied outside the tax entries. Fees can be levied in respect of a non-tax entry as well as for example, a state levy on public trusts is invalid as a tax as there is no such entry, but is valid as a fee under entry 47 of the concurrent list.

In *Shri Jagannath Ramanuj Das* v *State of Orissa*[149] the constitutional validity of the Orissa Hindu Religious Endowments Act, 1939, was challenged. This Act was passed for providing the better administration and governance of certain religious endowments. Section 49 of the aforesaid Act imposed on every *math* or temple having an annual income exceeding Rs. 250/- an annual contribution for meeting the expenses of the commissioner and the officers and servants working under him. Their lordships of the Supreme Court held that the levy of contribution under Section 49 of the Act, was regarded as a fee and not a tax. The payment was made for meeting out the administrative expenses. The collections made were not merged in the general public revenue and were not appropriated in the manner laid down for appropriation of expenses for other public purposes.

In the same year when Supreme Court delivered its judgment in *Jagannath* v *Orissa*[150] case another important judgment was delivered by the same court. The briefs, facts and the law laid down by the Supreme Court are discussed below. In this case the Supreme Court held that the contribution levied under the Madras Hindu Religious and Charitable Endowments Act, 1951 was in the nature of a tax and not fee.

The first case on religious freedom dealt with the validity of the Madras Hindu Religious and Charitable Endowments Act, (hereafter the Madras Act). This case was arose from an appeal preferred by the Commissioner, Hindu Religious and Charitable Endowments, Madras (hereafter the Commissioner) against the judgment of the Madras High Court invalidating some of the provisions of the Madras Act, which had repealed the old Act. When the mutt fell into debts caused by the expenditure incurred in connection with Pariyayam ceremonies, an agent was appointed under the old Act to manage the affairs of the mutt. The appellee, the mahant of the mutt, dismissed the agent when he insisted on having his own way in the management of the mutt and filed a suit in local court seeking various remedies. Later, when at the instance of the dismissed agent the Board, constituted under the old Act, informed the appellee that the settlement of a scheme was necessary for proper administration of the mutt and its endowments, he successfully challenged in a writ petition filed in the Madras High Court the validity of the Madras Act, which during this period replaced the old Act.

The Madras Act was applicable to religious and charitable institutions. The Act vested supervision of administration of religious and charitable institutions in the State of Madras in a department of the government with the Commissioner at its head and a network of branches spread over the state. It empowered some officials to enter any religious institution for purpose connected with the Act, authorised the inspection of trust property and forbade alienation of the immovable property of a trust, except on lease for not more than five years without the Commissioner's approval. It required the trustees to obey all lawful orders issued under the Act, administer the property with care, prepare registers and submit them for verification and supply the commissioner any information required by him.

The Act provided for regulation of utilization of the income and surplus of the institution. It prescribed a scale of expenditure and the procedure for its approval. The proposals for the scale of expenditure prepared by the trustee and published by the Commissioner for inviting suggestions could be modified by the Government at the instance of the Commissioner. The trustees, though permitted to spend personal gifts at their discretion and for purposes connected with the *math*, were required to keep regular accounts of the receipts and expenditure of the personal gifts. The Commissioner was authorised to require the trustee to appoint a Manager to look after the secular affairs of the institution. The Deputy Commissioner could if he deemed it necessary, frame a scheme for the better administration of the institution. This scheme would involve appointment of a Hindu as an executive officer, whose salary was payable from the institution's funds.

The doctrine of cypres was applicable when the objects of the trust failed. The Commissioner was entitled to take over and vest the administration of the institution in an executive officer appointed by him. The Act required the institutions to prepare budgets, get their accounts audited and pay to the Government annually a contribution not exceeding five per cent of their income on account of the services it rendered to them. Refusal as a trustee to comply with the provisions of the Act was made punishable.

It was alleged by mahant that his right to office was a protected constitutional guaranteed right to property. The Court first delineated the contours of Article 26 of the Constitution.[152] It was held that the language of Article 26 (b) suggests that besides 'affairs in matters of religion,' there could be other affairs not protected by it. To determine what are not matters of religion, the court analysed Article 26 and found that in clauses (c) and (d) the Article guarantees to a denomination the right to own and acquire property and the right to administer property according to law. The administration of its property by a religious denomination has thus been placed on a different footing from the right to manage its own affairs in matters of religion. The latter is a fundamental right which no legislature can take away, whereas the former can be regulated by laws which the legislature can validly impose. Therefore, questions relating to administration of property of a denominational institution were not 'matters of religion.'[153] The court, however, held that a mahant's right to protected right were the very same ones which had established the proprietary basis of religious offices in personal law terms. The Supreme Court held in Vidya Varuthi's case that a manager or custodian of the institution who has to discharge the duties of a trustee and is answerable as such, but he is not a mere manager and it would not be right to describe mahantship as a mere office.

It extended the protection of Article 25 and 26 to beliefs and practices of theistic and non-theistic religions and held that rituals and ceremonies like offerings of food to the idol, recitals of sacred texts, and oblations to the sacred fire, were despite the expenditure they involved matters of religion within the meaning of Article 26(b). The Court further held that a religious denomination or organisation enjoys complete autonomy in the matter of deciding as to what rites and ceremonies are essential according to the tenets of its religion and no outside authority has any jurisdiction to interfere with their decision in such matters.

The Court added :

> Of course, the scale of expenses to be incurred in connection with these religious observances would be a matter of administration of property belonging to the religious denomination and can be controlled by secular authorities in accordance with any law laid down by a competent legislature; for it could not be the injunction of any religion to destroy

the institution and its endowments by incurring wasteful expenditure on rites and ceremonies.

It should be noted, however, that under Article 26(b) it is the fundamental right of a religious denomination or its representative to administer its properties in accordance with law; and the law, therefore, must leave the right to administration to the denomination itself subject to such restrictions and regulation as it might choose to impose. A law which takes away the right of administration from the hands of a religious denomination altogether and vests it in any authority would amount to a violation of the right guaranteed under clause (d) of Article.

The court relief upon Sammontha Pandara Sellappah Chettiar[154] which was a case about the binding nature of debts on a succession to a mahant's office and *Giyana Sambandha Pandara Sannadhi*[154] v *Kandasami Tambiran* which involved a matter of succession.

Tripathi[155] says that the observation of the court that the state cannot take away the right to manage religious affairs while it can regulate by law the right to administer property is not wholly correct. Management of religious affairs of denomination being subject to public order, morality and health, is regulatable by the state on any of these grounds. Administration of denominational property, though subject to law, cannot be validly taken away altogether by the state. Thus, the state can take away neither of these rights, while it can regulate both of them.

The court seems to suggest that administration of property is not a matter of religion because it can be regulated by law. If this is so, ownership and acquisition of property, not being subjected by Article 26(c) to regulation by law, is entitled to be classified as a matter of religion. To identify and authenticate matters of religion the Court should have looked at the nature of the protected activity and not of the constitutional protection.

As the appellee, the Mathadhipati of the Shirur *math*, had sought protection of the fundamental rights guaranteed in Article 26 of a religious denomination or a section of it, the court considered whether this *math* was a denominational institution. The Court accepted the meaning of denomination given in the Oxford Dictionary. The Court found that the sects and sub-sects of Hinduism founded by religious leaders possessed a distinctive name, a common faith and a common spiritual organisation. The followers of each of these religious leader were, therefore, a religious denomination. And the Shirur *math*, reputed to have been founded by Madhawacharya and managed by a section of his followers—the Sivalli Brahmins—was a religious denomination.

The court then determined the position of the Matadhipati. It found that the opinion of the Privy Council on this question had been accepted in *Angurbala* v *Debabrala.*[156] The Privy Council had said that though the Mathadhipati discharged the duties of trustee and was answerable as such, he was not a mere Manager and it was not right to describe mahantship as a mere office. Besides, his duties connected with the endowment, he had in the trust property a personal interest of a beneficial character sanctioned by custom.[157] In Angurbala case the court held that like a Shebait, the Mathadhipati had a proprietary interest in the trust property.

In Angurbala's case, the court was required to pronounce on the nature of a Shebait's rights. The Shebaiti was to devolve on X, then on his wife XI and then on the heirs of XI'. X's second wife X2 claimed that after the death of XI and X (in that order)), she was entitled to sole rights in the Shebaiti. Alternatively, she claimed to share it with XS1 (X's son).

The court consisted of JJ Fazl Ali, Mahajan, Mukerjea and N.C. Aiyar. The court came to the following conclusions—

> In almost all such endowments the Shebait has a share in the usufruct of the debutter property which depends upon the terms of the grant or upon custom or usage. Even where no emoluments are attached to the office of the Shebait, he enjoys some sort of right or interest in the endowed property which partially at least has the character of a proprietary right. Thus in the conception of Shebaiti both the elements of office and property, of duties and personal interest, are mixed up and blended together and one of the elements cannot be detached from the other. It is the presence of this personal or beneficial

interest in the endowed property which invest Shebaitship with the character of proprietary rights and attaches to it the legal incidents of property.[158]

In Angurbala's case the court came to the conclusion that in almost all such endowments the Shebait has a share in the usufruct of the debutter property, which depends upon the terms of the grant or custom or usage. The court recognised the importance of custom. It held that in the absence of any direction to the contrary given by the founder the ordinary rule of succession under the Hindu law applies. This argument was also put before the Full Bench in *Manoher Mukerji* v *Bhupendranath Mukerji*.[159] The problem was whether the rule in *Tagore* v *Tagore*[160] applied where the founder laid down a line of succession. It was held that the said rule applied to the extent to which an estate unknown to the Hindu law was created.[161] The court held that a Shebait deals with the property in his custody or management as if he had some property, though not the full rights of property, in it, the legal property vesting in the idol. He has no right to alienate the property of the deity except for legal necessity, he may create proper derivative tenures and estates conformable to use.[162]

In *Kalipada* v *Palani Bala*[163] the Supreme Court was to decide whether the article applicable for recovery of Shebaitship was the one dealing with immovable property or the one dealing with hereditary office. Mukerjea J. with N.C. Aiyar and Ghulam Hasan JJ held that it was the later because a Shebaitship though property was not immovable property. The court defined the Shebait's interest in the office as a proprietary interest.

The court, therefore, held that the mahant's beneficial interest being property within the meaning of Article 19 (1) (f)[164] he was entitled to enjoy his property so long as he held that office. He is 'the head and superior of a spiritual fraternity and the purpose of the *math* is to encourage and foster spiritual training by maintenance of a competent line of teachers who could impart religious instruction to the disciple and followers of the *math* and try to strengthen the doctrines of the particular school or order of which they profess to be adherents. This purpose cannot be served if the restrictions (on his proprietary interest) are such as would bring the Matadhipati down to the level of a servant under state government.

Keeping in view all these observations, the court determined the validity of the challenged provisions of the Madras Act. The court invalidated Section 21 of the Act for authorizing the Commissioner and some of his subordinate officer to enter any religious institution for purposes connected with the spiritual functions of a temple had neither an unrestricted right to entry into it nor free access to the particularly sacred parts of it like the *sanctum sanctorum*.

The Court held that the power conferred by Section 56 on the Commissioner to require the trustee to appoint a manager and in the event of his failure to do so, to appoint the Manager himself, violated Article 26 (d). The Court said that under this section the Commissioner could deprive the mahant of his right to administer trust property even if there was no negligence or maladministration. 'The court also invalidated Sections 63 to 69 dealing with the taking over of administration of trust property by the Commissioner. The court struck down as violative of the mahant's right to property Section 30(2) and 31, which required the mahant to spend the surplus income for specified purposes with the prior approval of the secular authority. The court struck down the restrictions that Section 55 imposed on the mahant's power over personal gifts. The Court said that burdensome restrictions upon the right to property of the mahant impaired his dignity and efficiency as head of the institution. The court struck down the restrictions that Section 55 imposed on the mahant's power over personal gifts. The Court said that a mahant's power of disposal over personal gifts was absolute, though if he died without making any disposition, such gifts would form part of the trust property. Therefore, he could not be compelled to keep accounts of the personal receipts and expenditure of such gifts. It is therefore, clear that in 1954, the Supreme Court was quite content to apply the personal law connotation of property in the constitutional law context.

In *Ratilal Panachand Gandhi* v *The State of Bombay*[165] the Court reiterated its construction of Articles 25 and 26 in Lakshmindra's case and struck down the provisions of the Bombay Public Trusts Act, 1950, dealing with the appointment of a Charity Commissioner by a court as the trustee of a religious institution and application of the doctrine of cypres. The Court said that appointment of the Charity Commissioner by a court as the head of a *math* or the Shebait of a temple as provided in Section 44 and 47 (3) to (6) would amount to a flagrant violation of the right to manage affairs in matters of religion. The court held that as the object of a *math* was to maintain a competent line of religious teachers to propagate and strengthen the doctrine of a particular order or sect, the substitution of the Charity Commissioner for the Mathadhipati 'would mean a destruction of the institution altogether.'

Treatment of Parsis as a religious denomination within the meaning of Article 26 in Ratilal suggested that 'religion' and religious denomination' were synonyms. In *Ramchandra* v *State of Orissa* the Orissa High Court[166] rejected the argument that employment of these two expressions in Article 27 showed that they were not synonyms and said that this argument implied that Article 26 encompassed a religious institution of a sect or sub-sect only and not of a religious group as a whole. The Court held that like the Parsis, the Hindus, too, were a religious denomination. It said that in Lakshmindra the Supreme Court had not dissented from the observation made in the judgment under appeal that in a large sense a religious group as a whole constituted a denomination. But in appeal against the Orissa High Court's judgment in Ramachandra, the Supreme Court[167] said that it was not necessary for the Orissa High Court to go into that question and, because of the defective state of pleadings, declined to express any opinion on it, though in the Ratilal and Gurdwara case it had presupposed that Parsis and Sikhs were religious denominations.

In *Bira Kishore Deb* v *Orissa*[168] it was said by Justice Wanchoo and Sikri JJ that in the instant case only a right to management was involved. There had been a shift in Supreme Court's attitude. In the fifties Mukerjea, J's emphasis was on protecting personal law notions of property, office and control. In the early sixties Gajendragadkar J (later on became Chief Justice) appears to have reversed this emphasis and approved all these facts from the point of view of public law.

It is submitted that as there are religious institutions belonging to a religious group as a whole and also as there are religions that have no sects and sub-sects, a broad interpretation of 'religious denomination' that extends to such institutions and religions the freedom enshrined in Article 26 must be favoured. This is the duty of the courts to see that 'religious denominations' in Article 26 does not encompass castes and sub-castes. Extension of the hospitality of Article 26 to castes and sub-castes may perpetuate casteism and impair the operative vigour of all those provisions that seek to root out casteism from the Indian soil.

The present day position of the trusts including waqfs is not satisfactory. Most of the waqfs are mismanaged. These waqfs needs governmental control. Therefore, state legislature have directed these religious institutions to make a contribution to the government for services rendered by way of supervision. The matter of imposition of tax is not given either in List II or List III. Only Parliament could levy such a tax. Under entry 47 of List III a state can only levy a fee on religious trusts. According to Supreme Court a fee on religious trusts imposed to meet the expenditure of governmental supervision over their administration cannot be objected to under Article 27. The State does not impose contribution for fostering or preserving the Hindu religious on of any denomination within it. In fact the legislature intended to control secular administration of religious institutions.[169]

No separation between Church and State under the Indian Constitution

In *Narayanan Numbudripad* v. *State of Madras*[170] Section 76 of the Madras Hindu Religious and Charitable Endowments Act, 1951 was challenged as violating Articles 25 and 26 on the ground that under our constitution there was a wall of separation erected between the church and the state as there was in the United States. Justice Aiyar however, rejected this argument. It was said that the First Amendment to the U.S. Constitution falls into two parts : the first prohibits the establishment of any religion, and the second guarantees freedom of religion to all persons. In United States there was no unanimity of judicial opinion about the meaning of the word establishment The grammatic meaning of the word 'establishment' is the act of establishing. According to this meaning the state should not establish any religion by law. The other meaning of this word can be religious institution which had been established, so that the prohibition of the First Amendment would extend to any legislation in respect of a religious institution.

On the basis of decided cases of the United States it may be said that since both prohibitions were enacted in one amendment, it could not be that religion was a private purpose under the second part of the amendment and was a public purpose under the first.

The Indian Constitution does not contain anything corresponding to the first part of the First Amendment of the U.S. Constitution.

It has been argued that though our constitution had not expressly forbidden the establishment of a religion, it had done so impliedly. It is submitted here that the argument is not based on any authority. It is inconsistent with several express provisions of our constitution. In this connection the following observations of Justice Aiyer in the *Narayanan Nambudripad* v *State of Madras*[171] may be noted :

> ...there are provisions in our constitution which are inconsistent with the theory that there should be a wall of separation between church and state. Article 16(5) recognises the validity of laws relating to management of religious and denominational institutions. Article 28(2) contemplates the state itself managing educational institutions wherein religious instruction is to be imparted. Any among the subjects over which both the union and the state have legislative competence and are set out in List No. III of the 7th schedule to the constitution, entry

No. 28 is as follows : 'Charities and charitable institutions, charitable and religious endowments and religious institutions.'

Under Article 27 of the Constitution a tax cannot be imposed for the promotion of religion or religious denomination. Seervai[172] says that there is, however, a distinction between religion in its doctrinal and ritual aspects which is a private purpose, and the administration of property dedicated to the public for religious purposes which is a public purpose. It will be relevant here to discuss the facts and the law laid down by the Privy Council in *Amulya Chandra* v *Corporation of Calcutta.*[173] In this case the Corporation of Calcutta acquired certain land for building a dharmsala for accommodating pilgrims restoring to a Hindu temple. The Privy Council held that since the acquisition was for public purpose it was lawful.

Seervai says that the law as it stood before the constitution has not undergone a change.[174] It is submitted here that the above approach of Seervai is not correct. It is very difficult to maintain a difference between religion in its doctrinal and ritual aspects and the administration of property dedicated to the public for religious purposes. In fact, this is not the duty of the state to construct building of a religious institution for visitors. This work can be very well performed by the management committees of religious institutions. The duty of the state is only to see that these institutions are functioning properly. In case of Urs (annual fair *etc*). this is the duty of the state to make necessary arrangement for its proper conduct. Police personnel in sufficient number may be posted at such places and this will not amount to the promotion of any particular religion.

Article 28 guarantees as to attendance at religious instruction or religious worship in certain educational institutions[175]. There is a difference between educational institutions wholly maintained out of state funds and those recognised by the state or receiving aid out of state funds. In the educational institutions which are wholly maintained by state fund, no religious instructions can be given. Institution which are recognised by the state or receiving aid out of state funds, management can provide religious instruction. These institutions can also conduct religious worship. The attending of religious instructions or conduct of religious worship cannot be made compulsory. According to sub-clause 3 of Article 28 these institutions shall not give instruction to or make it compulsory upon a person unless such person gives his consent, or if he is a minor, consent of his parents has been obtained.

For properly understanding the background of Article 28 it is necessary to see the Constituent Assembly Debates on this subject. At the time of the framing of the Constitution the members of the Constituent Assembly were very well knowing the role played by the various religions in Indian politics. Therefore, the framers of the Constitution decided not to impart religious education in any educational institution wholly maintained by state fund. At the same time they were knowing the sentiments of minority communities. They, therefore, allowed the imparting of religious instructions in any educational institution recognised by the state.

In Constituent Assembly Dr. Ambedkar said that India is a country of multiplicity of religions. Hindus are in majority. Muslims, Christians, Jews and Parsis are in minority. Therefore, if public funds raised by taxes are allowed to be utilised for the benefit of any community this would have been against the policy of secularism. For example, if permission is accorded to impart any particular religious instruction, say, if a school established by a district or local board gives religious instruction, on the ground that the majority of the students studying in that school are Hindus, the effect would be that such action would militate against the provision contained in Article 27 of the Constitution. The district board would be making a levy on every person residing within the area of that district board. This levy will be collected from all inhabitants living in a particular area and, therefore, if religious instruction were imparted to the children of the majority community, it would be unconstitutional under Article 27, because the children of other community who do not agree to attend these religious instructions given in the schools would nonetheless be compelled by the action of the district or local board to contribute to the district or local board.

The other important factor for incorporating Articles 27 and 28 is the multiplicity of religions. Due to multiplicity of religions it is impossible to make necessary arrangements for imparting religious education to the children of all communities equally. For example, take a city like Bombay which contains a heterogeneous population believing in different creeds. Suppose, for instance, there was a school in the city of Bombay maintained by the Municipality. Obviously, such a school would contain children of Hindus believing in the Hindu religion, there will be pubils belonging to the Christian community, Zoroastrian community, or to the Jewish community. All these communities can again be divided into various sub-classes. For example, Hindus can mainly be divided into four sub-classes—Brahmins, Kshetris, Vaishs, Sudras. The sub-classes can again be divided into various sub-classes. It is, therefore, not possible for the educational institutions to treat all these children on a footing of equality and provide religious instruction in all the denominations.

Again, Indian religions are not merely non-social, they are anti-social. All the religions claim that their respective teaching and philosophy is only correct and its followers can only attain salvation, and all other religions are wrong. For example, according to Islamic faith a non-believer of Islam is *Kafir* and he is not entitled to brotherly treatment with the Muslims. Hindus believe that non-believers are *malich*. The Christians have a similar belief. Under these circumstances, if religious instructions would have been allowed in educational institutions it should be considerably disturbing the peaceful atmosphere of an institution of these controversies with regard to the truthful character of any particular religion and the erroneous character of the other were brought into just opposition in the school itself. The constitution makers, therefore, rightly provided that no religious instruction should be provided in wholly state owned institutions.[176]

Section 4 of the Guru Nanak Dev University Act empowered the State Government to make provision for the study and research on the life and teachings of Guru Nanak. The constitutional validity of this provision was challenged[177] on the ground that as the University was maintained wholly out of state funds it was abrogating the provisions of Article 28(1) and (2). Their Lordship of the Supreme Court rejected this contention. It was said that Section 4 of the aforesaid Act was not violative of the Constitution as it enjoined the University to encourage an academic study of the life and teachings of Guru Nanak and it did not amount to religious instruction or promotion of any particular religion.

Article 29 of the Indian Constitution guarantees protection of Interests of minorities.[178] It guarantees one's language. The scope of Article 29(1) may best be explained in the words of Dr Ambedkar,[179] Chairman of the drafting committee of the Constituent Assembly which drafted the constitution and himself a member of a minority community.

> It does not impose any obligation or burden upon the state. It does not say that when, for instance, the Madras people come to Bombay, the Bombay government shall be required by law to finance any project of giving education either in Tamil language or in Telugu language or in any other language. There is no burden cast upon the state. The only limitation that is imposed by the article is that if there is a cultural minority which wants to preserve its language, its script and its culture the state shall not by law impose upon it any other culture which may be local or otherwise. Therefore, this Article has really to be read in a much wider sense and does not apply only to what is called the technical minorities as we use it in our constitution. That is the reason why we eliminate the word 'minority' from the original clause.

In the year 1951, First Amendment Act was passed. This Act inserted clause (4) in Article 15 of the Constitution. Before this amendment the Madras High Court in *State of Madras* v *Champakam*[180], the State Government's order distributing seats among communities in state educational institutions was declared *ultra vires* the constitution. The court held that in matters of admission to educational institutions the backward communities are not protected and that

Article 29 (2) is not controlled by Article 46. After the First Constitutional Amendment by adding clause (4) to Article (4) made it constitutional for the state to reserve seat in public educational institutions for backward classes, scheduled castes and tribes. It also brought Articles 15 and 29 in line with Articles 16 (4), 46 and 340. It may be noted that Articles 15 (4) validates reservation for members of scheduled castes and tribes and backward classes only but does not validate reservation on communal grounds. Article 15 (4) was added as an exception to that part of Article 15 (1) which forbids discrimination on the grounds of race or caste and as an amendment of that part of Article 29 (2) which forbids denial of admission into educational institutions, on the same grounds[181]. However, since no such provision regarding educational institutions has been made in Article 15 in the case of the ground of sex, Article 29 (2) insofar as it does not mention sex as a forbidden ground of discrimination, in regard to admission into educational institutions, remains unaffected. It is submitted that the scheduled castes aud tribes and backward classes need these reservations. They may be helped on the basis of need without reference to their castes *etc.* There are many members of other communities who stand on exactly the same footing and hence need to be helped.

The idea behind Article 29 in the Constitution of India is to give cultural protection not only to the religious minority communities but also to linguistic minorities. The clause makes it clear that if there is a cultural or linguistic minority which wants to preserve its own language and culture, the state would not by law impose upon it any other culture.

Article 29 (2) is a counterpart of Article 15, the equality clause. It lays down for non-discrimination on the ground of religion, race, caste, language or any of them in the matter of admission into educational institutions provided they are maintained or aided by the State. In *State of Madras* v *Champakam*[182], the Madras High Court concluded that whereas clause (1) protects the rights of a section of the citizens, the rights conferred by clause (2) are given to individuals as such and not because they are members of a particular community. Article 29 (2) confers a fundamental right not only on members of minority groups but on every citizens. In *State of Bombay* v *Bombay Education Society*[183], the Supreme Court said to limit this right only to citizens belonging to minority groups will be to provide a double protection for such citizens and to hold that the citizens of the majority group have no special educational interest in the nature of a right to be admitted into an educational institution for the maintenance of which they make contributions by way of taxes. We see no cogent reason for such discrimination. The word 'aid' used in this clause has not been defined in the Constitution. It should, therefore, be given its ordinary meaning. It also includes a grant to an educational institution[184].

Article 30[185] guarantees right of minorities to establish and administer educational institutions. A minority community can effectively conserve its language only through educational institutions guaranteed in Article 30 is a necessary concomitant of Article 29 (1). This right is, of course, subject to Article 29 (2) if the educational institution gets state aid[186]. Grants-in-aid or recognition cannot, however, be offered on terms which involve the surrender of Fundamental Rights under Article 30 (1) of the Constitution. But Article 45[187] overrides this Article 30, although reasonable restrictions can be imposed as conditions of the aid or recognition[188].

The doctrine of minority educational rights has been used to hold *ultra vires* and void an order of the government interfering in the management of an educational institution[189]. This right is also interconnected with a minority's right to impart instructions in the language of its choice. It was said in the *State of Bombay* v *Bombay Education Society*[190], to hold otherwise will be to deprive Articles 29 (1) and 30 (1) of the greater parts of their contents. A state legislature has no legal competence to affect the medium of instruction.

The police power of the state to determine the medium of instructions must yield, indeed to this fundamental right to the extent it is necessary[191]. The educational institutions are not debarred from imposing beneficial conditions or limitations such as previous training, age, dissociations from injurious associations[192] *etc.* nor to refuse admission or[193] to expel a student on the ground of indiscipline[194] *etc.* provided there is no discrimination on the ground of religion, race, caste, language or any of them. In *Re* Kerala Education Bill the Court rejected the argument that the right to admission under Article 29 (2) was limited to members of the community for whose benefit the schools were established.

Article 26 guarantees to a minority the right to maintain religious and charitable institutions. Article 30 gives them the right to establish their own educational institutions is complementary to Article 29 (1) which gives a minority the right to preserve its language and script. It clearly implies a prohibition on the state not to ban the teaching of a minority community's language in an educational institution maintained[195] by it.

The above Article also implies a corresponding right in a person to attend such denominational institutions. In Re Kerala Education Bill[196], it was said that the right conferred by this Article would clearly be without any meaning if diploma/degree holder from such institutions were denied opportunities for higher learning in other institutions or for a useful career in life. It is not necessary that such institutions teach only the language or the religion of the minority community establishing it. They are free to give general education.

Article 30 not only gives to minorities the right to establish educational institutions but also the right to administer them. The claimant of such right has to claim following two things:—

(i) That it is minority; and
(ii) That the institution was established by it[197].

The right to administer is not an absolute right even though Article 30 lays down no specific limits. Therefore, an institution has no right to maladministration. Therefore, while granting aid, the state can impose the condition regarding competency of teachers and maintenance of proper discipline[198] etc. It may also be noted that the rights under Article 30 cannot be said to be available only so long as the community is in a position to run the institution from its own resources. While granting aid, or recognition, the state cannot impose any terms it consider fit. Article 30 (2) contains a prohibition against discrimination by the state in the matter of aid to educational institutions. Therefore, minority[199] educational institutions are entitled to state aid like any other educational institution.

Relationship between Arts. 29 (1) and 30(1)

The right to establish and administer an educaticnal institution under Article 30 is not confined only to the purposes specified in Article 29 (1)[200]. Under Article 29 (1) an educational institution may be established for conserving script, language and culture. However, under Article 30 (1) a religious and linguistic minority may establish an institution which may have no concern with the object of conserving its script, language or culture. The words of their choice occurring in Article 30 (1) qualify the words 'educational institutions' and this leaves vast options to the minorities in selecting the type of educational institution which they wish to establish. There is, therefore, under Article 30 (1) no limitation on any particular type of educational institution. The right includes the right to impart general secular education also for enriching the children of the minorities intellectually, morally and financially and enabling them to face the realities of life.

The view that the width of Article 30 (1) cannot be out down by importing into it the consideration on which Article 29 (1) is based on the following grounds :

(1) If the educational institutions referred to in Article 30 (1) must only be those institutions which have been established for the purpose of conserving language, script or culture, then it will render Article 30 (1) redundant, Article 30 (1) also grants rights to a religious minority to establish an educational institution which may be wholly unconnected with the conservation of language, script and culture.

(2) The rights under Article 29 (1) are available to 'any section of citizens'. This right can be enjoyed by minority as well as majority community. Article 30 (1) is applicable to all minorities whether based on

religion or language. This right cannot be enjoyed by any other section of citizens[201].

(3) While educational institution falling under Article 29 (1) can be set up only for the objectives mentioned therein, Article 30 (1) enables the religious and linguistic minorities to establish and administer any type of educational institution of their choice.

It may, however, be noted that the two articles create separate rights but it is possible that the rights might meet in a given case[202].

Recently, the Indian Supreme Court discussed in detail the above issues in *All Saints High School* v *Government of Andhra Pradesh*[203]. After briefly discussing earlier decisions the Supreme Court made the following observations :

(1) Article 30 (1) gives a fundamental right of the minority institution to manage and administer their educational institutions which is completely in consonance with the secular nature of democracy and the directives in the constitution itself.

(2) It is true that the rights guaranteed to minorities under the Constitution are absolute, unfettered and unconditional. But individuals are not given free licence for maladministration.

(3) Of course, the state or any other statutory authority has no right to interfere with the internal administration or management of the minority institution, the state can take regulatory measures to promote the efficiency and excellence of educational standards. The state can issue guidelines for the purpose of ensuring the security of the services of the teachers or other employees of the institution.

(4) Again, the state or any University authority cannot under the cover or garb of adopting regulatory measures tend to destory the administrative autonomy of the institution or start interfering willy nilly with the core of the management of the institution so as to render the right of administration of the management of the institution concerned nugatory or illusory.

(5) One of the salient feature of Article 30 (1) is that where affiliation is asked for, the University concerned cannot refuse the same unless there is a sufficient ground for refusing the same. The university cannot also impose such conditions as would destroy the autonomous administration of the educational institution.

(6) The introduction of an outside authority, however, high it may be either directly or through its nominees in the governing body or the managing committee of the minority institution to conduct the affairs of the institution would be completely destructive of Article 30 (1) and would reduce the management to a helpless entity having no real say in the matter and thus destroy the very personality and individuality of the institution which is fully protected by Article 30. The university can make rules for the better service conditions of the teachers. But the university should not take such steps which may ultimately control the voice in the matter and thus overshadow the power of the managing committee. Where educational institution have set up a particular governing body or the managing committee in which all the powers vest, such powers should not be curbed or taken away unless the government is satisfied that these powers are grossly abused and if allowed to continue may reduce the efficacy or the uselessness of the institution.

(7) The Government or the University can, therefore, make rules and regulations governing the service conditions of teachers in order to secure their tenure of service and to appoint a high authority to see that these rules are not violated. This will not amount to interference into the internal administration or autonomy of the institution. This step may be taken for improving the excellence and efficiency of the education. But while setting up such an authority care must be taken to see that the said authority is not given blanket and uncanalised and arbitrary powers

so as to act at their own sweet will ignoring the very spirit and objective of the institution.

(8) Where a minority institution is affiliated to a University the fact that is enjoined to adopt the courses of study or the syllabi or the nature of books, prescribed and the holding of examination to test the ability of the statements of the institution concerned does not violate the freedom contained in Article 30 of the constitution.

(9) The authority so appointed by the University must be provided with porper guidelines under the restricted field which they have to cover. Before coming to any conclusion the Head of the institution *etc.* must be associated and they should be allowed to have a positive say in the matter. It is not constitutionally valid that outside authorities should have absolute powers in taking decisions regarding the minority institutions without hearing them and these orders are binding on the institution.

Directive Principles of State Policy in a Nutshell

Articles 41[204], 45[205] and 46[206] of the Indian Constitution directs the state to promote education and to introduce free and compulsory education for all children up to the age of fourteen years. Unfortunately, the directions given in Article 45 could not be followed even though more than twice the prescribed period has elapsed. Education, especially in the state of Madhya Pradesh is a neglected subject. The Central Government has declared Madhya Pradesh as backward in education. In India, education is not a fundamental right, except for some educational rights of the minorities discussed above.

In Article 41 the use of term right to education is incorrect. The Indian Constitution does not recognise a right to education. The Chapter of Directive Principles of State Policy is not obligatory on the states to follow. The provisions of this chapter are directory and not enforceable. The maintenance of rights in a democracy, of the minorities as well as the majority depends to a very large extent upon a proper appreciation of the questions involved. Thus, having regard to the importance of education in a democracy the proportion of the national budget spent on education in India since independence seems to have been disproportionately meagre[207].

Establishment of Educational Institutions by minorities vs State's right to promote Hindi

Hindi is the national language of India. This is the duty of the union to promote the spread of the Hindi language. It may be developed in such a way that it may serve as a medium of expression for all the elements of the composite culture of India. Its enrichment may be developed without interfering with its genius, the form style and expressions used in Hindustani and in the other languages of India specified in the Eighth Schedule[208]. It is, therefore, clear that even though Hindi is the national language and Article 351 provides a directive to the state to promote its growth yet to achieve it the state cannot breach the rights given in Articles 29 and 30. It is submitted here that attempt should be made to reconcile Articles 41, 45 and 46 with the rights conferred by Article 30 even though the Directive Principles cannot override the Fundamental Rights in Article 30.

REFERENCES

1. For the definition of minority, please see—*Re* the Kerala Education Bill, 1857, *AIR* 1958 SC 956 ; *A.M. Patroni* v *E.C. Keshavan, AIR* 1965 Ker 75 ; *D.A.V. College Jullunder* v *State of Punjab, AIR* 1971 SC 1737 ; *Arya Samaj Education Trust* v *The Director of Education, Delhi Administration, AIR* 1976 Del. 207. For further detail the following articles may be seen M.P. Jain, Safeguards to Minorities, Constitutional Principles, Policies and Framework in M. Imam (ed), *Minorities and the Law* pp. 20-21(I.L.R., 1972); D.K. Singh, Cultural and Ecucational Rights in India, In G.S. Sharma (ed), *Educational Planning : Its Legal and Constituitonal Implications in India*, 136 at 137-138 (1967) ; I.P. Massey, Constitutional Protection to Educational Institutions of Minorities in India, in M. Imam (ed), ; *supra* K. Subbarao, *Social Justice and the Law* ; 95 (1974) ; K.K. Wadhwa, *Minority Safeguards in India*, 4-7 (1975) ; Report of the United Nations Sub-Committee on the Prevention of Discrimination and

Protection and Minorities ; *Year Book on Human Rights,* 490 (1950).

2. See Article 14 of the Indian Constitution.
3. See Article 15 ,, ,, ,,
4. See Article 16 ,, ,, ,,
5. See Article 19 ,, ,, ,,
6. See Article 25 ,, ,, ,,
7. See Article 26 ,, ,, ,,
8. See Article 27 ,, ,, ,,
9. See Article 28 ,, ,, ,,
10. See Article 29 ,, ,, ,,
11. See Article 30 ,, ,, ,,
12. Alan Gladhill. *Fundamental Rights in India*, (1956) pp. 35-36.
13. *Charanjit Lal Chowdhuri* v *Union of India, AIR* 1951 SC 41 ; (1950). SCR 869 ; *State of U.P.* v *Deoman, AIR* 1960 SC 1125, 1960 (2) SCA 371, 1960 ALJ 733.
14. *Heath and Millingan Mfg. Co.* v *Worst*, 207 U.S. 338.
15. *AIR* 1952 Mad 613.
16. *Namboodripad* v *C.D. Board. AIR* 1956 TC 19 (FB) ; C. Nair Secretary. C.B. Board, *AIR* 1957 Ker 188 (FB).
17. *AIR* 1959 SC 942 ; See also *Budhan Choudhry* v *The State of Bihar, AIR* 1955 SC 191, 1955 (1) SCR 1045 ; *Ram Krishna Dalmia* v *Justice Tendolkar, AIR* 1958 SC 538, (1959) (1) An WR 67, (1959) (1) MLJ 67. (1959) SCJ 147.
18. See J.D. Derrett, The reform of Hindu religious endowments in E.E. Smith (ed), *South Asian Politics and Religion*, (1966), p. 311 at 314.
19. P.K. Tripathi, *Secularism, Constitutional Provision and Judicial Review*, (1966) 8 JILI 10.
20. S C. Bhat, A note on the Report of the Hindu Religious Endowments Commission, *AIR* 1964 (Jr Sec) pp. 98-99.
21. In *Vikrama Das* v *Daulat Ram, AIR* 1956 SC 382 the Supreme Court said that it cannot allow a public trust to be left to the mercy of unauthorised persons who are scrambling for a position of vantage in its management. It may, however, be noted that the Indian Courts were not frequently interfering into the affairs of the Hindu religious institutions.
22. See the Report of the Commission on Hindu Religious Endowments, pp. 115-116.
23. Government of India, (1949).
24. See the Report of the Durgah Khwaja Saheb (Ajmer) Committee of Enquiry, Government of India, (1949), pp, 57, 63-65, 98-99.
25. Temple Funds—*The Times of India*, March 19, 1970, (Delhi ed), p 6, See also *The Hindustan Times*, April 20, 1970, Cols 1 & 2 p. 6 for a report on the controversy over the Tirupati Lord's wealth.
26. *Supra* note 22, pp. 31-35.

27. *AIR* 1962 SC 853.
28. See Article 25 of the Indian Constitution
29. *AIR* 1954 Mad 385, (1955) Mad 256 at p 377, (1953) 2 MIJ 699.
30. (1943) 67 CLR 116, 123.
31. S. 116 of the Commonwealth of Australia provides—'The Commonwealth shall not make any law for establishing any religion or for imposing any religious observance, or for prohibiting the free exercise of any religion, and no religious test shall be required as a qualification for any office or public trust under the Commonwealth.'
32. (1889) 133 US 333, 342, 33 L. ed. 637.
33. *Supra* note 30.
34 *AIR* 1954 SC 388.
35. (1909) 33 Bom 122 ; See also *Likji Nowroji Banaji* v *Bapuji Ruttonji Limbuwalla* (1887) 11 Bom 441. In this case the ceremonies of Mukted *etc.* where held as void.
36. *Commissioner of Hindu Religious Endowments, Madras* v *Sri Lakshmindra Tirtha Swamiar of Sri Shirur Mutt, AIR* 1954 SC 282.
37. *Durgah Committee, Ajmer* v *Hussain Ali, AIR* 1961 SC 1402.
38. *Article 26—Freedom to manage religious affairs* :—Subject to public order, morality and health, every religious denomination or any section thereof shall have the right—
    (a) to establish and maintain institutions for religious and charitable purposes ;
    (b) to manage its own affairs in matter of religion ;
    (c) to own and acquire movable and immovable property ; and
    (d) to administer such property in accordance with law. Entry No 10 of List III (concurrent list) of the Indian Constitution is *entitled* 'Trust and trustees' entry No 18 of the same list is entitled 'charities and charitable institutions, charitable and religious endowments and religious institutions'. Thus to protect and control the waqfs is the duty of both the central and state governments.
39. See Paul Procter, *Longman Dictionary of Contemporary English* p. 293.
40. See *Webster Dictionary.*
41. *Ibid*, p. 1022.
42. Roman Catholic Mission is a religious denomination. See *Chinnamma* v *R. Dy. D.P.I. AIR* 1964 A.P. 277.
43. See *Commissioner H R.E.* v *L.T. Swamiar, AIR* 1954 SC 282, 1954 SCR 1005. In this case, it was held that the Maths or the spiritual fraternity represented by it can legitimately come within the purview of Article 26.
44. *Ibid*, p. 1025.

45. *Durgah Committee Ajmer* v *Syed Hussain Ali, AIR* 1961 SC 1402 (1962) 1 SCR 383 ; *Venkataraman Devaru* v *State of Mysore, AIR* 1958 SC 255, (1958) SCR 895 ; *Jagannath Ramanuj De* v *State of Orissa, AIR* 1954 SC 400, 1954 SCR 1946 : *Commissioner H.R.* v *L.T. Swamiar, AIR* 1954 SC 282, (1954) SCR 1005.
64. *Supra* note 37.
47. *Sardar Syedna Taher Saifuddin Saheb* v *State of Bombay, AIR* 1962 SC 853, (1962) Supp 2 SCR 496 ; see also *Acharaj Singh* v *State of Bihar, AIR* 1967 Pat 114 ; *Sarwar Hussain* v *Addl. Civil Judge* ; *AIR* 1983 All 252.
48. *Sarwar Hussian* v *Addl Civil Judge, ibid.*
49. *Venkataramman Devaru* v *State of Mysore, AIR* 1958 SC 255, 268.
50. See *Seshammal* v *State of Tamil Nadu,* (1972) 2 SCC 11.
51. *AIR* 1948 PC 66, (1947) 75 I.A. 1. In this case the Privy Council held that the petitioner, who was the Dai-ul-Mutlal as the head of the Dawoodi Bohra community, was having the right to excommunicate any member of the community. The Privy Council also explained the term excommunication. It said that the term excommunication necessarily involves exclusion from the exercise of religious rights in places under the trusteeship of the head of the community in which religious exercises are performed.
52. The constitutional validity of the Act was challenged in *Sardar Syedna Taher Saifuddin Saheb* v *State of Bombay, AIR* 1962 SC 853, (1962) Supp 2 SCR 496, see also *Taher Saifuddin* v *Tyedbhai Noosaji, AIR* 1953 Bom 183, 55 Bom LR 1. The Bombay High Court declared the Act as unconstitutional.
53. The majority opinion was delivered by Das Gupta, Sarkar and Mudhlkar JJ.
54. *Ibid,* p. 537.
55. See H.M. Seervai, *Constitutional Law of India,* (1968) Vol 1, pp. 686-687.
56. *Commissioner H.R.E.* v *L.T. Swamiar, AIR* 1954 SC 282, (1954) SCR 1005, *Tilkayat Shri Govindlalji* v *State of Rajasthan, AIR* 1963 SC 1638, *State of Rajasthan* v *Sajjanlal Panjawat,* (1974) 1 SCC 500, see also *Raja Bika Kishore* v *State of Orissa, AIR* 1964 SC 1501, (1964) 7 SCR 32.
57. *Ibid,* p. 1029.
58. *AIR* 1958 SC 731, (1959) SCR 629, (1958) SCJ 975.
59. *Rati Lal Panachand Gandhi* v *State of Bombay, AIR* 1954 SC 38 392, 1954 SCR 1055 ; See also *Commissioner H.R.E.* v *L.T. Swamiar, AIR* 1954 SC 282, 295, 1954 SCR 1005. In this case section 56 of the Madras Hindu Religious and Charitable Endowment Act, 1951, authorised the Commissioner, at any moment he choose to deprive the mahant of his right to administer the trust property, even if there was no negligence or maladministration on

his part. It was held that the provision was opposed to Article 26 (d).

60. *Supra* note 37.
61. *Suryapal Singh* v *U.P. AIR* 1951 All 674.
62. *Khajamian Waqf Estates* v *State of Madras*, (1971) 2 SCR 790, (1970) 3 SCC 894.
63. *AIR* 1954 SC 282, 1954 SCR 1005.
64. *AIR* 1956 Mad 491.
65. *AIR* 1968 SC 1489. In this case reliance was made on *Roman Catholic Mission* v *State of Madras AIR* 1966 SC 1457.
66. *Sarwar Hussain* v *Addl Civil Judge*, Moradabad, *supra* note 47.
67. *AIR* 1959 SC 942. The Bench of the Supreme Court consisted of the following judges—S.R. Das, Chief Justice, P.B. Gajendragadkar, K.N. Wanchoo and M. Hidayatullah. This decision also covers the decision in *State of Bihar* v *Bhabapritanando Ojha* (1959) Supp (2) SCR 624, *AIR* 1959 SC 1073, (1959) SCJ 1197. (1960) 1 SCA 245. This case declared as lawful Sections 28 and 32, Bihar Hindu Religious Trusts Act, 1959 ; *Namoodripad* v *C.D. Board*, (1956) Tr. Co 74 (F.B.) *AIR* 1956 Tra. Co 19. It was held that it was within the competence of the legislature to make provisions for safeguarding religious institutions of a particular faith and for avoiding friction and mismanagement of the trust. It was a reasonable restriction in the interest of the general public.
68. *AIR* 1963 SC 1638. 1 SCR 561 ; See also *Raja Bika Kishore* v *State of Orissa*, *AIR* 1964 SC 1501, (1964) 7 SCR 32 ; Devraj v State of Madras, *AIR* 1953 Mad 149. (1952) 2 MIJ 487.
69. See H.M. Seervai, *Constitutional Law of India*, Vol 1 (1968) p 487.
70. *AIR* 1958 A P. 773 ; see also *Pubbiri* v *S. Govinda AIR* 1958 Mad 147, (1957) 2 MIJ 617 ; *Raja of Kozhikode* v *Commissioner H.R. & C.E. AIR* 1961 Mad 205.
71. *AIR* 1959 Ori 117, (1958) Cutt 666. In this case the opinion of the Supreme Court in Shirur Mutt and Ratilal Gandhi's cases was followed. See also *Mukundaraya* v *State of Mysore*, *AIR* 1960 Mys 18 ; *Narayan Prasad* v *State of Hyderabad*, *AIR* 1955 Hyd 82 ; *Rajendra* v *State of Andhra Pradesh*, *AIR* 1957 AD 283 ; *Narayan Doss* v *T. Neeladari Rao*, *AIR* 1959 AP 148, (1959) A.P. 67.
72. *R.* v *Dhyan Singh*, *AIR* 1952 All 53 ; H.M. Seervai, *Constitutional Law of India* Vol. 1 (1968) p. 490.
73. *AIR* 1957 SC 650, (1957) SCR 860, 867.
74. H.M. Seervai. *Constitutional Law of India*, Vol 1 (1968) p. 49.
75. *S. Veerabhadran Chettiar* v *E.V. Ramaswamy Naicker*, *AIR* 1958 SC 1032, (1959) SCR 1211, (1959) SCJ 1, (1958) SCA 1116 ; See also *Public Prosecutor* v *Ramaswami*, *AIR* 1964 Mad 258. In this case the court upheld the validity of Section 295A of the Indian Penal Code and held that the two articles written by him deliberately

and maliciously outraged the religious feelings of the Muslim community, as the articles contained insulting and abusive language about the *Quran* and about Allah.

76. *AIR* 1958 M.P. 115, (1957) M.P. 658.
77. *AIR* 1957 Cal 524, 61 CWN 717.
78. *AIR* 1958 SC 255, (1958) SCJ 382, (1958) SCR 895.
79. H M. Seervai, *Supra* note, p. 494.
80. *Supra* note 76.
81. *AIR* 1956 Mad 541, (1956) 1 MLJ 125.
82. See *State of Bombay* v *Narasu Appa Mali, AIR* 1952 Bom 84, (1951) Bom 775, 53 Bom LR 779 ; see also *Srinivasa Aiyar* v *Saraswathi Ammal, AIR* 1952 Mad 193, (1951) 2 MLJ 649, *Ram Prasad* v *State of U.P., AIR* 1961 All 334, (1961) ALJ 383. In this case rule 27, U.P. Government servants conduct rules which provided that a government servant may not marry a second wife during the existence of the first wife, without the permission of the state government was held constitutional and it did not infringe Art 25 of the Constitution.
83. *AIR* 1952 SC 252, (1952) SCR 889.
84. *AIR* 1954 Cal. 241, 88 CWN 73. See also *Chintamani Pratihari* v *State of Orissa, AIR* 1958 Ori 18, (1957) Cut. 328. In this case it was held that the acquisition of a Devadayan Inam under Section 3, Orissa Estates Abolition Act did not interfere with the fundamental rights guaranteed under Article 26.
85. *Anant Prasad* v *State of A.P. AIR* 1963 SC 853, 1 SCJ 615, (1964) Supp (1) SCR 844. In this case Sections 3 to 11, Hyderabad Endowment Regulations, 1940 was declared as lawful.
86. At p. 1068.
87. *Supra* note 56.
88. *AIR* 1959 AP 148.
89. At p. 1665.
90. p. 1665, Tilkayat case.
91. *Supra* note 88.
92. *Sarup Singh* v *State of Punab* , *AIR* 1959 SC.
93. At p . 866.
94. See *State of Bihar* v *Charushila Dasi, AIR* 1959 SC 1002 ; *State of Bihar* v *Bhabapritananda Ojha* , *AIR* 1959 SC 1073 ; see also *Labhchandra* v *State* , *AIR* 1969 Pat 209. In this case the Bihar. Swetambar Jain Religious Trusts Rules, 1955 framed under the Trusts Act, 1951 were held to be discriminatory and violative of Articles 14 and 26 of the Constitution.
95. (1962) 1 SCR 383.
96. At p. 414.
97. At p. 418.
98. *Supra* note 68.
99. *AIR* 1963 SC 966.

100. *AIR* 1970 SC 181, (1969) 1 SCC 844. In this case sections 46 and 47 of the Andhra Pradesh Act were held to be non-violative of Articles 14, 19 (1) (f) and 26 of the Indian Constitution.
101. *AIR* 1969 Pat 118, 119 and 124.
102. *AIR* 1971 SC 891 at p 897.
103. *AIR* 1957 SC 615, (1957) SCJ 714.
104. *AIR* 1965 All 333.
105. Article 19 (1) (f) of the Indian Constitution.
106. Article 300 A of the Indian Constitution.
107. Article 19 (5) says that nothing in Article 19 (1) (f) shall affect the operation of any existing law in so far as it imposes, or prevent the state from making any law imposing reasonable restrictions on the exercise of any of the rights conferred by the said sub-clause either in the interest of the general public or for the protection of the interests of any Scheduled tribe.
108. H.M. Seervai, *Constitutional Law of India*, (1968) Vol 1, p 353.
109. *AIR* 1954 SC 92, (1954) SCJ 127.
110. See *Rajindra Singh* v *Union of India*, *AIR* 1963 Punj 461.
111. See *Narayanan Nambudripad* v *State of Madras*, *AIR* 1954 Mad 385, (1953) 2 MLJ 699 ; followed in *Kumaran Nambudiri* v *Cochin Devaswam Board*. *AIR* 1954 Tr. Co 515 (F.B.) : *Nambudripad* v *C.D. Bord*, *AIR* 1956 Tr. Co. 741 ; *Chathu Madia* v *Commissioner H.R. & C.F.*, *AIR* 1958 Ker 57.
112. See however Justice Mathew's observations in *Kesavananda Bharti* v *State of Kerala*, (1973) 4 SCC 225, 884-85.
113. See *Guru Datta Sharma* v *State of Bihar*, *AIR* 1961 SC 1684, (1962) 2 SCR 292.
114. The courts have held the following as property within the meaning of article :
    (a) Liquor, *State of Bombay* v *E.N. Balsara*, *AIR* 1951 SC 318, (1951) SCR 682.
    (b) The office of Mahant, *Commissioner, H.R.F.* v *L.T. Swamiar*, *AIR* 1954 SC 282, (1954) SCR 1005.
    (c) Shebaitship, *Angurbala Mullick* v *Debarata Mullick*, *AIR* 1951 SC 293, (1951) SCR 1125.
    (d) Decree of the *Mahboob Begum* v *Hyderabad State*, *AIR* 1951 Hyd 1.
    (e) Hereditary trusteeship of Malabar Temple, *Kumaran* v *Cochin Devasam Board*, *AIR* 1954 TC 515.
    (f) Tenants interest in demised premises is property, *Bombay Corporation* v *Lala Pancham*, *AIR* 1965 SC 1008, (1963) SCR 342.
115. Mulla, *Transfer of Property Act*. (1973) 6th Ed. p 49.
116. *Jones* v *Skinner*, (1835) 5 IJ Ch. 87, 90 ; see also *Dwarkadas Shrinivas* v *Sholapur* Sp. and Wg. Co's, *AIR* 1954 SC 119, 139, (1954) SCR 674. The term property includes both corporeal and incorporeal rights.

117. *Nawab Zainyar Jung* v *Director of Endowments*, *AIR* 1963 SC 985, (1963) 1 SCR 469.
118. *Tilkayat Shri Govindlal i* v *State of Rajasthan*, *AIR* 1963 SC 1638, (1964) 1 SCR 561 ; see also *Shanti Bai* v *State of Bombay AIR* 1958 SC 532, 1959 SCR 265. It was held that the right of a bare licensee or to apply for winding up are not property.
119. *AIR* 1955 SC 493 ; see also *Mitta Kunth Adhicarry* v *Neerunjan Adhicarry*, (1875) 14 Beng L.R. 166.
120. *AIR* 1954 SC 92 ; 1954) SCR 587.
121. i.e. *Commissioner, H.R.E.* v *L.T. Swamiar*, *AIR* 1954 SC 282, 1954 SCR 1005. Their lordship of the Supreme Court affirmed this opinion in *S.M. Transport (Pvt)* v *Shankaraswamigal Mutt*, *ARE* 1963 SC 864, (1963) Supp. 1 SCR 282.
122. See *Gopal Narain* v *State of U.P.*, *AIR* 1964 SC 370 ; (1964) 4 SCR 869.
123. *Kastoorchandji* v *State AIR* 1967 MP 268 ; *K.T. Moopail Nai* v *State of Kerala*, *AIR* 1961 SC 552, (1961) 3 SCR 77.
124. *Jagannath* v *Union of India*, *AIR* 1962 SC 148, (1962) (2) SCR 118.
125. *Raj Ramkrishna* v *State of Bihar*, *AIR* 1963 SC 1667, (1964) 1 SCR 897 ; see also *Corporation of Calcutta* v *Liberty Cinema*, *AIR* 1965 SC 1107, (1965) (2) SCR 477.
126. *AIR* 1960 SC 1080, 1102, (1960)(3) SCR 887.
127. *Shiveshwar* v *District Magistrate*, *AIR* 1966 Pat 144 : *Ramkrishna* v *Radhamal*, *AIR* 1952 All 537 ; *Jeewan* v *State of Rajasthan AIR* 1952 Raj 137 ; *Ishwari Prasad* v *Sen*. *AIR* 1952 Cal 273.
128. See *Attar Singh* v *U.P. State*, *AIR* 1959 SC 564, (1959) (1) Supp. SCR 928.
129. See *Bhagirath Ram Chand* v *State of Punjab*, *AIR* 1954 Punj 167.
130. *State of Bombay* v *F.N. Balsara* , *AIR* 1951 SC 318 ; *Nashinwa* v *State of M.P.* (1975) (1) SCR 29 ; see also *Vibhuti Narain Singh* v *Improvement Trust*, *AIR* 1954 All 520. In this case limitations imposed on owners of land by Municipal by-laws to construct buildings was held as valid.
131. (1972) (1) SCC 70 ; see also *M.P. Sharma* v *Satish Chandra*, (1954) SCR 1077, *AIR* 1954 SC 300 ; *Prem Dulari* v *Raj Kumari*, *AIR* 1967 SC 1578, (1967)(3) SCR 273. In this case it was said that where the sale is of property having a common outer entrance with other properties, the right of prior purchase given to the owners of such property is a reasonable restriction under clause (5) of Art 19.
132. *AIR* 1961 SC 1602 at 1613.
133. *AIR* 1956 SC 432.
134. *AIR* 1954 SC 400. The judgment was read by J. B. K. Mukherjee.
135. *K.A. Samajam* v *Commissioner of H.R.* and *C.E*, Hyderabad, *AIR* 1971 SC 891, (1970) (3) SCR 359. In this case the court app-

roved the case of *Sambuda Murthi Mudaliar* v *State of Madras*, (1970) (2), SCR 424, (1970) (1) SCC 4 ; *Manthunain* v *Sundaralingam AIR* 1971 Mad 1 (FB).

136. *Amarsingh* v *Custodian*, Evacuee property, (1957) SCR 801. *AIR* 1957 SC 599, (1957) SCJ 574.
137. *Hafiz Mohammad* v *U.P.* S.C. Board of Waqfs, *AIR* 1965 All 333.
138. *Mahant Sri Jagannath* v *State of Orissa*, *AIR* 1954SC 400, (1954) SCJ 329 ; (1954) SCR 1046.
139. *State of West Bengal* v *Subodh Gopal Bose*, *AIR* 1954 SC 92, (1954) SCR 587, (1954) SCJ 127.
140. *Rajindra Singh* v *Union of India*, *AIR* 1963 Punj 461.
141. *Honnalige Gowda* v *State of Mysore*, *AIR* Mys 84, 106.
142. *Biswanath Prasad* v *Union of India AIR* 1965 SC 821, 825.
143. *See Bokaro & Rampur Ltd.* v *State of Bihar*, *AIR* 1963 SC 516, (1962) Supp (2) SCR 831.
144. *Aniyoth Kunhamina Uuna* v *Ministry of Rehabilitation*, *AIR* 1962 SC 1616, (1962) (1) SCR 505 ; (1961) (2) SCJ 621.
145. *Narayana* v *State of Andhra*, *AIR* 1959 AP 471.
146. Article 27. Freedom as to payment of taxes for promotion of any particular religion. No person shall be compelled to pay any taxes, the proceeds of which are specifically appropriated in payment of expenses for the promotion or maintenance of a particular religion or religious denomination.
147. *Lakshmindra* v *Commissioner*, *AIR* 1952 Mad 613 ; *Commissioner* v *L.T. Swamiar*, *AIR* 1954 SC 282. In this case Madras Hindu Religious Endowments Act, 1951, on account of the extra burden imposed on the state revenues by the Religious Endowments Boards required religious institutions to which it applied——
    (a) to pay a percentage of their income, and in the case of richer institutions.
    (b) to pay further sums for the audit of their accounts. The Madras High Court said that the former imposition was a tax used in part for the maintenance of religious institution, and so repugnant to Article 27.
148. M.P. Jain, *Indian Constitutional Law*, p. 281 ; see also *Jagannath* v *Orissa*, *AIR* 1954 SC 400 ; *Ratilal* v *Bombay*, *AIR*.
149. *AIR* 1944 SC 400, 403, (1954) SCR 1046.
150. *Ibid.*
151. *Commissioner, Hindu Religious Endowments, Madras* v *Lakshmindra*, *AIR* 1954, SC 282, (1954) SCR 1005.
152. The judgment was delivered by Justice B.K. Mukerjea, S.R. Das, Vivian Bose, Ghulam Hasan, Bhagwati and V. Ayyar. For the views of Justice T.L.V. Ayyar, see his book entitled *The Evolution of the Indian Constitution* (1970) 106.

153. *Supra* note 151. The court relied on *Angurbala* v *Debarata AIR* 1951 SC 293 ; and *Vidya Varuthi* v *Balusami*, (1921) 48 I.A. 302.
154. (1878) 2 Mad 175.
154A. (1887) 10 Mad 375.
155. P.K. Tripathi, Secularism, Constitutional Provision and Judicial Review, *Secularism, Implications for Law and Life in India*, Sharma GS (ed), pp 165, 178-180.
156. (1951) SCR 1125.
157. *Vidya Varuthi* v *Balusami*, s.n. 153.
158. See also *Manohar Mukerji* v *Bhupendranath*, (1933) 60 Cal 452; *Ganeshchunder* v *Lal Behary*, (1936) 63 I.A. 448 ; Babatrini Ashalata (1943) 70 I.A. 57; *Gossamee Sree Greedharrejee* v *Rumanlolljee Gossamee* (1989) 16 I.A. 137.
159. (1933) 60 Cal 452,
160. (1872) I.A. (Supp) 47.
161. The court overruled the opinion of JJ Greaves and Chakravarty in *Sreepati Chatterjee* v *Krishna Chandra Banerjee*, (1923) (41) Cal LJ 22.
162. See *Shibessure Debi* v *Mothoornath Acharje*, (1869) 13 MIA 270; *Abhiran Goswami* v *Shyama Charan Nandi*, (1909) 36 Cal.
163. *AIR* 1953 SC 125.
164. This article guarantees to every citizen the right to acquire, hold and dispose of property. (Omitted by the Constitution Forty-fourth Amendment) Act, 1978).
165. *Supra* note 34.
166. *Ramchandra* v *State of Orissa*, *AIR* 1959 Ori 5.
167. *Sarup Singh* v *State of Punjab*, *AIR* 1964 SC 860.
168. *AIR* 1964 SC 1501, 1511.
169. *Commissioner, H.R.E.* v *Lakshmindra*, s.n. 36 ; *Ratilal* v *Bombay*, s.n. 59; *Jagannath* v *Orissa*, s.n. 45 ; *Moti Das* v *Sahi*, s.n, 67; *Mukundarya* v *Mysore*, *AIR* 1960 Mys 18, 23.
170. *AIR* 1954 Mad 385, (1953) (2) MLJ 699. In this case the decisions of the U.S. Supreme Court were relied. The First Amendment to the U.S. Constitution provides Congress shall make no law respecting an establishment of religion, or prohibiting the free exercise thereof.
171. *Supra* note 170.
172. *Supra* note 55, p. 477.
173. *AIR* 1922 PC 333.
174. *Supra* note 55,
175. Article 28 (1)—No religious instruction shall be provided in any educational institution wholly maintained out of State funds.

    (2) Nothing in clause (1) shall apply to an educational institution which is administered by the State but has been established under any endowment or trust which requires that religious instruction shall be imparted to such institution.

    (3) No person attending any educational institution recognised by the state or receiving aid out of state funds shall be required to

take part in any religious instruction that may be imparted in such institution or to attend any or in any premises attached thereto unless such person or, if such person is a minor, his guardian has given his consent thereto.

176, *Constituent Assembly Debates*, Vol 7, pp. 883-84.

177. See *D.A.V. College, Jullunder* v *State of Punjab*, (1971) (2) SCC 269 ; (1971) Supp SCR 688 (per J Jaganmohan Reddy).

178. Article 29 (1)—Any section of the citizens residing in the territory of India or any part thereof having a distinct language, script or culture of its own shall have the right to conserve the same.

(2) No citizen shall be denied admission into any educational institution maintained by the State or receiving aid out of state funds on grounds only of religion, race, caste, language or any of them.

Note : The Constitutional First Amendment Act, 1951 by inserting clause (4) in Art 13 has since then controlled by Article 29 (2).

179. *Constituent Assembly Debates*. Vol VII, p. 923.

180. (1951) SCR 525.

181. *Anjali Roy* v *State of West Bengal*, 56 CWN 891.

182. *Supra* note 180.

183. (1955) 1 SCR 568.

184. See *Re Kerala Education Bill*, (1959) SCR 995.

185. Article 30 (1)—All minorities, whether based on religion, language, shall have the right to establish and administer educational institutions or their choice.

(2) The state shall not in granting aid to educational institutions, discriminate against any educational institution on the ground that it is under the management of a minority, whether based on religion or language.

186. *Supra* note 184.

187, Article 45—*Provision for free and compulsory education for children* The state shall endeavour to provide, within a period of ten years from the commencement of this constitution, for free and compulsory education for all children until they complete the age of fourteen years.

188. See *Rashid Ahmed* v *State Municipal Board*, Kairan, (1950) SCR 566 ; *Md. Yasin* v *Town Area Committee*, Jalalabad, (1952) SCJ 162 ; *State of Bombay* v *Bombay Education Society*, *Supra* note 183.

189. *Dependra Nath* v *State af Bihar*, ILR 40 Pat 783 (FB).

190. *Supra* note 183.

191. See *Srikrishna* v *Gujarat University*, *AIR* 1962 Guj 88 (FB).

192. Cooley, *Constitutional Law*, p. 294-95.

193. *Vikarrudin* v *Osmania University*, *AIR* 1954 Hyd 25.

194. *Ramesh* v *B.B. Intermediate College*, *AIR* 1953 All 90.

195. *State of Bombay* v *Bombay Education Society*, *Supra* note 183.

196. *Supra* note 184:

197. *Ramanikanta* v *Gauhati University*, *AIR* 1951 Assam 163.
198. *A.P. Subha* v *State of Bihar*, *AIR* 1958 Pat 359.
199. *Supra* note 184.
200. *State of Bombay* v *Bombay Education Society*, *Supra* note 183 ; *re* the Kerala Education Bill, *Supra* note 184 ; Rev. *Father Proost* v *State of Bihar*, *AIR* 1969 SC 465 ; *D.A V. College Jullunder* v *State of Punjab*, *supra* note 177 ; *St. Xaviers College* v *State of Gujarat*, *AIR* 1974 SC 1389.
201. See *Rev. Bishop S.K. Patro* v *State of Bihar*, *AIR* 1970 SC 259. In this case the Supreme Court held that the right under Article 30 (1) is available even to foreigners residing in India provided that they form a well defined religious or linguistic minority in India.
202. Rev *Father Proost* v *State of Bihar*, *Supra* note 200 ; see also the views expressed by P.B. Gajendragadkar, *Indian Parliament and the Fundamental Rights*, (1972) pp. 54-57.
203. *AIR* 1980 *SC* 1942, (1980) 2SCC 478.
204. Art. 41. *Right to work, to education and to public assistance in certain cases.* The state shall, within the limits of its economic capacity and development, make effective provision for securing the right to work, to education and to public assistance in cases of unemployment old age, sickness and disablement, and in other cases of undeserved want.
205. *Supra* note 187.
206. *Art 45 —Promotion of educational and economic interests of scheduled caste, scheduled tribes and other weaker sections.* The state shall promote with special care the educational and economic interests of the weaker sections of the people, and, in particular, of the Scheduled Castes and the Scheduled Tribes, and shall protect them from social injustice and all froms of exploitation.
207. *Jaipur Law Journal Studies in Law*. (1976-77), Vol 17, 2, p. 49 at 63.
208. Article 351 of the Indian Constitution.

10

Conclusion

In the ancient days the duty of the state was only to to maintain law and order. With the advancement of civilization the state is said to be a welfare state. A modern state is under the duty to prepare rules and enact laws regulating all aspects of human life. The rise of the welfare state proceeds from the political philosophy that the greater intervention of a government and the adoption of public measures must aim at general economic and cultural betterment. Those days have numbered when an individual was left free to live or languish. Modern state is very much concerned with the well-being of the individual as an integral part of the society. All round development of the human personality is dependent upon basic axioms of social justice, liberty and equality.

Now with the change of time the role of law has completely changed. The zeal and interest in the positive role of law in India is reflected in the quantitative and qualitative legislative output. The main aim of our legislature is to construct a just and equitable social set up on the anarchist and fascist backwaters of a caste ridden, strife-torn Indian society. It was on account of this reason that Indian Parliament and state legislatures passed numerous Acts. In addition to these Acts there are many other socio-economic reforms which have been introduced through the various Acts of Parliament and state legislatures.[1]

India is inhabited by various cultural, religious and ethnic groups that have their own characteristic attitude and approach. Muslim are one of them. In India, from the very beginning religion has been closely attached with the administration of the country. The Britishers realised this attachment of religion with administration and they therefore decided not to interfere into the personal laws of various communities of India. Warren Hastings, introduced the policy of non-interference into the personal laws of Hindus and Muslims. This policy of non-interference was pursued by the colonial rulers throughout their rule in the country. The Second Law Commission in its second report advised against the codification of these laws.

During the British rule English Common Law with its statutory modifications and the doctrine of the English courts of equity was introduced. The introduction of English common law and equity deeply coloured and influenced the law and the system of judicial administration of whole sub-continent inhabited by nearly four hundred million peoples. The massive stracture of Indian law and jurisprudence resembles the height the symmetry and the grandeour of the common and statute law of England.[2] After the advent of independence, there began an area of social legislations. But as far as the personal law of Muslims was concerned the Indian Parliament decided to continue this policy of non-interference. But the constitution makers introduced Article 44 in the constitution which directs the state to introduce uniform Civil Code as and when it becomes convenient for the state to introduce the same.

According to the Preamble of the Constitution, India is a secular state. Articles 25 to 28 of the Indian Constitution guarantees to all citizens freedom of conscience and religion. The Indian approach towards secularism is not anti God or anti religion. In India, religion has relevance and validity in the lives of many, though not necessarily all citizens, but it emphasises that while religion may be relevant in life, it cannot stall, hamper or frustrate the progress of Indian democracy in its allotted task of creating a new social order.[2] The introduction of a uniform waqf laws in India mostly depends on the success of secularism. Therefore, if we want a secular state then it is necessary that religion should be separated from other matters and secular laws be enacted applicable to followers of all religions.

It is, however, regrettably submitted that in this regard no serious attempt has so far been made. Even there is no Indian Waqf Act. The States of Bengal, Uttar Pradesh, Jammu and Kashmir and Maharashtra are having their own waqf laws. For the sake of convenience, certainty *etc.*, it is absolutely necessary that if we cannot have one common religious endowment Act prevalent throughout the country, we should at least have a uniform waqf law. It is the duty of the legislature to introduce a good system of laws, which is certain, simple, lucid and uniform without giving rise to disputes or fostering disharmony among the people that are governed by it.

In the modern world, a legal system binds together the citizens of a country and this creates among them a sense of national integration and unity. The role of a strong legal system has not been realised fully. If national integrity is to be a reality, one of the means would be the adoption of uniform system of law.

There is an urgent need of social change, especially among Muslims. For achieving a uniform waqf law the public and especially the intellectuals have to play a vital role. It is the duty of the intellectuals to see that the relevant laws are fully and faithfully implemented. It is also their duty to make a distinction between ethics, morality and faith on the one hand, religion on the other. There must be a new approach, a modern approach, moral and ethical approach. This programme is a must and should be undertaken immediately by the progressive intellectuals, particularly the Muslim progressive intellectuals, who believe in the paramount importance of creating a secular society.

It is the duty of progressive Muslim intellectuals to explain to the Muslim masses the true character of the Muslim personal law and philosophy and inculcate in their mind a spirit of tolerance towards all religions and an attitude of responsiveness to the call of modernising and rationalising the provision of personal law.

Mulims can come to terms with the contemporary world, only if they go straight back to *Quran* and renew their faith and belief by seeking direct inspiration and guidance from it.[3]

With the advancement of civilization from capitalistic societies to socialistic ones, from the individual liberty of man to the social liberty of all, the norm of *laissez-faire* has come to be displaced by the socialist school of thinking. Their social interest demands a prosperous society with evenly distributed income, wherein wants and sufferings stand alleviated. Norms of social security try to safeguard the socially and economically weaker sections of society. Our constitution has proclaimed a welfare state and the directive principles of state policy lay down the guidelines to usher in an era of socio-economic reforms and humanitarian measures for the welfare of the weaker sections of the society. Both Parliament and state legislatures are passing many laws for establishing a social order with that object in view.

With the march of time, crimes are becoming more and more sophisticated. It is, therefore, necessary that if the forces which have to meet the challenge of crime are to prove equal to the task they must keep abreast of and acquire the technique of handling and controlling such crimes. It is a matter of regret that during the last one or two decades, the individual crimes in India have not been receiving that much attention as it should have because of the onerous duties imposed upon the police force. The result has been that there is less time for investigation of the cases. The quality of investigation goes down in the process much to the anguish of those who are the victims of the quality of investigation are the actual offenders.

The functioning of our courts is linked with the image of our judicial system. Some of the questions which face us are — Does our judicial system satisfy the demand for justice ? Does it fulfil the expectations of the people ? Are courts of law looked upon as temples of justice, where it is administered without fear or favour, oblivious of the personalities of the litigants and without regard to their long purse or high status ?

Does common man have an abiding and unshaken faith in the process of justice as administered by the courts ? It is upon the answer to these questions that our judicial system would ultimately be judged. The image of the courts depend in the final analysis, upon the way the cases are handled, upon the extent of confidence the courts inspire in the parties to the cases before them, upon the promptness or absence of delay in the disposal of cases and upon the approximation of the judicial findings of fact with the realities of the matter.

No evolution of our judicial system would be complete and realistic unless we take into account some of infirmities which have crept into it or some of the drawbacks which have manifested themselves. Firstly, there is the question of delay in the disposal of cases. Linked with the delay in the disposal of cases is the question of right of successive appeals. All over the world the trend now is towards having one right of appeal and a revision or second appeal only on some substantial question of law. Provision for too many successive appeals and revisions has the effect of delaying the final disposal of cases. The need is to draw the final curtain on the course of litigation relating to a dispute within a reasonable time of the commencement of the litigation.

Another factor which led to the expeditious disposal of cases was that hardly any witness who came to court in obedience to summons went back without his evidence being recorded. To cope with larger number of cases, we must have either separate courts for separate disputes or larger number of courts. If this method is not adopted it would lead to the effect of tarnishing the image of the system because of the long meandering course of judicial cases. Notions of economy should not be allowed to stand in the way of prompt and expeditious disposal of cases.

Another question which might engage our attention is how far the judicial finding of fact accord with the realities of the situation. Judges have to give their findings upon the evidence adduced in the cases. Sometimes the witnesses do not tell the truth. On other occasions persons who could give the true versions are not willing to come forward and give evidence which would have the effect of antagonising one of the parties. The result is that a judicially finding of fact is sometimes entirely divorced from the reality of the situation. This is bound to shake the confidence of the people in the ability of the courts to ascertain the truth of the matter and thus to do substantial justice.

The personality of our judges is one of the most important factors to ensure the efficient working of our judicial system. The quality of justice depends not merely upon having well worded codes and statutes, but much more so upon the way they are administered and enforced. In this connection on the role played by the trial court judge is very important. He is the most important and influential participant in the dispensation of justice, He is the man with whom the members of the general public come into contact whether as parties or as witnesses. A trial court judge's ability, efficiency, tact or the lack of them can make all differences regarding the fate of cases handled by him. The best of laws and codes would not bring about reform and improvement in the functioning of our courts unless we have the judges of the right calibre, integrity and sense of devotion to their work.

The main object of procedural law is to ensure a just disposition of the dispute before the court. But because time, resources and the ability to determine what is just are limited, a procedural system inevitably represents a system of compromises. Justice to society is sometimes taken to require that a given case be used not only to deal with the situation immediately before the court but also to serve a larger public interest.

There are many drawbacks which have manifested themselves in the system and they have to be set right. National and local conditions may also necessitate changes in laws to make them suitable. Some changes in laws also become imperative with the passage of time and in the context of new thinking and fresh national developments. Change is the law of nature and human society also keeps changing. There is also the change in values and the change in ideas. Laws have to keep abreast of time if they are to serve the needs of society and prove useful instruments for social engineering. It is also submitted that unwanted pieces of legislation should be discontinued. These lagislations unnecessarily encumber the statute book and constitute a bewildering mess for all students and practitioners of law.

Functionally, a statute is no more than a skeletal framework for those operating it. It draws flesh and blood in the course of its operation. The operationalising process consists in activating one or more of the statute's verbal formulae, each of which is hopefully clothed with a settled meaning by the legislature framing it and collectively, designed to achieve certain socially preferred objectives. The efficiency of these verbal formulae is tested each time when a conflict situation has to be resolved through their incantation. This is best observed in court battles. But court level resolution of conflicts has its limitations like, among others, a case has to be taken to courts, to begin with. Moreover, having recourse to courts is usually a sign of failure of the statute's conflict-resolving mechanisms at the operational stage. For a legal scholar, therefore, the working of a statute below court level is equally, if not more, important.

Law in the institutional and the philosophical sense is a system of justification of all human behaviour in interaction. It is closely related to social and philosophical speculation in the h story of human thought.[4] Justification presupposes referential norms and standards. The continuing problem of all social and legal philosophy is reaching some judgment on the *inter se* validity of these norms and determining their priorities[5] in the dynamic processes of change in human life and environment. Before the secularisation of the law, in the post-feudal period, the inherent values of human life drawn from religion and theology were considered inviolable and were regarded as ultimate in the scheme of hierarchy of norms. The rise of utilitarian theories and later the triumph of culture of technology shifted the emphasis to the norms of expediency away from the ultimateness of inherent values of human life which get reflected through the modalities of culture of a society.

In societies like that of India which are today neither modern nor traditional, conflicts and tensions get accentuated to the pitch of a crisis or a trauma. Traditional institutiions lose their social cohesion value and get transformed into political pressure media, claiming immediate satisfaction of exaggerated demands without the self-sustaining ethos of either a truly democratic spirit or the truly Gandhian spirit of trusteeship and positive contentment. The projection by the constitution of the India of the egalitarian ideology and the dignity of men without a sustaining culture and environment further aggravates the social situation.

The American jurists have defined law as any set of norms which is capable of ordering, managing, handling and resolving conflicts and disputes in society. They take the disputed situation as a recurring social phenomena and their effort is to examine all societal attempts including those of tribes, traditional societies and modern secular societies and arrive at a universal theory of law in this wide sense. The law is a technology with a wide spectrum of rules, procedures and remedies brought into the service of social control and social change.

The Role of the Mutawalli

A Mutawalli is having legal, moral and religious duties. He is supposed to administer waqf property and its income in the same way as a prudent man would deal with his own property. He should be careful and vigilant in dealing with the waqf property.

The powers enjoyed by the Mutawalli under the Act are not absolute. There are exceptions to this rule. A Mutawalli is not the owner of the waqf property and, therefore, he cannot dispose of the waqf property according to his fancy. He is merely the manager of the waqf property. He is not the trustee of waqf property. The property vests in him only in a literal sense, so that he can only hold and manage it. He has no legal estate of his own.[6] He is under the duty to administer the waqf property according to the terms of 'waqfnama.' It is the duty of a 'mutawalli' to administer and protect waqf property in his charge to the best of his capabilities. He must discharge his responsibilities diligently, honestly, cautiously and with integrity. The waqf property belongs to God and the 'mutawalli' is its bailee and must act as such.

No right to sell *etc.*

A mutawalli has no right to sale or mortgage waqf property without an express provision in the 'waqfnama'[7] or the permission of the court.[8] The provisions of Section 36-A and 36-B of the Waqf Act, 1954, intends to control the power to mutawallis of alienation of waqf properties. Section 36-A provides that for the sale, mortgage, gift or exchange, or lease for a period exceeding three years in the case of agricultural land, or for a period exceeding one year in the case of non-agricultural land or building, the prior permission of the waqf board shall be necessary, even though the waqf deed may provide otherwise.

Recovery of Illegally Transferred Waqf Property

Similarly, Section 36-B lays down that if the Board is satisfied that any immovable property of a waqf entered as such in the register of waqfs has been transferred without the previous sanction of the Board, it may send a requisition to the Collector within whose jurisdiction the property is situated to obtain and deliver possession of the property to it. The Collector may pass an order directing the person concerned to make the delivery of the property to the Board within a period of thirty days from the date of the service of the order. The aggrieved party has been given the right of appeal. Any aggrieved person may within a period of thirty days prefer an appeal to the District Court. Under Section 36-B the decision of the court shall be final.

The need of this proviso was felt for a long time. Under the classical Muslim law and the Waqf Act, waqf properties cannot be transferred without the permission of the court or the State Board, 'Mutawallis' frequently make illegal alienations. Waqf Boards were having no alternative but to file a suit in the court of law for the recovery of the properties. Expenditure involved in the filing of the suit was very high. It was, therefore, not possible for the Board to file all the suits in the court of law for the recovery of waqf properties. Prior to the passing of the Waqf Act, 1954, Waqf Board was not having any sort of administrative control over the 'Mutawallis'. Most of them were abusing their power. It was, therefore, felt necessary that simple procedure for the recovery of properties should be laid down.

It may, however, be noted that the object for which this proviso was made could not be a success. The Collectors of the respective districts are already busy in maintaining law and order situation in their respective districts. They are required to perform several multifarious activities. They have, therefore, no time to look into waqf affairs. It will, therefore, be better if in each district a waqf cell is opened. This cell will be responsible for protecting the waqf property in the district.

Issue of Executions to the Collectors

It is a common experience of the Waqf Boards that barring a few, most of the Collectors do not pay the required attention to the communications of the Waqf Board. It is, therefore, submitted that the state government should issue necessary instructions to the collectors to treat matters of the waqf board at par with those of any government department or any similar institution.

A Mutawalli is free to spend money on all lawful purposes. Section 37 of the Waqf Act, 1954, says that a mutawalli is allowed to pay from the income of the waqf property any expenses incurred properly by him for the following purposes :

(a) enabling him to furnish any particular documents or copies ;
(b) or any accounts ; or
(c) any information or documents required by the Board ; or
(d) for the purpose of enabling him to carry out the directions of the Board.

The heads under which a mutawalli can spend money are vague. It means he can spend money on any item. It is, therefore, necessary that the heads under which a mutawalli can spend money should be made clear. It is proposed here that instead of mutawalli there should be a management committee of waqfs. This committee shall be responsible for spending money. The amount of more than Rs 50/- should be spent only after a resolution of two thirds majority has been passed by the Committee.

In the absence of any provision in the waqf deed *etc.*, he possesses no right to exchange or give on lease the waqf property. Under the Waqf Act, 1954, he cannot transfer or exchange waqf property without the previous sanction of the Waqf Board even if he is allowed to do under the waqf deed. In *Abdul Qayyum* v *Ali Bhali*[9] the Supreme Court of India said that once a mutawalli has accepted the responsibilities of his office he cannot renounce them afterwards except under certain specified conditions. It was also held that mutawalli cannot transfer their duties, functions and powers to some other body of men and create them trustees in their own place unless it is clearly allowed by the waqif in the waqf deed.

Normally, a mutawalli has no power to mortgage a waqf property. The mortgage of the waqf property by the mutawalli will be a breach of trust.[10]

A waqif can be the co-sharer in the property and at the same time he can become a mutawalli. After creating such waqf, he shall have no right to sale the same. In *Sabir Hussain* v *Smt Hashim*[11] the waqif was the co-sharer in a house. He created a waqf *alal-aulad* and became its mutawalli. Afterwards, she sold the house.

Justice Deoki Nandan of Allahabad High Court held that the waqif could not confer any higher right, title or interest in the property than what she had. The waqf created by her was valid to the extent of her title to the house in suit, and the sale deed in favour of another person would be invalid to the same extent on account of its being waqf property and inalienable as such.

In the case of permanent or long term lease of waqf property the rules applicable in the case of alienation or mortgage of waqfs property shall be applied. The following two considerations are necessary for granting lease :

(a) the grant of lease must be for the benefit of the waqf ; or
(b) the grant of lease is necessary[12]

The courts are competent to confirm such a lease retrospectively if it is for a legal necessity or for the benefit of the waqf or its beneficiaries.[13]

The courts are not in agreement with regard to the validity of the grant of lease in contravention of above directions. It is not clear whether such a transaction will be void *ab initio* or not. It was held that a lease in violation of these conditions will not be void *ab initio*. It will be only voidable at the option of the mutawalli or the beneficiaries of the waqf.[14]

Formerly, the Indian courts took the view that a permanent lease cannot be granted by mutawalli and is void *ab initio*.[15]

It is submitted that the view taken by the Allahabad High Court in *Shaida* v *Delhi Iron and Steel Co.*[16] case appears to be correct and it should be followed in such cases.

In *Sundra Murthi* v *Chotti*,[17] the Madras High Court said that if a mutawalli has granted lease permanently, it will bind the mutawalli personally during his life time and he cannot repudiate it or evict the lessee.

A mutawalli has no power to grant a lease of waqf property, if it is an agricultural land, for a period exceeding three years and if non-agricultural, for a term exceeding one year. It is not necessary for the mutawalli to obtain prior permission from the waqif or court for this purpose.[18] In *Shah Mohammad* v *Manzoor Ali*[19] the Patna High Court maintained that a permanent lease of agricultural (waqf) property granted by the mutawalli was not void *ab initio*, it remained wholly valid for three years and became voidable thereafter so that if after the expiry of three years no steps were taken to avoid it, the lessee could not be regarded as a trespasser.

A mutawalli is not competent to dispose of the waqf property by way of sale, mortgage *etc*. For this purpose, the permission of the court/waqf board is necessary. In this connection it may be pointed out that an alienation or mortgage without court's prior permission, if it is for the benefit of the waqf or necessary for its purpose is not void *ab initio* and may, therefore, retrospectively be confirmed by the court.

Mutawalli as a Beneficiary – The nature and incidence of his interest

The courts have made a distinction between the claim to the beneficial interest and the office of the mutawalli. In *Lokenath* v *Jahanial*[20] held that a right of fishery is not immovable property for all purposes but it is an interest in immovable property.[21] In Vidya Varuthi's[22] case the Privy Council said that waqf constitutes typing up of property in the ownership of God, the Almighty and the devotion of the profits for the benefit of human beings. It was also maintained that even a 'Sajjadanashin' who has a larger interest in the usufruct acquires no right to the property belonging to the waqf.

The matter again came for consideration before the Privy Council in *Abdur Rahim* v *Narayan*[23]. The Privy Council pointed out that on such an endowment the property itself is not chargeable according to the measure of interest which the beneficiary may have in the rents, and profits of the whole.

The Allahabad High Court followed the above opinion in *Mst, Zohra Khatoon* v *Janab Mohammad Jane Alam.*[24] In this case the plaintiff made two claims *i.e.* to act as mutawalli and also the interest of the beneficiary under the endowment. Justice Anil Sen of Calcutta High Court expressed the view that under the Muslim law, a waqf is a two-fold transfer simultaneously made perpetual in both its aspects with religious motive pervading, the transaction as a whole consists of a transfer (1) of the usufruct in favour of the beneficiary or objects of the waqf and (2) of the substance in reality a renunciation of the substance metaphorically spoken of as a transfer of the substance to God. Therefore, there can be no dispute that on such endowment under the Muslim law the ownership in the property is wholly renunciated or vested in the God and the benefits which the beneficiaries derive come only out of the usufruct. Muslim law, it must be remembered, makes a difference between 'Ayn' (corpus) and 'Manafi' (usufruct) and the beneficial interest under the endowment is generally created out of such usufruct. Such being the position, the beneficiary acquires no interest in the strict sense in the property itself though an interest in the usufruct arising out of such property is vested in the beneficiary. Though, therefore, the beneficiary acquires no right in the immovable property yet his right to share the usufructs which are to accrue from such property in years to come creates an interest of a particular nature in the immovable property. Such an incidence arises from a grant of this nature.

It was further held that under these circumstances the plaintiff's claim in respect of the beneficial interest under the endowment cannot be considered *de hors* the immovable properties covered by the endowment and the suit cannot but be held to be one coming under Section 16 (d) of the Code of Civil Procedure.

Mutawalli as a Beneficiary of private Waqf

For a considerable time it was said that in the case of a private waqf where the mutawalli is also the beneficiary, he is not a mere superintendent or manager but is the owner of the waqf property. Later on, it was said that the mutawalli acquires no right, title or interest in the property itself but he is merely the holder of the office of a manager under the Muslim law[25]. It is submitted that a mutawalli of a private waqf is the manager, governer, superintendent *etc.* He is not the owner of waqf property. It may be specifically provided in the Waqf Act that the mutawalli of a private waqf will not acquire any right, title or interest in the waqf property. He will be merely the holder of the office of a manager. He will have no beneficial interest in the waqf property.

A mutawalli is the manager of the waqf property. This is his duty to see that the beneficiaries are getting the advantage of waqf property. It is submitted here that the support and maintenance of the waqif's family cannot be a purpose recognised by the Muslim law as religious, pious or charitable. Unless and until a provision for help of the settlor's family is made in the waqf deed, they shall have no beneficial right in the property.

The Waqf Board is required to keep a very vigilant watch on the activities of the mutawalli of a private waqf. He should not be allowed to advance his own interest or the interest of his relations by virtue of the position held by him.

The scope of Section 43 has been broadened to enable a

Board to remove a mutawalli who is physically or mentally unfit for performing his job. Moral delinquency, in a mutawalli should never be tolerated, particularly in the cases of religious or charitable waqfs. A mutawalli addicted to drinks, gambling, sex *etc.*, has no place in such waqfs. Similarly, a person who does not offer prayers has no place in such waqfs. Similarly, a person who does not offer prayers regularly should not be allowed to act as mutawalli. Till the amendment of Waqf Act, 1954, the Board could supersede a committee appointed by itself but it cannot take action against any committee except the one appointed by a court of law.

Strict action should be taken against the mutawalli if he was negligent towards his duties. Where he has failed to repair the waqf premises and allows them to fall into ruins it should amount to breach of waqf. A mutawalli should be held grossly negligent if he knowingly and intentionally causes damages or loss to the waqf property and for this purpose he should be immediately removed. Similarly, if a mutawalli has failed to produce accounts or pay taxes without any reasonable cause, he shall be guilty of misconduct and shall be removed from his office.

In *Mohammad Mohideen* v *State Waqf Board*[26] the Madras High Court said that under Section 43 of the Waqf Act, 1954, the Waqf Board has jurisdiction to enquire into allegations, if made against some mutawalli, for his removal. The mutawalli shall not be having right to take the defence that until and unless the Board has not given its decision, the application shall be prematured and the High Court shall not have the jurisdiction to entertain the same.

A mutawalli is under an obligation to pay the contribution as may be fixed from time to time. If he refuses or neglects to pay such contribution, he shall be personally liable for the same.

The conviction of the mutawalli by a competent court of law under the Indian Penal Code is also a ground for the removal of a mutawalli.

A mutawalli is also liable to be removed if he is convicted of an offence involving moral turpitude or is required to furnish security under Section 109 or Section 110 of the Code of Criminal Procedure, 1973.

If a mutawalli had transferred the property without the prior permission of the appropriate authority he is liable to be removed from the office of the mutawalli.

Mismanagement of the waqf property by the mutawalli is also one of the grounds for the removal of the mutawalli. Similarly, misappropriation of waqf property is the ground for the removal of the mutawalli. Non-payment of contribution coupled with a false account either as to the receipt of the money or its disposal is conclusive evidence.[27]

Negligence on the part of the mutawalli is also one of the ground for the removal of the mutawalli. In *S. Buksh* v *Ghulam Nabi*[28] the Calcutta High Court said that if a mutawalli neglects to repair the waqf premises and allows them to fall into ruins it amounts to a breach of trust. He will be held grossly negligent if he knowingly and intentionally causes damages or loss to the waqf property and for this purpose, he can be removed. If a mutawalli has failed to produce accounts or pay taxes without any reasonable cause, he shall be guilty of misconduct and shall be removed from his office.[29]

A mutawalli may be removed by the Board on proof of misfeasance or breach of trust or if it is found that he is otherwise unfit to hold the office, though the founder may have expressly directed that he should not be removed in any case.

Before the amendment of the Waqf Act, 1954, a dismissed mutawalli was reappointed. There was no bar for his reappointment. This was considered not in consonance with the principles of justice, equity and good conscience. Now a dismissed mutawalli cannot be appointed to that office for a period of five years from the date of his removal.

It is submitted here that after the removal of the mutawalli on the grounds mentioned in the Act, he shall not be eligible for any appointment in any waqf for a period of five years. Merely removing a corrupt mutawalli will not be sufficient He should be prosecuted and punished according to the provisions of Indian Penal Code *etc.* A fine should also be imposed for doing unlawful acts. With a view to publicising his removal, a notification to this effect be published by the Waqf Board and a copy of the said notification be sent to all concerned persons.

Before the passing of U.P. Muslim Waqf Act, 1960, the procedure of removing a mutawalli was difficult. A mutawalli could be removed only when he was convicted by a magistrate. Now under the U.P. Muslim Waqf Act, 1960, a mutawalli can be removed by the Board itself. It is not necessary to move the court for this purpose. The Waqf Board now acts as a court and, therefore, the removal of mutawalli under Section 35 of the Act is a quasi-judicial proceeding.

Under the U.P. Muslim Waqfs Act, 1960, the Board can remove a mutawalli if he misappropriates, deals improperly with the properties of waqfs, wrongfully alienate or mortgage the waqf property, persistently neglects in complying with the directions of the Board and is fined on more than one occasion on these grounds, or he is of unsound mind or is suffering from other mental or physical defects or an infirmity rendering him unfit to discharge his duties and fails to pay without reasonable excuse for two consecutive years the contribution payable under the Act.

"The Board has no power to remove a mutawalli arbitrarily".

Section 32 of the Waqf Act, 1954, directs a mutawalli to prepare and furnish to the Board a full and true statement of accounts. The statement should contain complete information as may be described by the Board. It is, therefore, the duty of the mutawalli to maintain proper and true statement of day today account. Formerly there was no such provision and, therefore, most of the mutawallis were preparing accounts at the end of the year in order to submit a statement to the Board. Now under Section 32, it is imperative on the part of the mutawalli to prepare day today accounts.

It is the duty of the mutawalli to supply all information regarding waqf property or its management and other particulars as and when required by the Central Board. Where a mutawalli has wilfully neglected to do so, he may be removed from the post of mutawalli.

A mutawalli is bound to give assistance in enquiries and

investigations when called upon to do so by the Board. In case a mutawalli has failed to provide assistance, strict legal action may be taken against him.

A mutawalli is under an obligation to deliver possession of any waqf property if ordered by the Board to do so in case of failure, the mutawalli is liable to be removed.

A mutawalli may be removed from his office if he has failed to deposit any surplus income in his hands in any recognised bank.

A mutawalli is also under an obligation to obey the orders of the Board. In case he failed to follow the orders of the Board, he may be removed from his office.

Mutawalli plays pivotal role in the administration of waqfs. It is, therefore, necessary that their service conditions are made attractive and the defaulter mutawalli be punished severely. At present, in the State of Madhya Pradesh no pay scale has been prescribed for them. Generally, a mutawalli is paid from Rs. 50.00 to 200.00 p.m. This is a very meagre amount. They should be given proper salary according to the needs of the time. It may be seen that only educated people are appointed as mutawalli. This is one of the most important factor for properly maintaining and administrating waqf properties. They have to feel that they are holding a sacred trust and they must exhibit a high standard of rectitude. Similarly, a mutawalli who does not fulfil the terms and conditions of Section 43 of the Waqf Act, 1954, must be severely punished. After the passing of Amendment Act, 1964, the scope of Section 43 has been enlarged. Certain additional grounds have been added for the removal of mutawallis. It is proposed here that the provisions of Section 43 be strictly applied and a defaulter mutawalli be punished strictly. This will definitely have beneficial effect on the working of other mutawallis.

After the passing of the Waqf Act, 1954, the position of mutawalli has been changed. He is under the direct control of the Waqf Board and the court. He is bound to file regular accounts. It is submitted that any slackness on his part will deprive him of his office.

A mutawalli of public waqf is simply the manager of the

waqf property. The waqf property does not vest in him. He is answerable and responsible in case of mismanagement in the same manner as if he was the trustee thereof. A mutawalli must take legal action against those persons who have wrongfully taken waqf property. He is, therefore, required to see that the waqf property is used according to the provisions of the waqf deed. He must file civil suit for the eviction of them. He must see that the property is protected from decay. He must make necessary repair at appropriate time. The mutawalli must use his power reasonably. He should not be allowed to make, or expend on, mere improvements, *e.g.* the addition of a minaret to a mosque, unless it was necessary.

The waqf property shall not be liable to attachment and sale in execution of a personal decree against the mutawalli. Similarly his office should not be attached in execution of a personal decree against the mutawalli,

Muslim law does not prohibit a person belonging to a particular school of law to act as mutawalli for Waqf belonging to the followers of another school of law. The only condition which Islam imposes for the appointment of mutawalliship is that he should be trustworthy, major and be able to understand the things properly. A Sunni may be appointed mutawalli of a Shia waqf. Similarly, a Shia Muslim can be appointed mutawalli of a Sunni waqf. Again, there is no specific provision under which it can be said that ladies cannot be appointed as mutawalli. Muslim law does not exclude a woman from doing the temporal or non-religious duties of a mutawalli. A female or non-Muslim or a society may validly be appointed as mutawalli. Where the mutawalli is required to perform religious duties or spiritual functions which cannot be performed by a female, a lady or non-Muslim shall not be appointed a mutawalli.

Appointment of Minor as Mutawalli

A person who has not attained the age of majority according to Indian law and who is not of sound mind shall not be appointed as mutawalli. In most of the cases waqf had left a will for the appointment of minor as mutawalli. In such cases the intention of the waqif should be taken into consideration. It is presumed that the intention of the waqif must not be to appoint a minor as mutawalli. It is, therefore, submitted that a minor shall not be appointed to the office of mutawalli till he has attained the age of majority according to Indian Majority Act,

Mutawalli is not Property

Under the Muslim law mutawalliship is an office. It is not the property. The right to act as mutawalli is not heritable. He is, therefore, not allowed to sell, mortgage or lease the waqf property unless he has obtained the permission of the court.

Appointment of Mutawalli

The founder of the waqf posseses power to appoint the first mutawalli. He may also lay down scheme for the administration of the waqf and for succession to the office of mutawalli. Where the post of mutawalli is lying vacant and the waqf deed is also silent on the mode of succession of mutawalli, the waqif or his executor can appoint a successor.

Where the waqf and his executor are dead, and the waqf-nama is silent in respect of the appointment of mutawalli, the mutawalli for the time being may appoint a successor on his death bed. This power may, however, be used only if the mutawalli is lying on the death bed. Where the mutawalli is having sound health he shall have no right to appoint a mutawalli.

While appointing mutawalli the wishes of the waqif should be given paramount consideration. In the absence of express provision in the waqfnama, the office of mutawalli cannot go by hereditary right to the heirs of mutawalli.

Where the number of mutawallis is more than one and they were appointed jointly, the mutawalliship should go by way of survivorship.

Ordinarily, the courts are not expected to interfere with the intention of the founder as regards the objects of waqf, but the courts are having full discretion in the matter of management. Keeping in view the interest of the waqf, the court can appoint a junior member in preference to a senior one or a non-descendant in preference to a descendant.

A Waqf Board shall have right to require the tenant by notice to pay rent not to the mutawalli but to itself as he has failed to submit accounts to the Board.

The Board is not competent to interfere in the administration of a waqf during the pendency of proceedings for the removal of a Muslim.

Remuneration of Mutawalli

A provision should be made for the payment of adequate remuneration to the mutawalli. A proviso to this effect may be laid down in the Waqf Act. The remuneration paid to the mutawalli must be adequate. The courts can also fix the amount of remuneration. The waqif has the right to fix the amount of remuneration of the officers and servants of the waqf. The mutawalli shall have no power to enhance the remuneration of the officers and servants of the waqf.

Powers of Mutawalli

Under Muslim law a mutawalli has been given very wide powers. He is responsible for the proper administration of waqf property. He is free to do all those acts which are reasonable and necessary for the protection and administration of the waqf properties under his supervision. He can use the waqf property for purposes other then those originally intended by the waqif.

A mutawalli may be allowed to construct buildings on the waqf land. However, the construction must be beneficial to the objects of waqf. A mutawalli shall not have the right to sell, or mortgage waqf properties in spite of the contrary directions in the waqfnama. A provision to this effect may be provided in the Act. Any transaction in contravention of this provision will be treated as wholly void.

A mutawalli may be allowed to give the waqf land on lease if it was required for legal necessity. However, if a mutawalli has executed a deed which was not permitted under the Muslim law or exceeded the right given to him under the law the deed shall be treated as void *ab initio* It should not be treated as voidable.

Where it is not known when the permanent lease was granted, such lease may be treated as cancelled. Any appointment or nomination made during the life time of the mutawalli is recoverable like other testamentary disposition. The office of mutawalli is not legally saleable and any custom to the contrary is opposed to public policy and, therefore, shall be treated void.

A mutawalli has no power to appoint his successor's successor and so on and so forth.

De facto Mutawalli

Under the Muslim law the office of *de facto* mutawalli has been recognised. A *de facto* mutawalli can sue without establishing his *de jure* character.

A mosque is the place of worship. This is the fundamental right of all Muslims to enter into the mosque and offer Namaz. However, the decorum of mosque has to be maintained and nobody can disturb the peace of the mosque. Every sect has an inherent right to form a separate congregation and offer prayer.

The Indian courts are not in favour of sectarian practice. The Indian courts have not favoured reservations in dedications excluding other Muslims from the right to pray in any mosque.

At present, there are number of mosques under illegal possession of the trespassers. The various Waqf Boards in the country have taken legal action against these trespassers. However, due to lack of funds these Boards were not successful in their attempts. It is, therefore, necessary that both Indian Muslims and the state government should come forward to remove the occupiers. A District Waqf Committee be constituted in each district. This shall be the duty of such committees to make complete enquiry in all cases where waqf property has been unlawfully acquired. The Committee shall inform to the Waqf Board all such cases and with the approval of Waqf Boards, these Committees should file eviction suits in their respective districts.

The District Waqf Committees shall have a waqf fund. All the Muslims living in the district shall contribute generously in this fund. The District Waqf Committee shall have proper staff and office at district headquarters. Muslims of the respective area will have to come forward for the protection of their property.

The state government alone cannot remove all the trespas sers. This shall be the duty of the state government to resolve the difficulty by evicting the trespassers and handing over the possession of mosques to the Waqf Board.

Deserted Mosques

Muslim law prohibits the disposal by way of sale the used material of dilapidated mosques. It has been reported that iron girders, bricks, doors and other material of old and dilapidated mosques in the country are lying in large quantity. Much of such material has already been taken away by unauthorised persons. This matter was brought into the notice of the deserted mosques and graveyards committee of the Central Waqf Council. After careful consideration into the matter the committee made the following recommendations :—

> Where there are deserted mosques whether in good condition or dilapidated or whether what remains of them is only the sites on which they existed they must be protected at all costs. They can neither be transferred nor utilised for any other purpose.

(a) in case, material such as doors, windows, bricks and stones *etc.*, belonging to such mosques is lying as a result of dilapidation, it can be utilised for mosques at other places ;

(b) whether there is land, rooms, quarters *etc.*, apart from the site itself on which the main place of worship stood, it will be permissible to give them on the basis of exchange, or utilize them in any other manner.[30]

It is, therefore, submitted that the above recommendations may be incorporated in the Waqf Act, 1954. The lying material can be utilised for the mosques or other places. The wholly unwanted material can also be buried. The same can also be given to the needy Muslims.

Khanqah

A khanqah is also a place of importance for the common

man. People irrespective of their caste and creed visit this place. The main aim of this institution is to manage the property, receive offerings, instiate and instruct disciples and hold usr (annual fair). The property, offering *etc.* received in the khanqah should be treated as public property. At present, this institution is grossly mismanaged. State has so far not been able to take concrete steps to control their authority by democratising the scheme of administration and whenever government has tried to check the evils, the management reached to these efforts of government.[31] It is submitted that government should take some concrete steps in the matter. A Committee of management be constituted for each khanqah.

Imambara

A Shia may establish an Imambara and only Shias may be allowed to celebrate certain ceremonies. But such Imambaras cannot be treated as purely private. These are public institutions meant for a particular community. Therefore, an Imambara will come within the category of a public waqf and be governed under the Waqf Act.

Graveyards

In India, the position of public graveyard is far from satisfactory. Most of the land has been unlawfully acquired either by the government or by the public. In Punjab, there are several instances where graveyard land was unlawfully acquired by refugees who migrated from Pakistan. In most of the cases there is no boundary wall. Therefore, the common man of that locality is using the graveyard land as a common passage. Under the law they have acquired adverse possession. For this state of affairs Muslims are mainly responsible. They themselves are divided into groups and sub-groups. They have no idea to unite. The waqf property is the property of the Muslim community. They themselves have to protect waqf property. It is submitted that in every district they should from a committee, who will be looking after the waqf propery within their respective districts. Every Muslim should contribute some money to this committee. This shall be the duty of such a committee to protect waqf propety from unauthorised occupation and decay. The Committee should try to construct boundary line of graveyard as soon as possible.

In such cases the Indian courts have also not taken correct approach. In *Mohammad S. Labbai* v *Mohd Hanifa*[32] the Supreme Court of India held that the courts before whom the disputes came up for decision handed down judgments which were not strictly in accordance with the 'Shariat' and the essential tenets of Muslim law. It is, therefore, necessary that courts should decide such cases according to the provisions of Muslim law.

It is again submitted that if a particular piece of land is not used by Muslims as graveyard it does not mean that such a land has ceased to be a waqf land and any person can acquire such land. There are number of graveyards which are not in use after partition of the country *i.e.* from 1947 as most of the Muslims of that particular locality had already migrated to neighbouring country. It does not mean that a waqf by user once created has come to an end as no dead was buried there.

The Supreme Court in *Mohammad S Labbai* v *Mohd Hanifa*[33] held that for the validity of a graveyard it is necessary that there should be a conclusive proof to the effect that a particular piece of land was used as public graveyard.

It is submitted here that it is not always easy to produce conclusive proof of a particular graveyard. A piece of land may be used as a graveyard from time immemorial and there was no dispute regarding the use of such land as graveyard. Under such circumstances, it is not necessary at all to produce the conclusive proof of the graveyard. The courts are bound to declare such property as waqf. This is also the duty of the courts to pass order for the complete vacation of such land from unauthorised occupiers. Fyzee has rightly said that a graveyard once created continues to be so even though there remain no traces of the dead, not even the bones...(and) although there is no evidence of an express dedication.[34]

Sajjadanashin

The functions of the Sajjadanashin's office are not of spiritual or religious nature. They have no disciples and doctrines of sufism or anything to teach. They are required to offer annual *urs* and to offer *fathia* at tombs. The duties assigned to a Sajjadanashin can be performed by any person. He has the right to share in the offerings made at the tomb. The successive incumbents are also entitled to receive that share as long as he holds the office. Unfortunately, the office of Sajjadanashin does not come within the purview of Waqf Act, 1954. He is, therefore, immune from the jurisdiction of the Waqf Board. It is, therefore, necessary that the functions of the Sajjadanashin be properly controlled. He should have no right to share the offerings made at the tomb. These are the property of the tomb. This shall be the duty of the Sajjadanashin to keep a register of all the offerings. The register shall be open for inspection and any person can inspect the register.

Today the 'Dargah' is in distress. The Dargah Khwaja Sahib Act, the object of which was to remove the evils, has failed to achieve its object. The Dargah committee is paying too much importance to make collection of Nazars and nothing else more. The manner in which Dargah Committee is dealing with the affairs needs immediate check. Till now it could not solve the problem of begging, sanitation *etc.* The financial position of the Dargah is also not satisfactory. It is necessary that an honest, hard working Nazim should be appointed for looking after the Dargah.

The most important problem which a visitor faces immediately on reaching Ajmer is of boarding and lodging. The Dargah Committee should give top priority for this work. As soon as cheap and best boarding and lodging becomes available, the role of the 'Khadim' can also be eliminated. Today they take advantage of the situation only because of the boarding and lodging. The Chishti Chaman Project (a plan for the construction of a six storeyed building) should be taken up as soon as possible.

At present Dargah is paying 20 per cent administrative charges to the government. This amount is paid from the annuity payable to the Dargah. When the zamindari system was abolished in Ajmer by the Ajmer Abolition of the Intermediaries and Land Reform Act, No 3 of 1956, annuity was fixed in the case of Dargah properties affected by the Act. It is submitted that in view of the above discussion the Dargah should be exempted from paying this amount.

As noted earlier Dargah of Khwaja Muinuddin Chisti is governed by a central Act. This Act has failed to achieve its objects. People are paying lot of money in the name of great saint of India. Daily collection is made in the Dargah. Even today this amount is being misappropriated by the Khadims.

From the time of Prophet Mohammad, emphasis has been placed on democratic principles. One of the principle of democracy is free and fair election. Hazrat Imam Husain sacrificed his life only because he refused to submit himself before dictatorship. This can be the best example of democracy. Unfortunately, Muslims, have forgotten the principle. The office of Sajjadanashin is claimed on the basis of succession. From the Mughul period, Khadims, Sajjadanashin *etc.* are inheriting their office. This is totally against the Islamic principles. It is, therefore, proposed here that a Management Committee be constituted. Some of the members of the committee be sponsored by the government. Rest of the members be appointed on the basis of election. In this way only can the affairs of the Dargah be controlled.

It is submitted here that Khadims and Sajjadanashins have not judicially recognised customary right to receive Nazar. They are extracting heavy amount from innocent people. Nazars, whether in cash or kind, made at the Dargah is the property of the Dargah. The whole offering should be kept under the proper custody. Nobody, except the persons appointed by the Dargah committee, shall have right to receive offerings. The Committee shall maintain a register. The register shall contain full record of the offerings. This is the duty of the government to prevent the exploitation of visitors and pilgrims within the premises of the Dargah. Penal provision should also be made in the Act. Any person who tries to take illegal money should be awarded rigorous imprisonment up to five years and a fine up to Rs. 1000.00. Khadims should be totally excluded from the premises and the administration of the Dargah.

The concrete action can be taken by the government unless

and until public opinion especially of Muslims is in favour of such action. It is, therefore, necessary that public opinion should be created in favour of the proposed reforms. Muslim intelligentsia should come forward for the help of government then only government can made sincere efforts in the matter.

Begging is very common within the premises of Dargah and it has become a problem for the management. This problem was discussed in detail by the Enquiry Committee. The Enquiry Committee suggested that begging within the Dargah premises should be strictly prohibited. Beggars suffering from any infectious disease shall be ejected from the Dargah premises. Others shall be kept and maintained in a home especially provided for them.[35] There is a provision in the by-laws for ejectment of beggars with virulent disease.[36] There is also a provision for not allowing the beggars to loiter about or solicit alms within the Dargah compound.[37] It is, however, regretted that the Dargah Committee neither provides them with any shelter nor prohibits their entry into the Dargah premises.

Family Waqfs

Today, family waqfs (*waqfs-alal-aulad*) are faced with many problems. Neither is their number in the country known nor is there any effective administrative supervision over them. The callous indifference of beneficiaries and mutawallis towards the maintenance and improvement of such waqfs has thrown them into a pitiable condition. What really discourages Muslims to create family waqfs is the growing awareness of the disadvantages of tying up property in perpetuity where succeeding generation obtain smaller fractions of the income, part of which is often squandered in vexatious and frivolous litigation and duly absorbed by unscrupulous lawyers.[38]

The adverse effects of the laws of Estate Duty, Income Tax and land reforms *etc.*, are crippling the institutions of family waqfs. It is high time Muslim of India made a choice between this fast decaying institution and something more useful. Instead of abolishing this institution completely, family waqfs may be created for a spciefied time. This type of waqf should be created for period of two generations at the end of which it may be reconstituted provided the beneficiaries agree to do so.

The principles applicable to private chapels in England proceed on the same footing. A lord of the manor or any other who generally keeps a private chapel in his own mansion or house is at full liberty to divert or otherwise use the chapel at his own sweet will and pleasure. However, in England, the rule against perpetuities will apply universally to all gifts unless the gift be to a public charitable purpose. In India, the rule is different. The Hindu law recognises a gift to a family idol and any property can be dedicated in perpetuity for the worship of the idol or other religious purposes so as to be inalienable. The position will be same when a person merely makes a payment to a charity or spends for an idol out of his income or out of the income from a particular fund or property without dedicating the fund or property for the purposes.[40]

The Musalman Waqf Validating Act, 1913, enabled the Indian Muslims to create waqfs for an indefinite period, for the maintenance and support of his family, children or descendants, providing that the ultimate benefit was expressly or impliedly reserved for the poorer for any other purpose recognised by the Muslim law as religious, pious or charitable.[41] Section 4 of the Act says that no such waqf shall be deemed invalid merely because the benefit reserved therein for the poor or other religious, pious or charitable purpose of a permanent nature was postponed until after the extension of of the family children or descendants of the founder of the waqf.

By the Musalman Waqf Validating Act, 1913, the Muslims have been allowed to donate their properties perpetually. In fact, this is against the public policy. A property should not be made inalienable perpetually. In *Stanley* v *Leigh*[42] Sir Joseph Jekyll said :

> The law does abhor what is called a perpetuity...the reason of which is the mischief that would arise to the public from estates remaining forever or for a long time inalienable or untransferrable from one hand to another, being a damp to industry and a prejudice to trade, to which may be added the inconvenience and distress that would be brought on families whose estates are so fettered.

In the modern industrial age, it is necessary that the Mussalman Validating Act, 1913, should be repealed. The consequences of the Muslim Validating Act are devastating. The Act has blocked the initiatives which may be taken by the Muslim upper class in the direction of industry. It perpetuated a pathetic class of pensioners devoid of economic initiative who were bound in the long run to become a drag on the community. People are also realising the disadvantages of tying up property in perpetuity where succeeding generations obtain successively smaller fractions of the income, part of which—if not the whole—is often squandered by unscrupulous lawyers[43].

The ruling given by the Privy Council in *Abul Fata* v *Russomoy*[44] should be followed. It may not be out of the way to mention here that Kenya has followed in *Fatumabinti Mohammed* v *Mohammed bin Salim*[45] the rulings of Privy Council given in Abul Fata's case.

Now everywhere (including Muslim states) states are having control over waqf properties. In India, for example we are having various waqf acts and by these various acts, the state is controlling the waqf properties.

Family Waqfs to Strangers

As a matter of fact there cannot be a family waqf in favour of stranger. The Waqf Act is not specific on this point. It is submitted here that if family waqfs in favour of strangers are treated as valid, it will defeat the very purpose of the family waqf. It is, therefore, submitted that family waqfs in favour of strangers should not be treated as valid. A proviso to this effect may be made in the Waqf Act.

At present a pure private waqf will not come within the purview of the Waqf Act, 1954. For attracting the provisions of this Act, the object of a private waqf must be pious, religious or charitable[46]. It has been held that the provisions of the Act shall be made applicable only to the properties which have been dedicated by Muslim law as pious, religious or charitable. The waqf Board will have jurisdiction only to the extent to which property was dedicated for any purpose recognised by Muslim law as pious, religious or charitable and this must be in addition to the provision for the members of the family and descendants.

It is submitted here that every (including private waqf) waqf is created with an intent of charity *etc.* otherwise it cannot be a valid waqf. A settler is free to create a waqf or not to create a waqf. Once he decides to establish a waqf his main motive is charity as well as the help of his relatives. Therefore, all such waqfs will come within the purview of waqf legislation. The main idea in establishing these institutions is gaining religious recompense. Family waqfs are established to save the property from the wasting hands of squandering descendants. The movement which was started by Indian Muslims after the Privy Council judgment in 1894 was passed by the government and the family waqfs were recognised by this Act. The social consequences of this piece of legislation were devastating. The main effect of this enactment was that it blocked the initiative by the Muslim upper class in the direction of industry. The main ingredient of family waqf is that the children and children of the waqif are bound to derive income from the property of the waqf. In the words of Daniel Latifi,[47] the Act of 1913, perpetuated a pathetic class of pensioners devoid of economic initiative who were bound in the long run to become a drag on the community. The present writer, therefore, submits that the Act of 1913, be repealed immediately.

In the modern industrial age the dedication of property in waqf has stopped the natural growth and development of the national economy. During 1925, in Turkey, three fourths of the arable land, estimated at 50,000.00 Turkish pounds, was endowed as waqf. This resulted in the stagnation of Turkish economy. Consequently, the Turkish Government abolished the ministry of waqf. The whole property was given under the control of government.

In Egypt, at the end of the nineteenth century, one eighth of the cultivated soil was in the ownership of God. Mohammad Ali was the first man in Egypt, who confiscated all agricultural waqf and compensated the beneficiaries. In the year 1924, the waqf ministry came directly under the control of Parliament.

In Algiers one half and in Tunis one third of the cultivated land was dedicated in waqf. It was only in the beginning of 20th century that it was realised that dedication of property in the ownership of God is a handicap to the natural growth and development of the national economy. In 1930, therefore, the French government took over the haboos in Algiers and later in Morocco. In Kenya, the decision of the Privy Council in Abul Fata's case is the law of the land from 1894.

We are living in a fast changing world in which the established structures are becoming obsolete every moment. Alvin Toffler the author of *Future Shock* calls our world 'a turbulent, high change'. The incredible development in science and technology have so affected our modes of living that a new situation has been created, a situation to which all institutions have to respond appropriately if they are to stay relevant. In the west, society is going through a massive transformation. From the industrial it is becoming a super or post industrial society. This change also effected Muslims and Muslim states. Therefore, many Muslim countries either completely or partially abrogated the institution of family waqfs. In Middle East either the family waqfs have been abolished or they have been restricted.

In Aden, Kenya and Zanzibar the legislature passed special laws to validate family waqfs as was done in India through the Musalman Waqf Validating Act, 1913[48]. Professor Anderson says that it is unfortunate that the judges in these countries should feel themselves bound by the Privy Council's decision in Abul Fata's case despite the fact that it has been recognised by all competent persons as 'a wholly mistaken interpretation of the Islamic law'[49]. A similar opinion was expressed by Justice Hamilton of Kenya. He says while the Muslim law, uninfluenced from outside sources, permitted perpetuities and the erection of waqfs for family aggrandizement solely, the influence of English Judges of the Privy Council has gradually encroached on this position[50].

In Egypt, the *waqfs dhurri* were first made temporary and revocable[51] and then in 1952 were abolished altogether[52].

In Lebanon, the law of 12th March, 1947 restricted waqfs dhurri to two generations. After the expiry of this period the waqf for his heirs will become the owner of the property[53].

In Syria the creation of waqf *dhurri* has been abolished and all waqf *dhurri* created prior to that date was dissolved[54].

It is here submitted that in view of the evils in the family waqfs and the recent amendments introduced into the law of family waqf in various Muslim countries, Muslims should review their attitude and they should adopt a realistic approach. The government should also take necessary steps for abandoning the family waqfs. Indian Muslims can direct the income of these family waqfs in some of their welfare schemes.

Till today the exact number of family waqfs is not known. There is no administrative supervision over them. The passing of the Estate Duty Act, Income Tax Act, Land Reforms and other laws have adversely effected on the existence of this institution. Gradually this institution is extinguishing. It has become necessary that some concrete steps should be taken to save this institution. This institution should be saved from dying. In fact, those beneficiaries who are not working according to the directions of the creator of the waqf should not be allowed to draw benefit. They should be removed. It is wrong to say that there is every likelihood that the coming generation might be virtuous enough to be entrusted with the full ownership of properties. In this view of the matter, it would be far better to tie up the property for a specified period rather than in perpetuity, granting them all the privileges of a charitable waqf[55]. The problem will not be solved by tying up the property for a specified period. According to present author the best course is to deprive of the corrupt beneficiaries from enjoying the income of the waqf. There is a more effective check on their administration. The Waqf Act, 1954, be also amended on the lines of the Bengal and U.P. Waqf Acts.

Sub-section (3) of Section 2 of U.P. Muslim Waqfs Act, 1960 was omitted by Section 2 of the U.P. Act No 28 of 1971. The amended Act provided that the Act shall not be applicable to those waqfs in which more than 75 per cent of the income of the waqf has been reserved for waqif or his descendants. In case there remains no descendant of the waqf, the income from such waqf shall be applied for religious, pious or charitable purposes. Unless and until such waqfs get themselves registered with the Waqf Board their existence would not be safeguarded. It has, therefore, been provided that the above Act shall be applicable to all *waqfs alal-aulad* to the extent to the property, the subject of which is dedicated for religious, pious or charitable purpose[56]. The beneficiaries are entitled to receive the portion of the total income of the waqf only in the capacity of beneficiaries. They are not entitled to receive income in any other capacity[57].

Under classical Islamic law, the power to transfer the waqf property by a mutawalli vests in the Qazi. Now this power of Qazi has been taken over by the courts and the courts are competent to grant such permission. It can be granted on the application of the mutawalli; filing of a suit for this purpose is not necessary[58]. It has been generally seen that in number of cases, mutawallies have disposed of the property of the family waqf without obtaining necessary permission from the court. It is, therefore, submitted that thorough survey of such cases be made by the Waqf Board and the culprits be punished.

Waqf Board : It must be an Active and Vigilant Body

Of course, many mutawallis and other employees are corrupt, but at the same time the Waqf Boards also do not take full care of the waqf properties. It is, therefore, submitted that the Waqf Boards must pay adequate attention to the development of urban waqf properties. It is also necessary that the constitution of the waqf should be changed. Persons who are interested to work for the cause of waqf should be appointed. Persons who are interested to work for waqf cause should only be taken as the members of the Waqf Board. It has been observed that persons are appointed on the basis of political alliance *e.g.* if Congress party is in power then persons having contact with the Congress party are appointed as members and chairman of the Board. This practice should be abandoned immediately. Appointments should be made purely on the basis of merit, honesty and integrity.

After the fall of Mughals no proper attention was paid to the waqf property in the country. In fact, during British period no attention was made for the proper administration of waqfs in the country. The Musalman Waqf Validating Act, 1913, and its subsequent amendment were of very little help in the proper administration of waqfs in the country. It was only after independence that concrete steps were taken in this direction and the Waqf Act, 1954, was passed. The Waqf Act, 1954 lays down a comprehensive administrative structure to ensure proper administration of waqfs in the country. The Act provides for the establishment of Boards.[59] Under the Act the Board has been given wide powers to control the administration of waqfs. Under the Act mutawallis have been made responsible for their acts. In case of default they can be penalised. Under the Act the state governments are required to act as supervisor of these waqfs. The central government has been authorised to lay down the policies to be adopted by the Board.[60]

Nomination of Members

At present the members of the Board are appointed by the State Government.[61] Under the Acts the State Government is empowered to appoint members from categories of persons mentioned in Section 11 of the said Act. It is submitted that instead of nominating persons the members should be appointed through election. At the same time the state government may reserve the right to nominate one or two members from the persons having knowledge of law. At present, it is absolute discretion of the waqf minister of the state to recommend the name of any person to be appointed as the member of the Board. It has been seen that incompetent persons having political affinity to any particular party are generally appointed as the members of the Board. The result of this practice is that the Waqf Board consists mostly of incompetent persons. They are busy in their own affairs *etc.* and they have no time to serve the waqf cause. This state of affairs can be to a very large extent, of the waqf Board appointed by way of election. In this way interested and competent persons may become the members of the Waqf Board.

Salary *etc.* of the Members

At present, under the Waqf Act, 1954 there is no provision

for the payment of the salary of the Chairman and members of the Waqf Board. One of the reason for not taking interest in the waqf administration is that they are not entitled for any honorarium *etc.* as a member of the Board. A Chairman of the Board is required to work as a whole time employee. Under the Act he is required to perform several important duties. He is the head of the institution. It is, therefore, necessary that a provision of their salary *etc.* should be made in the Waqf Act. Unless and until this provision is made, there cannot be any hope of better waqf administration in the country.

According to Section 8-A of the Waqf Act, 1954, the Central Government may establish a Council to be called the Central Waqf Council. The members of this Council are appointed by the Central Government. This Council can play very important role in the administration of waqfs in the country. It is, therefore, recommended that the members of this council be appointed through election. It may also be seen that at least one member should be appointed from each state.

The existence of the Central Council depends on the amount of one per cent of the aggregate of the net annual income of the waqfs which every Waqf Board shall pay out of its waqf fund. There is no other source of income of the Council. It is necessary that the Central Government should come forward for its help and a lump-sum amount should be paid every year as grants-in-aid.

For the better administration of waqf it is necessary that members of the Waqf Board shall be given certain powers. Where a member comes to the conclusion that a mutawalli is not functioning properly or he is negligent, the member may be authorised to look after the waqf property. He may be allowed to file a suit for the eviction of waqf property. He may also be allowed to collect the rent from the tenants. However, such collected rent should be deposited in the Board's account immediately.

The jurisdiction of the Board is limited to administration of waqfs. A Board can exercise jurisdiction only to persons coming under waqfs. It has no jurisdiction over a stranger,

Appointment of non-Muslims as member of the Waqf Board/ Mutawalli

In all judicial or quasi-judicial proceedings, justice must not only be done but must manifestly be seen to be done. The Waqf Board may comprise men of high integrity and conscience. There can be no doubt these members of Waqf Board may be fully conscious of the obligation, imposed by holy *Quran*. Nonetheless, it is possible to believe that a non-Muslim alleged 'unauthorised occupant' of waqf property, would not feel the same confidence in the adjudication of his case by a purely Muslim body like the Waqf committee.

It is necessary that Waqf Board should consist of young and energetic persons. Where suitable Muslims are not available and they are not required to perform religious functions a non-Muslim may be appointed as member of the Waqf Board. A non-Muslim can also be appointed as Mutawalli. Muslim law nowhere says that non-Muslim cannot be appointed as mutawalli, member of the Waqf Board. Therefore, in appropriate cases, non-Muslims may also be appointed as Mutawalli/Member of the Waqf board.

Appointment of Retired Persons

It has been seen that generally retired persons are re-employed by the Waqf Boards. In M.P. Waqf Board Office in Bhopal majority of the employees is of retired persons. Some of them are in good health. However, rest of them are not able to perform their duties properly. Due to old age they are not able to perform their duties properly. It is submitted that the retired persons who are not able to perform their duties properly should not be appointed. The Board may prefer to appoint such persons who are between 30 to 55 years of age. The persons between this age group are young and cannot be taken in government service. Under such circumstances they will not try to join government service and they will serve the Board wholeheartedly.

Appointment of District Waqf Officers

For the proper administration of waqfs it is absolutely necessary that in each district a waqf and deputy waqf officer should be appointed. The district should be selected as the unit for the administration of waqf properties and collection of contribution *etc.* The Waqf Officer shall hold the office independently and he will not be under the control of the collector. As far as possible persons having sound knowledge of Islamic jurisprudence, secular outlook having knowledge of Urdu, Hindi and local language may be appointed to the posts. The knowledge of Urdu as well as local language is necessary as most of the waqf deeds are prepared by the waqif either in Urdu or in local language. It is not at all necessary that District Waqf Officers must be Muslims. Any person having knowledge of waqf matters can be appointed as District Waqf Officer.

The above officers so appointed shall be the employees of the government and their salaries, allowances, pensions and other remuneration shall be paid in the first instance out of the consolidated fund of the state and subsequently reimbursed from the Waqf Administration Fund.

Qualifications for appointment of Waqf Officer

A person to be appointed as the Waqf Officer shall be one (i) who is holding or has held a judicial office not lower in rank than that of a District Judge ; or (ii) who has been not less than ten years—

(a) an advocate enrolled under the Indian Bar Council Act, 1926, or the Advocates Act, 1961.

(b) an attorney of a High Court.

Deputy and Assistant Waqf Officer

The state government may also appoint Deputy and Assistant Waqf Commissioner in each district. A person to be appointed as a Deputy Waqf Commissioner shall be—

(a) an advocate enrolled under the Indian Bar Council Act, 1926 or the Advocates Act, 1961 ;

(b) an Attorney of a High Court ; or

(c) a person of repute who is having interest in waqf matters ;

A person to be appointed as an Assistant Waqf Officer shall be a person—

(a) who is holding or has held a judicial office not lower in rank than that of a civil judge, or any office which in the opinion of the state government is an equivalent office, for not less than four years, or

(b) who has been for not less than seven years—

(i) an Advocate enrolled under the Indian Bar Council Act, 1926 or the Advocates Act, 1961 ;

(ii) an Attorney of High Court, or

The Deputy and Assistant Waqf Officers shall exercise such powers and perform such duties and functions as may be provided by or under the provisions of the Act.

Appointment of Waqf Officer

The appointment of Waqf Commissioner *etc.* should be made by the government on such terms and conditions as the government might deem it fit.

The appointment of Deputy/Joint and Assistant Waqf Officer shall be transferrable from one place to another place within the state.

The Waqf Officers *etc.* shall have the same powers as are vested in a civil court under the Code of Civil Procedure, 1908, in respect of the following matters, namely—

(a) enforcing the attendance of any person and examining him on oath or affirmation and making local inspections ;

(b) compelling the production of documents ;

(c) issuing commissions for the examination of the witnesses and accounts and local investigations.

MANAGEMENT OF WAQF PROPERTY

Investment of waqf money

It is submitted here that all waqf monies other than monies required for the day-to-day expenditure of the waqf shall be kept in a scheduled bank or a post office savings bank or in any registered bank. The waqf money can also be deposited with any banker or person acting as a banker who has given such security for the safe custody and repayment on demand of the monies. The main aim of this submission is that the waqf money may be invested in such places or with such persons that its security and safe custody is not affected.[62]

It may also be provided that the waqf deed contrary to the provisions of this provision shall carry no force.

The power of delegation by the Board should not be subject to any contrary provision in the Act and further subject to such restrictions and conditions which may by rule be prescribed. Where only the powers are delegated and not the duties, but the duties and powers are so interconnected that one cannot be exercised without the other than alongwith the powers the duties must also be taken to have been delegated.

The Board may delegate to the Chairman or any other member or to the Secretary or any other officer or servant of the Board or any committee such of its powers and duties under the said Act as it may deem necessary. The section also provides that the delegation can only be done by an 'order in writing'. However, this expression has not been defined in the Act. This term should be constr ed strictly. A separate order in writing should be made by the Board after due application of its mind and not mere administrative direction in the nature of distribution memo.

Where the powers and duties are delegated by the Board to any authority prescribed under the Waqf Act, 1954, then on delegation such authority stands fully in the shoes of the Board. The authority concerned should have full powers and duties of the Board. The delegated authority acts in the same way as if it is the original appointed authority. Every act done, order passed, power exercised and duty performed by the delegated authority would be deemed to have been done by the authority who delegated.

Where the power has been delegated, such delegation would be absolute. However, the person delegating would still retain the authority. It was held in *Syed Shah* v *Commissioner of Waqfs*[63] that where the function of the Board is delegated to the Commissioner, the Commissioner acts for and on behalf of the Board and the appointment made by the Commissioner of a temporary mutawalli would be deemed to have been made by the Board itself who delegates the functions to the Commissioner.

Registration of Waqfs

Registration of waqfs both public and private be made mandatory. The power of registration may be given to District Waqf Officer. India is a very vast country. Naturally the area of those states is also very vast. Again the state of Madhya Pradesh is the biggest state in the country. Most of the waqf property is situated in villages. No proper control is exercised. It is, therefore, not always possible for a person living in Jagdalpur or Raigarh to go to Bhopal (where the Waqf Board office is situated) and to get waqf registered. It is, therefore, absolutely necessary that facility of registration should be made in each district. It is not always easy for the Waqf Board to make preliminary enquiries before granting registration.

Sub-section (3) of Section 25 of the Waqf Act, 1954, says that an application for registration can be made in such form and manner and at such place as the Board may prescribe and shall contain necessary particulars. It has been observed that sometimes it becomes difficult for the mutawalli to provide all such information, It is, therefore, submitted the rules may provide that in the case of any or all public/private waqfs it shall not be necessary to give the particulars of the waqf property of such value and such kind.

Sub-section (8) of Section 25 provides that in the case of waqfs created before the commencement of Waqf Act, 1954, every application for registration shall be made within three months from such commencement and in the case of waqfs created after such commencement, within three months from the date of the creation of the waqf. This is a mandatory provision and, therefore, must be fulfilled.[64] There are numerous waqfs which could not be registered due to negligence of the mutawalli *etc.* It is hereby submitted that the period of three months is not sufficient. It may be extended to one year.

The non-registration of waqf on the part of mutawalli or any other person should be made punishable. One of the tests evolved to decide whether a provision is mandatory or directory, is whether non-compliance thereof would incur penal consequences or not. There is no penal provision in the Waqf Act, 1954. It can, therefore, be said that the use of the word 'shall' in Section 25 of the Waqf Act, 1954, cannot be construed as mandatory.

It should be noted here that the limitation prescribed by the Act for making an application has not the effect of barring the application which is the general effect of law of limitation. If no application is made within three months of creation of waqf it cannot be said that a waqf has got an immunity from registration and no application can be made thereafter. What the limitation here means is that if the Mutawalli does not make any application within the prescribed period he would render himself liable to be punished. The intent and purport of three months' limitation is that a mutawalli is to act within this period otherwise it shall be the break of statutory duty cast upon him by the Act.

It is also relevant here to note down the provisions of the Limitation Act (No 36 of 1963). This Act provides that where under a special or local law, a period different from what is prescribed in the Limitation Act is provided, the provisions of the Limitation Act (from Section 4 to Section 24 of the Act) shall apply. It can, therefore, be said that if the application is not moved within three months and there is a sufficient cause for not making an application within the prescribed period, the period may be extended for making an application.

Sub-clause (7) of Section 25 of the Act says that on receipt of an application for registration, the Board may, before the registration of the waqf, make such inquiries as it thinks fit in respect of the genuineness and validity of the application. This provision of the Waqf Act 1954, is not mandatory. The Board may or may not make the enquiry before granting registration. It is not obligatory on the part of the Board to record these findings with reasons. It is submitted here that holding of enquiry should be made mandatory. It will help to ascertain the facts by judicial inquiry. The concept of inquiry clearly includes the notice to the other side who may be affected by it and after hearing all concerned, to arrive at conclusion. A duty should be imposed on the officer concerned to hold an inquiry and to arrive at the conclusion on all the relevant matters and then give judgment whether a waqf is public or not. It means an objective test which of necessity depends upon an inquiry. Inquiry includes hearing the concerned parties which is the principle of natural justice. It is, therefore, submitted that holding of enquiry before arriving into any conclusion regarding registration be made compulsory.

Issue of a public notice regarding enquiry shall also be made mandatory.

Determination of Public Waqf

The determination of the fact whether a waqf is public or not also necessarily involves a question whether there is any waqf at all in existence or it is merely a resemblance of waqf. Therefore, the determination of this question involves two aspects of the matter (i) whether there is any waqf, (ii) if so, whether it is a public waqf. The rough and ready test to determine the nature and character of waqf is as to who are the beneficiaries ? In case of a public waqf, the beneficial interest is vested in an uncertain and fluctuating body of persons such a body may be a sect following a particular religion or religious persuasion.

The porperties of a Public Waqf

The present Act does not contain any provision as to what are the properties of public waqf. Ordinarily where there is any documents or documentary evidence about the properties belonging to a public waqf, there is no difficulty in ascertaining its character, value and other details but the real difficulty arises when there is no document or written evidence or where the waqf is so old that the reliable and satisfactory evidence cannot be gathered or available. The absence of documents regarding waqf property is very common in India.

The dedication of property must be final and complete if the dedication is complete and absolute then only a public waqf may come into existence. If the dedication is not complete then no public waqf will come into existence. The dedication will be a charge over the property in favour of the charity.

The Officer-in-charge of waqfs in each district should also be authorised to ascertain the objects of the waqf. While judging the object of the waqf it is necessary to keep in mind the substantial object of the waqf as distinct from the ancillary or subordinate object of the waqf.

Transfer of Immovable[65] Property of Waqfs

Section 36-A of the Waqf Act, 1954, is identical to Section 36 of the Bombay Public Trusts Act, 1950. It is materially different from Section 14 of the M.P. Trusts Act, 1951. The present section provides that notwithstanding anything contained in the waqf deed, whereas Section 14 of the M.P. Trusts Act, 1951, says that the sale *etc.* can take place subject to the directions contained in the instrument of trust. The object of Section 36-A of the Waqf Act, 1954 is to put check upon the indiscriminate transfer of the properties belonging to the public waqf. The Waqf Board has been assigned power to examine every application for transfer of the waqf property and accord or refuse sanction to it. The power should be exercised judicially and not capriciously.

It may, however, be noted that Section 36-A of the Waqf Act, 1954, merely confers controlling power on the Waqf Board and the ultimate power and authority of transferring the waqf property vests in the mutawallis. Under the present section waqf Board has no right to auction any waqf property nor can grant any lease of the agricultural land for any period whatsoever. Such an act would be clearly outside the jurisdiction of the Waqf Board.

Immovable Property

It may be noted that the present section only deals with

immovable property and does not restrict transfer of movable property. The term 'immovable property' has not been defined by the Act and, therefore, the definition given under Section 3(18) of the M.P. General Clauses Act, 1957, (corresponding to Section 3(26) of the Indian General Clause Act, 1897) may be referred to. It defines 'immovable property' shall include land, benefits to arise out of land, and things attached to the earth, or permanently fastened to anything attached to the earth.

Section 3 of the Transfer of Property Act gives a negative definition *i.e.* 'immovable property' does not include immovable property. 'Immovable property' includes land, buildings, hereditary allowances, rights to waqfs, ferries, fisheries or any other benefit to arise out of land and things attached to the earth or permanently fastened to anything which is attached to but not standing timber, growing crops nor grass.

It is submitted that the definition given in the General Clauses Act would be of utility and use because the definition given under Section 3(26) of the General Clauses Act applies to all the M.P. Acts, wherever the terms defined by the Act are used.

Previous sanction of the Board

The words 'previous sanction' are very material in the Section 36-A of the Central Act. The expression lays stress and emphasis on the fact that a sanction has to be obtained by the mutawalli from the Board prior to the transfer. The word 'previous' preceding the word 'sanction' reinforces the conclusion that any sanction obtained after the transfer will not validate a transfer made prior to such sanction

The provision of the section pertaining to sanction may be compared with the provisions contained in Section 86 of the Code of Civil Procedure, wherein the consent of the Central Government is made necessary prior to the filing of the suit against Ruler *etc.* Although the word 'previous' does not precede the word 'consent' in Section 86 C.P. C. yet it was held that the consent has to be obtained prior to the insititution of the suit. A consent obtained subsequent to the filing of the suit would not validate the suit instituted without prior consent.[66] It was held to be a condition precedent and is not subject to any waiver.[67]

It can, therefore, be said that the provision for sanction is a condition precedent for valid transfer without which the transfer shall not be valid.

Power of Review

It is the general principle of law that unless the power of review is specifically conferred on any tribunal or court, it does not inhere in it. The power of review must be expressly granted by a statute. The Waqf Act, 1954, does not provide for review of an order of sanction passed by the Board, the Board can review the same either on his own motion or on the application of any party. After according sanction to the proposed sale of the house, the Board becomes *functus officio* and had no jurisdiction to recall or review the sanction given by him.[68] It is, therefore, necessary that the power of review be given to the Waqf Board.

Maintenance of Accounts[69]

The term 'accounts' in the Act has been used in a wider sense and not in the narrow or conventional sense of denoting books of account or account books. Account is a detailed statement of series of receipts and disbursements which have taken place between two or more persons. A registry of dates, credits and charges or a detailed statement of series of receipts and disbursements of money which have taken place between two or more persons (Wharton).

The provision of Sections 32 and 50 of the Waqf Act, 1954, are identical and mandatory in nature.

A mutawalli and the Board is bound (a) to keep clear and accurate accounts of the waqf property and (b) at all reasonable times, at the request of any person interested in the waqf property to furnish him with full and accurate information as to the amount and state of waqf property. The duty to keep account of waqf property, involves in it three-fold duty,

(i) the duty to keep accounts ;
(ii) the duty to deliver accounts ; and
(iii) the duty to vouch the accounts.

Out of this three-fold duty, the duty to keep accounts of waqf property is an essential and primary duty. The above principles are based on natural justice and fair play and therefore, these are applicable to public or private religious or charitable endowments.

Shall keep regular Accounts

This expression means that the accounts are to be kept in proper manner. If there is a fault in mode of accounting it will not be irregular within the meaning of section if it cannot be shown that the actual receipts are not entered or the expenditure entered is fictitious or excessive. The expression does not mean that the account are to be made from day today or from hour to hour but it merely denotes that the entries are to be made a systematic manner. Thus 'regular accounts' means a systematic form of accounts kept in regular course. It is relevant here to make reference to Section 34 of the Indian Evidence Act, 1872, wherein entries in books of accounts regularly kept in the course of business are made relevant.

Audit of accounts of waqfs—Accounting year[70]

Section 33 of the Waqf Act, 1954, provides that the accounts of waqfs shall be audited and examined annually or at such other intervals as the Board may determine by an auditor appointed by the Board. The Waqf Board may fix the accounting year for each public waqf. This is the discretion of the Board to fix any other day on which the accounts will be completed but in the absence of any other direction, the year will be the financial year.

Section 33 of the Waqf Act, 1954, makes annual audit of accounts compulsory. The audit of account serves following three purposes—

(i) It gives the true financial position at the time of audit of the accounts of a public trust.

(ii) It further brings to the notice of all concerned the facts as to whether there is malfeasance, misfeasance or non-misfeasance on the part of any trustee resulting in loss to the trust ;

(iii) whether the trustees have spent money contrary to or in excess to the trust ;

The above section does not lay down any qualification for the appointment of auditors. Any person can be appointed as auditor. It is submitted that this provision of the Act needs slight amendment. The following persons may be appointed as auditors—

(i) holder of a certificate granted under Section 226 of the Companies Act, 1956 ;

(ii) a member of an institution or association, the members of which have been declared under that section (*i.e.* under Section 226 of the Companies Act, 1956) to act as auditor of companies ;

(iii) any other person who has been authorised to act as an auditor by the State Government ;

(iv) auditors of local funds under the M.P. Local Funds Audit Acts, 1933.

The Board may be authorised to appoint any person as auditor only where a waqf was having annual income of not more than Rs. 1,000.00. Such waqfs are petty whose accounts of income and expenditure is simple in nature and does not require so much professional skills as an audit of a public waqf having large annual income and expenditure may require.

Unfortunately the Boards have failed in their duty to make proper use of the waqf income. Generally the Boards have taken the plea that on account of lack of funds they are unable to fulfil their obligation. It is submitted that the whole economy of the waqfs and Waqf Board's depend on the proper audit. It is, therefore, necessary that the Waqf Boards must perform this pious obligation well. It is only on account of failure of the Waqf Boards to perform their obligation that mutawallis could dare to misappropriate waqf fund. The Waqf Boards can at least audit the accounts of some important waqfs of their respective states.

Special Audit

Under the Waqf Act, 1954, there is no provision for special audit. It is submitted here that the Board may be authorised to direct a special audit of the accounts of any waqf which the Board considers necessary. The fee of special audit shall be paid out of the waqf property (fund) as per the scale to be provided in the rule. The determination of the fee shall not be left to the determination of the Board.

Penalty

Section 41 of the Waqf Act, 1954 deals with regard to penalty. This section is not complete. There are other grounds also which should be included in this section. Penalty shall be imposed if the mutawalli has failed to perform any of the following duties. These grounds may be inserted in Section 41 of the Act.

Failed to give information *etc.*

Penalty shall be imposed if the mutawalli of the management committee—

(i) has failed to give information of the changes in the waqf; or

(ii) has failed to give information of the proposed changes in the constitution of the waqf.

Executor failed to apply to the Board *etc.*

Penalty shall also be imposed if the executor of a will has failed to apply the Board/Waqf Officer for registration of a waqf which is created by the will, within six months from the day of testator's death or within one month of obtaining the probate.

Failed to deposit Waqf fund in Bank *etc.*

The obligation to invest waqf money with the scheduled bank shall be made a criminal offence. The enactment of this provision is necessary to safeguard the interest of the public regarding waqf money. The defaulter should be fined as well as convicted as it is a very serious default on the part of the mutawalli *etc.* The defaulter should be made absolutely responsible and their act should not depend upon the proof or disproof of criminal intention.

Non-maintenance of Accounts

This shall also be the duty of the management committee/ mutawalli to prepare and maintain accounts of the waqf regularly. In case of non-maintenance of accounts heavy fine should be imposed on the above persons.

Transfer without any Authority

Penalty shall also be imposed if the management committee/mutawalli has transferred waqf property without the prior approval of the Waqf Board.

Failed to get accounts Audited

Auditing of accounts is necessary for the proper maintenance of accounts. Where the management committee/mutawalli has failed to get the waqf accounts audited, heavy penalty shall be imposed on the defaulters.

Non-presentation of Budget

Preparation and presentation of budget is also a necessary duty of the management committee/mutawalli. Where the mutawalli has failed to prepare and present budget, he may be penalised.

It is further submitted that *mens rea* should not be made a constituent part of the offences created under the Act. For example, where a mutawalli has failed to keep waqf accounts in the approved form and get them audited as required by the Act, such omission would be an offence irrespective of the element of *mens rea*.

Under Section 45, the enquiry can be made either by the Waqf Board or by any person authorised by the Board for this purpose. This proviso of Section 45 is very widely worded. The Board can delegate the power to make necessary inquiry to any person. According to Section 45 (2) of the Waqf Act, 1954, the Board may authorise any person in this behalf to hold an inquiry, into any matter relating to a waqf and take such action as it thinks fit. It is submitted here that power of inquiry and to take suitable action by the authorised person is not desirable here. He should have been only given the power to make investigation. The plain meaning of investigation is the collection of evidence and materials in a particular case for the purpose of making an inquiry. It is a prelude to an inquiry. During the course of investigation whatever material is collected and evidence recorded that will form part of the record and the authorised person can take legal action against the defaulter. It is submitted that the power of penalising should have been retained by the Waqf Board. After the receipt of the report and the record of investigation, the Waqf Board should have come to its own conclusion and in case of necessity must record the evidence. The Waqf Board cannot delegate the essential duty and function of arriving at findings without applying his own mind to the case. This is the duty of the Waqf Board that before coming to any conclusion it should exercise its mind independently. The Board should not be bound in any way by the report. Where the Board agrees with the report, it must afford a reasonable opportunity of hearing to the parties concerned before a final order is passed. Where the Board has not accepted the report, it can adopt any of the following course :—

(i) a fresh inquiry should be made by the Board; or

(ii) a further inquiry may be made and an independent conclusion be drawn; or

(iii) the case may be again referred for re-investigation to the officer concerned with necessary directions.

It is further submitted that instead of authorising any person to make inquiry, the same may be done by any revenue officer not below the rank of Deputy Collector.

Under the Waqf Act, 1954, the Waqf Board has no power of search. The Board cannot, therefore, issue search warrants for the purpose of compelling the production of documents.

Under the Waqf Act, 1954, the Waqf Board is not empowered to issue commissions. It is submitted here that the Board may be empowered to issue commissions for the following purposes—

(a) to examine any person;

(b) to make a local investigation;

(c) to examine or adjust accounts;

(d) to make partition.

The issue of commissions for the purpose of examination of a witness may be issued in one of the following circumstances :—

(a) Persons who are exempted from personal appearance in court. Section 133 of the Code of Civil Procedure enumerates such persons :—

(i) the President of India;

(ii) the Vice-President of India;

(iii) the Speaker of the House of the People;

(iv) the Ministers of the union;

(v) the Judges of the Supreme Court;

(vi) the Governors of states and administrators of union territories;

(vii) the Speakers of the Legislative Assemblies;

(viii) the Chairmen of the State Legislative Councils;

(ix) the Ministers of states:

(x) the Judges of the High Courts ;

(xi) the persons to whom Section 87-B applies *i.e.* the rulers of former states recognised as such by the President of India.

(b) women who according to the customs and manners of the country, ought not to be compelled to appear in public are exempt from personal appearance in court. (Section 132 of the Code of Civil Procedure)

(c) person from sickness or infirmity is unable to attend the court (Rule 1 Order 16).

(d) any person resident beyond the local limit of the court's jurisdiction (Rule 4 Order 26).

(e) any person who is about to leave the jurisdiction of the court before the date of examination in court (Rule 4 Order 26).

(f) any person in the service of the government who in the opinion of the court cannot attend without detriment to public service (Rule 4 of Order 26).

(g) persons who cannot be compelled to appear in court under Order 16 Rule 19, Code of Civil Procedure *i.e.* person living beyond the local limits of the court or at a place beyond two hundred miles from the place where the court is situated.

Budget

Sections 31 and 49 of the Waqf Act, 1954[71] deals with regard to the budget of a waqf and Waqf Board respectively. The Act does not prescribe any time limit within which the budget must be prepared. Every budget shall make an adequate provision for—

(i) the due maintenance of the objects of the institution or endowment and the proper performance of and the remuneration for, the services therein;
(ii) the due discharge of all liabilities and subsisting commitments binding on the waqf;
(iii) the maintenance of the working balance;
(iv) the arrangement to be made for securing the health, safety or convenience of the disciples, pilgrims, or other persons resorting to the institution;
(v) a provision for the construction, repair, renovation and improvement of the endowment and the buildings connected therewith;
(vi) where the budget relates to a religious institution or endowment whose annual income exceeds twenty thousand rupees, the budget shall also make provision for the payment at five per cent to the welfare fund.

It is submitted here that it shall be the duty of all the waqfs having an income of at least Rs. 500.00 to prepare and submit a budget to the Waqf Board.

The Waqf Board may after giving notice to the mutawalli *ete.* and after considering his representation, if any, pass an order making such alterations, omissions or additions in the budget as he may deem fit.

The order passed by the Board shall be appealable to the government. The appeal may be filed within 30 days from the date of the receipt of the order.

If, in the course of a financial year, the mutawalli finds it necessary to modify the provisions made in the budget in regard to the receipt or to the distribution of the amounts to be expended under the different heads, he may submit to the Waqf Board his supplemental or revised budget.

This shall be the duty of the mutawalli to report forthwith every expenditure incurred in excess of the provision made in the budget together with the reasons.

The budget shall be presented in the prescribed form. It shall be prepared one month before the date on which the ensuing budget year of the waqf commences. The budget year or the accounting year shall be approved by the Board. The budget must relate to the probable receipts and disbursements of the waqf property during the following year. The duty to prepare and submit the budget shall be on the mutawalli of the waqf. It shall also be provided that the non-compliance of the above provision shall render the mutawalli liable to a penalty which may extend up to Rs. 500.00. The above provisions shall not be applied to waqfs whose gross annual income does not exceed Rs. 500.00.

Inspection of the Budget

The effectiveness of law lies in the implementation. Its non-enforcement is the negative aspect of such instrument of social control. Inspection is one of the means to enforce laws. There is, however, no such provision in the Act for the inspection of the budget. A similar provision exists in most of the Acts prevalent in the country[72]. It is submitted here that a provision may be made in the Act for the inspection of the balance sheet, the income and expenditure accounts. These documents shall be open to inspection in each district either in the collector's office or at some appropriate place. The right to inspection may be given only to those persons who are having interest in the waqf, to which the document relates.

Control

As stated earlier, waqf officers be appointed in each district. They shall be responsible for the protection and maintenance of the waqf property in their respective district.

The Waqf Officer shall have the right to enter into the waqf premises and inspect any property belonging to a waqf. He shall also have the power to call for or inspect any extract from any proceedings of the mutawalli of any waqf or any book or account in the possession or under the control of the mutawalli. He may also be empowered to call for any return statement account or report which he may think fit from the mutawalli or any person connected with the waqf. It is, however, submitted that the sacramental nature and character of the waqf property should be protected at all costs. The officer concerned must pay regard to the religious practices or usages. He should not enter a mosque or tomb wearing shoes nor he can smoke, drink, *etc.* It shall, however, be the duty of the concerning officer making the entry to give reasonable notice to the mutawalli. He shall also pay full regard to the religious practices or usages of the place where he intends to enter. The above power of Waqf Officer shall be exercisable in the following two ways —

1. He can himself enter and inspect any waqf property; or
2. He can authorise any other person to enter upon and inspect any property.

Before this power can be exercised it should be certain that the property in respect of which the power is sought to be exercised, belongs to the waqf. This power cannot be exercised with respect to a property which is not of waqf.

The power to enter on any waqf property includes the power to break open the lock, if despite reasonable notice the property is not kept open for entry and inspection of the waqf officer. The Waqf Officer can also employ reasonable force in exercising power of entry and inspection. While performing his duties, the waqf officer acts as a public servant in performance of his duties and in case of obstruction, he will be prosecuted and punished under Section 353 of the Indian Penal Code.

The above power can be exercised only by the Waqf Officer. He must obtain prior approval of the Waqf Board. He cannot delegate the function to any other person. The above powers are to be exercised within the framework of the scheme mentioned above. The power to call and inspect any document cannot be exercised by effecting seizure of the documents. The Waqf Officer shall have only the power to call for any book, account or proceeding in possession of or under the control of the mutawalli *etc*. While making enquiry he can compel production of documents including account books but he should not be able to seize or order the seizure of the account books of any waqf.

The power exercised by a waqf officer shall be quasi-judicial. He should be empowered to take appropriate action against the mutawallis who are found guilty of gross negligence, breach of waqf or other kind of misconduct, resulting in loss to the waqf. While exercising this power, the Waqf Officer shall call for the explanation of the defaulting mutawallis. He should also determine the loss caused to the waqf property, and the person who can be held responsible for such loss. The Waqf Officer shall have effective control over waqf property. It is submitted that a Waqf Officer may be able to take action only on the fulfilment of the following conditions :—

(i) that the auditor has submitted his adverse report;

(ii) that the auditor has disclosed material defects in the administration of the waqf;

(iii) that the Waqf Officer should be of the opinion that the audit report shows definitely the material defects in the administration of the waqf; and

(iv) that after coming to the conclusion the Waqf Officer should give a notice to the mutawalli asking him to submit his reply within a reasonable time.

This shall be the duty of the auditor to mention in his report all cases of irregularities, illegalities or improper expenditure or failure or omission to recover money or other property belonging to the waqf or waste or money or other property thereof. He should also mention whether such expenditure, failure, omission, loss or waste was consequential of an act or omission or breach of trust, misapplication or any other misconduct on the part of the mutawallis or any other person. The defects must be of substantial character and mere irregularity or technical defect would not constitute material defect. The satisfaction of the Waqf Officer must be judicious. It should not be arbitrary or capricious. The satisfaction is to follow the holding of any inquiry in the prescribed manner and after giving opportunity to the person concerned. If the Waqf Officer come to the conclusion that an inquiry is necessary then the principles of natural justice be followed. The enquiry to be conducted by the Waqf Officer must be judicial. It should not be an administrative inquiry. Mutawalli and other persons against whom action has been proposed to be taken must be given reasonable and proper opportunity. The Waqf Officer should record his findings with reasons. Here it is relevant to mention the provisions of Order 20 Rule 4 of the Code of Civil Procedure which require a judge to record his findings on each issue with reasons therefor.

This shall be the duty of the mutawalli and other responsible persons to obey the directions of the waqif except as modified by the consent of all the beneficiaries being competent to contract. Where the beneficiary is incompetent to contract his consent may be given by a principal civil court of original jurisdiction. A mutawalli cannot be expected to obey any direction when to do so would be impracticable, illegal or manifestly injurious to the beneficiaries.

A mutawalli is bound to deal with the waqf property as carefully as a man of ordinary prudence would deal with such property as if it were his own ; and in the absence of a contract to the contrary a mutawalli so dealing shall not be responsible for the loss, destruction, or deterioration of the waqf property. Where a waqf was created for the benefit of several persons in succession, and the waqf property is of a wasting nature or a future or reversionary interest, the mutawalli is bound to convert the property into property of a permanent and immediately profitable character.

It may also be provided in the Waqf Act that this shall be the duty of the mutawalli to prevent waste. A mutawalli must keep clear and accurate accounts of the waqf property. This shall also be his duty to furnish him with full and accurate information as to the amount and state of the waqf property.

It may also be provided in the Waqf Act that where the waqf property consists of money and cannot be applied immediately or at an early date to the purposes of the waqf, the early date to the purpose of the waqf, the mutawalli shall be bound to invest the money on the following securities, and on no others—

(a) in promissory notes, debentures, stock or other securities of any state government or of the central government or of the United Kingdom of Great Britian and Ireland ;

(b) in bonds, debentures, annuities charged or secured by the Parliament of India ;

(c) in stock or debentures of, or shares in, railway or other companies the interest whereon shall have been guaranteed by the Central government or in debentures of any recognised bank;

(d) in debentures or other securities for money issued under the authority of any Central Act or Provincial Act or State Act, or on behalf of any municipal body, port trust or city improvement trust in any Presidency town ;

(e) on a first mortgage of immovable property situated in any part of the territories ;

(f) on any other security expressly authorised by the instrument of waqf, or by any rule which the High Court may from time to time prescribe in this behalf.

This shall be the duty of the mutawalli to fulfil the purpose of the waqf and to obey the directions of the waqif. If the mutawalli goes beyond the directions in the waqfnama, he is guilty of breach of trust.

It shall also be the duty of the mutawalli to acquaint himself, as soon as possible, with the nature and circumstances of the waqf property ; to obtain where necessary a transfer of the waqf property to himself and to get in waqf moneys invested on insufficient or hazardous security.

This shall be the duty of the mutawalli or any other responsible person to maintain and defend all suits and to take such necessary steps which may be reasonably required for the preservation of waqf property and the assertion or protection of the title.

A mutawalli shall have no cl im or title adverse to the waqf. A plea of adverse title by the mutawalli shall be treated as breach of waqf. This shall also be the duty of the mutawalli to deal with the waqf property as carefully as a man of ordinary prudence would deal with his own property. He should not mix up his private property with the waqf property. A mutawalli should never keep waqf money in his own hands. This amount should be invested in approved securities. A mutawalli should avoid to introduce strangers as mutawalli or co-mutawalli. The neglect to repair the waqf property shall be treated as breach of waqf.

Power to Insure

A mutawalli may insure against loss or damage by fire any building or other insurable property to any amount including the amount of any insurance already on foot, not exceeding three fourths parts of the full value of the building or property, and pay the premiums for such insurance out of the income thereof or out of the income of any other property subject to the same waqfs without obtaining the consent of any person who may be entitled wholly or partly to such income. Failure to pay insurance premium and consequently lapse of insurance policy would be a breach of waqf.

Power to Delegate

Originally a waqif was expected, in theory, to perform all his duties personally. *Delegatus non potest delegare.* Whether or not this was ever a practical proposition, it early became complications of business life. A mutawalli shall have no right to renounce waqf nor can delegate his essential duties and if he renounces waqf or delegate essential duties it will amount to breach of waqf.[73]

Duty to Invest

It may also be provided that investment of waqf money,

otherwise than in accordance with the provisions of the Act, however, well intentioned and honest such investment may be, would be a breach of waqf. For this purpose the legislature should pass Waqf Investment Act. Similarly, the investment of funds by a mutawalli with himself would constitute breach of waqf.

A mutawalli shall not be allowed to draw overdrafts for his personal gains. Allowing overdrafts out of motives of personal gains and concealment of it from co-mutawalli shall amount to breach of waqf. Similarly, application of assets for objects other than those defined would amount to breach of waqf. A mutawalli may also not be able to commit any unlawful or prohibited act, with a view to causing gain to the waqf. This will also amount to breach of waqf.

Negligence

Section 33 (2) and 51 (2) of the Waqf Act, 1954, provides that the auditor shall make the report to the state government of all cases of negligence. The Act has not defined this term. Negligence means the comission to do something which a reasonable man, guided upon those considerations which ordinarily regulate the conduct of human affairs, would do, or doing something which a prudent and reasonable man would not do.[74] The general concept of reasonable foresight is the criterion of negligence and is fluid in its application ; it has to be fitted to the facts of the particular case.[75] Negligence is not established by proving that the loss might possibly and with extraordinary foresight and prudence have been avoided.[76] Negligence in a legal sense is negative rather than a positive term and in any given circumstances is the failure to exercise that care which the circumstances demand. What amounts to negligence depends on the facts of each particular case and the term negligence is, therefore, not susceptible of any precise definition which will be of unversal application. It may consist in doing something which ought either to be done in different manner or not at all or in omitting to do something which ought to be done. Where there is no duty to exercise care at all, negligence in the popular sense has no legal consequences. Knowledge or opportunity of knowledge that a particular course is fraught with danger does not necessarily render its adoption 'negligent' but such knowledge or opportunity of knowledge is frequently an ingredient of negligence.[77]

According to Winfield,[78] the following are the ingredients of negligence :

(a) a legal duty on the part of A towards B to exercise care in such conduct of A as falls within the scope of the duty ;
(b) breach of that duty ;
(c) consequential damage to B.

This term was also defined in *Sheikh Jumman* v *King Emperor*.[79] It was said that negligence does not mean absolute carelessness and indifference but want of such a degree of care as is required in particular circumstances. A negligent state of mind is consistent with one's intention to exercise as much care as one can to avoid the accident.

It is, therefore, clear that a mutawalli is required to take all necessary care for the protection of waqf property. If he has failed to take necessary care, he will be prosecuted and punished for negligence.[80]

Misconduct

This is a very wide term. It is not possible to give any exhaustive definition of the term. It means improper conduct, a conduct not befitting to a trustee. It embraces every act of non-feasance, misfeasance, and mal-feasance, on the part of trustees. The literal meaning of this word is wrong or improper conduct. It means misconduct is a conduct in violation of definite rule of action. It is the failure to perform a duty what a man is required to do. A person may be guilty of misconduct, although he has not acted wilfully or maliciously.[81] It may also amount to intentional doing of something, which the doer knows to be wrong or which he does recklessly not caring to know whether it is right or wrong.[82] The term misconduct includes some degree of *mens rea* on the part of the person concerned or at any rate a very grave degree of negligence or serious failure, to carry out instructions[83]. It is a conduct arising from some honest though erroneous breach and neglect of duty and responsibility on the part of the person concerned.[81]

As already noted an exhaustive definition of this term cannot be given. However, for the sake of convenience, this term may be grouped as under—

(a) negligence in performance of duties ;
(b) non-performance of duties or performance of the acts prohibited by law or not permitted by the waqf deed ;
(c) wrongful acts resulting in direct or indirect loss to the waqf property.

The following are the few instances which may come within non-performance of duties or performance of the acts prohibited by law. These instances may amount to misconduct:—

(i) Non-carrying out of directions given by the author of the waqf at the time of creation :
(ii) Non-acquaintance with the nature and circumstances of the waqf property ;
(iii) Non-obtaining the transfer of waqf property ;
(iv) Investment of waqf property on insufficient or hazardous security ;
(v) Non-maintenance of suits for preservation of waqf property or for the protection of the title ;
(vi) Non-defending of the suits against waqf property ;
(vii) Setting up of any title which is adverse to the interest of waqf ;
(viii) Setting up of title in third person of the waqf property adverse to the interest of the waqf ;
(ix) Dealing with the waqf property in imprudent manner ;
(x) Non-maintenance of clear and accurate accounts of waqf property.

A mutawalli shall be paid his salary according to his qualifications and experience. An unpaid mutawalli is expected to use such due diligence and care in the management of estate as man of ordinary prudence and vigilance would use in the management of their own affairs. A higher standard of diligence and knowledge is required from paid mutawallis. In the performance of his duties a trustee must use common sense, common skill, common prudence and common caution. If he acts honestly and bonafidely he is not guilty of any misconduct.[85] It may, however, be noted that a mutawalli cannot be held responsible for act of God *i.e.* fire, theft, tempest and other natural or like calamities resulting in loss to the waqf property. There shall be the statutory duties imposed on the mutawalli and the non-performance of the same shall be treated as misconduct or breach of waqf. Serious legal action may be taken against mutawallis who have (i) failed to apply for registration of waqf ; (ii) non-submission of budget, absence of audit of accounts, alienation of waqf property without prior permission from the Waqf Board *etc.*

A mutawalli shall be held responsible only for resultant loss to waqf. It means not only the above acts of non-feasance, is-feasance and malfeasance must be established but it must also be further proved that as a result therefore loss is caused to the waqf property which can be ascertained in the terms of money and no other losses would be covered by it. There should be reasonable nexus between the loss to waqf and guilty conduct of the mutawalli which occasioned the loss. Before any action could be taken it must be shown that the mutawalli was guilty of misfeasance, neglect or misapplication resulting in loss to the waqf property as a direct consequence of the act complained of.

Liability for breach of Waqf

A mutawalli shall be liable for breach of waqf. He shall be liable to make good the loss which the waqf property or the beneficiary has thereby sustained unless the beneficiary has by fraud induced the mutawalli to commit the breach, or the beneficiary has himself concurred in the breach with full knowledge of the facts of the case and of his rights as against the mutawalli.

Several liability of the Mutawalli and other Persons

Where the wrong was committed by the mutawalli and other persons jointly or where one of them by his neglect enables the other to commit a breach of waqf each shall be liable for the whole of the loss occasioned by such breach.

A mutawalli shall be respectively chargeable only for such money, stocks, funds and securities as he actually received and shall not be answerable the one for the other of them. He will not be answerable for any banker, broker or other person in whose hands any waqf property may be placed. He will also not be responsible for the insufficiency or deficiency of any stocks, funds or securities *etc.*

A guilty mutawalli shall be held liable to make good the loss by paying the amount of such loss. The amount of loss shall be fixed by the Waqf Board/Waqf Officer. This amount shall be fixed by making an inquiry as to the quantum of loss attributable to the misconduct of a mutawalli.

This shall be the duty of the mutawalli to deposit the levied amount within the prescribed time. If despite reasonable time given for compliance of the order, the amount is not deposited, the same may be recovered as land revenue.

Appeal

There is no provision of appeal under the Act. Under Section 56 of the Waqf Act, 1954, a suit can be instituted against the Board in respect of any act purporting to be done by it in pursuance of the Act or of any rules made thereunder. There is no right of appeal directly from the order of the Board, although the remedy is in substance analogous to the remedy of appeal. The provisions of this Section are identical to the provisions of Order 21 Rule 58, Code of Civil Procedure where also no right of appeal is given but an independent remedy of the suit is provided to an aggrieved person under Order 21 Rule 63 Code of Civil Procedure.

Management of Waqfs by Committees

It is proposed here that as far as possible instead of single mutawalli the management of waqfs be done through committees. This shall be the duty of the working committee, as soon as a vacancy occurs in the management to inform the Waqfs Board of such vacancy and the time within and the manner in which he proposes to fill the same. The Waqf Board may issue directions to the working committee regarding the filling of such vacancy not inconsistent with any instrument of waqf and the working committee shall comply with any such direction.

If the working committee has failed to give any such information or to fill the vacancy within the time specified by him or to comply with any direction issued by the Waqfs Board, the Board may appoint any person as the member of the committee. Any aggrieved person having interest in the waqf may apply to the court for setting aside the order of the Board within thirty days from the date of such order.

It may also be provided in the Waqf Act that whenever an appointed mutawalli disclaims, or any mutawalli dies or is for a continuous period of six months absent from India, or refuses or leave India for the purpose of abroad, or is declared an insolvent or desires to be discharged from the waqf, or becomes, in the opinion of a principal civil court of original jurisdiction unfit or personally incapable to act in the waqf, or accept an inconsistent waqf, a new mutawalli may be appointed in his place by—

(a) the person nominated for that purpose, by the instrument of waqfs ; or

(b) if there be no such person, or no such person able and willing to act, the author of the waqf if he be alive and competent to contract.

Under the present Act there is no provision for the appointment of mutawalli or members of the management committee by the court. It is submitted here that whenever any such vacancy or disqualification occurs and the Waqf Board has not appointed a mutawalli etc then the same may be appointed by the court.

Assumption of direct Management

Section 43-A of the Waqf Act, 1954 deals with regard to the assumption of direct management of certain waqfs by the Board. This section says where no suitable person is available for appointment as a mutawalli of a waqf, the Board may assume direct management of the waqf for such period or periods, not exceeding in the aggregate five years. Section 43-A of the Act confers executive or administrative power on the Board. The Board is also given certain supervisory and advisory powers for the smooth functioning of the waqf. This section does not deal with a situation wherein the intervention of the Waqf Board shall be necessary on account of improper functioning of waqf or mismanagement or maladministration of waqf property. Similarly, the Board is also not empowered to interfere if the original object has become impossible to be fulfilled. The present Section 43-A of the Act should be carefully and properly exercised otherwise its abuse may affect the functioning of a waqf.

It is not clear from the working of Section 43-A that it is also applicable to private waqfs or not. The provisions of this section should be made applicable to both public and private waqfs.

The Waqf Board has no power to appoint committee of persons to take charge of the waqf property. Under Section 43-A the Waqf Board may assume direct management of the waqf.

This is the direction of the Board to come to the conclusion that no suitable person is available for appointment as a mutawalli and, therefore, the management of the waqf be taken by the Board. This is the satisfaction of the Board that no suitable person is available to be appointed as the mutawalli. Section 43-A needs amendment. A Waqf Board should not be given arbitrary power to assume direct management of the waqf property as and when it deem fit. The following provisions may, therefore, be provided in the Act.

(i) before assuming management of the waqf the principle natural justice be followed strictly. Therefore, enquiry regarding the affairs of the waqf be made.

(ii) the Waqf Board shall make necessary enquiry into the affairs of the Board.

(iii) mutawalli concerned be given reasonable opportunity to explain his case. He should be given reasonable time within which he should submit his report.

In case mutawalli has failed to explain his case then only management of the waqf be assumed by the Board.

It is again submitted that instead of assuming direct management, the Board may appoint a fresh committee. This will be a more democratic principle and will definitely help in the better administration of waqfs in the country.

Bar against hearing and Decision of the Suit

It is submitted that no suit to enforce a right on behalf of a waqf which has not been registered under the Waqf Act shall be heard or decided in any court. This proposal of mine is based on public policy and matter of practical utility. This provision will help in the registration of waqfs. Mutawallis *etc.* will be constrained to get waqfs registered otherwise they will not be able to file a suit in the court of law. A reference may be made to Section 69 of the Indian Partnership Act, 1932, wherein a suit is barred on behalf of a firm which is not registered as a partnership firm under the Act.

It is further submitted that non-registration of a waqf shall only bar the hearing and decision of the suit. The prohibition be made in respect of suit not only for the benefit of waqf but it must be for the purpose of enforcing a right which inheres in a waqf. The right which may be enforced may be either a private right or a right enjoyed by a waqf as a public right. The right may not necessarily relate to status or character of waqf or any person related to waqf.[86]

In all such cases, where the bar or restriction is not on the very institution, presentation or filing of a suit but only for the hearing and the decision of it, the suit is validly instituted and in case of non-registration, the reasonable time may be granted to the plaintiff to get the requisite registration. It would be better if in all such cases the suit is adjourned or stayed and not dismissed. Where an objection on the ground of non-registration is successfully raised, the procedure to be adopted should be to stay the decision on merits to enable the party to obtain its registration.

Judicial Proceedings

At present a suit to obtain any of the reliefs mentioned in

Section 92 of the Code of Civil Procedure, 1908, relating to any waqf may be instituted by the Board. The remedy provided under the Act is not speedy. It is also not free from all those technicalities which precede the suit under Section 92 of the Code of Civil Procedure, 1908. An aggrieved person is required to file a suit for seeking remedy under Section 92, Code of Civil Procedure. Therefore, the remedy is not speedy exclusively and special in the nature. The remedy can be made easy if instead of filing the suit, application is allowed to be made in the nature of reference which shall be presented by or under the direction of the Waqf Board. The application shall be made by the Waqf Board or under his direction by the Mutawalli. The application shall be treated as an ordinary application in the nature of reference. It should not be treated as representative suit. The application should be made only before the court having jurisdiction in the area where the waqf is registered. Ordinarily a civil court cannot delegate the trial of the suit to any other court for the purpose of holding an inquiry. The result of this provision is that courts are overburdened with the work, and, therefore, no proper inquiry is possible. It is, therefore, submitted that the courts be authorised to delegate an inquiry to any other authority. It may also be provided that the sanction of Advocate General or Collector will not be necessary for the initiation of proceedings.

The title of Chapter VII of the Waqf Act, 1954, is entitled 'Judicial Proceedings' though the Act nowhere says that the proceedings held under the Act shall be judicial. The plain rule of interpretation is that when the things are not clear the heading may be taken into consideration. Therefore, the inquiries held under the Act shall be treated judicial. It will help the Board to exercise check and control against the fabrication and production of false evidence whether documentary or oral. This will help the Board to have full and effective administrative control and powers over the affairs of waqfs. In the absence of such a provision the Board cannot enforce the provisions of the Act with a tight grip.

The term judicial proceedings includes proceedings in the course of which evidence is or may be legally taken on oath.

The acts of the court which are done after hearing the parties would be covered by the expression judicial proceedings.

It is submitted here that all inquiries under the Waqf Act, 1954, shall be deemed to be juidcial proceedings within the meaning of Section 193, 219 and 228 of the Indian Penal Code.

The Waqf Board is a quasi-judicial tribunal. It is, therefore, the duty of the Tribunal to decide disputes in a judicial manner and declare the rights of parties in a definitive judgment. The Board is also under the duty to fulfil the requirements of natural justice *i.e.* the parties are entitled as a matter of right to be heard in support of their claim and to adduce evidence in proof of it. It is also the duty of the authority to decide the matter on a consideration of the evidence adduced and in accordance with law.

The sections of Indian Penal Code referred above deals with regard to the offences committed during or relating to judicial proceedings. It can, therefore, be said that any false evidence given by a person during an inquiry under the Act it can be punished under Section 193 on a complaint being made by the Board under Section 195 of lhe Criminal Procedure Code, after following the procedure mentioned in Section 476 of the Criminal Procedure Code.

The Waqf Board can also file a complaint under Section 228 of the Indian Penal Code if there is any intentional interruption, or insult shown during inquiry.

The Act nowhere prescribes the procedure, the forum and the person who can file the complaint. There is no mention of machinery for the launching of them. Prosecution and the trial of the offences to be tried under the Act. Under these circumstances the procedure prescribed under the Code of Criminal Procedure would apply. According to Section 5 of the Code all offences under any other law shall be investigated, inquired into, tried and otherwise dealt with according to the provisions of the Criminal Procedure Code but subject to any enactment for the time being in force regulating the manner or place of investigating, inquiring into, trying or otherwise dealing with such offences. One of the consequence of this approach will be that if there is any contravention of any provision of the Act amounting to an offence, the penalty cannot be imposed by the Waqf Board but it has to file a complaint in the ordinary criminal court and that court alone shall be responsible for the prosecution and conviction of the offence This will delay the very purpose of the penalty prosecution of the Act. It is, therefore, submitted that the proper procedure, the forum and the person who can file the suit should be elaborately mentioned in the Act.

At present, the maximum amount of fine can be Rs. 1000.00 only. Looking to the present day positon this amount is very meagre. It is proposed here this amount be increased from Rs. 1000.00 to 5000.00 or imprisonment upto six months or both. It may also be provided that the penalty shall be paid within the time fixed by the Waqf Board by the person against whom the order is made. He shall deposit the amout of penalty from his own pocket. Where the person concerned has failed to pay the amount of penalty the Collector of the district in which any property of the person against whom an order has been made is situated, shall on requisition made to him by the Waqf Board, recover the amount as an arrear of land revenue.

Proceedings

In Section 57 (2) of the Waqf Act, 1954 the word proceeding has been used. This is a term of very wide application and includes every proceedings of whatever nature before any civil or revenue court under any provision of law which either pertains to or which is likely to effect to a public waqf or its property or any matter recorded in register of public waqfs. The word proceeding in a general sense means 'the form and manner of conducting judicial business before a court or judicial officer'.[89] A suit, appeal or second appeal can come within the category of proceedings. The term proceedings means a prescribed course of action for enforcing or protecting legal right. It also means any suit, case or appeal. Therefore, it is a circumstance, situation or happening which is a subject matter of an investigation or any enquiry.

Civil Court

This term has not been defined in the Act. In its ordinary

meaning Civil Court means which is opposed to court of criminal jurisdiction. The term civil court includes every court, however, high or low in the hierarchy of courts which administers justice in its ordinary civil jurisdiction.

Section 3 of the M.P. Civil Courts Act has given the list of the following categories of civil courts :—

(i) The Court of the District Judge ;

(ii) The Court of the Additional District Judge ;

(iii) The Court of the Civil Judge Class I ; and

(iv) The Court of the Civil Judge Class II.

Apart from the above courts Section 8 provides that additional courts of Civil Judge Class I and Class II may be created in an area wherever the necessity so arises.

The word Civil Courts include all those courts exercising civil jurisdiction as opposed to criminal jurisdiction and, therefore, the term civil court includes the other country or tribunal exercising special jurisdiction conferring by or under special statutes. Therefore, the Compensation Tribunal under the M.P. Town Improvement Trusts Act, the Land Acquisition Officer under the Land Acquisistion Act, 1894, would be civil court within the meaning of the term civil court.

Dedication by Non-Muslims

Formerly, it was believed that a non-Muslim cannot dedicate his property in waqf. In 1964, therefore, the Central Waqf Act was amended.[87] It was provided that where any movable or immovable property has been given or donated by any person not professing Islam for the support of a waqf then such property shall be deemed to be comprised in that waqf.[88] To attract the provisions of this section two things are necessary. At the time of dedication there must be a waqf in existence and the dedication can be made in respect of (a) a mosque, Idgah, Imambara, Dargah, Khanqah or Maqbara ; (b) a Muslim graveyard ; (c) a choultry or a Musafirkhana. It was held that unless a grant made by a non-Muslim comes under any one of the classes mentioned in that section, it would not be a waqf.[89]

It is submitted here that Section 66-C of the aforesaid Act be construed liberally. The property dedicated by non-Muslims should be treated as part and parcel of waqf. A dedication should not only be allowed in respect of (a), (b) and (c) of Section 66-C of the Waqf Act, 1954. A non-Muslim may also be allowed to dedicate his property for religious, pious and charitable purposes according to Muslim faith.

At present, a non-Muslim can dedicate his property only in a waqf already in existence. He cannot establish a new waqf. It is submitted that non-Muslims should be allowed to establish and dedicate their property in a new waqf. The present author does not see any reason for not allowing non-Muslims to establish and dedicate property in a new waqf.

Rule making Power

Sections 67 and 68 of the Waqf Act, 1954, are very important, and these sections confer rule and regulation making power to the State Government. The state government may make rules to carry out the purposes of the Act other than those of Chapter 11-A.[90] Section 68 of the aforesaid Act gives power to the Waqf Board to make regulations. In such a case the previous sanction of the State Government is necessary and the regulations so made should not be inconsistent with the Act. In modern legislation such power is generally conferred by the legislature on the executive. This type of legislation is generally known as subordinate legislation or delegated legislation. In the present Act at several places minor details are left to the discretion of the State Government by providing 'as may be prescribed' which means the State Government and the Waqf Board shall make rules and regulations respectively.

The Waqf Act, 1954, is a very small piece of legislation. It contains only 70 Sections.[91] Therefore, the executive has been given much wider discretion. Now this is the duty of the State Government and the Waqf Board to make rules and regulations for carrying out the intention of the legislature. It may, however, be noted that the power given to the State Government is not absolute. The legislature has imposed certain fetters, limitations and conditions. The following are the main principles of the rule making power :—

1. The rule cannot enlarge the scope of statutory provision. If a rule goes beyond what the section contemplates, it must yield to the state.[92]
2. The rule making authority cannot make rule with a view to neutralising or contradict the provisions under which they are framed. The rules be made in such a way that the provision of the statute may be better carried into effect.[93]
3. The rules are made by a subordinate authority which is not the legislature. Therefore, the rules made under an Act of a competent lagislature cannot be made to depend upon act or omission of subordinate authority.[94]
4. Rules framed under an Act be treated for all purposes of construction or obligation exactly as if they are part and parcel of the Act. The effect of these rules be same as if contained in the Act. The rules are not administrative directions.[95]
5. The rule making authority cannot exceed the powers conferred on it by the Act and frame rules inconsistent with the provisions of the Act or rules neutralising, or contradicting or abridging a right conferred by the statute itself.[96]
6. A rule made under an enactment cannot be declared *ultra vires* unless it is found that the enactment does not confer any power at all to make the rule. A rule purported to have been made under a wrong provision of an Act would nonetheless be valid if it is shown to be within the four corners of the power conferred by any other provision of the Act.[97]
7. This is the rule of interpretation that the Act and the rules be read harmoniously and in such a way that the rules may not be in conflict with the Act under which they are framed.[98]
8. This is the basic principle of interpretation that if a rule is ambiguous and giving two meanings, one of

which is in consonance with the parent provision in the Act and the rule makings power, then the rule be construed in such a way as brings it in consonance with the provisions of the Act and the rule making power.[99]

9. A distinction was maintained between a rule which was enforceable because of a valid rule making power, and a rule which was declared to be a part of the Act itself under which it is made. In the first type of case the rule could be enforced provided it did not come in conflict with any provision of the Act. The rules, therefore, remained a separate entity and could be struck down, if they came into conflict with the Act. In the second type of cases the rule framed was as binding as the provisions of the Act itself. Therefore, the rules so framed could not be struck down for repugnancy with the Act and both *i.e.* rule and the section will receive the same treatment.[100] In *State of Kerala* v *M.C. Abdulla* the Supreme Court took a different view. This court held that a subordinate legislation does not lose its character and it will continue to be subordinate to the parent Act under which rules were made.[101]

According to Section 20 of the General Clauses Act, 1897 corresponding to Section 20 of the M.P. General Clauses Act, 1957, the expression used in the rules and forms shall have, unless a different intention appears, same meaning as in the Act conferring the power. Accordingly, all State Governments have framed the rules for the proper administration of the waqf in their respective states.

This Act is supreme on all matters for which provisions have been made under this Act and any contrary direction in any Act, rule or instrument is of no consequence or effect. The provisions of this section are in addition to any other similar provisions contained in any other Act. For instance, a public trust being an educational society is registercd under the M.P. Societies Registeration Act, such educational society if comes within the definition of the public trust, would still be required to be registered under this Act because the provisions under this Act for registration of waqfs are not subordinate to the provisions contained in the M.P. Societies Registration Act.

Section 69 of the Waqf Act, 1954, is the repealing Section. The provision of this Section says that such repeal shall not affect the previous operation of that corresponding law. The main effect of repeal is that the repealed Act was never in existence. However, Section 6 of the General Clauses Act, 1897 lays down that where an Act repeals another Act, then unless a different intention appears, the repeal shall not—

(a) revive anything not in force or existing at the time at which the repeal takes effect ; or
(b) affect the previous operation of any enactment so repealed or anything duly done or suffered thereunder ; or
(c) affect any right, privilege, obligation or liability, acquired, accrued or incurred under any enactment so repealed ; or
(d) affect any penalty, forfeiture or punishment incurred in respect of any offence committed against any enactment repealed ; or
(e) affect any investigation, legal proceeding or remedy in respect of any such right, privilege, obligation, liability, penalty, forfeiture or punishment as aforesaid.

'Anything done' or 'action taken'

The proviso to Section 69 of the Waqf Act, 1954, contains these words. In *Universal Imports Agency* v *Chief Controller of Imports and Exports*[102] the Supreme Court of India was required to interpret 'thing done' used in para 6 of the French Establishments (Application of Laws) Order, 1954. It was said that the word 'things done' was comprehensive enough to take into it not only the things done but also the effect of the legal consequences flowing therefrom. The inquiry held by the Registrar under the M.P. Act was indisputably 'a thing duly done' under that Act. The object of such a saving clause is to save what has been previously done under the repealed Act. Consequently, the pre-existing law continues to govern the thing done before a particular date from which the repeal of such a pre-existing law takes effect.[103]

Grant by the State Government to the State Waqf Board

There are in every state, a number of mosques and shrines, *etc.* which have no income of their own. The Waqf Board is not having surplus income to maintain and repair such institutions. Some of these institutions are of historical or traditional importance. The only alternative left for the State Government is to come to the rescue of such institutions.

It may not be out of place to mention here that the Government of Andhra Pradesh is maintaining Mecca Masjid, Hyderabad, the public Garden Mosque which do not have any income of their own. Similarly, a sum of Rs. 1 lakh was sanctioned by the Government of Tamil Nadu for the purpose for the financial year 1972-73. Further, a sum of Rs. 3 lakh has been provided by them for the year 1973-74.[104]

It is submitted that similar amounts may be provided by other state governments for this purpose and placed at the disposal of the State Waqf Boards.

Taxation

The exemption from taxation under various Acts is given to the property. The term property is a word of widest import and subject to any limitation or qualification which the context might require, it signifies every possible interest which a person can acquire, hold and enjoy.[105] The organisation and the undertaking as well as the fluctuating stock of yarn and cloth would constitute property within the meaning of this clause.[106] A partner's share in partnership property would constitute 'property' for a charitable trust.[107] It is, therefore, necessary that the legislature should define the term property.

Section 11 of the Income Tax Act, 1961 gives exemption to trusts. There is no mention of waqfs. In view of this the courts can refuse to grant exemption to waqfs. It is, therefore, necessary, that the term 'waqf' may also be inserted in Section 11 of the Income Tax Act, 1961.

It is further submitted that the position of income of family waqfs which is meant for public religious and charitable purposes should also be exempted from the purview of taxation laws.

It has also been seen that mosques *etc* are required to file return of income tax and then only exemption is granted by the Income Tax Commissioner. This creates problem to the management of the institutions. They are also required to engage lawyers for this purpose. It is, therefore, submitted that mosques *etc.* be totally exempted from income tax and these institutions need not be required to file income tax returns.

REFERENCES

1. Some of these Acts were—The Zamindari Abolition Acts, Land Reform Acts passed by the various state legislatures ; Kerala Land Reforms Amendment Act 35 of 1969 ; The Employees Provident Fund Act, The Workmen's Compensation Act, 1923 ; The Trade Union Act, 1926 ; The Minimum Wages Act, 1948. The Payment of Bonus Act, 1965 ; The Employees State Insurance Act, 1948 ; The Mines Act, 1952; The Employees State Insurance Act, 1984. The Monopolies and Restrictive Trade Practices Act, 1969 ; The Food Adulteration Act, 1954 ; The Orphanages and other Charitable Houses (Supervision and Control) Act, 1960 ; The Abolition of Whipping Act, 1955 ; The Essential Commodities Act, 1955.

1.A See the Mussalman Waqf Validating Act, 1913, the Mussalman Waqf Act, 1923 and the Waqf Act, 1954.

2. Gajendragadkar, *Secularism and the Constitution of India*, p. 83.
3. Tyabji (Badruddin), *The Self in Secularism*, (1971) p. 122.
4. Robert S. Summers, Legal Philosophy Today—An Introduction in *Sammer's Essays in Legal Philosophy*, Basil Blackwell, Oxford, 1986 p. 20.
5. Edgar Bodenheimer, *Jurisprudence*, 1974 ; Harvard University Press. p. 313.
6. *Rukheya Bano* v *Nazira Bano*, *AIR* 1928 Cal 130, 55 Cal 448.
7. *Mohammad Yusuf* v *Mohammad Sadiq*, *AIR* 1933 Lah 501.
8. *Jain Mohammad* v *Mahmood Ali*, *AIR* 1974 All 124.
9. *AIR* 1963 SC 309.
10. *Abdul Rahim* v *Narayan Das*, *AIR* 1923 PC 44.
11. *AIR* 1980 NOC 134 (All).
12. *Maiadhar* v *Orissa Waqf Board*, *AIR* 1966 Ori 208.
13. *Shaida* v *Delhi Iron and Steel Co.* (1971) ALJ 510.
14. *Ibid* ; see also *Ramdhan* v *Janki*, *AIR* 1972 All 553.
15. See *Radal Mirza* v *Tinkari*, 104 IC 345 ; *Abdul Rahman* v *Abdul*

Hossein, (1936) 4 CWN 585; *Alimunissa* v *Mohammad Abdul Rahman AIR* 1938 All 485 : 177 IC 205.

16. *Supra* foot note 13.
17. *AIR* 1942 Mad 641 ; see also *Arshad Hussain* v *Naresh*, 40 CWN 58.
18. *Majadhar* v *Orissa Waqf Board, AIR 1966* Ori 208 ; *Shaida* v *Delhi Iron & Steel* Co. (1971) AIR 510.
19. *Shah Mohammad* v *Manzoor Ali, AIR* 1966 Pat 45. See *Abdul Kadir* v *Kadiria Sabha, AIR* 1953 Mad 143.
20. (1911) 14 Cal LJ 572.
21. The identical case is *S.J. Sultan* v *State of Madras, AIR* 1954 Mad 949.
22. *AIR* 1922 PC 123.
23. *AIR* 1923 PC 44.
24. *AIR* 1978 Cal 133.
25. *Motahar Raza* v *The Joint Commissioner of Consolidation, AIR* 1973 All 509 ; *Nawab Zainyar Jung* v *Director of Endowment, AIR* 1963 SC 985.
26. *AIR* 1963 Mad 132.
27. Venkaatya Subbayya, *In re*, 1953 MWN 929.
28. 22 CWN 605.
29. *Shah Najibuddin* v *Ameer Hussain, AIR 1934* Pat 44.
30. The Central Waqf Council and Its Activities 1964-65 to 1968-70, Central Waqf Council, New Delhi, p 45.
31. For example in *Ikramul Haq Shah* v *Rajasthan Muslim Waqf Board AIR* 1973 Raj 57 the Miskeen Shah's dargah at Jaipur was badly mismanaged. Therefore, the government decided to improve the state of affairs of the dargah. The government appointed a receiver to look after the administration of dargah. The appointment of receiver was vehemently protested by the Sajjadanashin. The government was constrained to review the appointment.
32. *AIR* 1976 SC 1569.
33. *Supra.*
34. Fyzee (A.A.A.), *Outlines of Muhammadan Law* (3rd ed), London, 1964, p. 3185. Fyzee has cited the case of *Motishah* v *Abdul Gaffar, AIR* 1956 Nag 38.
35. See report of the Dargah Khwaja Saheb, p. 103.
36. See By-law No 19.
39. By law of the Dargah Khwaja Saheb B-4 Laws, 1958.
38. s.n. 35.
39. Majid S.A., Waqf as Family Settlement among the Muhammadans.
40. *Mst. Azeenuniza Khanum* v *Mst. Ashrufoonnisa*, (1872) 14 MIA 433.
41. Section 3.
42. 1732 All ER 917.
43. s.n. 35.
44. (1894) 22 IA 76.

45. (1952) AC 1.
46. See Ameer Ali, *Muhammadan Law, Vol 1*, See also *M. Afzal Din Mohammad, AIR* 1947 Lah 117.
47. Law of Family Waqf, Need for Reconsideration, *Islamic Law in Modern India*, p. 229-30.
48. The following Acts were passed—Aden, The Muhammadan Waqf Ordinance, 1939 ; Kenya, the Commissioners Ordinance, 1951, Zanzibar, The Waqf Validating (Amendment) Decree of 1951.
49. JND Anderson, Islamic Law in Africa : Problems of Today and Tomorrow in *Changing Law in Developing Countries*, edited by Anderson, London, (1963), p. 177.
50. See Hamilton J, in *Talibu bin Mwijaka* v *Executors of Siwa Hajk* (1907) 2 E.A.L.R. 33.
51. The Law No 48 of 12 June 1946 provided that the dhurri waqfs must be limited to not more than two generations, or sixty years from the date of the waqif's death. The waqif was given the right to revoke the waqf wholly or in part, and to alter its conditions.
52. The law No 180 of September, 1952, abolished any existing waqf, that is not presently and exclusively devoted to a charitable cause.
53. See articles 8 and 9 of the Law of 12 March 1949.
54. Legislative Decree No 97 of 26 November, 1949, p. 220, f.n. 13.
55. See S. Khalid Rashid, *Waqf Administration in India*, p. 146.
56. *Begum Asma Jaffar and others* v *The State of Bihar, AIR* 1975 Pat 48 ; see also *AIR* 1962 SC 1722 ; *AIR* 1968 Mad 243 ; *AIR* 1961 SC 1170 ; *AIR* 1959 SC 951 ; *AIR* 1952 SC 369 *AIR* 1947 Mad 176 ; *AIR* 1944 Bom 91 ; *AIR* 1940 Cal 501.
57. *Sheikh Karim Ullah* v *The Central Sunni Waqf Board of U.P.* 1971 AWR 224 *AIR* 1940 Cal 501.
58. *Jan Mohammad Khan* v *Mahmmod Ali, AIR* 1974 All 124.
59. See section 9 of the Act.
60. See section 8-A (i) of the Act.
61. Sections 8 and 11 of the Waqf Act, 1954.
62. *Mysore Board of Waqfs* v *Dr M. Channaba Saiah.*
63. Analogous laws on this point are—section 35 of the Bombay Public Trusts Act, 1950 ; section 13 of the M.P. Public Trust Act, 1951 ; section 30 of the Rajasthan Public Trusts Act, 1 section 20, Indian Trusts Act, 1882.
64. *AIR* 1961 SC 1095.
65. *Shah Mansur Peer Dargah* v *State AIR* 1980 Katt 118.
66. The following are the analogous laws on the point under discussion. Section 70, Andhra Pradesh Act No XVII of 1966 ; Section 14, M.P. Public Trusts Act, 1951 ; section 44, Bihar Hindu Religious Trusts Act, 1950 ; Section 36, Bombay Public Trusts Act, 1956 ; Section 77, Madras Act No 22, 1959 ; Section 31, Rajasthan Public Trusts Act, 1959 ; Section 86, Travancore Cochin Act No XV, 1950 ; section 7, U.P. Act No 8, 1965.

67. *Bai Shakart* v *Bapu Singhji Takhat Singhji*, *AIR* 1958 Bom 30.
68. *M. Usmanali Khan* v *Sagarmal*, *AIR* 1965 SC 1798 ; see also T.N. *Waqf Board* v *Syed Inam Saheb*, *AIR* 1983 Mad 297.
69. For the above views see *Laxmichand Modi* v *B.R. Mandal*, (1964) MPLJ 244.
70. The following are the analogous laws on the point under discussion. Section 51 (1), Andhra Pradesh Act No XVII, 1966 ; Section 32, Bombay Public Trusts Act, 1950 ; Section 87 (1), Madras Hindu Religious and Charitable Endowments Act, 1959 ; section 58 (1), Orissa Hindu Religious Endowments Act, 1951 ; section 32, Rajasthan Public Trusts Act, 1959 ; Section 81, Travancore Cochin Hindu Religious Institutions Act, 1950 ; section 12, Religious Trusts Bill, 1960 ; Section 15, M.P. Public Trusts Act, 1951 ; section 19, Indian Trusts Act, 1882.
71. The following are the analogous laws on the point under discussion. Section 52 (2) and (3), A.P. Charitable and Hindu Religious Institutions and Endowments Act, 1966, (No XVII of 1966) ; section 63, Bihar Hindu Religious Trusts Act, 1950 ; section 33, Bombay Public Trusts Act, 1950 ; Section 87, Madras Hindu Religious & Charitable Endowments Act, 1959, (No 22 of 1959) ; section 58, Orissa Hindu Religious Endowments Act, 1951 ; Section 33, Rajasthan Public Trusts Act, 1949 (No 42 of 1949) ; Section 102, Travancore-Cochin Hindu Religious Institutions Act No XV, 1950 ; Section 16, M.P. Public Trusts Act, 1951.
72. The following are the analogous laws on the point under discussion. Section 50 of the Andhra Pradesh Act No XVII, 1966 ; Section 50, Bihar Hindu Religious Trusts Act, 1950 ; Section 86, Madras Act No 22, 1959 ; section 57, Orissa Hindu Religious Endowments Act, 1951 ; Section 35, Rajasthan Public Trusts Act, 1959 ; section 33, Travancore-Cochin Act No XV, 1950 ; Rule 23, U.P. Rules, 1966 : section 19, M.P. Public Trusts Act, 1951.
73. Section 36, Rajasthan Public Trusts Act, 1959 ; Section 19, M.P. Public Trusts Act, 1951.
74. *Abdul Kayum* v *Ali Bhai*, *AIR* 1963 SC 309.
75. *Blyth* v *Birmingham Water Works Co.* (1885) (11) Ex. 781.
76. 1943 A.C. 98 at p. 106.
77. (1851) 18 LT 334.
78. Halsbury's *Law of England*, Vol 23, para 823, pp. 568-70, Hailsham edition.
79. Winfield, *Treatise on Tort*, 7th ed., p. 168.
80. 1944 NTL 451 (Nyogi. J.).
81. In this connection reference may be made to Sections 11, 12, 13, 15 16, 18, 19, 20 and 20A of the Indian Trusts Act, 1882.
82. *Mohd Sheikh* v *Governor-General-in-Council*, *AIR* 1954 Nag 337.

83. *Rasabai Bewa* v *Union of India, AIR* 1961 Ori 113 ; Dominion of *India* v *Ad Shaw, AIR* 1957 Pat 219.
84. *Gordhandas* v *G.G. AIR* 1952 Punj 191.
85. *Indian Minerals Co* v *The L.I. Lime Marketing Association, AIR* 1958 All 692 ; see also *Lalchand* v *Deoraj, AIR* 1951 Pepsu 115 ; *Surgunj Raigarh Karmachari Sangh* v *Managing Director, Surguja Raigarth Roadways,* 1968 JIJ 942.
86. *Subramania* v *Prayag Dossjee AIR* 1917 Mad 355 (2).
87. For identical provisions please see Section 11-A of the M.P. Money-Lenders Act, 1934 ; Section 32 of the M.P. Public Trusts Act, 1951, Section 69 of the Indian Partnership Act, 1932.
88. Section 66-C of the Waqf Act, 1954.
89. *Ibid.*
90. *Madras State Waqf Board* v *Khazi Mohideen Sheriff, AIR* 1974 Mad 225 at p. 228.
91. Section 67.
92. The U.P. Muslim Waqf Act, 1960 contains 85 sections : the Bengal Waqf Act, 1934 contains 96 sections ; the J & K Waqfs Act, 1959 contains 58 Sections.
93. *Central Bank of India* v *Their Workmen, AIR* 1960 SC 12.
94. *Somdutta* v *Janpad Sabha, Sohagpur,* (1962) J.L.J. 181.
95. *State of Bombay* v *United Motors Ltd., AIR* 1953 SC 250.
96. *State of U.P.* v *Baburam, AIR* 1961 SC 751.
97. *Employees State Insurance Corporation* v *State,* 1963 JLJ 370.
98. *P. Balakotiah* v *Union of India. AIR* 1958 SC 232 ; *Hukumchand Mills* v *State of M.P. AIR* 1964 SC 1329 ; *Gopal Narayan* v *Mahabiralal, AIR* 1964 SC 370.
99. *M/S Sainik Motors* v *State of Rajasthan, AIR* 1961 SC 1480.
100. *Kedarnath* v *CTO, AIR* 1966 SC 12.
101. See *Rewati Prasad* v *Central Cooperative Bank,* 1960 JIJ 234.
102. *AIR* 1965 SC 1588,
103. *AIR* 1961 SC 41.
104. See *Hasan Noorani* v *Assistant Charity Commissioner, AIR* 1967 SC 1742.
105. See letter No 17 (10) 74—Waqf dated 23.8.1974 written by Mr. Hisanuddin Ahmad, Officer on Special Duty, Waqf, Government of India, Ministry of Law, Justice & Company Affairs (Legislative Department) New Delhi.
106. See *J.K. Trust, Bombay* v *C.I.T., AIR* 1970 SC 846. Therefore, managing agency, stock and goodwill of a Press was held to be

property of a trust, see *Tribune Press, Lahore* v *C.I.T., Punjab, AIR* 1939 PC 208.

107. *All India Spinners Association* v *C.I.T., Bombay, AIR* 1944 PC 88 ; *Angurbala Mullick* v *Debbrate Mullick, AIR* 1951 SC 293 ; *Commissioner, H.E.E. Madras* v *Lakshamindra* Tirth Swamiar, *AIR* 1954 SC 282 : C.I-T. v *P. Krishna Warriar, AIR* 1965 SC 59,

108. *C.I.T., New Delhi* v *Hamdard Dawakhana, AIR* 1960 Pun 219 ; *J.K. Trust* v *C.I.T.* s.n. 8 ; *Dharma Vijay Agency, Bombay* v *C.I.T. Bombay, AIR* 1960 Bom 380 : *Vallabhdas Karsandas* v *C.I.T., AIR* 1947 Bom 382.

Table of Cases

Abadi Begum v *Kaniz Zainab*, *AIR 1927* PC 2, (1927) 51 IA 33, 6 Pat 259, 99 IC 669.

Abbas Ali v *Mohammad Shah*, *AIR 1951* MB 92.

Abdul Alim Abed v *Abir Jan Bibi*, *AIR 1928* Cal 368, (1928) 55 Cal 1284.

Abdul Awal v *Abdul Monaem*, PLD 1960 Dacca 90.

Abdul Aziz v *Mohammed Ibrahim AIR 1941* Bom 238, 196 IC 181, (1941) Bom 341, 43 Bom LR 126

Abedul Baqi v *Chitanya*. *AIR* 1971 All 328.

Abdul Edris v *Zain*, 13 Bom 555,

Abdul Fata Mahommed Ishak v *Russomoy Dehri Chowdury*, (1894) 22 IA 76 (PC), (1894) 22 Cal 619.

Abdul Ghafur v *Nizamuddin*, (1892) 17 Bom 1 (PC), (1892) 19 IA 170.

Abdul Ghafoor v *Rahmat Ali*, *AIR 1930* Ch 245, (1930) 122 IC 326.

Abdul Ghafoor v *Hakim Ali*, *AIR 1959* All 78.

Abdul Ghafoor v *Mohammed Kasam*, (1968) JIJ 225 (SC).

Abdul Ganne Kasam v *Hussen Miya Rahimtulla*, (1873) 10 Bom DCR 7.

Abdul Halim Abed v *Abir Jan*, *AIR* 1928 Cal 368, ILR 55 Cal 1284, 110 IC 416, 32 CWN 835, 22 CIJ 577.

Abdul Hamid v *Abdul Aziz*, *AIR 1935* Rang 112, (1934) 13 Rang 27.

Abdul Hamid v *Fateh Muhammed*, PLD (1958) Lah 824.

Abdul Kadir v *Salima*, (1886) 8 All 149.

Abdul Karim v *Abbas Subhan*, 39 Cal 146. 13 IC 243.

Abdul Karim v *Rahimabai*, *AIR 1946* Bom 342, (1946) 48 Bom IR 67.

Abdul Kasim v *Mahomed Dewood*, *AIR 1964* Mad 24.

Abdul Kadir v *Kediric Sabha*, *AIR 1953* Mad 143.

Abdul Mannan v *Mutawalli of Janebali*, *AIR 1956* Cal 584.

Abdul Ruavi v God Almighty through Asaf Ali Khan, *AIR 1962* All 364.

Abdul Qavi v *Ashraf Ali*, *AIR 1922* Cal 429.

Abdul Rahim Khan v *Mohammed Shafi*, *AIR 1927* Mad 69 (1970) MIJ **968.**

Abdul Rahim v *Narayandas*, (1922) 50 I.A. 84,
Abdul Rahim Khan v *Ramzan*, *AIR 1929* All 518, 118 IC 382.
Abdul Rahim v *Fakir Mohammod Shah*, *AIR 1946* Nag 401.
Abdul Rahman v *Abdul* v *Abdul Hossain*, 40 CWN 585.
Abdul Rahman v *Maung Mutu*, *AIR 1932* Rang 65, 138 IC 851.
Abdul Rajak v *Jimbabai*. (1911) 14 Bom 295, 14 IC 988.
Abdul Rauf v *Shamshulhaq*, *AIR 1969* All 35.
Abdul Razak v *Sheikh Ali Baksh*, *AIR 1946* Lah 200, (1948) 75 IA 172.
Abdul Salam v *Abdul Aziz*, *AIR 1944* Cal 299.
Abdul Sattar v *Advocate General of Bombay*, (1933) 35 Bom LR 18
Abdul Shakur v *Abdul Baqr*, *AIR 1930* Bom 191, (1929) 54 Bom 358.
Abdul Sobhan Bhuyta v *Wasim Bhuyta*, *AIR 1950* Dacca 10, Pak (1950) Dac 11.
Abdul Wahab v *Musammat Sughra*. *AIR 1932* All 248, (1932) 54 All 455, 136 IC 169, (1932) ILR 54 All 455.
Abdul Rahim v *Mahomed Barkat Ali*, *AIR 1928* PC 16, 55 IA 96, (1928) 55 Cal 519, 108 IC 361, 32 CWN 482, 48 CLJ 55, 26 ALJ 464, 30 Bom LR 744, 54 NLJ 609.
Ahedally Hyderbhal v *Advoeate General of Bombay*, (1946) 48 BLR 631.
Abhiram Goswami v *Shyama Charan Nandi*, (1909) 36 Cal 1003.
Abu Sayid v *Bakar Ali*, (1901) ILR 24 All 190.
Acharai Singh v *State of Bihar*, *AIR 1967* Pat 114.
Adam Sheikh v *Isha Sheikh*, (1894) 1 CWM 76.
Adamson v *Attorney General*, (1933) AC 257.
Adam Haji Omar v *Collector of Poona*, (1938) XVI Bom LJ 54.
Additional Commissioner of Income Tax v *Victoria Technical Institute*, (1979) 120 ITR 358.
——v *Sherwani Charitable Trust*, (1975) Tax LR 620.
Adelaide Company of Jehovah's Witnesses Inc v *The Commonwealth*, (1943) 67 CLR 116.
Advocate General v *Vishwanath Atmaram*, (1855) 1 BHCR 9.
Advocate General of Bombay v *Fatima Sultan Bagum*, (1872) 9 BHCR 19 (23-24).
Advocate General of Bombay v *Yusuf Ali Ebrahim*, *AIR 1921* Bom 338, (1922) 24 Bom LR 1960, 84 IC 759.
——v *Muhammad Hussen Huseni*, (1866) 12 Bom HCR 32.
——v *Hormuaji*, (1905) *ILR 29* Bom 375.
——*for Ontario* v *Advocate General for the Dominion*, (1896) Ac 348 (PC).
Afzal Hussain v *Cheddi Lal*, *AIR 1935* All 792, (1935) 57 All 727, 155 IC 791.
Aga Ali Khan v *Altaf Hasan Hussain*, (1892) 14 All 429.
Ahmed Hussain v *Kallu Mian*, *AIR 1929* 277, (1920) ALJ 460.
Ahmadi Begum v *Badrun Nissa*, *AIR 1940* Oudh 324 (FB), (1940) Luck 586, (1940) OWN 689, 189 IC 391,
Ahmad Yar v *Ghulam Nabi*, *AIR 1949* Lah 65, (1946) Lah 116.
Ahmed v *Rahim Bibi*, 30 All 233.

Ahmed G.H. Ariff v *Commissioner of Wealth Tax, AIR 1971* SC 1691.
Ahsanullah Shah v *Ziauddin*, (1937) ALJ 585.
Aisha Bibi v *Nabissa Sahib, AIR 1957* Mad 583.
AIS Association v *CIT, AIR 1944* PC 88, (1944) 12 ITR 482.
Akbar Ali v *Iftikhar Ali*, PLD 1951 Lah 368.
Akbarally Adamji Peerbcoy v *Mahomedally Adamji Peerbhoy, AIR 1932* Bom 356, 138 IC 810, (1932) 34 Bom LR 655.
Akbar Ali v *Mohamedali*, (1931) 57 Bom 551, 34 Bom L.R. 655.
Akhtar Ahmed v *State of Andhra Pradesh, AIR 1964* A.P. 244.
Akhtar Bano v *Kahayalal, AIR 1941* Oudh 492.
Allah Rakhi v *Mohammad Abdul Rasshim, AIR 1934* PC 77, (1933) 61 IA 50 (All).
Ali Asghar v *Fariduddin Hasan, AIR 1947* All 261, (1946) All 661.
Ali Bakhtiyar v *Khandkar Altaf Hussain, AIR 1933* Cal 581, (1933) 60 Cal 790, 145 IC 638.
Ali Husain v *Fazal*, (1914) 36 All 431, 23 IC 291.
Alimiya v *Syed Mohammed, AIR 1968* Guj 257.
Ali Muhammed Khan v *Ali Akbar Khan, AIR 1924* Lah 382, 4 Lah 133, 73 IC 613, 80 IC 765.
Ali Muhammed v *Mohammed Nasir*, (1929) 27 ALJ 517,
Ali Mohammed v *Mohammed Yusuf. AIR 1962* Cri 111.
Ali Shah v *Fateh Mohammed Mutawalli, AIR 1935* Lah 657, (1935) 159 IC 537.
Ali Zamin v *Akbar Ali Khan, AIR 1937* PC 127.
Altaf Hussain v *All Rasul Ali Khan, AIR 1938* PC 71, (1938) OWN 253, 172 IC 985.
Amar Singh v *Custodian Evacuee Property, AIR 1957* SC 599, 1957 SCR 801, (1957) SCJ 574.
Ambika Silk Mills Co Ltd v *CIT, Bombay*, (1952) 22 ITR 54.
Amir Ahmed v *Mnhammed Ejaz Hussain, AIR 1936* All 15, (1935) 58 All 464, 160 IC 354.
Amir Ali v *Syed Wazir*, (1905) 9 CWN 876.
Amir Begum v *Mehr Bibi*. 38 PR 1883.
Amir Bi v *Nilasandra Mosque, AIR 1969* Mys 103.
Amir Hussein Shah v *Hafiz Ghulam Rasul, AIR 1936* Pesh 65, (1936) 161 IC 652.
Amiraunessa Bibi v *Hatema Ali Khan, AIR 1933* Cal 739, (1933) 37 CWN 697.
Amir Jan v *Shaikh Sulaiman Sahib*, (1968) II MLJ 559.
Amjadulla Siddiqui v *Mirza Nizamuddin Baig, AIR 1982* AP 342.
Amruatlal v *Shaik Hussein*, (1887) 11 Bom 492.
Amulya Chandra v *Corporation of Calcutta, AIR 1922* PC 333.
A.M. Patroni v *E C. Keshvan, AIR 1965* Ker 75.
Anant Prasad v *State of U.P. AIR 1963* SC 853, 1 SCJ 615, (1964) Supp (1) SCR 844.
Andhra Pradesh Waqf Board v *Hidayatullah, AIR 1974* AP 287.
Andres v *Jeakim*, (1859) 2 Bom LR 148.

Angurbala Mullick v *Debarata Mullick, AIR 1951* SC 293, (1951) SCR 1125.

Anis Bano v *Muhammad Ibrahim, AIR 1925* All 720.

Aniyoth Kunhamina Unna v *Ministry of Rehabilitation*, (1962) 1 SCR 505, (1962) 2 SC 621.

Anjadulla Siddiqui v *Mirza Nizamuddin Baig AIR 1982* AP 342.

Anjali Roy v *State of West Bengal*, 56 CWN 891.

Anjvman Islamia Punjab v *Mubarak Ali Khan*, PLD 1967 Lah 1221.

Anjuman Islamia v *Latafat Ali, AIR 1950* All 109.

Anjuman Islamia v *Munshi Tegh Ali* (1970) U.J. (SCJ 131 ; (1971) 3 SCC 814.

Anjuman Islamia v *Nazim Ali, AIR* 1982 M.P. 17.

Anjuman-E- Islamia v *Sakeenabi, AIR* 1986 Kant 75.

Annapu Ramanna v *Ponduri Sreeramulu, AIR 1958* Pat 359.

A.P. Waqf Board v *Somaiah, AIR 1980* AP 199, (1980) 1 Andh L.T. 477.

A.P. Waqf Board v *Bowla Bibi, AIR 1983* A.P. 57.

A.P. Waqf Board v *K. Nagabhushushanam*, 1975 APHN 33.

Appaya v *Padappa*, (1898) ILR 23 Bom 122.

ARC Associatinn v *CIT Gujarat*, (1971) 3 SCC 475, 1973 Tax LR 78 (1971) 82 ITR 704, (1972) 1 SCJ 458.

Aruna Singh v *Badar Din, AIR 1940* Lah 119, (1940) 188 IC 877.

Aruna Group of Metates v *State of Punjab*, (1965) 55 ITR 642.

Arya Samaj Education Trust v *The Director of Educatian*, Delhi Administration, *AIR 1976* Del 207.

Asad Raza v *Waheedunnissa*, 57 IC 70.

Asghar Ali v *Delroos Banoo*, (1877) 3 Cal 324.

Asha Bibi v *Nabissa Saheb*. *AIR 1957* Mad 583.

Ashraf Ali v *Mohammad Nurajama*. 49 IC 355, 23 CWN 115.

Asheerooddeen alias Kalla Mian v *Drobn Moyee*, (1876) 25 WR 557.

Askari Hussain v *Chunnilal, AIR 1929* All 849, (1930) ALJ 205.

Assoabai v *Noorbai*, (1906) 8 BLR 245.

Ata-Ullah. v *Azim-Ullah*, (1889) 12 All 494 (FB), (1890) AWN 179.

Ataur Rehman Barlaskar v *State of Assam, AIR* 1986 Gau 19.

Attar Singh v *U.P. State, AIR 1959* SC 564, 1959 Supp (1) SCR 928.

Attorney General v *Carlton Bank*, (1899) 2 QBB 158.

——v *A.W. Gango Ltd.*, (1949) All ER 732.

Ayrshire Pullmau Motor Services. v *IRC*, (1928-29) 14 TC 754.

Asimuunissa Aegum v *Sirdar Ali, AIR 1927* Bom 387, (1927) 29 Bom LR 434, 102 IC 129.

Baba Kakaji v *Nassaruddin*, (1893) 18 Bom 103.

Babatrini v *Ashalata*, (1943) 70 I.A. 57.

Baboojun v *Mahmood Noorul Haq*. (1868) 10 WR 375.

Badrul Islam Ali Khan v *Mt All Begum, AIR 1935* Lah 251, (1935) ILR 16 Lah 782, 158 IC 465.

Balkrishna Saralram Pujari Waghmane v *Shree Dhyaneshwar Maharaj Sansthan, AIR 1959* SC 798.

Ballabh Das v *Nur Mahommed, AIR 1936* PC 83, (1936) 40 CWN 499, 70 Mad LJ 55.

Balwant Singh v *Firm Raj Singh, AIR 1969* Punj 197.

Banubi v *Narsinghrao*, (1907) 31 Bom 250.

Baonder Khan v *Raghvindra Pratap, AIR 1934* Oudh 263.

Baqaullah Khan v *Ghulam Siddique, AIR 1935* All 616, (1935) 33 AIJ 647.

Baqar Ali Khan v *Anjuman Ara Begum*, (1902) 25 All 236, 30 IA 94.

Batuk Prasad Singh v *Ambica Prasad Singh, AIR 1932* Pat 238.

Baqar Khan v *Babu Raghindra Pratap Sahi, AIR* 1934 Oudh 263, (1934) 9 Luck 568, 48 IC 433.

Bashir v *Abdul Jabbar, AIR 1968* Pat 29.

Bashiruddin Ashraf v *State of Bihar, AIR 1967* SC 645, (1957) SCJ 714.

Behari Lal Bhargava v *CIT*, 1941 ITR 24.

Bell v *Federal Commission of Taxation*, (1953) 87 CLR 548.

Bli Ram v *Afzal, AIR 1948* PC 168, (1949) ILR Lah 1, 50 BLR 674.

Bhagirath Ram Chand v *State of Punjab AIR 1954* Punj 167.

Bhurruck Chandra Sahu v *Ghulam Shurruff*, (1868) 10 WR 458.

Bibi Akhtari v *Diljan Ali, AIR 1923* PC 11, 28 CWN 545, 71 IC 621, 45 MLJ 359.

Bibi Jan v *Kalb Hussain*, (1909) 31 All 136, 1 IC 763.

Bibi Jinjira Khatun v *Mohammad Fakhrulla, AIR 1922* Cal 429.

Bibi Kubra v *Jainandan Prasad, AIR 1955* Pat 270.

Bibi Zohra v *Bibi Habibunnissa, AIR 1940* Pat 9, 186 IC 28, (1938) 18 Pat 417.

Bikani Mia v *Shuk Lal Poddar*, (1893) ILR 20 Cal 116.

Bira Kishore v *Orissa, AIR 1964* SC 1501.

Birjis Mahal v *Humayun Reza, AIR 1944* Pat 234, (1944) 23 Pat 203.

Bishop (Inspector of Taxes) v *Finsbunj Securities Ltd*, (1966) 1 WLR 1402.

Biswanath Prasad v *Union of India, AIR 1965* SC 821.

Blair v *Duncan*, (1902) AC 37.

Board of Muslim Waqfs for Rajasthan, Jaipur, v *Bhanwar Chand, AIR* 1981 Raj 98.

Bokaro and Rampur Ltd v *State of Bihar, AIR 1963* SC 516, (1962) Supp. 3 SCR 831.

Bombay Corporation v *Lala Pancham, AIR 1965* SC 1008, (1965) 1 SCR 542.

Bradury v *Enfield London Borough Council*, (1967) 1 WLR 1311.

Brothers Choudhary v *Mohammad Afzal, AIR 1948* PC 168, 50 BLR 674.

Budhan Choudhry v *State of Bihar, A 1955* SC 191, (1955) 1 SCR 104

Burnett v Wells, (1933) 289 US 670.

C.A. Abraham v *ITC, Kottayam, AIR 1961* SC 609.

C.C. Peeran v *State Waqf Board, AIR 1969* Mad 530.

Cadell v *Palmer*, (1833) 1 Cl, & F. 372.

C. Mohammad Yasin v *Rahmat Illahi, AIR 1947* All 520.

C.P. and Berar Provincial Cooperative Bank Ltd v *CIT, AIR 1946* Nag 216, 1946 ITR 479.

Capte Brandy Syndicate v *IRC*, (1921) 1 K.B. 64.
Carbetta Executors v *I.R.*, (1943) 2 All B.R. 218.
Cassamally v *Currimbhoy*, (1911) 36 Bom 214, 12 IC 225.
Chairman Auqaf Committee v *Suraj Ram, AIR 1976* J & K 14.
Charanjit Lal Choudhuri v *Union of India, AIR 1951* SC 41, (1950) SCR 869.
Charitable Gadodia Swadeshi Stores v *CIT, AIR 1944* Lah 465, (1944) ITR 385.
Charles James Partington v *Attorney General*, (1869-70), ULR ML 100.
Chatu Madia v *Commissioner H.R. & C.E. AIR 1958* Ker 57.
Cheney v *Conn.*, (1968) 1 W.L.R. 242.
Chichester Diocessan Board v *Simpson*, (1944) AC 341.
Chidambaram Chettiar v *CIT, Madras, AIR 1966* SC 1453.
Chidhoo v *Haider Khan*, 1955 MLJ 161.
Chief Administrator of Auqaf v *Rashid-ud-daula*, PLD 1961 (WP) Lah 993.
Chinnamma v *R. Dy. D.P.I., AIR 1964* A.P. 277.
Chinnaswami v *Pichai Maricar, AIR 1947* Mad 58.
Chintaman Rao v *State of M.P.*, (1971) Rev. Nirney 95.
Chintamani Pratihari v *State of Orissa, AIR 1958* Orissa 18, (1957) Cutt 328.
Chatko v *Gambhir, AIR 1931* Oudh 45, (1931) 6 Luck 452, 130 IC 117.
CHW (Hudderifield) Ltd v IRC, (1963) 1 WIR 767.
C. Kotaiah v *Waqf Board of A.P., AIR 1978* A.P. 34, (1977) APHN 182.
Collector of Murshidabad v *Bishwanath Rai*, (1807) 6 Ind Dec (Old Series) 170.
Commissioner of Hindu Religious Endowments, Madras v *Sri Lakshmindra Tirtha Swaminar of Sri Shirur Mutt, AIR 1954* SC 282.
Commissioner v *Malik*, 105 IC 155.
Commissioner of Income Tax v *Krishna Warrier, AIR 1965* SC 59.
——v *Andhra Chambers of Commerce, AIR 1965* SC 1281, 55 ITR 722.
—— v *R.C. Association*, 1973 Tax LR 1228.
——v *Ajay Products Ltd., AIR 1965* SC 1458, (1965) 56 ITR 741.
——v *Shahzada Nand and Sons, AIR 1966* SC 1342, (1966) 60 ITR 392, (1966)3 SCR 379.
——v *Provident Investment Co Ltd., AIR 1962* SC 664.
——v *Andhra Pradesh* v *Motors and General Stores (P) Ltd.*, (1967) 66 ITR 692.
——v *Andhra Pradesh Chamber of Commerce, AIR 1965* SC 1281.
—— *M. P. and Bhopal* v *Sodra Devi, AIR 1957* SC 832.
—— *Madras* v *Meenakshi Mills, Madurai etc. AIR 1967* SC 819.
—— *Gujarat* v *A. Raman and Co, AIR 1958* SC 49.
——v *Maharaja Vishweswar Singh*, 1935 ITR 216.
——v *Ramkrishna Deo, AIR 1959* SC 239.
——v *N.P. Sand Sangam*, (1975) Tax LR 246.

Commissioner of Income Tax v *Andhra Chamber of Commerce, AIR 1965* SC 1281.
—— *Jamal Mohammad, AIR 1941* Mad 535 (FB).
——v *G M. Association, AIR 1939* Bom 45, 6 ITR 427.
——*Beach Candy Swimming Bath Trust*, 1955) 27 ITR 279.
—— v *Keshari Singh Nahar*. (1963) 51 ITR 699.
——v *Trustees of S.M. M.C. Trust*, Trust, (1959) 37 ITR 419.
——v *Moosa Haji Ahmad*, 1964) 52 ITR 147.
——v *Takore Das Bhargava*, (1960) 40 ITR 301 (SC),
——v *W.D.J.* (1958) 34 ITR 228.
——*Punjab* v *Kulu Valley Transport Co Ltd, AIR* 1970 SC 1734.
——*Duke of Westminster* (1936) AC 1.
Commissioner of Wealth Tax v *P.P. Waqf Board: AIR 1966* Ker 108.
Commissioner of Inland Revenue v *Anges and Co.*, (1889) 23 QB 579.
——v *Fisher's Executors*, (1926) 10 Tax Cases 302.
Commissioner of Waqf v *Asraful Alam, AIR 1975* Cal 162.
——v *Haji Rashid Ali Din, AIR 1958* Cal 413.
——v *Mohammad Mohain*, , *AIR 1954* Cal *463, 48* CWN 252..
Congreve v *Inland Revenue Commissioner*, (1948) ITR 1229.
C. Nair v *Secretary, C.B. Board, AIR 1157* Ker 188 (FB).
Corporation of Calcutta v *Liberty Cinema, AIR 1965* SC 1107, (1965) 2 SCR 477.
D. Alton v *Gibbons*, (1917) 1 Ir. R. 448.
D. Arur v *CIT.*, (1945) 13 ITR 465.
D.A.V. College, Jullunder v *State of Punjab, AIR 1971* SC 1737, (1971) 2 SCC 269, (1971) Supp SCR 688.
D.A.V. College v *S.N.S. High School, AIR 1972* P & H 45 (FB).
Delroos Banu Begam v *Nawab Asghar Ally*, 15 Beng LR 167, 23 WR 453.
Dargah Choteh Abdul Kader Saheb v *A.P. Waqf Board*, (1981) 1 ALT 207.
Dalrymple v *Khoondkar Azeezul Islam*, (1885) SDA Cal 586.
Dargah Khwaja Saheb, Ajmer v *Syed Hussain*, (1962) 1 SCR 383.
Das Merces v *Hyde*, 6 Hyde 65.
Dasondhay v *Muhammad Abu Nasar*, 33 All 660, 11 IC 35.
Daud Shah v *Ismail Shah*, (1878) 3 Bom 72.
Davinder Singh v *Mst Lachmi Devi, AIR 1930* Lah 985.
Davis v *Benson*, (1889) 133 US 333.
Daw Ein v *Daw Chan Tha, AIR 1939* Rang 365, 186 IC 210.
Dayal Chand v *Karamat Ali*, (1871) 16 WR 116.
Deleur Banu v *Qazee Abdur Rahman*, (1875) 23 WR 453, 15 Beng LR 167
Dependra Nath v *State of Bihar*, ILR 40 Pat 783 (FB).
Devraj v *State of Madras, AIR 1953* Mad 149, (1952) 2 MIJ 487.
Dewar v *IRC*, (1935) 2 KB 351.
Dharam Singh v *State of Haryana, AIR 1974* Punj 99.
Dharma Vijaya v *Income Tax Commissioner, AIR 1960* Bom 380,

Dhirendra Singh v *Dhanai, AIR 1983* All 216.
Dhurrum Singh v *Kissan Singh,* 7 Cal 767.
Digyadarsan v *State of A.P.. AIR 1970* SC 181, (1969) 1 SCC 844.
Director of Public Works v *Ho Po Sang,* (1961) 2 All ER 721.
Dost Mahomed v *Chainrai, AIR 1940* Sindh 43, 187 IC 227, (1940) Kar. 174.
Dr. U.C. Mahammed Hashim v *Tamil Nadu State Waqf Board,* (1980) 93 L.W. 546, (1980) 1 MLJ 235.
Durgah Committee, Ajmer v *Syed Husain Ali, AIR 1961* SC 1402.
Dwarkadas Shrinivas v *Sholapur Spinning and Wg. Co., AIR* 1954 SC 119, 1954 SCR 674.
Eagle Oil v *R,* (1946) AC 119.
Eastword v *Henod,* (1968) 2 QBD 932.
Ebrahim Alibhai v *Bai Asi,* (1933) 58 Bom 254, *AIR 1934* Bom 21.
Ebratenessa Bibi v *Sarat Chandra, AIR* 1934 Cal 14, (1934) 37 CWN 892, 150 IC 386.
Ehsan Beg v *Rahmat Ali, AIR 1935* Oudh 47, 152 IC 798, (1934) 10 Luck 547.
Ejaz Ahmed v *Khatun Begum,* (1916) 39 All 288, 37 IC 885.
Elahi Baksh v *Mahomed Ghaus, AIR (1933)* Iah 27, 34 PLR 81, (1933) 141 IC 169.
Emda Ali Choudhari v *Tubulla, AIR 1937* Cal 313.
Escorts (Agents) Private Ltd v *Commissioner for Income Tax, AIR 1959* Raj 364.
Faiz Mohd v *Kanahiyalal,* (1964) *ILR* 14 Raj 1044, (1964) Raj L.W. 567.
Fakruddin v *Ackenni.* 2 Mad 197.
Fakruddin v *Kiyat-ul-lah.* 1910) 7 *ALJ* 1095. 8 IC 578.
Fakhrunnisa v *District Judge of 24 Parganas,* (1920) 47 Cal 592, 56 IC 479.
Fakir Mahomed Nanji v *Agha Khan, AIR 1930* Sindh 204.
Fakira v *Meher Singh,* 6 PR 1911.
Fanesh Chunder v *Lal Behary,* (1936) 63 IA 448.
Faqir Mohammad v *Abda Khatoun, AIR 1952* All 127.
Farid-un-Nissa v *Mukhtar Ahmed, AIR 1925* PC 204.
F.A. Shihan v *Abdul,* (1930) 58 Cal 474.
Fateh Mohammad v *Sardar Ali Shah AIR 1936* Lah 48.
Fatheuddin Ahmad v *State Waqf Board, AIR 1966* Mad 307.
Fathmabai v *Ghulam Hussain,* (1907) 9 BLR 1337.
Fatima Bibee y *Ariff Ismailjee,* (1881) 9 CLR 66.
Fatmabibi v *Advocate General of Bombay,* (1882) 6 Bom 42.
Fatma binti Mohammad v *Mohammad bin Salim,* (1952) AC 1 (PC).
Fazal Din v *Karam Hussain, AIR 1936* Lah 81, (1936) 162 IC 404.
Fazale v *Zainul Abdin, AIR 1932* Lah 359, LIR 13 Lah 162, 131 IC 632, 32 PIR 400.
Fazlul Rabbi Pradhan v *State of West Bengal, AIR 1965* SC 1722, (1965) 3 SCR 307.

Fazlur Rahman v *Anath Bundhee*, (1911) 16 CWN 114.

Fazlur Rahim v *Mahomad Obedul*, (1903) 30 Cal 666.

Fazul Marim v *Kawla Baksh*, (1891) 18 Cal 448, 458, 18 IA 59.

Fegrado v *Mahomed*, (1871) 15 WR 75.

Ganesh Singh (Mudeesur) v *Ram Gopal*, 5 Beng LR App 55.

Ganga Bai v *Thavar*, (1863) 1 Bom H.C. CC 71.

Garib Das v *Munshi Abdul Hamid*, *AIR 1970* SC 1035,

Ghafar Ali v *Mohiuddin*, *AIR* 1932 Bom 65, 33 Bom *LR 1575*, 135 IC 896.

Greedhari Doss v *Nundikshore Doss*, (1867) 11 MLA 405.

Ghanasambandhu Pandara Sannadhi v *Velu Pandaran* 27 IC 69.

Ghaniur Rahman v *Abdus Salam*, PLD 1965 (WP) Pesh 27.

Ghazanfar Husain v *Ahmadi Bibi*, *AIR* 1930 All 169, 1930 ALJ 109, 123 IC 369, (1930) 52 All 368.

Gholam Hussain Shah v *Syed Altaf Hossain*, *AIR 1934* Cal 328, (1934) 61 Cal 80, 149 IC 1215.

Gholam Hossain Sherazee v *Province of East Pukistan*, (1967) PLD Dacca 1.

Ghulam Ali v *Mahomed Ali*, *AIR 1934* Lah 342, (1933) 144 IC 467, 34 PLR 763.

Ghulam Hussain v *Ali Ajam Talladah Saib* and *vice versa*, (1860) 4 Mad HCR 44.

Ghulam Mohammad v *Abdul Rashid*, (1933) 14 Lah 558, 144 RV 636, *AIR 1933* Lah 905.

Ghulam Mohammad v *Ghulam Hussain*, *AIR 1932* PC 81, 136 IC 454.

Ghulam Mohideen Khan v *Abdul Majid Khan*, *AIR 1957* AP 941, (1956) Andh WR 922. (1956) Andh L.T. 673.

Ghulam Rasul v *Ghulam Qatab ud-din*, *AIR 1942* Lah 142.

Ghulam Rasul v *Chief Administrator of Auqaf*, PLD 1986 Lah 978.

Ghulam Rasool v *Mst Noor Jahan* *AIR 1982* All 511.

Ghulam Sankadani v *A.P. Waqf Board and other*, 1974 (2) An (WR 372, (1974) 2 APLJ 118,

G M.A. Bhaimia v *The Madras State Waqf Board*, (1968) 1 MLJ 410.

Gobinda Chandra v *Abdul Majid*, *AIR* 1944 Cal 163, 48 CWN 225, 78 CLJ 48, (1944) 1 Cal 329, 216 IC 143.

Gokul Prasad v *Mahadevi Kaur*, *AIR 1941* Oudh 341.

Golam Hussain Shah v *Altaf Hussain*, *AIR 1934* Cal 328, (1933) 61 Cal 80.

Gopal Narain v *State of U.P.*, *AIR 1964* SC 370, (1964) 4 SCR 869.

Goppumal Kanhaiyalal v *Commissioner of Income Tax*, 1950 ITR 584.

Gossamee Sree Greedhareejee v *Raman Lolljee Gossamee*, (1890) 16 I.A. 137.

Gott v *Nairne*, (1876) 2 Ch. D. 278.

Gregory v *Helvering*, 1935) 293 US SC 465.

Grey v *Pearson*, (1857) 6 H L C 61, 26 L J Ch 473, 5 W R 454. 108 R R 19.

Grimond v *Grimond*, (1905) AC 124.

Gulam Mohammed Mir Yassen Ali v *A.P. Waqf Board*, Hyderabad, *AIR* 1983 (NOC) 43, (1982) (1) A L T 70 (NRC) (1982) 2 An L T 79.
Gulam Ali v *Sultan Khan*. *AIR 1967* Ori 55.
Gulzari Lal v *Collector of Estate*, 58 I.A. 460, 53 All 910.
Guru Datta Sharma v *State of Bihar*, *AIR 1961* SC 1684, (1962) 2 SCR 292.
G. Venkataswamy v *Mir Zahid*, *AIR 1973* Mys 145.
Habib Ashraf v *Syed Wajiluddin*, *AIR* 1933 Oudh 222, (1933) 144 IC 654.
Hafiz Mohammad v *U.P. S.E. Board of Waqf AIR 1965* All 333.
Haidaitoonissa v *Syed Afzal*, 2 NW 422.
Haider Hussain v *Sudama Prasad*, *AIR 1940* Oudh 18, (1939) OWN 858.
Hajee Sheikh Ali v *Mohammad Yusuf*, *AIR 1962* Ori 111.
Hakim Khalil v *Mailk Israfi*, (1917) 2 Pat L J 108, 37 IC 302.
Hakim Khan v *Sahebjan Sahib*, *AIR 1935* Mad 1040, (1935) 69 MIJ 722, 159 IC 694.
Halima Khatun, In re, (1909) 37 Cal 870. 7 I C 33.
Hamid Khan v *Gowhar Bibi*, (1977) A P L J 39 (NRC), 1977 APHN 317.
Hamid Ali v *Mujawar Husain*, (1902) 24 All 257.
Humira Bibi v *Zubaida Bibi*, (1916) 43 IA 294, 301-302.
Hanoraj Laddashet v *Anant Pad Manabh Bhat*, 4 I C 514. 42 Bom 742.
Haq v *Anjuman-i-Islamia*, PLD 1962 (WP) Lah 462.
Hardatt Singh v *Block Development and Panchayat Officer*, *AIR 1976* P & H 122.
Har Prasad v *Mohammad Usman*, *AIR 1943* All 2.
Har Prasad v *Fayaz Ahmed*, *AIR 1933* PC 83, (1933) 60 I.A. 116, 142 IC 217.
Hasan Sab v *Mohidinsab*, *AIR 1923* Bom 42, 70 IC 150.
Hasanali v *Mansoorali*, *AIR 1948* P C 66, (1947) 75 I.A. 1.
Hashim v *Ahmed Raza*, *AIR 1974* All 305.
Hashim Ali v *Hamidi Begum*, *AIR 1942* Cal 180, (1942) 46 CWN 561, 74 CLJ 261.
Hashim Haroon v *Gounsalishah*, *AIR 1942* Sindh 137, ILR 1942 Kar 179
Hari Krishna Das v *Commissioner of Income Tax*, 5 I T C 275.
Harland v *Trigg*, (1782) 1 Bro C C 142.
Harnarayan v *Surja Kunwari*, *AIR 1921* P C 20.
Hazera Khatoon v *Abdul Latif*, 75 C W N 114.
Hazrat Pirmohamed v *Commissioner of Income Tax*, (1965) 58 ITR 360.
Haji Abdul Razak v *Ali Baksh*, *AIR 1946* Lah 200, I L R 1945 Lah 554.
Haji Abdul Razak v *Shaikh Ali Baksh*, *AIR 1948* P C 163, (1948) 75 I A 172.
Haji Abdul v *Haji Hamid* (1903) 5 B L R 1010.
Haji Abdul Razak v *Haji Adam*, (*1935*) 37 B L R 603.
Haji Ali Mohammad v *Anjuman-i-Islamia*, *AIR 1931* Lah 379, (1931) 12 Lah 590, 135 I C 56.

Haji Anwar Khan v *The Punjab Waqf Board, AIR 1980* P & H 306.
Haji Mohammad v *Abdul Ghafoor, AIR 1955* All 688.
Haji Nizamuddin v *State of Uttar Pradesh, AIR* 1978 All 271.
Haji Nyee v *U Nag We Zin, AIR 1937* Rang 524.
Haji Syed Md Hussain v *State of Bihar, AIR 1979* Pat 103.
Heath and Milligan Mfg Co v *Worst*, 207 U S 338.
Hebbert v *Purchas*, (1871) LR 3 PC 605.
Hemant Kumari v *Gori Shanker, AIR 1941* P C 38.
Hidaitoannisa v *Mammanna Ravuthan*, (1912) 35 Mad 681.
Hirdey Narain v *Emperor, AIR 1929* All 850.
Honnalvge Gowda v *State of Mysore, AIR 1964* May 84
Husseinbhai v *Advocate General Bombay*, (1920) 22 BLR 846, 57 IC 991.
Hussain Shah v *Gul Muhammad, AIR 1925* Lah 420, (1925) 6 Lah 140, 81 I C 816.
Hya-tu-nissa v *Mufulkkir-ul-Islam*, (1815) 1 SDA Cal 106.
Ibrahim Khan v *Ahmed Said Khan*, (1910) 7 A L J 761, 6 I C 219.
Imam Baksh Munawar Din v *Narsingh, Puri AIR 1938* Lah 246, (1938) 175 IC 1005.
Imdad Ali v *Ashiq Ali, AIR 1929* Oudh 25, (1929) 4 Luck 101, 113 IC 494.
Imdad Ali Khan v *Sardar Khan, AIR 1954* Ori 15.
Indira Sohanlal v *Custodian of E.P., AIR 1956* S C 77,
Inche Noriah v *Saaik Aly*, (1929) A C 127.
IRC v *Wolfen*, (1949) 1 All E R 865.
IRC v *Broadway Cottages Trust*, (1955) 1 Ch. 20.
——v *Luke*, (1960) 40 TC 630.
——v *Hinchy*, (1960) AC 748.
——v *Cliffornia Investment Ltd*, (1963) 1 W L R 396.
——v *Coutts and Co.*, (1964) A C 1393.
Irfan Ali v *Official Receiver, AIR 1930* All 837.
Ishtiaq Ahmed v *Saiyid Masood*, (1908) 6 ALJ 632.
Ishwri Prasad v *Sen, AIR 1952* Cal 273.
Ismail Haji v *Umar Abdulla, AIR* 1942 Bom 155, (1942) 44 B L R 256,
Ismail v *Mohammed*, (1893) 20 Cal 834.
Iqbal Begum v *Mt Syed Begum, AIR 1933* Lah 80.
Jaafar Mohiuddin v *Haji Mohiuddin*, (1864) 2 Mad Had HC 19.
Jaffar El Edroos v *Mohammed El Edroos, AIR 1937* Bom 217, 36 Bom LR 277.
Jagadinra Nath Roy v *Hemanta Kumari Debi*, (1904) 31 I A 203.
Jagannath v *Kajoria, AIR 1951* Raj 167.
Jagannath Ramanuj Das v *State of Orissa, AIR 1954* SC 400, (1954) SCR 1046.
Jagannath Ramanuja v *P.K. Patra, AIR 1959* Ori 117. (1958) Cutt 666.
Jagannath v *Union of India, AIR 1962* SC 148, (1962) 2 SCR 118.
Jamaluddin Nasar v *Mujataba Hussain*, 33 All 660, 635.
Jamia Masjid Magadi Town v *Karnataka Board of Waqfs, AIR 1981* Karn 37.

Jamshedji v *Soonabai*, (1909) 33 Bom 122.
Janabali Sardar v *Smt. Sabeha Khatun*, *AIR 1938* Cal 257, (1938) 177 IC 307.
Janab Walad Ahmed v *Jamal Walad Jallal* (1877) 1 Bom 633.
Jan Ali v *Ram Nath Mudal*, 8 Cal 32.
Jan Mohammad v *Mahmood Ali*, *AIR 1974* All 124.
Jangu v *Ahmadullah*, (1889) 13 All 419 (FB).
Jani v *Bishan Singh*, *AIR 1935* Lah 698.
Jawaharbeg v *Abdul Aziz*, *AIR* 1956 Nag 257.
Jawahar v *Akbar Husain*, 7 All 178 (FB).
Jaybunnessa Bibi v *Mujibullah Mahomed Pramanik*, 81 IC 850.
Jee Ram v *Director of Panchayats*, (1974) Punj L J 52.
Jethanand v *State of Delhi*, *AIR 1960* SC 89.
Jeewan v *State of Rajasthan*, *AIR 1952* Raj 137.
Jewan Doss v *Shah Kubeer-oo-deen*, (1840) 2 MIA 390.
Jhaolal v *Ahmedullah*. *AIR* 1934 All 335, (1934) All L J 248, 149 IC 966.
Jinjira Khatoon v *Mohammad Fakhrulla*, *AIR 1922* Cal 429, (1922) 49 Cal 477, 67 IC 77
J.K. Trust v *Commissioner of Income Tax*, *AIR 1953* Bom 232, (1953) 23 I T R 143.
J.K. Trust v *Commissioner of Income Tax*, *AIR 1957* SC 816.
Jogendra Nath Naskar v *Commissioner of Income Tax*, (1969) 1 SCC 555.
Jones v *Skinner*, (1935) 5 LJ Ch. 87.
Jotindranath v *Province of Bihar*, *AIR 1949* P C 175.
Judah v *Judah*, (1890) 5 Bom L R 433.
Jugatmoni v *Ramjani*, (1884) 10 Cal 533.
Juggatsundary v *Manickchand*, (1857) 1 Boulnois 266.
Juggur Mohinder v *Sakheemoney*, (1871) 14 MIA 289.
Jyoti Pershad v *Union Territory*, *AIR 1961* SC 1602.
Kadir Bux v *Sadullah*, *AIR* 1938 Oudh 77, (1938) 173 IC 260.
Kadir Ibrahim Rowther v *Mahomed Rahi Mudolla*, (1909) 33 Mad 118, 4 IC 136.
Kadir Murtuza Hussain v *Mohamad Murtuza Hussain*, *AIR 1943* Mad 234, (1942) 2 MLJ 672.
Kailashchand v *Bhupal Nath*, *AIR 1973* All 238.
K.K. Kochuni v *State of Madras*, *AIR 1960* SC 1080, (1960) 7 SCR 887.
Kalandar Batch v *Jailani Sahib*, *AIR 1930* Mad 554.
Kale Khan v *Karim Rahman*, *AIR 1935* Bom 207 (1935) 37 Bom LR 207, 156 IC 203.
Kali Bux Singh v *Ramgopal Singh*, 41 IA 23.
Kalipada v *Palani Bala*, *AIR 1953* SC 125.
Kalyana Venkataramana Ayyangar v *Kasturiranga Ayyangar*, 40 Mad 212, 31 MLJ 777.
Kamla Port Trust, *Kanpur* v *CIT*, 1975 Tax L R 829.
Kaniz Mehdi Begum v *Mirza Rasul Beg*, *AIR 1918* Oudh 379, 48 IC 39.
Kaniz Zohra v *Saiyd Mustapha Hussain*, *AIR 1925* Pat 576, (1923) 2 Pat 899, 77 IC 209.

K.A. Samajan v *Commissioner of H.R. & C.E.*, Hyderabad, *AIR 1971* SC 891. (1970) 3 SCC 359.

Kastoor Chandji v *State, AIR 1967* MP 268

Kasamkhan v *Kazi Abdulla, AIR 1926* Bom 153, (1926) 50 Bom 133, 93 IC 135.

Kasim v *Hazera Begum, AIR 1920* Cal 800, (1920) 32 Cal L J 151.

Kassimiah Charities v *Secretary, M.S. Board, AIR 1964* Mad 18.

Kerala Waqf Board v *Alam Aboobacker Sait, AIR* 1987 Ker 176.

Keshavlal v *Bai Girja*, (1899) ILR 24 B.U.

Keshavan v *State of Bombay, AIR 1951* SC 128.

Khader Shariff v *T.N. State Waqf Board. AIR* 1987 Mad 40.

Khagum Khan v *Mohammad Ali Sahib, AIR 1955* A.P. 209, (1955) Andh W.R. 1.

Khalil Ahmed v *Malka Mehar Nigar Begum, AIR 1954* All 362 (FB).

Khalil Ahmed v *Sheikh Mohammad Askari, AIR 1965* All 320.

Khalil-ud-din v *Shri Ram, AIR 1934* All 43, (1934) 56 All 293, 148 IC 294.

Khaliq Ahmed v *Siddiq Ahmed, AIR 1974* All 382.

Khajah Hossein Ali v *Shahzadee Hazra Begum*, (1869) 12 WR 344.

Khajah Salimullah v *Abdul Khair*, (1909) 37 Cal 263.

Khajah Solehman v *Nawab Salimullah*, (1922) 49 IA 153(Cal), *AIR 1922* PC 107.

Khajamian Waqf Estates S. v *State of Madras*, (1971) 2 SCR 790, (1970) 3 SCC 894.

Khati v *Mitrza Hussain, AIR 1962* Ori 95.

Khatizabai v *Controller of Estate Duty, AIR 1960* Bom 61.

Khwaja Mahmud v *Khwaja Hamid, AIR 1928* Lah 778, 23 PR 1917.

Khuda Bux v *Manager Caledonian Press, AIR 1954* Cal 484.

Khurshid Jahan Begum v *Qamquan Ali, AIR 1947* Oudh 17.

Khushalchand v *Mahadevji*, (1875) 12 Bom HCR 244.

K.T. Moopil Nair v *State of Kerala, AIR 1961* SC 552, (1961) 3 SCR 77.

Kishwar v *Zafar, AIR 1933* All 186, (1933) 55 All 164, 146 IC 733.

Kulsambi v *Mohammad Abdul Sattar, AIR 1948* Nag 183.

Kulsom Bibi v *Golam Hossain*, (1905) 10 CWN 449.

Kumaran v *Cochin Devasam Board, AIR 1954* TC 515.

Kumaran Nambudiri v *Cochin Devaswom Board, AIR 1954* Tr Co 515 (FB).

Kumari Shaida Begum v *Delhi Iron Company*, Lucknow, (1971) ALJ 510.

Kuttayan v *Mamanna Rauthar*, (1922) 35 Mad 681.

Labhchandra v *State, AIR 1969* Pat 209.

Lachman Das v *Arya Pritinidi Sabha, AIR 1932* Lah 603.

Ladha Danani v *Hasan Ismail, AIR 1949* Kutch 17.

Lakshmindra Thirtha Swamiar v *Commissioner, H.R.E., AIR 1952* Mad 613.

Lakshmiratan Cotton Mills v *CIT, U.P., AIR 1969* SC 817.

Lala Hem Chand v *Peareylal*, (1943) MLJ 11 at 14 (PC).

Latafatunnissa v *Shaharbanu*, *AIR 1932* Oudh 108, (1932) 139 IC 292.
Latifunnisa v *Najimudd.n*, *AIR 1935* All 856, (1935) 156 ID 609.
Latilla v *IRC*, (1943) AC 377, (1943) 1 All ER 265.
Laung v *Moolji*, (1919) 21 Bom LR 1111, 54 IC 455.
Levenet v *CIR*, (1928) AC 217.
Limji Nowroji Banaji v *Bapuji Rattonji Limbuwala*, (1887) 11 Bom 441.
Lokamanya Tilak Jubilee National Trust Fund Bombay, In re, *AIR 1942* Bom 61, 43 Bom L R 1027.
Lord Howard de Walden v *CIT*, (1942) 1 KB 389.
Lt Commissioner v *P Krishna*, *AIR 1965* SC 59.
Lucas v *Earl*, (1930) 281 US 111.
Luchmiput v *Amir Alam*, (1882) 9 Cal 176
Madras Provincial Cooperative Bank Ltd v *CIT*, (1933) ITR 158.
Madras Waqf Board v *Khazi Mohiudden Shariff*, *AIR 1974* Mad 255, 1974 MCJ 253.
Ma E. Khin v *Maung Sein*, *AIR 1925* Rang 71, (1924) 2 Rang 495, 88 IC 167.
Mahabir Prasad Marwari v *Syed Shah Mohammad Yehyea*, (1936) ILR 15 Pat 88, *AIR 1936* Pat 390, 163 IC 869.
Mahabir Prasad v *Syed Mustafa Hussain*, *AIR 1937* PC 174, (1937) 41 CWN 933.
Mahant Sri Jagannath v *State of Orissa*, *AIR 1954* SC 400, 1954 SCJ 329, (1954) SCR 1046.
Maharaja of Kapurthala v *CIT*, (1945) ITR 74.
Maharajadhiraj Sir Kameshwar Singh v *CIT*, *AIR 1964* Pat 231.
Mahbub v *Hyderabad State*, *AIR* 1951 Hyd 1.
Mohamed Hamidulla v *Lotful Huq*, (1881) 6 Cal 744.
Mahommad Ahmad Shah Mubarak Shah v *Pir Aita Khan*, *AIR* 1934 Pesh 57, 152 IC 523.
Mohamed Ahsanulla v *Amarchand Kundu*, 17 IA 28, (1899) 17 Cal 498
Mohammad Eshaq v *Mohammad Amin*, *AIR* 1948 Cal 312.
Mahomed Hasan v *Mohammad Ibrahim*, (1903) 5 B L R 624.
Mohammad Hashim v *Iffal Ara*, (1947) ILR 2 Cal 16.
Mahomed Hussein v *Collector of Broach*, *AIR 1945* Bom 157, 46 BLR 925, 219 IC 449, (1945) Bom 257.
Mahmud Illahi v *Dawn Trust*, *PLD 1950 Kar, 15*, (1950) Pak Sindh 25.
Mahomed Ibrahim v *Abdul Latiff*, (1923) 37 Bom 447, 17 IC 689.
Mahomed Ismail Ariff v *Ahmed Moola Dawood*, *AIR 1916* PC 732, 35 IC 30, (1916) 43 I.A. 127.
Mahomed Kazim v *Syed Abi*, *AIR 1932* Pat 33, 136 IC 417, (1932) ILR 11 Pat 238.
Mahomed Mohin v *Madras State Waqf Board*, *AIR* 1968 Mad 243, (1967) 1 Mad LJ 65.
Mahomed Oosman v *Essak Salemohamed*, *AIR 1938* Bom 184, (1937) 39 Bom LR 502.
Mahommad Safi v *Khadim Ali*, *AIR 1944* Oudh 291.

Mahomed Shafiuddin v *Chatur Bhuj*, (1958) Raj L.W. 461.
Maktumsab v *Dadabhai, AIR 1934* Bom 495, (1934) 36 BLR 1098, 154 IC 684.
Ma Mi v *Katlander Ammal*, (1926) 54 IA 23.
Manijan v *Khadem Hussain*, 32 Cal 273
Manohar Ganesh Tembekar v *Lakhimra, Govindram*, (1887) ILR 12 Bom 27.
Manohar Mukerji v *Bhupendranath Mukerji*, (1933) 60 Cal 452.
Manthunainathu v *Sundaralingam, AIR* 1971 Mad 1 (FB).
Maqsood Ali v *Zahid Ali, AIR 1954* All 385.
Mariambi v *Fatmabai, AIR* 1929 Bom 127, (1928) 31 Bom LR 135. 116 IC 242.
Mariamma v *Andhuni*. (1979) KIT 231.
Mariam Bi v *M,J. Abdur Rahman, AIR 1973* Mad 191.
Maryam Bai v *Mohammad Jaffar, AIR 1972* PC 985.
Maryam Begum v *Nawab Sahib Mirza*, (1889) 16 IA 175.
Masihuddin v *Ballabh Das*, (1912) 35 All 68, 17 IC 471.
Masjid-e-Islamabad v *The Karnataka Board of Waqf, AIR 1981* Karn 154.
Masjid Shahidgunj v *Shiromani Gurdwara Prabandhak Committee, AIR 1940* PC 116, 116 ILR (1940) Lah 493, 67 IA 251.
Maryana Murthy v *Achayya*, *1925 AIR* Mad 411.
Masuda Khatun v *Mohammad Ebrahim, AIR 1932* Cal 93, (1932). 50 Cal 402, 133 IC 657.
Masud Alam v *Commissioner of Police, Calcutta*, (1955) 59 CWN 293.
Maulana Mohd Ibrahim Riza Malek v *CIT, AIR 1930* PC 226.
Maula Baksha v *Amir-ud-din*, *AIR 1920* 384, (1920) ILR 1 Lah 317.
Maula Bax v *Hafizuddin, AIR 1926* Lah 372, 94 IC 7.
Maule Shah v *Gul Mohammad*, (1924) 6 Lah 140.
Maule Shah v *Ghane Shah, AIR 1938* PC 202, (1938) 40 Bom LR 1071.
Maulvi Saiyid Mohammad Munawwar v *Razia*, (1905) 32 I.A. 86.
Mayadhar v *Orissa Board of Waqfs*, *AIR1966* Ori 208.
Mazhar Ali v *Ghulam Murtaza, AIR 1958* A.P. 8.
Mazhar Hussain v *Adiyasaran, AIR 1948* PC 42, (1948) 1 MIJ 259.
Mazhar Hussain v *Abdul*. (1911) 33 All 400, 9 IC 753.
Mazhurool Haq v *Puhraj Ditaree*, (1870) 13 WR 235.
Meer Mohammad Ismail Khan v *Sashichurn Ghose*, (1892) 19 Cal 412.
Mehraj Din v *Ghulam Mohammad, AIR 1931* Lah 607, 134 IC 492, (1931) 12 Lah 540.
Mercantile Bank of India (Agency) Ltd, *In re*, (1942) 10 ITR 512.
Meredith v *Heneage*, (1824) 1 Sin. 542.
Metropolitan Police Commissioner v *Hammond*, (1964) 2 All ER 772 (H.L.) 780.
Meyyappa Chettiar v *CIT*. Madras, *AIR 1951* Mad 50.
Mian Jan v *Faqir Mohammad* PLD 1960 (WP) Kar 420.
Mir Mahbuballi v *Ahmada, AIR 1933* Nag 266.
Mir Mardan Lal v *Zarim Khan, AIR 1926* Nag 337.

Mirza Fida Rasool v *Yakub Beg*, *AIR 1925* PC 101, 87 IC 70.
Mirza Yakub v *Mirza Rasul Baig*, *AIR 1923* Oadh 254.
Mittakunth Adhicarry v *Neerunjah*, (1875) 14 Beng LR 166.
M.M. Husa'n Faroki v *Syed Abdul Haq*, *AIR* 1942 Mad 485.
Moattar Raza v *Joint Director of Consolidation*, U.P. Camp at Bareilly, *AIR* 1970 All 509.
Moazzam v *Raza*, *AIR* 1924 All 818. (1924) 46 All 856, 81 IC 851.
Mohabur Rahman v *Haji Abdur Rahman*, *AIR* 1921 Cal 210, 48 Cal 53.
Mohammad v *Salamat Ali*, *AIR* 1933 All 407.
Mohammad Abbas Ali v *Waqf Board*, *AIR* 1979 A.P. 117.
Mohammad Abdul Aziz v *Mahbub*, *AIR* 1936 All 202.
Mohammad Abdul Aziz v *G. Bhumavva*, *AIR* 1982 A.P. 357.
Mohammad Abdul Gani v *Mt Kulhaun Nisa*, *AIR* 1954 Cal 328, (1954) 49 CWN 273.
Mohammad Abdulla Jitaker v *Abdul Rahman*, (1907) 9 BLR 998.
Mohammad Abu Zafar v *Israr Ahmad*. *AIR 1976* All 366.
Mohammad Afzal v *Din Mohammad*, *AIR 1947* Lah 117, (1945) 27 Lah 300, 354-356.
Mohammad Ahmed Saeed v *Kishorilal*, (1932) 30 AL 44.
Mohammad Ali Khan v *Ahmed Ali Khan*, *AIR 1945* All 261, 221 IC 515, (1945) All 818.
Mohomedally v *Akbarally*, *AIR* 1934 PC 53, (1934) 36 Bom LR 386.
Mohammad Ali v *Mt. Bismillah Begum*, *AIR 1930* PC 255, (1930) 35 CWN 324, 128 IC 647.
Mohammad Ali v *Dinesh Chandra Roy*, *AIR 1940* Cal 417.
Mohammad Ayub v *Amir Khan*, *AIR 1939* Cal 268.
Mohammad Aza v *Hamid*. *AIR 1947* All 137.
Mohammad Badrul v *Shah Hasan*, *AIR 1935* All 278.
Mohammad Baqar v *Mohammad Qasim*, *AIR 1932* Oudh 210, 138 IC 725.
Mohammad Bhai v *Wazirbi*, *AIR 1947* Nag 31, (1946) Nag 646, 224 IC 338.
Mohammed Dilawar Ali v *A.P. Muslim Waqf Board*, *AIR 1967* AP 281, (1968) 1 AIT 165, (1967) 1 An WR 221.
Mohammad Eshaque v *Maimuna Bibi*, (1969) 1 ILR Cal 333.
Mohammad Esuf v *Maulvi Abhul Sathur*, (1918) ILR 42 Mad 162 (FB).
Mohammad Ghous v *Mohammad Yusuf*, *AIR 1976* Mad 371.
Mohammad Hanif Qureshi v *State of Bihar*, *AIR 1958* SC 731, (1959) SCR 629, (1958) SCJ 975.
Mohammad Hameed v *Mian Mahmud*, *AIR 1922* PC 384, (1922) 4 Lah 15, (1922) 50 I.A. 92.
Mohammad Hussain v *Syed Abdul Haq*. *AIR 1942* Mad 485,
Mohammad Ibrahim v *Commissioner*, *AIR 1930* PC 226, 57 IA 260, 32 Bom L R 1538.
Mohammad Ibrahim Sait v *Kerala Waqf Board*, *AIR 1964* Ker 310.
Mohammad Irfan Ali Khan v *Mohammad Tabiz Ali Khan*, *AIR 1933* All 277, (1933) 31 ALJ 97.

Mohammad Isak Saheb v *Najaruddin*, *AIR 1962* Mys 253,
Mohammad Ismail v *Mohammad*, *AIR 1921* All 224.
Mohammad Ismail v *Sabir Ali*, *AIR 1962* SC 1722.
Mohammad Jacoo Sait v *District Collector of Trichur*, *AIR 1962* Ker 343.
Mohammad Kasam v *Abdul Gafoor*, *AIR* 1964 MP 227.
Mohammad Khan Saheb v *Kadir Batcha Sahib*, *AIR* 1926 Mad 466, 92 IC 950.
Mohammad Mazaffr-al-Musavi v *Bibi Jabeda Khatun*, *AIR* 1930 PC 103.
Mohammad Mohin v *Madras State Waqfs Board*, *AIR* 1968 Mad 243, (1967) 1 Mad L J 65.
Mohd-Fasih v *Munir Khan* (1987) All LJ 617.
Mohd Mohidden v *State Waqf Board*, *Madras*. *AIR* 1963 Mad 132.
Mohammad Qmar v *Salamat Ali*, *AIR* 1933 All 407.
Mohammad Qasim v *Mohammad Mehdi*, *AIR* 1937 Oudh 465, 170 IC 629, 1937 OWN 85.
Mohammad S Labbia v *Hanifa*, *AIR* 1976 SC 1569.
Mohammad Sabir Ali v *Tahir Ali*. *AIR* 1954 All 94, (1954) 2 All 556.
Mohammad Sadiq Ali Khan v *Kazim Ali Khan*, *AIR* 1934 Oudh 188 11 OWN 323, 150 IC 193.
Mohammad Sadiq v *Fakhr Jahan Begum*, *AIR* 1922 PC 281, 49 IA 195.
Mohammad Shah v *Fasihuddin*. *AIR* 1956 SC 713.
Mohammad Shah v *Shamsuddin*, *AIR* 1948 Cal 159.
Mohammad Shareef v *The Superintendent* (*Waqfs*), *AIR* 1971 Mad 243.
Mohammad Soleman v *Tasaddaq Hussan*, *AIR* 1935 Cal 623, (1935) 158 IC 544.
Mohammad Usuf v *Mohammad Afzal*, *AIR* 1949 Lah 514.
Mohammad Wasi v *Bachan Singh*, *AIR* 1955 All 68.
Mohammad Yasin v *Town Area Committee*, *Jalalabad*, (1952) SCJ 162.
Mohamad Yusuf v *Azimuddin*, *AIR* 1941 All 235, (1941) ALJ 269, 196 IC 324, (1941) All 443.
Mohammad Zahur v *Najibulla*, 154 PR 1881.
Mohinder Singh v *Mohommad Ibrahim*, *AIR* 1982 H.P. 95.
Mohiuddin v *Sayiduddin*, (1893) 20 Cal 810.
Mohiuddin Ahmed v *Sofia Khatun*, *AIR* 1940 Cal 501, (1940) 2 Cal 464, 44 CWN 974, 192 IC 693.
Mohiuddin v *Hafiz Abdul Rashid*, *AIR* 1947 All 127, ILR (1947) All 334.
Moinuddin Bibi v *Ratnavali*, 51 ML J 598, (1947) ALJ 232.
M.N.R. v *MacInes*, (1954) Ex CR 181.
Morice v *Scott*. (1914) Bom 281.
Mohammad Sadik v *Mohammad Ali*, (1798) 1 SDA (Cal) 17.
Morice v *The Bishop of Durham*, 1804) 10 Ves 522.
Mosten v *Commissioner of Income Tax*, *AIR* 1955 NOC 3639.
Moti Das v *S.P. Sahi*, *AIR* 1959 SC 942.
Motishah v *Abdul Khan*, *AIR* 1955 Nag 1000.

Moulvi Mohammad Fahim-ul-Haq v *Jagat Ballav Ghosh*. 74 IC 403.

Moulvi Shah v *Ghare Shah*, (1938) 40 Bom LR 1071.

M P. Sharma v *Satish Chandra*, *AIR* 1954 SC 300, (1954) SCR 1077.

Mt Niamatul Nissa v *Hafizul Rahman*, *AIR* 1933 Oudh 261, 8 Luck 422, 10 OWB 393, 144 IC 473.

Mt Ali Begum v *Badul Islam Ali Khan*, *AIR* 1938 PC 184, (1938) 65 IA 198.

Mst. Alimunnissa Bibi v *Mohammad Abdur Rahim*, *AIR* 1938 All 485, (1938) ALJ 727, 177 IC 205.

Mt Allah Rakhi v *Shah Mohammad*, *AIR* 1934 PC 77, (1934) 61 IA 50.

Mst Bismilla Begum v *Mohammad Ali*, *AIR* 1927 Oudh 162.

Mt Kammon v *Allah Baksha*. *AIR* 1941 Lah 36, (1941) 193 IC 323.

Mst Khorsheed Jehan v *Kasim Ali*. *AIR* 1947 Oudh 17.

Mst Manik Devi v *Habibullah*, *AIR* 1936 Lah 876.

Mst Moideen Bibi Ammal v *Rathnavelu, Mudali*, *AIR* 1927 Mad 69.

Mt Mubarak Jan v *Mt Tej Begum*, *AIR* 1938 Lah 453, ILR (1938) 19 Lah 435.

M/s Mathraprasad and Sons v *State of Punjab*, *AIR* 1962 SC 745.

Mst Mundaria v *Shyam Sunder*. *AIR* 1963 Pat 98.

Mst Peeran v *Hafiz Mohammad* *AIR* 1966 All 201.

M/s Ram Krishna v *Janpad Sabham*, *AIR* 1962 SC 1073.

Mt Ruqia Begum v *Sarajmal*, *AIR* 1936 All 404, (1936) ALJ 231, 163 IC 344.

Mt Zohra Khatoon v *Janab Mohammad Ilias Khan*, *AIR* 1973 Cal 133.

Mubarak Ali v *Ahmed Ali*, *AIR* 1935 Lah 414.

Muhammad Ahsan v *Umardaraz*. (1906) ILR 28 All 633.

Muhammad Ali Muhammad v *Mst. Bismillah Begum*, (1930) 35 CWN 325, 332 (PC).

Muhammad Azizuddin Ahmad v *Leg Ram*, (1893) 15 All 321.

Muhammad Aziz-ud-din v *The Legal Remembrancer*, 15 All 321.

Muhammad Esuf v *Maulvi Abdul Sattar*, (1988) 42 Mad 161.

Muhammad Ibrahim v *Gulam Ahmed*, (1962) BHCR 236.

Muhammad Ibrahim v *Ahmad*, (1910) 32 All 503, 6 IC 219.

Muhammad Imdad v *Mt Bishmillah*, *AIR* 1946 All 468, (1947) 227 IC 50.

Muhammad Ismail, In *re*, *AIR* 1944 Sindh 183.

Muhammad Jafar v *Muhammad Taqi Khan*, *AIR* 1933 Oudh 517, (1934) 9 Luck 170, 145 IC 1003.

Muhammad Kazim v *Abi Saghir*, *AIR* 1932 Pat 35, 11 Pat 288, 136 IC 417

Muhammad Mumtaz v *Zubaida Jan*, (1889) 11 All 460, 16 I.A. 205.

Muhammad Raza v *Yadgar Hussain*, *AIR* 1924 PC 109, 51 IA 192, LIR 51 Cal 446

Muhammad Rustom Ali v *Mushtaq Hussain*, (1920) 47 IIA 224, 42 All 609, 57 IC 329.

Muhammad Shafiq v *Muhammad*, *AIR* 1928 All 660, (1929) 51 All 30, 111 IC 93.

Muhammad Yakub v *Ali Muhammad*, *Pak* (1957) Lah 544.

Mhammad Yusuf v *Muhammad Sadiq*, *AIR* 1933 Lah 501, (1933) 14 Lah 431, 144 IC 271.

Muhammad Zain v *Nur-ul-Hasan*. *AIR 1924* All 113, 74 IC 142, (1925) 45 All 682.

Muhammad Yusuf v *Muhammad Shafi*, *AIR* 1934 All 1013, (1935) ALJ 40. 153 IC 344

Muhassam Abdul Khan v *Kalu*, 21 All 187.

Mujib-un-nissa v *Abdul Rahim*, (1900) 28 IA 15, 23 All 233.

Mukarram v *Anjuman un-Nissa*, *AIR* 1924 All, 223, (1923) 45 All 152.

Mukundaraya v *State of Msyore*, *AIR* 19 0 Mys 18.

Mumtaz Qadar v *Advocate General*, *AIR* 196 Oudh 244, 225 IC 21.

Munnalal v *Tara*, *AIR* 1929 All 850.

Munnalal Tiwari v *Premchand Jain*, 1970 ALJ 718.

Munnavarul Begum v *Mahapalli*, (1918) 41 Mad 1033.

Murtuzabai v *Jamuna*. (1890) 13 All 261.

Musa Baba v *Badesaheb*, (1937) 39 BLR 1108, *AIR* 1938 Bom 84.

Musahib Khan v *Raja Kumar Bakshi*, *AIR* 1938 Oudh 238, (1938) NWN 937, 177 IC 718.

Mussett v *Bingle*, (1876) W.N. 170.

Musharraf Begum v *Sikander*, *AIR* 1928 All 516, (1929) 51 All 40, 111 IC 583.

Mustafa v *Amina Begum*, 2 *AIR* 519.

Mutukana Ana Ramanadhan Chettiar v *Veda Levvai Marakayar*, (1909) 34 Mad 12, 14 IA 21.

Mutu Ramandan v *Vava Levvai*, 39 IC 235, (1917) 44 IA 21 ILR 40 Mad 116.

Muthu v *Gangathara*, 17 Mad 95.

Muzhurool Huq v *Puhraj Ditarchy*, (1870) 13 WR 235.

Mysore Board of Waqfs v *K.S.L. Setty*, *AIR* 1874 Kart 28.

Mysore Board of Waqfs v *Mahboob Ali*, *AIR* 1962 Mys 128.

Nabinnissa v *Liaqat Ali* (1928) 50 All 830.

Nagamani Achi v *Alamelu Achi*, *AIR* 1957 Mad 401.

Najhuddin Ahmed v *Amir Hasan*, *AIR* 1934 Pat 443, (1934) 153 IC 557.

Namboodripad v *C.D. Board*, *AIR* 1956 Tr Co 74.

Namhoobeg v *Gulam Hussain*, *AIR* 1951 Nag 327.

Narasimhan v *Venkatalingam*, (1927) 50 Mad 687 (FB).

Narayan v *Chintamani*, (1881) ILR 5 Bom 393.

Narayan Dass v *T. F. Neeladar Rao*, *AIR* 1959 A.P. 148.

Narayanan Nambudripad v *State of Madras*, *AIR* 1954 Mad 385, (1955) 2 MLJ 699.

Narayana v *State of Andhra*, *AIR* 1959 A.P. 471.

Narayan Singh v *Niranjan Chakravarti*, (1923) 51 I.A. 37.

Narayan Prashad v *State of Hyderabad*, *AIR* 1955 Hyd 82.

Narsingh Das v *Safiullah*, *AIR* 1954 All 773.
Nashinwar v *State of M.P.* (1975) 1 SCC 29.
Nasrullah Khan v *Mafil Ali* (1930) 54 All 167.
Nasrullah Khan v *Wajid Ali*. *AIR* 1932 All 362.
Nawab Bahadur Murshidabad v *Karmani Bibi*, (1931) 59 Cal 1 (PC) (1932) 58 I.A. 215.
Nawab Hyder Hussain v *Nawab Faghfur Mirza*, (1905) 32 I.A. 135.
Nawab Zainyar Jung v *Director of Endowments*, *AIR* 1963 SC 985 (1963) SCR 469.
Netram v *Bhagwan*, *AIR* 1941 Nag 159.
Nawab Ahmed Khan v *Hasmuddin Ahmed*. *AIR* 1936 Cal 262, (1936) 162 IC 762.
Nimai Chand Addya v *Golam Hussain*, (1909) *ILR* 37 Cal 179, 3 IC 353.
Nizam-ul-Haq v *Mohammad Ishfaa*, *AIR* 1936.
Nizam's R.E. Trust v *CIT*, (1963) 1 An WE 205, 361.
North Sylhet Local Boord v *Gazanfar Ali*. (1949) 54 Cal WR 53,
Nosh Ali v *Shamsunnissa Bibi*, *AIR* 1939 All 319.
Nwen Thomas v *IRC*, (1971) 2 WLR 39.
Palani Muslim Dharmabaripalana Sangam v *Waqf Board*, (1957) 1 Mad LJ 201.
Palanjappa Chetty v *Devasikamony*, (1917) 44 IA 197.
Pandara Sannadhi v *Kandasami*, *Tambiran*, (1887) 10 Mad 375.
Pandi Saligram Acharya v *Pandi Raghvacharya*. *AIR* 1969 Pat 118.
Pande Nar Narayan v *Suraj Kanwari*, (1921) 48 I.A. 143.
Panjab Waqf Board v *Amala Panchayat Garhi Brahmin*, *AIR* 1969 Pan 344.
Pathu Kutti Umma v *Nedungudi Bank Ltd*, *AIR* 1937 Mad 731, 173 IC 699.
*P.B.*N.*C. Committee* v *Government of Andhra Pradesh*, *AIR 1958* AP 773 Pemsel case, (1891) AC 531.
Pettingall v *Pettingal*, (1842) 11 L.J. Ch. 176
P.G. Venkataswamy v *Mir Zahid Hussain*, *AIR* 1973 Mys 148.
Pirbright v *Salway*, (1896) W.N. 86.
Philip John Plasket Thomas v *CIT*, *AIR* 1964 SC 587.
Phate Saheb Bibi v *Damodar Premji*, (1879) 3 Bom 84.
Phatmabi v *Haji Musa*, (1915) 38 Mad 491, 21 IC 964.
Phra Phraison Salarak v *CIT*, 3 ITC 237.
Phul Chand v *Akbar Yar Khan*, (1896) 19 All 211.
Pir Ahsanullah v *Pir Ziauddin*, (1937) 41 CWN 624 (PC) Sindh.
Pir Baksh v *Mohammad Ibrahim*, *AIR 1922* Lah 493 (2), 138 IC 69, 33 PLR 468.
Pirbux v *Sher Mohammed*, (1969) All LJ 169.
P. Majilisa-e-Islamia v *Sheikh Muhammad Nagoor*, *AIR 1963* Ker 49.
Pott's Executors v *IRC*, (1951), 1 AC 443.
Pragdas Mathura Das v *ITO*, *1950* ITR 757.
Pramathanath v *Pradumma Kumar*, 1925) I.A. 245.

Prankrishna v *Junior Assessor, AIR 1954* Cal 241, 88 CWN 73.
Prem Dulari v *Raj Kumari. AIR* 1967 SC 1578. (1967) 3 SCR 273.
P.S. Charya v *State of Madras, AIR 1956* Mad 541, (1956) 1 MLJ 125.
Prithipal Singh v *Magh Singh, AIR 1982* P & H 137.
Pryce v *Monmouthshire Canal and Railway Companies*, (1879) 4 AC 197
Pubbiri v *S. Govinda, AIR 1958* Mad 147, (1957) 2 MLJ 617.
Public Prosecutor v *Ramaswami, AIR* 1964 Mad 258.
Punjab Sindh Bank v *Anjuman Himayet Islam, AIR* 1935 Lah 596, (1935) 158 IC 937.
Punjab Waqf Board Ambala v *Gram Sabha AIR* 1986 HP 23.
Punjab Waqf Board v *Panchayat Deh, AIR* 1971 Punj 482.
Punjab Waqf Board v *Commissioner, Patiala Division* (194) PLR 467.
Punjab Waqf Board v *Mohar Singh, AIR* 1975 SC 1891.
Punkalu v *Shanker Kalu, AIR* 1961 MP 348.
Putti Kunwar v *Janki Das*, (1924) 46 All 813,
Queen Empress v *Ramzan*, (1885) 7 All 461 (FB).
R v *Dhyan Singh, AIR* 1952 All 53.
R v *Ellis* (1921) 125 L.T. 397.
R v *Wicks*. (1946) 2 Ali E R 529.
Radhakanta Deb v *The Commissioner of Hindu Religious Endowments, AIR* 1981 SC 798.
Rahiman Begum v *Baqridan*, (1936) 11 Luck 735. 160 IC 264.
Rahim Baksh v *Chaman Din, AIR* 1921 Lah 390.
Rahima Bibi v *S. Mustafa*, (1938) 178 IC 83.
Rahim Khan v *Fakir Muhammed Shah, AIR 1964* Nag 401.
Rahman v *Baqridan*, (1936) 11 Luck 735, 160 IC 495.
Rahmat Bi v *State Waqf Board, AIR 1982* Mad 202.
Rai Ramkrishna v *State of Bihar, AIR 1963* SC 1667, (1964) 1 SCR 897.
Raj Kali Kuer v *Ram Rattan, AIR* 1955 SC 493.
Raia Bika Kishore v *State of Orissa, AIR* 1964 SC 1501, (1964) 7 SCR 32.
Raja of Kozhikode v *Commissioner HR & C.F., AIR 1961* Ker 87.
Raja Nilomoni Singh v *Pakranath Singh*, (1882) 9 I.A. 104.
Rajab Mutt Ramalinga Setupati v *Perianayagam*, Pillai, (1874) 1 IA 209.
Raj P.C. Lal Choudhary v *CIT*. (1959) 31 ITR 226.
Raja Valad Shivapa v *Krishnabhat*. (1878-79) ILR 8 Bom 232.
Rajindra Narain v *Suroda*, (1871) 15 WR 548.
Rajendra v *State of Andhra, AIR* 1957 A.P. 283.
Rajindra Singh v *Union of India, AIR* 1963 Punj 461.
Ramalinga v *Perianayagum*, (1874) I.A. 209.
Ramandhan v *Vada Pevvai*, (1911) 34 Mad 12.
Ramanandan Chettiar v *Vada Levvi*, (1916) 40 Mad 116 (PC),
Ramanikant v *Gauhati University, AIR* 1951 Assam 163.
Rama Nayar v *Dy Commissioner*, HR & C.E., *AIR* 1963 Mad 205.
Ramaswami v *Madras Hindu Religious Endowments Board, AIR* 1935 Mad 755.

Ramchandra v *State of Orissa, AIR 1959* Ori 5.
Ram Dhan v *Janki Rai Singh, AIR 1972* All 553.
Ramesh v *B.B. Intermediate College, AIR 1953* All 90.
Rameshwar Pagode, 1 I.A. 299.
Ramji Lal Modi v *State of U.P., AIR 1957* SC 650, (1957) SCR 860, 867.
Ramkrishna v *Rahamal, AIR 1952* All 537.
Ram Krisdhna Dalmia v *Justice Tendolkar, AIR* 1958 SC 538, (1959) 1 An WR 67, (1959) 1 MLJ 67, 1959 SCJ 147.
Ram Lal v *Khashi Ram, AIR 1949* E.P. 233.
Ram Prasad v *State of U.P. AIR 1961* All 334, (1961) ALJ 383.
Ramrao Narayan Bellang v *Rustomkhan*, (1901) 26 Bom 198.
Ram Rupe v *Saran. AIR* 1936 Lah 283.
Ramshan Din v *Muhammad Shariff*, (1936) 161 IC 650.
Ramzan v *Mohammad Ahmad Khan, AIR* 1936 Oudh 207, 165 IC 104.
Ramzan Momin v *Dasrath Raut, AIR* 1953 Pat 138.
Ranchordas v *Parvatibai*, (1899) 23 Bom 725.
Ranchordass v *Parvati*, (1899) 26 IA 71.
Rangal Shah and others v *Mula Jadal*, PLD 1960 Kar (W.P.) 312.
Rani Amrit Kanwar v *CIT*, (1946) ITR 567.
Rashid Ahmed v *State Municipal Board, Kairan*, 1950 SCR 566.
Rashidunnissa v *Ata Rasool, AIR* 1958 All 67, 72.
Ratilal Panna Lal Ghandi v *Bombay State, AIR 1953* Bom 242.
Ratilal Panchand v *State of Bombay, AIR* 1954 SC 388, 1954 SCR 1055.
Raushan Din v *Mahomed Shafiff, AIR* 1936 Lah 87.
Razika Binti v *Sharifa Binti Mohammad*, 1964 AC 15.
Re Slevin, (1891) Ch 393.
Rev Bishop S.K. Patro v *State of Bihar, AIR 1970* SC 259.
Re Cassamally v *Peerbhai*, (1906) 30 Bom 391.
Re Chardon, (1928) Ch 464.
Re Dean, (1889) 41 Ch D 552.
Re Hain's Settlement, (1961) 1 WLR 440.
Re Hoyles Row v Jagg, (1911) 1 Ch. 179, 187.
Re Kerala Education Bill, 1957, *AIR* 1958 SC 956.
Re Macduff, (1896) 2 Ch. 463.
Re Riland, (1881) W.N. 173.
Re Sutton, (1885) 28 Ch. D. 464.
Re Thompson, (1934) 1 Ch 342.
Re Waqf Paramathi Nemakkal Taluk, *AIR* 1946 Mad 146.
Re Wilson, (1913) 1 Ch. 314.
Rev Father Proost v *State of Bihar, AIR* 1969 SC 465.
Rex v *Lady Portionton*, (1712) 1 Salk 162.
Roman Catholic Mission v *State of Madras AIR* 1966 SC 1457.
Rugghan v *Dhanno, AIR* 1927 All 257, (1927) 49 All 437.
Rukeya Banu v *Najira Banu, AIR 1928* Cal 130, (1928) 55 Cal 448.
Rupa Jagshet v *Krishnaji*, (1885) 9 Bom 169.
Russell v *Scott*, 1948 AC 422,

Ruqayya v *Surajmal*, *AIR 1936* All 40.
Saadat Ramel Hanum v *Advocate General for Palestine*, *AIR* 1939 PC 185, (1939) AC 508 (PC).
Sabir Hussain v *Smt. Hashmi Begum*, *AIR* 1980 NOC 134 (All).
Sadesib Prakash v *State of Orissa*, *AIR* 1956 SC 432.
Sadiq Ali v *Jai Kishore*, (1928) 30 BLR 1346.
Saheb Baksh v *Ghulam*, 22 CWN 605.
Sain Maule Shah v *Ghane Shah*. *AIR* 1938 PC 202.
Saiyad Hussain Matira v *Collector*. (1897) 21 Bom 48.
Saiyad Naher Hussein v *Haji Ali Mohammad*, (1933) 36 BLR 526, 534.
Sajjad Ali v *Jagmohandas*. *AIR 1927* Oudh 534.
Sajjada Shah v *Shah Habib*, (1919) 53 IC 677.
Saklat v *Bella*, (1925) 55 I.A. 45.
Saleb Khan v *Mader Sahnb*, *AIR* 1954 Ori 239.
Saliquan-Nissa v *Moti Ahmad*, (1903) 25 All 418.
Saliuddin Ahmad v *Mohiuddln Ahmad*, *AIR* 1948 Pat 374, (1948) 26 Pa 531.
Sambuda Murthi Mudaliar v *State of Madras*, (1970) 2 SCR 424, (1970) 1 SCC 4.
Sammantha Pandara v *Sellappa Chettiar*, (1878) 2 Mad 175.
Sanjib Kumar v *Principal St. Paul's College*, *AIR* 1957 Cal 524 61 CWN 717.
Sankaranmurti v *Chidambara*, (1864) 17 Mad 143.
Saruswawathi Ammal v *Rajgopal*, *AIR* 1953 SC 491, (1954) SCR 297, 297.
Sardar Ali Shah v *Fateh Mohammad*, *AIR* 1953.
Sardar Ali v *Gahana Shah*, *AIR* 1933 Lah 444, (1933) 142 IC 847.
Sardar Syedna Taher Saheb v *State of Bombay*, *AIR* 1962 SC 853.
Sarkum v *Rahaman Buksh*, (1896) 24 Cal 83.
Sarup Singh v *State of Punjab*, *AIR* 1964 SC 860.
Sarwar Hussain v *Additional Civil Judge*, *AIR* 1983 All 252.
Sattar Ismail v *Hamid Sait*, *AIR* 1944 Mad 504, (1944) 2 MLJ 92.
Sattappa v *Mohomed Sahib*, (1935) ILR 60 Bom 516.
Saunders v *Vautier*, (1841) 4 Beav, 115.
Sayad Mahomed v *Sayad Gobar*, (1881) 6 Bom 88.
Savedna Taher Saifuddin In re, *AIR* 1934 Bom 169.
Seaford Court Estates Ltd v *Saher*, (1949) 2 KB 481,
Secretary Bihar States Sunni Waqf Board v *Leela Devi*, *AIR* 1980 Pat 141.
Secretary of State v *Syed Ahmad Badsha*, (1921) 41 MLJ 278.
Secretary of State v *Mohiuddin*. (1900) 27 Cal 674.
Seshammal v *State of Tamil Nadu*, (1972) 2 Sec 11.
Sibte Rasul v *Sibte Nabi*, *AIR* 1943 All 74, (1942) ALJ 722.
Siddique Ahmed v *Syed Ahmed*, *AIR* 1945 Cal 418, 49 CWN 311.
Siddique Fatima v *Mohomed Hasan*, *AIR* 1978 SC 1368.
Sitat Ali Man, *AIR* 1933 All 248.
Sikandar v *Badruddin*, *AIR* 1935 Cal 792.
Sir Dinsha Manakji v *Sir Jansetji*, Jini Bhai, 33 Bom 509, 2 IC 701,

Sivayya v *Reddi*, 22 Mad 223.

S.J. Jafri v *Aziz and others*, (1962) 2 APLJ 206, ILR 1971 A.P. 558.

S.H. Hussain v *S.A. Raza*, 1973 ALJ 843,

Shabbir Hussain v *Ashiq Hussain*, *AIR* 1920 Oudh 225, (1929) 4 Luck 429, 117 IC 739.

Shabhan Mohd v *Hemraj, Raghvaji*, *AIR* 1942 Sindh 14, ILR (1941) Kar 474, 197 IC 884.

Shafiq-ud-Din v *Mahbub*, *AIR* 1930 Lah 714.

Shahabuddin v *Sohanlal*, (1907) PR 75.

Shah Mansur Peer Dargah and another v *State of Karnataka and others*, *AIR* 1980 Karn 118.

Shah Mohammed Nain v *Mohammed, Shamsuddin*, *AIR* 1927 Oudh 113 (1927) ILR 2 Luck 109.

Shah Najibuddin Ahmed v *Amir Hasan, Khan* *AIR* 1934 Pat 44.

Shahadul Hamid v *Qazi Mohammad Hussain*, *AIR* 1941 Mad.

Shahar Banoo Aga Mahomed, (1907) 34 IA 46, 34 Cal 118.

Shahi Jama Masjid Merta v *K.L. Bhagat*, *AIR* 1973 Raj 322.

Shahrukh v *Enayet Hussain*, *AIR* 1975 All 452.

Shaikh Muhammad v *Bibi Mariam*, *AIR* 1929 Pat 410, (1929) 8 Pat 484 117 IC 638.

Shailendranath v *Hade Kaza*, *AIR* 1932 Cal 356.

Shakul Hameed v *Mohamed Hussain*, *AIR* 1941 Mad 42.

Shantibai v *State of Bombay*, *AIR* 1958 SC 532, 1959 SCR 265.

Sheikh Abdul Manna v *Mutawalli of Sir Jabebali*, *AIR* 1956 Cal 584.

Sheikh Karimdin v *Nawab Mir Sayad*, (1885) 10 Bom 119.

Sheikh Master Sahib v *Balarani, Reddi*, *AIR* 1953 Mad 959.

Sheikh Muhammad Mushtaq v *Zubaida*, (1889) 11 All 460, 16 IA 205.

Sheikh Ramzan v *Mst Rahmani*, *AIR* 1932 Oudh 71, (1932) 7 Luck 300 135 IC 372.

Sheikh Ramyan v *Rahman*, *AIR* 1932 Oudh 71.

Sheoratan Kunwari v *Ram Parkash*, 18 All 227.

Shibessure Devi v *Mothoornath Acharje*, (1869) 13 MLA 270.

Shilandranath Patil v *Hadi*, (1931) *ILA* 59 Cal 586.

Shiv Dinshah Monekji v *Shiv Jonetji*, 33 Bom 509, 2 IL 701.

Shiva Sambhu v *Raj Mohan*, *AIR* 1966 Tripura 16.

Shiveshwar v *District Magistrate*, *AIR* 1966 Pat 144.

Shri Ishwari Bhuwaneshwari Thukrani v *Brojonath Dey*, *AIR* 1937 PC 185.

Siraj Ahmad Khan v *Gaya Prasad*, *AIR* 1939 All 219, (1939) ALJ 115, 180 IC 942.

Sirajul-Haq v *Sunni Central Board, U.P.*, *AIR* 1959 SC 198, (1959) SCR 1287, 1959 SCJ 367.

Sk. Abdul Latif v *Commissioner of Waqfs*, *AIR* 1982 Cal 288.

S.M. Transport (Pvt) v *Shankaraswamigal Mutt*, *AIR* 1963 SC 864, (1963) Supp 1 SCR 282.

Sonatu Bysack v *Juggal Kishore*, (1859 a MIA 66.

Sonilal v *Kanhaiyalal*, (1913) 19 IC 291 (FC).

Spencer v *Hooton*. (1920) 37 TLR 280.

Spindles School v *Sati Tahilramani*, *AIR* 1969 Delhi 7.

Sreepati Chaterjee v *Krishna Chandra Banerjee*, (1923) 41 Cal LJ 22

Srinivasa Aiyar v *Saraswathi Ammal*, *AIR* 1952 Mad 193, (1951) 2 MIJ 649.

State of Bihar v *Kamesawhr Singh*, *AIR* 1952 SC 252.

State of Bihar v *Bhabapritanando Ojha*, *AIR* 1959 SC 1073, (1959) Suppl 2 SCR 624, 1959 SCJ 1197, (1960) 1 SCA 245.

State of Bombay v *F.N. Balsara*, *AIR* 1951 SC 318, 1951 SCR 682.

State of Bombay v *Narasu Appa Mali*, *AIR* 1952 Bom 84, (1951) Bom 775, 53 Bom LR 779.

State of Bombay v *Bombay Education Society*, (1955) 1 SCR 568.

State Bombay v *A and A Indussries Corporation*, (1961) 12 STC 122.

State of Madras v *Champakam*, 1951 SCR 525.

State of Madras v *Mahalingaswamy Devastan*. *ILR* 1957 Mad 752.

State of Madras v *Mohmmad Sahib Quraishi*. *AIR* 1963 Mad 39.

State of Orissa v *Bhupendra Kumar*, *AIR* 1962 SC 945.

State of Orissa v *M.A. Tullock and Co*,, *AIR* 1964 SC 1284.

State of Punjab v *Sajjanlal Canjawat*, (1974) 1 SCC 500.

State of U.P. Deoman, *AIR* 1960 SC 1125, (1960) 2 SCA 371, 1960 AIJ 733.

State of West Bengal v *Subodh Gopal Bose*, *AIR* 1954 SC 92, 1954 SCR 587, 1954 SCJ 127.

Steavenson v *Lier*, (1841) 151 ER 1024.

Styles v *Middle Temple*, 4 Tax Cases 123.

St. Xaviers College v *State of Gujarat*. *AIR* 1974 SC 1389.

Subbaraya v *Chellappa*, (1881) ILR 4 Mad 315.

Subrat Shanker Bahadur v *The Bihar Sunni Waqf Board*, *AIR* 1976 Pat 271.

Sudhindra v *H.R.E. Commissioner*, *AIR* 1963 SC 966.

Sughra Bibi v *Haji Kummu Mian*. *AIR* 1969 SC 884.

Sudhindra v *H.R. and Commissioner*, *AIR* 1956 Mad 491.

Sujiada Shah v *Shaw Habit*. (1919) MWN 662, (1919) 53 IC 677.

Sundaramurthy v *Chhotti Bibi*. *AIR* 1942 Mad 641.

Sunni Central Board of Waqfs, v *Sirajul Haq*, *AIR* 1954 All 88.

Sudhindra v *H.R. and Commissioner*, *AIR* 1956 Mad 491.

Surjit Devi v *CIT. Kanpur*, 1974 Tax LR 586.

Suryapal Singh v *U.P.*, *AIR* 1951 All 674.

Swami Parmatmanand Sarswati v *Ranii Tripathi*, *AIR* 1979 SC 2141.

S. Veerabhadran Chettiar v *E.V. Ramaswamy Naicker*, *AIR* 1958 SC 1032, (1959) SCR 1211.

S.V. Patel v *CIT Gujarat*, 1972 Tax LR 1069.

Srikrishna v *Gujarat University*, *AIR* 1962 Guj 88 (FB).

Sri Venkataramana Devaru v *State of Mysore*, *AIR* 1958 SC 255, (1958)

SCJ 382, (1958) SCR 895.
Syeda Bibi v *Mughal Jan*, (1902) 24 All 231.
Syed Abdullah v *Syed Zamin*, (1889) 13 Bom 555, 560.
Syed Ahmad v *Hafiz Zahid*, *AIR* 1934 All 732.
Syed Ahmad v *Julaikha Bibi*, *AIR* 1947 Mad 176, (1947) Mad 480, (1946) 2 MLJ 335.
Syed Ali Mohammad v *Collector of Bhagalpur*, *AIR* 1927 Pat 189.
Syed Ali v *Bibi Akhtari*, *AIR* 1931 Pat 354, (1931) 10 pat 506, 134 IC 417.
Syed Ali v *Syed Muhammad Ali*, *AIR* 1928 Pat 441. (1928) 7 Pat 426, 116 IC 525.
Syed Ali Zamin v *Syed Mohammad Akbar Ali Khan*, (1937) 64 IA 158, 16 Pat 344, 41 CWN 709, 167 IC 884.
Syed Altaf Hussain v *Diwan Syed Ali*, *AIR* 1938 PC 71.
Syed Amjadullah Khodir v *Muslim Waqf Board*, (1962) 2 An W.R. 28 (NRC).
Syed Arshad Hussain v *Smt. Naresh Nandini*, (1936) 40 CWN 584.
Syed Diljan v *Bibi Akhtari Begum*, AIR 1925 Pat 544, ILR 4 Pat 741, 88 IC 1035.
Syed Hasan v *Mir Hasan*, 1917) 40 Mad 941.
Syed Hasan Ali Shah v *Dargah Committee*, *Ajmer*, *AIR* 1959 Raj 177.
Syed Ismoil v *Hamidi*, *AIR* 1921 Pat 125.
Syed Ismail Saheb v *Ethikasha Sargura*, (1941) Mad 897.
Syed Mazhar Husain v *Haji Ali Mohammad Jalauddin*, *AIR* 1934 Bom 257, 152 IC 50, 36 Bom LR 526.
Syed Mahamed Ghouse v *Sayabiran Sohib*, *AIR* 1635 Mad 638, (1925) 68 MLJ 684, 156 IC 757.
Syed Mohd v *Syed*, (1881) 6 Bom 88.
Syad Mustafa Peeran Snhib v *Waqf Board*, *AIR* 1969 Mad 66.
Syed Niammutulla Quadri v *A.P. Waqf Board*, 1675 APHN 34.
Syed Saulat Husain v *Syed Ilmuddin*, *AIR* 1981 Raj 29.
Syed Shah Mahomed Kazim v *Syed Abi Saghir*, *AIR* 1932 Pat 33, 11 Pat 288, 136 IC 417.
Syed Shah Abdul Latif Mohideen Kadiri Sajjatha Sahiba Hadullah Sahib v *Mohammad Lebbai*, (1958) 2 MLJ 199.
Syedun v *Allah Ahmed*, (1864) WR 327.
Syed Shah v *Syed Ali*, *AIR* 1932 Pat 33, (1932) 11 Pat 288.
Tafazzal Begum v *Majid Ullah*, *AIR* 1924 Lah 432, (1924) 5 Lah 59.
Taft v *Bowers*, (1929) 278 US 470.
Tagore v *Tagore*, (1872) I.A. Suppl. 1, 47.
Taher Saifuddin v *Tyebhi Moosaj*, *AIR* 1953 Bom 18 , 55 Bom LR 1.
Taken Steam Navigation Co Ltd v *CIT*, (1941) 2 All ER 111.
Tamil Nadu Waqf Board v *M. Ebrahim Musuee*, *AIR* 1979 Mad 231.
Tamil Nadu Waqf Board v *Sannasi Munayathiriyan*, *AIR* 1982 Mad 293.
Tejraj v *State of Madhya Bharat*, *AIR* 1958 M.P. 115.

Tengamail v *Fathima*, *AIR* 1960 Mad 487.
Tilkayat Shri Govindlalji v *State of Rajasthan*. *AIR* 1963 SC 1638 (1964) 1 SCR 561.
Thakarlal v *Nathulal*, *AIR* 1964 Raj 140.
Thanga Pappa, *AIR* 1960 Mad 318.
Thangachi v *Ahmad Hussain*, *AIR* 1957 Mad 194.
The Trustees of Charity Fund v *Commissioner of Income Tax*, *AIR* 1959 SC 1060, 61 Bom LR 1452.
T.K. Lakshmana v *State of Madras*, *AIR* 1968 SC 1489.
Udhavadas Kewalram v *GIT*. (1967) 66 ITR 462.
Umedi Bhai v *Collector*, 1969 MPLJ 680.
Usman Sahib Shiraj Saheb v *The Karnataka Board of Waqfs*, Bangalore, *AIR* 1981 Kart 206.
Upper India Chamber of Commerce v *CIT*, 1947 ITR 263.
U.P. Sunn' Central Board of Waqf v *Smt. Hasan Jehan Begum*, *AIR* 1977 All 18.
Velayudham v *Subramania*, *AIR* 1941 Nad 709.
Venkataranya Charlu v *Krishnama Charlu*, 37 Mad 184, 20 IC 515.
Venkataramana Devaru v *State of Mysore*, *AIR* 1958 SC 255.
Venkata Narayan v *Deputy Registrar of Cooperative Societies*, Eluru, ILR 1975 AP 242.
Vestey's Executors v *IRC*., (1949) 1 All ER 1108.
Vibhuti Narain Singh v *Improvement Trust*, *AIR* 1954 All 520.
Vidya Varuthi Thirtha v *Balusami Ayyar*, *AIR* 19'2 PC 123, 48 IA 302, 44 Mad 831, 65 IC 161.
Vikaruddin v *Osmania University*, *AIR* 1954 Hyd 25.
Vikrama Das v *Daulat Ram*, *AIR* 1956 SC 382.
Vinarjak v *Collector Bombay*, (1900) 26 Bom 339.
V.J. Mahmood Naina v *State of A.P. AIR* 1976 A.P. 169.
V. Mohamad Mohin v *Waqf Board, Madras*, *AIR* 1968 Mad 243.
Vivian Joseph Ferreria v *Bombay Municipality*, (1972) 1 SCC 70.
V.V.V.R.K Yachandur Varu v *The Andhra Pradesh Waqf Board*, *AIR* 1978 AP. 156.
Wajid Ali v *Dadannessa Bibi*, *AIR* 1947 Cal 282, (1947) 51 CWN 111.
Waqf Board, Hyderabad v *Parvati Bai*, *AIR* 1972 A.P. 333.
Walayat Shah v *Sardera*, PLD 1952 Lah 249, (1952) Lah 624.
Warburton v *Loveland*, (1832) 2 D and Cl. 480, 1901 (4) Eng Reports 806.
Waris Ali v *Sheikh Shamsuddin*, (1936) 63 CLJ 573,
Watson and Co v *Ram Chund Dutt*, (1890) 18 I.A. 18, 18 Cal 10.
Wazir Ali v *Ladley Begum*, *AIR* 1938 Cal 437, (1938) 177 IC 417.
Wazir Khan v *Hussain*, *AIR* 1929 Oudh 65.
W.M. Cory and Sons Ltd v *IRC*, 1965 AC 1088.
Woozatunnessa, In the matter of, (1908) 36 Cal 21.
W.T. Commissioner v N.S. & *R.E. Trust*, 1973 Tax LR 1020.
Williams v *Kershaw*, (1935) 5 Cl & F 111.

Yakoob Ali v *Lachman Dass*, (1874) 6 NW 80.
Yora Karaddi Mallareddi v *Syed Amanullah Hussain*, (1972) 2 An WR 327.
Yunus Mia v *Firoz Ahmad*, PLD 1952 Dacca 206, (1951) Dacca 576.
Yusufally v *Yusufally*, *AIR* 1953 Bom 92, (1952) 54 Bom LR 702.
Zafarbhai v *Chaganlal AIR* 1942 Bom 21.
Zafar Hussain v *Mahomed Ghasuddin*, *AIR* 1937 Lah 552, (1937) 18 Lah 276.
Zafrul Hasan v *Farid-ud-din*, *AIR* 1976 All 177, 47 BLR 239.
Zain Yar Jung v *Director of Endowments*, *AIR* 1963 SC 985.
Zoolekha Bibi v *Syed Zynul Abedin*, (1904) 6 Bom LR 1056-58, 1067.
Zubaida Sultan Begum v *Dawood Ismail Makra*, *AIR* 1937 Cal 402, (1937) 1 Cal 99.

Bibliography

Books

Aziz Abdul, *Fatawa-i-Azizi*, Delhi (1894).

Baillie, *Digest of Moohummudan Law*, Part I, (2nd Ed) (1875).

Chaturvedi and Pithisaria's, *Estate Duty Law*.

Chopra *et al*, *Estate Duty*.

Cooley, *Constitutional Law*.

C.R. Datta, *Estate Duty*, (1974) (Eastern Law House, Calcutta).

C.V. Vaidya, *History of Mediaeval Hindu India* (Poona), (1926).

D.E. Smith (ed), *South Asian Politics and Religion* (1966).

Elliot, H.M. and John Dowson, *The History of India as told by its own Historians*.

Encyclopaedia of Islam, (New Ed) Vol II.

Fath-ul-Kadir, Vol II.

Father F. Catrou, *History of the Mughal Dynasty*.

Fatawa-i Alamgiri, Vol II.

Fatwa-i Kazi Khan.

Fazl Abul, *Ain-i-Akbari*, translated by H. Blochmann.

Friedmann, *Law in a Changing Society*, (1959).

Fyzee, Asaf A.A. *Outlines of Muhammadan Law*, (Fourth Ed) (1974), (Oxford).

Ganapati Iyer, *The Law relating to Hindu and Mahomedan Religious Endowments*.

George W. Keeton, *The Law of Trusts*, (Ninth Ed).

Gledhill, Alan *Fundamental Rights in India*, (1956) Tripathi, Bombay.

Gerald Dworkin Odger, *Construction of Deeds and Statutes*, (1967).

G.S. Sharma (ed), *Educational Planning: Its legal and Constitutional Implications in India* (1967).

Gulzar Ali, *Tardid Maswada Qanoon Waqf Khandanee Ahle Islam*, (Patna).

Hamilton, *Hedava*.

Harbans Mukhia, *Medieval Indian History and the Communal Approach*.

Hassumani, A.P. *Some Problems of Administrative Law in India*, (1964).

H.M. Seervai, *Constitutional Law of India*, (1968) Vol I.

Hunter, *Roman Law*.

Husein and Rashid, *Waqf Administration in India*, Eastern Book Co., Lucknow (1973).

Husein Hilmi Isik, *The Religion Reformers in Islam*, (1978) Waqf Ikhlas Publications.

Ibn Hasan, *The Central Structure of Mughal Empire*, London, (1936).

I.H. Qureshi, *The Administration of the Sultanate of Delhi*, Lahore, (1944).

Lahore Abdul Hamid, *Badshah Namah*, 1868, Vol II.

Irfan Habib, *The Agrarian System of Mughal India*.

I.T. Pritchard, *The Administration of India from 1859 to 1868*, Vol II, London (1869).

I.V. Rangacharya, *The Indian Trusts Act*, 1882 (MLJ)

J.B. Kanga and N.A. Palkhivala, *Law and Practice af Income Tax*, (6th Ed. 1969).

J.N.B. Bagchi, *Trust in Taxation and Tax Planning*.

J.R. Riazuddin, *Law of Waqfs*.

J.M. Shelat, Traditions of Indian Historiography and the problems arising from them, inaugural address to the annual session of the Madhya Pradesh Itihasa Conference, (1970).

J.N.D. Anderson, *Changing Law in Developing Countries*, London, (1963).

Kamila Tyabji, *Limited Interests in Muhammadan Law*, (1946).

K.A. Nizami, *Tarikh Mashaikh-e-Chist*. Delhi, (1952).

K.D. Gangrade, *Social Legislation in India*, Vol II, (1978), Concept Publishing House, New Delhi.

Khan Bahadur Moulvi Mohammad Yusoof, *Review of the Mohammadan Law of the Waqf*, Calcutta, (1906).

Khaduri *et al*, *Law in the Middle East*, Vol I, (Washington DC), (1955).

Khan, Bakhtawar, *Mirat-i-Alam*.

K.K. Wadhwa, *Minorities Safeguards in India*, (1975).

K.P. Saxena, *Muslim Law*, (1963) Eastern Book Co. Lucknow.

K. Subbarao, *Social Justice and the Law*, (1974).

Kremer Von, *The Orient Under the Caliphs* (tr. s. Khuda Baksh), University of Calcutta, (1920).

Laws of Jammu and Kashmir. Vol. 5 (1974) J & K Government Publications.

Macnaghten, *Considerations on the Hindoo Law*, (1824)

——–, *Principles and Precedents of Mohammadan Law*.

Mahli Abdul Hai Firanghi, *Majmoo-i-Fatawa*.

Majid Khadduri (ed)., *Law of Waqf in the Middle East*, (1955), Washington DC.

Mani, Abdul Bari, *Asnad-ul-Sanadid*, (1952) Sultan Press, Bombay.

M.B. Ahmad, *Administration of Justice in Medieval India*, Aligarh, (1941).

Maxwell, *Interpretation of Statutes*. (12th Ed), (1969).

M. Imam (ed), *Minorities and the Law*, ILI, (1972).

M.A. Qureshi, *Marriage and Matrimonial Remedies*, (1978) Concept Publishing House, New Delhi.

Mulla, *Mohamedan Law*, (18th Ed) (1980).

——— *Transfer of Property Act*, 1973 (6th Ed).

M.P. Jain, *Indian Constitutional Law*.

Nanavati *et al.*, *The Estate Duty Act*.

Nelson, *Madura Mannual*, Part III.

Nizami, A.K., *Some Aspects of Religion and Politics during the Thirteenth century*.

N.P. Aghinides, *Mohammadan Theories of Finance*, Lahore, (1961).

Paras Diwan, *Modern Hindu Law*,

—— , *Muslim Law in Modern India*.

P.B. Gajendragadkar, *Indian Parliament and the Fundamental Rights*, (1972).

P.K. Tripathi, *Constitutional Provision and Judicial Review*
Radd-ul-Mukhtar, Vol III.

Rahm Ali Al Hashmi, *A Guide to Moral Rectitude*, (1972), The Board of Islamic Publications, Delhi.

Rahim, Abdur *Muhammedan Jurisprudence*, (1963).

Rajendra Prasad, *India Divided*, (Bombay), (1946).

Ram Prasad Khosla, *Mughal Kingship and Nobility*, (1976).

R.C. Kochatta, *Madhya Pradesh Public Trusts Act*, (1951).

R.P. Gupta *et al*, *Estate Duty Law and Practice*, (Thirteenth Ed), (1972) Mira Prakashan, Agra.

R.P. Tripathi, *Some Aspects of Muslim Administration* Allahabad (1936) and (1964).

Rauzat-us-Safa

R.H. Maudsley and E.H. Burn, *Trusts and Trustees, Cases and Materials* (2nd Ed) (1978), Butterworths.

Rustom Ali, *Tarikh-i-Hindi*, (Reign of Mohammad Shah).

S. Athar Husain, *Waqf Laws and Administration in India.*

Syed Ameer Ali, *Mohammadan Law*, Vol I (3rd Ed).

Rashid, *Waqf Administration in India*, Vishal Publications, Kurukshetra (19/6).

——, *Waqf Administration in India. A Social-Legal Study*, Vikas.

Sahih Bukhari, Vol III (Urdu Tr. Mirza Hairat, Karachi).

Samsul Haq Firanghimahli, *Tardid Maswada Qanoon Waqf Khandanee Islam*, (Patna).

Sir Ronald Wilson, *Anglo-Mohammadan Law*, (Sixth Ed) (1930) (London).

Sir Thomas Roe, *His Pilgrims.*

Shamsul Ghani Khan, *The khadima of the Khawaja Saheb of Ajmer and the Baneful Effects of the Dargah Khwaja Saheb Bill on their Rights.*

Shams Siraj Arif, *Tarikh-e-Firoz Shahi* (Elliot and Dowson).
Sharaiul Islam.

Shibli Numani, *Waqf-e-aulad*, *Maqalat-e-Shibli*, Vol I, Azamgarh, (1930).

—— *Seerat-un-Nabi*, Vol II, (Azamgarh).

S.M. Ikram, *Muslim Civilization in India*, Columbia University Press, (1964).

S. Sulaiman Nadvi, *Hayat-e-Shibli*, (Azamgarh), (1943).

Syed Abul Mansur Habibullah, *The Law of Waqfs*, Dilkushan Chambers, (Calcutta).

Syed Asghar Husain, *Fatawa Mohammadi*, Sharah Deobandi, Deoband (1928).

Tara Chand, *Influence of Islam on Indian Culture*, (1946), (Allahabad).

Tarikh-i-Jahan Gusha, Vols I & II.

T.L.V. Ayyar, *The Evolution of the Indian Constitution*, (1970).

Tudor, *Charities*, (4th Ed) (1906).

Tyabji, *Muslim Law*, (4th Ed).

V. Balasubramanian's, *Law and Practice of Estate Duty.*

V.N. Shukla, *Constitution of India*, (Sixth Ed), (1979), Eastern Book Co, Lucknow.

V.P. Sarathi, (ed). *The Law of Hindu Religious and Charitable Endowments*, (1977).

V.S. Agarwal, *A Note on Medieval Temple Architecture*,

Waqf Administration, Ministry of Irrigation & Power, New Delhi, (1962).

Waqf Laws in Andhra Pradesh, (Second Ed), Asia Law House, Hyderabad.

W. Foster (Ed)., *Early Travellers in India.*

Zahiruddin Faruki, *Aurangzeb and his Time.*

Brochures

Extract of Opinions on the Scheme for *Co-ordination between English Education and Deeni Taleem*, Central Waqf Council, New Delhi.

An Explanation, Mr. M.N. Masud, Central Waqf Council, New Delhi.

An Account of the Survey of Waqf Properties and Allied Matters in Rajasthan, 1957-64.

Activities of the Punjab Waqf Board, 1965-70, Punjab Waqf Board, Ambala Cantt.

Amendments to the Waqf Act, 1954, Recommended by the Amendment Committee, Central Waqf Council, New Delhi.

Waqf Administration, 1961, Waqf Section, Government of India Review of Waqf Administration for the years 1962-63.

The Central Waqf Council and its Activities (1964-65) to (1969-70) Central Waqf Council, New Delhi, 1971.

Journals

Jaipur Law Journal Studies in Law, (1976-77).

K.D. Gaur, "Judicial Attitude to tax avoidance in the United Kingdom and India", 1975, *Journal of Indian Law Institute Law Quarterly Review*, No 57 (1941).

Leolin Price, More about Unclean Hands, 1959, *British Tax Review*.

M.C. Bijawat, *Taxation*, (1978) 50 Taxation.

Parikh, Kumar *et al*, Tax Planning *via* Trust, (1977-78), 82 *Calcutta Weekly Notes*, (1978) 1 *Madras Law Journal*, (1978) II *Supreme Court Weekly Notes*.

Peter G. Whiteman, The Meaning of the Term Arrangement, (1966) *British Tax Review*.

P.K. Tripathi, *Secvlarism, Constitutional Provision and Judicial Review*, (1966) 8 JILI.

S.C. Bhat, A note on the Report of the Hindu Religious Endowments Commissioner, *AIR* 1964 (Jr. Section).

Sir Syed Ahmed Khan's proposed Bill on Waqf-al-aulad, 1 *Aligarh Law Society Review*, (1970).

Tripathi *et al*, Twarikhe Daulate-e-Sher-Shah, *Medieval India Quarterly* Vol I, No 1, July-September, 1950.

V.S. Agarwal, A note on Medieval Temple Architecture, *Journal of the United Provinces Historical Society*, (1943) July issue.

Constituent Assembly Debates

Constituent Assembly Debates, Vol 7.

Gazette

Gazette of India, Part II, Section 2, 26th July, 1952.

Newspapers

Curzon Gazette, Delhi, September, 1902.

Ahsan-ul-Akbar, Calcutta, 24 October, 1902.

Dawat, Delhi.

Hindustan Times, April 20, 1970.

Rehnuma, Hyderabad.

Times of India, 19th March, 1970.

Watan, Lahore, 22nd August, 1902.

Reports

(both government and semi-government).

Report of the Select Committee on The Muslim Waqfs Bill, 1952.

The Concept and Purpose of the Central Waqf Section, Government of India.

Orissa Native Commission and Madras Hindu Religious Institutions Bill, 1878.

Report of the Dargah Khwaja Saheb (Ajmer) Committee of Enquiry, Government of India, New Delhi, 1949.

Administration Report of the Dargah Hazrat Khwaja Saheb, Ajmer, (1961-62, 1962-63 and 1963-64).

Report of the Religious Endowments Commission, 1960-62, Government of India.

Report of the Archaeological Survey of India, 1909-10 and 1923.

Interim Report of the Waqf Inquiry Committee, 1973.

Fourteenth Report of the Law Commission, of India, New Delhi.

Report of the United Nations Sub-Committee on the Prevention of Discrimination and Protection of Minorities, *Year Book in Human Rights*, 1950.

Report on Tax Administration in India's Foreign Tax Assistance, U.S. AID India, 1964.

Report of the Royal Commission on Taxation, Canada, Vol 3, (1966).

Report of the Dargah Khwaja Saheb, Ajmer, (from 1956-1964).

Proceedings of the Inter-State Waqf Conference, 1960.

Agenda and Notes of the Inter-State Waqf Conference, 1960, Ministry of Irrigation and Power.

Proceedings of the Meetings of the Central Waqf Council, 1965,

Agenda and Minutes of the Fourteen Meetings of the Central Waqf Council, (1965 and 1976).

Table of Enactments

Administrative of Evacuee Property Act, 1950.

Ajmer Abolition of the Intermediaries and Land Reform Act, 1956.
Ancient Monuments Archaeological Sites and Remains Act, 1958.
Bengal Waqf Act, 1934.
Bihar Land Reforms Act, 1950.
Bihar Waqf Act, 1947.
Bombay Public Trusts Act, 1950.
Charitable Endowments Act, 1890.
Charitable and Religious Trusts Act, 1920.
Civil Procedure Code, 1908.
Dargah Khwaja Sahib Act, 1936.
Dargah Khwaja Sahib Act, 1955.
Dargah Khwaja Sahib (Emergency Provisions) Act, 1950.
Dargah Khwaja Sahib (Amendment) Act XX, 1964.
Delhi Muslim Waqf Act, 1943.
Displaced Persons (Compensation and Rehabilitation) Act, 1954.
Estate Duty Act, 1953.
Gift Tax Act, 1958.
Hyderabad Endowment Regulation, 1939.
Income Tax Act, 1961.
Indian Evidence Act, 1872.
Indian Succession Act, 1925, S. 118.
Indian Stamp Act, Art. 64.
J & K Muslim Act 1959.
Kazees Act, 1864.
Land Acquisition Act, 1894.
Limitation Act, 1963.
Madras Code, (Regulation VI) 1817.
Madras Hindu Religious and Charitable Endowments Act, 1959.
Madhya Pradesh Societies Registration Act, 1959.
——Accommodation Control Act.
——Dharmadaya Funds Act, XVIII. 1951.
——Ghoshala Act No 4, 1953.
——Public Trust Act, 1951.
Madhya Bharat Shri Mahakaleshwar Temple Act, 1954.
——Gangajali Fund Trusts Act, 1954.

---(Bomay Amendment to the Mussalman Waqf Act, 1923) Act 1935.

Mussalman Waqf Validating Act, 1913.

Nanded Sikh Gurdwara Sachkhan Shri Hazur Apchalnagar Sahib Act, 1956.

Official Trustees Act, 1913.

Public Premises (Eviction of Unauthorised Occupants) Act, 1958.

Public Waqfs (Extension of Limitation) Amendment Act, 1969

Regulation XII of 1793.

Regulation III of Bengal Code, 1810.

Regulation VI of Madras Code, 1817.

Religious Endowment Act, 1863.

Religious Trusts Bills, 1960.

Religious Societies Act, 1880.

Transfer of Property Act, 1882, s 18.

Sikh Gurdwara Act, 1925.

U.K. Finance Act, 1894.

U.P. Land Revenue Act, 1910.

U.P. Land Laws (Amendment) Act, 1960.

U.P. Muslim Waqf Act, 1936.

U.P. Muslim Waqf Act, 1960.

U.P. Muslim Waqf (Amendment) Act, 1974.

U.P. Zamindari Abolition and Land Reforms Act, 1950.

Waqf (Amendment) Act, 1964.

Waqf (Amendment) Act, 1969.

Index